# AGRICULTURAL ECOLOGY OF SAVANNA
## A STUDY OF WEST AFRICA

To the memory of my wife Pam, whose love and courage inspired and sustained me throughout our long West African safari.

J.K.

# Agricultural ecology of Savanna

## A STUDY OF WEST AFRICA

J. M. KOWAL

AND

A. H. KASSAM

1478
1978

CLARENDON PRESS · OXFORD

*Oxford University Press, Walton Street, Oxford* OX2 6DP

OXFORD LONDON GLASGOW NEW YORK
TORONTO MELBOURNE WELLINGTON CAPE TOWN
IBADAN NAIROBI DAR ES SALAAM LUSAKA ADDIS ABABA
KUALA LUMPUR SINGAPORE JAKARTA HONG KONG TOKYO
DELHI BOMBAY CALCUTTA MADRAS KARACHI

© J. M. Kowal and A. H. Kassam 1978

**British Library Cataloguing in Publication Data**

Kowal, J M
    Agricultural ecology of Savanna.
    1. Savannas — Africa, West    2. Agriculture —
    Africa, West
    I. Title    II. Kassam, A H
    630'.966      S472.W/     77-30412

    ISBN 0-19-859462-3

Typeset by Hope Services, Wantage
Printed in Great Britain
by J. W. Arrowsmith Ltd., Bristol

# Preface

This book is intended as a source of reference for those engaged directly or indirectly with the development of agriculture and the efficient utilization or conservation of natural resources in the Savanna of West Africa. It is therefore hoped that it will be used by a variety of readers including university students, agricultural scientists, extension officers, administrators and planners, and those who need to know more about West Africa.

Although the basic principles of agricultural practice are universal, an informed understanding of local environment is essential in order to synthesize agricultural technology which meets local needs for improved production practices or efficient exploitation of production resources. Quantitative assessment of environmental resources, or the understanding of the physical processes in the environment affecting agricultural production in the seasonally arid tropics of West Africa is scarce. Intense efforts to quantify environmental variables that relate to agricultural production have occurred only recently. One of the most recent contributions in this field *An agro-climatological atlas of the Northern States of Nigeria* by Kowal and Knabe (1972), has generated interest surpassing all expectations. This, and a vastly increased volume of research information originating in West Africa (e.g., Institute for Agricultural Research (IAR), Nigeria; Office de la Recherche Scientifique et Technique Outre-Mer (ORSTOM) and Institut de Recherches Agronomiques Tropicales (IRAT), Senegal and elsewhere) on management of soil fertility, plant breeding, crop nutrition, agroclimatology, crop ecology, pests and diseases, and socio-economics, has prompted us to write an integrated account linking quantified variables of the total environment to agricultural production.

The book stresses what is specific or unique in the environments of the West African Savanna for efficient crop production and agricultural development therein, and considers some of the important aspects of the transition from traditional agriculture (dominantly subsistence based) to modern agriculture (dominantly commercial based) which involve economic, social, and political considerations. It is hoped that this book will provide in some measure an understanding of the agricultural ecology of the West African Savanna, stimulating improved production practices that will not only lead to an increase in food production beyond the level of subsistence, but also to an achievement of better living standards. Indeed, it will be seen that an enormous potential for agriculture exists within this region which modern science and technology could develop to an exceptionally high level of productivity.

We are deeply indebted to Dr. I. S. Audu, former Vice-Chancellor of Ahmadu Bello University, Zaria, Nigeria, for his support, and to Professor A. D. Bradshaw, Head of Botany Department, Liverpool University, for reading the manuscript and making many valuable suggestions and for his continous encouragement and advice.

We are most grateful to the following people for reading and commenting on the whole or various parts of the manuscript: Mr. D. J. Andrews, Dr. C. Charreau, Professor M. B. Russell (whole manuscript), Professor A. H. Bunting (chapters 3 and 7), Dr. J. C. Davies (chapter 7, pests), Dr. P. J. Dart (chapter 4), Mr. J. Derrick (chapter 2), Dr. H. Doggett (chapter 7, cereals), Dr. R. W. Gibbons (chapter 7, groundnut), Dr. Y. L. Nene (chapter 7, diseases), and Mr. G. A. F. Rand (chapter 7, tobacco).

We wish to thank Miss Christine Kowal for her help in the preparation of the text and illustrations, and to Mr. V. S. Raju for typing the manuscript.

Finally our thanks are due to the Inter-University Council for Higher Education, London, for providing JMK with financial support during the period when this work was prepared, to the International Crops Research Institute for the Semi-Arid Tropics (ICRISAT), Hyderabad, India, for paying the travel expenses incurred by AHK, and to Liverpool University for computer and library facilities and for drawing the illustrations.

*May* 1976

J.M.K.
A.H.K.

# Contents

# 1 Introduction

History may well record the twentieth century as being the 'period of exponential change'. Certainly this is true of the human population increase, the exhaustive use of non-renewable resources and scientific exploration. The present acute world food shortage, the energy crisis, and revaluation of basic world commodities are clearly direct consequences of the exponential increase in the human population and the exhaustive use of non-renewable resources.

Agriculture, man's chief activity for producing renewable resources, lags behind technological development and in most areas of the world agriculture remains surprisingly primitive and grossly underdeveloped. It is a certainty that a vast application of science and technology needs to be directed towards an increase in the world's consumer goods from renewable resources.

The most fundamental agricultural consideration in our immediate future is

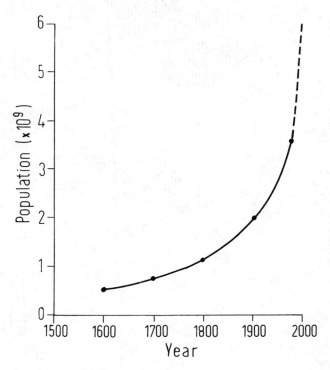

Fig. 1.1. World population growth.

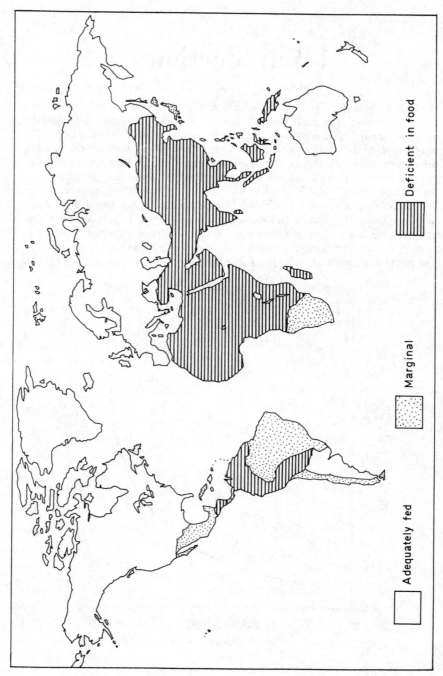

Fig. 1.2. The geography of hunger (Penman 1968).

Deficient in food

Marginal

Adequately fed

that of the enormous growth in the world's population (Fig. 1.1). According to the F.A.O. estimates the present world population of $3.6 \times 10^9$ will increase to about $6.5 \times 10^9$ by A.D. 2000 with nearly four-fifths of mankind existing in what are now developing countries where food shortages and malnutrition or nutritional imbalances are at present most prevalent. Geographical distribution of areas deficient in food supply is illustrated in Fig. 1.2. The bulk of food deficient areas falls within the tropics and sub-tropics. This is a paradox since the greatest asset of tropical and sub-tropical areas is the large amount of solar radiation that could be utilized to yield a high agricultural production. Assuming nutrients, water and crop health are adequate, the relative potential productivity of different regions of the earth is summarized in Table 1.1, clearly illustrating a very high agricultural potential in the tropical and sub-tropical regions including the West African Savanna (Fig. 1.3).

**Table 1.1**

*The potential productivity of the earth and the population
it could support (de Wit 1967)*

| North latitude (degrees) | Land surface (ha $\times 10^8$) | Number of months with mean temp. above 10°C | Carbohydrate (kg $\times 10^3$/ ha/year) | Population ($\times 10^9$) |
|---|---|---|---|---|
| 70 | 8 | 1 | 12 | 10 |
| 60 | 14 | 2 | 21 | 30 |
| 50 | 16 | 6 | 59 | 95 |
| 40 | 15 | 9 | 91 | 136 |
| 30 | 17 | 11 | 113 | 157 |
| 20 | 13 | 12 | 124 | 105 |
| 10 | 10 | 12 | 124 | 77 |
| 0 | 14 | 12 | 116 | 121 |
| –10 | 7 | 12 | 117 | 87 |
| –20 | 9 | 12 | 123 | 112 |
| –30 | 7 | 12 | 121 | 88 |
| –40 | 1 | 8 | 89 | 9 |
| –50 | 1 | 1 | 12 | 1 |
| Total | 131 | | 1122 | 1022 |

Crop production, which is the basic agricultural activity, can be defined as an organized exploitation of the environmental resources of solar energy, carbon dioxide, water and nutrients into economic products. However, the response of crop plants to these environmental factors in terms of such important processes as photosynthesis, the partition of photosynthates into economic and non-economic plant parts and the use of water and nutrients depends a great deal on their genetic make-up. Since the Second World War much has been achieved in the understanding of physical processes in the environment which influence agricultural production. This had led to development of biophysical models which allow one to analyse and predict crop responses to environmental variables in terms of the biological and physical components of the whole system. From the wealth of information accumulated from research in various disciplines

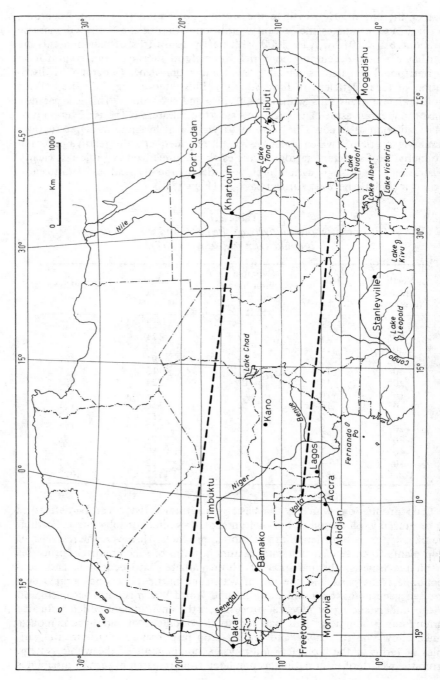

Fig. 1.3. Approximate northern and southern boundaries of the West African Savanna region.

of the agricultural sciences conducted in both the developing and developed areas of the world it has become clear that inherently the environments of the tropics are potentially productive, provided the right kind of management practice is available to reap the genetic potential of cultivars being bred for these environments.

The level and stability of crop yields depends on the environment, the cultural practice and the cultivar. There is little doubt that the application of improved techniques and inputs does result in a substantially increased agricultural production in the seasonally arid tropics of the West African Savanna (Arnon 1972). The consistently high yields of crops on large experimental plots at Samaru in northern Nigeria match the high yield levels of the most productive areas of the world. For example, a crop of 117-day maize produced 7200 kg/ha of grain and 19 000 kg/ha of dry matter, equivalent to efficiency of energy conversion of 1·4 per cent (Kowal and Kassam 1973a).

In reality, however, the improvements in technology of crop production in underdeveloped regions directed towards an intensification of food production nearer the potential of the natural environment is only one of the essential requirements that must be considered. Of equal importance in agricultural development are the provisions that must be directed towards the improvement of the farmer's economic and socio-institutional environment. The resources of a subsistence farmer are low and improvements in production techniques inevitably depend on the availability of inputs and incentives. First, the farmer has to be convinced of the value to him of a new technology. Then he needs to have the means to adopt that technology, which usually means money to purchase inputs: the inputs of seed, fertilizer, chemicals, etc., need to be available at the right place and at the right time; and finally he needs to be able to sell his produce in order for there to be an adequate incentive for him to expend his labour.

The constraints on a higher level in an economic and socio-institutional environment are even more considerable, requiring huge capital resources for investment and educational facilities. Roads, transport, communications, credit facilities, distribution centres, storage, marketing, the stability of prices, extension services, etc., must be developed in parallel with technological innovations at farm level. This in fact implies that there must be a replacement of the present subsistence farming and drastic changes in its social and economic structure.

In the past and to a large extent up to the present time, the productivity of subsistence farming in West Africa has been on a reasonable equilibrium with the farmer's total environment. The traditional method of farming which relies basically on the farmer's own meagre resources of hand labour, natural soil fertility (largely maintained through bush fallow or through the addition of manure†) and intercropping practices still largely satisfies the farmer's security and profit motives. Most farms provide little more than a subsistence and their size is restricted to the area that can be cultivated by hand. Also, the period of cultivation is limited to the rainy season and this imposes another restriction in the size of farm that one man can operate. Both these are labour restrictions

†Manure refers to sources of plant nutrients (e.g., animal manure, compost, refuse) which have not been through an industrial process to differentiate it from fertilizer which has.

rather than land restriction *per se* and force the farmer to limit the area under cultivation to a size which he knows he can handle effectively. Because nearly the whole of the rural population is engaged in subsistence farming, labour for hire is not readily available during the periods of peak demands even if a farmer had money available to hire labour. The average farmer is therefore limited to the labour of his own family and the size of the farm is governed primarily by the size of his family. Since the farmer is limited in the amount of land he can cultivate and has to produce all the food for the coming year during the wet season, he has evolved the technique of multiple cropping largely based on the principle of growing more than one crop simultaneously on one piece of land and thereby achieving a land equivalent ratio† (LER) (Andrews and Kassam 1975) of greater than one. However, because of the subsistence nature of the agricultural economy, the farmer gives first thought to the production of food to satisfy the needs of his family. Consequently, this natural and primary pre-occupation with food crops has resulted in a situation whereby cash crops occupy a second place, are given attention only after the farmer is satisfied of his food supplies, are planted late and do not receive comparable level of husbandry (Ramsey 1968). All these factors reduce the yields of the cash crops. However, the present system of farming offers great advantages to the farmer within his subsistence setting.

At any location climate and the genetic make-up of the plant defines the potential yield that may be possible. However to what extent the potential is realized depends on the availability to the crop of nutrients and water in the soil on the one hand and the control of diseases, pests and weeds on the other. Soil fertility is concerned with the availability of the soil to supply nutrients and water to enable crops to maximize the climatic resources of a given location, but productive capacity of a location or site also depends on how free it is from diseases, pests, and weeds during the growth of crops.

The productivity of a site without interference from man can be defined as its capacity to support the climax population of plants and animals above the soil and the associated flora and fauna in the soil (Cooke 1967). When land is taken over for agriculture man uses his skill to manipulate the aerial, edaphic and biotic elements of the natural environment to his advantage for production of food and other raw material required to sustain life. Shifting cultivation and nomadic pastoralism are simple forms of agriculture where the farmer and herds-man rely on natural soil fertility for food and other products. In these systems man shifts locations continuously to allow the exploited site to replenish its productive capacity. There is a continuous selection for plants and animals which have adequate tolerance or resistance to diseases and pests, and the farmer also imposes a certain measure of control through his cropping and herding time-table. As opportunities for shifting locations become restricted due to population growth and other reasons, maintenance of the required production demands greater skill. The aim of management is to utilize available production resources skilfully so that the required production can be obtained on a sustained basis.

†LER is the ratio of the area needed under sole cropping to one hectare of intercropping, at the same management level, to give an equal amount of produce. LER is the sum of the ratios or fractions of the yield of the intercrops relative to their sole crop yields.

However, the concept of long-term returns from the same piece of land is alien to farmers practising shifting cultivation and to nomadic herdsmen. It is only when farming communities become tied permanently to a given location that a need arises for the use and management of resources in a manner which will produce sustained yields.

In the West African Savanna one of the major consequences of population growth has been the evolution, from shifting cultivation, of grass or bush fallow rotation systems of cultivation. In these systems farmers live in stationary villages and small yields of crops are taken annually on the same piece of land, usually with periods of rest fallow. Consequently, the land is used more intensively† compared to shifting cultivation. The amounts of plant nutrients removed in the crop are small and can be replaced by slow weathering of soil minerals, the natural processes of nitrogen fixation, and the return of crop residues normally in the form of ash. The bush fallow rotation system in the past and to a large extent up to the present time has enabled the farmer to obtain small but adequate yields and maintain soil fertility. However in areas of high population density the area under continuous cropping is expanding and the cropping intensity of the land under bush fallow rotation is increasing to the point where the fallow periods are not long enough to maintain soil fertility although there has been an increase in the use of animal manure, household refuse, and crop residues as ash, to maintain fertility under continuous cropping. However, the supply of these sources of nutrients is always very limited with the consequence that in some areas of high intensity soil fertility under continuous cropping has already suffered (Baker and Norman 1975). Also, the introduction and expansion of cash cropping, which has paralleled the increase in population growth, has further encouraged the exploitation of soil resources.

The other important consequence of population growth has been the expansion of the total area under cultivation, and because the area of land that can be handled by a farmer using simple hand tools is limited, the increase in population has led to an almost proportionate increase in the number of small subsistence farmers. Further, because herding and arable farming are largely separate activities, the increase in area under cultivation and cropping intensity has led to a decrease in grazing area; and consequently the herdsman is being increasingly forced to intensify the exploitation of the area available for grazing.

The above social and economic pressures have already forced farmers into land use pattern where the natural soil fertility is being increasingly strained. It is clear that if husbandry practices do not improve with further increases in population, more land including marginal land will be brought under cultivation in the future; and the land already under cultivation with or without fallows, but using traditional resources only, will inevitably lead to further depletion of soil fertility. The changes which are presently occurring in the traditional pat-

† The word *intensively* is used here to mean that the production per unit area per unit time is greater. Production per unit area during the annual cropping season may be still the same or lower than that in shifting cultivation but because of an increase in cropping intensity, which is a normal feature of the bush fallow rotation system, time allowed for the land to replenish its natural productive capacity is reduced. Cropping intensity is defined as years of cultivation multiplied by 100 and divided by the sum of the numbers of years with cultivation plus the numbers of years with fallow.

terns of land use cannot be reversed; and unless technical improvements are made in the use and management of resources the present low production per unit area is not likely to be maintained indefinitely. It is very possible that the conditions of overcrowded villages and impoverished soils must be attained before better farming methods can spread.

Farming technology employed by farmers, at any level of desired production, involves the use of several kinds of resources. Some of these resources are site specific while some are imported. It is the job of management to integrate the use of these resources into farming methods or technology in order to achieve economically viable cropping systems and production on a sustained basis. Management of resources on the farm implies that the important aerial, edaphic and biotic elements, both natural and artificial, are under the control of the farmer. It is this feature which, when accompanied by high production per unit area, differentiates the high input and high production intensive farming from the low input and low production farming. In the former, all developments in the use and management of resources are made to make farming more productive; and there is no doubt that socio-economic, political, educational, institutional and other forces greatly influence production enhancing development both off- and on-the-farm. This is an area where blue-prints for inducing innovations and change in farming methods are not yet available for the West African Savanna. However, improved farming methods involve multiple inputs which are often interdependent. For example, it is known that if cotton production in the West African Savanna is to increase, improvements are needed as a 'package' involving early sowing of improved variety with better crop nutrition and protection. Improvement in crop nutrition alone without proper crop protection is not likely to produce the desired effect.

Fig. 1.4 is a simple conceptual presentation of some major, on-the-farm, technical components which relate to the use and management of resources for

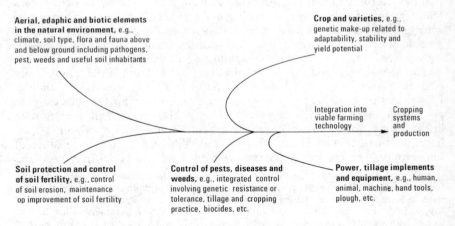

Fig. 1.4. A simple conceptual presentation of major, on-the-farm, technical components which relate to the use and management of resources for crop production.

cropping systems and production. It is generally recognized by agriculturists working in the West African Savanna that if production is to improve major technical changes required in farming methods are those related to better control of soil erosion, improvement in soil fertility, timeliness of operations, use of high yielding improved cultivars, better control of diseases, pests and weeds, and change from hand cultivation techniques to animal and machine cultivation supported by suitable implements and equipment. However, it should be appreciated that technical improvements used to intensify production generally have multiple effects on crop ecology; and unless the total effect is a positive one, sustained improvements cannot be achieved. For example, if hand tillage as practised in the present traditional system is replaced with power tillage to improve timeliness of operations, soil physical conditions and weed control, the total effect on the soil conditions for crop growth may be a negative one if no consideration is given to the effect it may have on the nutrient status of the soil. Power tillage is certainly a means to improve soil physical condition but it also increases the oxidation and decomposition of soil organic matter and availability, in soil solution of nutrients to plant roots thereby decreasing the natural fertility of the soil. If no fertilizer or manure is applied to replace the loss of nutrients in plants and leaching, the total effect on the crop ecology will be a negative one. It should also be realized that improvements in farming methods for increased production require a capital outlay which increases proportionately with the level of production. Innovations in farming methods in the Savanna regions must therefore lead to reliable cash returns to satisfy the farmer's security and profit motives.

However, whether it is considered from the point of view of the nation, the farm owner or the occupier, there is no condition (except that farming is attended with profit) of greater importance than that the fertility of the soil be maintained or increased because upon this mostly depends the power of the soil to produce future crops (Robinson, D. H. 1965). In the West African Savanna this condition cannot be achieved independently of protection measures against soil erosion and leaching.

There is an increasing number of unsatisfied young people in the agricultural sector who drift into towns seeking better opportunities. This is reflected by the rapid increase in urban population and unemployment. A demand for an increased food supply due to the population increase and a lowering of productivity due to the decline in soil fertility, overgrazing and soil erosion, has been met in the past by bringing new areas under cultivation. However, the demand for an increased food supply in the future will have to be met more and more by an increase in agricultural productivity per unit area. At present there are large areas in the West African Savanna which are not under arable farming. However, rural population in these areas will continue to increase for many years to come and if their well-being is to improve within the framework of general economic development of the area, agriculture will have to improve not only to provide more and better food the year round than it does now but to provide productive work for the rural population, food for the urban population, raw material for industries and export, markets for the products of indigenous industries, and provide funds for general rural development (Bunting 1972a). To achieve the above objectives, much will depend on the rate of increase in agricultural productivity per unit area or the area to yield transition (Brown and Finsterbusch 1972).

Chapter 2 provides a general impression and outline of some of the features of the West African Savanna that influence the agricultural scene. In the subsequent six chapters the dominant resources are analysed in some detail in relation to productivity. Chapter 8 is a contribution by Professor D. W. Norman on the farming systems in the West African Savanna and problems of improving them.

# 2 Savanna, history, economy, and background

Between the humid equatorial High Forest and the Desert bioclimates of Trans-Saharan Africa there lie a variety of tropical regions having in common a number of physical and biological similarities. The natural vegetation in these regions is dominated by grassland with varying densities of scattered trees or shrubs (Phillips 1959). Ecologically, the varied assemblages of vegetation within these regions are described as Savanna. Differentiated by variables of climatic gradients but particularly by a seasonal amount and distribution of rainfall resulting in water regimes with marked rainy and dry seasons of varied duration and intensity, these regions carry their own characteristic vegetation. For the greater part the natural vegetation is conditioned by the climate, but there are numerous and significant examples of edaphic control, e.g., the Vertisols. Because the dominant climatic factors and elements affecting the distribution of Savanna vegetation have very pronounced gradients along the north-south axis, the area of West African Savanna is in consequence a strip of territory lying nearly parallel with the equator.

## 2.1 Savanna area

The area can be defined as follows: it extends from the Atlantic Ocean in the west to Central Sudan in the east. The uniformity of the pattern is broken further east by the influence of the Ethiopian mountains and the Red Sea. Because of the uncertainty as regards the boundary of the Derived Savanna successional to the High Forest, the southern limit of the Savanna area cannot be sharply defined. However, from the vegetation maps of the Savanna regions (Phillips 1959) the approximate limit of the southern boundary in respect of latitudinal ($LA$) and longitudinal ($LO$†) position may be described by the equation: $LA = 8 \cdot 2 - LO/11 \cdot 9$. Thus, for example, at $LO = 0$, the southern boundary is approximately at $8 \cdot 2°N$ latitude. This approximate equation excludes the coastal land belt of some 350–400 km wide east of the Atlantic Ocean which is covered by High Forest.

The northern boundary of the Savanna area lies along the fringes of the arid zone of the Sahel-Sahara sub-desert with ground cover that varies locally from open to sparse, supporting woody and sometimes spinose elements, xerophytic grasses and various lowly sub-shrubs and herbaceous vegetation: perennial grasses being short and widely spaced while annual grasses and herbs occurring after the rains (Phillips 1959). Similarly, as with the southern boundary, the northern boundary may be described approximately by the equation: $LA = 18 \cdot 9 - LO/9 \cdot 4$.

†Throughout the book $LO$ is algebraically positive east of Greenwich and negative west of Greenwich.

The total area of the West African Savanna can be thus defined as a strip of territory between the 16°W and 30°E longitude (some 4500 km long) with the southern and northern boundaries described by the equations, averaging about 1100 km in width. Fig. 1.3 is a map of the portion of Africa which contains the area described (Phillips 1959) while the bold lines delineate the approximate northern and southern boundaries of the West African Savanna area. This area of some 4 950 000 km$^2$ includes portions of the territories of the following countries: Senegal, Mali, Mauritania, Upper Volta, Ivory Coast, Togo, Ghana, Niger, Dahomey (Benin), Nigeria, Chad, and Cameroon.

## 2.2 History

### 2.2.1 *Early history*

Because of its geographical position much of the area of the West African Savanna and many of its people during their early history remained isolated and less accessible to the influences of the outside world. Sheltered by the formidable barrier of the Sahara Desert along its northern boundary and the Atlantic Ocean at its western boundary, the area by and large remained impregnable to invaders. Away from the great trade routes of early civilizations, far from the principal centres of technological development, the people of the Savanna developed their own social and political organizations, characterized by a centralized political structure and a hierarchical society.

Although the earliest history of the area is obscure and lacks documentation (both due to the lack of written record and archaeological findings) it has been established that between the fourth and the sixteenth century, there were a succession of kingdoms, their economic and cultural development in no respect inferior to that of many contemporary European or Arab countries. Located at the southern end of the Saharan caravan routes, the prosperity of these states was based on trade in gold, ivory, slaves, and cola-nuts in exchange for salt, copper, glass, and linen (Crowder 1962). According to Arab chroniclers, the oldest and most powerful of these states, the kingdom of Ghana, was founded in the fourth century by Berbers from the south-west Sahara.

The greatest and most decisive event influencing the history of the West African Savanna people was the emergence of Islam and the Arab influence beween the seventh and eleventh century. Thus after the decline of the kingdom of Ghana, the much more powerful and extensive Islamic Empire of Mali emerged. The Mali Empire founded at the beginning of the thirteenth century saw its zenith during the fourteenth century under the reign of Kango Moussa who became famous for his pilgrimage to Mecca in 1324 and his distribution of gold dust to crowds in Cairo. During the end of the fourteenth century the Mali Empire declined enabling the vassal states to break free and extend their own power. A powerful Songhay Empire centred on Gao, and organized under Askia Mohammed (1439–1529) emerged in succession to the Mali Empire, extending from the Air to lower Senegal and from Upper Niger to Central Sahara. At the end of the sixteenth century, a Moroccan expedition overthrew Songhay.

In the central parts of the West African Savanna (south of the loop of the river Niger) Mossi kingdoms were established in the thirteenth and fourteenth centuries. These resisted Islam and continued to do so until recently.

Further east, two great political groups developed during the twelfth century: (1) The kingdom of Kanem-Bornu in northern Nigeria expanding as far as Tibesti to the north and the Nile to the east. Its decline after the end of the sixteenth century enabled the vassal states to become independent. (2) The Moslem state of Baguirmi in Southern Chad and to the east the kingdom of Darfur.

In what is today northern Nigeria the 'Seven Hausa States' were converted to Islam during the fourteenth century. In spite of pressure from Bornu in the east and Songhay in the west in the sixteenth century, these states managed to preserve their independence until the Fulani conquest in the nineteenth century. During the fourteenth century, the Fulani nomads of Western Sudan (thought to be of Caucasian stock) began to move westwards and under the leadership of Manga Diallo reached Hausa country. By the early nineteenth century they had been converted to Islam and had established a great Fulani Empire ruling over most of the Savanna of northern Nigeria.

The spread of Islam since the eleventh century was accompanied by a growth in Arabic learning and culture throughout the Savanna. The main occupation of people was agriculture, their subsistence crops being millet and beans. Over the ordinary peasant farmers was placed a hierarchy of village and district heads, collecting taxes for the support of the central authority, which does not appear to have been absolute, but limited by the power of certain hereditary officials. Although the political and social system approximated the system prescribed by the Koran it included many pagan practices and traditions. (For example, women in society were far more influential.)

The trade carried across the Sahara desert by the caravans of the Berbers helped to introduce domesticated animals and new plants and undoubtedly largely contributed to wealth. The struggle to hold the position of the terminus for the trans-Sahara caravans became a factor that dominated politics (Bovill 1933, 1955).

## 2.2.2 *Modern history*

The second half of the nineteenth century marks the beginning of rapid changes throughout the whole of Africa, because of the European interference and conquest. The rapid growth of population and industrialization in Western Europe was responsible for the search of raw tropical materials and new markets and for the disposal in Africa of the manufactured products which could not be absorbed by their own markets in Western Europe. This led after 1875 to the European scramble and conquest of Africa.

Although the first European contacts with West Africa date back to the middle of the fifteenth century through the progressive establishment of coastal trading posts and chartered companies, these had only an indirect influence on the inland Savanna regions. Penetration inland was too hazardous due to the hostility of both climate and people and the high risk of disease. The major points of coastal colonization were in Senegal (French), in Gambia, Sierra Leone, Gold Coast, Nigeria (British), and Angola (Portuguese). Initially gold and peppers were the major trading commodities which were later on extended to include tropical products such as palm oil and timber. However, with the discovery of the New World the most profitable trade was in Negro slaves. Thus began one of the most remarkable forced migrations in history whereby the pattern of the world's population was radically altered. Some estimates (Crowder 1962) put the total number of slaves exported from West Africa and Angola as high as 24 000 000, of which probably only 15 000 000 survived the notorious Middle Passage across the Atlantic. In the sixteenth century about 1 000 000 slaves were transported to the Americas, in the seventeenth century some 3 000 000 and in the eighteenth century some 7 000 000.

The Congress of Vienna in 1815 forbade trade in Negro slaves but slavery was not abolished until 1833 in British possessions and 1848 in French possessions. In the United States slavery was abolished in 1865 and in Brazil in 1888. The West African slave trade was slowly replaced, after the second quarter of the nineteenth century, by trade in commodities and led to the European penetration into the interior of the African continent as British, French, and German explorers removed the mystery of the 'dark continent'. However, one of the main effects of slave trading on the Savanna of West Africa was the depopulation of its southern parts resulting in a diminished agricultural production that is apparent even today.

The exploration of the interior of the West African Savanna began in 1795 when Mungo Park reached the river Niger at Segou from Gambia. In 1818 Mollien explored the interior of Senegal. The Lake Chad region was explored between 1823–1825 by the Englishmen Gordon, Laing, Denham, and Clapperton and the Frenchman Lyon. Timbuktu was reached by Caille in 1829 and the Sudanese regions between Niger and Chad were explored between 1850–1855 by the German Barth.

The intense competition for raw materials and markets for industrial goods in Europe as well as the concern for a strategic position and prestige finally led to the Berlin Conference and Treaty of 1885 which decided the spheres of influence in Africa. The conference established the right of European powers which already had a foothold on the coastal regions of Africa to annex the hinterland subject to actual occupation. This led to the accelerated activity of European powers through treaties and military conquests to secure colonies. By the beginning of this century the colonial occupation of all Africa was completed and only two independent states remained: Ethiopia and Liberia. Since then the map of colonial Africa changed but little until the Second World War although Germany lost all her colonies after the First War.

In British possessions traditional rulers and chiefs were maintained and allowed to run 'local government' under the supervision of British officials. This had a particular effect on the Savanna region of Nigeria where original institutions of government and traditions were largely left intact and preserved. In the French Empire, on the other hand, administration was always direct and exercised by French officials with a strong tendency towards central control. Much of the French culture and identity with Metropolitan France was implanted.

Economically, the interest of colonial powers was directed towards the exploitation of resources and the control of markets. However, colonialism, particularly British, brought about considerable benefits to the inhabitants: the tribal wars were stopped, law and order was introduced, communications (railways, roads, harbours and telecommunications) developed, modern education and the principle of respect for human rights, fair play and individual merit were propagated, and medical facilities were provided. Modern research, particularly into agriculture, accompanied by the introduction of new crops, improved varieties and modern technology, was introduced and remarkably expanded. The introduction of export crops initiated the evolution from a subsistence production to a commercial commodity economy.

All this progress was comparatively very rapid and must be considered as a foundation stone for the development of modern states. Colonialism however denied the dignity of self-respect in its fullest sense and the desire of people to be responsible for their own affairs and future.

Changes in public opinion after World War II, particularly in Britain, towards the 'glory of imperial rule', preoccupation with the domestic economic problems, and changes in the world balance of power prompted Britain to disengage herself from colonial involvement. This and the rising nationalism in Africa towards self-rule resulted in the grant of independence. Within a few months of 1960, seventeen African countries gained their independence. Ten years later, almost all of Africa was independent.

## 2.3 Population

Statistically, the continent of Africa holds a record of extremes with regard to its population. It is the least populated continent but one undergoing a most rapid growth. The estimated density in 1970 of its inhabitatns was 330 millions averaging 11 persons/km$^2$. Both the birth rate and death rate of 46 and 23 per thousand respectively are amongst the highest in the world. The more recent decline in infant mortality and the dynamic increase in birth rate has resulted in a natural growth rate of 27 per thousand, the highest in the world for the continent as a whole. Further, Africa is populated by young people with 55-60 per cent of the population being under the age of 20 and only 5 per cent over the age of 60. Fifty years ago one out of every 13 inhabitants of the earth was African, today one out of every 10 is African.

The dramatic growth of the African population since the end of the nineteenth century and increase in the rate of natural growth is shown in Table 2.1. This rapid growth of population is attributed to the control of endemic diseases, the improvement in social amenities such as medical care, a clean water supply,

**Table 2.1**
*Estimated population and natural growth rate*

| Year | Estimated population (millions) | Natural growth rate/1000 |
|------|-------------------------------|--------------------------|
| 1900 | 110–120 | |
| 1930 | 165 | |
| 1940 | 191 | |
| 1950 | 222 | 15 |
| 1960 | 377 | 21 |
| 1965 | 310 | 25 |
| 1970 | 330 | 27 |

the spread of education and to the fact that fertility remains one of the most important of feminine virtues. If the present trend is unchecked the population of Africa will double within the next 20–30 years presenting serious economic, social and political problems.

The population density is by no means uniformly spread (Fig. 2.1) but is related to the natural environment that can support the human burden, the level of agricultural technology, the development of transport and communications, and trade and commercial activities. It is estimated that north of the Equator the population is about 220 million or two-thirds of the total population in Africa, of which 113 millions live in West Africa. At least 90 per cent of the population in the West African Savanna live in rural settlements which range from nomadic encampments, dispersed settlements, and hamlets to agricultural villages.

In West Africa urban growth is mainly associated with the coastal areas, and the development of new industries that absorb growing unemployment, trade, and commercial and administrative activities. In the Savanna of West Africa the distribution of population is still largely related to an ancient civilization based on agriculture and the varied activities of trade and crafts.

The desert and sub-desert areas contain a scattered and mobile population constantly seeking pasture and a water supply for its livestock of cattle, camels, goats, and sheep. The density of population rapidly increases southwards reaching an average concentration of more than 50 persons/km$^2$ between the 10°–15° latitude. The highest concentrations of 100–600 persons/km$^2$ are found in Nigeria in Kano State, in Moshi in Upper Volta and in Western Senegal reflecting historical influence and a healthy environment. In many of these areas intensive and continuous cropping presents serious problems with regard to the maintenance or conservation of soil fertility and land degradation. Further south, between 9°–12° latitude, the Woodland Savanna is sparsely populated averaging about 8 persons/km$^2$. This is in spite of the fact that the potential productivity for annual grain crops in West Africa is the highest in this region (Kassam and Kowal 1973, Kassam, Kowal, Dagg, and Harrison 1975a). The area is particularly suitable for intensive cereal production. Its past history, particularly that of the slave trade, and the high incidence of disease in man and stock is largely responsible for a low density of population. The population density increases again further south, e.g., in the Niger valley it is about 20 persons/km$^2$. Although the area has a high amount of annual rainfall, its distribution is bimodal which is less suitable for intensive grain production. Its natural potential is in the production of root crops and pasture.

An interesting example of the edaphic effect on population density is the occurrence of Vertisols, a black heavy clay soil that is highly fertile but too difficult to develop by traditional hand cultivation. Vertisols occur in the Chad basin, the Gombe area in Nigeria, and the Accra Plains in Ghana, and carry an estimated density of population of 5 persons/km$^2$.

Finally, it must be pointed out that the West African Savanna has a very great diversity of people that, eludes a comprehensive classification. These diverse groups or types of people are linked by language and culture. The most important language groups are: Arabic, Hausa, Mossi, Bambara, Tomachek, and Teda.

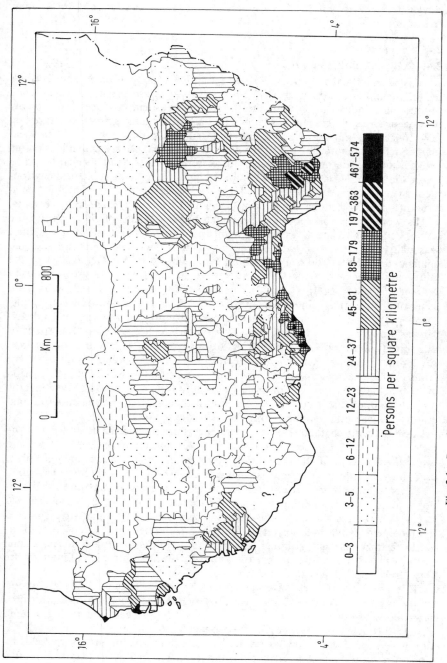

Persons per square kilometre

| 0-3 | 3-5 | 6-12 | 12-23 | 24-37 | 45-81 | 85-179 | 197-363 | 467-574 |

Fig. 2.1. Population distribution in West Africa (Morgan and Pugh 1969).

However the most unifying factor throughout the area is Islam and the Islamic civilization.

## 2.4 Economy

### 2.4.1 *Agricultural economy*

It is estimated that at least 90 per cent of the population in the Savanna region, including a greater part of the people in towns, are engaged in subsistence production. Under this system, the farmer or herdsman produces food for his own needs and supplements this largely by barter for other essential goods necessary to sustain him and his family while surplus production is sold in local markets. The economy of the subsistence farmer is exclusively dependent on his own resources. The main resource at his disposal is labour and his adaptation to his habitat in order to maintain a complex equilibrium of the ecological environment at an acceptable level of productivity. Consequently, the specific social structure and traditions have been developed to meet these requirements.

His work and daily routine are dictated by the seasons of the year and the labour required to meet seasonal agricultural demands. Because of the distinct seasonality of rainfall on which crop production depends, there is a seasonal demand for labour. The peak of labour requirements occurs at the start of the rainy period for land preparation and sowing and later on in the growing season for weeding (Norman 1967, 1972). Since all the work on land is done by hand using the hoe as the main implement, the work is laborious and time consuming. These peaks of labour demand have a direct bearing on the area of land that can be brought under cultivation and on the production volume. The effect of this serious constraint is reduced by traditionally collective labour arrangements. All work on land is performed collectively either by families, traditional age groups or contractual associations set up for specific tasks. However, the period of high activity on farms during the wet season follows a period of long inactivity forced upon them during the dry season that is often associated with community festivals and temporary migrations to the towns.

An important characteristic of subsistence farming and the adaptation of the farming community to the habitat is communal land tenure. In general, the land is a collective asset of the community, the farmer only possesses the right of its use. However, the Islamic land law which recognizes individual tenure has modified this tradition. The current trend towards the individual control of land does not equate to a freehold concept and modern commercial attitudes are not strongly developed in land transactions. There is no direct incentive for land improvement while soil fertility is largely maintained by periods of fallow. Little fertilizer is used, although ashes of burnt refuse or crop residues, animal manure and household refuse are used in maintaining soil fertility. Livestock are very rarely integrated with arable farming.

This non-intensive system of agriculture in the past resulted in little opportunity for trade. However, since the First World War the traditional system of subsistence farming based mainly on food crops has been undergoing a rapid change through the introduction of commercial (cash) crops grown in association with food crops. This has resulted in creation of an important source of income for growers and governments and in an enormous increase of internal trade. The production of groundnuts and cotton in the Savanna regions has expanded rapidly and is at present not only an important source of industrial raw materials earning foreign exchange but also provides a basis for new local industries. The introduction of fertilizers, improved crop material and modern techniques (including irrigation) have had the further drastic effect of modifying or replacing the economy of subsistence production and leading to greater areas under cash crops. However, in spite of the rapid increase in population and the greatly increased area under cash crops, production per unit area of both food and cash crops is low and food production only manages to meet rural needs and part of urban needs with periodic shortages.

### 2.4.2 *Economic growth*

In common with the rest of the developing areas of Africa the Savanna region in West Africa is one of the lowest production and income areas of the world. The average gross national product in Africa amounts to only $160 per head as compared with $4246 in North America, $2071 in Europe, $430 in South America, $200 in South-East Asia. Judging by the economic conditions of those states which are wholly in the Savanna environment, the gross national income of the Savanna region is much lower than the average for the continent, e.g., $49 per capita in Upper Volta.

In spite of the fact that Africa is the principal provider of raw materials for industrialized Europe, all African countries apart from those with large oil revenues have a trade and balance of payments deficit. This is due to the unfavourable price of raw materials in the world markets which showed a tendency to decline during the post-war period. It is also due to lack of industrialization caused by shortages of capital and expertise. Mineral resources are still largely unexploited but without industrialization, the development of mineral resources is unlikely to affect the economy significantly.

The future economic growth in the West African Savanna depends undoubtedly on the rate of change from its largely subsistence production and on the efficiency of the utilization of all natural resources available. In all this, agriculture will have to improve not only to produce more food but to provide employment, raw material and funds for rural and urban economic development.

## 2.5  Relief and hydrography

There are three major drainage systems in the West African Savanna; the Senegal-Gambia drainage in the west, the inland drainage basin of Lake Chad dominated by the Lagone and Chari rivers in the east, and the huge central basin of Niger-Bain-Tilemsi-Benue.

The main characteristic of the river systems is that only a few (the largest) sustain a permanent flow throughout the year. The network of tributaries is extensive, but only a few sustain a flow during the dry season. This characteristic is of major importance to agriculture since it excludes the possibility of using a direct stream flow for large scale irrigation during the dry season.

Larger rivers, such as the Niger, are characterized by vast swampy flood plains. In general the flow regimes of large rivers are influenced by the flow patterns of small rivers, e.g., a rapid drop in flow rates during the dry season.

However, the delaying effect of flood plain storage results in large rivers taking appreciably longer than small ones to recede from the high wet season to the low dry season flow. None the less the flow of most rivers during the fourth month of the dry season is either greatly reduced or stops entirely. In Nigeria for example, towards the end of the dry season, only the Niger with its two tributaries, the Rima and Kaduna rivers, shows a significant flow. In the Chad basin, the Yobe dries in April and the Logone's flow is greatly reduced. Further south, in the Benue basin, the length of the dry season does not exceed 5 months. Consequently, major tributaries of the Benue flow throughout the year, including the Gongola river which is the most northerly tributary.

The most important river of the region is the Niger. The third largest river in Africa, it is some 4200 km long and of great economic importance to the region. It provides an enormous hydroelectric potential, a water reserve for agriculture, a communication line, and fisheries. Rising in the heights of the Guinea Dorsal, it flows towards the centre of the Sahara forming the Sotuba rapids downstream at Bamako in Mali, spreading out further north into a vast inland delta of swamps and lakes. On reaching Timbuktu (about 17° N latitude) it makes a wide bend in the middle of the Sahelian zone and flows south-east towards the Gulf of Guinea. At Lakoja in Nigeria where the Benue joins the Niger, the river is about 3 km wide. Its average flow is estimated to be 7000 $m^3$/sec with a maximum flow of 30 000 $m^3$/sec. The Niger is navigable in stretches between Kauroussa and Bamako, Koulikoro and Asongo, Tillabery and Gaya and south of Jebba.

## 2.6  Geology and geomorphology

A number of accounts on the geology and geomorphology of the region are available (e.g., Haughton 1963, Furon 1963, Dixey 1963). In common with the rest of the African continent, the region of the West African Savanna is much affected by differential erosions of the pre-Cambrian 'shelf' which was planed down, flattened, and transformed into peneplains. Geologically the region could be described as consisting of central basins corresponding to the depressed or subsidence portions of the primitive foundation, flanked by discontinued line and elevated plateau that coincide with the surface of the 'shelf' and its sedimentary covering.

The main basins that have been built up to a great thickness over the course of several geological ages, by marine and continental sediments and of more recent river deposits include: the Senegalo-Mauritanian basin, the western middle Niger basin, the eastern middle Niger basin and the Chad basin. The flat monotony of these plains is broken only by the great Saharan swellings to the north that include Mauritanian Adrar, Iforas Adrar, the Air Mountains and the volcanic Tibesti Mountains. The southern flank includes the Fouta Dyalon Mountains, the Guinea Dorsal, the Nigerian high plateaux of Jos and Bauchi and the Adamawa Mountains. Most of the elevated plateaux rise steeply out of the horizon forming flattened terraces with residual hills of hard rocks exposed by erosion. One of the characteristics of non-sedimentary areas is the occurrence of inselbergs that break the monotony of flat or of a slightly undulating landscape.

The recent quaternary, tertiary, and cretaceous sediments form the bulk of the Savanna region. Primary formations mainly of pre-Cambrian and magmatic rocks that occur largely in the southern parts of the Savanna region account very roughly for about one third of the area.

The geological differences have a profound influence on agriculture affecting soil properties including fertility, and influence drainage and aquifer characteristics. Weathering in primary formations has taken place on a very irregular scale seldom extending to more than 10 m depth of decomposed rock and clay material to serve as an efficient aquifer. The soil surface is often capped by cellular or concretionary laterite that renders the soil infertile.

The mineral resources include high grade iron, bauxite, tin, manganese, phosphate, columbite, uranium, titanium, and gold.

In conclusion it must be stressed that most of the land surface of the Savanna region consists of ancient peneplains of flat-topped plateaux often capped with laterite exposed by recent erosion. Vast areas are covered by transported materials forming clay, loess, or sand plains. Consequently the landscapes are very flat and uniform over long distances lending themselves to intensive agriculture. This large scale uniformity is compensated by surface irregularity (sometimes extreme) caused through ancient termitaria.

## 2.7 Soils

### 2.7.1 *Distribution of soil types*

The distribution of soil types in the Savanna region, described using the terminology of d'Hoore (1964), is presented in Fig. 2.2. Since the d'Hoore classification is essentially climatogenic it is not surprising to see that the distribution of main soil types is closely associated with the climatic and vegetation zones that can be approximately defined by their latitudinal position.

The approximate proportion of various soil types in the West African Savanna estimated from Fig. 2.2 is shown in Table 2.2. It will be seen that the dominant soil of the Savanna is the Ferruginous Tropical soil which covers about 60 per cent of the region. This compares with 11 per cent for the whole of Africa (d'Hoore 1964). Next in extent, about 17 per cent of the area, is occupied by a belt of Ferrallitic and Ferrisols soils which are usually found in more humid areas. A belt of Brown and Reddish-Brown Arid soils bordering the Sahara

**Table 2.2**

*The relative distribution of soil types in the West African Savanna*

| Soil type | Area (%) |
|---|---|
| 1. Ferruginous tropical soils and associated soils | 60 |
| 2. Ferrallitic soils | 10 |
| 3. Ferrisols | 7 |
| 4. Brown and Reddish-Brown soils of Arid and Semi-Arid Areas | 5 |
| 5. Vertisols | 2 |
| 6. Other soils (mainly Hydromorphic) | 7 |
| 7. Rock, debris, ferruginous crusts | 9 |

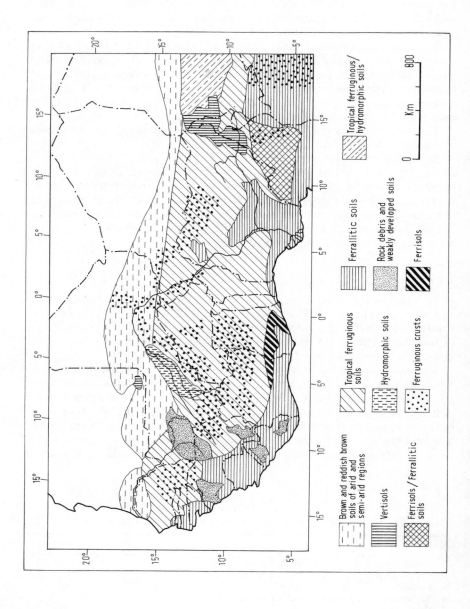

| | Brown and reddish brown soils of arid and semi-arid regions | | Tropical ferruginous soils | | Ferrallitic soils | | Tropical ferruginous / hydromorphic soils |
| | Vertisols | | Hydromorphic soils | | Rock debris and weakly developed soils | | |
| | Ferrisols / Ferrallitic soils | | Ferruginous crusts. | | Ferrisols | | |

desert accounts for about 5 per cent. The Vertisols which are more extensive in the eastern parts of the Savanna occupy only 2 per cent. However, if the study area is extended further east into the Sudan the proportion of Vertisols would be much greater.

Since the classification is based on the mode and intensity of soil evolution, only broad generalizations can be made about the main properties of recognized soil types. The following is a brief description of the main properties of Savanna soils but it should be appreciated that within each soil type there are wide variations. The analytical data are shown in Table 2.3.

(a) *The Brown and Reddish-Brown soils of the Arid and Semi-Arid Regions.* These are soils bordering the desert region and are formed under a hot and dry climate with rainfall rarely exceeding 500 mm. The parent material is often aeolian in origin. Weathering and leaching are slight, so that these soils often contain appreciable amounts of 2:1 lattice silicates. Their physical properties are moderately good but tend to deteriorate rapidly on cultivation. Despite the low content of organic matter and clay in the top soil, exchange capacities are moderate. The agricultural potential of these soils is limited by aridity and thus best utilization is probably extensive grazing.

(b) *Ferruginous Tropical soils.* Considered to be the zonal soils developed under 500–1200 mm annual rainfall and sharply marked by dry and wet seasons, these are highly weathered soils and markedly laterised by the loss of silica. They are usually formed on parent material rich in quartz but not on volcanic, ultrabasic, or calcareous rocks.

A common feature of these soils is the downward movement of clay within the profile, a process which tends to produce a sandy surface soil, rather low in organic matter and base exchange capacity, and compact subsoil where the clay has accumulated. A second feature is the separation of free iron oxides which are deposited in the profile in the form of mottles, concretions, or a ferruginous hardpan.

The soils have usually fairly shallow profiles, most profiles extending to less than 150 cm depth. The clay fraction is predominantly kaolinitic often with small amounts of illite. In the surface horizon clay contents are low but very variable (0–25 per cent) depending on parent material. Cation exchange capacities are therefore also low (1–10 me/100g soil) and depend closely on the soil organic matter status. The soil organic matter is related to rainfall, soil clay content and previous land use, but rarely exceeds 2–3 per cent carbon. In the more arid areas it may be less than 0·5 per cent.

The physical condition of the soils is poor. The bulk density of the surface soil is seldom less than $1·4–1·5 g/cm^3$. The soil aggregates are usually very small and very unstable, with tendency to compact under wet conditions. The water holding capacity of the soil is moderately good, but depends primarily on its structural condition. Most of these soils have a tendency to form surface crusts and are highly erodible.

The agricultural value of these soils is usually rated as poor to average. Nutrient levels, particularly that of phosphate, are low and the soil has a very low buffering capcity.

**Table 2.3**

*Analytical data of major Savanna soils (0–15 cm depth)*

| Soil type | Clay (%) | | pH | | Organic C (%) | | TEB† (me/100 g) | | P (ppm) | |
|---|---|---|---|---|---|---|---|---|---|---|
| | Range | Average | Range | Average | Range | Average | Range | Average | Range | Average |
| 1. The Brown and Reddish-Brown soils of the Arid and Semi-Arid Regions | 4–20 | 7 | 5·9–7·2 | 6·8 | 0·07–0·44 | 0·25 | 1·1–9·3 | 4·3 | 40–194 | 92 |
| 2. Ferruginous Tropical soils | 0–34 | 9·2 | 4·8–8·2 | 6·2 | 0·09–2·84 | 0·62 | 0·7–11·8 | 3·1 | 13–560 | 125 |
| 3. Ferrallitic soils | 0·4–28·1 | 10 | 4·8–7·3 | 6·0 | 0·21–1·79 | 0·83 | 0·4–10·5 | 2·3 | 44–314 | 127 |
| 4. Vertisols | 22–75 | 50 | 4·6–8·8 | 7·1 | 0·35–3·47 | 1·0 | 8–57 | 26 | 75–590 | 194 |

†Total exchangeable bases

(d) *Ferrallitic soils.* These are the climatogenic soils of areas more humid and more strongly leached than the Ferruginous soils. These are the soils of much of the High Forest zone of West Africa, but there are extensive outliers in the Savanna, notably in Nigeria.

The soils reflect the final stages of weathering and leaching, wherein only the least mobile and weatherable constituents remain. Ironstone gravel in the profile is more common and the influence of parent material and slope on the soil profile is much more pronounced. The soils are deeper, better structured, and more fertile than Ferruginous soils but it is most important to appreciate that the maintenance of even a moderate level of available nutrients is dependent on the maintenance of organic matter in the top soil and the return of nutrients in the forest litter. Drainage is good and clay content, consisting of kaolinite, and iron and aluminium oxides, increases only gradually with depth. The cation exchange capacity of the clay fraction is generally below 20 me/100 g. The more sandy members of this soil unit are among the poorest soils in Africa, e.g., some soils in the Derived Savanna of Eastern Nigeria, described by Obihara, Badwen, and Jungerius (1964), have less than 1 me/100 g total exchangeable bases in the top soil.

(d) *Ferrisols.* These are transitional soils between the Tropical Ferruginous and Ferrallitic soils, and are characteristically forest soils. Their occurrence under Savanna is almost entirely limited to a broad area over Basement Complex rocks in the Ivory Coast, Guinea and Southern Mali.

Ferrisols are generally more fertile than either Ferruginous or Ferrallitic soils, have a higher content of exchangeable bases, a better structure and high biological activity (d'Hoore 1964).

(e) *Vertisols.* These are dark coloured heavy clay soils that expand on wetting and are formed from basic materials under poor drainage conditions. The clay fraction contains a high proportion of 2:1 lattice clay and consequently has a high exchange capacity.

The soils are rich in calcium but are usually deficient in phosphate. Because Vertisols contain only small amounts of organic matter (0·5–2·0 per cent carbon), total nitrogen levels are also low and the annual production of mineral nitrogen is usually not sufficient for more than very moderate crop yields.

The development and productivity of these soils depends on heavy investment in drainage, farm mechanization and irrigation. These soils are too heavy for large-scale hand cultivation, the main agronomic problem being the maintenance of aggregates that are formed on cultivation but are unstable, and the provision of effective drainage. The control of salt formation under irrigation management is also important.

### 2.7.2 *General physical and chemical characteristics of soil*

It must be pointed out that the above classification is very broad and includes only major soil types of the West African Savanna. Important variations occurring in these soils are not discussed. Soils that have only a limited distribution within the Savanna, such as Eutrophic Brown soils, are not included either. There is also a large area under Juvenile soils, and quite extensive and economically important Hydromorphic soils which occur in valley bottoms which are widely used during the dry season.

All the soils are extremely weathered, and are physically and chemically friable. They are markedly laterised by the loss of silica, and the resulting free metal oxides often coat the quartz and clay particles, immobilize phosphate, and help to cement or compact the soil, not only at the surface but also in the lower layers where clay accumulates to form a pan-like horizon.

With the exception of Vertisols and Eutrophic Brown Soils, the chemical status of Savanna soils is poor or very poor. Kaolinite dominates the clay fraction which in a cultivated layer of the soil averages about 12 per cent (range up to 60 per cent). The soil organic material level is also low averaging 0·7 per cent of soil carbon within the range 0·08–4·70 per cent. Consequently most soils have a very limited exchange capacity. Phosphate deficiency is widespread, and amounts of oganic nitrogen, phosphorus and sulphur mineralized annually are often well below the requirement for high crop yields, and so need to be supplemented by manures and fertilizers. However, the soils are poorly buffered against changes induced in it by agricultural activities and require very careful management. For example, high and frequent doses of ammonium sulphate reduce the soil pH rapidly to the extent that crop failure may result. The low buffering capacity of the soils is often responsible for nutrient imbalance resulting from a very heavy application of fertilizers under continuous and intensive cropping, inducing micronutrient deficiencies.

The total content of available plant nutrients and bases in soils and ecosystems is small because soluble products of weathering and mineralization are readily and rapidly removed by leaching and because nitrogen, sulphur and other elements may be lost in fires.

Agronomic studies have shown phosphate deficiency in nearly all crops in most parts of the Savanna. Phosphate in conventional fertilizers is often immobilized although acidity, and calcium and sulphur contents are often as important as the phosphate content in determining the shape of response curves. The residual effects of phosphate over several seasons were recorded even from modest fertilizer dressings, an important factor under a non-intensive and low productivity system.

Available nitrogen, approximately proportional to total nitrogen, is generally low, and responses to nitrogen fertilizers have been obtained widely on cereal crops and cotton. In most soils, the peak of nitrate accumulation occurs early in the rains, and four-fifths of the total nitrogen may be in the nitrate form. As the season proceeds, precipitation soon consistently exceeds evaporation and most of this soluble nitrogen is very rapidly lost by leaching unless it is taken up by plant roots. Since in the later part of the season the soil supplies virtually no nitrogen (what little is left may be lost by denitrification as the soils become waterlogged and the water table rises) early planting is important to capture as much as possible of the soil nitrates before they are leached. This is one of the main reasons for the pronounced labour peak at the start of the season, when land (previously too dry to work) has to be prepared, crops planted and weeded in a very short period (Bunting 1972b). Under these conditions the timing of a nitrogen fertilizer application is critical. Under heavy leaching split application is beneficial.

The sulphur status is delicate due to loss through burning and leaching that can be greater than the small contribution from the atmosphere. However, sulphate is conserved by absorption on the clay of textural B-horizons. Sulphur deficiency occurs in groundnuts and cotton and would be more common under experimental conditions but for the fact that phosphate fertilizers applied generally contain sulphur thus masking the deficiency.

The status of soil potassium is usually sufficient and crop responses to potash are rare except under intensive continuous production on soils formed on non-crystalline parent materials.

Deficiencies of calcium and magnesium are rare but may be brought about by the prolonged cropping of poor soils. Lack of calcium is responsible for a low shelling percentage in groundnuts. Of trace elements, boron is often deficient in cotton, and less often, molybdenum in groundnuts.

The physical properties of the Savanna soils have been much less investigated than their chemical properties. In general, however, the soils could be described as having a weak structural development. The aggregates are usually very small and quite unstable in wet conditions. The pore size distribution in cultivated soils changes during the season so that soil water characteristics are more directly related to soil texture than to structure. The surface soil tends to pack early in the season and most soils tend to form surface crusts that reduce infiltration, encourage surface run-off and impede gas exchange. Clay and fine soils are readily mobilized by rain-splash in cultivated soils, and washed away so that with time the texture of the surface layer becomes lighter and less fertile. This process is particularly accelerated under ridge cultivation. Penetration of soil by roots is often superficial but little as yet is known about its cause or effect. Because of heavy rain-splash and the high intensity of storms cultivated land presents a high risk of accelerated erosion. In soil derived from the Basement Complex there is a seasonal rise in the height of the water table. This often results in water-logging and floods affecting crops on the lower slopes of the topography. Consequently crops may lodge, roots die and fertilizer may be washed away. Under such environmental conditions the management of terrain and soil surface requires special techniques and attention.

The chemical and physical properties of Savanna soils are described in more detail in Chapter 4. Good accounts are also given in Charreau (1974a) and Jones and Wild (1975).

## 2.8 Vegetation zones and bioclimatic regions

### 2.8.1 *General*

Nearly all the vegetations of the West African Savanna are fire climaxes consisting of mixed formations of grass and fire resistant trees and shrubs. The density of woody growth varies greatly according to the severity of the annual burn and also with the degree of man's interference, i.e., with the intensity of cultivation, the method of clearing and intensity of grazing.

The existing vegetation in most areas bears little resemblance to the true climatic climax. None the less there is an unmistakable climatic influence on vegetation that is apparent even to a superficial observer. Thus, moving northwards from the 'edge' of the High Forest there is at first densely wooded and vigorous grassland with fire resistant shrubs and trees up to 17 m tall, often referred to as Woodland Savanna. Further north, the Woodland Savanna gradually gives way to less wooded Tree Savanna (with numerous protected trees) resembling parkland. Still further north in more arid areas is Grass Savanna with trees and shrubs either absent or very sparse.

The earliest botanical description and classification of the Savanna vegetation in West Africa was provided by Chevalier (1900), who described three broad zones which he termed the Guinea, the Sudan and the Sahel. The zones are still recognized although they have been modified to include variants by the introduction of new zones (Shantz and Turner 1958, Clayton 1958, Keay 1959, Phillips 1959, Rains 1963, Naegele 1967).

A brief account of the distribution of the natural vegetation in the West African Savanna forming distinct bioclimatic regions is given in the following pages. The account is based on the terminology and the vegetation map (Fig. 2.3) of Phillips (1959).

### 2.8.2  *Bioclimatic regions*

(a) *Desert–Southern Saharan Fringe (Fig. 2.3).* This agriculturally marginal area with very scanty rainfall and no distinct rainy season is a transition zone between northern Sahel and the central true desert. The vegetation is very widely spaced or wholly lacking in some parts. Characteristic plants vary from west to east, consisting mainly of annual grasses and herbs in dry riverbeds and depressions that flush into leaf and flower just after the rains.

Among the most prevalent grasses are *Aristida papposa, Panicum* spp., *Cymbopogon* spp. and *Cenchrus catharticus*. Woody shrubs of importance include *Fagonia cretica, Indigofera* spp., *Leptadenia spartium, Cassia* spp. and *Acacia* spp.

(b) *Sub-desert Wooded Savanna.* Over the distance separating the Atlantic Ocean and the Red Sea many variants of the transitional zone between the Arid Wooded Savanna and the desert region occur; they include most of the Sahel zone defined by Chevalier (1900). This region is characterized by a very prolonged dry season and is largely populated by nomads and pastoral people but also includes some settled agricultural land. The area is strongly influenced by desiccating winds (the Harmattan†) bearing a load of sand and silt that has physiological effects on most forms of life causing discomfort in man and beast alike. The region receives less than 500 mm of annual rainfall that diminishes northwards; it is most irregular in amount and distribution, thus presenting high risks to arable agriculture. The open water evaporation (Penman's $E_0$) ranges from 2100–2800 mm/annum. The greatest agricultural constraint is however the length of the rainy season, the northern half of the region having less than 55 days of the rainy period which is considered to be the minimum required for settled millet farming (Kowal and Adeoye 1973).

The vegetation of the region has been described by Chevalier (1900) and

† Harmattan is the dust-laden wind which blows from NE from the Sahara during the dry season.

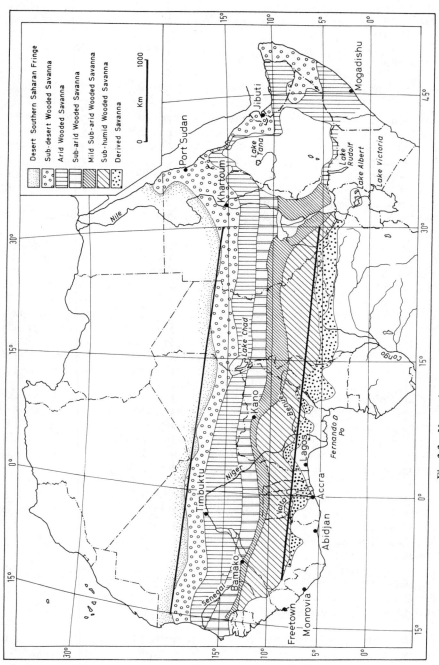

Fig. 2.3. Vegetation map of the Savanna region (Phillips 1959).

Desert Southern Saharan Fringe
Sub-desert Wooded Savanna
Arid Wooded Savanna
Sub-arid Wooded Savanna
Mild Sub-arid Wooded Savanna
Sub-humid Wooded Savanna
Derived Savanna

Km
0          1000

Port Sudan
Khartoum
Nile
Lake Tana
Jibuti
Mogadishu
Lake Rudolf
Lake Albert
Lake Victoria
Lake Chad
Kano
Benue
Congo
Lagos
Fernando Po
Accra
Volta
Niger
Timbuktu
Bamako
Senegal
Abidjan
Freetown
Monrovia

Aubreville (1959). Typical species include *Acacia raddiana*, *A. senegal*, a valued yielder of gum-arabic, *A. laeta, Balanites aegyptiaca, Commiphora africana*, and *Maerua crassifolia*. Important grasses are species of *Aristida, Chloris* and *Eragrostis*. As grass is rarely abundant—especially where it is grazed—fires are less common.

(c) *Arid Wooded Savanna.* Synonymous with Chevalier's (1900) Savane de la zone soudanaise, this region is characterized by open grassland and a rather favourable climate and soils for agricultural production. Owing to a relative freedom from a number of serious human diseases there are high densities of population in many areas. Similarly the absence of certain animal diseases results in large number of domestic livestock. The major climatic features of the region are: 500–800 mm annual rainfall; $E_0$ of about 2200–2000 mm/annum; the duration of the rainy season 70–125 days; considerable water surplus over potential evapotranspiration demands during the peak of the rainy season. These characteristics offer opportunities for a greater diversity of agriculture at acceptable risks.

The natural vegetation include tree species of *Guiera senegalensis*, *Combretum glutinosum*, and *Piliostigma reticulata*, and associated with water courses, *Hyphaene thebaica*. However, the combination of indiscriminate burning and uncontrolled grazing has resulted in the disappearance of perennial grasses from many areas in this zone. The number of perennial species adapted to withstand the long dry season is small, but they are vigorous and compete successfully with the annuals provided that grazing is regulated. Perennials which grow vigorously include *Andropogon gayanus, Anthophora nigritane, Aristida stipoides, Hyparrhenia* spp., *Pennisetum setosum,* and *Urelytrum giganteum*. Commonly occurring annuals include *Andropogon pseudapricus, Aristida* spp., *Cenchrus* spp., *Ctenium elegans, Hyparrhenia* spp., and *Loudetia* spp.

The southern boundary of this zone is economically and agriculturally important. It separates the less productive sub-desert and Arid Wooded Savanna regions sometims referred to as the spiny steppe (van Chi-Bonnardel 1975), from the potentially productive Sub-arid and Sub-humid Wooded Savanna. This boundary can be fairly accurately described in respect of longitudinal (*LO*) and latitudinal (*LA*) position by the equation: $LA = 13 \cdot 7 - LO/8 \cdot 5$.

(d) *Sub-arid Wooded Savanna.* This is a transitional zone of the Northern Guinea and Sudan zones and synonymous with the Sub-Sudan zone of Rains (1963) in Nigeria. The region is still free of tse-tse fly and is intensively farmed. The rainfall is much more reliable but still within the range of 650–800 mm/annum.

The tree cover is extremely variable with the dominant species of *Acacia* and *Balanites aegyptiaca*. The commonest grasses in this zone found in Nigeria are *Hyparrhenia subplumosa* and *H. cynanescens* and annuals such as *Euclasta condylotricha, Loudetia annua, Sorgastrum bipinnatum*..

(e) *Mild Sub-arid Wooded Savanna.* The area receives between 7507–1000 mm rainfall distributed over a period of 120–140 days, and $E_0$ is about 2200 mm/

annum. The region in most areas is intensively cultivated and has a very high potential for grain production.

The region is open woodland with tall grass dominated by *Hyparrhenia* spp., *Brachiara* spp., and *Cymbopogon giganteus*. In Nigeria the region roughly corresponds to part of the Northern Guinea Savanna zone which is essentially an *Isoberlinia–Hyparrhenia* association, and is discussed also in the next section.

(f) *Sub-humid Wooded Savanna.* This is the most extensive and important region of the West African Savanna with a very high potential agricultural productivity. It is much less populated than the adjacent northern regions. At present cattle are excluded from much of the area at least during the rains because of the presence of tse-tse. It is a perennial tall grass country associated with *Isoberlinia* and *Daniellia* tree species.

The northern part of this region is often referred to as the Northern Guinea Savanna (Keay 1959). Here the dominant perennial grass is *Hyparrhenia* in association with *Isoberlinia* and may be regarded as a western extension of the *Isoberlinia–Brachystegia* woodland of Central Africa. Physiognomically, however, it is more like the open woodland of the drier northern areas of Rhodesia than the denser *Brachystegia* woodland of Zambia. Trees commonly occurring in the zone include *Isoberlinia doka, I. dalzielii*, and *Monotes kerstingii*. Around towns and villages it is usual for only the economically valuable trees to have been preserved. Grasses include *Hyparrhenia rufa, H. dissoluta,. H. cynanescens, H. subplumosa, Andropogon* spp., *Cymbopogon giganteus, Brachiaria* spp., and *Pennisetum* spp. The zone is associated with one peak rainfall of between 1000–1400 mm/annum, a 140–190 days duration rainy period and $E_0$ of about 1800 mm/annum. There is very considerable excess of precipitation over evapotranspiration demands during the main period of the growing season. The drought hazards are very low.

The southern part of this region is referred to as the Southern Guinea Savanna zone. It has a more luxuriant vegetation, the tree cover varies from light forest to open Savanna woodland. Among the main trees are *Daniellia oliveri, Lophira alata, Terminalia glaucescens. Isoberlinia* spp. are normally absent. Grasses are numerous in species and rich in bulk, the genera *Adropogon, Cymbopogon, Hyparrhenia, Pennisetum,* and *Setaria* being significant. The re-leafing of the trees—which are largely deciduous—and th ˙ shooting of grasses normally occur before the rains, the hottest period. The rainfall pattern is bimodal with an annual precipitation of 1300–1500 mm, $E_0$ of about 1500 mm/annum, and a rainy season of 190–240 days.

(g) *Derived Savanna.* This region is considered to represent a closed forest which has been reduced as a result of farming activity. It carries atypical vegetation that is mainly influenced by the intensity of man's activity through cultivation, fire and a regeneration period.

## 2.9 Land use and crops

In spite of the low natural fertility of most Savanna soils, the traditional farmer was in the past able to adapt his subsistence farming system in order to maintain an equilibrium with envirionment. His demands on soil fertility were light, most of the land being allowed to revert to bush fallow for a long period after only a few years of cropping. His crop varieties were adapted to low fertility, planting densities were low, and ashes and organic residues were generally returned to the fields. Using fire and hoe, the land was made into ridges which saved him much labour (only half the land area was lifted by hoe). Moreover, through ridging the relatively rich top soil, ashes and plant residues were concentrated within the area of plant roots thereby aiding fertility. Erosion hazards were slight since most of the eroded soil and run-off were intercepted by the surrounding bush.

Today, the population and economic pressures have already changed this pattern in many areas. Fallows have been shortened or have entirely disappeared and the introduction of cash crops has encouraged the exploitation of soil resources. The agglomeration of large areas through continuous cropping results in greatly accelerated soil erosion and since the use of fertilizers is low or non-existent, the soils are being rapidly degraded and are becoming less productive.

The distribution of crops and cropping patterns is largely dependent on the amount and distribution of rains and the resulting length of the growing period. In contrast with the East African Savanna, the rainfall in much of West Africa is very reliable and has a definite pattern regarding the amount and the length of the rainy period. This is reflected in the distribution of crops which in broad terms conforms to the following pattern:

Yams and maize are the principal crops in the wetter areas, cotton and sorghum where it is drier, and millet and groundnuts are found in the areas with low rainfall.

The rural landscape of the Savanna often gives the appearance of disorganized activity with scattered and small fields that are irregular in shape, have ill-defined borders, and include scattered tree stumps. Such a landscape represents a non-intensive system. However, in many of the Northern Guinea and Sudan areas, agriculture is 'intensive' and the countryside presents an orderly look totally committed to arable agriculture.

Arable farming and herding are usually separate activities, although crop residues are utilized by stock animals which are owned and handled by special tribes. Livestock remains a major economic asset much to be desired, with livestock herding (cattle, camel, goat, and sheep) mainly confined to the northern areas free of tse-tse.

The northern parts of the Sahel Savanna and sub-arid areas, between about 19° and 16° N latitude and extending from 0 mm isohyet to the 350 mm isohyet, have a rainy season of less than 70 days. This area is utilized for rangeland grazing. The productivity of this region is low and economically the area must be regarded as marginal for efficient arable production.

The southern parts of the Sahel Savanna, between about 16° and 14·5° N latitude and extending from the 350 mm isohyet to the 5500 mm isohyet, have a rainy season of between 70 days and 100 days. In this region settled arable farming is practised, based on millet, but farmers run the risk of failure due to drought.

Extending from about 14·5° to 9·5° N latitude in the Sudan and Northern Guinea Savanna lies the main cereal production area of the West African

Savanna. Here millet and sorghum are the main food crops. The rainfall in the Sudan Savanna is between about 5500 mm and 900 mm, in the Northern Guinea Savanna it is between about 900 mm and 1250 mm. Millet and sorghum are seldom grown in pure stands but are interplanted with cash crops and other food crops. The principal cash crops in the area are groundnut and cotton. Cowpea, pepper and vegetables are also grown to supplement the cereal diet. Rice, both paddy and upland, is produced in some areas. During the dry season temperatures are low enough for the production of temperate crops such as wheat using irrigation. In upland areas, potato is grown as a cash crop but by far the most important cash crops grown during the dry season are onion, tomato and sugar cane.

South of the 9·5° N latitude, in the Southern Guinea Savanna, increased amounts of root crops are grown, forming a mixed cereal–root zone. Yam, cassava, cocoyam are the predominant root crops either as intercrops with cereals such as sorghum or in pure stands. Yams usually follow the sorghum crop, stalks of the previous sorghum crop serving as a support for the yam vines, and cassava usually occupies the end of the rotation particularly on less fertile soils. This cereal–root zone also includes a variety of crops normally not grown outside the zone such as sesame and soya bean. In addition to cowpea and minor crops such as groundnut and cotton, the zone also supports larger areas of rice and maize.

In the Derived Savanna, bordering the High Forest areas root crops predominate. Maize (sold green on cobs), cowpea and various vegetables are also produced.

# 3 Climatic resources

Climate plays a dominant part in most human activities. Being made up of a variety of elements, active both in respect of intensity and time, climate determines the natural environment which within an ecosystem affects men's agricultural and economic activity. Seasonal rhythms in the climatic elements are reflected by climax vegetation formations, the distribution of soil types and the level of potential and actual agricultural production. Climatic elements have positive and negative effects on the biological processes which contribute towards agricultural productivity. The skill with which climatic elements are manipulated for agricultural production, therefore, greatly determines the extent to which climate becomes an economic asset: the object being that of making an efficient use of the climatic elements which contribute positively to production while minimizing the adverse effects of those contributing negatively.

## 3.1 Maximizing returns from climatic resources

Yet up to the period of about the Second World War, agro-climatology remained mostly a descriptive subject, mainly detailing the relationship of vegetation to climate based on the average values of temperature and precipitation (Griffiths 1966). The application of climatology to agriculture in the developing world is of even more recent origin and has been stimulated by the advances in plant physiology and crop ecology. The main contributing factor to the neglect of climatology in agriculture in the past has been the common misconception that studies of the relationship between climatic elements and crop production have only a limited practical applicability. It was considered that man could not change the weather through an application of his technology; and the adjustment of crop characteristics and agricultural practices to manipulate the climate in tropical areas was considered not to be of significant importance to affect productivity. Emphasis was placed on the exploitation of natural soil fertility, supplemented by manures and fertilizers where available, as a practical means of increasing productivity with little regard to potential crop productivity as determined by climate. Consequently, recommendations for agricultural developments were based more on the use of soil management under low fertility level than on fully exploiting the climatic and plant genetic resources.

This in the past has led to slow progress in exploiting agricultural potential of the Savanna areas, and some large scale development projects produced disastrous results. The failure of the Tanganyika Groundnut Scheme, for instance, is now partly attributed to a lack of climatological information and its correct interpretation. Further, the use of fertilizers in the under-developed tropics was economically not justifiable under the conditions of subsistence farming; and fertilizer technology introduced from temperate climate conditions without adjustments to a tropical environment requiring special forms of fertilizers, improved cultivars, and soil and crop management, gave disappointing results.

Furthermore, research emphasis and meagre research resources in the under-developed tropics were directed towards soil classification, which was supposed to reflect indirectly the climatic resources, but to our knowledge has proved to be of little immediate practical application. The traditionally accepted prac-tice of defining the so-called 'climatic analogues' primarily in terms of monthly means of temperature and precipitation (Nuttonson 1947) or the use of an eco-logical classification of natural vegetation and soils as a guide to plant introduc-tion or land use planning, can no longer be regarded as a sufficiently accurate index.

In order to minimize empiricism in selecting crops and cultivars for a parti-cular area or choosing an area best suited for the production of specific crops or analysing and synthesizing farming systems, a detailed analysis of climatic variables together with an intimate knowledge of plant responses to climatic parameters is required. Although there are still large gaps in our knowledge regarding the eco-physiological bases of crop productivity, a great deal has been achieved in the last ten years. Whereas earlier the climatic resources of the Savanna areas were considered marginal for crop production, today this is no longer the case. However, to maximize the return from climatic resources, the genetic make-up of the crops and the pattern of their growth requirements must match as far as possible the available pattern of the climatic elements which con-tribute to productivity.

An excellent example and indeed pioneering work in this respect is provided by Cocheme and Franquin (1967) in their book, *A study of agro-climatology of the semi-arid area south of the Sahara in West Africa* and the subsequent publica-tion by Brown and Cocheme (1969) *A study of the agro-climatology of the high-lands of East Africa*. Their work provides an assessment of climatological vari-ables with specified confidence limits so that a reliable inventory of climatic resources can be matched to known requirements of crops and cultivars. Of course, crop performance is also influenced by soil fertility, cultural practice, pests, and diseases, but no crop can achieve real importance in an agricultural system unless it is well adapted to the existing climatic conditions.

Climate assumes significance in nearly every phase of agricultural activity: from long-range planning to daily operation and the selection of sites for agrono-mic experiments. Many agronomic experiments and fertilizer trials conducted in West Africa for decades took little account of the variation in the climatic potential for growth in different regions. Consequently, the variations in the results obtained have been difficult to interpret. An example of variation in biological responses to climatic variables in Nigeria is given by Kassam and Kowal (1973) who demonstrated that the rates of dry matter production and economic yields of certain crops in the Savanna areas are twice as high as they are in the High Forest environment. This clearly indicates that the assessment of agronomic treatments or fertilizer response in substantially different environ-ments without an adjustment for differences in climatic variables could be mis-leading.

Of dominant interest is the water regime since the extent of crop growth and duration in the Savanna is entirely dependent on the availability of water. Para-doxically, during the growing period crops are exposed to drought, leaching, and flooding. Thus the control and management of water in rain-fed and irrigated farming through the management of drainage, the terrain, and the soil surface is far more important in the Savanna than in temperate regions.

The water regime can be assessed from an analysis of rainfall characteristics, crop water requirements, soil water storage, and evaporation rates by means of a water balance account. This technique allows one to estimate and identify the amount and periods of water deficiency or water surplus, and the length of the growing season with a reasonable accuracy. The length of the period of water availability in any particular area can then be matched with the growth cycle of crops or cultivars ensuring an increased efficiency of production and providing the agronomist or plant breeder with information to serve as a basis for further improvement.

Since 1970 a considerable amount of work has been done at the Institute for Agricultural Research, Samaru, Nigeria (representing the climatic conditions of the Northern Guinea Savanna) on the pattern of availability of water and water use of several crops: sorghum (Kowal and Andrews 1973), maize (Kowal and Kassam 1973a), cotton (Kowal and Faulkner 1975), groundnuts (Kassam, Kowal, and Harkness 1975b), millet (Kassam and Kowal 1975). These studies were conducted at one lysimeter site during five different seasons. The pattern of water use by crops during the growing season was assessed from the continuous function of the ratio $ET/E_0$ plotted against the time (Dagg 1965, 1970). In the ratio, $E_0$ is the Penman (1948) estimate of open water evaporation and $ET$ is the actual evapotranspiration of the crop measured by the weighing lysimeter. The pattern of crop water use determined at Samaru can be used to determine crop water requirement for other areas in the Savanna region. Further, these crop water use studies were complemented by measurements of radiation and energy balances and crop growth analyses, allowing an assessment of assimilation rates and efficiency of production.

Several quantitative models have been recently developed (de Wit 1959, Monteith 1965, 1972, Duncan 1967) to describe the potential photosynthesis of crops. The concept links rationally several meteorological and plant factors with crop production, on the assumption that water, nutrients, and crop health are not limiting growth. The value of the concept is not unlike that of potential evapotranspiration (Thornthwaite 1948) in providing an insight into the basic relations between climate and crop production. It provides a means of replacing statistical and descriptive relations between climate and crop performance with a quantitative solution in which cause and effect can be identified and adequately assessed. Field experiments can be designed using the potential photosynthesis approach as a guide to exploring environmental and physiological limits on the rate of production of dry matter and yield; and a comparison between the measured rates of growth and potential photosynthesis can be used to assess the efficiency of production (actual/possible) indicating the extent of the gap that may exist between the actual production on farms or experimental stations and the possible utilization of environmental resources for primary and secondare production (de Wit 1965, Chang 1970, van Ittersum 1972, Monteith 1972). This may suggest means of increasing production by changes in crop husbandry and/or by breeding of new crop cultivars.

In the following pages of this chapter the climatic activity of the West African Savanna is described and assessed in relation to agriculture.

## 3.2 Climatic factors and elements

In order to describe the climatic activity and resources of a region in a logical manner it is convenient to draw a clear distinction between the factors and elements of applied climatology. By the definition of Griffiths (1966), 'a factor is a determining cause of a phenomenon, an aspect that gives rise to certain effect, while an element is a component part of that effect'. The recognized climatological factors are: air masses and ocean currents. The major elements of applied climatology are: solar radiation, sunlight, cloudiness, temperature, precipitation, humidity, wind, and evaporation.

The circulation of air masses and ocean currents is a function of an astronomical (geometry of the solar system) and geological (land–sea configurations) nature, and of fundamental importance to weather characteristics. The theory and detailed description on general circulation of ocean currents and air masses is beyond the scope of this book, and readers are referred to Brunt (1941) and Byers (1959). Let it suffice here to point out that the dominant climatic factor affecting the seasonality and climatic activity of the West African Savanna is the circulation of two predominant air masses, the Harmattan and the Monsoon. The circulation and interaction of these two air masses has a dominant effect on the pattern of occurrence, duration and intensity of individual climatic elements. The ocean current has only a minor effect on the inland Savanna; its main influence is on irregularity in the pattern of the distribution of climatic elements in certain coastal areas, e.g., Accra Plains, Mauritania, and Senegal.

To simplify the discussion on the climatic activity, the above climatic factors and elements are examined separately with some consideration given to important interactions.

## 3.3 Circulation of the atmosphere over West Africa

The most significant feature of atmospheric circulation over West Africa is the interaction of three major air masses (Walker 1962). Of these, two are normally in contact with the ground, meeting along the Inter Tropical Convergence Zone (ITCZ) that oscillates along the south–north axis, determining seasonality of the dry and rainy periods and the distinct climatic characteristics of each period.

The first air mass flowing from the sub-tropical anticyclones of the south Atlantic ocean inland in a general south-west to north-east direction, referred to as the Monsoon or the Tropical Maritime, has a long history of sea tract and consequently is laden with moisture evaporated from the ocean. For example Warri, in the Niger delta, and lying under this air mass throughout the year, has mean monthly values of relative humidity in the range 95–99 per cent at 0600 hr and 65–85 per cent at 1200 hr. The relative humidity of this air mass remains relatively constant with altitude to about 2000 m but falls off sharply above it. The decrease in temperature with height in this air mass is small.

The second air mass flowing from the sub-tropical Azores anticyclone and its extension over the Sahara is referred to as the Harmattan or the Tropical Continental. It has a long history of desert track before reaching the Savanna region as north-easterly winds. The surface layers of this air mass are dry with a large decrease in temperature with height. The relative humidity is low at all levels. For example, Sokoto in northern Nigeria during the five months from December to April shows mean monthly values of relative humidity in the range 23–38 per cent at 0600 hr and 10–17 per cent at 1200 hr.

These two winds blow alternately over the Savanna region and largely condition the weather. The Tropical Maritime and the Harmattan approach the tropics from opposite sides of the equator flowing towards each other. The belt into which they flow is known as ITCZ, a region of ascending air. The air rising through decreasing pressure is cooled by expansion, condensation takes place, thick clouds are formed and precipitation occurs. The rainfall is seasonal due to the northward movement of the rain bearing ITCZ within which the humidity accumulated in the Monsoon stream is precipitated. The ITCZ oscillates north and south tending to follow the zenithal position of the sun with a time lag of four to six weeks.

Within this system of ITCZ it is important to recognize the distinct weather zones of particular significance to agriculture. In general, going from north to south the following pattern emerges (see a, b, c, d in Figs. 3.1 and 3.2).

(a) At the actual boundary of the two air masses little rainfall occurs because the lifted air is too dry to cause precipitation (Fig. 3.2). The Harmattan air overrides the Tropical Maritime to give the latter a wedge shape which increases in thickness southwards. Rain does not usually occur unless the wedge is about 2000 m thick, several hundred kilometers to the south of the location of the ITCZ on the ground surface. However, the humidity of the air is sufficiently increased to trigger off the biological activity in the natural vegetation. The environment is hot and unpleasant for humans.

(b) Further south a zone is met that might be some 400 km wide where rainfall occurs mainly from localized cumulus clouds as scattered showers of medium intensity, originating the start of the rainy period. The irregularity of rainfall in this zone due to the advance and recession of the moist air currents has a very serious consequence for arable agriculture in the Savanna region. The start of rains coincides with the most intensive and critical period in agricultural management and peak labour requirements. Because of the rainfall irregularity during this period, the start of the rainy season is seldom sharp and the frequent occurrence of 'false starts' results in high hazards for seedling survival that is reflected in poor crop establishment leading to serious economic loss. Furthermore, variations in time of the onset of rains affect the duration of the growing period (the retreat of rains being much less variable) and has serious repercussions on crop productivity due to the shortening of the growing period. This is of particular importance at higher latitudes where the growing period in average years is characteristically of much shorter duration.

(c) Still further south there is a zone of about 1000 km wide where disturbance lines predominate. Here clouds are composed of bands of active cumulonimbus bringing rain to hundreds of thousands of square kilometres. The rainfall is usually an intensive downpour lasting for a few hours and sometimes followed by several hours of less intensive rain. Between 8° N and 16° N, the annual

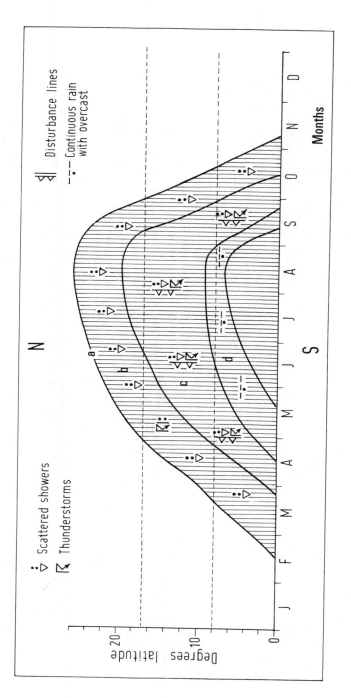

Fig. 3.1. The seasonal movement of the ITCZ system over West Africa (Cocheme and Franquin 1967).

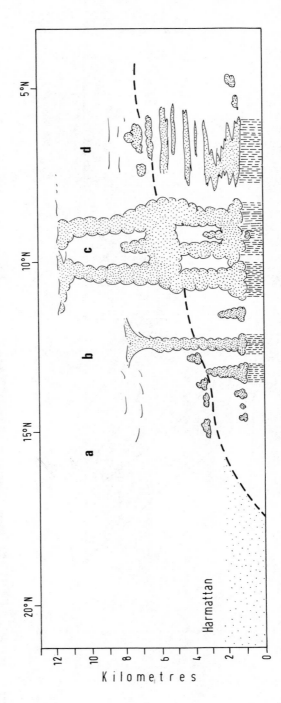

Fig. 3.2. Diagrammatic vertical cross section of air circulation from north to south. The dotted line represents the surface boundary between the two air masses, the Harmattan and the Tropical Maritime (Cocheme and Franquin 1967).

characteristic of rainfall distribution is one peak (unimodal). Because of the lack of geographical diversity the rainfall regime is one of pronounced uniformity and regularity when viewed on a broad scale. The drought hazards are minimal and conditions during the wet season are exceptionally favourable for arable agriculture.

(d) Lying to the south of the zone in c and beyond the limit of the convergence zone is a belt some 300–400 km wide characterized by more prolonged precipitation of lesser intensity but less regular with some rainless periods. The characteristics of annual rainfall distribution is marked by two peaks (bimodal). The skies are cloudy to overcast for most of the time. Although this zone has a prolonged rainy period, the rainfall distribution is less favourable for arable production. Crop water requirements are more difficult to match to the pattern of rainfall distribution; cloudiness reduces radiation income, resulting in lower daily assimilation rates while day and night temperatures show little variation inducing higher respiration losses and excessive vegetative growth.

The seasonal movement of the ITCZ over West Africa is presented graphically in Fig. 3.1. It will be noted that there is some correlation between the latitudinal position and the onset, retreat or duration of the influence of ITCZ. It is therefore not surprising that such a relationship with the latitudinal position also exists with the other climatic elements.

## 3.4 Influence of ocean currents

The ocean currents have direct or modifying effects on the climate. Warm ocean currents reinforce tropical humidity along the coast and have a moderating influence on the temperature. On the other hand, cool sea currents enhance aridity.

The main sea currents along the West African coast (Figs. 3.3 and 3.4) are the Benguela and Canaries currents carrying *cold* water from the south and north respectively flowing towards the equator. The South Equatorial current which is a *warm* current flows from the west towards the African continent but is deflected southwards at too great a distance from the shores to affect the climate directly.

The inland regions of the Savanna are too distant from the direct influence of the sea except for the western parts. Thus the southern Mauritanian coast and northern Senegal are subject to the influence of the cool Canaries current that moderates the temperature of the coastal area and causes climatic abnormality as evident by the increased aridity in these areas.

Indirectly, however, the climate of the Savanna region is influenced by the sea since most of the recharge of atmospheric humidity occurs at sea. The prevailing winds from the south Atlantic ocean, already very moist, become even wetter on contact with the warm sea currents. As the rain-bearing air mass moves inland the distance from the sea becomes important. The air mass gives progressively less total rainfall, firstly because it is continually losing moisture as rainfall along its path northwards, and secondly because the duration of its influence decreases from south to north.

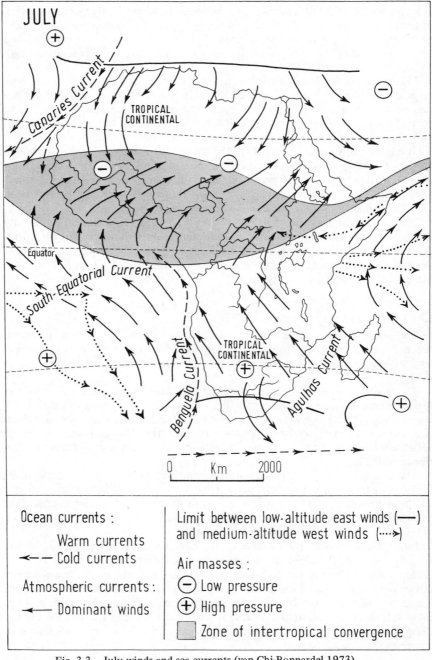

Fig. 3.3. July winds and sea currents (van Chi-Bonnardel 1973).

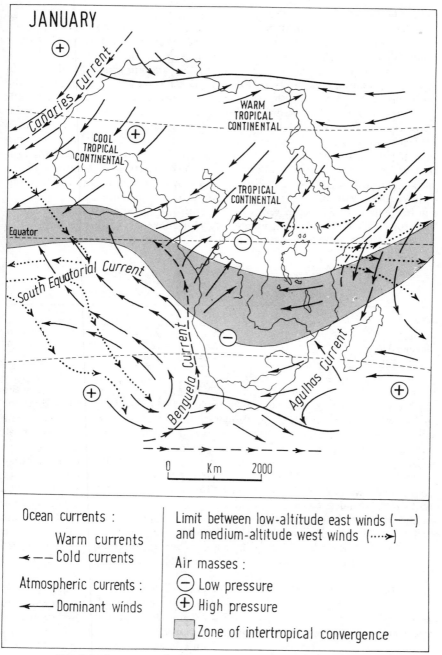

**JANUARY**

Canaries Current

WARM
TROPICAL
CONTINENTAL

COOL
TROPICAL
CONTINENTAL

TROPICAL
CONTINENTAL

Equator

⊖

South Equatorial Current

Benguela Current

Agulhas Current

⊕          ⊖          ⊕

⊕

0          Km          2000

Ocean currents :

    Warm currents

◄——Cold currents

Atmospheric currents :

◄———Dominant winds

Limit between low-altitude east winds (——)
and medium-altitude west winds (····➤)

Air masses :

⊖ Low pressure

⊕ High pressure

▨ Zone of intertropical convergence

Fig. 3.4.  January winds and sea currents (van Chi-Bonnardel 1973).

### 3.5  Solar radiation

Solar radiation is the most important and basic asset of the natural environment. Its variation during the seasons gives rise to differences in temperature and pressure affecting the circulation of the air masses, ocean currents, precipitation and evaporation regimes. In agriculture, the amount and distribution of incoming radiation sets limits to the dry matter production of crops and the productivity of agricultural systems. Radiation provides the two essential needs of plants: the light required for photosynthesis, and thermal conditions for normal physiological functions. The sun gives out radiation at an approximately constant rate equivalent to about 2·0 cal $cm^{-2}$ $min^{-1}$ (8·4 J $cm^{-2}$ $min^{-1}$) on a surface normal to the beam and at the earth mean distance from the sun. This solar flux varies ±3 per cent with changes in the distance from the sun due to the earth's elliptical orbit. The combined motions of the rotation of the earth about its own tilted axis and its revolutions round the sun produce an annual north–south oscillation of the apparent daily orbit of the sun above the local horizon. This results in differences of radiation receipt above the earth's atmosphere in respect of its latitudinal position on earth.

**Table 3.1**

*Solar radiation at the top of the atmosphere (kcal/$cm^2$)*

| Lat. °N | 5° | 10° | 15° | 40° | 50° |
|---|---|---|---|---|---|
| Annual | 311·6 | 307·3 | 301·9 | 241·1 | 213·0 |
| Summer half-year | 160·9 | 164·9 | 167·7 | 167·6 | 156·0 |
| Winter half-year | 149·6 | 142·4 | 134·2 | 81·5 | 57·0 |

The magnitude of annual and seasonal amounts of radiation receipt above the earth's atmosphere in kcal/$cm^2$ at latitudes within the West African Savanna region and at Mediterranean and temperate latitudes are given in Table 3.1. The annual receipt of radiation within the Savanna region is fairly similar for all latitudes averaging about 307 kcal/$cm^2$ which is about 20 and 30 per cent greater than at 40° and 50° N latitudes representing the Mediterranean and temperate zones respectively. During the summer period the radiation income of about 160 kcal/$cm^2$ is similar in all latitudes including the Mediterranean and temperate latitudes. During the winter period the radiation is much lower than in the summer period. Furthermore, the values sharply decrease with increase in latitude. In the Savanna region the values are reduced by 10–20 per cent as compared with the values during the summer period, dropping to about 30 and 50 per cent in the Mediterranean and temperate latitudes respectively.

### 3.5.1  Depletion and sacttering of short-wave radiation

As solar radiation passes through the atmosphere it is depleted and scattered in a number of ways. About one-third is usually reflected back to space, mainly from clouds, and smaller amounts are absorbed and scattered diffusely by various atmospheric components, so that on average only about half of the sun's radiation finally reaches the earth's surface. However, the proportion of depletion varies markedly in different climates, reaching as high as 60 per cent in tropical rainy climates, and as low as 40 per cent in the arid regions with little clouds. The amount of depletion also depends on the solar air mass (the length of the beam's path through the atmosphere) since the highest concentration of dispersing and absorbing materials are found near the ground level. Thus high altitude areas receive a relatively greater proportion of the total incoming radiation.

The radiation reaching the earth's surface is referred to as incoming short-wave radiation or global radiation. It comprises of two components, a direct solar beam and diffuse sky radiation. Under clear sky conditions the direct beam generally accounts for about 90 per cent of the total intensity with the sun overhead to about 80 per cent with the sun at 20° elevation. Under overcast skies all radiation received at the surface is diffuse radiation. The distinction between direct and diffuse short-wave radiation in agricultural research is of some importance since there are differences in the photosynthetic response and the albedo (reflection coefficient).

The direct measurements of global radiation $(R_i)$ in West Africa are few, and for the assessment of radiation income in the Savanna region it has been necessary to use the Angstrom (1924) empirical formula, $R_i = R_A (0.18 + 0.55 \, n/N)$, where $R_A$ is the radiation at the top of the atmosphere and $n/N$ the observed fraction of total possible sunshine hours. Because the Campbell–Stokes sunshine recorder used in the estimation of sunshine hours fails to record diffuse radiation under cloud cover and also underestimates sunshine at low solar altitudes, the calculated $R_i$ values are underestimated by about 7 per cent as compared with measured values (Kowal 1972a).

There are distinct patterns in the distribution of short-wave radiation in respect of geographical position and the seasons.

### 3.5.2 Annual values of short-wave radiation

There is a very pronounced tendency for the annual radiation receipt at the earth's surface to increase northwards along the north–south axis. There is also a strong tendency for the similar values of the annual radiation receipt to be aligned along lines slightly inclined to latitudinal parallels. The isolines therefore tend to incline northwards as one moves from west to east.

Because of these pronounced tendencies it is possible to describe quantitatively the annual short-wave radiation in different parts of the Savanna region by means of a multiple regression equation. The relationship between the amount of annual radiation $(R_i)$ and any geographical position described by latitude $(LA)$ and longitude $(LO)$ in degrees and decimals of a degree, estimated from 51 stations within the Savanna region is:

$$R_i(\text{annual}) = 307.4 + 11.46 \, (LA) + 1.67 \, (LO) \text{ cal cm}^{-2} \text{ day}^{-1}$$

(correlation coefficient, $r = 0.74$)           (3.1)

In spite of the scatter of values and distinct anomalies particularly in the extreme eastern and western parts of the region the equation describes adequately the amount and regional distribution pattern of annual radiation. The values range from 388 cal cm$^{-2}$ day$^{-1}$ (142 000 cal cm$^{-2}$ annum$^{-1}$) along the southern boundary to 480 cal cm$^{-2}$ day$^{-1}$ (175 000 cal cm$^{-2}$ annum$^{-1}$) along the northern boundary.

The average gradient in the radiation receipt along the north–south axis is 11·5 cal cm$^{-2}$ day$^{-1}$ (4197 cal cm$^{-2}$ annum$^{-1}$) per degree latitude. Assuming an annual conversion efficiency of solar radiation into primary production of one per cent, the increased gain from the radiation receipt per one degree latitude northwards is equivalent to about 1050 kg/ha of plant dry matter. This might be taken to represent the relative differential in productivity in the region along its north–south axis.

The alignment of the radiation isolines in respect of longitudinal parallels averages about 1·67 cal cm$^{-2}$ day$^{-1}$ (610 cal cm$^{-2}$ annum$^{-1}$) per degree. The values increase from west to east, and approximately for every 6·8 degrees longitude there is a corresponding change in the annual radiation receipt equivalent to a change in one degree latitude.

### 3.5.3 *Seasonal values of short-wave radiation*

Since agricultural activity in the Savanna region is largely seasonal, depending on rainfall, it is important to distinguish between radiation receipt during the growing period and radiation income during the dry season.

It is obvious that certain assumptions and definitions are required in order to describe a season before assessing the seasonal radiation regimes. Thus the growing season is defined as a consecutive number of ten-day periods in the year in which the evapotranspiration demand of crops is met. Assuming that crops can mature without ill effects after the end of the rains on 10 cm of water stored in the soil profile, the growing season can be taken to be the number of consecutive ten-day periods between the start† and the end‡ of the rains plus the number of ten-day periods after the end of the rains which is equivalent to the evapotranspiration losses not exceeding 10 cm.

The above definition of the growing season emphasizes the moisture availability to crops and is therefore a practical assessment of the length of the period for successful crop production. The units of ten-day periods used in the definition of the growing season are large and consequently introduce an error in the assessment of seasonal radiation regimes, but it is doubtful whether the use of shorter periods would be more meaningful in practical terms.

(a) *Short-wave radiation during the growing season.* The radiation data from 51 stations within the region was used to assess the distribution of seasonal radiation in respect of the latitudinal and longitudinal position using the multiple regression technique. The regression line was found to be:

†The assumption is made that a recharge of the surface soil by 2·5 cm of water will allow for the cultivation of land, and an amount of rainfall in the following decades of at least half the potential evapotranspiration ($E_t$) will sustain crop growth. The start of the rains is defined therefore as the standard ten-day period in which rainfall is greater than 2·5 cm and with two subsequent ten-day periods of precipitation greater than half the potential evapotranspiration.

‡End of rains is defined as the last ten-day period of the rainy season with at least 1·25 cm of rainfall and $E_t$ in the prevous ten-day period not less than precipitation.

$R_i$ (growing season) $= 163\ 591 - 7686\ (LA) - 375 \cdot 7\ (LO)$ cal/cm$^2$ per season

$$(r = -0 \cdot 90) \tag{3.2}$$

The multiple correlation coefficient for equation (3.2) is much higher than in the case of annual $R_i$ in equation (3.1). It will be noted, however, that the values decrease northwards along the north–south axis which is in contrast to the pattern of annual distribution of $R_i$. The values range from about 38 000 cal/cm$^2$ per season along the northern boundary to about 100 000 cal/cm$^2$ per season along the southern boundary (Fig. 3.5). This large difference in seasonal values within the southern and northern boundaries of the Savanna region is due to large differences in the growing period. The values are indicative of the potential productivity of various parts of the Savanna region under rain-fed agriculture for the growing season as a whole. Again, assuming one per cent conversion efficiency into net photosynthesis the values correspond to 9·5 tonnes and 25 tonnes of dry matter along the northern and southern boundary respectively (see section 15.2 for the definition of the northern boundary for arable production).

The average gradient in the radiation isolines along the north–south axis is 7686 cal/cm$^2$ per season per degree latitude. Thus, again, assuming a photosynthetic conversion efficiency of one per cent, for each degree latitude southwards there is an increase in the potential dry matter production of about 1921 kg/ha per season due to the increase in the length of the growing period.

The radiation values when expressed as radiation per day of the growing period gave the following regression equation:

$$R_i \text{ (growing season)} = 322 \cdot 5 + 9 \cdot 66\ (LA) + 0 \cdot 02\ (LO) \text{ cal cm}^{-2} \text{ day}^{-1} \tag{3.3}$$

Thus, there is in actual fact a slight increase of about 10 cal cm$^{-2}$ day$^{-1}$ for each degree latitude northward. However, although there is a significant increase of radiation income with increase in latitude the increase is much less than the radiation gain due to the increase in the length of the growing season southward.

(b) *Short-wave radiation during the dry season.* Because there is a considerable surplus of water in the Savanna region that could be utilized in supplementary or dry season irrigation, the radiation regime during the dry season is of considerable agricultural interest.

The amount of short-wave radiation receipt during the dry season is positively correlated with latitude. The multiple regression equation is:

$R_i$ (dry season) $= -51\ 375 + 11\ 869\ (LA) + 982\ (LO)$ cal/cm$^2$ per season

$$(r = 0 \cdot 93) \tag{3.4}$$

The radiation isolines along the northern and southern boundaries of the Savanna region are about 142 000 and 49 000 cal/cm$^2$ per dry season respectively. This enormous amount of solar energy which is presently largely unused during the dry season is equivalent to 35 and 12·5 tonnes of dry matter along the northern and southern boundaries respectively, assuming a net photosyn-

thetic energy conversion efficiency of one per cent. The gradient along the
north–south axis is about 11 870 cal/cm$^2$ per dry season per degree latitude
while the gradient from west to east is about 980 cal/cm$^2$ per dry season per
degree longitude, increasing eastwards.

### 3.6  Radiation balance

On reaching the vegetation and/or ground surface, the incoming short-wave
radiation, is partly reflected and partly back radiated. The remaining, known as
the net radiation $(R_n)$, is the most important quantity of incoming radiation
dominating the microclimate in which plants grow, providing energy input for
all biological processes.

Quantitatively the net radiation is described as the difference between
downward and upward radiation fluxes as:

$$R_n = R_i(1 - \alpha) \pm R_b \qquad\qquad (3.5)$$

Here, $\alpha$ is the short-wave reflection coefficient (albedo) and $R_b$ is the net long-
wave radiation exchange between the surface and atmosphere.

In other words the equation describes the energy input and output resulting
from all the radiation fluxes to and from the ground/vegetation surface during
the day-time and night-time. It must be emphasized that $R_n$ is a surface phenomenon and its values depend not only of $R_i$ but on $\alpha$ and $R_b$ both of which are
surface dependent.

### *3.6.1  Reflection coefficient ($\alpha$)*

The short-wave reflection coefficient ($\alpha$) is defined as the ratio of the amount
of $R_i$ reflected by a surface to the amount of incident $R_i$ upon it. The proportion of reflected radiation depends on solar elevation, surface colour and
moisture content, crop cover and canopy structure, and cloud cover.

At low solar elevations the $\alpha$ is high but decreases with increase in sun angle.
This is reflected by diurnal variations during the day when at a low sun angle
during the early morning and early evening the values are high and may reach
30–40 per cent, levelling off to lower values at higher sun elevations (Rijks
1967). Similarly changes in solar altitude in respect of latitudinal position affect
$\alpha$. Similar surfaces have different values at different latitudes. The comparatively
low reflectivity in the tropics is a consequence of the greater solar elevations.

In general reflection increases with the brightness of the surface. The darken-
ing effect caused by wetting of a light coloured surface lowers the reflection
coefficient. This is particularly evident in the Savanna region. Thus, for example,
at Samaru the reflection coefficient of dry soil is about 28 per cent but on wetting decreases to between 10–14 per cent.

The reflectivity of a cropped surface is particularly affected by the canopy
development and structure. During the early stages of crop development when
ground cover is incomplete the coefficient is high because of the high reflectivity
of the soil. The values decrease gradually as the canopy develops and ground
cover increases due to the reduction in the area of exposed soil and because part
of the radiation is trapped by the leaves of the developing canopy. A dense

canopy structure with erect leaves significantly traps more radiation and due to multiple reflection within the canopy reduces the reflection coefficient. Typical changes in the reflection coefficient during the growing season measured at Samaru for maize and millet crops are shown in Table 3.2. Reflection coefficient measured over a lake at Samaru was 0·08. Values of $\alpha$ for different surfaces and climatic zones of Nigeria are given in Oguntoyinbo (1974) while typical values of $\alpha$ measured world over are given in the Smithsonian Meteorological Tables (SMT 1951), Brooks (1959), van Wijk (1966), and Monteith (1973).

**Table 3.2**

*Reflection coefficient ($\alpha$) of maize and millet crops at Samaru (Kowal and Kassam 1973a, Kassam and Kowal 1975)*

| Period | Maize | Millet |
|---|---|---|
| 21–31 May | | 0·26 |
| 1–10 Jun | | 0·25 |
| 11–20 | 0·26 | 0·26 |
| 21–30 | 0·21 | 0·23 |
| 1–10 Jul | 0·19 | 0·15 |
| 11–20 | 0·18 | 0·15 |
| 21–31 | 0·17 | 0·13 |
| 1–10 Aug | 0·16 | 0·14 |
| 11–20 | 0·16 | 0·13 |
| 21–31 | 0·15 | 0·14 |
| 1–10 Sep | 0·15 | 0·17 |
| 11–20 | 0·14 | 0·15 |
| 21–30 | 0·14 | |
| 1–10 Oct | 0·13 | |

Cloud cover reduces the reflectivity by proportionately increasing the diffuse radiation which is almost independent of solar elevation thus modifying and/or reducing the diurnal changes and daily values.

### 3.6.2 Long-wave radiation ($R_b$)

Since all bodies above absolute zero temperature radiate continuously, the earth radiates too, and some of the $R_i$ absorbed is re-radiated with long-wave-length characteristics into the atmosphere and space. However, atmospheric absorption and therefore the emission of radiation is much greater for the long-wavelength than for the short-wavelength, and much terrestrial radiation is absorbed by the atmosphere and re-radiated back to the earth surface. The atmospheric absorption of terrestrial radiation depends in a complex manner on radiation wavelength. Apart from a low absorption within the $0 \cdot 8 – 1 \cdot 4\mu$ wave-length band which escapes freely into outer space ('spectral window'), about 90 per cent of the radiation from the earth surface is absorbed in the atmosphere by water vapour, clouds, ozone and carbon dioxide. This 'atmospheric blanket' mechanism is very efficient so that the *net* long-wave radiation lost from the earth surface is appreciably less than that originally emitted.

It will be now appreciated that both the heating and cooling of the surface by radiation are intensified by clear skies, dry air, and a lack of vegetation. Consequently $R_i$, $R_n$, $R_b$, and $\alpha$ during the wet and dry seasons are expected to have different regimes and will be considered separately in respect of the two seasons.

Estimates of the net outgoing radiation can be obtained with sufficient accuracy using the Brunt (1941) equation which relates the downward long-wave radiation from clear skies with vapour pressure measurements at screen height:

$$R_b = \sigma T_k^4 (0.56 - 0.079 \sqrt{e})(1 - aC) \tag{3.6}$$

In the equation $\sigma$ is the Stefan-Boltzman constant, $T_k$ is the absolute mean air temperature, $e$ is the vapour pressure of the air in millibars, $C$ is the cloudiness and $a$ is a constant depending on cloud type. If data for cloud type is not available the term $(1 - aC)$ can be roughly approximated in terms of actual $(n)$ and possible $(N)$ hours of sunshine by $(1 - n/N)$ as used in the Penman equation:

$$R_b = \sigma T_k^4 (0.56 - 0.079 \sqrt{e})(0.10 + 0.9 \, n/N) \tag{3.7}$$

The $R_b$ values estimated from the above formula for a period of the growing season at Samaru are very similar to the values derived from the direct measurements of components in the equation $R_b = R_n - R_i (1 - \alpha)$.

Measurements at Samaru indicate that during the growing period the long-wave radiation averages between 18–21 per cent of the incoming radiation. This is not excessive and results in only a moderate nocturnal cooling of the soil and air. However, when the air is very dry and skies are clear as in the dry season the $R_b$ is expected to be much higher. Consequently diurnal variations in the soil and air temperatures are expected to be and indeed are very pronounced. This has a very important consequence in agriculture, limiting the choice of crops that can be grown efficiently under irrigation during the dry season. Such crops must be adaptable to high day and low night temperatures. The hazards of frost damage although very infrequent are real and have been witnessed by the authors near Samaru. In the low lying area (*fadama†*), used extensively for irrigation, the combined effect of rapid cooling due to excessive $R_b$, evaporation, and the sinking of cool air from the upper areas results in very low night temperatures which can adversely affect crop growth.

### 3.6.3 Net radiation $(R_n)$

Direct measurements of net radiation in the West African Savanna are few. However, measurements at Samaru, northern Nigeria (Kowal 1972a, Kowal and Kassam 1973a, Kassam *et al.* 1975b, Kassam and Kowal 1975) indicate that during the growing period, the measured values of day-time net radiation over various crop surfaces range between 50–65 per cent of the short-wave radiation.

Kowal (1972a) found that the average regression line for measured day-time net radiation during the growing period was: $R_n = 0.65 \, R_i - 36$. A similar

---

†*Fadama* is low-lying land which is seasonally flooded or has a high water table and can be cropped during the dry season as well.

regression line, $R_n = 0.612\,R_i - 28$ for West Africa is quoted by J. A. Davies (1967).

Measured data of $R_n$ for the dry season in the Savanna region are not available. The reason for this is that without water the dry season is unproductive and there is also some difficulty in generalizing or describing the characteristics of the land or crop surface. However, as a result of the pronounced aridity and changes in the land cover that ranges from bare land and burnt vegetation surfaces to surfaces covered with dried up grassland with few scattered green trees and bushes, the reflection coefficient and the net long-wave back radiation increases considerably, resulting in very low dry season $R_n$ values.

Since there is a lack of measured net radiation data in the Savanna region an assessment of the pattern of net radiation in the region must be based upon calculated values. These are derived using the assumed reflection coefficient of 0.25, the Brunt equation for estimating $R_b$ values, and the Angstrom equation for estimating $R_i$ values. It must be emphasized that the $R_n$ values thus derived are strongly dependent upon the assessment of sunhsine hours $(n/N)$ and because of a number of assumptions or empirical relationships, the values must be regarded only as approximations.

(a) $R_n$ *during the growing season.* The regression analysis of the calculated net ratiation values in respect of latitudinal and longitudinal positions gave the following equation:

$$R_n \text{ (growing season)} = 127\,126 - 6010\,(LA) - 268\,(LO) \text{ cal/cm}^2$$

$$(r = -0.82) \tag{3.8}$$

The negative correlation is the result of a decrease in the length of the growing period with increase in latitude. The gradient in $R_n$ along the south–north axis is 6010 cal/cm$^2$ per season for each degree latitude. This amount of net radiation is equivalent to energy required for the evaporation of about 10 cm of water. The net radiation isolines for the growing period are about 20 000 cal/cm$^2$ per season along the northern boundary and about 80 000 cal/cm$^2$ per season along the southern boundary of the Savanna region.

The $R_n/R_i$ ratio, calculated from the $R_n$ and $R_i$ regression equations, is about 0.44. This low ratio is probably due to an under estimation of the $R_n$ values resulting from assuming the reflection coefficient of 0.25. The more realistic $\alpha$ during the crop cycle is nearer 0.15–0.17 that would increase the $R_n/R_i$ ratio to within the expected range of values.

(b) *Annual values of* $R_n$. There is little to be gained from the analysis of calculated annual $R_n$ values since they would be largely dependent upon the characteristics of the intercepting surface. Thus the values would be affected by the management of land during the dry season, e.g., fallow, irrigation, mulch. Those interested in the distribution of monthly $R_n$ values in relation to time and geographical position are referred to Cocheme and Franquin (1967) and Kowal and Knabe (1972).

### 3.7 Energy balance

By applying the principle of energy conservation through equating all incoming and outgoing energy flux densities at the earth surface, an energy balance can be drawn up, indicating how available energy is being used.

Net rate of incoming energy per unit area is equal to net rate of outgoing energy per unit area as described in the equation:

$$R_i (1 - \alpha) \pm R_b = G + H + LE + P_n \tag{3.9}$$

where  $G$  =  ground heat flux density
$H$  =  atmosphere sensible heat flux density
$LE$  =  evaporation heat flux density
$P_n$  =  photochemical energy flux density

Since $R_i (1 - \alpha) \pm R_b = R_n$, the energy budget equation can be written as:

$$R_n = G + H + LE + P_n \tag{3.10}$$

showing that the net radiation energy is dissipated in four ways. Seasonal values of the various components of the energy balance at Samaru for a well managed crop of maize is shown in Table 3.3.

### Table 3.3

*Seasonal values for the components of the energy balance
for maize during the period 11 June to 10 October at Samaru
(Kowal and Kassam 1973a)*

| Components | cal cm$^{-2}$ day$^{-1}$ | Per cent of $R_n$ |
|---|---|---|
| Net radiation ($R_n$) | 319 | 100 |
| Transpiration ($E_p$) | 174 | 54·5 |
| Soil evaporation ($E_s$) | 73 | 22·9 |
| Evapotranspiration ($ET = E_p + E_s$) | 247 | 77·4 |
| Air heat flux ($H$) | 54 | 16·9 |
| Soil heat flux ($G$) | 12 | 3·8 |
| Net photosynthesis ($P_n$) | 6 | 2·0 |

Two thirds of the net energy was dissipated as latent heat while about 17 and 4 per cent of the energy was used for heating the air and the soil respectively. Consequently the day temperatures during the wet season are not too high and show relatively little fluctuation. The night temperatures during the wet season are not far different from the day temperature because of low net losses from back radiation due to cloud cover and relatively low surface temperatures due to wetter soil.

During the dry season, when the land lies bare or is under scanty natural vegetation cover, with little water available for evaporation and transpiration, the bulk of net energy is used in heating the air and soil. This causes a rise in air and soil temperatures during the day. It is not uncommon to find the surface temperature on bare soil under these conditions to be 70–80°C at noon. The high surface soil temperature is of some significance. It serves, for example, as a very effective sterilization agent for various pests and pathogens but at the same time may have an adverse effect on the useful soil inhabiting micro-organisms.

Since the skies are relatively clear and day-time air and soil temperatures high, there is much back radiation at night with a consequent drop in night temperatures. The low night temperatures are below optimum temperature conditions required for satisfactory production of tropical crops and restrict the choice of crops which can be grown efficiently under irrigation.

Between the extreme conditions of the well watered vegetation during the growing season on the one hand and the arid conditions during the dry season on the other, there is a wide range of conditions. Consequently the variation in the components of the energy budget is also wide.

Special mention must be made of irrigated areas during the dry season. Considerable difficulties are encountered in assessing the energy balance under irrigation conditions due to the horizontal divergence of advective energy from the surrounding semi-desert conditions. The magnitude of the advective term in small irrigated fields may equal the net radiation term and becomes responsible for excessive evapotranspiration rates. Measurements at Samaru of an irrigated plot of maize forming an 'oasis' in a very arid area gave evapotranspiration rates of about 10–12 mm/day, resulting in poor growth. Measurements over lake Makwaye, Samaru, indicated that a fetch of 60–75 m is required to nullify completely the advective influence.

## 3.8 Sunlight

Most of the radiant energy from the sun is contained in the wavelength spectrum in the range $0 \cdot 3$–$4\mu$. However, not all the wave bands within the spectrum have a direct effect on plants. The most important wave band which is used in photosynthesis is the range $0 \cdot 4$–$0 \cdot 7\mu$ and is known as 'photosynthetically active radiation' (PAR). The human eye is also sensitive to radiation in this spectrum band and it is therefore referred to as light or visible radiation. In general, wavelengths greater than $1\mu$ have no known direct effects on plants while those shorter than $0 \cdot 3\mu$ are detrimental; and radiation of less than $0 \cdot 28\mu$ wavelength rapidly kills plants.

Analyses of theoretical calculations and a range of experimental measurements (Sceicz 1974) including some at Samaru (Monteith 1972) have shown that PAR as a fraction of the total (direct + diffuse) radiation is almost independent of atmospheric conditions and is nearly constant at $0 \cdot 50 \pm 0 \cdot 03$. Thus, measurements of total solar radiation can be used confidently in estimating efficiencies of photosynthesis and crop growth.

The length of day varies with latitude and time of the year; and the time of flowering in many crop plants in the Savanna region is influenced by the relative duration of day and night. This effect is referred to as photoperiodism which is essentially a photo-stimulus process as against photosynthesis which is a photo-energy process. The influence of photoperiod on the time of flowering, growth and yield in photoperiodic plants is discussed in chapter 7 on crop resources.

### 3.8.1  *Photosynthesis*

Photosynthesis in plants is the basic thermodynamic step which agriculture exploits to convert and store solar energy into chemical energy both in plant and animal products. About 90 to 95 per cent of the dry weight in the plant is derived from photosynthesis. During photosynthesis, electromagnetic energy present in the visible portion of the solar radiation is converted into the chemical energy needed by green leaves to reduce carbon dioxide and synthesize plant carbohydrates. Photosynthesis takes place in the chloroplast, and the overall process can be described by the equation:

$$CO_2 + 2H_2O + \text{Light} \longrightarrow (CH_2O) + H_2O + O_2 + 112 \text{ kcal/g-atom of C} \quad (3.11)$$

The photochemical energy is used in the first stage to remove electrons from water and produce oxygen and a weak reductant. A second photoact is involved in the further transport of electron to nicotinamide adenine dinucleotide phosphate (NADP); the reducing power, ultimately in the form of NADPH, together with adenosine triphosphate (ATP) produced by photophosphorylation during electron transport, is used to reduce carbon dioxide to the level of carbohydrate $(CH_2O)$. Therefore, the process of photosynthesis consists of two quite separate series of reactions: those related to the trapping of light energy (the light reactions), and those concerned with carbon fixation (the dark reactions). The conversion of carbon dioxide into complex organic compounds during the dark reactions is therefore accomplished using the ATP and NADPH generated energy, initially trapped during the light reactions. Carbon fixation is thus not directly dependent on light but only on the products of the light reactions. Accounts of various aspects of photosynthesis are given in Fogg (1968), Hatch, Osmond, and Slatyer (1970), Zelitch (1971), Hall and Rao (1972), and Zelitch (1975).

The two most important pathways of carbon fixation in crop plants are the $C_3$-pathway (Calvin and Bassham 1962) and the $C_4$-pathway (Hatch and Slack 1966); and plant species can be classified into two distinct groups based on several distinct characteristics related to the pathway of carbon fixation (Black 1971). These two groups are, 1) the high capacity producers or the $C_4$ species, and 2) the low capacity producers or the $C_3$ species (Table 3.4). Leaves of efficient crop species such as sorghum, millet, maize, and sugar cane have rapid rates of net carbon dioxide assimilation (40–80 mg $CO_2$ per hour for each square decimetre of leaf area) at high light intensity in normal air at 25° to 40°C or more (Zelitch 1971). These species produce malate or aspartate (4–carbon compounds) as the first detectable product (Hatch and Slack 1966). Hence, they are referred to as the $C_4$ species. Leaves of most other crop species such as rice, wheat, tobacco, groundnut, cowpea and cotton, with few exceptions, assimilate carbon dioxide at rates about one half or less of the $C_4$ species. The first product of carbon dioxide fixation in the species belonging to the low capacity producers group is 3–phosphoglyceric acid which is synthesized by the operation of the Calvin cycle pathway (Calvin and Bassham 1962).

The difference between gross photosynthesis and net photosynthesis or growth rate is due to respiratory losses; and two sources of respiratory losses of

## Table 3.4

*Characteristics which distinguish high and low capacity producers (Black 1971)*

|  | High capacity producers ($C_4$) | Low capacity producers ($C_3$) |
|---|---|---|
| 1. General type of plant | Herbaceous and mostly grasses or sedges | Herbs, shrubs or trees from all plant families |
| 2. Morphology: leaf characters | Bundle sheath cells around vascular bundles packed with chloroplasts | No chloroplasts in the bundle sheath cells |
| 3. Physiology: rate of photosynthesis | 40–80 mg $CO_2$ $dm^{-2}$ $h^{-1}$ in full sunlight. Light saturation at full sunlight or greater | 10–35 mg $CO_2$ $dm^{-2}$ $h^{-1}$ in full sunlight. Light saturation at 10–25% full sunlight |
| 4. Response to temperature | Growth and photosynthesis optimal at 30°–45°C | Growth and photosynthesis optimal at 10°–25°C |
| 5. $CO_2$ compensation point | 0–10 ppm $CO_2$ | 30–70 ppm $CO_2$ |
| 6. Sugar transport out of leaves | Rapid and efficient, 60–80% in 2–4 h at high temperature | Slower and less efficient, 20–60% in 2–4 h |
| 7. Water requirements (g $H_2O$ to produce 1 g dry matter | 260–350 | 400–900 |
| 8. Carbon fixation | Predominantly $C_4$ pathway but also $C_3$ | $C_3$ pathway only |
| 9. Photorespiration | Not present or negligible | Present |

dry matter in plants have been recognized; one, due to dark respiration known to occur in mitochondria (James 1953, Stiles and Leach 1960, Beevers 1961), the other, due to photorespiration believed to occur in peroxisomes (Tolbert and Yamazaki 1969, Frederick and Newcomb 1969, Hatch *et al.* 1970, Zelitch 1971). Photorespiration differs biochemically from dark respiration and is entirely dependent on current photosynthesis for substrate (Zelitch 1975). It therefore occurs in the photosynthetically active tissue during photosynthesis only. However, the exact function of photorespiration is still unknown. Dark respiration, on the other hand, occurs in all living parts of the plant, day and night, and is necessary for the provision of energy for essential biochemical reactions concerned with growth, maintenance and synthesis of ATP.

However, it appears that the maximum rates of gross photosynthesis between some of the $C_3$ and $C_4$ species are similar, e.g., tobacco and maize (Zelitch 1971), indicating that a greatly different gross photosynthetic capacity is not responsible for the large difference in net photosynthesis of leaves and crop growth rate usually observed between the $C_3$ and $C_4$ species (see also Table 3.5). Most of the difference is explained by the fact that photorespiration in $C_3$ species is considerable, whereas in $C_4$ species it is negligible or small. Although the exact

## Table 3.5

*Net energy conversion efficiency ($\epsilon$) as per cent of total radiation of some experimental crops at Samaru during the growing season (Kassam 1972)*

| Crop | Fixation pathway | $\epsilon$ (per cent) Seasonal | At maximum growth rate | Source |
|------|------------------|----------|-------------------------|--------|
| Millet: Ex-Mokwa | $C_4$ | 2·24 | 4·80 | A. H. Kassam, unpublished |
| Ex-Bornu | $C_4$ | 2·08 | 3·20 | A. H. Kassam, unpublished |
| Sorghum: Farafara | $C_4$ | 1·90 | 2·30 | Goldsworthy (1970a) |
| Short-Kaura | $C_4$ | 1·28 | 2·00 | Goldsworthy (1970a) |
| Samaru Hybrid | $C_4$ | 1·18 | 2·22 | Goldsworthy (1970a) |
| NK 300 | $C_4$ | 1·22 | 2·78 | Goldsworthy (1970a) |
| Maize: 096 | $C_4$ | 1·34 | 2·15 | Kowal and Kassam (1973) |
| Biu Yellow | $C_4$ | 1·31 | – | A. Abdullahi, unpublished |
| Bomo Local | $C_4$ | 1·34 | – | A. Abdullahi, unpublished |
| Cowpea: 593 | $C_3$ | 0·25 | – | A. H. Kassam, unpublished |
| Wheat: Indus 66 | $C_3$ | 0·37 | – | D. J. Andrews, unpublished |
| Groundnut: S38 | $C_3$ | 0·48 | 0·98 | A. Bromfield (1973) |
| Cotton: Okra Leaf | $C_3$ | 0·56 | 1·33 | J. B. Smithson, unpublished |
| Normal Leaf | $C_3$ | 0·78 | 1·85 | J. B. Smithson, unpublished |
| Kenaf | $C_3$ | 0·91 | 3·68 | E. F. I. Baker, unpublished |
| Roselle | $C_3$ | 1·20 | 3·44 | E. F. I. Baker, unpublished |

magnitude of photorespiration in the $C_3$ species is not known, it is thought to be between 20 to 50 per cent of gross photosynthesis (Hatch 1970, Zelitch 1971, K. J. Treharne, private communication 1975). In general, seasonal crop growth rate of the $C_4$ species is two to three times the crop growth rate of the $C_3$ species; and maximum growth rates of the $C_4$ species are in the range of 30–60 g dry weight per square metre of land per day, while those of the $C_3$ species are 10–30. Consequently, for a unit of water transpired during photosynthesis, the $C_4$ species can produce two to three times more dry matter than the $C_3$ species.

The difference in the rate of photosynthesis between the leaves of the $C_3$ and $C_4$ species is shown in Fig. 3.6. In $C_3$ species the maximum rate of net photosynthesis is 10–30 kg dry matter $ha^{-1}$ land $h^{-1}$ while in $C_4$ species 30–60. Also the saturation light intensity of leaves of the $C_3$ species is reached in the range of 1000–4000 foot candles (1 cal $cm^{-2}$ $min^{-1}$ of total solar radiation = 6000–7000 foot candles of visible radiation) while with leaves of the $C_4$ species it is difficult to reach saturation even at full sunlight. This does not mean that a high efficiency of energy conversion cannot be achieved with the $C_3$ species. For example, the fibre crops, kenaf and roselle, sown at a very high density for fibre production can have high energy conversion efficiency values (see Table 3.5)

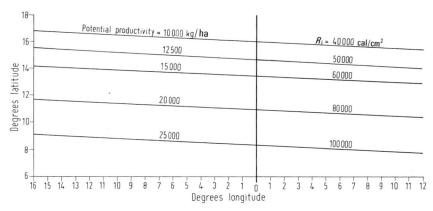

Fig. 3.5. Distribution of radiation during the growing season and potential productivity at energy conversion efficiency of 1·0 per cent.

because of their better canopy structure which allows light to penetrate deeper into the crop canopy without over-saturating the top most leaves.

One of the consequences of the high optimum temperature for the $C_4$ species is that they do not perform efficiently during the dry season when temperatures are low. However, breeding high yielding $C_4$ species particularly maize and sorghum for low temperature and highland conditions has met with very good success; therefore although maturity is delayed in maize and sorghum, high yields are possible under cooler conditions. On the other hand, some $C_3$ species such as cotton, groundnut, and cowpea perform better in the more warmer conditions during the wet season than in the dry season, while some such as wheat, potato, and onion perform better during the dry season. Therefore, although there is a large difference in the photosynthetic capacity between the $C_3$ and $C_4$ species, the range in temperature requirement in $C_3$ species is wide and some species perform better under medium temperature conditions (25–30°C). However, temperature conditions (30–45°C) best suited for the $C_4$ species are generally too high for the $C_3$ species. Temperature requirements for vegetative and reproductive growth for individual crops are discussed in chapter 7 on crop resources.

For rational and efficient utilization of the climatic resources of temperature, radiation and water, a choice of crops should be based as far as possible on matching the physiological adaptability characteristics to the pattern of distribution of these climatic elements. In general, the temperature and radiation conditions during the wet season in the Savanna region favour the production of the $C_4$ species and the $C_3$ species with higher temperature requirements (Kassam, Kowal, and Sarraf 1977, Kassam 1977). During the dry season under irrigation conditions, temperature conditions favour the production of the $C_3$ species which are temperate in their requirements.

### 3.8.2 Efficiency of energy conversion

The radiation in the wavelength range 0·4–0·7μ (PAR) is utilized by the

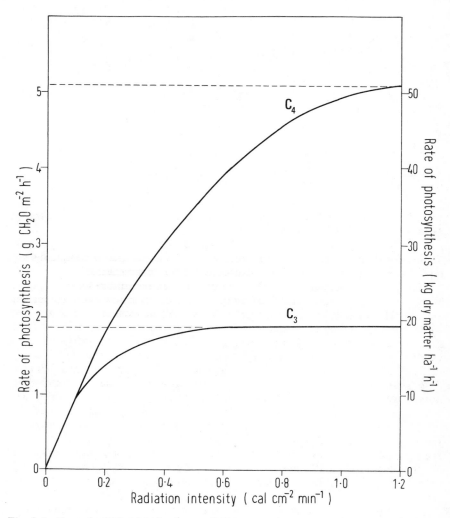

Fig. 3.6  General relationship between radiation intenstity and rate of photosynthesis for leaves of $C_3$ and $C_4$ plants (Black 1971).

chlorophyll to assimilate carbon dioxide during photosynthesis. As a photochemical process, photosynthesis is subject to the photochemical law which states that each molecule taking part in a chemical reaction induced by exposure to light absorbs one quantum of radiation causing a reaction. In actual fact the synthesis of one molecule of plant dry matter ($CH_2O$) requires one molecule of carbon dioxide and energy of 10 light quanta (Hill, R. 1970), since additional light energy is needed to form complex intermediate products.

Blue and red regions of the PAR are very strongly absorbed by the chlorophyll while green is reflected and transmitted. Taking into account the quantum difference between the radiation of different wavelength within the $0.4-0.7\mu$ range, it can be shown that the average energy content of one quantum of visible radiation is $8.57 \times 10^{-20}$ cal (Monteith 1972). Since the energy stored in one molecule of $CH_2O$ is $1.84 \times 10^{-19}$ cal, and assuming that 10 quanta are required for the photosynthesis of one molecule of plant dry matter, the theoretical amount of light energy which can be converted into chemical energy of plant carbohydrate is:

$$\frac{(1.84 \times 10^{-19}) \times 100}{10 \times 8.57 \times 10^{-20}} = 21.5 \text{ per cent} \tag{3.12}$$

This assumes complete absorption of light by leafy pigments. However, under field conditions some 15 per cent of incident radiation ($R_i$) is lost in reflection and a further 15 per cent is transmitted and absorbed by the inactive parts of the foliage. Further, measurements show that PAR on average is about 50 per cent of the incoming radiation (Sciecz 1974). Therefore, the maximum conversion efficiency is $0.215 \times 0.85 \times 0.85 \times 0.50 = 0.078$ or about 8 per cent of the total incoming radiation.

(a) *Estimation of net assimilation rate.* In an assessment of the efficiency of energy conversion it is convenient to deal with the biological or total yield, and to regard the separation into useful and non-useful parts as a separate problem. Any measure of plant biological yield can be converted into an energy equivalent using 4000 cal/g as a general average for all kinds of plant material (Westlake 1963, Sestak, Catsky, and Jarvis 1971). Accepting the theoretical efficiency of energy conversion as 8 per cent of total radiation, the relationship between the gross rate of dry matter production ($P_g$) in a g m$^{-2}$ day$^{-1}$ and $R_i$ in cal cm$^{-2}$ day$^{-1}$ is:

$$P_g = \frac{0.08 \, R_i \times 10\,000}{4000} = 0.2 \, R_i \tag{3.13}$$

To calculate the net photosynthesis from the gross photosynthesis, a measure of respiratory losses is required. Unlike photosynthesis which takes place mainly in the leaves and only during the day, respiration proceeds throughout the plant, day and night. It has been shown that respiration increases with temperature, and within the temperature range 15-35°C, the coefficient of increase in respiration for each 10°C increase in temperature ($Q_{10}$) is about 2 (Chang 1968, Monteith 1972). Further, it is accepted that at a mean temperature of 15°C respiration accounts for 25 per cent of the gross photosynthesis (Stiles and Leach 1960). Hence, when $T$ is 15°C, $R = 1.667 \, T$ per cent; and at any temperature $T$ in °C within the 15-35°C range the percentage of the gross photosynthesis lost through respiration ($R$) is approximately:

$$R = \frac{1 \cdot 667 \times 15 \times 2^{T/10}}{2^{15/10}} = 8 \cdot 84 \times 2^{T/10} \qquad (3.14)$$

Since the gross photosynthesis $(P_g)$ was estimated to be about $0 \cdot 2 \, R_i$ in equation (3.13), the maximum net dry matter production $(P_n)$ can be calculated from $R_i$ and $T$ data as:

$$P_n = 0 \cdot 2 \, R_i (1 - 0 \cdot 0884 \times 2^{T/10}) \, \text{g m}^{-2} \, \text{day}^{-1} \qquad (3.15)$$

The proportion of assimilates used for respiration is expected to be larger in the Savanna regions than in temperate regions because the temperature coefficient for respiration of green tissue exceeds the coefficient for photosynthesis over the range of temperature in which the plants grow during the wet season. At $25\,^{\circ}$C, an appropriate daily mean temperature in the Savanna regions during the wet season, $R$ calculated from equation (3.14) is about 49 per cent of the gross photosynthesis. At $R_i$ of 500 cal cm$^{-2}$ day$^{-1}$, $P_n$ is calculated from equation (3.15) is about 51 g m$^{-2}$ day$^{-1}$ equivalent to energy conversion efficiency of $4 \cdot 1$ per cent of $R_i$.

(b) *Measured energy conversion efficiency.* It is clear that provided the management of growth factors including water, temperature, and nutrients do not limit crop growth, the maximum amount of plant dry matter that can be produced depends on the amount of incoming solar radiation and the type of plant employed to exploit the radiation (de Wit 1959; Monteith 1965, 1972; Chang 1970; van Ittersum 1972). However, although the maximum possible gross energy conversion efficiency of crops is about 8 per cent and net conversion efficiency is about 4 per cent, for many crops growing under improved farming conditions in a wide range of environments, the seasonal net conversion efficiency is approximately 1 per cent (Lemon 1966, 1967, 1970). In areas in the tropics, including the Savanna regions, under the subsistence farming systems of production energy conversion efficiencies are much lower, about $0 \cdot 1$–$0 \cdot 3$ per cent, due to major genetic, biotic, and husbandry limitations (Penman 1968).

Net energy conversion efficiency of some experimental crops during the growing season at Samaru are given in Table 3.5. These chapters illustrate the high potential of the Savanna region, particularly for cereals, which is not lower than under temperate or tropical climates elsewhere under good management (Bonner 1962, Loomis and Williams 1963, Lemon 1966, 1967). In fact, a production of more than 100 tonne/ha of dry matter per year has been obtained in the Savanna region under irrigation with sugar cane and *Pennisetum purpureum* (Charreau 1974a). The Savanna has probably the highest potential productivity in dry matter in the world, but also probably the lowest actual productivity at present. The gap that exists between the actual production and possible utilization of the climatic resources to produce dry matter including saleable or edible products is enormous.

### 3.9 Temperature

As has been pointed out previously, the temperature of the environment (air and soil temperatures as well as the temperature of leaf surfaces) is mainly a manifestation of the radiation and energy balance. Because of the high radiation income which is relatively evenly distributed throughout the year, the Savanna region has a warm environment that is seasonally modified by changes in water regimes and surface conditions. Consequently there is no winter season as experienced in the temperate regions and the growth of vegetation or crops is not limited by low temperatures. However, temperatures do vary significantly with the seasons and within the seasons affecting the level of crop production and choice of crops.

The mean annual temperatures are some 10–20°C warmer than in temperate regions and all chemical and many biological processes are consequently more rapid. Chemical reactions are about 2–4 times faster in the hot environment of the Savanna as compared with cool temperate regions. For example, the mineralization of the soil organic matter and the decomposition of crop residues occur very rapidly (e.g., the flush of nitrates at the beginning of the rainy period), if moisture conditions are favourable. Biological processes tend to be rapid and crops tend to grow faster if water and nutrients are not limiting. Air temperature is closely linked with the rate of growth and development. Increases in leaf size, as well as rates of unfolding and expansion, are temperature dependent, and the relative leaf growth rate is positively correlated with the mean day temperature (Monteith and Elston 1971). Biochemical processes associated with photosynthesis and respiration are temperature dependent affecting the rates of net assimilation and crop growth. However, the temperature response differs greatly in plants characterized by a low and high photosynthetic capacity, as shown in Fig. 3.7 and Table 3.4. The optimum temperature for high photosynthetic capacity plants ($C_4$ species) is the range of 30–45°C, with carbon dioxide uptake decreasing rapidly at lower temperatures. The high photosynthetic capacity plants are far more sensitive to low temperatures than to high temperatures provided there is sufficient moisture supply. In contrast, the optimum temperature for carbon dioxide assimilation of low photosynthetic capacity plants ($C_3$ species) is in the broad range of 10° to 25°C with a decrease often noted as the temperature increases above 25°C. Lower temperatures are much less damaging and indeed sometimes beneficial.

### 3.9.1 Annual temperature

The assessment of thermal regimes dominating the Savanna region is based on long-term records obtained at 51 stations. The temperature values for the growing period and the dry season are shown as mean seasonal maximum, mean seasonal minimum and mean seasonal temperatures in Table 3.6. The mean seasonal values have a tendency to smooth out daily variations particularly at maximum and minimum temperatures, but this is considered to have little consequence in assessing thermal regimes. Temperatures at a given place and time of the year vary relatively little, the coefficient of variability being 5–7 per cent (Cocheme and Franquin 1967).

The main thermal features of the region are a consistently high mean annual

**Table 3.6**

*Temperatures (°C) during the growing and dry season*

| Place | Location | Growing season | | | | Dry season | | | |
|---|---|---|---|---|---|---|---|---|---|
| | | Mean max. | Mean min. | Mean | Range | Mean max. | Mean min. | Mean | Range |
| Agadez | 16·98°N, 7·98°E | 38·1 | 23·3 | 30·7 | 14·8 | 35·4 | 18·1 | 26·8 | 17·3 |
| Gao | 16·27°N, 0·05°W | 37·2 | 24·8 | 31·0 | 17·4 | 37·3 | 20·7 | 29·0 | 16·5 |
| St. Louis | 16·05°N, 16·45°W | 30·1 | 24·4 | 27·3 | 5·7 | 27·0 | 17·8 | 27·4 | 9·2 |
| Matam | 15·63°N, 13·22°W | 35·1 | 24·1 | 29·6 | 11·0 | 36·8 | 18·5 | 27·7 | 18·3 |
| Tahoua | 14·90°N, 5·25°E | 35·1 | 22·8 | 29·0 | 17·3 | 36·4 | 20·2 | 28·3 | 16·2 |
| Thies | 14·80°N, 16·95°W | 31·5 | 22·6 | 27·1 | 8·9 | 32·6 | 17·5 | 25·1 | 15·1 |
| Dakar | 14·73°N, 17·50°W | 30·0 | 24·6 | 27·3 | 5·4 | 26·0 | 19·5 | 22·8 | 6·5 |
| Mopti | 14·52°N, 4·10°W | 34·0 | 23·3 | 28·7 | 10·7 | 35·6 | 19·0 | 27·3 | 16·6 |
| Kayes | 14·43°N, 11·43°W | 34·5 | 23·8 | 29·2 | 10·7 | 37·9 | 21·6 | 29·8 | 16·3 |
| N'Guigmi | 14·25°N, 13·12°E | 34·8 | 23·4 | 29·1 | 11·4 | 34·7 | 18·4 | 26·6 | 16·3 |
| Abeche | 13·85°N, 20·85°E | 34·5 | 21·3 | 27·9 | 13·2 | 39·4 | 20·7 | 30·1 | 18·7 |
| Zinder | 13·80°N, 9·00°E | 34·5 | 22·7 | 28·6 | 11·8 | 35·5 | 19·8 | 27·7 | 15·7 |
| Birni N'Konni | 13·80°N, 5·25°E | 34·9 | 22·9 | 28·9 | 12·0 | 36·8 | 20·1 | 28·5 | 16·7 |
| Tamba-conda | 13·76°N, 13·68°E | 33·3 | 21·4 | 27·4 | 11·9 | 37·5 | 19·1 | 28·3 | 18·4 |
| Niamey | 13·48°N, 2·17°E | 34·3 | 23·3 | 28·8 | 11·0 | 37·4 | 20·3 | 28·9 | 17·1 |
| Maradi | 13·47°N, 7·08°E | 33·5 | 21·5 | 27·5 | 12·0 | 36·0 | 17·5 | 26·8 | 18·5 |
| Segou | 13·43°N, 6·15°W | 32·9 | 22·5 | 27·7 | 10·4 | 35·8 | 19·8 | 27·8 | 16·0 |
| Sokoto | 13·02°N, 5·25°E | 32·6 | 22·0 | 27·3 | 10·6 | 36·1 | 19·7 | 27·9 | 16·4 |
| Katsina | 13·02°N, 7·68°E | 33·2 | 21·2 | 27·2 | 12·0 | 34·3 | 17·3 | 25·8 | 17·0 |
| Nguru | 12·88°N, 10·47°E | 33·4 | 23·0 | 28·2 | 10·4 | 35·5 | 18·4 | 27·0 | 17·1 |
| Bamako | 12·63°N, 8·03°W | 33·5 | 22·5 | 28·0 | 11·0 | 36·1 | 20·7 | 28·4 | 15·4 |
| Ouagadougou | 12·35°N, 1·52°E | 33·6 | 22·0 | 27·8 | 11·6 | 36·5 | 20·2 | 28·4 | 16·3 |

| | | | | | | | | | |
|---|---|---|---|---|---|---|---|---|---|
| Mongo | 12·18°N, 18·68°E | 33·8 | 22·0 | 27·9 | 11·8 | 38·3 | 22·7 | 30·5 | 15·6 |
| Gusau | 12·17°N, 6·70°E | 32·3 | 20·4 | 26·4 | 11·9 | 34·9 | 17·8 | 26·4 | 17·1 |
| F. Lamy | 12·13°N, 15·03°E | 33·8 | 22·3 | 28·1 | 11·5 | 36·8 | 19·0 | 27·9 | 17·8 |
| Kano | 12·05°N, 8·53°E | 32·4 | 21·5 | 27·0 | 10·9 | 33·8 | 18·2 | 26·0 | 15·6 |
| Maiduguri | 11·85°N, 13·08°E | 33·2 | 21·7 | 27·5 | 11·5 | 35·9 | 17·2 | 26·6 | 18·7 |
| Potiskum | 11·70°N, 11·03°E | 32·1 | 21·5 | 26·8 | 10·6 | 35·1 | 16·8 | 26·0 | 18·3 |
| Bobo D. | 11·17°N, 4·30°W | 31·9 | 20·8 | 26·4 | 11·1 | 35·2 | 19·1 | 27·2 | 16·1 |
| Samaru | 11·18°N, 7·63°E | 30·0 | 18·7 | 24·4 | 11·3 | 32·2 | 16·8 | 24·5 | 15·4 |
| Am-Timon | 11·03°N, 20·28°E | 33·0 | 20·3 | 26·7 | 12·7 | 37·2 | 16·6 | 26·9 | 20·6 |
| Navrongo | 10·88°N, 1·08°W | 32·5 | 22·4 | 27·5 | 10·1 | 36·6 | 22·0 | 29·3 | 14·6 |
| Yelwa | 10·88°N, 4·75°E | 32·5 | 22·2 | 27·4 | 10·3 | 37·5 | 16·9 | 27·2 | 20·6 |
| Kaduna | 10·50°N, 7·45°E | 30·4 | 19·3 | 24·9 | 11·1 | 33·0 | 16·6 | 24·8 | 16·4 |
| Bousso | 10·48°N, 16·71°E | 33·4 | 22·0 | 27·7 | 11·4 | 37·9 | 19·0 | 28·5 | 18·9 |
| Maroua | 10·47°N, 14·27°E | 33·8 | 21·6 | 27·7 | 12·2 | 35·6 | 20·5 | 28·1 | 15·1 |
| Bauchi | 10·28°N, 9·81°E | 32·3 | 19·6 | 26·0 | 12·7 | 34·4 | 16·9 | 25·7 | 17·5 |
| Kaele | 10·08°N, 14·45°E | 33·2 | 21·8 | 27·5 | 11·4 | 36·3 | 21·3 | 28·8 | 15·0 |
| Jos | 10·86°N, 8·90°E | 26·2 | 16·9 | 21·6 | 9·3 | 28·8 | 16·4 | 22·6 | 12·4 |
| Minna | 9·61°N, 6·20°E | 31·3 | 21·9 | 26·6 | 9·4 | 35·6 | 21·4 | 28·5 | 14·2 |
| Mokwa | 9·30°N, 5·07°E | 32·2 | 21·7 | 27·0 | 10·5 | 36·0 | 18·4 | 27·2 | 17·6 |
| Garoua | 9·33°N, 13·38°E | 32·7 | 22·0 | 27·4 | 10·7 | 37·2 | 21·5 | 29·4 | 15·7 |
| Pala | 9·37°N, 14·91°E | 31·6 | 21·3 | 26·5 | 10·3 | 35·8 | 20·2 | 28·0 | 15·6 |
| Yola | 9·23°N, 12·47°E | 32·7 | 22·2 | 27·5 | 10·5 | 36·9 | 19·8 | 28·4 | 17·1 |
| F. Archamb. | 9·13°N, 18·38°E | 32·7 | 21·8 | 27·3 | 10·9 | 37·5 | 19·7 | 28·6 | 17·8 |
| Bida | 9·10°N, 6·02°E | 32·3 | 22·0 | 27·2 | 10·3 | 36·0 | 22·2 | 29·1 | 13·8 |
| Lokoja | 7·80°N, 6·73°E | 31·7 | 22·7 | 27·2 | 9·0 | 34·7 | 22·2 | 28·5 | 12·5 |
| Moundou | 8·61°N, 16·07°E | 33·3 | 21·5 | 27·4 | 11·8 | 34·5 | 17·4 | 26·0 | 17·1 |
| Ilorin | 8·48°N, 4·58°E | 31·8 | 21·0 | 26·4 | 10·8 | 34·6 | 19·8 | 27·2 | 14·8 |
| Ibi | 8·18°N, 9·75°E | 31·6 | 22·3 | 26·9 | 9·3 | 35·8 | 19·9 | 27·9 | 15·9 |
| Makurdi | 7·73°N, 8·53°E | 31·6 | 27·2 | 26·9 | 9·4 | 35·4 | 20·6 | 28·0 | 14·8 |

*Climatic resources*

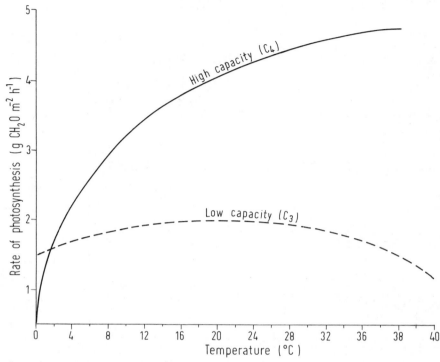

Fig. 3.7. General temperature response curves for high and low photosynthetic capacity plants (Black 1971).

temperature and relatively small seasonal variations, especially in the southern parts of the region. The pattern of thermal fluctuations during the year is presented graphically in Fig. 3.8 demonstrating extreme conditions found in the region as represented by Agades (northern part of the region) and Ilorin (southern part of the region). The mean monthly temperature fluctuations during the year range from 19-33°C at Agades and from 25-29°C at Ilorin. The lowest mean monthly minimum temperature was 10·7°C at Agades and 18·3°C at Ilorin. Clearly temperature cannot be considered as limiting agricultural production.

The annual temperature increases from south to north and corresponds with the gradients of increase in solar radiaion and decrease in annual rainfall. There is also a pronounced difference in temperature regimes during the growing period and the dry season which is of paramount importance to agriculture.

### 3.9.2  *Temperature regime during the growing period*

Disregarding the oceanic influence near the west coast and the atypical conditions of the high plateaux, the average seasonal values of mean monthly temperatures range from 26-30°C. The regression equation describing the relationship between the geographical position and the mean seasonal temperature during the

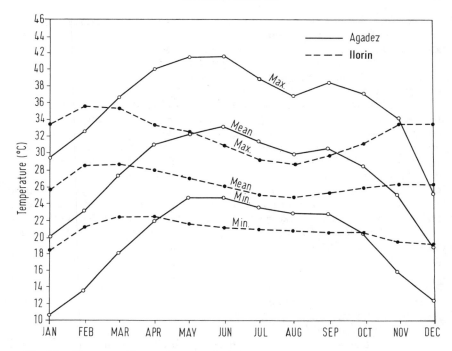

Fig. 3.8. Mean monthly, maximum, and minimum temperatures at Agades and Ilorin.

growing season is:

$$T \text{ (growing season)} = 22\cdot81 + 0\cdot38(LA) + 0\cdot02(LO)°C \quad (r = 0\cdot60) \quad (3.16)$$

This range in the average temperatures during the season, particularly at higher latitudes, is near optimal for assimilation by the high photosynthetic capacity plants ($C_4$ species).

The thermal climate is even more favourable for the production of the $C_4$ crops when one considers the ranges of the mean maximum and the mean minimum temperatures during the growing period. The average maximum and minimum temperatures for the growing season are described by the regressions:

$$T_{\max} \text{ (growing season)} = 25\cdot94 + 0\cdot54(LA) + 0\cdot08(LO)°C$$

$$(r = 0\cdot61) \quad (3.17)$$

$$T_{\min} \text{ (growing season)} = 19\cdot67 + 0\cdot22(LA) - 0\cdot04(LO)°C$$

$$(r = 0\cdot56) \quad (3.18)$$

The mean maximum temperatures during the growing season varies from about 36°C at the northern boundary to about 30°C at the southern boundary.

These high values can be taken to represent day-time temperatures that occur during the high rates of insolation, thus creating favourable conditions for assimilation. Furthermore, the average minimum temperatures for the growing season, roughly representing night temperatures, are relatively low averaging between 21–23°C and consequently favour a reduction in respiration losses, thus resulting in higher net assimilation rates.

It could therefore be concluded that the thermal regime and radiation during the growing period creates a very favourable climate for the production of $C_4$ crops such as sugar cane, maize, sorghum, and millet as well as for numerous grasses such as *Cynodon, Digitaria, Setaria, Cyperus,* and *Amaranthus* (Holm 1969, Black 1971). Indeed Kassam and Kowal (1973) and Kassam *et al.* (1975a) have demonstrated that the rates of dry matter production and economic yields of certain crops, but in particular maize in the Savanna, are twice as high as they are in the humid High Forest environment. This is mainly a consequence of higher radiation and day-time temperatures favouring high assimilation rates and of low night-time temperatures decreasing respiration losses. The temperatures during the growing season also favour the production of $C_3$ crops such as cotton, groundnut, rice.

### 3.9.3  *Temperature regime during the dry season*

The dry season is characterized by wide fluctuations in the day-time and night-time temperatures (Fig. 3.8). The range in the temperature fluctuation is much more pronounced at the higher than at the lower latitudes.

The lowest temperatures occur in January and December involving a delayed growth for irrigated crops such as rice, sugar cane, and cotton. The germination of most crops during that time is poorer as compared with the rainy season. Because of low monthly minimum temperatures that range from 10–25°C, and very wide fluctuations in the mean monthly temperatures, the thermal regime is more favourable for the production of $C_3$ crops such as wheat, barley, and temperate vegetables. Cotton, rice and groundnuts which are $C_3$ crops of tropical origin do not grow satisfactorily under these conditions.

The day-time temperatures may exceed 44°C, but the usual range of the mean monthly maximum temperatures is 38–44°C in the northern part and 37–39°C in the southern part. These high temperatures occur at the end of the dry season, and directly affect the rates of photosynthesis of $C_3$ crops. Indirectly, however, coupled with high dry winds, the high temperatures cause high transpiration rates resulting in moisture stress, the closure of stomata and consequently reduced rates of assimilation.

Finally it must be emphasized that there is a considerable gap in our knowledge regarding the effect of temperature regimes on crop production under irrigation during the dry season conditions prevailing in the Savanna. The mean data here considered hide the variation and particularly the effect of extreme values on crop performance. The large irrigation schemes now under development in the West African Savanna region face many technical problems but probably the most important is the choice of suitable crops or varieties that will match the dry season climate satisfactorily, but particularly in regard to temperature.

### 3.9.4 Soil temperature

Soil temperature affects both the rate of the mineralization of soil organic matter and the physiology of crops. The average soil temperatures are much higher than in temperate climates ranging from 25°C to 35°C at 30 cm depth. Surface soil temperatures at the start of rains reach 45°–55°C. As an example, seasonal changes in soil temperatures at 5, 30, and 120 cm depth are shown in Table 3.7.

There is a lack of experimental evidence that high soil temperatures are detrimental for optimum root growth and seed germination although Lal (1973) working at Ibadan (in the Forest zone) obtained a significant benefit from protecting maize seedlings from high soil temperatures during the hot March–May period.

It is generally held that increases of soil temperature up to a maximum of between 20–30°C increases dry matter production (Monteith and Elston 1971). This is attributed to a more rapid intake of water and nutrients by warmer roots as well as a faster formation and movement of growth regulators. Soil temperatures above 30°C have an adverse effect on dry matter production (Brouwer 1962). On this basis soil temperatures during the growing period are unlikely to affect crop production adversely in the Savanna region.

### 3.9.5 Thermoperiodicity and crop production

Pronounced differences in temperature regimes during the rainy and dry seasons have important consequences on the economy and crop production. The following summary of conclusions is drawn:

(i) The temperatures of the environment throughout the year are high and do not restrict crop production to any particular period during the year. Consequently, the available high radiation income can be exploited by year round cropping provided there is adequate water supply.

(ii) In the southern parts of the region, temperatures are favourable for the year round production of high photosynthetic capacity crops. However, because of lower radiation intensities and relatively high night-temperatures, the actual production rates of dry matter and economic yield are inherently lower than in the northern parts of the region.

(iii) In the northern parts of the region the temperatures are suitable for the production of high photosynthetic capacity crops during the rainy period. Higher radiation income and lower night temperatures provide an ideal environment for the $C_4$ crops. However, during the dry season crop growth under irrigation may be held back by low temperatures and especially by the wide difference in the maximum and the minimum temperatures. The diurnal temperature variation is too great for the production of high photosynthetic capacity crops while some of the $C_3$ crops such as cotton, groundnut and rice also do not perform well due to low temperatures.

(iv) The matching of crops to temperature regimes is of very great importance and until recently little attention had been paid to this important factor.

**Table 3.7**

*Mean monthly soil temperatures (°C) at 5, 30, and 120 cm depth*

| Depth | Station | J | F | M | A | M | J | J | A | S | O | N | D |
|---|---|---|---|---|---|---|---|---|---|---|---|---|---|
| 5 cm | Samaru (11·18°N) | 26·2 | 29·6 | 34·0 | 35·1 | 33·4 | 29·8 | 27·6 | 26·7 | 28·3 | 28·9 | 27·1 | 26·2 |
| 30 cm | Gusau (12·17°N) | 24·5 | 27·7 | 30·5 | 32·0 | 32·9 | 29·5 | 29·6 | 26·8 | 27·5 | 28·0 | 27·1 | 25·8 |
| | Samaru | 23·7 | 25·7 | 29·0 | 20·4 | 29·7 | 27·7 | 26·4 | 25·6 | 26·2 | 26·8 | 25·2 | 23·9 |
| | Mokwa (9·30°N) | 29·1 | 31·2 | 34·4 | 34·2 | 32·5 | 30·2 | 28·8 | 28·2 | 28·3 | 29·2 | 29·9 | 29·1 |
| 120 cm | Gusau | 27·2 | 28·1 | 29·7 | 31·4 | 31·9 | 31·3 | 29·5 | 28·4 | 28·4 | 28·7 | 28·7 | 28·2 |
| | Samaru | 25·5 | 26·0 | 27·8 | 29·4 | 29·7 | 28·7 | 27·6 | 26·7 | 27·3 | 27·3 | 26·9 | 25·9 |
| | Mokwa | 29·3 | 30·3 | 32·6 | 33·7 | 32·8 | 31·4 | 30·1 | 29·2 | 29·0 | 29·3 | 29·8 | 29·7 |

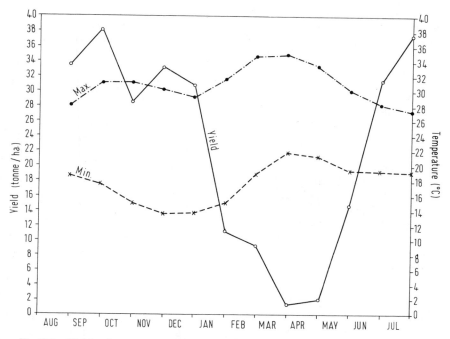

Fig. 3.9. Yields of tomato crops planted at monthly intervals at Samaru (Quinn 1974).

An excellent example of thermal effect on crop production in the Savanna region is illustrated by the dramatic fluctuation in the yield of tomatoes in relation to planting date (reflecting thermal regime) at Samaru, Nigeria (Quinn 1974). Tomato is a $C_3$ crop and particularly sensitive to a relatively narrow range of day and night temperatures. It will be noted from the pattern shown in Fig. 3.9 that the tomato crops planted during the January to May period gave very unsatisfactory yields, while those planted outside that period produced exceptionally high yields. This pattern in yield fluctuation is attributed to increases in day and night temperatures to levels regarded as deleterious for tomato growth, and fruit setting. The results indicate that day temperatures with maximum mean monthly temperatures above 32 °C and night temperatures with minimum mean monthly temperatures 20 °C appear to be critical and drastically reduce production. As a result of these findings the planting of the industrial crop in northern Nigeria is restricted to the June–December period, thus assuring a high level of production from late August until April.

## 3.10 Rainfall

Rainfall is the main source of moisture supply to crops and of dominant interest to farmers. The principal features of rainfall in the tropics are its seasonal character and its variability from year to year. In contrast to a temperate climate, where seasonality is radiation and temperature dependent, seasonality in the tropics is determined by rainfall distribution (duration and pattern). The duration of rainfall and its pattern determines the growing season which can range from 12 months in the year through single and double rainfall maxima of various duration to virtually rainless conditions. Depending on the duration, amount and reliability of rains the crop cycle can be matched to the pattern of water availability so as to meet crop water requirements. Under the conditions of a long growing season several crops can be taken per year.

For proper soil and water management mean values of tropical annual rainfall receipt cannot be interpreted fully without information on seasonal distribution, storm characteristics and evaporation rates. The atmosphere in the tropics can hold greater volume of moisture because of higher temperatures. The weather cells contain more energy and consequently the amount of water they hold and the rates at which it can be shed is also large. Therefore, rainstorms are generally of high intensity/high volume kind. The rainstorms are rarely prolonged and the average duration of rainstorms is in the range of 2–3 hours although heavy storms of 5 cm or more with an intensity reaching 20 cm/h over short periods are not uncommon. This tends to result in problems of rainsplash, soil compaction, surface crusting, and sheet or gully erosion, requiring special management of the soil and terrain largely unknown under the gentler rainfall conditions of a temperate climate (Bunting 1972b).

### 3.10.1  Mean annual rainfall

On a broad scale the rainfall pattern shows a distinct and fairly regular south–north gradient in which the mean annual rainfall decreases from the south inland. The isohyets run nearly parallel, with a tendency to dip southwards as they extend eastwards (Toupet 1965). Because of this regular pattern in the distribution of isohyets it is possible to describe with some precision the distribution of the mean annual rainfall ($P$) in mm by a multiple regression equation in respect of its latitudinal ($LA$) and longitudinal ($LO$) position. The regression equation derived from the long term means at 52 stations within the region is:

$$P \text{ (annual)} = 2470 - 130 \cdot 9(LA) - 8 \cdot 6(LO) \text{mm} \quad (r = 0 \cdot 91) \qquad (3.19)$$

The regression equation suggests the following:

(i) The average decrease in annual rainfall is 131 mm per degree latitude northwards or $131/111 = 1 \cdot 18$ mm rain per km inland suggesting that the distance from the source of moisture is the dominant factor. The rain-bearing southerly air mass gives progressively less total rainfall inland, first because it is continually losing moisture in precipitation along its path northwards, and secondly the duration of its influence decreases from south to north.

(ii) The tendency of the isohyets to dip southwards as they extend eastwards averages 8·6 mm per degree longitude. This is mainly due to the land and sea configuration. The agricultural significance of this tendency is that the same amount of rainfall and approximately the same length of the growing period are associated with different variations of length of day during the year, since day-length depends only on latitude. Thus, for example, the 600 mm isohyet in west

Senegal corresponds to a yearly variation of 100 minutes in daylength whereas around Lake Chad, two degrees further south, it is 70 minutes.

(iii) The intercept suggests that about 2470 mm of rain per year would fall at the source of moisture if there were no other factors affecting precipitation.

(iv) The closeness of the association between the distance from the source of moisture and the amount of annual precipitation is shown by the high correlation coefficient of 0·91 taking into account 82 per cent of the observed variability in the annual rainfall.

(v) Annual rainfall ranges from about 1500 mm at the southern boundary of the region to about 370 mm near latitude 16° N. No rainfall is expected at latitudes greater than 18·9° N at 0° longitude.

### 3.10.2 Annual variability

Experience has shown that mean annual rainfall even when derived from a large number of years is at best an unreliable guide to the variations that occur from year to year and might be quite misleading for agricultural purposes. A statement specifying the *reliability* of rainfall, i.e., the least amount and the greatest amount likely to be received over a specified number of seasons is essential for an evaluation of crop risk either from too dry or too wet conditions. This can readily be calculated for any chosen level of probability which provides additional information of confidence limits to the averages of the expected rainfall. Satisfactory statistical methods exist for calculating confidence limits that are based on normal frequency distribution curves and readers are referred to Manning (1951, 1956) for details particularly with regard to the treatment of skewness in distribution.

De Brichambaut (1956) and Griffiths (1960, 1966), have demonstrated that in about 75 per cent of cases the tropical rainfall has a normal distribution curve so that standard deviations can be used directly for estimates of the chosen confidence limits. In the remaining cases the values are log-normally distributed.

An example of the close agreement between the theoretically expected and actual values of the distribution curve in the Savanna region is given in Fig. 3.10 showing the frequency of distribution of annual rainfall at Kano for the period 1905–1973 (Kowal and Kassam 1975). The frequency of the distribution of annual rainfall about the mean is very close to normal. Expressed in terms of 4:1 confidence limits ($P = 0·2$) values outside the range 676–1062 mm occur only twice in 10 years for the theoretical population. In fact these limits were exceeded 15 times in 69 years, which is equivalent to 2·2 times in 19 years. Moreover, the theoretical deviations fall equally above and below the prescribed limits so that exactly once in 10 years is rainfall less than 625 mm; in the actual population the frequency is 1·3 times in 10 years.

On the assumption that crop failure, due to inadequate rainfall, once in ten years (the lower limit at 4:1 confidence) is a level of risk acceptable to most farmers, the 4:1 confidence limit was chosen as appropriate in defining the annual rainfall regime in the Savanna region. The data, calculated for 52 stations within the region, were used in the multiple regression analysis to describe the distribution of lower and upper limits of rainfall in respect of latitude and longitude. The results are presented graphically in Fig. 3.11 while the regression equa-

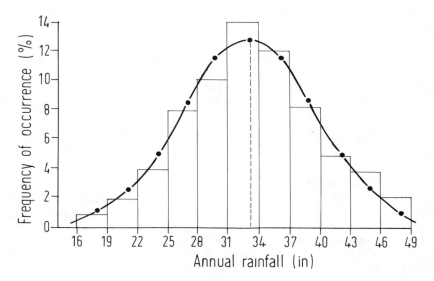

Fig. 3.10. Frequency distribution of annual rainfall at Kano for the period 1905–73 (Kowal and Kassam 1975).

tions for the upper and lower limits are:

$$P_{4:1} \text{ upper limit} = 2966 - 154(LA) - 11(LO)\text{mm} \ (r = -0.90) \qquad (3.20)$$

$$P_{4:1} \text{ lower limit} = 2050 - 113(LA) - 7(LO)\text{mm} \ (r = -0.89) \qquad (3.21)$$

The high correlation coefficients accounted for about 80 per cent of the observed variability in the upper and lower confidence limits. The regression equations suggest that $16°N$ latitude and $0°$ meridian, the mean annual rainfall of 376 mm is expected to have a range in seasonal variations within the 242–502 mm. Rainfall below the 242 mm limit is expected to occur only once in ten years as is the rainfall above the 502 mm limit. At $7°N$ and $0°$ meridian the mean annual rainfall of 1544 mm has a range of seasonal variations between 1259–1888 mm and seasonal variations resulting in a precipitation lower than 1259 mm or greater than 1888 mm is expected to occur only once in 10 years.

The validity of confidence limits calculated using established methods can be in doubt if the observed rainfall pattern is one in which climate is consistently changing, or years with similar rainfall tend to be grouped together. Great concern was expressed by many regarding the below-average annual rainfall received during the 1972–3 seasons in the Sudan and Sahel Savanna region of West Africa (Dalby and Harrison Church 1973). Claims were made by some climatologists that the area was possibly undergoing a significant climatic change as a result of

Fig. 3.11.(see opposite)   Regression line for annual rainfall at zero longitude showing 4:1 confidence limits.

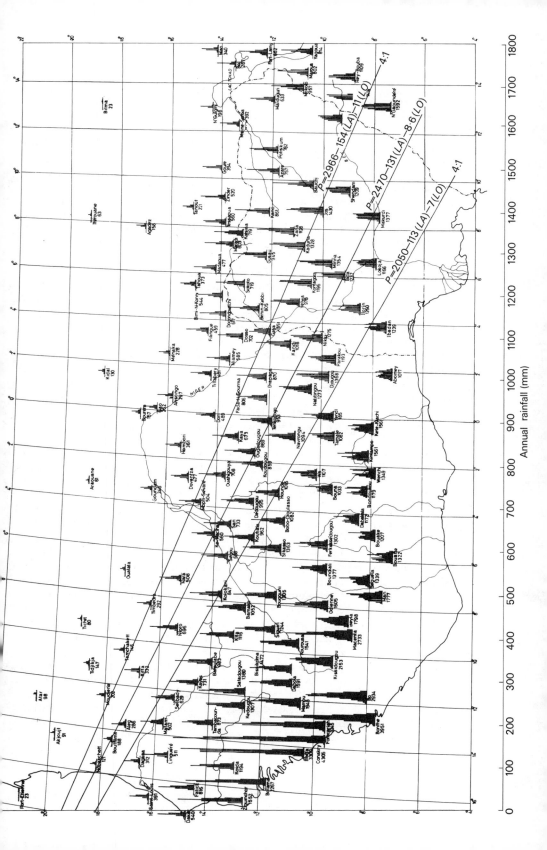

Annual rainfall (mm)

both long-term and short-term cyclic variations in annual rainfall (Lamb 1972; Gribbin 1973, Jenkinson 1973, King, J. W. 1973, Winstanley 1973). However, there is no conclusive evidence that this is so (Goudie 1972, Grove 1973, Bunting, Dennett, Elston, and Milford 1976). A statistical analysis of the long-term rainfall records of the region by Bunting *et al.* (1976) failed to detect any established trends or periodicities in annual rainfall. They concluded that the recent succession of drought years fell within statistical expectation and did not indicate a changing climate in the region. Further, there is no conclusive evidence to show that years with similar rainfall tend to be grouped together. In the West African Savanna, analysis of long-term rainfall records has indicated that the variations from year to year are essentially random (Kowal and Kassam 1975; M. D. Dennett, personal communication 1977).

*3.10.3  Seasonal distribution pattern*

The greater part of the region, roughly extending north of the 1300 mm isohyet, has a rainfall distribution characterized by a single peak (unimodal). Here the rains increase gradually in frequency and amount to a maximum in August, when the full effect of the inter-tropical convergence is felt. After the peak of precipitation is reached there is a relatively rapid decline and determination of rains. The frequency distribution based on monthly or ten-day periods shows a normal or log-normal distributions though with a greater variability than for annual rainfall. For details readers are referred to Kowal and Knabe (1972) who have provided a detailed analysis of rainfall distribution and rainfall histograms for a number of stations in Nigeria.

Immediately south of the 1300 mm isohyet there is a transitional area rather ill-defined with one or two peak characteristics. However, further south the rainfall pattern changes to a more distinct two-peak (bimodal) characteristic. The first peak occurs in June–July and the second peak in September, with August being relatively dry. For an inspection of the bimodal rainfall characteristic see Kowal and Knabe (1972).

The important factor to appreciate is that the rainfall pattern with one peak characteristic has a far more reliable distribution than the two-peak rainfall. This is an important factor when considering the adequacy of rainfall in relation to crop water requirements. The second important factor is that in the initial part of the season precipitation is variable in amount and irregular in frequency, when considered over ten-day periods, having some zero values that do not fit a simple normal or a log-normal distribution curve. However, once the increase in the amount of precipitation has reached the rate of about 25 mm per ten-day period, there is a regular increase in the frequency and the amount of precipitation in the succeeding ten-day periods. Rainfall becomes reliable and adequate to the extent that it exceeds potential evapotranspiration demand so that there is a surplus which rapidly replenishes the soil water deficit in the dry soil profile. Hence, the first ten-day period in the season in which the amount of rainfall is equal to or greater than 25 mm but with a subsequent ten-day period in which the amount of rainfall is at least equal to half the potential evapotranspiration demand, is taken as the start of rains. Further justification for this is based on observations that the irregularity and the amount of precipitation per ten-day period prior to the start of rains are inadequate to wet the soil surface to a sufficient depth to allow for cultivation. Furthermore, work conducted at Samaru on water use of a range of crops during five seasons (Kowal and Andrews 1972, Kowal and Kassam 1973a, Kowal and Faulkner 1975, Kassam *et al.* 1975b, Kassam and Kowal 1975) has shown that the actual evapotranspiration (*ET*) at sowing for good establishment is on average $0.48 E_t$. Therefore as long as rainfall is equal or greater than $0.5 E_t$ crop water requirement will be met.

### 3.10.4   Onset of rains

A reliable estimate of the start of the rainy season is very important in tropical agriculture. First, the start of rains coincides with the highest demand for labour and equipment presenting a major constraint to management. Reliable information as regards to the time the growing season begins contributes greatly to the correct planning of farm operations. Secondly, the establishment of crops early on in the season means higher yields (Stanton and Cammack 1953, de Geus 1970, Jones and Stockinger 1972, van Rheenen 1973, Kassam and Andrews 1975) and there is a tendency in good farming to plant early. A reliable knowledge of the onset of the rains eliminates the risk of a poor crop establishment or crop failure, where early planting is necessary. Furthermore, the correct assessment of the length of the growing season, which is an important parameter in matching crops or cropping sequences to the climate, depends on a knowledge of the start of the rains.

There is a well marked pattern in the onset of the rains in the Savanna region. The southern area on average has an early start, from the middle of March. In the northern part of the region there is a late start, beginning in June. Therefore, there is a difference of about three months in the start of the rains between the extreme southern and northern parts of the region.

The regular pattern of the distribution of the start of the rains within the region (Fig. 3.12) is described by the following multiple regression equation based on the data of 51 stations.

$$\text{Start of rains (decade)} = -1.16 + 1.34(LA) + 0.07(LO)$$

$$(r = -0.94) \qquad\qquad (3.22)$$

About 88 per cent of the variability can be explained by the geographical position of stations or by the distance from the source of moisture. The regression equation indicates that the rain belt advances at a mean rate of 1.34 decade (13.4 days) per degree latitude. The Longitudinal position has a very small effect of about 0.68 days per degree longitude. It also suggests that the hypothetical start of the rains, at the source of moisture, falls at about the middle of December.

### 3.10.5   Termination of rains

The end of rains here is defined as the last ten-day period of the rainy season with at least 1.25 cm of rainfall and $E_t$ in the previous ten-day period not less than precipitation. The end of the rains signals the approaching end of the grow-

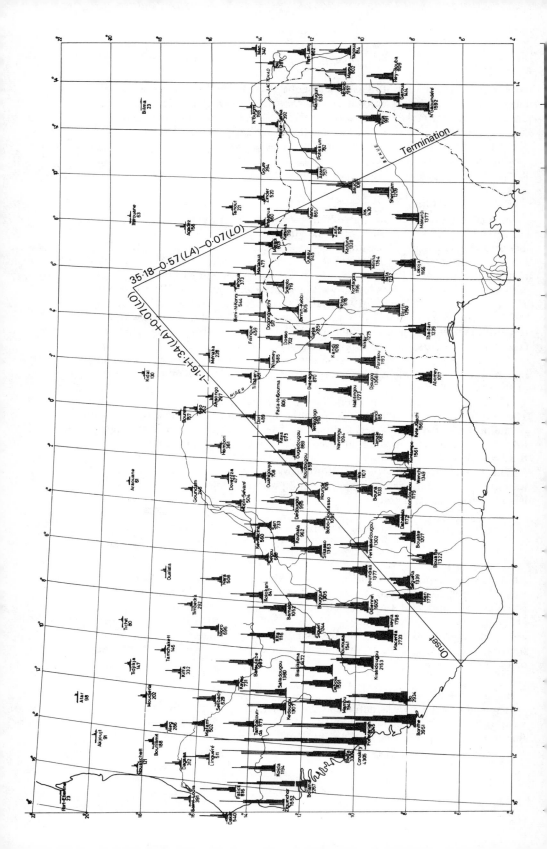

ing season and is of considerable interest to agriculture. The timing of the end of the rains is essential in defining the length of the rainy season. It is also of interest in planning farm management, e.g., lifting of groundnuts, incorporation of plant residues, land fallowing, before the surface soil sets too dry for these operations.

The end of the rains is sharp and begins earlier in the year in the northern parts of the region (mid-September) than in the southern parts (end of October). The difference between the northern and southern boundary of the region is about one and a half months.

Similarly, as with the start of the rains, the time of termination of the rains is described by the following regression equation, using coded ten-day periods and the latitudinal and longitudinal position (Fig. 3.12).

$$\text{End of rains (decades)} = 35 \cdot 18 - 0 \cdot 57(LA) - 0 \cdot 07(LO)$$

$$(r = 0 \cdot 84) \tag{3.23}$$

The correlation coefficient indicates that the closeness of association is still high accounting for about 70 per cent of the variations in the regression equation. The retreat of the rains is much faster than their advance, averaging about 5·7 days per degree latitude. The longitudinal position has apparently only a minor effect averaging 0·7 days per degree longitude. The intercept suggests that the hypothetical end of the rains, at the source of moisture, falls during the middle of December.

### 3.10.6 The length of the rainy period

The difference between the end of the rains and the beginning of the rains at any particular station represents the length of the rainy period (Fig. 3.12). The regression equation describing the duration of the rainy period in coded ten-day periods in respect of latitude and longitude is:

$$\text{Length of rainy period (decade)} = 36 \cdot 34 - 1 \cdot 91(LA) - 0 \cdot 14(LO)$$

$$(r = 0 \cdot 94) \tag{3.24}$$

The rainy period decreases northwards by about 19 days per degree latitude and eastwards by about 1·3 days per degree longitude. At the 350 mm isohyet the duration of the rainy period is 55 days, at the 1500 mm isohyet it is 220 days. At the hypothetical source of the moisture it is raining all the year round.

The precise knowledge of the duration of the rainy period is of paramount importance to rain-fed agriculture. As well as being of practical use to the farmer in planning farm operations and labour requirements, the knowledge of the duration of the rainy period is basic for the rational and efficient exploitation of climatic resources.

The full advantage of the knowledge of the duration of the rainy period could

Fig. 3.12. (see opposite) Onset of rains, their termination, and the length of the rainy season at zero longitude.

be applied in order to delineate areas suitable for stable arable farming at a chosen level of risk in respect of crop water requirement. Areas with an insufficient length in rainy period and with erratic rainfall could be identified for pastoral activity (Kowal and Adeoye 1974). The choice of crops and cultivars could be safely matched according to the availability of water and to the physical environment, thus assuring a greater efficiency in the exploitation of climatic resources. The exact matching of the length of the crop growth cycle to the length of the rainy period is important in several aspects. For example if a sorghum crop has too long a growth cycle and sets seeds after the end of the rainy period, relying entirely on residual moisture in the soil to fill the grain, the yields are significantly reduced (Curtis 1968a, 1968b, Kassam and Andrews 1975). On the other hand if the crop matures considerably earlier before the end of the rains it suffers in quality due to attack by diseases and insects.

The regression equation (3.24) can be used to assess quantitatively the potential productivity of various regions in the Savanna at any chosen level of efficiency of assimilation as demonstrated by Kowal and Davies (1975). It could also be used in assessing effects of drought on crop yield in the northern parts of the Savanna (Kowal and Kassam 1973b).

### 3.10.7  The growing season

Crops which have not matured by the time rains have ended have to rely partly or completely on residual soil moisture for yield formation and maturation. Photosensitive sorghums and millets form their yields and mature on residual soil moisture because they are susceptible to head mould and insect damage when they mature before the end of the rains. In cotton first boll-opening must be timed so that it occurs as the rains are ending, to avoid problems with pests and low quality of lint. A large portion of the total yield in cotton is therefore formed on residual soil moisture. Crops such as groundnut, cowpea, maize and photoinsensitive Gero millet when sown on time do not generally rely on residual soil moisture for maturation in the Guinea Savanna areas. Where the rainy season is short (e.g., in parts of the Sudan Savanna) or when sowing is late these crops may rely on residual moisture for maturation. Gero millet is resistant to head mould, and maize cobs are protected against rain damage by husk. For good groundnut crops maturation must occur as the rains are ending; if the yield is formed largely on the residual soil moisture, lifting of the crop becomes a problem.

The amount of residual moisture which a crop can utilize at the end of the rainy season therefore depends on a number of crop, soil, and climatic variables; and crop type, growth stage and crop cover, rooting depth and density, soil type and depth, evaporative demand of the atmosphere all influence the extent to which crops can utilize the residual soil moisture for growth and maturation. The duration of the growing season is therefore clearly crop and location specific depending on the total situation.

For the purpose of describing regional differences the duration of the growing season here is notionally calculated for a soil with 10 cm available water in 100 cm soil depth. The growing season is therefore defined as the number of ten-day periods in which the evapotranspiration demand is met during the length of the rainy period plus the time required to exhaust 10 cm of soil water. Water use by individual crops is discussed separately in section 3.14.3.

The regression equation describing the end of the growing season in terms of coded ten-day periods is:

$$\text{End of growing season (decade)} = 40 \cdot 58 - 0 \cdot 82(LA) - 0 \cdot 06(LO)$$

$$(r = -0 \cdot 89) \tag{3.25}$$

The equation signifies the estimated optimum time of maturation and harvest for crops which rely on 10 cm residual moisture during the maturation period. Crops maturing after the date specified in equation (3.25) are likely to suffer from moisture stress and would be expected to have reduced yields.

The regression equation describing the length of the growing season in ten-day period is:

$$\text{Length of growing season (decade)} = 41 \cdot 74 - 2 \cdot 16(LA) - 0 \cdot 01(LO)$$

$$(r = -0 \cdot 94) \tag{3.26}$$

At the 350 mm isohyet the duration of the growing season is about 70 days, at 1500 mm isohyet it is about 260 days.

## 3.11 Energy load and the instantaneous intensity of rainstorms

The intensity of rainfall and energy load of individual rainstorms systems in the West African Savanna is much greater than that of temperate and sub-tropical rainstorms and presents special problems in agricultural management and land conservation. Thus, Charreau (1974a) states that the mean intensity of rainfall in the Savanna is two to four times greater than in Western Europe or in the Mediterranean basin. At Bambey (central Senegal) half of the rains fall with an intensity higher than 27 mm/h and a quarter with an intensity greater than 52 mm/h. At Sefa (southern Senegal) the corresponding values are 32 and 62 mm/h. In northern Nigeria, individual rainstorms of greater than 50 mm precipitation with peak intensities of 120–160 mm/h are not uncommon (Kowal and Kassam 1976).

This is consistently reflected in the concentrated nature of the precipitation in the tropics which is heavier and of shorter duration (Ellison 1952, Hudson 1971). Using high speed photography, Ellison (1944) showed the erosive nature of raindrop splashes and the heavy batttering effects of individual raindrops on the soil surface. These characteristics of rainfall, particularly under the tropical conditions of heavy rainstorms, high intensities, and high energy loads, result in the breaking up of soil aggregates, compaction and sealing of the soil surface, a decrease in infiltration and increase in run-off and soil erosion. All this leads to the problems of of soil, water, and crop management unknown under the gentler rainfall conditions of temperate and sub-tropical regions and justifies a detailed account of the physical characteristics of rainfall such as drop size distribution, kinetic energy, and rate of rainfall.

Kowal and Kassam (1976), using a specifically designed instrument that gives a continuous record of the number and size of rainfall drops on a time scale (Kowal, Kijewski, and Kassam 1973), analysed individual storms at Samaru and described the kinetic energy and instantaneous rate of rains. They also related the amount and intensity of rainfall to the energy load of rains. The summary of their results is presented in the following pages.

### 3.11.1  Drop size distribution

The drop size distribution of individual rainstorms varies considerably depending on the amount or volume, duration and intensity of rainfall. At Samaru, drizzles which occur infrequently are of prolonged duration, low volume and intensity and composed of small drops. On the other hand, short duration rainstorms are of high volume and intensity, and composed of relatively larger drops. The drop size distribution of selected rainstorms at Samaru is shown in Fig. 3.13. The extent of the variation in drop size distribution between different types of rainstorms is clearly demonstrated. In particular, the greater the rainfall, the greater the proportion of larger drops.

A record of drop size distribution in a typical 20 mm, 18 minute duration rainstorm is given in Table 3.8. The drop size ranged from 2.34 to 4.86 mm diameter. The predominant drop size diameter was 2·34 mm while the mean drop

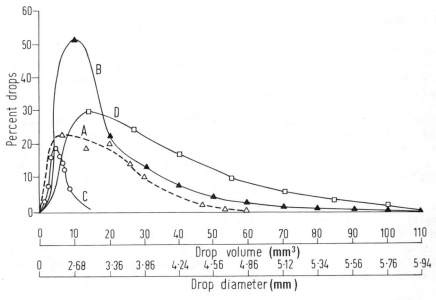

Fig. 3.13.  The drop size distribution of selected rainstorms at Samaru (Kowal and Kassam 1976).
  A—typical rainfall (20·1 mm, 96 drops/cm²),
  B—composite (storm and drizzle) rainfall (6·0 mm, 528 drops/cm²),
  C—drizzle (6·6 mm, 135 drops/cm²),
  D—heavy rainfall (40·6 mm, 1228 drops/cm²).

## Table 3.8

*Number and size of drops and kinetic energy load distribution of a 20 mm, 18 minute duration rainstorm on 21 August 1973 at Samaru (Kowal and Kassam 1976)*

| Drop size class | Drop No. per cm² | Drop No. (%) | Volume (mm³/cm²) | Average drop volume (mm³) | Drop diameter (mm) | Kinetic energy (ergs/cm²) | Kinetic energy (%) |
|---|---|---|---|---|---|---|---|
| 1 | 21·81 | 22·7 | 144·88 | 6·64 | 2·34 | 34,672 | 5·0 |
| 2 | 17·84 | 18·5 | 236·78 | 13·28 | 2·94 | 70,585 | 10·2 |
| 3 | 19·59 | 20·3 | 390·23 | 19·92 | 3·36 | 131,185 | 18·9 |
| 4 | 14·68 | 15·2 | 389·10 | 26·56 | 3·70 | 141,846 | 20·4 |
| 5 | 9·92 | 10·3 | 327·68 | 33·20 | 4·00 | 111,809 | 16·1 |
| 6 | 9·43 | 9·8 | 374·10 | 39·84 | 4·24 | 146,119 | 21·1 |
| 7 | 2·08 | 2·2 | 88·64 | 46·41 | 4·46 | 36,583 | 5·3 |
| 8 | 0·80 | 0·8 | 46·75 | 53·13 | 4·66 | 17,290 | 2·5 |
| 9 | 0·16 | 0·2 | 9·56 | 59·75 | 4·86 | 3,897 | 0·6 |
| Total | 96·31 | 100·0 | 2007·74 | | | 693,986 | 100·0 |
| Average | | | | 20·85 | 3·42 | | |

diameter for the rainstorm was 3·42 mm. Compared with values of temperate rainfall (Bean and Wells 1953, Hudson 1971) the Samaru rainfall is composed of much larger drops.

### 3.11.2  Drop number

The number of rain drops of various sizes in successive one minute intervals in a typical 20 mm, 18 minute duration storm at Samaru is given in Table 3.9. The total number of drops per cm² intercepted in each successive one minute interval ranged from 2·65 to 6·77 with a mean of 5·35. Compared with the number of drops reported by Bean and Wells (1973) for temperate rains, the values are similar except that the bulk of drops for temperate rains were of much smaller size.

### 3.11.3  Rainfall intensity

(a) *Instantaneous intensity*. A detailed analysis of a typical storm at Samaru shows that rainfall intensity during successive one minute intervals (Table 3.10) ranged from 36 to 111 mm/h. The average rate for an 18 minute period was 67 mm/h. These values are typical for the Savanna regions and several times greater than in temperate regions.

Perhaps of particular interest are the positive correlations between the intensity (within the range of 40-80 mm/h) and the drop number ($r = 0·64$) and between the intensity and the average drop volume ($r = 0·70$), suggesting that about 41 per cent of the increase in the rainfall intensity may be attributed to the increase in drop number and about 49 per cent to the increase in drop size.

(b) *Peak intensity*. Analysis of 157 rainstorms for which peak intensity was recorded by a 68·6 cm diameter Jardi recorder, has shown a positive correlation ($r = 0·78$) between the peak intensity and the amount of rainfall. For each increase of 1 mm rainfall there is a corresponding increase of 0·23 mm/h in peak intensity.

### 3.11.4  Energy Load

The energy load of rainfall, which is a function of the drop size distribution and the number of drops, is an energy source used in all the phases of soil erosion—in breaking down soil aggregates, in splashing them in the air, in causing turbulence and washing away soil nutrients in surface run-off, in scouring and carrying away soil particles.

The energy load distribution of a typical rainstorm in successive one minute intervals is shown in Table 3.11. The kinetic energy ranged from 32-38 J cm⁻² mm⁻¹ rainfall while the average kinetic energy load for the whole rainfall was 34·6 J cm⁻² mm⁻¹. These values are much higher than those quoted by Elwell and Stocking (1973) for Rhodesia or Hudson (1971), and are a reflection of the greater proportion of large volume drops, i.e., 59 per cent of all drops being greater than 3 mm diameter.

Of particular· interest was a positive and highly significant correlation ($r = 0·99$) between the amount of rainfall and the kinetic energy load, and between the rainfall intensity and the kinetic energy load obtained from an analysis of drop size and number in eighteen rainstorms. This suggests that the kinetic

**Table 3.9**

*Distribution of drop number per $m^2$ per second, total drop number per $cm^2$ per minute and average drop volume ($mm^3$) in successive one minute intervals in a 20 mm, 18 minute duration rainstorm at Samaru (Kowal and Kassam 1976)*

| Drop size class | Time interval (min) | | | | | | | | |
|---|---|---|---|---|---|---|---|---|---|
| | 1 | 2 | 3 | 4 | 5 | 6 | 7 | 8 | 9 |
| 1 | 147 | 198 | 332 | 238 | 358 | 332 | 385 | 198 | 212 |
| 2 | 173 | 67 | 93 | 120 | 185 | 198 | 160 | 292 | 278 |
| 3 | 398 | 212 | 147 | 265 | 185 | 80 | 93 | 80 | 278 |
| 4 | 238 | 147 | 185 | 93 | 93 | 133 | 53 | 146 | 147 |
| 5 | 107 | 107 | 67 | 173 | 120 | 53 | 13 | 80 | 93 |
| 6 | 27 | 160 | 147 | 80 | 40 | 80 | 40 | 53 | 13 |
| 7 | 0 | 80 | 27 | 0 | 0 | 0 | 0 | 0 | 0 |
| 8 | 0 | 53 | 13 | 0 | 0 | 13 | 0 | 0 | 13 |
| 9 | 0 | 27 | 0 | 0 | 0 | 0 | 0 | 0 | 0 |
| tal drop ./m²/sec | 1090 | 1051 | 1011 | 969 | 981 | 889 | 744 | 849 | 1034 |
| tal drop ./cm²/min | 6·54 | 6·30 | 6·07 | 5·81 | 5·89 | 5·33 | 4·46 | 5·09 | 6·20 |
| erage drop lume (mm³) | 20·31 | 26·97 | 20·90 | 20·52 | 16·89 | 17·60 | 13·44 | 18·22 | 18·27 |

| | Time interval (min) | | | | | | | | | Average drop No./m²/sec |
|---|---|---|---|---|---|---|---|---|---|---|
| | 10 | 11 | 12 | 13 | 14 | 15 | 16 | 17 | 18 | |
| | 225 | 120 | 198 | 252 | 133 | 147 | 120 | 40 | – | 201·9 |
| | 212 | 352 | 185 | 225 | 80 | 173 | 120 | 40 | 13 | 165·1 |
| | 265 | 318 | 198 | 173 | 198 | 147 | 66 | 120 | 40 | 181·3 |
| | 185 | 147 | 212 | 53 | 173 | 93 | 160 | 67 | 120 | 135·8 |
| | 67 | 93 | 120 | 13 | 160 | 40 | 147 | 80 | 120 | 91·8 |
| | 93 | 93 | 93 | 93 | 80 | 53 | 13 | 67 | 345 | 87·2 |
| | 0 | 0 | 0 | 0 | 27 | 0 | 27 | 27 | 160 | 19·3 |
| | 0 | 0 | 0 | 0 | 0 | 0 | 0 | 0 | 40 | 7·3 |
| | 0 | 0 | 0 | 0 | 0 | 0 | 0 | 0 | 0 | 1·5 |
| | )47 | 1129 | 1006 | 809 | 851 | 653 | 653 | 441 | 838 | 891·4 |
| | 6·28 | 6·77 | 6·04 | 4·85 | 5·11 | 3·92 | 3·92 | 2·65 | 5·03 | 5·35 |
| | 19·52 | 20·04 | 20·91 | 16·94 | 23·76 | 19·56 | 22·36 | 24·86 | 36·81 | 20·85 |

## Climatic resources

### Table 3.10

*Distribution of rainfall volume (mm³/cm²), average amount of rainfall (mm) and average rainfall intensity (mm/h) in successive one minute intervals in a 20 mm, 18 minute duration rainstorm at Samaru (Kowal and Kassam 1976)*

| Drop size class | Time interval (min) | | | | | | | | | | | | | | | | | | Total volume (mm³/cm²) | Total volume (%) |
|---|---|---|---|---|---|---|---|---|---|---|---|---|---|---|---|---|---|---|---|---|
| | 1 | 2 | 3 | 4 | 5 | 6 | 7 | 8 | 9 | 10 | 11 | 12 | 13 | 14 | 15 | 16 | 17 | 18 | | |
| 1 | 5·8 | 7·9 | 13·2 | 9·5 | 14·3 | 13·2 | 15·3 | 7·9 | 8·4 | 9· | 4·8 | 7·9 | 10·0 | 5·3 | 5·8 | 4·8 | 1·6 | 0 | 144·8 | |
| 2 | 13·8 | 5·3 | 6·6 | 9·6 | 14·7 | 15·8 | 12·7 | 23·2 | 22·2 | 16· | 28·5 | 14·7 | 17·9 | 6·4 | 13·8 | 9·6 | 3·2 | 1·1 | 236·1 | 1 |
| 3 | 47·6 | 25·3 | 17·5 | 31·7 | 22·1 | 9·6 | 11·2 | 9·6 | 33·3 | 31· | 38·0 | 23·7 | 20·7 | 23·7 | 17·5 | 8·0 | 14·3 | 4·8 | 390·2 | 1 |
| 4 | 38·0 | 23·4 | 29·5 | 14·9 | 14·9 | 21·5 | 8·5 | 23·4 | 23·4 | 29· | 23·4 | 33·7 | 8·5 | 27·6 | 14·9 | 25·5 | 10·6 | 19·1 | 389·9 | 1 |
| 5 | 21·2 | 21·2 | 13·3 | 34·5 | 23·9 | 10·6 | 2·7 | 15·9 | 18·6 | 13· | 18·6 | 23·9 | 2·7 | 32·9 | 8·0 | 29·2 | 15·9 | 22·2 | 327·7 | 1 |
| 6 | 6·4 | 38·0 | 35·1 | 19·1 | 9·6 | 19·1 | 9·6 | 12·7 | 3·2 | 22· | 22·3 | 22·3 | 22·3 | 19·1 | 12·7 | 3·2 | 15·9 | 81·1 | 374·1 | 1 |
| 7 | 0 | 22·3 | 7·4 | 0 | 0 | 0 | 0 | 0 | 0 | 0 | 0 | 0 | 0 | 7·4 | 0 | 7·4 | 4·3 | 44·1 | 92·9 | |
| 8 | 0 | 17·0 | 4·2 | 0 | 0 | 4·2 | 0 | 0 | 4·2 | 0 | 0 | 0 | 0 | 0 | 0 | 0 | 0 | 12·7 | 42·5 | |
| 9 | 0 | 9·6 | 0 | 0 | 0 | 0 | 0 | 0 | 0 | 0 | 0 | 0 | 0 | 0 | 0 | 0 | 0 | 0 | 9·6 | |
| Total volume (mm³/cm²) | 132·9 | 170·0 | 126·0 | 119·2 | 99·5 | 93·8 | 60·0 | 92·8 | 113·3 | 122· | 135·6 | 126·3 | 82·1 | 121·4 | 72·8 | 87·6 | 65·9 | 185·1 | 2007·7 | 10 |
| Average rainfall amount (mm) | 1·33 | 1·70 | 1·27 | 1·19 | 0·99 | 0·94 | 0·60 | 0·93 | 1·13 | 1· | 1·36 | 1·26 | 0·82 | 1·21 | 0·73 | 0·88 | 0·66 | 1·85 | 20·07 | |
| Average rainfall intensity (mm/h) | 79·7 | 102·0 | 76·1 | 73·6 | 59·7 | 56·3 | 36·0 | 55·7 | 68·0 | 73· | 81·4 | 75·8 | 49·3 | 72·9 | 43·7 | 52·6 | 39·5 | 111·1 | 66·92 | |

## Table 3.11

*Distribution of kinetic energy (KE) in ergs/cm² and total kinetic energy in J m⁻² mm⁻¹ of rainfall in successive one minute intervals in a 20 mm, 18 minute duration rainstorm at Samura (Kowal and Kassam 1976)*

| Drop size class | KE per drop (ergs) | 1 | 2 | 3 | 4 | 5 | 6 | 7 | 8 | 9 | 10 | 11 | 12 | 13 | 14 | 15 | 16 | 17 | 18 | Total KE |
|---|---|---|---|---|---|---|---|---|---|---|---|---|---|---|---|---|---|---|---|---|
| 1 | 1590 | 1399 | 1892 | 3164 | 2273 | 3418 | 3164 | 3672 | 1892 | 2019 | 2146 | 1145 | 1892 | 2400 | 1272 | 1399 | 1144 | 381 | 0 | 34672 |
| 2 | 3957 | 4115 | 1582 | 2215 | 2849 | 4392 | 4708 | 3798 | 6924 | 6608 | 5025 | 8507 | 4392 | 5342 | 1899 | 4115 | 2849 | 949 | 316 | 70585 |
| 3 | 6697 | 16005 | 8505 | 5893 | 10648 | 7433 | 3214 | 3750 | 3214 | 11183 | 10684 | 12791 | 7969 | 6964 | 7969 | 5893 | 2678 | 4821 | 1607 | 131185 |
| 4 | 9663 | 13818 | 8503 | 10725 | 5411 | 5411 | 7730 | 3092 | 8503 | 8503 | 10725 | 8503 | 12272 | 3092 | 10049 | 5411 | 9276 | 3865 | 6597 | 141846 |
| 5 | 11272 | 7214 | 7214 | 4508 | 11722 | 8115 | 3607 | 901 | 5410 | 6312 | 4508 | 6312 | 8115 | 901 | 10821 | 2705 | 9919 | 5410 | 8115 | 111809 |
| 6 | 15496 | 2479 | 14876 | 13636 | 7438 | 3719 | 7438 | 3719 | 4958 | 1239 | 8677 | 8677 | 8677 | 8677 | 7438 | 4958 | 1239 | 6198 | 32076 | 146119 |
| 7 | 17589 | 0 | 8442 | 2814 | 0 | 0 | 0 | 0 | 0 | 0 | 0 | 0 | 0 | 0 | 2814 | 0 | 2814 | 2814 | 16885 | 36583 |
| 8 | 21613 | 0 | 6916 | 1729 | 0 | 0 | 1729 | 0 | 0 | 1729 | 0 | 0 | 0 | 0 | 0 | 0 | 0 | 0 | 5187 | 17290 |
| 9 | 24360 | 0 | 3897 | 0 | 0 | 0 | 0 | 0 | 0 | 0 | 0 | 0 | 0 | 0 | 0 | 0 | 0 | 0 | 0 | 3897 |
| Total KE (ergs/cm²) | | 45030 | 61827 | 44684 | 40341 | 32488 | 31590 | 18932 | 30901 | 37593 | 41729 | 45935 | 43317 | 27376 | 42262 | 24481 | 29919 | 24438 | 71143 | 693986 |
| Total KE (J m⁻² mm⁻¹) | | 33·9 | 36·4 | 35·2 | 33·8 | 32·7 | 33·7 | 31·6 | 33·3 | 33·2 | 34·0 | 33·2 | 34·3 | 33·3 | 34·0 | 33·6 | 34·1 | 37·1 | 38·4 | 34·6 |

energy load of rainstorms may be estimated with equal accuracy from either the rainfall intensity or rainfall amount. It is of course much more convenient to assess the kinetic energy of rains from the rainfall amounts rather than from the accepted intensity relationships. The regression equation derived for estimating the kinetic energy load (*KE*) of rains (*P*) in mm for the Savanna areas (Kowal and Kassam 1976) is:

$$KE = (41 \cdot 4\,P - 120) \times 10^3 \text{ erg/cm}^2 \quad (r = 0 \cdot 99) \qquad (3.27)$$

### 3.11.5 Seasonal distribution of energy load

As an example of the seasonal distribution pattern of the energy load of rains in the Savanna region, the rainfall records at Samaru were analysed in terms of

*Climatic resources*

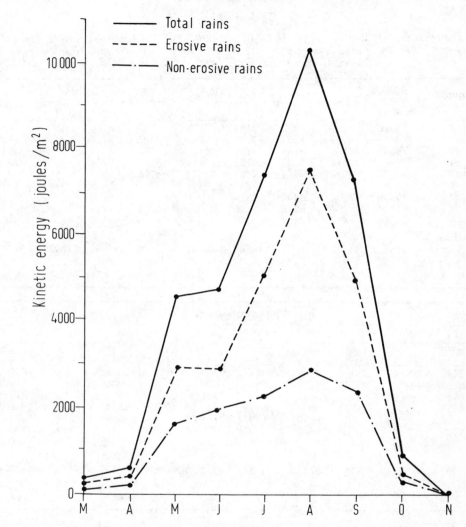

Fig. 3.14. Seasonal distribution of energy load of rains at Samaru. Energy load of total rainfall of 1091 mm = 35 975 J/m²; energy load of erosive rainfall of 635 mm = 24 180 J/m²; energy load of non-erosive rainfall of 456 mm = 11 790 J/m² (Kowal and Kassam 1976).

energy load using equation (3.27) and the results are presented in Figs. 3.14 and 3.15.

The annual kinetic energy load of 1090 mm rainfall was 36 000 J/m². This is twice as large as the amount estimated by Elwell and Stocking (1973) for the Henderson station, Rhodesia. The seasonal distribution of the kinetic energy load is similar to the seasonal distribution of the amount of rainfall, culminating

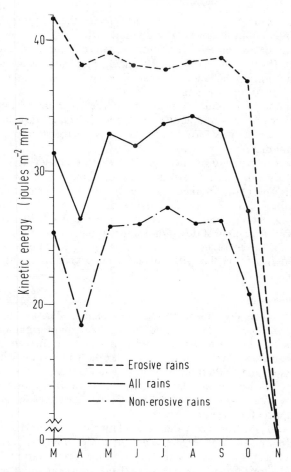

Fig. 3.15. Wet season distribution of kinetic energy of individual storms (monthly average) at Samaru. Annual average energy load of all storms, erosive storms, and non-erosive rain storms equal to 33·0, 38·1, and 25·9 J m$^{-2}$mm$^{-1}$ respectively (Kowal and Kassam 1976).

in a peak in August at 10 300 J/m$^2$ when the precipitation is 302 mm.

The average kinetic energy of rains was about 33 J m$^{-2}$ mm$^{-1}$, suggesting that the predominant drop size is about 3·3 mm diameter.

### 3.11.6 *Erosiveness of rainstorms*

Kowal (1970c, 1970d), studying the surface run-off and soil erosion from cultivated areas of gentle and long slopes at Samaru, found that out of an average of 85 rainy days in the wet season, 32 rainstorms (30 per cent) produced run-off. The water from the remaining 53 rainstorms was wholly accepted by the soil. All rainstorms greater than 20 mm precipitation resulted in run-off: the degree of run-off depending on the rainfall duration and intensity. A distinction, therefore, could be made between erosive rains (greater than 20 mm) and non-erosive rains with precipitation of less than 20 mm.

On this basis, about 58 per cent of annual rainfall (635 mm) was erosive and had a total energy load of about 24 200 J/m$^2$ (Fig. 3.15), corresponding to an average of 38 J m$^{-2}$ mm$^{-1}$. This suggests that the predominant drop size of the erosive rainfall is about 4 mm diameter.

Non-erosive rainfall was about 42 per cent of the total annual rainfall and contained 33 per cent of the total annual energy load. The average energy load of the non-erosive rainfall was 25·9 J m$^{-2}$ mm$^{-1}$ which suggests a predominant drop size of 2·5 mm diameter.

From the seasonal distribution of the erosive rainstorms (Figs. 3.14 and 3.15) it is evident that the hazard of soil erosion is about the same throughout the wet season. However, the frequency of occurrence of erosive rains is much higher in the months of July, August, and September.

Charreau (1974a) who gives a comparison of the rerosive power of tropical rainfall with the U.S.A. rainfall states, 'Whatever the method of study, dry tropical climates have six to ten times more erosive power than temperate climates. It can be assumed from this that risks of accelerated erosion are very high in these areas.'

### 3.12  Wind and advection

Wind speeds are generally low in the Savanna regions. The average speed is under 8 km/h. Speeds are less at night and during the early morning with a high percentage of calm during these periods. Speeds are greater during the middle of the afternoon when average values rise to 8–16 km/h. The highest wind speeds occur as gusts, associated with thunderstorms. The maximum speeds recorded at Samaru were of the order of 110 km/h. Gusts of 80 km/h or more may be expected three times a year. Damage to crops by gusts is however infrequent and blow-down of crops seldom occurs.

During the growing season the winds are relatively cool and dry, becoming progressively hotter and drier towards the end of the growing season. The physiological effect of winds consists mainly in increasing transpiration. The extra heat brought into crops from relatively dry land, adjacent or at a distance, increases the rates of transpiration even in humid weather. Towards the end of the growing season this effect is very pronounced exposing crops to water stress that might affect their yields.

During the Harmattan season the wind direction changes and blows from the Sahara. The Harmattan is relatively cool and dry at the beginning of the season, becoming progressively hotter and drier as the rainy season approaches. Because of its extreme dryness the relative humidity may drop to 5–10 per cent.

The ratio of the wind speed in the Harmattan season to that in the rainy season increases gradually northwards and wind speeds at higher latitudes may be more than double at the height of the Harmattan.

Little is known of the physiological effect of the Harmattan on crop production. However, the Harmattan wind is laden with dust particles which reduce the visibility and intensity of radiation, affect the quality of light, and form deposits on the leaf surface clogging stomatas and interfering with photosynthesis.

Perhaps the most serious adverse effects of the Harmattan on crop production are the greatly increased transpiration rates. These might be considerably greater than could be accounted for by total net radiation receipt, because of the extra energy carried in the hot and desiccating wind. The rates of evapotranspiration can be as high as 8 mm/day inducing a high water deficit in the plant leading to stomatal closure, low assimilation and wilting even when soil moisture is adequate.

Lastly at higher latitudes and on lighter sandy soils strong winds cause soil erosion and the land has to be protected by the planting of trees as windbreaks.

### 3.13 Evaporation and evapotranspiration

Evaporation and evapotranspiration are usually considered together in spite of the fact that they are two distinctly different elements of the climate.

Evaporation $(E_o)$ (synonymous with the 'open water evaporation') relates to the evaporative power of the air and the loss of liquid water as vapour to the atmosphere from an extended open water surface. $E_o$ serves as a standard yard-stick for comparing the evaporative power of the air in various regions and provides a means of describing and measuring several important agro-hydrological parameters, e.g., assessing crop-water requirements for particular climatic areas, assessing water loss from water reservoirs, irrigation needs.

Since there is a conspicuous lack of reliable and standard instrumentation for measuring evaporation, $E_o$ is almost invariably calculated and assessed indirectly from the temperature and a number of meteorological parameters. $E_o$ is very sel-dom measured directly by observation from lakes (Kohler 1954, Kohler, Nordensen, and Fox 1955), and evaporation pans have been found unreliable and lacking in standardization (Dagg 1968).

Evapotranspiration, or the combined transfer of water by evaporation from the soil and by transpiration from the plant, is a very different element depend-ing on the availability of water in the soil, evaporative demand of the atmos-phere, crop density and cover, and the stage of growth. Actual evapotranspira-tion $(ET)$ or crop water use can be measured by the use of lysimeters (Dagg 1970, Kowal and Stockinger 1973a). However, it is not always easy or practical to obtain $ET$ data for different crops in different regions because of the nature of the lysimeter set-up. On the other hand if $ET$ values measured throughout the growth of a crop at a given location are related to the evaporative power of the atmosphere (which is dependent on only meteorological variables), then the measured $ET$ could be used to predict or deduce water requirement of the crop in another location. As mentioned above, $E_o$ as calculated by the Penman (1948) equation is an estimation of the evaporative power of the atmosphere; and the continuous function of $ET/E_o$ with time during crop growth cycle has been used to deduce seasonal pattern of crop water requirement (Dagg 1965, 1970).

Thornthwaite (1948) introduced the concept of potential evapotranspiration $(E_t)$, and defined it as the amount of water that would be transpired or evapora-ted under conditions of unlimited soil moisture supply and complete vegetation cover. $E_t$ represents the 'maximum need of water' of any crop in a given climate, and is only dependent on climate. It relates to the evaporative demand of the

atmosphere in a manner similar to that of $E_o$. $E_t$ can be calculated from meteorological parameters using Penman (1948) equation by using reflection coefficient of 0·25. It is therefore lower by 21 per cent than the calculated $E_o$
which assumes in its calculation reflection coefficient of 0·05. The ratio $ET/E_t$
has also been used to deduce the seasonal pattern of water requirement of crops,
and $ET/E_t = 1·26\, ET/E_o$.

In West Africa both $E_o$ and $E_t$ have been calculated using the Penman (1948)
equation which has been found reliable and valid over a very wide range of
climatic conditions. One of the main difficulties for the user of the Penman
equation is not so much the rather large number of climatic parameters involved
in the formula, as the computation itself, and readers are referred to Frere
(1972) for a simplified procedure for calculating $E_o$ and $E_t$.

### 3.13.1  Annual evaporation and potential evapotranspiration

The pattern of the potential evapotranspiration ($E_t$) during the year is presented graphically in Fig. 3.16. $E_t$ has a distinct bimodal distribution with peaks
occurring in March/April and October/November when values of over 7 and
5 mm/day respectively are reached. According to Slatyer (1967) transpiration
rates in excess of 7 mm/day can cause plant water stress high enough to induce

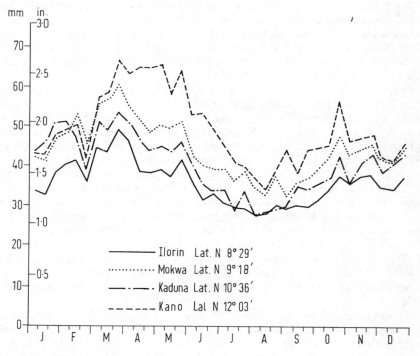

Fig. 3.16. The pattern of potential evapotranspiration (in ten-day periods) during the year
(Kowal and Knabe 1972).

stomatal closure and a reduction or stoppage of assimilation. The minimum $E_t$ occurs in August and December averaging between 3 and 4 mm/day.

During the growing season the energy component is the dominant factor contributing to evaporation (Fig. 3.17) while during the dry season the main component of evaporation is the aerodynamic term.

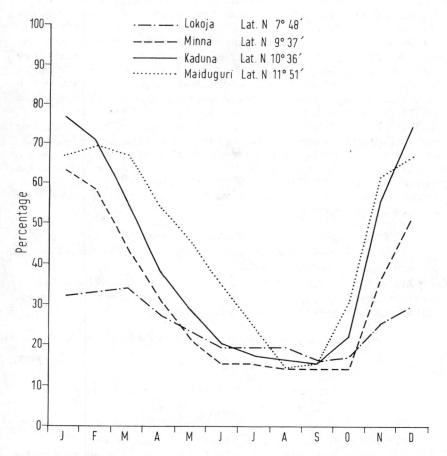

Fig. 3.17. Contribution of the aerodynamic term to total potential evapotranspiration (Kowal and Knabe 1972).

The relationships between the annual amounts of $E_o$ and $E_t$ and the geographical position are described by the following regression equations:

$$E_o \text{ (annual)} = 996 + 95{\cdot}26(LA) + 4{\cdot}44(LO)\text{mm} \ (r = 0{\cdot}69) \qquad (3.28)$$

$$E_t \text{ (annual)} = 758 + 74{\cdot}53(LA) + 3{\cdot}46(LO)\text{mm} \ (r = 0{\cdot}70) \qquad (3.29)$$

The positive correlations are significant and indicate a distinct increase in aridity northwards. The average annual $E_0$ increases by about 95 mm for each degree northwards. The evaporation isolines incline from west to east in respect of the latitudinal position, i.e., the eastern part of the region is more arid in respect of latitude than the western part. The annual $E_0$ along the 350 mm and 1500 mm isohyet is 1700 mm and 2540 mm respectively. At a hypothetical source of evaporation in the South Atlantic Ocean the mean annual $E_0$ is about 996 mm or 2·7 mm/day.

Of particular interest, however, is the intercept of the regression lines of the annual rainfall (equation 3.19) and annual $E_t$ (equation 3.29). The difference between the two regression equations, $P - E_t = 1712 - 205·43(LA) - 12·06(LO)$, is a measure of the balance between precipitation and potential evapotranspiration and can be regarded as an index of aridity in respect of the geographical position. The position of the line at which annual $P - E_t = 0$ runs along 8°19′N, 9°16′W–7°23′N, 0°–7°23′N, 16°E or the 1380 mm isohyet. North of this line the annual deficit between $P$ and $E_t$ increases by about 200 mm per degree latitude while south of this line there is a surplus precipitation over potential evapotranspiration demands that increases some 200 mm per degree latitude. It is therefore to be expected that south of the line the stream flow would be perennial and that the climate can support evergreen vegetation and perennial crops such as cocoa, coffee, citrus, oil palm, and hard woods.

### 3.13.2 *Seasonal evaporation and potential evapotranspiration*

From the agricultural standpoint is is essential to analyse evaporation on a seasonal basis and in relation to rainfall.

(a) *Growing season.* The average total open water evaporation ($E_0$) and potential evapotranspiration ($E_t$) for the growing season in respect of the geographical position can be described by the following regression equations:

$$E_0 \text{ (growing season)} = 1807·4 - 76·5(LA) - 4·9(LO) \text{mm}$$
$$(r = 0·86) \tag{3.30}$$

$$E_t \text{ (growing season)} = 1407·5 - 59·6(LA) - 3·84(LO) \text{mm}$$
$$(r = 0·86) \tag{3.31}$$

$E_0$ during the growing season decreases northwards by some 76 mm per degree latitude. This negative association is the result of the decrease in the length of the growing period and does not imply decrease in rates of daily evaporation. In fact, the regression line for the average rate of evaporation per day during the growing season with latitude has a positive correlation and is:

$$E_0 \text{ per day} = 2·18 + 0·28(LA) + 0·009(LO) \text{mm} \quad (r = 0·79) \tag{3.32}$$

indicating that the average daily rates of evaporation per season increase northwards by some 0·28 mm per day per degree latitude. The average daily rates of evaporation per growing season are not excessive, ranging from about 3·8 to

6·6 mm per day (equivalent to about 3 to 5·2 mm per day of $E_t$).

Of interest, however, is the difference between precipitation (equation 3.19) and $E_t$ during the growing period (equation 3.31), $P - E_t$ (growing period) = 1062·4 − 71·3($LA$) − 4·71($LO$), suggesting that north of the line 15°36'N, 10°W–14°12'N, 10°E or the 520 mm isohyet the precipitation is insufficient to match the potential evapotranspiration demands of crops through the whole growing season.

(b) *The dry season.* The regression equation describing the amount of evaporation during the dry season is:

$$E_o \text{ (dry season)} = -803\cdot3 + 170\cdot5(LA) + 9\cdot6(LO)\text{mm} \quad (r = 0\cdot89) \quad (3.33)$$

The range of $E_o$ within the Savanna region is roughly between 460 mm at the 350 mm isohyet and 1960 mm at the 1500 mm isohyet; and there is an increase in evaporation of about 170 mm per season per degree latitude northwards.

The average potential evapotranspiration during the dry season is described by the equation:

$$E_t \text{ (dry season)} = -625\cdot9 + 132\cdot8(LA) + 7\cdot5(LO)\text{mm} \quad (r = 0\cdot89) \quad (3.34)$$

### 3.14 Water regimes

The interaction between precipitation and evaporation and the resulting water regime is undoubtedly the dominant factor which affects productivity and management of crops, land and terrain in the agricultural environment of the Savanna. The water regime determines the seasons, their relative duration and intensity.

The typical water regime of the Savanna region is the mirror image of the water regime in a temperature climate (Bunting 1972b). Thus during the dry season evaporation is high and in the absence of rainfall, soil water reserves are used up rapidly, vegetation tends to dry up, and the soil surface approaches air dryness. No cultivation can take place because soils are too dry and compact to be worked on without damage to the soil structure and to implements. Because of extreme dryness, fires often break out affecting the soil microflora and fauna and may result in a partial sterilization of the soil. In contrast, during the corresponding period (winter) in the temperate climate evaporation is lower than precipitation, and rain water or snow-melt fills the soil profile with water during the winter.

The first rains in the Savanna fall on air dry, bare, hard, and warm soil, and unless the volume of individual rains is sufficiently large to penetrate the soil to a sufficient depth, water is rapidly lost by evaporation rendering rainfall ineffective. For example, it is estimated that 10 mm rainfall would bring the surface soil to field capacity at a depth of only 4-5 cm. Under the high evaporative conditions prevailing during this period most of the water would be evaporated in a day or two.

At the start of the season, i.e., once the rains have become established and soil moisture is recharged to a depth allowing for cultivation, there is a labour peak for seed-bed preparation and planting that has no parallel in temperate climate conditions, where soil preparation is usually done well in advance of planting. If field operations at the start of the rainy season are delayed, there are usually serious and adverse consequences: the increased amount and frequency of rains with the advancing season may prevent field operations, particularly under a mechanized system, due to excessively wet conditions. Late planting means a reduction in the effective length of the growing season and often results in a decreased productivity. Nitrogen economy is drastically affected. The nitrate flush due to rapid mineralization occurs early in the rainy season. Crops planted late lose the beneficial effects of the flush due to pronounced leaching. Since leaching cannot be prevented, the fertilizer effect on late planted crops is reduced. On the other hand, at the start of the season the water reserves in the profile are very low, and crops rely almost entirely on the frequency of rainfall. Consequently, even relatively short rainless periods may affect the establishment of crops.

During the rainy season in the Savanna, evapotranspiration decreases and precipitation increases, so that the surplus of precipitation results in leaching which becomes increasingly pronounced with crop development. This eventually leads to a temporary rise in the height of the water table which may even appear at the surface, killing roots or adversely affecting the physiology and nutrition of crops (Palmer 1968, Kowal 1970a). Thus leaching and flooding, which in temperate regions are features of winter, occur during the growing season in the Savanna regions. Accordingly, the management of crops, land and terrain must be adjusted. The end of rains is sharp, annual crops exhaust the available water within their root range and die.

Agriculture in the West African Savanna is thus paradoxically caught between the extreme conditions of dryness and marginal soil water reserves on the one hand, and the excessively wet conditions of leaching, waterlogging and flooding on the other. Therefore the control of water and water movement by irrigation, as well as by drainage and management of the terrain and the soil surface is far more important in the Savanna regions than in temperate regions.

A precise time-tabling of farm operations imposed by the water regime is of paramount importance for the timely and successful preparation of land and for the establishment of crops, weeding, the efficient use of fertilizers and for productivity. Delayed farm operations not only adversely affect subsequent operations (weeding, spraying of crops) but result in a reduction of the growing period and an increased risk of water stress during the period of maturity leading to reduced yields. Specialized types of cultivation and land protection, against damage of excessive run-off, waterlogging and soil erosion are necessary. Crops must be handled so as to lessen the effects of drought, withstand waterlogged soil and flooding, and be able to regenerate roots rapidly after the end of waterlogged conditions.

On the other hand the dry season modifies the biology of weeds, pests, and diseases of crops and farm animals and should be taken advantage of by suitable management.

In order to assess quantitatively the water regime for any particular ecological zone in the Savannas, a distinction is made between the *hydrological phases* which allow a numerical description of the water regime during the annual water cycle, and the *water availability periods* that relate to the agronomic management of crops and terrain.

### 3.14.1 Hydrological phases

A quantitative description of water regimes is conveniently based on the analysis of the amount and the pattern of distribution of rainfall and evaporation. The simplest model that allows the identification of distinct hydrological phases in the Savanna environment, and a quantitative assessment of water surplus or water deficit, is based on two dates during the annual water cycle when rainfall is equal to potential evapotranspiration ($E_t$, calculated according to Penman formula using 0.25 reflection coefficient) (Fig. 3.18). These dates objectively define the characteristics of the annual water cycle in terms of pre-humid, humid, and post-humid phases.

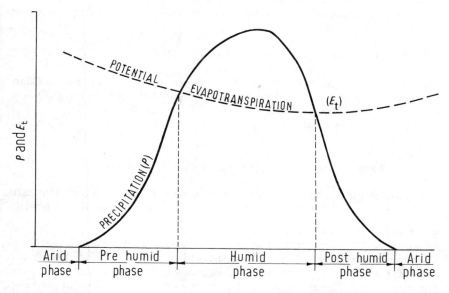

Fig. 3.18. Distribution of rainfall and potential evapotranspiration with time and the resulting hydrological phases.

(a) *Pre-humid phase.* The pre-humid phase represents an intermediate period in the annual water cycle during which changes from the dry to wet season occur. During this phase the rains are being established by the increased amount and frequency of precipitation, the soil moisture deficit being gradually and sufficiently replenished to allow for cultivation, seed germination, and crop establishment.

(b) *Humid phase.* The humid phase is the part of the rainy season during which rainfall exceeds potential evapotranspiration. During this phase most of the vegetative growth of crops occurs and lack of water is very unlikely to limit crop growth. The surplus water might be excessive and detrimental to crop production presenting serious problems in the management of crops and land. Nutrient loss due to leaching and soil erosion is heavy during this phase. Both the duration of the phase and the amount of excessive precipitation can be described quantitatively by multiple regression equations.

Regression equations describing the start and the end of the humid phase in the Savannas (in coded ten-day periods) are:

$$\text{Start of humid phase} = 2\cdot13 + 1\cdot30(LA) + 0\cdot07(LO) \ (r = 0\cdot90) \quad (3.35)$$

$$\text{End of humid phase} = 35\cdot6 - 0\cdot68(LA) - 0\cdot04(LO) \ (r = 0\cdot87) \quad (3.36)$$

The resulting duration of the humid phase ranges from few ten-day periods at higher latitudes in the Savannas to about 16 ten-day periods at lower latitudes.

The regression equation describing the duration of the humid phase in the Savanna in ten-day periods is:

$$\text{Duration of humid phase} = 33\cdot49 - 1\cdot98(LA) - 0\cdot11(LO) \quad (3.37)$$

The water surplus, i.e., the difference between precipitation and potential evapotranspiration, increases from little or none at higher latitudes of the Savannas to about 600 mm at lower latitudes.

The magnitude of water surplus in mm is described by the following regression equation:

$$\text{Water surplus} = 1116 - 66\cdot94(LA) - 3\cdot11(LO)\text{mm} \ (r = 0\cdot73) \quad (3.38)$$

The equation may be used to assess the magnitude of leaching at different parts of the Savanna, and for the assessment of water storage or irrigation potentials.

(c) *Post-humid phase*. The post-humid phase is a mirror image of the pre-humid phase and represents an intermediate period during which pronounced environmental changes occur marking the end of the wet season. During this phase the amount and frequency of precipitation diminishes, and rains cease. There is a rapid increase in the aridity of the environment, and an increased dependence of vegetation on reserves of stored moisture in the soil profile.

(d) *Arid phase of the dry season*. The post-humid phase is followed by the arid phase of the dry season. During this phase crops or natural vegetation are entirely dependent on reserves of moisture stored in the soil profile. Arid conditions lead to a rapid drying up of soil moisture reserves and a termination of the growing period. If irrigation water is available crop production is possible.

### 3.14.2  *The water budget*

The annual pattern of precipitation and evaporation lends itself to a detailed numerical analysis by means of simple water budget accounting. The water budget account provides an opportunity to monitor the water status in the environment of any locality or wider areas, throughout the year. Further, it provides a means for theoretical estimates of the amount of water surplus or water deficit and periods of their duration, for monitoring changes in the soil water status, deep drainage and for an estimate of effective rainfall. This information is basic to the planning of good farm management, for the assessment of drought hazards and for matching the pattern of crop water requirements to the pattern of water availability.

The water budget account is made first by grouping the rainfall and potential evapotranspiration ($E_t$) data into standard (ten-day) periods. Water balance is calculated for each standard period by subtracting $E_t$ values from rainfall values: positive values of this parameter are entered in a separate column as 'water surplus' (*WS*), indicating the extent to which the soil profile is being recharged with water or the amount of rainfall contributing to ground water or stream flow. Negative values are entered in another column as 'water deficit' (*WD*), indicating the extent to which the vegetation with complete ground cover must depend for transpiration on water reserves stored in the soil profile. The entries are arranged further to allow for the monitoring of changes in soil water storage within an assumed storage capacity of the soil profile. These include 'ground charge' (*GC*), i.e., the amount of water passing into or out of assumed soil water storage; 'cumulative charge' (*CC*), i.e., cumulative water surplus and water deficit within assumed soil water storage; and estimates of goundwater (*AW*), i.e., the water surplus above the assumed soil water storage capacity. Lastly, effective rainfall (*EP*), i.e., the amount of rainfall which has neither evaporated early in the season nor percolated beyond the reach of roots, and therefore is avail-available for crop production, is assessed for each period and the season.

The entries allow one to identify water budget components and their periods at a glance, and to evaluate the magnitude of the recharge or depletion of soil water storage, to assess the amount of rainfall contributing to leaching and groundwater, and to assess drought or flood hazards. The accuracy of estimating various components of the water budget depends on correct assumptions, particularly in respect of the soil water storage capacity which is largely dependent on the depth and efficiency with which the soil profile is being exploited by roots. Also, evapotranspiration during the whole period under consideration is assumed to be equal to $E_t$ whereas under crop situation actual evapotranspiration (*ET*) during the pre-humid and post-humid phase is less than $E_t$ while during the humid phase it is greater than $E_t$ (see next section for details). Nevertheless, the water budget account provides an excellent means of assessing water regimes during various hydrological phases that can be related to management practices and improved crop production.

A comparison of calculated components of the water budget with measured components in catchment basin studies (Kowal 1970b) show a very close agreement. Details of the water budget account in ten-day periods for Nigeria are given by Kowal and Knabe (1972), while Cocheme and Franquin (1967) provide accounts in monthly periods for the northerly areas of the West African Savanna. A typical example of water budget account for Kano is given in Table 3.12.

*Climatic resources*

## Table 3.12

*Water budget† account for Kano with 100 mm soil moisture storage
All values are in mm. (Kowal and Knabe 1972)*

| Decade | Period | | $E_t$ | P | WD | WS | IP‡ | GC | CC | AW | EP |
|---|---|---|---|---|---|---|---|---|---|---|---|
| 1 | Jan | 1–10 | 43 | | 43 | | | | | | |
| 2 | | 11–20 | 43 | | 43 | | | | | | |
| 3 | | 21–31 | 48 | | 48 | | | | | | |
| 4 | Feb | 1–10 | 49 | | 49 | | | | | | |
| 5 | | 11–20 | 50 | | 50 | | | | | | |
| 6 | | 21–28 | 42 | | 42 | | | | | | |
| 7 | Mar | 1–10 | 58 | | 58 | | | | | | |
| 8 | | 11–20 | 59 | | 59 | | | | | | |
| 9 | | 21–31 | 67 | 1 | 66 | | 1 | | | | |
| 10 | Apr | 1–10 | 64 | 1 | 63 | | 1 | | | | |
| 11 | | 11–20 | 65 | 4 | 61 | | 4 | | | | |
| 12 | | 21–30 | 65 | 4 | 61 | | 4 | | | | |
| 13 | May | 1–10 | 66 | 13 | 53 | | | | | | 13 |
| 14 | | 11–20 | 59 | 23 | 36 | | | | | | 23 |
| 15 | | 21–31 | 64 | 34 | 30 | | | | | | 34 |
| 16 | Jun | 1–10 | 53 | 32 | 21 | | | | | | 32 |
| 17 | | 11–20 | 53 | 48 | 5 | | | | | | 48 |
| 18 | | 21–30 | 50 | 54 | | 4 | | +4 | 4 | | 50 |
| 19 | Jul | 1–10 | 46 | 54 | | 8 | | +8 | 12 | | 46 |
| 20 | | 11–20 | 41 | 66 | | 25 | | +25 | 37 | | 41 |
| 21 | | 21–31 | 40 | 89 | | 49 | | +49 | 86 | | 40 |
| 22 | Aug | 1–10 | 37 | 102 | | 65 | | +14 | 100 | 51 | 37 |
| 23 | | 11–20 | 34 | 104 | | 70 | | | 100 | 70 | 34 |
| 24 | | 21–31 | 39 | 108 | | 69 | | | 100 | 69 | 39 |
| 25 | Sep | 1–10 | 44 | 60 | | 16 | | | 100 | 16 | 44 |
| 26 | | 11–20 | 39 | 48 | | 9 | | | 100 | 9 | 39 |
| 27 | | 21–30 | 44 | 25 | 19 | | | −19 | 81 | | 44 |
| 28 | Oct | 1–10 | 45 | 11 | 34 | | | −34 | 47 | | 45 |
| 29 | | 11–20 | 46 | 1 | 45 | | | −45 | 2 | | 46 |
| 30 | | 21–31 | 54 | | 54 | | | − 2 | | | 2 |
| 31 | Nov | 1–10 | 46 | | 46 | | | | | | |
| 32 | | 11–20 | 47 | | 47 | | | | | | |
| 33 | | 21–30 | 47 | | 47 | | | | | | |
| 34 | Dec | 1–10 | 42 | | 42 | | | | | | |
| 35 | | 11–20 | 41 | | 41 | | | | | | |
| 36 | | 21–31 | 45 | | 45 | | | | | | |
| Total | | | 1775 | 882 | 1208 | 315 | 10 | − | − | 215 | 657 |

†Water budget equation: $P - E_t + WD - WS = 0$
‡$IP$ = ineffective precipitation

### 3.14.3  Water availability periods

The importance of the precise time-tabling of farm operations imposed by water regimes for timely land preparation, the successful establishment of crops, weeding, the efficient use of fertilizers, and increased productivity justifies the recognition of periods in the annual water cycle that are specific to management and crops. Applying a criteria of practical interest to the agronomist that are specific to management and crops and conform to definitions and assumptions adopted in this book (e.g., the start and the end of the rains, the length of the rainy and growing periods), five distinct '*water availability periods*' in the annual water cycle can be recognized and related to agronomic management. These periods closely relate to the components in the water budget account and thus provide means for a quantitative description of each period in terms of time and amount.

The pattern of water availability periods with latitude at zero longitude for the West African Savanna is shown in Fig. 3.19 and the individual periods are described below.

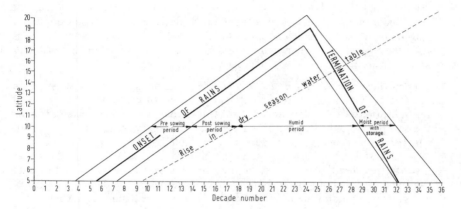

Fig. 3.19. The pattern of water availability periods with latitude at zero longitude in the West African Savanna. Upper and lower 4:1 confidence limits are shown for onset and termination of rains.

(a) *The pre-sowing period (land preparation period)*. Assuming that a recharge of the surface soil of 25 mm water will allow for the cultivation of land, the pre-sowing period coincides with the start of the rains which by definition is the ten-day period with rainfall greater than 25 mm and with two subsequent decades of precipitation greater than half the potential evapotranspiration.

The pre-sowing water availability period is identified primarily in order to indicate the earliest time with sufficient rainfall permitting cultivation but not sowing. In practice, however, land cultivation can start at any time during the first decade when rainfall is about 25 mm and continue according to needs, overlapping with the subsequent water availability periods. The examination of rainfall data in Kowal and Knabe (1972) indicates that the *average* amount and frequency of rain distribution in the Savanna received after the first decade with precipitation of 25 mm is almost always greater than half the potential evapotranspiration. Thus, the onset of the rains can be taken as being identical to the first decade receiving 25 mm of precipitation.

However, it must be emphasized that annual variations in the occurrence of the first decade receiving 25 mm or precipitation are considerable and the regression equation (3.23) for the onset of rains $= -1 \cdot 16 + 1 \cdot 34(LA) - 0 \cdot 07(LO)$, gives only a 'best estimate' of when the start of the rains is expected to occur. The standard error of the estimate is $1 \cdot 09$ ten-day periods. For example Samaru, which is situated at $11 \cdot 18°$ latitude and $7 \cdot 63°$ longitude, the mean date at which the onset of the rains occurs is $14 \cdot 2$ decade or 12th May. At a confidence limit 9:1 the actual dates in which 25 mm of precipitation is expected to occur will lie within $\pm 1 \cdot 64 \times 1 \cdot 09$ ten-day periods or about $\pm 18$ days of the mean date of the onset of the rains (12 May), ranging from about 24 April to 30 May. Only once in 20 years the first 25 mm of rainfall is likely to occur later than the 30 May. Similarly, only once in 20 years the first 25 mm of rainfall is likely to occur earlier than 24 April.

At more northern latitudes, around 700–500 mm isohyets, the uncertainty of the occurrence of the onset of the rains places a severe constraint upon management when the rains are late. This fact underlines the research emphasis that has been given by Francophone workers to soil preparation and in particular to soil cultivation at the end of the growing season.

(b) *Post-sowing pre-humid moist period.* This period represents a stage in the annual water cycle when there is an increasing excess of precipitation over actual evapotranspiration ($ET$) demands of crops, resulting in a gradual recharge of the entire soil profile with water to field capacity. The end of this period is marked by the rise in the level of the dry season water table.

The earliest safe sowing time could be defined as the date set by the upper 9:1 confidence limit of the start of the rains because subsequent to this date rainfall will be equal or greater than actual evapotranspiration demands of crops. The regression equation describing the earliest and safest time for sowing at the upper 9:1 confidence limit is similar to the regression equation (3.22) describing the average onset of the rains but includes an additional 18 days. The lysimeter work conducted at Saramu on a range of crops (Kowal and Andrews 1973, Kowal and Kassam 1973a, Kowal and Faulkner 1975, Kassam *et al.* 1975b, Kassam and Kowal 1975) has shown that the $ET$ at the time of sowing is on average $0 \cdot 48\ E_t$ or $0 \cdot 38\ E_o$ (Fig. 3.20). Therefore, as long as rainfall is equal or greater than $0 \cdot 5\ E_t$ water requirements of for crop establishment should be met. On accepting the above definition of the earliest safe sowing time, a farmer would risk a possible failure in crop establishment once in twenty years, and the time available for land preparation would vary in the range 0–36 days. The definition may be regarded as overcautious but it can be adjusted to the needs or risks the farmer is prepared to take. Moreover, as has been pointed out earlier, in practice the pre-sowing and post-sowing periods may overlap considerably depending on the region, crop, labour and management resources at the farmer's disposal.

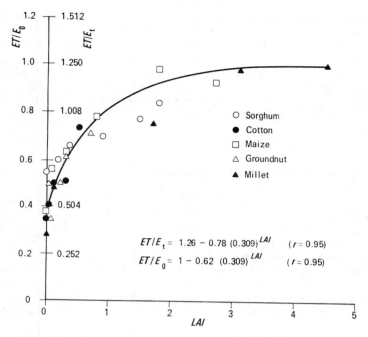

Fig. 3.20. Relationship between leaf area index (*LAI*) and relative evapotranspiration (*ET*/*E*$_t$); also between *LAI* and relative evaporation (*ET*/*E*$_o$) during the post-sowing, pre-humid moist period (i.e., from sowing to the time of rise in water table); based on data from Kowal and Andrews (1973), Kowal and Kassam (1973a), Kowal and Faulkner (1975), Kassam *et al.* (1975b), and Kassam and Kowal (1975).

The ratio $ET/E_t$ during the period increases from 0·48 at sowing to about 1·26 or $ET/E_o = 1·0$, and as expected is greatly influenced by the leaf area index (*LAI*) of the crop (Fig. 3.20). the lysimeter studies at Samaru on sorghum, maize, cotton, groundnut and millet has shown that the relationships between $ET/E_t$ or $ET/E_o$ and *LAI* in the LAI range 0–4·5 is asymptotic as follows:

$$ET/E_t = 1·26 - 0·78 \, (0·309)^{LAI} \quad (r = 0·95) \qquad (3.39)$$

$$ET/E_o = 1 - 0·62 \, (0·309)^{LAI} \quad (r = 0·95) \qquad (3.40)$$

If the change in LAI with time of a crop is known then using equation (3.39) or (3.40) it is possible to deduce the pattern of water requirement of the crop in any area during the post-sowing period from calculated values of $E_t$ or $E_o$.

The complete recharge of soil water deficit in the entire soil profile is marked by the rise in the dry season water table that can be easily observed by monitoring the height to the water table in wells. Unfortunately, only few such data are available. However, the time of complete recharge of soil water deficit can be estimated indirectly from the analysis of the water budget account. Indeed, comparisons of the observed times at which the level of the dry season water table rises at Samaru and Kano with the calculated dates of water surplus occurrence, showed a very close agreement if soil water deficit is assumed to be 100 mm.

Using the calculated values of water surplus in the multiple regression analysis, the average time of the rise in the dry season water table can be estimated for any location in the Savanna region in coded ten-day periods of the dry season from the equation:

$$\text{Rise in water table} = 13 \cdot 9 + 0 \cdot 68(LA) + 0 \cdot 05(LO) \ (r = 0 \cdot 58) \qquad (3.41)$$

There is therefore a delay in the time of rise in water table of about 7 days per degree latitude northwards.

The practical significance of the start of the post-sowing water period lies in the fact that it provides approximate mean data for the safest and earliest planting. Although during this period potential evapotranspiration rates gradually decrease and precipitation increases in the amount and frequency of falls, the surplus rainfall is entirely retained by the soil to nullify the soil water deficit. Consequently, there is no significant leaching, an important factor in plant nutrition and nitrogen fertilizer economy. Further, the volume of individual rains during this period tends to be low, consequently the energy load of individual rainstorms is low and there is little surface run-off and accelerated soil erosion.

Except for the initial part of the period when the soil water reserve is very low and when the successful establishment of crops depends on the favourable frequency of the rains, lack of water will seldom limit crop production. Both the amount and the distribution of rainfall are usually sufficient and reliable enough to sustain good crop growth rates and to recharge the soil profile completely.

(c) *Humid period.* This period represents a stage in the annual water cycle when there is a substantial excess of precipitation over evapotranspiration demands and begins when the soil profile is completely recharged to its storage capacity. The surplus precipitation over evapotranspiration demands is stored temporarily as ground water or flows directly as surface run-off into streams or rivers. The period extends from the observed rise in the dry season water table to the time when the average precipitation is equal to or greater than potential evapotranspiration. The period lies within the humid phase of the water regime but is shorter because of the time taken to recharge the soil profile completely.

During the period a lack of water very seldom affects crop growth. However, farm management is presented with the serious problems of excessive water accumulation and its disposal particularly in the Guinea Savanna. Pronounced leaching, high surface run-off, persistent high water tables, flooding, and soil erosion present serious hazards to crop production and problems in managing land and crops. These problems, singularly or in combination, may and often do affect crop production adversely.

The conditions during the humid period are so wet that the influence of *LAI*

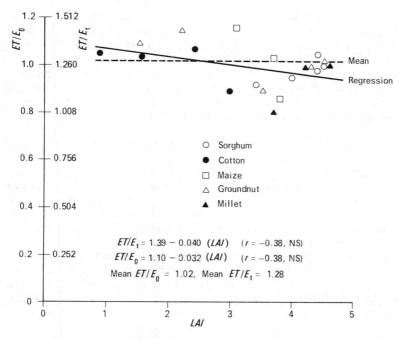

Fig. 3.21. Relationship between leaf area index (*LAI*) and relative evapotranspiration (*ET*/*E*$_t$); also between *LAI* and relative evaporation (*ET*/*E*$_0$) during the humid period (i.e., the period, starting from the time of rise in water table, when precipitation is equal to or greater than potential evapotranspiration); based on data from the same sources as Fig. 3.20.

on $ET/E_t$ or $ET/E_o$ is not significant (Fig. 3.21), and $ET/E_t$ = 1·28 and $ET/E_o$ = 1·02 over the *LAI* range 0·9–4·6.

The estimated amount of rainfall which goes into deep drainage or surface run-off ranges from 0–660 mm (Kowal and Knabe 1972), depending on the region but in the abnormally wet years it is much higher. Under these conditions the leaching of soil nutrients is excessive and the efficient utilization of highly mobile nitrogen supplied in fertilizers presents particular problems. The mechanical cultivation of land is often difficult due to too wet soil conditions. During the peak of the rains and indeed during the whole of the humid period the high humidity and wetness of the environment encourages the spread and attack of pests and diseases. In areas where the length of the growing period is sufficiently long to produce two crops per season, the harvest of the first crop and land preparation and sowing of the second crop falls during the humid period and presents serious and practical difficulties in the harvesting the first crop and establishing the second crop. These difficulties are so serious that at present the full utilization of areas with a sufficiently long growing period for the production of two fast growing crops per season is attempted on a very limited scale. Traditional multiple cropping based on the simultaneous principle (e.g., intercropping) and involving crops with different growth periods (Andrews and Kassam 1975) is better adapted to utilize more fully the areas with a prolonged growing season than multiple cropping based on sequential cropping of mono crops.

During the humid period stream flow occurs and it is the only period during the year in which a substantial water harvest from small catchment basins is possible for conservation and water storage. The end of the humid period in decade can be estimated from the equation:

$$\text{End of humid period} = 35 \cdot 6 - 0 \cdot 68(LA) - 0 \cdot 04(LO)\ (r = 0 \cdot 87) \quad (3.42)$$

(d) *post-humid moist period with water storage.* The period as defined here extends from the time precipitation is equal or less than potential evapotranspiration to the termination of rains plus the time required to evaporate 100 mm water (representing 100 mm of soil water reserve). In reality however, the end of the period varies with crop type and the influence of soil moisture deficit on the rate of canopy senescence.

The period is a mirror image of the post-sowing period and signifies a drying up stage in the annual water cycle. During the period little rainfall is received and crops are mainly dependent on the reserves of water stored in the soil profile. The period begins when rainfall receipt is below potential evapotranspiration demands and lasts until the crops reach maturity and are harvested.

The period is characterized by rapid and drastic changes in microclimate and environmental conditions. There is a rapid reduction and termination of the rains, an increase in potential evapotranspiration rates, a rapid fall in the height of the water table and a gradual increase in the moisture deficit in the soil profiles. The relative humidity of the environment decreases, day-time temperatures increase and night-time temperatures decrease. The radiation receipt is considerably increased when compared with the humid period, and so is potential photosynthesis. In general, the environmental conditions favour high assimilation rates during the grain filling period provided crops are able to exploit water reserves stored in the soil profile.

The relationship between $LAI$ and $ET/E_t$ or $ET/E_o$ (Fig. 3.22) obtained from the lysimeter studies at Samaru are quadratic as follows:

$$ET/E_t = 0 \cdot 030 + 0 \cdot 622(LAI) - 0 \cdot 078(LAI)^2\ (r = 0 \cdot 95) \quad (3.43)$$

$$ET/E_o = 0 \cdot 024 + 0 \cdot 494(LAI) - 0 \cdot 062(LAI)^2\ (r = 0 \cdot 95) \quad (3.44)$$

The regression equations indicate that at a given $LAI$, $ET/E_t$ or $ET/E_o$ are lower than at similar $LAI$ during the post-sowing period, particularly at $LAI$ values less than 2. The equations hide the interactions between crop characteristics (e.g., rooting depth and density, physiological age of the crop, canopy status), soil type and depth, and soil moisture deficit. However, they do show clearly that $ET/E_t$ or $ET/E_o$ are still strongly related to $LAI$ and the influence of increasing soil moisture deficit during the period or evapotranspiration is mediated through $LAI$.

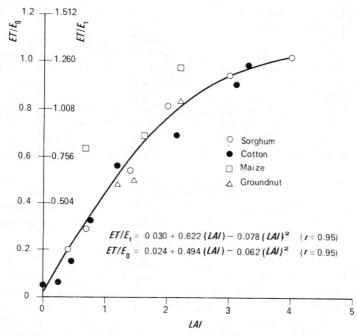

Fig. 3.22. Relationship between leaf area index (*LAI*) and relative evapotranspiration (*ET/E*$_t$); also between *LAI* and relative evaporation (*ET/E*$_0$) during the post-humid moist period with storage (i.e., from the time when precipitation is less than potential evapotranspiration till harvest); based on data from the same sources as Fig. 3.20.

In general, a crop during its reproductive phase goes through a physiological change which induces senescence and sets the crop on a path towards physiological maturity. If during this period there is a soil moisture deficit, the process of senescence and maturity is hastened, the effect depending on the extensiveness of the root system and the physiological age of the crop. In Gero millet grown at Samaru the crop is physiologically mature during the humid period (Kassam and Kowal 1975) but its *LAI* decreased from a maximum of 4·6 to 3·5 although there was no rainfall deficit. The maximum *LAI* of 3·8 in maize was reached during the humid period but had already declined to 2·5 at the start of the post-humid period (Kowal and Kassam 1973a) because of the advance physiological age of the crop. Similarly for groundnut (Kassam *et al.* 1975b). On the other hand *LAI* in sorghum and cotton was maximum during the humid period but the decrease in *LAI* occurred during the post-humid period (Kowal and Andrews 1973, Kowal and Faulkner 1975). This indicates that soil moisture stress induced senescence in these crops and once having induced it, probably hastened it. However, despite the differences in the pattern of senescence the change in *ET/E*$_t$ or *ET/E*$_0$ remained closely related to the change in *LAI* (Fig. 3.22) brought about through the above interactions. The relationships provide an opportunity of deducing water requirement of crops for any region from the available data of *LAI* and calculated values of $E_t$ or $E_o$.

During the later part of the post-humid moist period there is a strong influence of the Harmattan, the rate of evaporation and evapotranspiration increases due to a flow of advective energy, natural vegetation dries up, and crops that mature late are exposed to exceptionally high rates of evaporation demand. In isolated fields, late sown crops can show rates of evapotranspiration twice as high as can be accounted for by the receipt of net radiation. The end of the period in decade can be estimated from the equation:

$$\text{End of post-humid moist period with storage} = 40 \cdot 6 - 0 \cdot 82(LA) - 0 \cdot 06(LO)$$
$$(r = 0 \cdot 89) \qquad (3.45)$$

(e) *Dry period.* During this period crops cannot be grown without irrigation. Some species of natural vegetation with a deep and efficient root system, i.e., mangoes, and some exotic species, e.g., *Eucalyptus camaldulensis*, can withstand severe dry conditions, but in general the growth of most species is severely restricted.

The soil water deficit that develops during the dry season ranges from about 100 to 270 mm depending on vegetation cover. Typical values of the actual moisture deficit under various vegetation covers at Samaru are shown in Table 3.13. The smallest deficits occurred in soils under bare fallow and under crops harvested early, and the greatest deficit under natural vegetation, especially where this included deep rooted trees and bushes which continue to transpire through part or all of the dry season.

**Table 3.13**

*Typical values of soil moisture deficit under various vegetation covers at Samaru (Kowal 1969)*

| Vegetation cover during the rainy season | Moisture deficit in the soil profile at the end of dry season (mm) |
|---|---|
| Bare fallow | 100 |
| Sorghum | 140 |
| Groundnuts | 160 |
| Cotton | 199 |
| Grass | 239 |
| Natural vegetation | 271 |

Differences in the amount of soil water deficit at the end of the dry season affect the water budget and water regime of the following growing season. The greater the soil moisture deficit, the longer the time and the more rainfall required to restore the soil water deficit. Charreau and Fauck (1970) provide an example of the radical modification of the water regime following a change in vegetation cover and land utilization. Thus, during the fifteen years following the clearing of woodland for arable cropping at Sefa (Senegal), there was a drastic increase in the height of the water table and a modification in the soil profile showing accentuated hydromorphism and changes towards a Ferruginous type displaying mottles and concretions. There was also a general increase in the compaction and hardness of the soil.

### 3.15 Bioclimatic regions

The most striking result that has emerged from the analysis of climatic elements in West African Savanna is that their distribution, amount or intensity can be described accurately by regression equations. This has several important implications, but particularly it enables numerical assessment of climatic resources in each recognized bioclaimtic region, identification of various forms of constraints, and assessment of potential productivity. Above all, selection of crops and their cultivars can be made according to their environmental requirements particularly in respect of matching crop water requirement to water availability, thus ensuring more efficient exploitation of resources and higher productivity.

Recognized bioclimatic regions of West African Savanna have already been described in terms of natural vegetation but so far these have not been related quantitatively to various climatic elements. Using the multiple regression equations, describing distribution of various climatic elements within the Savanna, and vegetation maps delineating various vegetation zones, bioclimatic regions are now described quantitatively in terms of more important climatic elements.

Undoubtedly, the duration of the rainy period and the amount of annual rainfall are the dominant climatic elements affecting the distribution of natural vegetation and characteristics of bioclimatic classification. The characteristics of the bioclimatic regions of the West African Savanna are summarized in Table 3.14.

### *3.15.1 Desert–Southern Saharan Fringe*

Delineation of the desert boundary can be derived by equating the regression equation for annual rainfall with zero, i.e., $2470 - 131(LA) - 8\cdot6(LO) = 0$. This indicates that no rainfall is expected north of the $18\cdot9°$ latitude at $0°$ longitude. The zero isohyet dips southwards by $0\cdot07°$ for each degree east of $0°$ longitude so that at the $16°$ west longitude it is at about $20°$ latitude and the at $16°$ east longitude it is at about $17\cdot8°$ latitude.

Similarly, the equation for the length of the rainy period equated to zero, i.e., $36\cdot4 - 1\cdot9(LA) - 0\cdot14(LO) = 0$, indicates that the 0 isohyet runs approximately from $20\cdot9°$ latitude in the extreme west to about $18\cdot6°$ latitude at the $16°$ east longitude.

In actual fact the desert begins fairly abruptly along the 200mm isohyet with rare vegetation but with occasional islands of green in fossil valleys where underground water is found near the surface. Except in these cases no sedentary life is possible: only nomadic herdsmen can exist, basing themselves at the occasional water points and in the Sahel-Sudan transition zones. The area is covered sometimes by sand and sometimes by pebbles and dune basins of shifting sand. In the desert, wind erosion dominates. Rainfall is rare but when it occurs, due to temporary depressions, it is extremely violent and always brief.

**Table 3.14**

*Characteristics of the bioclimatic regions of the West African Savanna*

| Characteristics | Bioclimatic regions | | | | |
| --- | --- | --- | --- | --- | --- |
| | Sahel | | Sudan | Guinea | |
| | Northern | Southern | | Northern | Southern |
| Boundary: Northern | $2470 - 131(LA) - 8·6(LO) = 0$ | $2470 - 131(LA) - 8·6(LO) = 350$ | $2470 - 131(LA) - 8·6(LO) = 500/600$ | $2470 - 131(LA) - 8·6(LO) = 880$ | $2470 - 131(LA) - 8·6(LO) = 1200/1300$ |
| Southern | $2470 - 131(LA) - 8·6(LO) = 350$ | $2470 - 131(LA) - 8·6(LO) = 500/600$ | $2470 - 131(LA) - 8·6(LO) = 800$ | $2470 - 131(LA) - 8·6(LO) = 1200/1300$ | $2470 - 131(LA) - 8·6(LO) = 1500/1600$ |
| Range in annual precipitation (mm) | 0–350 | 350–500/600 | 500/600–880 | 880–1200/1300 | 1200/1300–1500/1600 |
| Length of the rainy period (days) | 0–68 | 68–95/102 | 95/102–140 | 140–187/200 | 187/200–229/244 |
| Solar radiation during the rainy period (cal cm$^{-1}$ day$^{-1}$) | 523–478 | 478–464/460 | 464/460–439 | 439–416/408 | 416/408–394/386 |
| Evaporation ($E_o$) during the rainy period (mm/day) | 7·3–6·6 | 6·6–6·2/6·1 | 6·2/6·1–5·6 | 5·6–4·9/4·7 | 4·9/4·7–4·3/4·1 |
| Main soil types | Sands–Arid brown | Arid brown | Non-leached Ferruginous | Leached Ferruginous | Concretionary Ferruginous, Ferrisols, Ferrallitic |
| Main tree species | — | Acacia spp. Commiphora spp. | Combretum spp. Acacia spp. Terminalia spp. | Combretum spp. Isoberlinia spp. | Daniellia oliveri |
| Main grass species | — | Cenchrus spp. | Andropogon gayanus | Andropogon spp. Hyparrhenia spp. | Andropogon tectorum Imperata cylindrica |
| Main food crops | — | Millet | Millet, Sorghum | Sorghum | Yams, Maize, Sorghum |
| Main export crops | — | — | Groundnut | Cotton | Soya bean, Sesame |
| Physiognomy | Open thorn Savanna | Open thorn Savanna | Shrub woodland | Open Savanna woodland | Light forest open woodland |

### 3.15.2 Sahel bioclimate

This can be best described as a transitional zone from desert to Sudan bioclimate. The southern boundary of this region is difficult to define precisely, as it moves according to the prevailing variations of weather or years, drier or wetter than the average (see section 3.10.2). However, according to most vegetation maps the southern boundary of Sahel roughly corresponds to the isohyet for 500–600 mm annual rainfall. Thus, the Sahel bioclimatic zone forms a belt of some 500 km wide extending its southern boundary along a line from about 16° latitude in the west to about 14° latitude at 16° east meridian.

From the agricultural standpoint Sahel zone consists of two distinct regions:

(i) Northern region, bordering on the Sahara, where rainfall and growing season are insufficient in amount or duration for crop production. Here pastoral (nomadic) agriculture is dominant form of land use. However, the vegetation cover is very sparse, growth seasonal, and it can therefore support only limited amount of livestock. For this reason the area must be considered as agriculturally of marginal value.

(ii) Southern region where sedentary agriculture is the main source of livelihood. Here low and erratic rainfall limits the number and variety of crops that can be grown, as well as their yields. The risks of crop production are high due to frequent occurrence of drought. Millet and sorghum are the main crops grown but also some groundnut and cotton as cash crops.

The northern boundary for arable farming can be assessed using method described by Kowal and Adeoye (1973). The criteria chosen for delineating the boundary are the climatic characteristics corresponding to requirements for millet production under 'intensive' farming with regard to: (i) minimum rainfall providing the water requirements of a 75-day millet; (ii) minimum length of the rainy period of 55 days (see Kowal and Adeoye 1973 for details); (iii) reliability of rainfall and length of rainy period in terms of acceptable risk to the farmer.

The minimum rainfall required to meet water requirements of a 75-day millet crop is readily calculated by the regression equation for potential open water evaporation during the rainy period:

$$E_o = 1524 - 63 \cdot 8(LA) - 5 \cdot 6(LO) \text{mm} \qquad (3.46)$$

and the average ratio of $ET/E_o = 0 \cdot 71$ for the growing period (Kassam and Kowal 1975). Substituting $E_o$ with $ET/0 \cdot 71$ in equation (3.46) gives

$$ET = 1082 - 45 \cdot 3(LA) - 4 \cdot 0(LO) \text{mm} \qquad (3.47)$$

Equation (3.47) provides a value for the minimum water requirement which must be matched by at least an equal amount of rainfall using the regression equation (3.19) for annual rainfall. Equating $ET$ in the equation (3.47) with P in equation (3.19):

$$1081 - 45 \cdot 3(LA) - 4 \cdot 0(LO) = 2470 - 131(LA) - 8 \cdot 6(LO) \qquad (3.48)$$

and solving for latitude at zero longitude provides an estimate of latitudinal boundary position at which the minimum water requirement for a 75-day millet crop during average years are met.

The boundary at which these conditions are met corresponds to the average annual rainfall isohyet of 348 mm. However, the estimate does not take into account long term crop risk due to the considerable variation in annual rainfall. It is therefore necessary to apply confidence limits to specify risks of obtaining rainfall values that lie outside prescribed limits. Taking 4:1 confidence limits as appropriate to the circumstances of the subsistence farmer, which mean a risk of failure through inadequate rainfall (the lower limit) not more than once in ten years, the boundary at which these conditions match the minimum water requirement of millet is estimated from the equation:

$$2050 - 112 \cdot 7(LA) - 6 \cdot 6(LO) = 1082 - 45 \cdot 3(LA) - 4 \cdot 0(LO) \qquad (3.49)$$

where $2050 - 112 \cdot 7(LA) - 6 \cdot 6(LO) = P$ at 4:1 lower confidence limit. The boundary corresponds to isohyet of 588 mm rainfall thus indicating that nowhere in the Sahel region is annual rainfall reliable enough to ensure adequate water requirement at the specified risk level and that failure of 75-day millet crops in the southern parts of the Sahel is predicted to occur more frequently than once in ten years.

As for the adequacy of the length of the rainy period at 4:1 confidence limit, the regression equation describing the length of the rainy season is:

$$\text{Length of rainy season} = 366 - 18 \cdot 5(LA) - 1 \cdot 3(LO) \pm 10 \cdot 6 \text{ days}$$
$$(3.50)$$

Allowing for the minimum length of rainy period of 55 days required to grow the short season millet cultivars, the average length of the rainy period at lower confidence limits of 4:1 is $55 + (10 \cdot 6 \times 1 \cdot 28\dagger) = 69$ and coincides with the approximate boundary separating northern and southern regions of the Sahel.

It is of interest to note that the 588 mm isohyet representing the southern boundary at which rainfall requirements are met for production of millet at lower 4:1 confidence limit also corresponds to 100 days duration of the rainy period.

### 3.15.3 Sudan bioclimate

South of the Sahel, between isohyets of 550 and 880 mm annual rainfall, lies the Sudan bioclimatic region. This region is some 280–300 km wide and supports high density of settled population. The amount of rainfall, its greater reliability and duration of the rainy season that ranges from 100–140 days, allows wide range of crops to be grown. The drought hazards are relatively low. During the peak of the rains there is a surplus of rainfall over potential evapotranspiration that is stored as groundwater. Most of the region is under continuous cultivation and natural soil fertility is low. Yields can be improved by

---

† At 4:1 confidence limit ($P = 0 \cdot 2$), the corresponding $t$ value is $1 \cdot 28$.

timely and early sowing, application of fertilizers and choice of suitable cultivars whose life cycles match the rather short duration of the rainy period (Kassam *et al.* 1975a, Kassam, Dagg, Kowal, and Khadr 1976).

Natural vegetation consists of an open grassland Savanna with scattered deciduous trees comprising of a mixture of broad-leaved and fine-leaved species (some of them thorny).

### 3.15.4 Guinea bioclimate

This is agriculturally the most important and most extensive bioclimatic region of West African Savanna. It extends from about 880 mm isohyet some 500 km southwards to about 1500–1600 mm isohyets. The southern bounday is very ill defined due to the influence of the sea, inclination of coast and man's interference.

Because of its size and climatic diversity, particularly in regard to rainfall distribution characteristics, the region is subdivided into Northern and Southern zones. The dividing line of the two zones is approximately at the 1200–1300 mm isohyets. North of 1200–1300 mm isohyets lies the area characterized by one-peak rainfall while to the south lies the area with two-peak rainfall.

(a) *Northern Guinea bioclimate.* Agriculturally the region is most interesting, having the highest photosynthetic potential for one crop per season. It has reliable rainfall and is virtually free of drought hazards. There is a large water surplus which can be conserved. The average duration of the rainy period ranges from 140 to 200 days, allowing for a wide choice of crops and intensive arable production. The region at present has a relatively low density of population.

(b) *Southern Guinea bioclimate.* In contrast with the rest of the Savanna which is characterized by two distinct seasons a year, the wet and the dry seasons, the Southern Guinea bioclimate is transitional towards a bioclimate characterized by 4 seasons a year.

The two rainfall peaks in June and September are separated by a relatively dry period in August often referred to as the 'little dry season' Although the little dry season in the Southern Guinea region is not very pronounced, it does separate the rainy period into two growing seasons of unequal duration. The effect becomes more pronounced in the southern parts of the region where it affects the cropping pattern of arable crops. Neither the amount of rainfall nor the duration of the two rainy seasons can be easily matched to crop water requirements. Because of lower radiation and higher night temperatures, potential net photosynthesis per day is lower than in the Northern Guinea Savanna. Also because of the prolonged total rainy period and not so severe main dry season there is greater incidence of pests and diseases of crops and livestock. The area has a relatively low population density. The main food crops grown here are yams, sorghum, maize and main export crops soya bean and sesame.

The area would be most suitable for livestock production and range farming if tse-tse fly could be adequately controlled. The dominant grass species of the region is *Andropogon tectorum* and *Imperata cylindrica* which is a serious weed of cultivated areas.

### 3.15.5  High plateau and montane bioclimates

Although flatness and uniformity of physical geography of the West African Savanna are its most characteristic features, there are comparatively minor areas of high plateau and montane areas that have distinct bioclimatic characteristics and do not conform to the pattern of major bioclimatic regions already described.

The most important areas are Jos and Fouta Djallon plateau and Cameroon montane areas. Here temperature and rainfall regimes are strongly influenced by high altitudes (above 2000 m) forming complex but distinct bioclimatic regions. Because of lack of data the bioclimatic characteristics of these areas cannot be described. The areas are not extensive to be important economically. The climate is favourable for production of cash crops such as coffee, tea, and potato.

## 3.16  Concluding remarks

There is little doubt that the climatic resources of the West African Savanna with the exception of Sahel, are favourable for high crop production, although there are some constraints that need to be controlled by skilful management and new technology.

The main positive and negative factors of climatic resources in respect of agricultural production are summarized as follows.

(a) *Positive factors.*

(i) Solar radiation and thermal regimes are favourable for the production of $C_4$ and/or $C_3$ crops throughout the year thus resulting in a very high annual potential productivity.

(ii) The rain-fed agriculture in the middle latitudes has an exceptionally favourable and reliable moisture condition for crop production. At higher and lower latitudes the rainfall and water regime is less reliable and more difficult to match to crop water requirements.

(iii) There is considerable excess of precipitation over evapotranspiration that could be conserved and used for irrigation schemes.

(iv) The dry season is effective in controlling epidemics of pests and diseases.

(b) *Negative factors.* These are mainly related to water regimes or water availability.

(i) The need for water is relatively high. The average crop water use rate during the rainy period is just above 4 mm/day.

(ii) Evaporation rates during the dry season, and at the beginning and the end of the growing period are high and occasionally excessively high and may limit assimilation rates.

(iii) The high energy load of rainfall and high intensities result in high erosion risks.

(iv) During the humid period there is a high leaching of nutrients and a risk of waterlogging.

(v) At high latitudes, corresponding to the Sahel zone, the amount of rain and length of the rainy season is insufficient for reliable arable production.

(vi) At latitudes where the two peak rainfall pattern occurs the matching of crop water requirements to the pattern of rainfall distribution is difficult.

(vii) To fully exploit the high potential productivity of the Savanna region, either irrigation or supplementary irrigation is required.

(viii) The Harmattan and the dust it carries is not conducive to good crop growth. However, few quantitative data are available for a full assessment of the damaging effect.

Finally it must be pointed out that the great diversity of climate in the Savanna, particularly in the length of the rainy period, requires a diversity of crops and their cultivars so that the cycles of crops approximately match the different moisture regimes.

# 4 Soil resources

As a medium in which roots grow and as a reservoir for water and nutrients on which crops continuously draw during their life cycle, soils have long been recognized as an important national resource and valuable economic asset requiring protection, conservation and improvement through good husbandry.

The adequate agricultural exploitation of the climatic potential or sustained maintenance of productivity in any region largely depends on soil fertility. This is particularly true in tropical regions where the natural soil fertility seldom matches the high agricultural climatic potential, and where crop performance or productivity is often limited by a lack of water or nutrients, or by a nutrient imbalance.

Soil fertility is concerned with the ability of the soil to supply nutrients and water to enable crops to maximize the climatic resources of a given location. The fertility of a soil is determined both by its physical properties and by its nutrient status. An understanding, therefore, of the physical and chemical properties of soils is essential to the effective utilization of climatic and crop resources for increased productivity of regions.

This chapter looks briefly at the physical and chemical properties of soils, their interactions with the climate, and some agronomic consequences.

## 4.1 Physical characteristics

### 4.1.1 Soil depth

In general the bulk of the Savanna soils, particularly those formed on aeolian deposits, isohumic soils, and slightly leached Ferruginous soils, have a sufficient depth for the production of arable crops. Stoniness is rare, except in young and weakly developed soils in areas of more rugged topography, e.g., Eutrophic Brown Soils. However, there are extensive areas in which the soil contains considerable quantities of Ferruginous concretions and ironstone fragments derived from erosion and the reworking of ironstone outcrops and Ferruginous subsoils. Iron concretions and hardpans restrict the rooting of crops and render cultivation difficult. The fertility of these soils is very poor. The most extensive areas where iron concretions and hardpans occur are associated with the grey Ferruginous leached soils.

Compact plinthite layers in soil profiles are one of the major factors affecting the afforestation of the Savanna. The plinthite layer restricts the root penetration of trees to the deeper strata of the soil profile and the fuller utilization of water reserves stored in deep sections of the soil profile. Only a few species (e.g., *Eucalyptus camaldulensis*) have roots capable of penetrating the plinthite barrier.

### 4.1.2 Texture

The bulk of the Savanna soils is predominantly sandy, at least at the cultivated depth, and this underlines many of the problems associated with soil fertility, soil water availability, and soil management. Textures of the surface layers range from sandy to sandy loam.

Most of the sands are fine (0·05–0·20 mm) often constituting as much as 70 per cent of the soil. This is particularly true of soils formed over aeolian deposits. The proportions of coarse and fine sands are variable, but coarse fractions are dominant in soils derived from Basement Complex rocks.

The distribution of clay content within soil profiles of major Savanna soils is illustrated in Fig. 4.1. The clay content in the Brown and Reddish Brown Subarid soils and in the slightly leached Ferruginous soils on aeolian deposits is very low throughout the profile, ranging from 2 to 8 per cent. In the leached Ferruginous soil and Ferrallitic soil the clay content increases with depth. Depending on the parent material, the clay content in general ranges from about 8–10 per cent in the 0–10 cm surface soil, increasing progressively to between 30–40

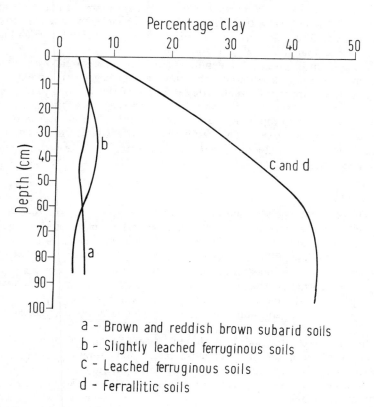

a - Brown and reddish brown subarid soils
b - Slightly leached ferruginous soils
c - Leached ferruginous soils
d - Ferrallitic soils

Fig. 4.1. Distribution of clay content within soil profiles of major Savanna soils (Charreau 1974a).

per cent at about 50–70 cm depth (B horizon) and remains fairly constant below this depth.

The reason for the sandy nature of the topsoil is due to several factors: the widespread occurrence of sedimentary, granitic and gneissic parent materials; the downward eluviation of clay; differential soil erosion due to the high kinetic energy of rainstorms tending to remove fine particles in run-off water; and the possible chemical destruction of kaolinite in the topsoil (Kowal 1968a, Charreau and Nicou 1971, Ahn 1974).

### 4.1.3 Soil consistency

Because of the sandy nature of soils, the consistency of the surface soil is non-sticky and non-plastic when wet, and friable to very friable when moist.

A distinctive feature of the Savanna soils is a very marked hardening and cementation of soils with decrease in soil moisture. This process of increased cohesion and hardening does not start until about half of the moisture content at field capacity has been lost, but thereafter it increases with time for as long as evaporation continues. From the evidence of penetrometric studies in Senegal (Charreau and Nicou 1971), the degree of hardness appears to be related to clay content, and the forces of resistance to penetration are five to ten times higher in the dry season than in the rainy season.

The mechanism involved in hardening is not fully understood. Whatever the mechanism, it results in a serious constraint on land management, since it makes land preparation almost impossible after the end of the growing season. Consequently, seed bed preparation cannot be carried out during the labour-slack dry season, and all farm operations are suspended till soil is moistened by first rains in the following season. This results in a bottleneck in the use of labour and equipment, and a reduction of the effective length of the growing season when sowing is delayed.

### 4.1.4 Clay fraction

The clay fractions of soils are either colloidal or colloidal-like, and are the centres of most chemical and physical reactions taking place in the soil. The three principal groups of clay minerals which occur in various proportions in most soils are kaolinite, illite, and montmorillonite.

Kaolinite consists of silica and alumina sheets, in a 1:1 ratio, which form a non-expanding crystal lattice. It has a low surface area (7–30 $m^2/g$) and low exchange capacity (3–15 me/100 g clay). Soils in which kaolinite predominates show little swelling or shrinking, and have a very limited capacity to hold nutrients.

In illite, in which the silica and alumina sheets are in 2:1 ratio, potassium bonds occur between the adjacent silica plates and prevent water molecules from expanding the structures. The surface area of illite is between 65 and 100 $m^2/g$ whilst the exchange capacity is between 80 and 150 me/100 g clay.

In montmorillonite the ratio of silica to alumina sheets is also 2:1 but the chemical bond between the plates is absent so that with hydration the clay swells and on drying shrinks considerably. The surface area of particles is in the range 600–800 m$^2$/g and is similar to that of humus, while the exchange capacity is similar to that of illite.

In addition to the above crystalline clay minerals, the fine particle fraction of the Savanna soils contains noncrystalline iron and aluminium oxides, the presence of which modifies the physical and chemical properties of soils. The cementing action of 'active' hydrous oxides of iron and aluminium influences structure formation, soil structure stability, and the water retention properties of the soil. The amount of water held at a given moisture tension is much higher in soils having noncrystalline fine material than in soils composed mainly of kaolin in its fine fraction. The free aluminium and iron oxides fix phosphate, rendering most of the Savanna soils deficient in available phosphate. Many soils of the Savanna have exchange capacities that are higher than can be accounted for on the basis of the measured amounts of kaolin. This higher capacity may be due to the presence of noncrystalline material.

Except in the more arid areas and in Vertisols, the clay minerals of the Savanna soils consist mainly of kaolin associated with free aluminium and iron oxides. Consequently the soils show a remarkable uniformity in their chemical and physical properties. Because of the low content of clay in the cultivated soil layer and the low exchange capacity of the clay fraction, the content of cations is closely related to the amount of soil organic matter and the pH.

The occurrence of different clay minerals in the Savanna soils (Charreau 1974a, Jones and Wild 1975) can therefore be summarised as follows:

The leached Ferruginous and Ferrallitic soils have only kaolinite and a considerable amount of amorphous iron hydroxide. The slightly leached Ferruginous soils are dominantly kaolinitic with some montmorillonite. The Vertisols, Brown and Reddish Brown soils, and Eutrophic Brown soils are dominantly montmorillonitic with small fractions of kaolinite–illite admixture. These latter soils and the slightly leached Ferruginous soils also have amorphous iron hydroxide in the clay fraction but in smaller amounts compared to the leached Ferruginous and Ferrallitic soils.

### 4.1.5 Soil structure

Soil structure is defined as the arrangement or grouping of individual soil particles into units or aggregates forming a porous medium. It influences water infiltration, retention of moisture, free movement of air, and penetration and ramification of the root system. In assessing soil structure two major factors which should be considered are (a) the size and stability of aggregates, and (b) the shaping or orientation of the aggregates forming the macrostructure.

(a) *Size and stability of aggregates.* Experience indicates that there is a close relationship between the fertility of the soil and the size and stability of aggregates. In general, aggregates smaller than 1 mm diameter tend to form compact soil which reduces pore space and restricts air movement. Aggregates larger than 5–6 mm diameter form soils with excessively large pore space which reduces the water holding capacity and prevents an intimate contact between roots and soil particles.

Most of the surface Savanna soils under natural vegetation, particularly in

more humid areas, have a good porous structure, as reflected in the high infiltration rates (Wilkinson 1975). The aggregates are water stable, and there is no surface crust formation due to rainfall impact. This is undoubtedly due to the
higher soil organic matter content, the effect of vegetation and leaf fall and the
effective interception of raindrops by the canopy of wooded vegetation.

Subsoils are generally compact, often massive, and there is a high mechanical
resistance to the penetration of roots. Thus, at Samaru for instance, it was observed that deeper roots tended to follow termite tracks and old root channels
in the soil profile; and that in the case of maize and sorghum the rooting depth
was mainly restricted to between 45 and 60 cm depth of soil profile although a
greater rooting is possible.

In soils brought under cultivation the soil structure rapidly deteriorates
(Charreau and Tourte 1967). This feature is attributed to a low clay content of
the surface sils, a predominance of kaolin in the clay fraction, and a rapid reduction in soil organic matter content. Using infiltration rates as an indicator of
changes in the physical properties of soils, Pereira (1955) in East Africa showed
that the deterioration in soil structure occurs during the first cropping year.
Most of the improvement in the physical properties of soil by fallows is lost after
two or three years of cultivation (Wilkinson 1975).

Generally, cultivation produces at best only unstable aggregation with little
or no resistance to heavy rains. After few rainstorms, the aggregates are broken
down in rainsplash and the smoothed soil surface dries out as a crust, restricting
infiltration and aeration and increasing surface run-off (Lawes 1961, Kowal
1972b). On further cultivation, the soil structure tends to become single-grained
(Martin 1963, Siband 1972a). Dusty soils are a common sight on fields that have
been farmed for many years and in more arid areas these soils bear a high risk of
serious wind erosion.

Francophone workers using Henin's index (Henin, Monnier, and Combeau
1958) of structural stability ($I_s$) defined as

$$I_s = \frac{\text{dispersed fraction}}{\text{stable fraction}} \tag{4.1}$$

have assessed stability of soil aggregation numerically. Values of $I_s$ generally
range from 0·5 for soils wih a very stable structure to 10 for soils with a very
unstable structure. Morel and Quantin (1972) reported that $I_s$ increased from an
initial value of 0·4 under Savanna vegetaton to 1·9 after eight years of cropping.
At Sefa, Senegal, $I_s$ increased from 0·4-0·7 under woodland to 1·2-1·6 after
cropping for six years. The increases were greater in Ferruginous than in Ferrallitic soils (Charreau and Fauck 1970), and there was a linear logarithmic relationship between permeability and structural instability. Interestingly enough, the
$I_s$ index was found to be related to the non-humified organic matter (Combeau
and Quantin 1964) and to the free iron oxides (Martin 1963).

(b) *Shaping and orientation of aggregates.* The flow of air or water through
soils is determined by the configuration of the flow path. The factor for the tortuosity of the flow path and the degree of ramification of the network of capil-

laries represents the geometrical parameters of soil structure.

In a cubical arrangement of soil particles each pore has for one entrance five exits. In a tetrahedral arrangement there are only three exits. Unfortunately work on the geometrical parameters of the soil structures of the Savanna soils is lacking except for the Francophone work describing the structure as angular blocky in Ferrallitic soils and fine subangular blocky in soils over aeolian deposits.

### 4.1.6 Soil physical indices

The soil is composed of three distinguishable phases: the solid, the gaseous and the water phase. The solid phase may be called the 'matrix' because this phase controls the form or distribution in space of the other two phases.

In order to define the recognized physical indexes or parameters of the soil and to clarify some of the relationships between the phases the reader is referred to Fig. 4.2 which represents a simple model upon which are based the definitions and soil-water-pore space relations described in this section.

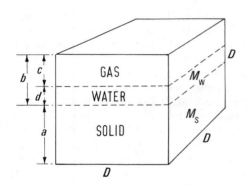

$D$ = Length of the edge of the cube

$a$ = Depth of the soil

$b$ = Depth of water plus gas

$c$ = Depth of the gas

$d$ = Depth of the water

$M_s$ = Mass of the soil

$M_w$ = Mass of the water

Fig. 4.2. A simple model of the soil–water system.

(a) *Soil moisture percentage.* The most commonly used index for the moisture content of soil is the soil moisture percentage $(P_w)$. This is defined as a ratio of the mass of the water $(M_w)$ to the mass of oven dried soils $(M_s)$.

$$P_w = (M_w/M_s) \times 100 \qquad (4.2)$$

(b) *Water depth ratio.* A more practical index of soil moisture content adaptable in agro-climatology and irrigation is the water depth ratio $(R)$. This expresses the moisture content of soil in terms of the equivalent depth of water $(d)$ per unit depth of soil $(D)$

$$R = d/D \qquad (4.3)$$

$R$ is also equal to the mass of water $(M_w)$ per unit volume of soil $(D^3)$.

(c) *Particle density*.  Particle density of soils ($\rho_p$) refers to the density of the soil particles collectively. It is expressed as the ratio of the total mass of the solid particles to their total volume excluding pore spaces between particles:

$$\rho_p = M_s/aD^2 \tag{4.4}$$

where *a* is the depth of the solid phase (Fig. 4.2). The values of particle density are required in calculations of porosity, particle size analysis that employs a sedimentation method, and for calculations involving particle movement in wind and water.

The range of particle density values found in the Savanna soils is between 2·6 and 2·7 g/cm³ (Kowal 1968a).

(d) *Bulk density*.  Soil bulk density ($\rho_B$) is the ratio of the mass to the bulk volume of soil particles plus pore spaces in the soil sample.

$$\rho_B = M_s/D^3 \tag{4.5}$$

The values of bulk density are widely used for converting moisture-percentage by weight to content by volume and for calculating porosity when the particle density is known. The values are frequently used to describe soil compaction and to assess comparative changes in soil structure.

In the Savanna soils poor structure, compaction, and a small total volume of pore space is reflected by high values of bulk density. The values range from about 1·5 to 1·8 g/cm³ (Kowal 1968a, Samie 1974). There is no apparent pattern in the values of bulk density with the increasing depth of the soil profile as can be seen in Table 4.1 which gives the values of bulk density of eight Ferruginous soil profiles at Afaka Forest Reserve near Kaduna, Nigeria. In certain profiles, plinthite layers with a bulk density about 2·0 g/cm³ occur. These layers form an effective barrier to the root penetration of most tree species, but roots of some *Eucalyptus* spp. are able to penetrate it.

On cultivation the bulk density of soils is reduced to about 1·2–1·3 g/cm³ but this reduction is only temporary and by the end of the growing season the values revert to the original high bulk density values of 1·5–1·55 g/cm³ (Lawes 1965, Kowal 1968a).

The effect of bulk density on rooting and yields of various crops in Senegal has been described by Blondel (1965), Nicou and Thirouin (1968), and Charreau and Nicou (1971). The weight or density of roots decreases rapidly as bulk density increases; the relation is linear for sorghum and hyperbolic for groundnut (Fig. 4.3). At some sites at Samaru, Nigeria, where the bulk density of soils at harvest time is about 1·50–1·55 g/cm³, about 75–80 per cent of the maize roots have been found (Table 4.2) to be at depths less than 30 cm from the soil surface and approximately 90 per cent at a depth of less than 45 cm; similarly in sorghum, 60 per cent of roots were found at a depth of less than 30 cm while about 80 per cent of the roots were at a depth of less than 45 cm.

High bulk density in the cultivated layer of the Savanna soils therefore can affect crop production adversely due to a reduction of root density. In sorghum

## Table 4.1

*Bulk densities in eight Ferruginous soil profiles from Afaka
Forestry Reserves near Kaduna, Nigeria (Samie 1974)*

| Profile depth (cm) | Bulk densities (g/cm³) | | | | | | | |
|---|---|---|---|---|---|---|---|---|
| | 1 | 2 | 3 | 4 | 5 | 6 | 7 | 8 |
| 0–15 | 1·53 | 1·61 | 1·29 | 1·51 | 1·52 | 1·48 | 1·73 | 1·66 |
| 15–30 | 1·49 | 1·69 | 1·72 | 1·66 | 1·48 | 1·48 | 1·66 | 1·50 |
| 30–45 | 1·43 | 1·62 | 1·72 | 1·64 | 1·59 | 1·48 | 1·61 | 1·64 |
| 45–60 | 1.46 | 1.56 | 1·72 | 1·68 | 1·54 | 1·41 | 1·56 | 1·64 |
| 60–75 | 1·45 | 1·53 | 1·77 | 1·64 | 1·57 | 1·45 | 1·57 | 1·65 |
| 75–90 | 1·39 | 1·77 | 1·63 | 1·62 | 1·44 | 1·60 | 1·65 | 1·68 |
| 90–105 | 1·39 | 1·74 | 1·65 | 1·63 | 1·44 | 1·62 | 1·79 | 1·68 |
| 105–120 | 1·35 | 1·73 | 1·64 | 1·68 | 1·48 | † | 1·84 | 1·70 |
| 120–135 | 1·41 | 1·66 | 1·53 | 1·63 | 1·42 | † | 1·73 | 1·76 |
| 135–150 | 1·48 | 1·74 | 1·61 | 1·70 | 1·43 | † | 1·72 | 1·71 |
| 150–165 | 1·63 | 1·75 | 1·54 | 1·61 | 1·57 | † | 1·76 | 1·66 |
| 165–180 | 1·65 | 1·64 | 1·53 | 1·59 | 1·55 | † | 1·78 | 1·75 |
| 180–195 | 1·77 | 1·68 | 1·49 | 1·57 | 1·55 | † | 1·78 | 1·73 |
| 195–210 | 1·61 | 1·65 | 1·47 | 1·48 | 1·53 | † | 1·79 | 1·69 |
| 210–225 | 1·65 | 1·68 | 1·43 | 1·49 | 1·69 | † | 1·79 | 1·69 |
| 225–240 | 1·67 | 1·65 | 1·43 | 1·52 | 1·72 | † | 1·74 | 1·61 |
| 240–255 | 1·65 | 1·55 | 1·51 | 1·50 | 1·79 | † | 1·69 | 1·61 |
| 255–270 | 1·66 | 1·65 | 1·44 | † | † | † | 1·61 | 1·48 |
| 270–285 | 1·73 | 1·62 | 1·49 | † | † | † | 1·69 | 1·37 |
| 285–300 | – | 1·57 | 1·55 | † | † | † | 1·69 | 1·50 |

†Plinthite layers with values ranging from 2·05 to 2·37 g/cm³

## Table 4.2

*Per cent of total measured root length above specified depth
(Nofziger 1974)*

| Depth (cm) | Maize | Sorghum |
|---|---|---|
| 15 | 45 | 46 |
| 30 | 77 | 61 |
| 45 | 89 | 71 |
| 60 | 96 | 80 |
| 75 | 99 | 91 |
| 90 | 100 | 100 |

(Fig. 4.3), grain yield decreased from 1·2 tonne/ha at bulk density of 1·4 g/cm³ to 0·6 tonne/ha at bulk density of 1·6 g/cm³.

(e) *Porosity.* Total porosity of the soil ($E$) is the fraction of the soil space occupied jointly by water and the gaseous phase.

$$E = bD^2/D^3 = b/D \qquad (4.6)$$

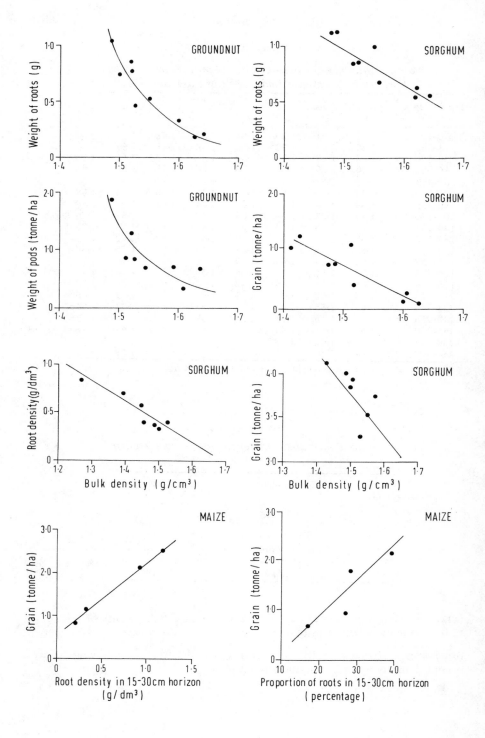

where $b$ is the sum of the water and gaseous phases. The total porosity is calculated from the measured values of particle density and the bulk density as:

$$E = (\rho_p - \rho_B)/\rho_p = 1 - \rho_B/\rho_p \qquad (4.7)$$

Total porosity is regarded as the simplest characterization of the soil pore system. In fertile soils total porosity has values greater than 50 per cent. In the Savanna soils the values usually range between 32 and 44 per cent, corresponding to bulk density values of 1·8 and 1·5 g/cm$^3$ respectively.

In cultivated fields the values vary with the cultivation history. Tillage creates a high surface porposity, often between 55 and 60 per cent, but the aggregates formed are unstable, and exposure to rain quickly leads to the formation of a surface cap and a gradual reduction of porosity to the original values of uncultivated land (Henin *et al.* 1958, Kowal 1972b).

Studies in Senegal (Blondel 1965, Nicou and Thirouin 1968) have shown the serious effects of low porosities on root growth and crop yield. A relationship was found between porosity and rooting density, and between rooting density and yields, and also between porosity and yields of major crops grown in the Savanna region. The adverse effect of low porosity has been attributed to the mechanical resistance to root extension rather than to poor aeration. Whatever the reason might be, low porosity resulting from structural instability is very often a limiting factor for root extension and growth, seriously affecting crop production in most of the Savanna soils.

To assure better and consistent yields, soil management practices should aim at improving the stability of aggregates in order to maintain a reasonable porosity, at least during the life cycle of crops.

(f) *Pore size distribution.* Information on total porosity is of limited direct use since it does not describe the complexity of the pore system in terms of pore size, pore configuration, tortuosity and continuity. However, the measurement of pore size distribution does enable a quantitative assessment of soil water storage and availability and movement of water and gases. In conjunction with information on the moisture release curves, it provides information on the intensity or energy aspects of available water. Furthermore, the concept of pore size has led to the use of soil water constants such as field capacity and soil moisture at 15 atmospheres tension which have direct practical applications to agriculture and relate soil water content to its energy status.

The concept of pore size distribution as a soil characteristic is based on the capillary model described by the equation:

$$h = \frac{2\gamma \cos \theta}{\rho g r} \qquad (4.8)$$

where $h$ is the height to which water will rise in a capillary tube of radius $r$,

Fig. 4.3. (see oposite) Relationships between soil bulk density, root density, and yield for sorghum, groundnut, and maize (Blondel 1965, Nicou and Thirouin 1968, Charreau and Nicou 1971).

$\gamma$ is the surface tension of water, $\rho$ is the soil density, $\theta$ is the contact angle and $g$ is the force of gravity.

If water is extracted from an initially saturated soil sample by a suction equivalent to $h$, the volume of water extracted is equal to the volume of pores having an effective radius just greater than $r$ and corresponding to the selected value of $h$ in the capillary equation. Applying a range of suctions and recording the corresponding soil water content, a moisture release curve is obtained from which the pore size distribution can be calculated.

(g) *Soil moisture characteristics.*  Water is retained in the soil in the same way as in a porous matrix by capillary forces and by physical absorption on solid surfaces. The former are dominant in wet soils, whilst the latter is dominant after most of the water has been removed from the pores and only films adhere on the soil particle surfaces.

The availability of water to plants does not correspond to the water content of soil as such but the suction force or water potential gradient in the plant in relation to soil water potential. The work required to move water from the soil to overcome forces of attraction is known as matric potential and is calculated using the free energy of pure water as a reference (Rose 1966, Slatyer 1967). It is equivalent to soil moisture tension and is often expressed in terms of soil $pF$ (the logarithm of the soil moisture tension expressed in centimeters height of a column of water).

A second factor, which increases the amount of work required by the plant to move water from the soil, is the concentration of salts in the soil solution. Presence of ions decreases the free energy of soil water because water molecules are attracted by the ions. The work required to overcome these forces of attraction is known as osmotic potential. This is of particular interest in the irrigated arid Savanna areas where the concentration of soluble salts in soil solution tends to be high, adding to the total amount of work required by plants to move water from the soil. The soil water potential therefore has two major components, matric potential and osmotic potential but the latter is generally assumed to be negligible. The plant water potential must be less than the soil water potential if water is to move from the soil into the plant.

For most practical purposes in assessing soil water storage and the availability of water to crops, it is sufficient to examine and interpret the $pF$ (moisture release) curves.

(h) *Moisture release curves.*  Typical $pF$ curves for distinct morphological horizons of a Ferruginous soil profile derived from Basement Complex rocks are given in Fig. 4.4. The curves are sigmoid. The vertical displacement of these curves is principally a reflection of soil texture while the shape of the curves is related to the structural characteristic of the soil.

Assuming that the water held between $pF$ 2 and 4·2 is available, the curves show that the bulk of the availabile water is loosely held, particularly noticeable in the 31 cm top of surface soil, implying that it is readily available to plants, but can also be readily lost by direct evaporation from the soil. About 75 per cent of available water in the cultivated surface of this soil is released at tensions of less

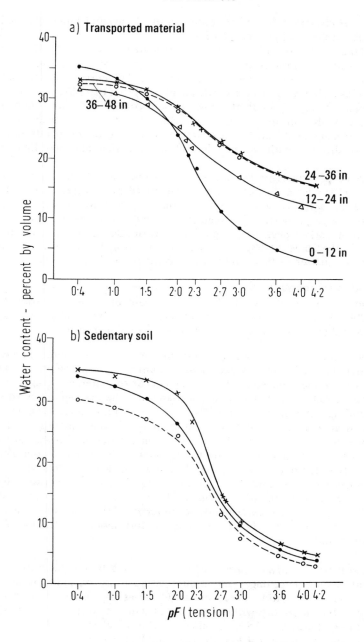

Fig. 4.4. Typical *pF* curves for a Ferruginous soil profile representing distinct morphological horizons (Kowal 1968a).

than *pF* 3 (equivalent to soil water potential of −1 bar) indicating that the bulk of pores have a diameter greater than $1.9\mu$.

Below the top 31 cm soil horizon, the curves are very similar showing a fairly uniform release of moisture per increment of applied suction, suggesting that there is no marked peak in pore size distribution. The curves indicate that the amount of available water decreases with depth and that there is a comparatively large amount of water held at *pF* above 4·2 and consequently not readily available. There is also an appreciable proportion of water in the available range which is strongly held, and the extraction of this water by plants becomes increasingly difficult with increase in soil water deficit and may limit plant growth.

At the deeper layers of the soil profile (below the 170 cm depth) the *pF* curves are all similar in shape and are characterized by a decreasing amount of available water with increasing depth. The bulk of the available water is loosely held with a large proportion between *pF* 1·5 and 2·7, suggesting that the soil matrix has a marked peak in the pore size distribution corresponding to pore diameters in the range $29-60\mu$. This is consistent with the presence of a higher proportion of coarser particles and low clay content (20–25 per cent).

### 4.1.7 Soil water constants

The soil water constants based on the concept of upper and lower limits of available water are important in understanding soil-plant-water relationships, and of direct practical importance in agricultural management.

(a) *Upper limit of available water.* Normally there is little interest in any soil state wetter than field capacity except when considering drainage problems. The field capacity values conveniently serve as one of the reference points for the estimation of soil water deficit, available water and the macroporosity of soils.

The drainage of soils to an equilibrium under definite tensions is used extensively as an indirect estimate of field capacity. However there is no unique tension which corresponds to field capacity value for all soils. The Samaru soils, drained to an equilibrium on tension tables, show moisture values equivalent to field capacity at tensions between *pF* at 2·15 and 2·4. Measurements with tensiometers *in situ* have indicated lower tensions at field capacity of between 80 and 125 cm of water column (*pF* 1·9 and 2·1). In the surface layers of sandy to loam soils, field capacity corresponds to about *pF* 2·0; in the lower layers of leached Ferruginous and Ferrallitic soils, it corresponds to about *pF* 2·3 (Charreau 1974a).

(b) *Lower limit of available water.* At the lower limit of available water, or the permanent wilting percentage, the amount of water in the soil is insufficient to supply the transpiration needs of turgid leaves. Its value is conveniently estimated in the laboratory without the use of indicator plants by draining soil samples to equilibrium at 15 atmosphere tension (Richards and Weaver 1943, Veihmeyer and Hendrickson 1949, Richards and Wadleigh 1952).

The 15 atmosphere percentage is a relatively stable value of soil since it represents an absorption stage for the soil water rather than pore water. Its value therefore is dependent upon the specific surface area of a soil. Since the specific surface area depends on the clay content, there should be a close relation between the 15 atmosphere percentage and the amount of clay. This was found in Samaru soils, where 15 atmosphere percentage values ranged from 6 to 20 per cent by volume (Kowal 1968b). According to Charreau (1974a) the 15 atmosphere values for sandy soil is in the range 3–4 per cent by volume for soils over aeolian deposits and 7–9 per cent for other Savanna soils.

(c) *Range of available water*. The capacity of soil to store large amounts of available water within the root zone of crops is of obvious importance, particularly in the more arid areas. Irregularities in rainfall distribution or a short rainy season often need to be buffered by the water reserves stored in the soil.

The amount of the water reserves in the soil profile available to plants depends not only on the soil available water but also on the depth of the soil profile to which roots extend, and root density within this depth. This is very variable depending on the plant, the soil, and the season, and is difficult to assess with precision. However, it is generally assumed that under the rain-fed conditions of the Savanna, the effective rooting depth of most crops does not extend beyond the depth of one metre. The notable exception is cotton which normally extends roots to greater depth.

Assuming that the effective rooting depth for most crops is one metre, the storage of available water within this depth ranges from about 80 to 110 mm in sandy soils over aeolian deposits and from 120 to 150 mm in Ferruginous and Ferrallitic soils (Charreau 1974a). The latter range, found by Francophone workers in more arid areas, is slightly higher than the range of 80–120 mm quoted by Lawes (1965), Kowal (1968b) and Samie (1974) for Ferruginous soils with weakly developed texture in B horizon, occurring in the more humid areas (Table 4.3).

The above values are relatively small when compared with those from soils with a well developed and stable structure. However, considering the amount and frequency of rainfall in the Guinea and Sudan Savanna the amount of available water stored within the effective root depth of well established crops is adequate to sustain them during rainless periods of 13 to 20 days. (Assuming the maximum water use by crops with fully developed canopy as 6 mm per day, the reserves of available water in soil profile are sufficient in the absence of rainfall to sustain crop growth for a period of 80/6 = 13 days to 120/6 = 20 days).

(d) *Macroporosity*. The amount and proportion of the total pore space that drains rapidly in the field is important for providing a suitable soil environment for plant growth. Provided the soil contains an adequate amount of available water, macroporosity is an index of soil fertility as far as aeration and rapid water movement are concerned. Macroporosity is measured as the difference between total porosity and the pore space occupied by water at field capacity.

The aeration requirements of different plants vary widely, but arbitrary values of macroporosity, assessed in terms of plant growth can be taken as, 0–4 per cent, poor; 4–7 per cent, moderate; and 7–10 per cent, good aeration levels (Stirk 1957). On this basis, the macroporosity values obtained for the soil profile at Samaru can be regarded as moderate to good (Table 4.4).

## Table 4.3

*Range of available water in two Ferruginous soils
(uncultivated land) at the Savanna Forestry Research Station
at Afaka, Nigeria (Samie 1974)*

| Depth of profile (cm) | Bulk density (g/cm³) | Water content at tension | | Available water (mm) |
|:---:|:---:|:---:|:---:|:---:|
| | | 1/3 Atm (mm) | 15 Atm (mm) | |
| 0–15 | 1·52 | 29 | 18 | 11 |
| 15–38 | 1·52 | 61 | 45 | 16 |
| 38–122 | 1·48 | 277 | 197 | 80 |
| 122–152 | 1·43 | 93 | 67 | 26 |
| 152–178 | 1·56 | 77 | 57 | 20 |
| 178–256 | 1·62 | 249 | 180 | 69 |
| 256–305 | 1·79 | 168 | 122 | 46 |
| Total | | | | 268 |
| 0–12 | 1·73 | 26 | 14 | 12 |
| 12–40 | 1·64 | 66 | 45 | 21 |
| 40–91 | 1·59 | 146 | 107 | 39 |
| 91–234 | 1·78 | 485 | 384 | 101 |
| 234–304 | 1·68 | 257 | 181 | 76 |
| Total | | | | 249 |

## Table 4.4

*Macroporosity and other related data for the soil profile at Samaru
(Kowal 1968b)*

| Depth of profile (cm) | Clay content (%) | Water at field capacity (% vol.) | Water at 15 Atm (% vol.) | Average water (% vol.) | Average water (mm) | Macro-porosity (%) |
|:---:|:---:|:---:|:---:|:---:|:---:|:---:|
| 0–8 | 12·7 | 15·4 | 6·2 | 19·2 | 15·2 | 21·5 |
| 8–15 | 14·4 | 25·4 | 5·7 | 19·7 | 30·5 | 22·0 |
| 15–23 | 20·3 | 25·9 | 8·9 | 17·0 | 43·2 | 15·3 |
| 23–30 | 25·7 | 25·9 | 11·7 | 14·2 | 53·3 | 15·3 |
| 30–38 | 28·5 | 27·3 | 13·8 | 13·5 | 63·5 | 13·5 |
| 38–46 | 33·4 | 27·3 | 16·6 | 10·7 | 71·2 | 14·1 |
| 46–53 | 37·9 | 28·4 | 18·6 | 9·8 | 78·7 | 12·3 |
| 53–61 | 39·3 | 28·4 | 20·3 | 8·1 | 86·4 | 13·6 |
| 61–69 | 38·1 | 29·6 | 21·9 | 7·7 | 91·4 | 13·0 |
| 69–76 | 42·7 | 29·6 | 20·5 | 9·1 | 99·0 | 11·9 |
| 76–84 | 41·7 | 30·1 | 20·0 | 10·1 | 106·1 | 11·1 |
| 84–91 | 40·6 | 30·1 | 19·9 | 10·2 | 114·9 | 12·0 |
| 91–100 | 41·3 | 30·0 | 20·2 | 9·8 | 121·9 | 12·4 |

The depth of the soil profile to the dry season water table is comparatively shallow in soils derived from Basement Complex rocks. Further, the fact that during the growing season rainfall greatly exceeds evapotranspiration demands, the macropores of the soil profile fill with water during the height of the rains causing a temporary rise in the water table. The effect of this at lower topographical slopes adversely affects crop production, cotton and maize being particularly susceptible. The rise of the water table occurs annually causing mottling of the clay subsoil and a seasonal flow of streams. Apart from its significance in terms of aeration, macroporosity affects the rate of water movement through the soil. Under field conditions this relates directly to rainfall acceptance.

### 4.1.8  Gaseous phase or soil atmosphere

The proportion and composition of the gaseous phase of the soil directly affects crop production. Crops require a constant and balanced supply of air for root respiration. If the soil atmosphere is inadequate with excessive carbon dioxide or corresponding oxygen deficiency, the growth of most crops and aerobic soil micro-organisms is adversely affected. An increase in the carbon dioxide concentration of soil air above one per cent or a reduction in oxygen content below 10 per cent usually results in damage to the root system.

The proportion of the gaseous phase present at any time in the soil depends on the pore size distribution and the amount of water held by the soil. Macroporosity is usually taken as an index of soil aeration and on this basis aeration in most of the Savanna soils is regarded as good. Exceptions to this are Vertisols with restricted drainage and prone to waterlogging.

Under waterlogged conditions, the escape of carbon dioxide and renewal of the air supply ceases, and as a result undesirable biological activity occurs which can be recognized by toxic concentration of methane, hydrogen sulphide or other toxic substances. Waterlogged conditions in the Savanna occur in soils derived from the Basement Complex rocks due to the rise in the dry season water table. Usually only lower slopes are affected and the waterlogging is temporary. Unfortunately it occurs during the later part of the growing season, thus adversely affecting crop production. A fluctuation in groundwater during the growing season within the rooting zone may seriously disturb the transport of gasses in the soil since gas diffusion mainly takes place in air filled pores. The limited exchange of gases not only decreases the soil oxygen content but also increases carbon dioxide content directly affecting a number of physiological processes such as nutrient and water absorption.

Apart from these direct effects on plants, a deficiency of oxygen in the soil results in a number of changes in the soil itself. Thus prolonged rise in the dry season water table favours an increase of divalent ions such as iron (Lawton 1945) and manganese (Leeper 1947) which may be toxic to plant roots in addition to any affect caused by the inadequate aeration of the root surfaces.

Experiments at Samaru (Palmer 1968) have shown that the water table within the root zone restricts root growth and, if persistent, causes asphysixation of deeper roots. Although plants can develop certain adaptations under fluctuating water table conditions, i.e., formation of thicker and shorter roots with air spaces, the growth of crops at Samaru in these conditions was well below the optimum. Cotton and maize were particularly sensitive to waterlogging while sorghum and millet were relatively tolerant.

### 4.1.9 Infiltration and hydraulic conductivity

Water intake through the surface of the Savanna soils varies greatly depending on surface soil conditions. Under natural vegetation, and particularly where surface organic mulch is present, the infiltration rate can be very high and soils can cope with very high intensity of rainfall without losing water in surface run-off (Kowal 1970c). This suggests that the hydraulic conductivity of soil profile is high. Indeed the hydraulic conductivity measured for a whole soil profile in Samaru area using pumping test method gave the surprisingly high value of 25 cm/h (Kowal 1968a).

In cultivated soils, the initial intake rates are rapidly reduced due to rain drop splash, destruction of unstable surface aggregation, clogging of pores by single grain particles and formation of surface crust (Kowal 1972b). Measurements of infiltration rates or rainfall acceptance in cultivated soils in the Savanna are few. Lawes (1961, 1964), using small catchment gauges at Samaru, recorded infiltration rates that varied from 120 mm/h under mulch or good grass cover to less than 100 mm/h for undisturbed bare fallow.

Wilkinson (1975) using field infiltrometers, recorded the equilibrium infiltration in grass fallows, and the effective hydraulic conductivity $K$ (i.e., when the driving force $i$ in Darcy's equation $V = Ki$ was approximately unity). His results show that under Gamba grass fallow $K$ values ranged from 29 to 58 mm/h, a range similar to that reported by Kowal (1970c). Under Gamba grass fallow the rates of infiltration increased proportionally to the square root of time. However, most of the increase was eliminated during the first seed bed preparation and all the increase was eliminated by the end of the first cropping season. Wilkinson (1975) stresses the fact that increases in infiltration rates in fallow were primarily associated with the activity of earthworms in the soil. A similar conclusion was recorded by Hurault (1971) working on the Savanna grassland in Northern Cameroon. However, it is likely that termite activity may also have been involved.

Chauvel and Tobias (1969) and Charreau and Nicou (1971), give comparative mean values of permeability under forest and cultivate land, showing a marked decrease of values under cropped soils where permeability was reduced to 1/3 or 1/6 of original values. This poses serious difficulties for soil management control of surface run-off and soil erosion in more humid areas, and conservation of rainfall in more arid areas.

## 4.2  Chemical properties

One of the main functions of soils is to provide an adequate reservoir of plant nutrients for crops. The availability of nutrients depends upon the amount and nature of inorganic and organic colloids present in the soil.

In most Savanna soils, inorganic colloids consist of kaolinitic minerals and amorphous iron and aluminium hydroxides derived from the parent material during weathering. Kaolinite and amorphous iron and aluminium oxides have a low exchange capacity.

The organic colloids are complex intermediate products formed during decomposition of organic matter by soil micro-organisms. These colloids have a high capacity to retain plant nutrients and their amount in the soil affects the fertility of the Savanna soils.

The soil colloids can absorb cations or anions in amounts directly proportional to their surface areas. The surface of soil colloids is normally negatively charged and this is neutralized by cations such as $H^+$, $Ca^{2+}$, $Mg^{2+}$ and $Na^+$. These cations can be readily replaced through simple exchange by other cations in solution and are therefore referred to as exchangeable cations. The proportion of cations replaced depends on the concentration of the replacing cation in the soil solution. The capacity of the soil to retain and exchange cation is an important soil property and a measure of the ability of the soil to store 'available' nutrients for gradual release to crops.

Anions are also held and exchanged in the soil. Anion exchange capacity increases with decreasing $p$H, being the opposite to the process of cation exchange (Arnon 1972). Phosphates and sulphates are more strongly held than chlorides and nitrates. The Savanna soils have a relatively high $p$H and a low capacity for anion absorption. Therefore, anions with the exception of phosphates, are easily leached from the soil. The predominant anion present in the Savanna soils is bicarbonate.

In the arid areas where leaching is limited, the accumulation of mineral salts may be much greater than that which can be absorbed by the soil exchange complex. Salts such as chlorides and carbonates of sodium and magnesium can accumulate in amounts harmful to crop growth. In general, when the concentration of the soluble salt content in the soil exceeds 0·5 per cent, soil productivity is reduced.

## 4.2.1 Cation Exchange Capacity (CEC)

In most Savanna soils, the cation exchange capacity is low. The exceptions are the Vertisols, Ferrisols and Eutrophic Brown soils which occupy only a small proportion of the Savanna areas.

The CEC values measured at $p$H 7·0 with molar ammonium acetate, are usually in the range 3–8 me/100 g. Under field conditions these values are expected to be lower since the charge characteristics in the colloidal complex are $p$H dependent, and most of the soils have the $p$H values below 7 used in the determination of the CEC. Further, iron-rich kaolinitic soils have a lower CEC in low electrolyte concentration than in the one molar concentration used in the analytical procedure (Barber and Rowell 1972).

The CEC values are closely related to the soil organic matter and clay contents of the soil. However, because the clay content of soils is low and mainly kaolinitic, the contribution of the clay to the cation exchange capacity is not greater than 1–2 me/100 g soil and the CEC is mainly related to the organic matter content of the soil. Jones (1971) in Nigeria calculated that an increase in soil carbon content from 0·1 to 1·0 per cent would increase the exchange capacity from 0·08 to 4·28 me/100 g soil and increase the contribution of the organic matter to the exchange capacity from 38 to 68 per cent.

Jones and Wild (1975) list the following implications of low exchange capacity of the Savanna soils:

(i)   Many soils are low in the exchangeable cations required as crop nutrients, and under cropping systems where nutrient demand is high they will quickly become unable to meet these requirements.

(ii)   A low content of exchangeable cations may lead to nutrient imbalances from conventional fertilizer practices, in which only one or two nutrients are applied. It may therefore become necessary to balance the nutrient supply by using more complete fertilizers.

(iii)   Nutrients applied as cations, ammonium, potassium, magnesium, etc., are weakly held and leaching may occur from the surface soil. Calculations show that a soil with a cation exchange capacity of 1 me/100 g would be saturated to depth of 15 cm by the ammonium ions given as an application of 280 kg N/ha, and although these are extreme conditions they are not entirely unrealistic.

(iv)   Rapid soil acidification occurs where ammonium sulphate and, to a lesser extent, urea are used. Other changes from traditional practices, for example the abandonment of burning or of the fallow, may also accelerate acidification.

These implications are particularly important under continuous system of cropping with high production demanding large fertilizer inputs. At a very high level of productivity they present a major management problem for which a practical solution has yet to be found.

## 4.2.2   Soil reaction

Soil reaction or $pH$ may affect crops by its influence on the availability of certain elements, by exerting a toxic effect on the root system, and by inhibiting desirable micro-organisms.

Under the natural Savanna vegetation and traditional farming systems the $pH$ values, measured in 1:1 soil:water, range between 6·0 and 6·8. This range is favourable for crop production and is maintained by the low net rate of removal of bases associated with the low level of production and return to the soil of some of the crop residues, by the effect of burning, and by very small or no application of ammonium and urea fertilizer. Further, a significant net transfer of some nutrients from the subsoil to the topsoil during a period under fallow tends to make good the net loss from the topsoil that occurred during the previous cropping period. Also the leaching of bases under fallow or non-intensive cropping is restricted by the low anion content of the soil solution.

In contrast, under continuous cropping, the soil reaction tends to fall with the increasing intensity of production; the application of large amounts of fertilizer, particularly ammonium sulphate and urea accelerate the process. For example, at Sefa, Senegal, exchangeable calcium and soil $pH$ declined by as much as 1 me/100 g soil over six years of cultivation, involving a loss which is only slowly, if at all, reversible (Fauck, 1956). The buffering capacity of the soil under these conditions diminishes and nutrient imbalance may become apparent. Exhausted soils have very low $pH$ values (less than $pH$ 4) and sometimes may include aluminium toxicity as for instance in some overcropped/degraded fields of the Kano Agricultural Experiment Station.

Low soil reaction reduces the availability of phosphates in soils high in iron and aluminium, and a decline in the availability of molybdenum with decreasing soil pH was observed by Heathcote (1972a) and Heathcote and Fowler (1977) in Nigeria.

The soil pH is easily determined and can serve as an excellent indicator of the general soil condition.

### 4.2.3 Nitrogen

About 99 per cent of the nitrogen naturally present in the soil is bound in organic materials having been fixed once by the assimilation of free nitrogen from air by soil organisms. The nitrogen status of soil is therefore closely associated with the soil organic matter, and is a function of relative rates of gain and loss which under stable conditions tends towards an equilibrium value. Unfortunately there is as yet no comprehensive account of the full nitrogen balance (Greenland 1975), particularly in the Savanna environment and only an approximate account of the gain, losses and availability of soil nitrogen can be presented.

Total soil nitrogen in the Savanna ranges from 0·008 to 2·90 per cent with an average value of 0·051 per cent in the upper layers (0–15 cm) of cropped soils or soils under grass fallows (Jones 1973). The smallest amounts of soil nitrogen are found in the northern part of the Sahel region where annual rainfall is less than 400 mm. The largest amounts occur at the southern boundary of the Savanna. The amounts in the High Forest areas further south are 30 to 80 per cent higher.

The total nitrogen content of the Savanna soils is influenced by annual rainfall and soil clay content. Using data from all the Savanna regions (350–1905 mm rainfall per annum), Jones (1973) obtained the relationship:

$$N\% = 0·00116 + 0·00175 \text{ (clay \%)} + 0·0000348 \text{ (rain mm)} \quad (r = 0·76) \quad (4.9)$$

Therefore, soil nitrogen status is also related to latitudinal position, and using equation (3.19) can be described by the following regression in terms of clay content, latitude and longitude:

$$N\% = 0·084796 + 0·00175 \text{ (clay \%)} - 0·00455(LA) - 0·0003(LO) \quad (4.10)$$

The equations show the general trend at equilibrium between rates of gains and losses. Losses will predominate under cultivation and will relate to the intensity of cropping. Gains will predominate under fallows, and conditions favouring a build up in the soil organic matter.

In the following paragraphs an account is given on gains, losses and the availability of nitrogen to crops.

(a) *Gains of nitrogen.* These arise from the following activities:

(i) Fixation as one of the oxides of nitrogen by electrical discharges allows some nitrogen to reach the soil dissolved in rainfall. These amounts are small.

Jones and Bromfield (1970) reported the annual content of nitrogen in rainfall at Samaru as being 4-5 kg N/ha. Higher values were reported (Thornton 1965), increasing southwards towards the sea. Measurements at Senegal ranged from 5 to 10 kg N/ha per annum (Charreau 1974a).

(ii) Fixation by nodules and bacterial root associations is the primary pathway by which atmospheric nitrogen is converted to forms usable by higher plants is fixation by *Rhizobium* and other micro-organisms which live symbiotically in nodules on the roots of leguminous plants and certain non-leguminous plants. Soil bacteria are also active in fixing nitrogen when closely associated with root which supply the carbohydrate for the energy this process needs. It appears that this fixation in the rhizosphere may also be regarded as a form of symbiotic fixation (Dobereiner, Day, and Dart 1972a, 1972b, Dommergues, Balandreau, Rinaudo, and Weinhard 1973, Dart and Day 1975, van Berkum, Dart, Day, Jenkinson, and Witty 1975, Joachim, von Bulow, and Dobereiner 1975, Rinaudo, Hamad-Fares, and Dommergues 1975, Day and Dobereiner 1976).

Fixation associated with nodules occur both with legumes in fallows and with crop legumes. Under natural vegetation there are many leguminous wood and herbaceous plants that exhibit root nodules which when cut show a reddish colour normally associated with leghaemoglobin and nitrogen fixation. In parts of the northern Sudan and Sahel zones, the traditionally protected tree *Acacia albida* is reported to be a vigorous nitrogen fixer. Dancette and Poulain (1969) reported that the amount of mineralized nitrogen in soils under *A. albida* was 15-20 kg N/ha greater than under sorghum. Dommergues (1966) in Senegal reported a fixation of about 60 kg N/ha by a stand of *Casuarina*, a non-leguminous species.

The fixation in crop legumes, the most important being groundnut, cowpea, and soya bean, is thought to be low by many agronomists. Certainly there is nothing comparable to the high rates of fixation and adaptability to different management of clover and lucerne grown in temperate regions. However, it is estimated that a groundnut crop of 3 tonne/ha of dry matter fixes about 150 kg of nitrogen (Bromfield 1973). Since the haulms of groundnut make very good fodder and are rarely returned to the soil immediately, about 30 to 40 kg N/ha is retained in the soil in roots and dry leaves.

Recent work on rhizospheric fixation (Dobereiner *et al.* 1972a, 1972b, Dommergues *et al.* 1973, van Berkum *et al.* 1975) has shown that roots of over 40 species of agronomically important tropical grain crops (including rice, maize, millet, and sorghum) and forage grasses stimulate much root associated nitrogen fixation (Table 4.5), as indicated by measurements of nitrogenase activity in reducing acetylene to ethylene. It is probable that this rhizospheric fixation makes or has the potential of making considerable contribution to the nitrogen economy under both fallows and crops. However, the extent and importance of the phenomenon are still to be assessed.

(iii) Nitrogen fixation in soils is also brought about by certain free-living organisms which include many species of the blue-green algae on the soil surface and certain free-living bacteria in the bulk of the soil. The most numerous

## Table 4.5

*Nitrogenase activity associated with the roots of some tropical grasses and cereals (Van Berkum et al. 1975)*

| Country and species | Nitrogenase activity (nmol $C_2H_4$/g root/h) |
|---|---|
| Brazil: | |
| *Brachiaria mutica* (Para grass) | 150–750 |
| *Brachiaria rugulosa* | 5–150 |
| *Cynodon dactylon* (Bermuda grass) | 20–270 |
| *Cuperus rotundus* (Nut grass) | 10–30 |
| *Digitaria decumbens* (Pangola grass) | 20–400 |
| *Hyparrhenia rufa* (Jaragua grass) | 20–30 |
| *Melinis minutiflora* (Molasses grass) | 15–40 |
| *Panicum maximum* (Guinea grass) | 20–300 |
| *Paspalum notatum* (Bahia grass) | 2–300 |
| *Pennisetum purpureum* (Napier or Elephant grass) | 5–1000 |
| *Saccharum officinarum* (Sugar cane) | 5–20 |
| *Sorghum bicolor* (Sorghum) | 10–100 |
| Nigeria: | |
| *Andropogon gayanus* (Gamba grass) | 15–270 |
| *Cenchurus ciliaris* (Buffel grass) | 16 |
| *Cymbopogon giganteus* | 60–85 |
| *Cynodon dactylon* (Star grass) | 10–50 |
| *Cyperus* sp. (Sedge) | 2 |
| *Hyparrhenia rufa* (Jaragua grass) | 30–140 |
| *Hypothelia dissoluta* | 10–15 |
| *Panicum maximum* (Guinea grass) | 75 |
| *Paspalum virgatum* | 3 |
| *Pennisetum purpureum* | 60 |
| *Pennisetum coloratum* | 13 |
| *Setaria anceps* | 1–120 |
| *Pennisetum typhoides* (Pearl millet) | 3–195 |
| *Sorghum bicolor* (Sorghum) | 22–83 |
| Ivory Coast: | |
| *Andropogon* sp. | 50–380 |
| *Brachiaria brachylopha* | 100–140 |
| *Bulbostylis aphyllanthoides* | 74 |
| *Cyperus obtusiflorus* | 30–620 |
| *Cyperus zollingeri* | 50–160 |
| *Cyperus* sp. (Sedge) | 1150–1900 |
| *Fimbristylis* sp. | 80–190 |
| *Hyparrhenia dissoluta* | 2–4 |
| *Loudetia simplex* | 54 |
| *Oryza sativa* (Rice) | 1040–2360 |
| Australia: | |
| *Setaria anceps* | 68 |
| *Pennisetum clandestinum* (Kikuyu grass) | 21–140 |
| France: | |
| *Oryza sativa* (Rice) | 1040–2360 |
| *Zea mays* (Maize) | 100–3000 |
| U.S.A.: | |
| *Zea mays* (Maize) | 14–16 |
| Philippines: | |
| *Oryzea sativa* (Rice) | 8–80 |

bacterium species found in the Savanna is *Clostridium*, an anaerobic saprophyte, followed by *Azotobacter* and *Beijerinckia* which are aerobic saprophytes (Meiklejohn 1962). There has been considerable speculation about the amounts of nitrogen actually fixed by these free living bacteria, but the aerobic nitrogen fixation has been reported to be about 6 kg N/ha per annum (Odu 1967). Little is known of the activities of the *Clostridia*, which need anaerobic conditions for nitrogen fixation. These free-living organisms require a source of available energy which is present in the form of organic residues. Part of the energy from the oxidation of these residues is used to fix elemental nitrogen. Bartholomew (1972) points out that one tonne of carbohydrate is needed by bacteria to fix 10 kg N/ha. He suggests that because of this very high energy requirement very little non-symbiotic nitrogen fixation occurs in most tropical soils.

The blue-green algae occur under a wide range of environmental conditions including rocks and semi-desert conditions. Since they are completely autotrophic, the energy required for the fixation of nitrogen is supplied by light. Therefore one would expect their contribution in the Savanna areas to be greater than from the free living bacteria.

(b) *Losses of nitrogen.* In order to appreciate fully the factors controlling the nitrogen status of the soil it is essential to know not only the gains from biological fixation and rainfall but also the magnitude of losses particularly those influenced by management. Losses arise from the following activities:

(i) The main factor contributing to a substantial nitrogen loss in the Savanna is the burning of residues from crops and fallows. Various estimates give the magnitude of nitrogen loss due to burning ranging from about 20 to 40 kg N/ha per annum (Nye and Greenland 1960, Vidal and Fauche 1962).

(ii) The magnitude of nitrogen loss due to leaching depends on the rate of mineralization and nitrification, amount and type of nitrogenous fertilizer added (Blondel 1971a), soil type (Jones and Wild 1975), vegetation cover (Tourte, Vidal, Jacquinot, Fauche, and Nicou 1964), and the amount of rainfall percolating through the soil (Charreau 1974a). From the lysimeter studies in Senegal it is estimated that leaching in the Savanna environment in 1 m soil depth may account for between 5 and 30 kg N/ha per annum depending on the situation (Charreau 1974a). Ammonium nitrigen is leached only slightly. However, it appears that leaching of nitrate nitrogen out of the topsoil may not necessarily mean permanent loss. In leached soils, with a high amount of amorphous material in the subsoil, nitrate tends to accumulate in the 1–2 m depth by adsorption on the positive changes in the textural B horizon (Jones and Wild 1975). This nitrogen can be recovered in a rotation involving deep rooting crops. Measurements of leaching rates (Blondel 1971c, 1971d, 1971e, 1971f, Wild 1972a, Jones 1975, Jones and Wild 1975) indicate that 1 cm of rainfall move nitrate nitrogen down the profile by 7 cm in the slightly leached Ferruginous sandy soil, 0·2–1·6 cm in the leached Ferruginous soil, and 1·7 cm in the Ferrallitic soil.

(iii) Gaseous losses of nitrogen. Nitrogen may be lost by denitrification which is the biochemical reduction of nitrates under anaerobic conditions, by chemical reactions involving nitrites under anaerobic conditions and by the volatile loss of ammonia gas from the surface of alkaline soils.

Loss by denitrification or by the successive transformation of $(NO_3^-) \rightarrow (NO_2^-) \rightarrow (N_2)$ by certain anaerobic organisms which can obtain their oxygen from nitrates and nitrites with the accompanying release of $N_2$ and $N_2O$, is enhanced by high moisture level of the soil, low amount of oxygen in soil atmosphere and low soil $pH$.

Losses by denitrification may be high in the soils flooded for rice cultivation, but also under the rain-fed conditions. Bartholomew (1972) estimated losses due to denitrification in the rain-fed soils to be of the order of 5–15 per cent of the available nitrogen in the course of a single cropping season. Lysimeter studies at Samaru (J. M. Kowal, unpublished) have shown that 15–20 per cent of the soil nitrogen may be lost due to denitrification.

Loss of gaseous nitrogen from well drained soils relate to the decomposition of $NO_2^-$ ion. Although there is no concensus regarding the mechanism of the decomposition process there are three pathways by which the reaction may take place:

$$NH_4 \, NO_2 \rightarrow 2H_2O + N_2$$

$$RNH_2 + HNO_2 \rightarrow ROH + H_2O + N_2$$

$$3HNO_2 \rightarrow NO + HNO_3 + H_2O$$

These reactions have not been determined experimentally in soil but are at present regarded as advanced explanations of the observed losses of nitrogen from the soil.

The losses by volatilization of $NH_4^+$ ions from the application of ammonium sulphate and urea are low in spite of the high temperature, and humidity and evaporation rates which favour the process. In central Senegal, under conditions most favourable for volatilization losses of $NH_3$ were only 5–10 kg N/ha (Blondel 1967). Normally, volatilization can be greatly reduced or prevented by placing fertilizers several centimeters under the soil surface.

(c) *Availability of nitrogen to crops.* The store of organic nitrogen in the soil only becomes available to crops when it is converted into ammonium and nitrate forms. The amount becoming available in any one period depends upon the rate at which soil organic nitrogen is mineralized and on the balance of gains and losses of soil nitrogen already discussed. The rate of mineralization of the soil organic matter depends on the activity of soil micro-organisms which in turn is affected by a variety of factors such as the seasonality, temperature, moisture, effect of wetting and drying, aeration, $pH$, and the chemical nature of the humus or organic matter. The relative importance of these factors will be now considered.

(i) Seasonality. Microbial activity in the Savanna soils ceases during the dry season, due to severe desiccation of the soil surface. For this reason there is a distinct seasonal pattern in the activity of the micro-organisms and the content of soil mineral nitrogen. In general, the level of mineral nitrogen is at its peak at the beginning of the rainy season, at its lowest at the height of the rains, and at a low–medium level during the dry season.

(ii) Temperature. Kowal (1954) working at Ibadan, Nigeria, and Cooper (1971) at Samaru, Nigeria, showed a close correlation between soil temperature and the rate of nitrification under steady moisture conditions. Moureaux (1967) working in Senegal reported a high level of biological activity at temperatures as high as 55-65 °C with maximum mineralization occurring at about 50 °C.

At the start of the rains when surface soil temperatures are at their highest level, the change in the soil moisture results in an explosion of soil microbial activity and consequent high rates of mineralization and nitrification.

The prolonged exposure of the surface soil to high radiation, high temperatures and extreme desiccation during the dry season results in a partial sterilization of the surface soil. This might have two consequences: the release of immobilized nitrogen locked in dead microbial nitrogen rich tissue, and the enchancement of the mineralization rate due to a reduction in microbial competition at the start of the following rainy season.

(iii) Moisture. The level of soil moisture has a large effect on the rates of mineralization (i.e., ammonification) and nitrification (i.e., nitrate formation from ammonium). During the prolonged and excessive periods of wetness not only high mobile $NO_3^-$ ions are leached away but the reduced diffusion of oxygen into soils with generally low macroporosity inhibits mineralization and nitrification and most likely encourages denitrification. Nitrification is inhibited more easily than ammonification by high and low soil moisture content. Thus in Nigeria Wild (1972b) found that ammonification continued at moisture contents below the wilting point but nitrification was arrested at low moisture tension.

The ratio of the quantity of $(NO_3^- - N)$ to the quantity of $(NH_4^+ - N)$ is thought to influence growth of crops. The ratio tends to be small during the dry season but increases when soil becomes sufficiently wet to permit nitrification. The most favourable $NO_3^-/NH_4^+$ ratio for crop growth for millet in controlled environment was found to be near 2 (Jacquinot 1973) but this is not commonly found in the Savanna soils.

(iv) Birch effect. Birch (1958) reported that repeated cycles of soil wetting and drying led to repeated flushes of mineralization at each rewetting, the magnitude of which declined only slowly with repetition. A similar effect of wetting and drying on mineralization of organic sulphur was reported by Bromfield (1974a) for the Savanna soils in Nigeria.

The amount of mineral nitrogen in the flush is of agronomic importance. Reported values from Senegal range from 58 kg N/ha at Bambey to 157 kg N/ha at Sefa (Blondel 1971c, 1971d). At Samaru Wild (1972b) found that the amount at the time of planting was about 7 kg N/ha after cotton, sorghum or groundnut when no manure had been applied; but where 12·5 tonne/ha of manure had been applied the amount after groundnut was about 70 kg N/ha.

A pronounced response of crops to early planting in the indigenous system in the Savanna is often attributed to an efficient use of this early mineralized nitrogen, before it is lost by leaching or taken up by weeds.

(v) Aeration. At the start of the growing season the soil macroporosity is at its optimum. As the season progresses rainfall increases in frequency and quantity, and the pore space in the soil becomes filled with an increasingly larger proportion of water. As the season advances the pore size distribution is modified, resulting in a greatly reduced macroporosity. Consequently most of the pore space is occupied by water thus reducing soil aeration and affecting rates of nitrification and denitrification.

(vi) Immobilization. Mineral soil nitrogen that is assimilated into microbial tissue and temporarily unavailable is referred to as immobilized nitrogen. This process occurs when the amount and frequency of incorporation of organic residues poor in nitrogen is increased. Under the Savanna conditions where loss of nitrogen due to leaching is rapid, a mechanism which conserves fertilizer nitrogen by holding it in organic form and releasing it slowly may be of considerable benefit. Undoubtedly the practice of frequent returns of crop residues under continuous cropping will be accepted as good farming and an essential part of the improvement of soil physical condition and soil fertility. Under this practice immobilization may become an important factor in soil management. In Senegal Fauche, Moureaux, and Thomann (1969) and Charreau and Fauck (1970) adopted incorporation of plant residues immediately after the end of the growing season as a means minimizing the effect of immobilization on the subsequent crop.

(d) *Nitrogen requirement of crops.* The nitrogen requirements of crops differ and vary with cultivar, stage of crop development and environment. In general, the total uptake of nitrogen is roughly proportional to the dry matter produced but the proportionality coefficient varies with crop and cultivar. Also, as the ratio of grain to straw is different between crops, similar amounts of nitrogen taken up may produce different yields. For example uptake of 130 kg N/ha approximately corresponds to yield of about 3 tonne/ha of millet but about 5 tonne/ha of maize (Charreau 1974a). In general there is a fairly close correlation between grain yield and nitrogen uptake. Increase in uptake increases yield more due to increases in the total plant dry matter than due to increases in harvest index.

Some examples of total nitrogen uptake of cereals are shown in Table 4.6. Not only the total uptake but also uptake per tonne of grain differs substantially between crop and variety. The percentage of nitrogen uptake per tonne of grain produced, nitrogen use efficiency (weight of grain produced per kg of nitrogen taken up) is roughly correlated with the maximum rate of nitrogen uptake. Genetically improved varieties generally have higher ratios of grain to straw, high maximum rates of nitrogen uptake, and high nitrogen use efficiencies.

In general, the pattern of nitrogen uptake by crops is such that plant nitrogen content follows a sigmoid curve similar to the dry matter accumulation curve (Fig. 4.5). The minimum requirement during the early stages of growth in millet increases as the rate of growth accelerates to reach a maximum during the period between panicle initiation and panicle emergence. Under the prevailing climatic and soil conditions in the Savanna, this pattern of crop nitrogen requirement is poorly matched to the availability of mineral nitrogen in soils, and in order to satisfy crop nitrogen requirements a supplementary nitrogen fertilizer must be applied in adequate amounts at the right time.

**Table 4.6**

*Nitrogen uptake by cereals in Senegal (Blondel 1971b)*

| Crop | Location | Grain (kg/ha) | Total nitrogen uptake (kg/ha) | Uptake per tonne of grain | Grain nitrogen / Total nitrogen (%) | Maximum rate of nitrogen uptake (kg/ha/day) | Grain to straw ratio | Nitrogen use efficiency (kg grain per kg N) |
|---|---|---|---|---|---|---|---|---|
| Pearl millet (PC 28) | Bambey | 1930 | 79 | 41 | 39 | 2·8 | 0·24 | 23 |
| Pearl millet (PC 11) | Bambey | 2200 | 92 | 42 | 35 | 1·5 | 0·18 | 23 |
| Pearl millet (Local) | Sefa | 3130 | 132 | 42 | 34 | 2·4 | 0·17 | 23 |
| Sorghum (51–69) | Nioro | 4066 | 134 | 33 | 54 | 2·2 | 0·36 | 30 |
| Maize (ZM 10) | Sefa (1967) | 4466 | 121 | 27 | 62 | 3·4 | 0·72 | 37 |
| Maize (ZM 10) | Sefa (1969) | 5440 | 138 | 25 | 71 | 5·0 | 0·75 | 40 |
| Rice (63–83) | Sefa | 3360 | 84 | 25 | 50 | 2·1 | 0·56 | 40 |
| Rice (TN 1) | Sefa | 4240 | 74 | 17 | 68 | 3·5 | 1·22 | 58 |

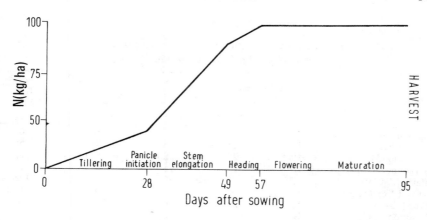

Fig. 4.5. Cumulative nitrogen uptake curve for millet (Blondel 1971c).

Charreau (1974a) draws attention to the fact that the nitrogen use efficiency markedly differs with various crops. He considers that the total uptake of nitrogen by crops may not be a good index of the needs of plants for nitrogen and that crop nitrogen requirements are better assessed when the maximum rates of uptake are also taken into account. To illustrate the point, the total uptake of nitrogen by a maize and a long season local millet crop at Sefa were found to be similar (Blondel 1971b). However, the uptake of this amount by the millet crop was met by the rate of mineralization of nitrogen in the soil and no fertilizer nitrogen was needed. On the other hand a heavy application of fertilizer nitrogen was required on the maize crop to meet crop demand. This is explained by the differences in the maximum rates of nitrogen uptake by these two crops which were 2·4 kg N/ha per day for millet and 5·0 kg N/ha per day for maize. Charreau (1974a) stresses the need for information on the quantitative patterns of nitrogen uptake in relation to time and stages of crop development for all crops and their cultivars as essential for interpretation and assessment of crop nitrogen requirement.

Theoretically it would be possible and desirable to add nitrogen as close as possible to the requirement of the crops as dictated by its growth pattern. However, in practice additional factors need careful consideration such as the pattern of soil nitrogen availability, prevention of excessive leaching and adverse effect of excess nitrogen on crop yield and quality. Excessive nitrogen in cereals can lead to lodging. In cotton nitrogen application can increase pest infestation and could lead to greater crop damage when the crop is not protected against pests (Palmer and Heathcote 1970, Hayward 1972).

In the Francophone areas split application of nitrogenous fertilizers and precise time of application has been defined and recommended to meet nitrogen requirements of crops and nitrogen use efficiencies. This is summarized in Table 4.7.

## Table 4.7

*Recommended nitrogen fertilization rates for the main crops in Senegal (IRAT 1972, Charreau 1974a)*

| Crop | Application (kg N/ha) | | | Times of application (days after sowing) | Total (kg N/ha) |
|---|---|---|---|---|---|
| | 1st (NH$_4$)$_2$SO$_4$ | 2nd (Urea) | 3rd (Urea) | | |
| Early millet | 10 | 25 | 25 | 0–15–15 | 60 |
| Late millet | 10 | 25 | 25 | 0–15–50 | 60 |
| Sorghum (51–69) | 10 | 25 | 50 | 0–15–50 | 85 |
| Sorghum (SH–60) | 10 | 25 | 25 | 0–15–65 | 60 |
| Maize (ZM 10) | 25 | 50 | 50 | 0–27–41 | 125 |
| Rice (I Kong Pao) | 10 | 50 | 50 | 0–20–55 | 110 |
| Rice (63–83) | 10 | 25 | 0 | 0–20 | 35 |
| Groundnut | 10 | 0 | 0 | 0 | 10 |
| Cowpea | 10 | 0 | 0 | 0 | 10 |
| Cotton–Centre | 11 | 22 | 0 | 0–50 | 33 |
| Cotton–South | 24 | 22 | 0 | 0–50 | 43 |

(e) *Conclusions.* Nitrogen is one of the two most important crop nutrients in the West African Savanna. In the presence of adequate phosphorus a lack of nitrogen may limit growth and yield of all crops. Amounts required are large, exceeding 100 kg N/ha for good cereal and legume crops. The main sources of crop nitrogen are as follows:

(i) Soil native mineral nitrogen (i.e., ammonium and nitrate nitrogen, mineralized from soil organic matter). Crop uptake from this source is in the range 10–40 kg N/ha per annum. Amounts are closely related to the values of organic matter in the soil which in the Savanna areas are generally low.

(ii) Rain water. Contributions from this source are of the order of only 4·4 kg N/ha per annum and of little practical importance.

(iii) Biologically fixed nitrogen. In crop legumes nitrogen fixation in nodules can meet crop requirements if other factors are not limiting. There is no doubt that nitrogen is fixed by bacteria in the rhizosphere of some plant although the amount is not known sufficiently accurately. The amount fixed by blue-green algae on the soil surface and free-living bacteria in the bulk of the soil are not known accurately.

(iv) Nitrogenous fertilizer. Under subsistence agriculture crop nitrogen is largely supplied by biological fixation and is sufficient for only very modest yields.

For substantially higher yields crop nitrogen requirements are higher and inputs of native mineral nitrogen are unlikely ever to meet crop demands. The rain water contribution is not amenable to any great change. Any increase in availability of nitrogen to the crop therefore must come from biologically fixed nitrogen or nitrogenous fertilizer. These two sources should not normally be regarded as competitive, but rather complementary. Nevertheless, it is pertinent to note that while nitrogenous fertilizer must be paid for and laboriously applied, biologically fixed nitrogen is free and is supplied just where it is needed.

Clearly biological nitrogen fixation has a dominant place to play in the economy and productivity of Savanna agriculture. Unfortunately as yet this aspect does not play any significant part in the management and economy of the Savanna agriculture comparable to long established practices in the temperate agriculture of crop relations involving legumes.

Little is known about the magnitude of nitrogen derived from biological fixation. The recent development of a comparatively simple, rapid, sensitive method for measuring nitrogen fixation, which measures the activity of the nitrogenase enzyme, bears much promise for making up this deficiency in the present knowledge. Nitrogenase, which is responsible for reduction of molecular nitrogen to ammonia, is equally capable of reducing acetylene to ethylene and these two gases are readily estimated by gas chromatography. Thus nitrogenase activity, and hence the current rate of nitrogen fixation, may be determined by measuring the rate of ethylene production of a sample placed in a closed vessel containing acetylene (Dart, Day, and Harris 1972, Hardy, Burns, and Holsten 1973). The sample may consist of nodules, and complete root systems, the soil only, or the whole plant-soil systems.

## 4.2.4 *Phosphorus*

The generally small quantities of phosphorus in the Savanna soils and its tendency to react with soil components to form compounds relatively insoluble and therefore unavailable to crops, results in widespread phosphate deficiency. In some soils the deficiency is so acute that crop growth stops as soon as the seed reserves of phosphate have been used up.

Because of its importance in tropical agriculture phosphorus has been more thoroughly studied than other nutrients. Relevant literature was recently reviewed by Olson and Engelstad (1972) and for Francophone areas by J. Bouyer (1970) and Pichot and Roche (1972).

(a) *Total phosphorus.* The average content of total phosphorus in the surface of the Savanna soils ranges from about 80 to 150 ppm (Nye and Bertheux 1957, Goldsworthy and Heathcote 1963, Bouyer and Damour 1964, Enwezor and Moore 1966). Exceptions are soils derived from Basalt and Vertisols where total phosphorus may be of the order of 1250 and 300 ppm respectively. This range is substantially lower than the average content of 1500 ppm P in the humid warm temperate region and 3000 ppm P in the sub-humid cool temperate region.

Although the total phosphorus content of soils is not a good measure of crop requirements, the exceptionally low values indicate widespread phosphate deficiency in the Savanna. In general, the Savanna soils with less than 220–390 ppm P respond to phosphate dressings (Bouyer, S. 1958, Berger 1964).

(b) *Forms of phosphorus.* The phosphorus in soils is generally classed as either organic or inorganic. The organic phosphorus is available through mineralization of the organic matter and constitutes usually only 15–40 per cent of the total phosphorus. Organic phosphate levels in most of the Savanna soils are low, in the range 15–60 ppm P (Goldsworthy and Heathcote 1963, Enwezor and Moore

1966, Ipimidum 1972). If one accepts an annual organic matter decomposition constant of 4 per cent in the cultivated Savanna soils, 15-60 ppm of organic phosphorus releases only 2-10 kg/ha from a depth of 30 cm. Work in the Francophone Savanna areas suggests that additions of humified organic matter has beneficial effect increasing phosphate concentration in the soil solution and the content of soluble phosphate.

The inorganic fraction of phosphorus in soils occurs in numerous combinations with aluminium, iron, and calcium phosphates (Bouyer and Damour 1954, Pichot and Roche 1972). The proportion of these forms in the soil depends mainly on the soil reaction. At $pH$ 7 calcium and aluminium phosphate predominate; in the $pH$ range 5·5-6·8, aluminium phosphate prevails; at $pH$ values lower than 5·5 iron phosphate and phosphorus linked with organic matter predominate. Only calcium phosphate and aluminium phosphate are thought to be directly available to plants. A high proportion of aluminium and iron phosphates occurs in occluded concretions and coatings in the Ferruginous and Ferrallitic soils. These are thought to be only slightly available to crops.

(c) *Availability of soil phosphate to crops.* Most of the soil phosphorus is taken up by crops in the form of $H_2PO_4^-$ ion or $HPO_4^{2-}$ ion. Compared with nitrogen or potassium the amount required by crops is relatively small being roughly about 1/10 of the nitrogen requirement or 1/5 of the potassium requirement.

Losses of soil phosphate by leaching are very small. Thus, in Senegal, the amount of phosphorus annually leached is estimated to range from 0·04 to 0·22 kg/ha (Charreau 1974a).

There is no loss of phosphorus due to burning of crop residues, although the phosphorus content in the ash is usually small and generally contributes little to soil phosphate status. On clearing the Savanna vegetation by burning, about 10-14 kg P/ha is returned to the soil. This compares with 120 kg P/ha found in a 40 year old High Forest vegetation (Greenland and Kowal 1960). One of the reasons for the widespread practice of land ridging might be to concentrate the ash containing phosphate in a narrow band of ridge so as to concentrate phosphate supply to crops (Kowal and Stockinger 1973b).

The main loss of phosphorus under arable conditions in the Savanna occurs in removal of crops and in soil erosion. Under high levels of production total uptake of phosphorus by crops may range from about 20 to 40 kg/ha. For example, a 9400 kg/ha maize crops removes 39 kg/ha of phosphorus in grain and 8 kg/ha in stover. Because the greater part of the phosphorus taken up by crops is accumulated in the saleable portions of the crop, the crop residues can contribute little if returned to the soil. Under moderate production levels total uptake by crops may range from about 10 to 15 kg P/ha for groundnuts, millet, sorghum and cotton to about 15-20 kg P/ha for maize and rice.

Losses due to accelerated soil erosion are estimated to be in the order of 5-10 kg P/ha per annum. These values however vary with soil type, rainfall, topography and management and can be much greater.

Changes from available to less available or unavailable forms of phosphorus in the soil also affect the uptake of phosphate by crops. Under acid or neutral soil conditions *adsorption* of phosphorus occurs by exchange reaction with hydroxyl ions coordinated with iron and aluminium. This reaction is thought to hold phosphate against leaching and is responsible for the pronounced residual effects of phosphate fertilizers in most of the Savanna soils. Adsorption is positively correlated with the soil clay content and exchangeable aluminium and iron, and negatively correlated with the soil *p*H. In general the adsorption capacity of the Savanna soils is moderate to low. It is most pronounced in the Hydromorphic soils, much less in Ferrallitic soils and is low in Ferruginous soils (Bouyer and Damour 1964).

Changes from available to less available or unavailable forms of phosphorus in the soil are of particular interest when phosphate fertilizer is added. It is important to make a clear distinction between non-solubility and non-availability of the soil phosphate. Rapid decrease in the availability of phosphorus applied to soils does not prevent the non-soluble form from gradually contributing phosphate into soil solution. The part of the phosphate fertilizer not taken up by the crop might be considered as an investment remaining in the soil as the 'labile pool'. Its presence will enable the subsequent addition of phosphate fertilizer to increase the soil phosphorus potential.

The uptake of phosphorus by crops is controlled by intensity, quantity, and rate factors. The intensity factor or the concentration of phosphate in soil solution is very low in most of the Savanna soils. In the Ferruginous soils the values range from 0·01 to 0·02 mg/l and are insufficient to meet crop demands for high yields (Bache and Rogers 1970).

The adequate maintenance of concentration of phosphate in soil solution largely depends on the labile phosphate, that is, the pool of readily desorbed phosphate (quantity factor). This is usually assessed using the method of isotopic exchange and signifies the fraction of phosphorus in the soil which is in equilibrium with soil solution. As long as adsorbed phosphate remains exchangeable, that is, it can undergo isotopic exchange, it is available to plants (Larsen 1967). In the Samaru soils the isotopically exchangeable phosphorus was found to range from 7 to 11 ppm (Bache and Rogers 1970). These amounts are low in comparison with 50 to 150 ppm P in the unfertilized soils of England (Larsen, Gunary, and Sutton 1965).

The rate factor depends mainly on the phosphate concentration in soil solution. For the usual amounts of phosphate application, phosphate concentrations will be low in soils with high adsorption capacities. However, since most of the Savanna soils have low to moderate adsorption capacity phosphate concentrations maintained at root surface of crops usually match crop demands. Obviously for fast growing improved cultivars the rate factor will need to be high to meet crop requirements at high yield levels, and appropriate amount of fertilizer must be added to increase phosphate concentration in soil solution.

Adsorption should not be confused with fixation of phosphate. Fixation is the process whereby adsorbed phosphate is changed into unavailable forms of complex aluminium and iron phosphates. At present there is little information on the nature and rate of this reaction nor is it known how it is affected by soil properties such as *p*H. However, the conversion of adsorbed phosphate into fixed unavailable form appears to be generally very slow. Under conditions of the Savanna environment fixation is considered to be of little importance since applied phosphate remains available over prolonged periods of time and total phosphorus recoveries are high.

Contrary to general assumptions fixation is not a serious obstacle to agricultural development of the Savanna soils. What constitutes the main limiting factor in crop production under the Savanna environment is the generally very low content of native phosphate in soils necessitating high dressing of phosphate fertilizers. Often 45 kg P/ha or more are needed to satisfy deficiency of soil in respect of intensity, quantity and rate factors already discussed, to meet high levels of crop production.

### 4.2.5  Potassium

Recognition of potassium deficiency in the Savanna is relatively recent. Charreau and Poulain (1963) and Bockelee-Morvan (1964) reported responses to potassium fertilizer on a number of crops in Senegal. Heathcote and Stockinger (1970) and Heathcote (1972b) found deficiencies of potassium in Nigeria but only under conditions related to intensive and lengthy cropping.

(a) *Amounts.*  The total content of potassium in the Savanna soils varies widely with parent material but is generally much lower than in temperate climates, ranging from 0·2 to 2 me/100 g of soil.

No satisfactory fertility scale based on total content of mineral soil potassium has been established and its significance only lies in the fact that exchangeable potassium can be quickly renewed in tropical soils from these reserves.

Amounts of exchangeable potassium tend to be low and mainly depend on the clay content and the intensity of mineral decomposition. The mean values range from 0·18 to 0·25 me/100 g and the mean ratio of total to exchangeable potassium is about 100 (Wild 1971).

(b) *Availability.*  The availability of potassium cannot be judged by exchangeable values alone. Many soils with exchangeable values as low as 0·1 or even 0·07 me/100 g do not respond to addition of potassium fertilizer. Wild (1971) measured the availability of potassium in soils of northern Nigeria in terms of quantity/intensity relationships. He found that the intensity of potassium expressed as K concentration (moles/litre solution) in Ferruginous and Ferrallitic soils was high, whereas the quantity of potassium measured by exchange with ammonium acetate was low, and buffer capacities for potassium were generally very low. Hence, under intensive cropping most of the soils will rapidly become depleted of readily available potassium, a conclusion that was supported by the results of exhaustive cropping in pots (Jones and Wild 1975). Indeed this conclusion is supported by field trials (Heathcote 1973). Wild's further investigation showed that there was only small uptake of non-exchangeable potassium in soils rapidly depleted of exchangeable potassium.

(c) *Gains and losses.*  Removal by crops constitutes by far the largest loss. A crop of 9400 kg/ha maize will remove 39 kg K/ha in grain and 157 kg K/ha in stover, a total of 196 kg K/ha. In contrast with phosphorus, potassium accumulates mainly in straw and therefore return of crop residues to the soil is important in conserving potassium in crop nutrition. Charreau (1974a) gives uptake of potassium by various crops under indigenous production, and these range from 21 to 29 kg K/ha for millet and sorghum, 25 to 42 for groundnuts, 33 to 50 for rain-fed rice and maize, and 21 to 50 for cotton. He also draws attention to luxury consumption of potassium by crops, which might be of particular importance in forage production when grasses are cut several times during the cropping cycle and demand on potassium being exceptionally heavy.

Leaching losses range from 8 to 17 kg K/ha per year and are not too excessive. Charreau and Fauck (1970) reported that as a result of combined losses through removal by crops and leaching under 15 years continuous cropping the exchangeable potassium in the 20 cm deep surface soil had decreased from 0·15–0·20 me/100 g of soil to 0·02–0·05.

Losses by accelerated soil erosion and surface run-off were estimated by Kowal (1970d) to range from 7·5 to 13·4 kg K/ha per annum.

Additions of potassium to soil occur from three sources: (i) atmospheric contribution which includes an estimated 5 to 15 kg K/ha per annum in rainfall, and an unspecified amount of exchangeable K in the Harmattan dust; (ii) the contribution from incorporation into the soil of plant residues which are high in potassium content; and (iii) the transformation of non-exchangeable to exchangeable potassium, which under drying and wetting cycles might be considerable. However, the supply of potassium from natural sources are rather limited and replenishment of potassium reserves in the soil under intensive cultivation can only be achieved through application of fertilizer.

## 4.2.6 *Sulphur*

Sulphur deficiency occurs widely in the Savanna and has been observed in groundnuts (Greenwood 1951, 1954, Goldsworthy and Heathcote 1963), in cotton (Gillier 1960, Braud 1967, 1969) and in cereals (Poulain 1967).

Most of the sulphur in the surface soils is found in organic combinations and because of the low organic matter content, the sulphur content of most of the Savanna soils is low. For the Savanna soils in nrothern Nigeria a range of 18–132 ppm (mean 45ppm) was reported by Goldsworthy and Heathcote (1963).

Natural vegetation depends almost entirely on the atmosphere for the addition of sulphur, and sulphur dioxide can be taken up directly by leaves or brought to the roots dissolved in rain water. Vegetation gradually accumulates atmospheric sulphur which is converted into organic sulphur in the soil when plants die and decay.

Studies on the components of the sulphur balance have been conducted in northern Nigeria (Bromfield 1974a, 1974b, 1974c, 1974d) and Senegal (Charreau 1972, 1974a). Sulphur in the rain water ranged from 0·5 to 1·9 kg S/ha per annum (mean: 1·14 kg/ha). The mean amount for Samaru was 0·9 kg S/ha (Bromfield 1974b). The annual deposition of sulphur in the dust ranged from 0·099 to 0·429 kg S/ha (mean: 0·226 kg/ha) (Bromfield 1974c). The atmospheric sulphur deposited on soil directly from the air was found to be 0·8 kg S/ha per annum. Bromfield (1974d) calculated that about 0·5 kg S/ha could be abosrbed by leaves of crops during the 120 days of crop growth.

There is little reliable evidence of losses of sulphur by leaching. Depending on soil type, crop, rainfall, and additions of sulphur, the magnitude of leaching reported from Senegal ranges from 5 to 30 kg S/ha per annum (Tourte *et al.* 1964; Charreau 1972). Burning of natural vegetation and harvest residues results in annual losses in the range of 5–10 kg S/ha (Charreau 1974a). This is probably an underestimate but is no doubt the main contributing factor in the widespread sulphur deficiency in the Savanna soils. A crop of groundnut consisting of 1 tonne/ha of haulm and 600 kg/ha of pods, an average farmer's unfertilized yield, removes 2·5 kg S/ha (Bromfield 1973). At higher levels of productivity the uptake by crops ranges from 10 to 25 kg S/ha.

Thus the annual accession of about 2 kg S/ha is insufficient to counterbalance sulphur losses and crop demands. The difference required to sustain high crop yields depends entirely on fertilizer use. Deficiency in sulphur in the Savanna has been masked for a long time because nitrogenous and phosphate fertilizer carriers contained much sulphur. More recently other non-sulphur containing carriers have been introduced and this has resulted in frequent and severe sulphur deficiency in most crops. However, small amounts of sulphur, usually no more than 20 kg/ha, are sufficient to correct soil deficiency.

### 4.2.7 *Calcium and magnesium*

Because of the low exchange capacity of the Savanna soils the amounts of exchangeable calcium and magnesium are low, usually ranging from 0·3–3·0 me/100 g of exchangeable calcium and 0·2–2·0 me/100 g of magnesium.

Calcium and magnesium are the dominant exchangeable cations accounting for between 25 and 85 per cent and 15 and 60 per cent of the exchangeable cations respectively. In the Vertisols and Eutrophic Brown soils, exchangeable calcium and magnesium values are much higher.

(a) *Availability to crops.* Little work has been done on measuring availability of calcium and magnesium and it is often difficult in acid soils to separate the detrimental effects on plant growth due to lack of calcium or magnesium as nutrients and the indirect effect of acidity or aluminium toxicity.

Deficiency of calcium in groundnuts causes 'blind nuts', and low shelling percentages are common when soil exchangeable calcium is 0·04–0·08 me/100 g (Meredith 1965). No direct effect of magnesium deficiency has been recorded to affect any of the crops in the Savanna areas. Uptake by crops of calcium and magnesium is moderate. A maize crop of 9400 kg/ha removes about 39 kg Ca/ha and 45 kg Mg/ha, most of it (70–80 per cent) being in the stover.

Losses due to leaching are high but depend on rainfall and water regimes. Charreau (1972) estimates annual loss due to leaching to be in the range 29–107 kg Ca/ha and 9–24 kg Mg/ha. Losses of calcium and magnesium in the drainage water increase significantly after mineral fertilizer additions. Under intensive cropping, the level of exchangeable calcium and magnesium falls because of repeated removal of the nutrients in crop produce, leaching losses, and the acidifying effect of added fertilizer. As a consequence the $p$H of the soil falls rapidly. Because of the very low buffering capacity of the Savanna soils, even moderate losses of exchangeable calcium and magnesium have a large effect on the soil $p$H.

(b) *Liming.* Lowering the soil pH has a pronounced effect on crops. In general when the soil reaction declines below pH 5·0, liming is often essential to correct nutritional disorders of crops but particularly aluminium toxicity in groundnuts and other legumes. Charreau (1974a) lists the following adverse effects of low soil reaction on crop production in the Savanna:

  (i) Depressing effect on crop yield below pH 5·0 due to desaturation of exchangeable bases and nutritional impoverishment of soils and nutrient imbalance.

 (ii) Decrease in availability of various mineral elements but particularly calcium, phosphate and molybdenum.

(iii) Increase in solubility of aluminium and manganese, concentration of which in soil solution becomes toxic to crops.

(iv) Depression of soil microbial activity in the rhizosphere affecting nitrogen nutrition.

In contrast with temperate experience, liming practice in the tropics has been in disfavour and is not generally adopted as an agronomic necessity. Certainly under non-intensive cropping there is little evidence of crop response to liming. This, however, does not apply to the conditions under continuous and intensive cropping where massive doses of nitrogenous fertilizer rapidly reduce the soil pH and cause nutritional imbalance. There is still little experimental evidence regarding the thresholds of pH at which liming is necessary to prevent soil acidification below which crop yield is depressed, but there is no doubt that liming has an important if not an essential place under continuous and intensive farming practice.

At present the main reason for liming in the Savanna areas on a routine basis would be the prevention of aluminium toxicity rather than to raise soil pH to 7·0. Pieri (1974) estimated that about 20 per cent of the cultivated area in Senegal requires liming to correct low soil reaction in order to prevent mobilization of aluminium. The low exchange capacity of the Savanna soils requires relatively small amounts of lime and on the average 0·5 to 1·0 tonne/ha of CaO is sufficient to increase the soil pH by one unit; and experiments in Senegal (Poulain 1967) indicate that there is no danger in overliming, and even at pH greater than 8 the availability of minor elements was not affected.

### 4.2.8 *Micronutrients*

Systematic study of micronutrients in the Savanna soils is of very recent origin and the present knowledge is far from being satisfactory. Micronutrients can affect crop production by either being deficient or by being in excess in the soil solution resulting in toxic effects. For some of the micronutrients, the margin of concentration between two limits of deficiency and toxicity is narrow, hence there are some difficulties in correcting deficiencies (Charreau 1974a). (Charreau 1974a).

In general, soils over crystalline and metamorphic rocks give rise to soils richer in trace elements than those over sedimentary rocks. Under non-intensive subsistence farming, micronutrient deficiencies were seldom recorded in the past because of the low rate of nutrient removal, burning of crop residues and return of ashes, and the effects of the fallow period. Under intensive and continuous cropping where large doses of fertilizers are applied, affecting soil $pH$ and soil nutrient balance, the micronutrient disorders are much more pronounced and the frequency and severity of micronutrient deficiencies may be expected to increase with the intensity of production.

(a) *Boron*. The most widely spread deficiency of micronutrients in the Savanna is boron affecting production of cotton, forest tress (*Eucalyptus* spp.), and in some areas groundnut (Braud, Fritz, Megie, and Ossillon 1969, Vaille and Goma 1972, Heathcote and Smithson 1974, FAO 1974). Heathcote and Smithson (1974) reported widespread deficiency of boron in farmers' fields in Nigeria (in some localities very severe), being well below the critical minimum of $0\cdot1$–$0\cdot2$ ppm of hot-water-soluble boron. However, values of hot-water-soluble boron at which deficiency may be expected vary according to crop and soil. Similarly, toxicity of boron varies according to crop and soil, the acceptable upper limit for sensitive crops being about 2 ppm B. Toxic rates of boron application are quoted as between 2 and 4 kg B/ha, but the recommendations for northern Nigeria are well below these values, being $0\cdot7$ kg B/ha for June sown cotton and $0\cdot35$ kg B/ha for July sown cotton.

Savanna Forestry uses very heavy dressings of borate fertilizers in *Eucalyptus* plantations: 144g (14% B) fertilizer per tree being applied.

(b) *Molybdenum* Molybdenum deficiency has been reported in Senegal (Martin and Fourrier 1965) and in northern Nigeria (Heathcote and Fowler 1977) on groundnut. Deficiencies are expected in acid soils high in active iron oxides. Addition of ammonium molybdate to seeds or by foliar application resulted in greatly increased haulm yield and an increase of pod yield of 300 kg/ha (Heathcote and Fowler 1977).

(c) *Zinc deficiency and aluminium toxicity*. Continuous use of ammonium sulphate and other acidifying nitrogenous fertilizers leads to gradual replacement of calcium, magnesium and potassium by hydrogen and aluminium ions. At the same time the availability of some of the trace elements declines. Deficiency of boron and molybdenum have been already described. Deficiency of zinc in rice in the Vertisols near Lake Chad has recently been identified. However, an application of $4\cdot5$ kg/ha of zinc sulphate eliminated the deficiency symptoms.

In very acid soils the increase in solubility of aluminium and manganese results in toxicity. Although most crops show a certain degree of tolerance to these changes in very acid soils, nodulation of legumes is reduced and there is a general decline in crop yields.

Amounts of exchangeable aluminium are usually negligible at $pH$ values higher than $5\cdot5$–$5\cdot8$, but increase with decreasing $pH$. At Kano, on exhausted soils with $pH$ of nearly $4\cdot0$ the aluminium toxicity prevented establishment of crops. Symptoms of aluminium toxicity consist of yellowing, reduced growth and depression of root growth. The severity of these symptoms is correlated with the ratio $Al^{3+}$/CEC rather than with the absolute content of $Al^{3+}$ and usually appear at about $pH$ $5\cdot4$ (Coleman, Weed and McCracken 1959, Charreau 1974a). Liming to increase soil reaction to higher $pH$ values eliminates aluminium toxicity.

**4.3 Termites and their effects on the soil physical and chemical properties**

One of the most characteristic features of the West African Savanna soils is the abundance of termites. Since most of the termites are entirely subterranean, their activity greatly affects the physical and chemical characteristics of soils. Extensive network of galleries, runways and nest systems often extend to depths of 2–3 m or more, significantly affecting soil macroporosity, drainage characteristics, the wetting pattern of soil profile and to some extent soil structure. The channels and network of subterranean passages are very stable and crops utilize the disused portions of these channels to extend their roots to a greater volume of the soil profile. The channels are enriched by excreta, organic debris and fungi, and this is probably an additional reason for root growth along the channels.

The frequency of termite channels in a soil profile at Samaru was investigated by the authors. It was estimated that the average number of channels in the 230 cm depth of soil profile was one per 300 cm$^3$ soil volume. However, the frequency was much greater in the surface soil, averaging one channel per 90 cm$^3$ soil volume within the 0–10 cm depth and one channel per 120 cm$^3$ soil volume within the 10–20 cm depth. The size of the channels varied greatly but the predominant size was 1·8–2·3 mm diameter.

The termites of the West African Savanna belong to some 11 recognizable genera with many species. The most important ones are:

(i) The species *Macrotermes bellicosus* forms tall (up to 8 m) cathedral like mounds, presenting serious hindrance to land development, cultivation and drainage control. On the other hand the greater amount of clay and bases in the soil around the mounds often does improve the soil nutrient status. The species mainly feeds on wood and grass and is not considered a serious pest of crops.

(ii) *Trinervitermes* spp. These species, particularly *T. geminatus*, are widely distributed throughout the Savanna. They form small domed mounds as their nests. These species are considered as one of the most important natural modifiers of soil physical properties. The mounds are easily destroyed by cultivation but are extensive in their number. It is estimated that under natural conditions of the Northern Guinea Savanna of Nigeria, the average density of mounds is about 143 per ha with a termite population of between 2 and 10 million per ha. The termites travel from their mounds through subterranean gallaries and emerge from foraging holes at the soil surface. Columns of several hundred individuals travel 2–4 m from the holes and cut down grass which is carried back down the foraging holes to the mounds. Up to 2500 holes per ha may be opened when foraging is active. On average about 0·4 kg/ha per day of grass is stored in the nests. The effect of termites in modifying the soil physical properties by burrowing and nest building, and on the soil chemical properties through deposition of organic debris and excreta is therefore apparent.

(iii) With few exceptions, crop-damaging termites are entirely subterranean, belonging to a group which relies on a symbiotic relationship with a fungus to break down the lignins and cellulose in their food into simpler carbohydrates which can be assimilated. At Samaru, the 'fungus gardens' were found at depths of 0·5 to 1 m in cultivated soils and nearer to the surface in soils under fallow. The termites belonging to this group may attack roots of crops which are often eaten away up into the stem. The most important termites belonging to this group of crop pests appear to be several species of *Trinervitermes* and certain species of *Ancistrotermes, Odontotermes* and *Amitermes*. Reports from various experimental stations in Nigeria indicate variable losses due to termite attack: maximum losses range from 20–40 per cent in cassava, groundnut and sorghum, and up to 60–70 per cent in maize and yams.

It might be concluded that although certain termites are serious crop pests and those feeding on wood cause damage to buildings, fences, etc., the majority of termites might be regarded as beneficial agents in improving the soil physical condition and the soil nutrient status. Unfortunately there is as yet little quantitative data on which to base a full assessment. However, there is not the slightest doubt that under the Savanna environment, contributions by termites to 'biological porosity' of soils is of very important significance in the agronomy of crops.

## 4.4　Organic matter

The amount of organic matter in a soil is a product of a number of diverse factors, acting over a period of time, on the relative rates of addition of organic residues to the soil and their subsequent breakdown. For an uncultivated soil carrying natural vegetation, the relative rates of addition and breakdown of organic matter are related to the type, extent and duration of growth of the vegetation and activity of soil organisms, all of which are influenced by soil and climatic conditions. If the vegetation is cleared and the soil cultivated, the cropping practice has a substantial influence on the level of organic matter in the soil, and similarly so can fire and grazing.

Organic matter in the Savanna and other soils in the tropics has attracted considerable attention because of the important role it plays in fertility in the traditional systems of farming where yields, although low, are obtained with little or no use of fertilizer. Further, the beneficial effects of organic matter on soil physical and chemical properties in the Savanna soils have been shown to be substantial. Although the natural level of organic matter in the Savanna soils is low and can be built up slowly under the natural Savanna vegetation or periods of rest fallows (Nye and Greenland 1960), crop residues under improved farming practices are undoubtedly more effective as evident from crop research already conducted. Francophone workers have shown that the maintenance of fertility using fertilizers is intimately interlinked with the physical status of the soil which can be improved or held in a favourable condition depending on the rate of turnover of soil organic matter and appropriate soil cultivation techniques. It may be argued that crop nutrient requirements can be fully met in absence of organic matter by application of balanced fertilizers. However, experience has shown that generally crops are easier and less expensive to grow when it is present. Further, production of crop residues and other organic waste products generally increase with increase in crop yields. Jones and Wild (1975) pointed out that the question frequently asked, whether the fertility of the Savanna soil can be permanently maintained with fertilizers alone, is an unrealistic one, if it ignores the management aspect. Also, in addition to the improvement of soil physical and chemical properties, the return of crop residues and organic wastes conserves plant nutrients and the conservation of nutrients and their recycling within the cropping system is an asset to any viable fertilizer policy.

### 4.4.1 *Level of organic matter and factors affecting it*

The organic matter content of surface soils in the Savanna is generally low compared with that in the Forest soils of West Africa (Nye and Greenland 1960, Ahn 1974) and in soils of the temperate regions (Cooke 1967). Mean values reported (Jones and Wild 1975) for 0–15 cm soil depth are about 0·5 per cent carbon in the Brown and Reddish soils, 1·2 per cent in the Ferruginous soils, and 2 per cent in the Vertisols, Eutrophic Brown and Hydromorphic soils.

Differences in organic matter content between a soil under a closed forest and that under open Savanna are largely due to the much greater weight of vegetation in the forest, and the annual burning of the above-ground parts of Savanna grasses. Much of the above-ground parts of the Savanna grasses may be also eaten by grazing animals. The organic matter in Savanna soils is therefore mainly derived from the roots.

(a) *Rainfall.* Within the tropics, soil organic matter content increases with increase in mean annual rainfall (Birch and Friend 1956, Jenny and Raychauduri 1960). A similar relationship has been reported in West Africa by Gavaud (1968) in Niger, over the range 230–875 mm per annum, and by Kadeba (1970) in forest-reserve sites in northern Nigeria. For well-drained soils Jones (1973) shows that the organic matter in the 0–15 cm depth increased significantly with increase in rainfall in the range 350–1905 mm. He obtained the relationship:

$$C\% = 0·137 + 0·000856 \, (\text{Rainfall, mm}) \, (r = 0·51) \qquad (4.11)$$

The equation indicates that for every 100 mm increase in annual rainfall, organic matter content increases by 0·17 per cent, assuming that soil organic matter contains 50 per cent carbon.

The strong relationship between soil carbon and rainfall is largely due to the fact that annual rainfall is related to the length of the growing season, and hence, the amount of organic residues returned to the soil. Also, the risk of fire generally decreases with increase in the length of the growing season because of the decrease in the length and severity of the dry season. Further, as the annual rainfall decreases the drying of the soil during the dry season becomes more intense and leads to a more rapid decomposition on subsequent rewetting. This effect is greater when the dry season is longer and hotter (Birch 1958, 1959, Enwezor 1967).

(b) *Temperature and atitude.* Within the tropics, soil organic matter increases with decrease in temperature (Birch and Friend 1956, Jenny and Raychauduri 1960). Temperature can affect organic matter levels by its effect on the rate of synthesis of organic matter or decomposition or both; and as other factors such as soil moisture status influence rates of synthesis and decomposition, it has been difficult to determine the specific effect of temperature on organic matter levels in the Savanna. However, in general, the rate of decrease in organic matter with increase in temperature in the Savanna is much greater than in the temperate climates mainly due to higher rates of decomposition. Further, the intensity of the dry season increases with latitude, and soil temperatures at the time of subsequent wetting the following season are higher where the dry season is longer, leading to a more rapid flush of mineralization of organic matter.

Within the tropics, soil organic matter has been shown to increase with altitude (Birch and Friend 1956, Jenny and Raychaudhuri 1960). A similar trend has been shown in West Africa (Gavaud 1968). Increase in altitude is accompanied by increase in rainfall and decrease in temperature, both of which lead to increase in organic matter through increase in organic matter returns and decrease in decomposition. However, the relationship between soil carbon and altitude can be influenced by parent material as demonstrated by Jones (1973) for soils on basic rocks, where soil carbon depended greatly on altitude, and soils on acid rocks where it did not.

(c) *Parent material.* Soil parent material can influence the organic matter content because it may determine soil texture, particularly the nature and size of its clay fraction, and also availability of nutrients.

The influence of texture on organic matter content of the Savanna soils has been reported by Fauck (1960), Gavaud (1968), and Kadeba (1970). For a wide range of well-drained soils in the Nigerian Savanna, Jones (1973) found that the carbon content in 0–15 cm depth was significantly related to the clay content in the range 0–50 per cent as described by the equation:

$$C\% = 0.341 + 0.0273 \,(\text{Clay}, \%). \ (r = 0.54) \tag{4.12}$$

Therefore, for each 10 per cent increase in clay content the organic matter increases by 0.55 per cent. In Vertisols, Jones (1973) found that the relationship between carbon content and clay content in top soils was nonsignificant and negative over the total range in clay content examined. However, there was a significant negative correlation between soil carbon and clay content for top soils with clay content greater than 35 per cent. Therefore, whereas in the well-drained non-Vertisolic soils there was a strong tendency for soil carbon to increase linearly with soil clay content, in the Vertisols this appeared to be true only up to a clay content of about 35 per cent. Above this value soil carbon contents tended to decrease from approximately 1.4 per cent at 35 per cent clay to about 0.6 per cent at 80 per cent clay (Jones 1973).

In their study of East African soils, Birch and Friend (1956) concluded that rainfall was one major factor which had an overall influence on soil organic matter while temperature and clay content exercised a modifying influence as minor factors. From the various surveys conducted in the West African Savanna, it is clear that rainfall is of great importance. However, as the soils are predominantly sandy, clay content also assumes a major role (Jones 1973). The predominant clay mineral in most of the soils in the West African Savanna is kaolinite, and this too is likely to have an influence because in soils formed on basic rocks and thought to contain clays other than kaolinite, amounts of organic matter tend to be lower. In contrast, organic matter content in Vertisols examined by Jones (1973) declined above 35 per clay content. The relationship between clay and organic matter content is therefore not a simple one, although the ability of clay to absorb humus is widely accepted (Russell 1973).

Nutrient availability can be important because it can influence the kind of natural vegetation developed. Soils formed on Shales tend to contain larger amounts of organic matter than the sandy soils developed on Granites and Sandstones because the former have a higher clay content. However, most of the well-drained soils of the West African Savanna are formed on acid Basement Complex rocks and Sandstones. Those formed from the former have a much higher total potassium content (Wild 1971) while those formed from the latter are poor in exchangeable bases (Fauck 1963). If similar differences occur with other nutrients then it is probable that the return of organic matter is likely to be greater where the natural availability of nutrients is greater. Thus Jones (1973) found a small but significant difference in the organic matter content between soil derived from Basement Complex and those from Sandstones in northern Nigeria.

(d) *Drainage.* In the poorly-drained soils in the Savanna, mean carbon and clay contents in the top soil are greater than in the well-drained soils, and Jones (1973) found that organic matter content of the poorly-drained soils was considerably higher than for the well-drained soils at all rainfall levels. However, the difference tended to be less in soils of high clay content. Increase in organic matter due to poor drainage is likely to be due to a prolongation of the period during which the soil is moist thereby increasing the organic matter returns and reducing the severity and frequency of the flush of decomposition (Birch 1959). It is also likely that the microbial activity is reduced due to poor drainage (Jones and Wild 1975).

(e) *Burning, clearing and cultivation.* Despite the obvious relationship between the West African vegetation belts and rainfall, it apepars that the present Savanna vegetation is not as natural as was once supposed, and that the climate in the Savanna areas could support a more woody vegetation than at present (Ahn 1974). Further, it is likely that much of the land in the Savanna region of West Africa has been cultivated at some time. Therefore the present day Savanna largely reflects the influence of man, particularly the annual fires which sweep across large areas of the Savanna every dry season. Grass or bush-burning both deliberate and accidental, has probably been a feature of the Savanna for a very long period. The organic matter levels in the Savanna soils reported earlier therefore reflect conditions intermediate between those under natural bush or wooded Savanna and those under interference from fire, grazing, and cultivation.

One of the effects of burning is that the above-ground parts of the Savanna vegetation are not returned to the soil, but merely provide ash; and although the nutrients in ash are later washed into the soil, some of the nutrients in the vegetation are lost in burning (particularly nitrogen and sulphur) while some are lost through leaching and in run-off before they can be taken up by plants the following wet season. Burning therefore decreases the organic matter input into Savanna soils resulting in the generally very low organic matter contents of the Savanna soils. If a mature *Andropogon* high grass in the moist Savanna (1400 mm rain per annum) in Ghana is taken for illustration, about 9 tonne/ha of dry leaves and stem is produced in a season (Greenland and Nye 1959), but very little of this is added to the soil, most being lost as carbon dioxide during the annual grass burn. The addition from root material was estimated to be about one-third the amount above the ground. Thus while the production of total organic matter is about 12 tonne/ha per annum, in the moist Savanna grass-land areas only about 3 tonne/ha becomes available to the soil (Nye and Greenland 1960). Values for drier areas are likely to be much lower and about 1 tonne/ha per annum of root residues from grass fallows have been found in Senegal (Charreau 1974a). Values for natural grass or bush fallows of short duration on cultivated soils are likely to be lower still.

The effect of cultivation which involves clearing and burning of vegetation results in lowering of the organic matter level in the soil. Siband (1972b) has reported the effect of clearing an open deciduous forest (Coastal Savanna) in Senegal followed by continuous cropping on soil organic matter. Over the 80 years since clearing the organic matter content decreased from about 2·4 per cent to about 1·3 per cent. The decrease in the first fifteen years was very rapid. Also, there was a decrease in the clay content from about 9 per cent to about 6 per cent. In general, soils under the present system of cultivation or under bush fallow following cultivation, for all the Savanna regions in Nigeria, have a mean carbon content in 0–15 cm depth of 0·58 per cent while soils which do not appear to have been cultivated recently the mean carbon content is 1·03 per cent (Jones 1973). However, it is likely that these figures underestimate the full cultivation effect because it is not easy to establish the extent of human interference on the soil and vegetation.

### 4.4.2 *Changes in soil organic matter*

Changes in soil organic matter with time depend on the balance between the rates of addition of organic matter to the soil, and losses of organic matter from the soil. The amount of fresh material added depends on the type of vegetation established and climate, and in the case of a rest fallow the initial rate of establishment and growth of the fallow vegetation is also very important. Cultivation reduces the amount of organic matter, depending on the intensity of cultivation and cropping sequence. Further, addition of crop residues, green manures and animal manures also greatly influences soil organic matter depending on the quantities involved and their quality.

When fresh organic matter is added to the soil, processes involved in its decay and decomposition convert it into a complex colloidal organic residue which is collectively known as humus. The formation of humus appears to be a complex process but humus is distinct from the organic matter from which it is derived, and also from the products of its later breakdown and eventual mineralization. Organic soil colloids are therefore only temporary end-products although mineral nutrients contained in them as components of humus remain in the soil considerably longer (Ahn 1974). According to Nye and Greenland (1960) good-quality humus has at least the following properties: (1) it breaks down readily to yield the available forms of mineral nitrogen, sulphur, and phosphorus, but does not decompose so rapidly that excessive losses of humus or of nutrient occur; (2) it has a high cation exchange capacity; (3) it improves the constitution of the soil, thereby improving its water relationships and diffusibility of carbon dioxide and oxygen through the soil; and (4) it provides food for the soil micro-organisms, particularly the nitrogen fixers.

A reduction in the amount of humus in the soil results in a deterioration in soil structure, a lowering of the cation exchange and water storage capacities of the soil, and the loss of the potential nutrients contained in the humus itself. In the Savanna, a reduction in the amount of humus may lead to a decline in the productivity of the soil and an increase in soil erosion. This is because humus levels in the Savanna soils in the traditional system can be only built up slowly. Once the productivity of the top soil is lost and erosion sets in, the power of the soil to recover depends on the nutrients remaining in the subsoil which is often relatively sterile while the rotting rock zone where fresh nutrients might be liberated may be out of reach of most plant roots (Ahn 1974).

Under the present indigenous system of farming, increases in the humus content of the Savanna soils occur mainly during bush or grass fallow periods, but the quantities which can be added are small while the rest fallow periods are getting shorter because of population pressure. In most areas household refuse and animal manure is used on the land under continuous cropping but again the quantities involved are small and at best can support 500–700 kg/ha of sorghum and millet yield.

(a) *Changes under fallow.* When a soil in the Savanna region is left to fallow, water shortage at the end of the cropping period generally prevents immediate regrowth, and the establishment of a grass or bush cover only begins the following season and deyelopment of a proper cover may take more than one season, if the soil was previously cropped for a long period. In the Savanna region the annual production of dry matter depends greatly on the length of the wet season and the radiation level. Actual annual production at different latitudes have not been measured, although as indicated earlier about 1 and 3 tonne/ha per annum of fresh organic matter, largely root material, from established fallows becomes available to the soil in the northern and southern parts of the Savanna respectively. This represents a decrease of about 10 per cent per latitude northwards from 8° to 14°N. (The decrease in potential dry matter production during the growing season with latitude was earlier shown in Chapter 3 to be about 8 per cent per latitude). Therefore, at Samaru (11° 11′N), in the Northern Guinea Savanna, the amount of root dry matter returned would be about 2 tonne/ha per annum. Under open deciduous forests in Senegal, annual production of litter is in the range 4–5 tonne/ha (Dommergues 1963), about half of those reported by Greenland and Nye (1959) (8 to 12 tonne/ha) for the humid High Forest areas.

Of the fresh organic material added, only a fraction becomes incorporated with the soil humus. Some is lost through oxidation and erosion, and the rest temporarily remains in the non-humic form. The soil humus itself is also subject to oxidation through the activities of soil micro-organisms. The proportion of fresh organic material converted to soil humus is therefore less than the added amounts. The actual proportion depends on factors such as composition of the material added, the extent to which the material decomposes on the soil surface or within the soil after burial by soil animals, temperature and moisture conditions during decomposition and soil clay content. Little is known about how all these factors operate and interact with each other. Figures for this humification factor or 'isohumic coefficient' for root material have not been accurately measured in the Savanna. However, Greenland and Nye (1959) found that the equilibrium level of humus carbon attained under a long well established grass fallow in the southern moist Savanna in Ghana was about 55 tonne/ha in the top 30 cm or 1·22 per cent carbon. They estimated that about 3 tonne/ha of root residues per year was being added to the soil, and the decomposition rate of soil humus was 1 per cent per annum. Therefore, to maintain equilibrium there was about 550 kg/ha of humus carbon being added to the soil per annum. This amount is equivalent to isohumic coefficient of about 35 per cent. For 23 sites under 'undisturbed' natural Savanna vegetation in the Northern Guinea Savanna in Nigeria, Jones (1973) found a mean carbon content of 1·03 per cent in the top 15 cm or 0·78 per cent in the top 30 cm, assuming that the carbon content in the 15–30 cm depth is half of that in the 0–15 cm depth. This amount is equivalent to about 35 tonne/ha of humus carbon in the top 30 cm. If the carbon level was near equilibrium then it would represent an annual addition of root residues of about 1950 kg/ha. Assuming an average annual isohumic coefficient of 35 per cent then the humus carbon added per annum would be 350 kg/ha or 0·0078 per cent carbon in the top 30 cm of soil. In areas further north at about 13° to 14°N, annual additions of root residues for established grass fallows in Senegal are reported to be about 1 tonne/ha, corresponding to about 18 tonne/ha of humus carbon in the top 30 cm or 0·4 per cent at equilibrium. At 35 per cent isohumic coefficient, the annual addition to soil humus would be about 180 kg/ha or 0·0004 per cent carbon in the top 30 cm of soil. The fact that equilibrium conditions are eventually established under long fallows suggests that for a given set of environmental and soil conditions and the kind of organic residues added, there must be a relationship between the level of humus carbon, the rate of addition of fresh organic residues, the rate of humification and the rate of decomposition, otherwise humus carbon would increase indefinitely. Very little work has been done on the optimum rate of additions of fresh organic matter in relation to rate of turnover of humus organic matter in the soil. This can be very important when management of crop residues is geared towards increasing the humus pool in the soil.

It is generally assumed that the rate of decomposition is directly proportional to the amount of humus carbon (Jenny 1941). The most commonly used equation for describing changes in the soil humus content with time under fallow is:

$$\mathrm{d}H_f/\mathrm{d}t = A_f - k_f H_f \qquad (4.13)$$

where    $H_f$ = humus content of the soil under fallow
         $A_f$ = addition of humus to the soil per unit time
         $t$ = time
         $k_f$ = decomposition constant under fallow

The applicability of the equation involves three assumptions: (a) there is a continuous formation of humus in the soil, (b) $A_f$ is a constant, and (c) $k_f$ is a constant fraction of the humus content. Although $A_f$ and $k_f$ are not constant over short intervals of time, the equation can be accepted as being generally valid over a long enough interval (several years) within a long fallow period.

The equation states that after a period of time the humus content of the soil will approach the value $A_f/k_f$ asymptotically. Integrating the equation (4.13) gives:

$$H_f = A_f k_f - (A_f/k_f - H_o)\, e^{-k_f t} \qquad (4.14)$$

where $H_o$ is the initial humus content of the soil and $A_f/k_f$ is the equilibrium level of humus in the soil ($H_{ef}$). From the knowledge of the equilibrium level of humus in very long-fallowed Savanna soils in which humus level had ceased to build up, Greenland and Nye (1959) calculated that the decomposition constant for the top 30 cm was between 0·5 and 1·5 per cent per annum. For soils under tropical lowland High Forest the decomposition constant was between 2 and 5 per cent per annum.

The logarithmic increase in soil humus carbon with time means that the rate of increase of humus depends on how far removed the soil is from its equilibrium level. Thus, at Samaru for example, the rate of increase in humus carbon for changes at 25, 50 and 75 per cent of the equilibrium level would be in the range 150–375, 100–250 and 50–125 kg/ha per annum respectively, assuming $k_f = 1$ per cent and equilibrum humus carbon level of 35 000 kg/ha. Therefore, humus in the soil is not likely to be subject to large fluctuations because the net additions per annum are small compared to the equilibrium level.

The calculation of the rate of increase of soil humus by the above method involves a number of assumptions concerning the quality of organic residues produced, the fraction of carbon in the residues incorporated into soil humus, and the relationship between the rate of decomposition and the level of humus carbon. Direct experimental attempts to verify equation (4.13) for Savanna conditions are rare and very few studies on changes in organic matter of soils under long natural fallow have been reported.

(b) *Changes under cropping.* From equation (4.13) it can be seen that if the rate of addition of humus to the soil is less than the rate of loss of soil humus, then the net effect would be a fall in the soil humus content. However, the rate of decomposition of humus under fallow is generally less than the rate of decomposition when the soil is cropped (Nye and Greenland 1960). Therefore, even if the additions under successive periods of fallow and crop were similar, there would be a decrease in the humus content with time. Also, when a virgin land is brought under continuous cultivation, the soil humus is not likely to disappear completely, because under cultivation, additions of organic matter to the soil still continue, at least from root residues even when the above ground parts of the crop are removed or burnt.

The rate of fall in the humus content under cropping can be described by the following equation assuming that there is an exponential decrease with time.

$$dH_c/dt = A_c - k_c H_c \qquad (4.15)$$

where $H_c$ = humus content of the soil under cropping
$\quad\quad A_c$ = addition of humus to the soil per unit time
$\quad\quad t$ = time
$\quad\quad k_c$ = decomposition constant under cropping

The equation states that after a period of years, the humus content of the soil will approach some equilibrium level defined by the asymptot $A_c/k_c$. Integrating the equation (4.15) gives:

$$H_c = A_c/k_c - (A_c/k_c - H_o)\, e^{-k_c t} \tag{4.16}$$

The equilibrium level and the rate at which it is reached therefore depends on the rate of addition and the rate of decomposition of humus.

The traditional cropping practice in the Savanna is the bush or grass fallow rotation, and in some areas the cropping is continuous. It is possible to relate the level of humus that will eventually be established at any cropping intensity to the level that is attained after a long rest fallow $(H_{ef})$. The rate of increase in humus content during the fallow period is given by equation (4.13). If the rate of addition of humus $(A_f')$ in any relatively short fallow period of $t_f$ years within the rotation is equal to the rate of addition during a long rest fallow $(A_f)$, then there will be a positive change in the humus content given by the equation:

$$dH_f'/dt = \Delta H_f'/t_f = A_f' - k_f'H_f' \tag{4.17}$$

Assuming that the rate of addition of humus during the cropping period $(A_c)$ of $t_c$ years in the rotation is equal or less than the amount during the fallow period, then there will be a negative change in the humus carbon during the cropping period given by the equation:

$$-dH_c/dt = -\Delta H_c/t_c = -(A_c - k_cH_c) \tag{4.18}$$

Therefore, the net change in one cycle of fallow and crop is:

$$\Delta H = t_f(A_f' - k_f'H_f') + t_c(A_c + k_cH_c). \tag{4.19}$$

When equilibrium is established, there is no net change in the humus content for a given cycle and $H = 0$ and $H_f' = H_c = H_{cf}'$. Substituting $H_{cf}'$ in equation (4.19) and dividing by $H_{ef}$ we have

$$\frac{H_{cf}'}{H_{ef}} = \frac{t_fA_f' + t_cA_c}{t_fk_f' + t_ck_c} \tag{4.20}$$

If the rate of addition during the cropping period is negligible, then

$$\frac{H_{cf}'}{H_{ef}} = \frac{t_fA_f'}{t_fk_f' + t_ck_c} \tag{4.21}$$

The rate of decomposition of humus under fallow in the Savanna was established to be about 1 per cent per annum, and when cropped it was estimated to be about 4 per cent (Nye and Greenland 1960). Francophone work has shown that $k_c$ for humus carbon to be within the range 2–5 per cent with a mean value of about 4 per cent (Charreau and Fauck 1970, Siband 1972b). Recently Jones and Wild (1975) indicated similar values for a cultivated soil at Samaru.

Using equation (4.20), the length of the fallow period $(t_f)$ required within the crop/fallow rotation after one year of cropping to maintain humus carbon at 25, 50, and 75 per cent of equilibrium level attained under natural vegetation or long established grass fallow $(H_{ef})$ calculated for $k_c = 2$, 4 and 6 per cent, $k_f' = 1$ per cent, $A_f' = A_f$, and $A_c = 0$, $1/3$ $A_f$, and $A_f$ is shown in Table 4.8. At $A_c = 1/3$ $A_f$, and $k_c = 4$ per cent, it would require 1, 3 and 11 years fallow period after each year of cropping to maintain humus level at $0.25$ $H_{ef}$, $0.50$ $H_{ef}$ and $0.75$ $H_{ef}$ respectively; at $A_c = 1/3$ $A_f$, equal periods of cropping and fallow would reduce the level of humus to about 25 per cent of $H_{ef}$. The effect of change in $k_c$ on humus level that could be maintained at a given $A_c$ is considerable. For example, to maintain humus level at $0.75$ $H_{ef}$ at $k_c = 2$ per cent would require a fallow period of 5 years when $A_c = 1/3$ $A_f$, but the period would be 17 years if $k_c$ increased to 6 per cent.

**Table 4.8**

*Length of fallow period ($t_f$) required to maintain $H_{cf}'/H_{ef}$ at 25, 50, and 75 per cent after one year of cropping for $k_c = 2, 4$, and 6 per cent, $k_f' = 1$ per cent, $A_f' = A_f$, and $A_c = 0$, $(1/3)A_f$ and $A_f$*

| $A_c$ | $k_c$ | $t_f$ (years) to maintain $H_{cf}'/H_{ef}$ at | | |
|---|---|---|---|---|
| | | 25% | 50% | 75% |
| 0 | 2 | 0.7 | 2.0 | 6.0 |
| | 4 | 1.3 | 4.0 | 12.0 |
| | 6 | 2.0 | 6.0 | 18.0 |
| $1/3$ $A_f$ | 2 | 0.2 | 1.3 | 4.7 |
| | 4 | 0.9 | 3.3 | 10.7 |
| | 6 | 1.6 | 5.3 | 16.7 |
| $A_f$ | 2 | – | 0 | 2.0 |
| | 4 | 0 | 2.0 | 8.0 |
| | 6 | 0.7 | 4.0 | 14.0 |

Values for soil organic matter reported by Jones (1973) for 'undisturbed' and cultivated soil of $1.03$ and $0.58$ per cent carbon respectively in the Northern Guinea Savanna in Nigeria represents $H_{cf}'/H_{ef}$ of about 50 per cent. If $A_c = 1/3$ $A_f$ and $k_c = 4$, the period of fallow required to maintain the humus content in the cultivated soils would be 4 years; at $k_c = 2$ and 6 per cent, it would be 2 and 7 years respectively. However, as the fallow takes one or more years to establish, the actual period would be longer.

## 4.4.3  Organic residues

Annual additions of root residues in the traditional cultivated fields are not likely to exceed those obtained under well established long rest fallow. However, even if they were similar, it is unlikely that humus carbon levels in the cultivated field with $H_{cf}'/H_{ef}$ of 50 per cent can be increased close to $H_{ef}$. This is because the annual additions in the range 1–3 tonne/ha root residues would add 0·003–0·012 per cent carbon to the top 30 cm. The soils in the Northern Guinea Savanna presently at 0·50 $H_{ef}$ (Jones 1973) would require a fallow period of about 30 years to attain 0·75 $H_{ef}$ level at an annual addition of 2 tonne/ha of fresh organic residues, isohumic coefficient of 35 per cent, and $k_f = 1$ per cent.

During cropping periods in the traditional practice nearly all the above ground parts of the crop are removed or burnt, so that only roots contribute to soil humus. The amount of crop residues (roots and tops) available from various crops under traditional practice in the Northern Guinea Savanna is estimated to be 0·6 tonne/ha for cowpea, 1·2–1·4 tonne/ha for groundnut and cotton and 1·8–2·1 tonne/ha for upland rice, maize, sorghum and millet. However, corresponding figures for roots alone are 0·2, 0·5 and 0·6–0·8 tonne/ha respectively. If 0·6 tonne/ha is taken as an average value then during cropping periods about 110 kg/ha of the fresh organic matter could be added to soil humus. This is about a third of that likely to be added under a long rest fallow or natural vegetation, i.e., 350 kg/ha estimated earlier. Also during short fallow periods within the rotation it is likely that the additions of fresh organic matter to the soil would be less than that under a long rest fallow or natural vegetation and $A_f'$ may be within 1/3–2/3 of $A_f$. The level of humus which would eventually establish within the crop/fallow rotation $(H_{cf}')$ as a fraction of the equilibrium humus level in the long rest fallow $(H_{ef})$ at different $A_c$ and $A_f'$ are given in Table 4.9. It will be seen that to maintain $H_{cf}'$ at about 0·50 $H_{ef}$ would require

**Table 4.9**

*Levels of humus that would eventually establish in crop/fallow cycles*
$(H_{cf}')$ *as a fraction of the equilibrium humus level in long fallow* $(H_{ef})$
*at different* $A_c$ *and* $A_f'$, *and* $k_f' = 1$ *per cent, and* $k_c = 4$ *per cent*

| $A_f'$ equal to | Crop:fallow ratio | $H_{cf}'/H_{ef}$ at $A_c$ equal to | | |
|---|---|---|---|---|
| | | $1/3\,A_f'$ | $1/2\,A_f'$ | $2/3\,A_f'$ |
| $1/3\,A_f$ | 1:1 | 0·13 | 0·17 | 0·20 |
| | 1:4 | 0·21 | 0·23 | 0·25 |
| | 1:7 | 0·24 | 0·26 | 0·27 |
| | 1:10 | 0·25 | 0·27 | 0·28 |
| $1/2\,A_f$ | 1:1 | 0·17 | 0·20 | 0·23 |
| | 1:4 | 0·29 | 0·31 | 0·33 |
| | 1:7 | 0·35 | 0·36 | 0·38 |
| | 1:10 | 0·38 | 0·39 | 0·40 |
| $2/3\,A_f$ | 1:1 | 0·20 | 0·23 | 0·26 |
| | 1:4 | 0·37 | 0·39 | 0·41 |
| | 1:7 | 0·45 | 0·47 | 0·48 |
| | 1:10 | 0·50 | 0·51 | 0·52 |

a crop to fallow ratio of 1:10 at $A_f' = 2/3\ A_f$. The magnitude of $A_c$ within this cycle would have a very small effect on $H_{cf}'/H_{ef}$ ratio, although the effect increases with decreases in the crop:fallow ratio.

Under a higher level of crop yields, the amount of crop residues is also greater. For example, at 3 to 5 tonne/ha cereal yields, the amount of stover would be about 3 to 5 tonne/ha and root residues would probably be similar. Isohumic coefficients for crop residues in the Savanna have not been studied in any detail. Isohumic coefficients for mulches and organic manures have been reported to be in the range 10–20 per cent in Ghana (Nye and Greenland 1960) and Nigeria (Jones and Wild 1975). However, mean isohumic coefficient for cereal stover in temperate conditions was reported by Monnier (1965) to be about 15 per cent. If this is applicable to Savanna conditions and if the isohumic coefficient for cereal root dry matter is about 35 per cent, then 6 to 10 tonne/ha of stover and root dry matter from a good cereal crop would mean an addition of about 765–1275 kg/ha of humus carbon to the soil. This would be equivalent to about 0·017–0·028 per cent carbon in the top 30 cm.

Little work has been done on the question of equilibrium humus level under different levels of additions and decomposition constants. Little is known about the isohumic coefficient of different kinds of crop residues and factors affecting it. It is widely accepted that a soil under a given set of conditions eventually attains equilibrium value because the ability of the soil to accept humus additions from fresh organic matter in any one season is limited. Further, little is known about the minimum level of humus carbon which will maintain favourable soil physical conditions, and there is evidence that structural stability of soil depends on the non-humified fraction of the total organic matter in the soil (Combeau and Quantin 1964). Therefore, it is likely that there may be a need to return organic residues to the soil in amounts large enough to meet the needs of both the humic and non-humic fractions of the soil. However, the decomposition constant for total organic matter is greater than that of humus, and values reported are 4·5–6·0 per cent during three years of cropping of land previously under *Imperata cylindrica* fallow at Bambari, Central African Republic (Quantin 1965), 6–7 per cent per annum during six years of cropping after clearing at Sefa, Senegal (Fauck 1956), and 10 per cent per annum during cropping after fallow in the Gamba grass fallow rotation experiment at Samaru (Jones 1971).

### 4.4.4 *Organic matter and soil fertility*

Much has been said and written about the beneficial effects of organic matter on fertility of tropical soils and in particular the Savanna soils where natural levels of organic matter and clay contents are low. However, the issue still continues to arouse considerable controversy. The early work on maintenance and improvement of soil fertility was very much tied up with trying to understand how fertility was maintained under traditional systems of farming which used no fertilizers and little or no organic manure. Much of this work was reviewed by Nye and Greenland (1960) who discussed the reasons behind the practice of shifting cultivation in the High Forest areas, and the bush or grass fallow rotation system in the Savanna areas. Decline in yields during the cropping period in these systems were due to deterioration in the soil physical and chemical properties, erosion of the top soil, and increase in the pest, disease and weed infestation. Rest fallow periods, during which soil nutrient and organic matter reserves built up, were essential to counterbalance the yield-reducing physical and chemical changes, which were found to be closely linked with changes in the soil organic matter content.

This early work was expanded in the Guinea Savanna areas into long-term rotation and continuous cropping trials involving manures and fertilizers at yield levels much higher than those obtained under the traditional practice. The results showed that in general the short-term beneficial effects of organic matter on physical and chemical properties of the Savanna soils were not essential for good yields provided crop nutrient requirements including trace elements were fully met by application of fertilizer. However, recent results from these experiments have shown that the long-term ability to maintain fertility under continuous cropping by application of fertilizer alone depends greatly on its effect on soil acidity and on the number of nutrient elements contained in it (Bache 1965, Bache and Heathcote 1969, Heathcote and Stockinger 1970, Jones and Wild 1975). In these experiments no special cultivation techniques were used to incorporate the organic matter into the soil.

On the other hand, long-term rotation and continuous cropping trials involving cultivation practices and soil incorporation of crop residues, and fertilizers have been conducted by the Francophone workers in the Sudan Savanna areas where soils are sandy. Here significant differences have been obtained in yield whch have been attributed partly to the effects of organic matter on the soil physical and chemical (other than nutrient supply) properties (Blondel 1965, Nicou and Thirouin 1968, Charreau and Fauck 1970, Charreau and Nicou 1971).

Favourable effects of soil organic matter at high yield levels under continuous cultivation has been attributed to various causes. These include the effects on soil structure, slow release of balanced nutrient reserves, amelioration of acidifying effects of nitrogenous fertilizers, and an increasing supply of trace elements. It is the difficulty of experimentally assessing each of these components of the total effect individually at different yield levels under different soil and climatic conditions that has been mainly responsible for much of the controversy regarding the importance of organic matter in the Savanna soils.

On balance it appears that the unique effect of organic matter on the soil physical properties is of particular importance for soils which are sandy and have a poor inherent constitution because of low clay and iron oxide contents. In such soils in Senegal incorporation of green manure crops was beneficial, although the green manure often adds little to the soil humus pool. Therefore it is likely that part of the beneficial effects of incorporating residues may be due to the unhumified organic debris mechanically preventing soil compaction (Russell 1973). However, the beneficial effects of returning crop residues to the soil is closely tied to the cultivation technique which actually incorporates them into the soil often by ploughing. This is clearly not suitable in the traditional hand tool system of farming, and greater return of crop residue will require the replacement of burning, presently used for land clearing, by ploughing and incorporation of crop residues.

The beneficial effect of organic matter on the soil chemical properties will continue to remain important. This will be a reflection of lack of information on long-term changes in these properties under continuous cultivation and lack of effective fertilizer technology to deal with such changes. Until very recently fertilizer experiments have been mainly conducted on an annual basis using fertilizer containing one or two major nutrients. Fertilizer policy for continuous intensive cropping based on results from such experiments will therefore inevitably lead to deficiencies of minor and trace elements. Further, the Savanna soils are low in cation exchange capacity and exchangeable bases, and during the growing season they experience heavy periodic leaching. The use of narrow-spectrum and often acidifying fertilizers in absence of liming or calcium is likely to lead eventually to problems of soil acidity, toxicity and nutritional imbalance. The role of wide-spectrum fertilizer in the maintenance of fertility of the Savanna soils will therefore assume greater importance in the future.

The effect of organic matter on soil physical properties and chemical properties (i.e., soil $pH$, CEC, exchangeable bases) was discussed earlier. Only the supply of nutrients in relation to organic matter is discussed here.

Under the present bush rotation system nearly all the source of nitrogen for non-leguminous crops resides in the soil organic matter which is mineralized during the wet season. When the C:N ratio is not excessively high, the availability of nitrogen increases with soil organic matter. During cultivation changes in soil N parallel changes in soil carbon although during long fallow the C:N ratio increases with increasing rainfall and the C:N ratio in the very dry parts of the Savanna region can be very low. For the well-drained soils in the Savanna regions in Nigeria, Jones (1973) obtained the relation:

$$\text{C:N} = 7\cdot72 + 0\cdot0047 \,(\text{Rainfall, mm}) \,(r = 0\cdot48) \qquad (4.22)$$

for the top 15 cm. Therefore the C:N ratio at the 300 mm isohyet is $0\cdot1$ and at the 1500 mm isohyet it is $14\cdot8$. Jones (1973) also found that soil nitrogen was related to rainfall and nitrogen in the top 15 cm increased from $0\cdot026$ per cent to $0\cdot089$ per cent over the range in annual rainfall of 400 to 1500 mm. If the annual rate of mineralization for organic nitrogen was 4 per cent, then these would correspond to about 23 to 80 kg N/ha per year. Mean soil nitrogen content for the Savanna region as a whole is about $0\cdot05$ per cent and would yield about 45 kg/ha of nitrogen per season. In the local millet and sorghum cultivars the grain nitrogen to total nitrogen taken up is about 30 per cent. If all the soil nitrogen were taken up by the crop, it would support sorghum and millet yields of about 800 kg/ha at 12 per cent grain protein.

The ratio of organic phosphorus to carbon in well-drained soils has been shown to be about 45–55, 60–110, 130–180 in the Southern Guinea, Northern Guinea, and Sudan Savanna respectively, corresponding to organic phosphorus content of about $0\cdot006$, $0\cdot004$ and $0\cdot0013$ per cent respectively (Enwezor and Moore 1966, Ipimidun 1972). At 4 per cent mineralization rate, $5\cdot4$, $3\cdot6$ and $1\cdot1$ kg P/ha would be released from the 0–15 cm depth per season in these regions respectively.

Most of the sulphur in surface soils is found in organic forms. In northern

Nigeria about 80 per cent or more of the soil sulphur was in the organic matter (Bromfield 1972). In general, the N:S ratio for well-drained soils is about 10 and C:S ratio about 100 (Charreau, 1974a). Sulphur in the top 15 cm soil would therefore range from 0·0026 to 0·0089 per cent. Mineralization rates of organic sulphur appear to be similar to that of nitrogen. Taking a mean value of 0·0045 per cent and 4 per cent mineralization rate, about 4·5 kg/ha would be released per season.

The amounts of plant nutrients, particularly nitrogen, phosphorus, and sulphur, released from soil organic matter every season, although low compared to levels required for high yields, none the less have allowed adequate yields to be obtained by the traditional farmers over many years. As population pressure has increased and fallow period decreased over the years, continuous cropping of land in the immediate vicinity of towns and villages has relied more and more on the additions to the soil of organic matter from animal manure and household refuse to maintain soil nutrient status. However, as long as animal and crop husbandry remain separate enterprises as they do now, availability of animal manure as a source of plant nutrient is going to limit yields; and the practice of removal and burning crop residues will remain a liability on the nutrient balance sheet until such time as burning is replaced by ploughing and crop residues are incorporated into the soil as husbandry practices and yields improve.

### 4.5  Soil erosion

The major problem of management under continuous cropping and intensive system of farming is the control of soil erosion. This is particularly true under conditions of mechanized farming where large areas of land brought under cultivation cause an increase in soil loss leading to a decline in soil fertility or land degradation. Standard conservation practices developed for temperate climate conditions are often inadequate under the Savanna environment to protect soils which are subjected to the exceptionally high intensity and kinetic energy load of rains. For these reasons, it is important to have a qualitative and quantitative appreciation of the factors affecting the rate of soil erosion so that appropriate control measures can be adopted or synthesized.

There are two forms of soil erosion in the Savanna region. At lower latitudes, in areas of high rainfall, water erosion is dominant; at higher latitudes approximately north of the 900 mm isohyet wind erosion also becomes increasingly more important. North of the 350 mm isohyet, i.e., in the northern Sahel bioclimatic region, severe aridity associated with steady winds, occasional violent air currents, and a flat topography with light sandy soils favour large scale movement of sand.

#### 4.5.1  Erosion by water

Water erosion is most significant in the Sudan and Guinea bioclimatic regions. Risks of accelerated soil erosion increase with the increased amount of annual rainfall and surface run-off and decreased vegetation. The most important forms of soil erosion through water agency are splash and gully erosions.

Splash erosion (often referred to as sheet erosion) occurs when soil particles detached from the surface soil by the splash of rain-drop impact are removed by run-off water flowing over the surface soil. It is less spectacular than gully erosion and very difficult to recognize, but it is the most widespread and important form of erosion in the Savanna region. Its significance is that it gradually removes the top soil which is most fertile. It is particularly serious where a shallow top soil overlies iron-pan or ironstone concretionary layers, and may cause complete degradation of the soil.

Gully erosion is spectacular and widespread throughout the Savanna region. It is usually associated with splash erosion and occurs where run-off has become concentrated in channels. It also occurs on steeper slopes, along roads and footpaths and around settlements where run-off from compounds and bare ground has concentrated in drains and ditches. Gully erosion is of less agricultural significance than splash erosion since comparatively it affects agricultural production much less. However, once the gully erosion has developed, its control is difficult and expensive. The cost of reclamation usually exceeds the value of land. Gully erosion is important as a source of high sediment in streams and may cause rapid siltation of water reservoirs.

### 4.5.2 Natural soil erosion

Under natural environmental conditions and the restricted activity of man, soil erosion in the Savanna region is not much greater than under the gentler climatic conditions of temperate environments.

The annual rate of erosion under natural bush vegetation at Sefa, Senegal, (1150mm rainfall) was estimated to be between 0·1 to 0·2 tonne/ha (Roose 1967). At Samaru, Nigeria, with a similar amount of precipitation, annual soil erosion from fire protected and annually burnt plots, measured over a period of 10 years, was found to be negligible due to the absence of surface run-off (Kowal 1970d). The absorptive capacity of soil, aided by floor litter impeding the flow of surface run-off, was able to retain water even from exceptionally heavy storms. The small amount of surface run-off that very occasionally occurred was completely free of sediment and very low in dissolved bases.

It is estimated that the rate of soil formation under natural conditions in the Savanna is about 1·8 tonne/ha (Bennett 1939). On this basis the rate of natural soil formation exceeds the rate of natural soil erosion by a factor of between 9 and 18.

### 4.5.3 Accelerated soil erosion

When natural conditions of the Savanna are disturbed by the increased activity of man, as happens when vegetation is cleared to make way for farming or woody vegetation reduced for fuel use or due to stock rearing activities, the rate of soil erosion is greatly accelerated.

Accelerated soil erosion is a consequence of several interrelated factors. The removal of the protective canopy and litter layer exposes the soil surface to the direct impact of rain drops which shatter the soil aggregates causing the detachment and hurling of soil particles into suspension in the run-off water. The micro-climate is drastically changed due to direct insolation. This adversely affects the biotic activity of the soil and causes a rapid decomposition of organic matter. As a consequence, the physical condition of the soil deteriorates, particularly affecting soil porosity, infiltration rates and the stability of aggregates. All this diminishes the sponge-like properties of the surface soil to absorb water thus leading to increased run-off and accelerated soil erosion.

In quantitative terms soil erosion is a function of the erosivity of the rain and erodibility of the soil. The erosivity or the potential ability of rain to cause erosion is very high under the climatic conditions of the Savanna. Both the exceptionally high kinetic energy load of rains which causes the detachment of soil particles, and frequent high intensity and high volume of rains that result in much surface run-off thus providing transport for the removal of detached soil particles, are responsible for a very high index of erosivity. The erodibility of Savanna soils or their vulnerability to erosion is high since the soils are sandy, low in organic matter and of unstable soil structure. The ease with which the soil particles disperse in water render Savanna soils particularly vulnerable to accelerated erosion.

There is substantial experimental data on the magnitude of accelerated erosion under various agronomic conditions in the West African Savanna. In general, the clearing of land from natural Savanna vegetation results in an accelerated erosion that is some 20 to 100 times greater than the rate of natural erosion under natural environment (Charreau 1974a).

Referring to Tables 4.10, 4.11, 4.12 and 4.13, it will be noted that soil erosion from cultivated land tends to increase with increase in rainfall and is influenced by vegetation cover, length and inclination of slope and particularly by management (land forms and roughness of cultivated surface). The actual magnitude of annual loss of soil by splash erosion from cultivated fields under very wide range of conditions varied from about 0·1 to 99 tonne/ha (Table 4.10). Under improved farming conditions, the annual loss of soil from land supporting various crops ranged from about 7 to 10 tonne/ha (Table 4.12). Assuming the bulk density of surface soil as $1·52$ g/cm$^3$, losses of 7 and 10 tonne/ha represent a loss of one centimetre soil depth in 22 and 15 years respectively. Such losses can be regarded as moderate. The actual acceptable limits of soil erosion vary but in the USA the acceptable upper limit is between 0·4 and 1·8 tonne/ha per year and in East Africa 1·5 tonne/ha per year for sandy soils and 1·8 tonne/ha per year for clay soils. Factors which influence magnitude of accelerated soil erosion are described in the following paragraphs.

(a) *The effect of rainfall.* In general the greater the rainfall the greater is the risk of soil erosion. This is because areas with higher rainfall receive a much higher total load of raindrop energy that detaches and disperses soil particles in splash. In addition higher rainfall areas are likely to have higher run-off thus providing greater opportunity for the removal of soil particles. Cocheme and Franquin (1967) suggest that significant run-off begins to occur wherever the mean annual rainfall exceeds 500 mm. Moreover, the effect of land management and cultivation techniques on run-off and erosion are complex and there is no simple relationship between the amount of rainfall, surface run-off, and soil erosion.

(b) *Soil texture.* In soils of light texture, soil particles easily detach and move, depending on the transport capacity of run-off water. In contrast, heavy

**Table 4.10**

*Magnitude of accelerated erosion under various vegetative cover (Charreau 1974a)*

| Country | Locality | Period of study | Slope (%) | Mean rainfall (mm) | Soil erosion (tonne/ha) | | | Source† |
|---|---|---|---|---|---|---|---|---|
| | | | | | Natural vegetation | Cropped land | Bare fallow | |
| Upper Volta | Ouagadougou | 1967–70 | 0·5 | 250 | 0·1 | 0·6–8·0 | 10–20 | 1 |
| Senegal | Sefa | 1954–68 | 1–2 | 1300 | 0·2 | 7·3 | 21 | 2 |
| Ivory Coast | Bouake | 1960–70 | 4·0 | 1200 | 0·1–0·2 | 0·1–26·0 | 18–30 | 3 |
| Ivory Coast | Abidjoss | 1954–70 | 7·0 | 2100 | 0·03 | 0·1–99·0 | 108–170 | 4 |
| Nigeria | Samaru | 1965–68 | 0·3 | 1070 | Negligible | 4–21 | 4 | 5 |

†Sources are as follows: 1. ORSTOM Ivory Coast and CTFT Upper Volta; 2. ORSTOM and IRAT in Senegal; 3. ORSTOM and IRAT in Ivory Coast; 4. ORSTOM in Ivory Coast; 5. IAR Nigeria.

textured soils are more resistant to soil erosion and the amount of material detached and removed depends on the violence of the rainfall. Most surface
Savanna soils after a number of years under cultivation become distinctly lighter
because fine clay particles are removed in splash erosion.

(c) *Slope gradient.* The steeper the slope, the greater the amount of run-off
and the rate of flow of run-off. Records from run-off plots at Sefa, Senegal,
during seven years showed that the mean run-off was almost twice as much from
a slope of 2 per cent as from one of 1·25 per cent and the erosion rate was
greater by a factor of 2·5 (Table 4.11).

**Table 4.11**

*Effect of slope on run-off and erosion at Sefa, Senegal
(seven year means) (Roose 1967)*

|                         | Slope (%)       |        |        |
|-------------------------|-------|-------|--------|
|                         | 1·25  | 1·50  | 2·00   |
| Annual rainfall (mm)    | 1235  | 1235  | 1186   |
| Run-off (%)             | 16·3  | 21·9  | 30·0   |
| Erosion loss (tonne/ha) | 4·75  | 8·62  | 11·81  |

(d) *Length of slope.* The longer the slope the greater is the build-up of surface
run-off, in volume, velocity, and depth. This results in scour erosion which
would not occur on a shorter length of slope. At Samaru, Nigeria, the maximum
safe length at 1·4 per cent slope was estimated to be about 55 metres. The length
of slope free of erosion is of particular practical interest in soil conservation
since it provides information needed on the required spacing of graded terraces
or erosion banks (Kowal 1970d). Both the inclination and the length of the
slope are recognized factors that are included in all numerical estimates of soil
erosion.

(e) *Crop cover.* Because of differences in the time of sowing and harvesting,
and in the rate of crop growth and growth habits, crops differ in their ability
to intercept the kinetic energy of rain drops. There is a considerable difference
in the rate of accelerated soil erosion in relation to crop cover (Table 4.12).

(f) *Land forms.* The effect of management on the rate of soil erosion can be
quite dramatic (Table 4.13). In general flat cultivation results in much less
erosion compared with ridge cultivation. The utilization of crop residues in the
form of mulch or by incorporation with the soil drastically reduces soil erosion
to acceptable low levels.

Cultivation practices which can produce a rough soil surface and the practice
of ploughing the land immediately after harvest (provided the soil moisture
is not too low for cultivation), reduces surface run-off and soil erosion.

**Table 4.12**

*Annual rate of accelerated erosion under various vegetative cover*
*at Sefa, Senegal (Roose 1967)*

| Treatment | Soil erosion (tonne/ha) |
|---|---|
| Natural vegetation (burnt) | 0·2 |
| Natural vegetation (unburnt) | 0·1 |
| Fallow (sparse vegetative cover) | 4·9 |
| Groundnuts | 6·9 |
| Cotton | 7·8 |
| Sorghum | 8·4 |
| Maize | 10·3 |
| Millet | 10·3 |

### 4.5.4 Erosion and soil fertility

The introduction of intensive methods of agricultural production into the Savanna environment, such as continuous cropping, the elimination of natural fallows, complete land clearing and mechanized farming, have drastic and far reaching effects on soil fertility that have no counterpart under the conditions of a temperate environment. The main agency responsible for this drastic effect on soil fertility is an acceleration in soil erosion. The soil fertility is reduced by selective removal of the smallest and lightest particles thereby reducing the proportion of soil colloids (organic and inorganic) thus directy affecting the physical and chemical properties of the soil.

By washing away the finer particles of the soil through rain-splash and dispersion, surface run-off reduces the nutrient status of the surface soil and changes its texture. Under more severe conditions, tillage becomes more difficult and less efficient, the exposed subsoil being relatively more compact and lacking in aggregation and available nutrients. Because of the low organic matter and clay content, the soil is very weakly buffered and therefore difficult to manage. If the top soil is removed by erosion, then even long after the addition of fertilizers and manures the subsoil remains less fertile than the original top soil.

The amount of nutrients lost in run-off water and eroded soil material from cultivated soils at Samaru, Nigeria, measured over a period of four years was described by Kowal (1970d). The average annual loss of about 10 tonne/ha soil and average annual run-off of about 200 mm contained about 22·7 kg/ha of cations (Na, K, Ca and Mg) and about 13·7 kg/ha of nitrogen (Table 4.14). A similar magnitude of annual nutrient loss by run-off and soil erosion reported by Bertrand (1967) at Baoule in the Ivory Coast included 240 kg/ha organic matter and 3·2 kg/ha of P.

It will be noted that nutrient loss in the run-off water comprises a large proportion of the total loss. Considering the total nutrient resources of the Savanna soils, the annual loss of nutrients in run-off water and soil erosion is very considerable.

## Table 4.13

*Magnitude of splash erosion from cultivated plots 183 m long, 8 m wide,
and 0·3 per cent slope, as affected by various land form treatments
at Samaru (five year means) (Kowal 1970d)*

| Treatments | Annual erosion (tonne/ha) | Rate of erosion† |
|---|---|---|
| Flat cultivation, crop residues ploughed in, under crop rotation | 2·2 | 69 |
| Flat cultivation, crop residues left on the surface, under crop rotation | 3·0 | 50 |
| Flat cultivated, bare fallow | 8·3 | 18 |
| Flat cultivated, under crop rotation | 8·9 | 17 |
| Flat cultivation, minimum tillage, under crop rotation | 9·4 | 16 |
| Ridge cultivation (91 cm centre) with alternatively tied ridges, under crop rotation | 12·6 | 12 |
| Ridge cultivation (91 cm centre), under crop rotation | 43·1 | 4 |
| Ridge broadlands with alternatively tied ridges, under crop rotation | 46·2 | 3 |

† Loss of 1 cm depth of soil in years, assuming bulk density of surface soil as 1.52 g/cm³.

## Table 4.14

*Average annual loss of nutrients by erosion at Samaru (Kowal 1970d)*

| | Na | K | Ca | Mg | N |
|---|---|---|---|---|---|
| Nutrients in run-off water and suspended material (kg/ha) | 2·27 | 7·65 | 4·9 | 2·1 | 7·4 |
| Nutrient in eroded soil material (kg/ha) | 0·33 | 1·0 | 3·2 | 1·2 | 6·3 |
| Total | 2·60 | 8·65 | 8·1 | 3·3 | 13·7 |

### 4.5.5 Erosion by wind

In the drier parts of the Savanna, but particularly in the northern Sudan and
Sahel regions, soil loss by wind erosion affects agricultural production. This is
particularly evident during the early stages of crop establishment; and in areas
with light surface soils, where natural vegetation has been depleted by overgrazing or the removal of woody vegetation for fuel, wind erosion is a more
serious problem than water erosion.

Torrential downpours on exposed soil and excessive drying during the dry
season lead to the depletion of soil organic matter, the crystallization of iron
and aluminium hydroxides and the hardening of the soil. The surface soil is
dusty and easily shifted by air currents.

Wind erosion is restricted to dry soils and the amount of soil which will be blown depends on wind velocity and the roughness of the soil surface. There are no data available on the qualitative and quantitative aspects of wind erosion in the West African Savanna.

## 4.6  Soil conservation

Continuous cropping and mechanical soil tillage methods are comparatively new introductions into the Savanna environment presenting a high risk of accelerated soil erosion that leads to a lowering of productivity, and if uncontrolled may result in a rapid soil degradation. An increase in area under continuous cropping and/or mechanized tillage usually results in an amalgamation of cultivated areas into continuous large blocks of exposed and unprotected soil. Because of the larger block size and the increased length of slope, the surface run-off is greatly accentuated, causing an increase in loss of soil, rill or gully erosion, or flood damage.

Of immediate concern is the fact that there is no tradition or experience in soil conservation methods and that farmers lack resources to participate in simple and inexpensive techniques of soil protection. Further, the introduction of standard conservation techniques that are successful in temperate environments often do not stand to a test under the more severe condition of the Savanna environment. The fact is that there is still a lack of a tested technology for this important sector of the management of soils which are subjected to an exceptionally high kinetic energy load and high intensity of rains. For example, termiteria, which are widely spread throughout the Savanna not only present difficulty in the normal mechanical tillage of land but interfere with normal soil conservation measures. Usually termiteria when levelled form areas of high clay content that shed water rapidly, causing ponding, and obstruct water disposal where land has been ridged to a gradient. This leads to breaches and reduces the effectiveness of any standard system of soil conservation.

Since the amount of run-off from high volume and high intensity rains is much larger than in a temperate environment, the engineering aspects of run-off management are much more expensive and costly and must be applied to complete drainage units, if waterlogging or flooding is to be completely avoided.

### 4.6.1  The universal soil loss equation

Soil erosion is influenced by a number of variables, identification and quantification of which are essential for the numerical assessment of erosion and for the adoption or synthesis of suitable management to control it.

The most widely used guide for soil conservation planning is the universal soil loss equation (Wischmeier and Smith 1960):

$$A = R \times K \times L \times S \times C \times P \qquad (4.23)$$

where  $A$  =  soil loss,
$R$  =  the rainfall erosivity index, measuring the erosion power of rains,
$K$  =  the soil erodibility factor,
$L$  =  the length of slope,

$S$ = the slope factor,

$C$ = The crop management factor (characteristic of vegetative cover protecting the soil against erosion),

$P$ = the conservation practice factor, i.e., the effectiveness of land forms such as ridges, terraces, etc.

Details and examples of working out the equation are described by Hudson (1971) to whom readers are referred.

The Francophone work has established that the values of the soil erodibility factor $K$ in the Sudan and Sahel regions range from 0·04 to 0·17. These values are low compared with those reported for American soils which range from 0·10 for the most erosion resistant soils to 0·50 for the most erosion susceptible soils. It therefore appears that the light Savanna soils are relatively resistant to erosion. However, by far the most important factor influencing erosion under the Savanna environment is R, the rainfall erosivity index, which is six to ten times greater than for temperate climates.

### 4.6.2  The control of run-off and soil erosion

Bearing in mind the components of the universal soil loss equation, the control of erosion is conveniently considered here under three headings. (a) The employment of large scale mechanized protection for the catchment basin or farms by means of the construction of contour bunds, terraces, contour cultivation and grass strips and artificial water courses. (b) The control by various forms of surface micro-relief, e.g., ridges, flat cultivation, mulches, etc. (c) The control by agronomic practices affecting land cover and structural condition of the soil.

(a) *Large scale conservation measures.* Experience indicates that well constructed contour banks are an effective safeguard against major erosion and probably the most practical means of controlling run-off and erosion in the Savanna environment. The size and spacing of banks as well as adequate provision for the discharge of intercepted run-off into a grassed watercourse is critical for the proper functioning of this conservation measure.

The method for the control of surface drainage and soil conservation at the farm belonging to the Institute for Agricultural Research, Samaru, Nigeria, can serve as an example of a simple conservation method that can be adopted throughout the Guinea Savanna. Graded banks about 360 m long, laid out at a changing gradient of 1:500 for the first 120 m and at gradients of 1:330 and 1:250 for the second and third 120 m respectively, form the basis of a system for intercepting run-off water. The average topographical slope at the farm is approximately 1·5 per cent. The terraces are laid out at a horizontal interval of about 76 m apart which is equivalent to a vertical interval of about 114 cm. The catchment area per terrace is therefore about 2·8 ha. On steeper topographical slopes, terraces would be narrower. The terrace discharges into a grass water course some 15 m wide at the top where the gradient is 1·8 per cent, widening gradually to some 56 m at the bottom of the valley. The water course drains about 100 ha and is designed to discharge water at the rate of 20 m$^3$/sec (Kowal 1970e).

The main disadvantage of land terracing is the high precision required in their construction, and the high cost in the provision of equipment and the necessary skill of execution. It is therefore clear that some national agency is required for the planning, financing and execution of the measure to be widely adopted.

Strip cropping, with strips of different crops planted on the contour alternating down the slope or grass strips on the contour between wider strips of cropped land, is a much simpler method of soil conservation. The method provides less protection than the contour bank and under certain conditions tends to aggravate drainage problems. Grass strips tested at Baoule, Ivory Coast, and at Allokoto, Niger, by Roose and Bertrand (1971) were successful in preventing erosion, each grass strip serving as a water absorption terrace from which run-off occurred only in exceptional circumstances.

(b) *Control by various forms of surface micro-relief.* Work at Samaru (Kowal 1970d) provides a good example of the pronounced effect of various land forms on the rate of soil erosion. In general any treatment that results in surface roughness and obstructs or slows down the movement of the water on the soil surface results in a marked reduction of soil loss.

The ridging of land along the contour may serve in the absence of other soil conservation methods as a useful means of avoiding large scale soil erosion. However, ridges concentrate the flow of water into a relatively narrow channel, increasing run-off velocity. This has a scouring effect on the ridge and increases the dispersion of weak aggregates. Consequently, ridges tend to accelerate the loss of soil colloidal matter and nutrients, and in the presence of major mechanical soil conservation works such as graded terraces, their use should be avoided.

Flat cultivation is preferred where graded terraces or other major conservation works exist. The improvement of surface micro-relief by the incorporation of soil residues, mulching, and the greatest roughness of surface that is compatible with being able to sow the crop, results in very low erosion. An additional advantage of flat cultivation is that, unlike ridges, it imposes no limitation on planting geometry. Crops may be therefore sown at spacings that ensure optimum utilization of radiation and provide maximum soil cover.

The tying of ridges certainly keeps water and soil in place but is not suitable for all crops, and should a ridge overtop the effect may be worse than if no protection were provided. Furthermore, ridging does not provide year round protection and thus a storm burst before ridging is conducted or after harvest could lead to severe damage. Annual ridging can be dangerous, and a ridge freshly thrown up, at centre spacing of 71 to 91 cm commonly used, is not sufficiently robust to withstand the high intensity and volume of rainfall to which it is subjected so frequently.

Tying of ridges is usually associated with water conservation, and so much attention is often focused on the need to conserve excess water where it falls that waterlogging can result. For this reason the tying of all ridges should be avoided in the Guinea Savanna region (Kowal 1970d). The tying of alternative furrows results in a more balanced management between the conservation of soil and water by run-off control, and the avoidance of surface waterlogging and excessive leaching during wet years. In the more arid areas in the Sudan and

Sahel Savanna where there is a stress on water conservation, the tying of ridges will retain most of the rainfall, provide soil protection and is likely to benefit crop growth.

Finally, the most effective control of run-off and soil erosion at the farmer's disposal is by the control of the size of fields. Irrespective of whether the crop is planted on the flat or on the ridges, or whether major physical protection such as terraces or grass strips are provided, run-off must pass the length of the land to the outlet. The volume and velocity of run-off will largely depend on the slope, length and the size of the field. Kowal (1970e) has discussed the length of the slope and size of fields affecting soil erosion in the context of one exceptionally heavy storm at Samaru.

(c) *The control of erosion by crop management.* Land productivity may be improved or it can be depleted by the management of crops. In general any management practice that results in a high productivity favours soil conservation.

Fertile soils that support closely grown crops expose a minimum area of soil to rainfall impact and suffer much less erosion than soils which due to their low fertility support only widely spaced stands which afford little cover. Early planting with crop geometry designed to intercept the maximum amount of radiation, contributes to soil protection through the early establishment of cover and a reduction of soil exposure.

Tillage practices such as moderately deep ploughing, particularly if it is done in the autumn before the dry season sets in, or trash farming, i.e., ploughing in crop residues after the harvest, are most effective measures of erosion control.

The effect of rotations on soil erosion has not been clearly documented in the West African Savanna. However, results obtained by Hudson and Jackson (1959) in East Africa show the effectiveness of rotations in contributing to higher yields and lower soil loss when compared with the continuous cropping of monocultures.

There is no direct experimental evidence to indicate that intercropping contributes to the control of erosion. However, it is reasonable to expect that a good protective cover established early in the season and the different habits of growth of various crops grown at the same time, reduce soil exposure and thus contribute to soil conservation.

### 4.6.3 *The control of wind erosion*

The damaging effect of wind erosion is recognized and measures of control were initiated in many parts of the arid Savanna by planting shelter belts and by afforestation. At farm level, emphasis is being placed on avoiding clean tillage, and the introduction of grass 'hedges' as a conservation measure is encouraged.

In general, there is an extensive programme being carried out to establish windbreaks of cashew (*Anarcardium occidentale*) and in Nigeria large scale development of shelter belt establishment is under way to protect the more arid parts of the Savanna. Of special value in these areas is *Acacia albida* which retains its leaves during the dry season thus providing shade and leaf fodder at a time when grass is scarce. It is also a soil improver (Jung 1967), and often creates a favourable micro-climate for crop growth (Dancette and Poulain 1968, 1969, Charreau 1974a). Certain *Eucalyptus* spp., and Neem (*Azadirachta indica*) do well as shelter belt species providing shade and shelter, as well as a source of fuel and employment.

## 4.7 Soil tillage

The principal objective of land tillage under the conditions of a temperate environment is directed towards the control of weeds, and the burial of stubble or manure through ploughing, resulting in a clean and relatively smooth surface which by further light cultivation turns into fine tilth, highly favouring seed germination and seedling establishment. The resulting seed-bed is highly porous, absorptive and in most soils, free draining. The soil aggregates are stable and their size distribution is relatively little affected by rainfall during the season. Tillage has a very minor role to play in soil conservation.

In contrast, under the environmental conditions of the Savanna, soil tillage has much wider objectives. These, in addition to weed control, include the modification of the physical state of soils within the rooting depth of crops, and under the system of continuous cropping at high production, tillage is an integrated part of soil management to control the safe disposal of surplus run-off water and the protection of land against excessive soil erosion.

This is a completely new aspect in the indigenous agricultural practices associated with settled farming. The traditional system of shifting cultivation provided an adequate protection of the land. However, rapid changes that occur in the physical environment when there is a change from shifting cultivation to continuous cultivation increases the risks of soil erosion. In the West African Savanna this changeover has been already occurring. The emerging problem is to find a means which would encourage farmers to participate in an effective programme of soil conservation and drainage. There is no tradition to guide farmers in the practice of soil conservation and there is very little practical information about methods which have been tried extensively in everyday farming.

### 4.7.1 Traditional methods of tillage

Under the undisturbed conditions of natural Savanna vegetation, particularly if it has been protected over a prolonged period of time against fire, the soil surface is porous and fairly well structured. This is due to a high organic matter content, the protection of aggregates against rainsplash by forest canopy and surface leaf mulch and by very high biological activity of earthworms, termites and other soil inhabitants. The biological activity of termites is particularly significant and partly responsible for the 'biological porosity' of the soil that greatly facilitates rapid rainfall infiltration and soil drainage. An extensive network of termite galleries and 'garden cavities' was found by the authors to extend 2–3 metres deep into the soil, facilitating extension of roots to deeper layers of an otherwise compacted soil profile. The channels, believed to extend to the dry season water table, facilitate soil drainage.

Both fire and cultivation rapidly destroy the natural structure of the surface soil due to a reduction in the biological activity of the soil, a decrease in soil organic matter, rain splash, and soil erosion.

Under the traditional systems of farming, associated with subsistence economy, all tillage is done by hand. The only means at the farmer's disposal for seed-bed preparation are cutlass, fire and hoe. The land is cleared by cutting and burning *in situ*. Clearing is rarely complete, trees of economic value being spared. When a return to bush fallow within a few years is expected, stumps of trees and shrubs are allowed to remain to facilitate rapid regeneration. The land is not levelled and termiteria mounds are not interfered with. Tillage is carried out by hand using only the hoe, and most crops are grown on ridges. The practice of ridge cropping is not entirely related to the climate, soil, topography, or land conservation to which it is often attributed. It is in fact a practical solution, presenting the farmer with the following advantages (Kowal and Stockinger 1973b).

(i) It saves hand labour in seed-bed preparation since only half the land area is worked, and the soil is lifted by hoe to form a furrow and deposited on top of the adjoining undisturbed soil surface to form a ridge.

(ii) In the process of ridge preparation, top soil enriched with ash and plant residues is concentrated in the area of plant roots. This increases the effective thickness of the top soil, thereby aiding fertility.

(iii) It gives protection against accelerated soil erosion when used on the contour. Ridging across a slope is usually the only soil conservation practice used by farmers in the Savanna areas. If finer soil fractions are washed out, they are caught by neighbouring tracts of vegetation. Under these conditions, ridging makes cultivation possible on steeper slopes.

(iv) During excessive wet periods, ridges provide a controlled means for a safe disposal of surplus water: the furrows acting as open drains. Ridges improve aeration during these wet periods for the roots. In water-deficient areas, ridges are often cross-tied to conserve both water and soil.

(v) Ridges facilitate the growth of the underground pods in groundnut and tubers of certain crops such as yams, in the softer more friable soil of the ridge and make harvesting of the crop easier.

Under conditions of shifting cultivation and bush fallow rotation, where plots are small and surrounded by tracts of regenerating fallow, ridging apparently has some disadvantages. Ridges tend to erode in the furrow, and weeding sometimes knocks them down. This results in a poor plant support and an increase in lodging of tall crops such as maize or sorghum. Extra labour may also be needed to maintain ridges. The soil in the ridges tends to be drier because water runs off into the furrow and the greater surface area exposed results in greater evaporation. Early in the season, when rains are not as frequent or regular, this can result in poor crop establishment. Ridges tend to concentrate water in the furrow and if the ridges are not on a contour, which is the case in most fields, run-off and erosion increase considerably. The estimated rate of erosion in a 200 m long ridged plot with a 0·25 per cent slope was about 25 mm of soil in 20 years compared with a loss of 25 mm of soil in 110 years on non-ridged land (Kowal 1970d). However, under shifting cultivation and bush fallow rotation, small patches of land surrounded by undisturbed or regenerating vegetation are used for only 2 or 3 years. Consequently, erosion losses are not great and sediment is trapped at field perimeters (Kowal and Stockinger 1973b).

## 4.7.2 *Traditional methods of tillage under continuous cropping*

Near large population centres or along the main trunk roads where pressures on land do not allow the restoration of soil fertility through fallow periods, continuous cropping is now increasingly being practised. This can be regarded as a transition from rotational bush fallowing and subsistence economy to semi-permanent or permanent cultivation relying increasingly on the use of manure and fertilizer, the expansion of cash cropping and a commercially orientated economy. Hand labour using the hoe and ridge cropping still form the basis of tillage. Most of the stumps are eliminated and only a few economic trees are allowed to grow. In general there is a rapid decline in soil fertility and a consequent fall in productivity where application of manure and fertilizer is not adequate.

The elimination of fallow areas that surround cultivated land and intercept run-off, and the amalgamation of small plots into large, continuous, tracts of cultivated land increases slope lengths on unprotected land. Consequently, run-off increases and soil erosion accelerates. Since hand tillage is in general use in the Savanna regions, the land is ridged to reduce labour requirements. Because of the low natural soil fertility, the ridges are spaced too far apart to allow crops to form a protective canopy, thus contributing further to run-off, soil erosion and weed infestation. During heavy storms furrows often become incipient erosion gullies.

All this contributes to rapid land degradation and the lowering of productivity because there is no tradition of coping with the changing conditions which are presently occurring, and the farmer lacks means to participate in an effective system of maintaining soil fertility and controlling soil erosion.

## 4.7.3 *Improved methods of tillage*

The improved cultivation methods in the savanna are based on the introduction of power (animal or mechanized) and light to heavy implements and equipment.

The introduction of animal or mechanical traction into farming has a drastic effect on soil properties and management. It destroys the whole basis of subsistence farming whether based on shifting cultivation, bush fallow rotation, or continuous cultivation. First, the land must be cleared of all large roots and stumps from which bushes regenerate during fallow under the traditional systems. Secondly, the land must be protected against soil erosion, and soil fertility must be maintained with fertilizers. Thirdly, to be economically feasible, socio-economic and institutional changes are required to replace the subsistence economy with a commercial economy.

Power cultivation using draft animals or tractors is as yet in its infancy, but it is strongly encouraged by all the West African governments as an effective means for improving living standards and food production. In most Savanna areas, both large and small projects in which the keynote has often been the necessity for a mechanized approach to land clearing and crop production, have been launched; and although the machine has not yet provided the productivity hoped for or needed to justify its economic use, mechanization is being used increasingly both for land clearing and crop production.

The use of power, for tillage and other operations, replacing partly or entirely hand tillage, is an inevitable consequence of evolution from the traditional hand tool system of subsistence farming to a commercial farming based on continuous cropping. There are clear advantages in mechanized farming, perhaps the most important being the incentive it could offer to the members of the younger generation who are presently becoming increasingly reluctant to engage in heavy hand cultivation. Further, the increased area that can be brought under cultivation, timely farm operations, the high promise of increased yields and the necessity of introducing standard soil conservation measures into large areas already under continuous cropping, favour the expansion of mechanized farming.

According to Charreau (1974a) the rate of work by one man using hand and power cultivation is as follows:

| | |
|---|---|
| Hand cultivation (hoe) | 0·8 to 1·2 ha |
| Power cultivation: | |
| draft animals | 2 to 3 ha |
| tractor | 15 to 25 ha |

Power cultivation is therefore much faster than hand cultivation providing the farmer with much greater opportunity to perform tillage operations easily and at the right time. Land which is too dry to work during the dry season has to be prepared as a seed-bed, planted and weeded in a very short period during the 'pre-sowing' and 'post-sowing' water availability periods. If sowing and weeding is delayed, the capture of mineralized nitrogen by crops may be lost (by leaching and/or weeds), and with crops whose life span is fixed the dry season may arrive before accumulation of yields is completed. Yield increases due to early planting can be very considerable and timely sowing often determines the response of other production inputs (Baker 1975).

However, the main benefit from power cultivation is that it makes possible the use of the plough for basic tillage operations. Ploughing drastically modifies soil structure, and positive yield responses to ploughing have been obtained at many sites throughout the West African Savanna. In general, yield increases with cultivation depth: tractor ploughing > ox ploughing > hand hoeing. The effect of ploughing on soils and crops is discussed in the next section.

There are serious problems imposed by introduction of power tillage and the plough in particular. To start with, the land must be 'developed', i.e., cleared of stumps and other obstructions such as termiteria mounds, and it often has to be levelled before mechanical cultivation is possible. The protection of land against erosion must be included in any land development scheme right from the start and means of maintaining soil productivity through crop rotation and judicious fertilizer application must be assured. Further, a capital outlay is required for the purchase of draft animals, their housing, feeding, maintenance of health, and training. Introduction of tractors and tractor drawn implements implies an even greater capital outlay presently outside the means of the ordinary farmer. The use of tractors at present is only feasible through collective farms or tractor-hire schemes now operating in a few areas in West Africa. Apart from being far more expensive than in industrial countries, tractors and equipment wear much more rapidly in the tropics and their spare parts are more costly. The provision for repair workshops, spare parts stores, and specialized personnel (mechanics, operators, and administrative staff) adds greatly to the total cost. In order to justify this high capital investment, much of the potential productivity inherent in the climatic resources of the West African Savanna must be realized through efficient intensive farming and high productivity. Further, a range of economic and institutional reforms are needed to provide incentives to farmers to exploit production-enhancing technological innovations. Reforms relating to land tenure and education are obvious but also the provision of attractive markets, credit facilities, inputs (i.e., fertilizers, improved seed, biocides, etc.) must be made.

### 4.7.4 *Modification of the physical properties of soil by power cultivation*

There are wide gaps in our knowledge regarding the effect of power cultivation on soil properties and the yield of crops, particularly with regard to various kinds of implements used and moisture conditions during tillage operations. However, there is no doubt that mechanical cultivation, particularly ploughing, has beneficial modifying effects on the physical properties of Savanna soils, and positively affects yields, soil conservation, and soil water status. Based mainly on the research findings of the Francophone workers in West Africa, the following facts regarding the modification of the physical properties of soils by mechanical cultivation has emerged.

(a) *Effect on soil structure.* Since the cultivated layers of the Savanna soils are predominantly sandy, low in organic matter content, and exposed to the high kinetic energy of rains as well as to prolonged periods of excessive desiccation, the soil structure is poor and soils have a tendency to compact. Consequently most Savanna soils particularly those under continuous cropping have high bulk density, low porosity, and a poor rooting medium.

Tillage performed under favourable moisture conditions and to a moderate depth (10 to 30 cm) aids root growth by increasing the total soil porosity and reducing mechanical impedance to root penetration, resulting in root ramification into a greater volume of soil. Increased porosity through tillage is also reflected by improved infiltration and permeability and in an increase in the amount of available water.

The durability of improved porosity and lowered bulk density following ploughing can be variable. Charreau and Nicou (1971) reported the residual effect of ploughing with the incorporation of organic matter lasting four years. However, in most Savanna soils the bulk density of the ploughed soil layer steadily increases as the growing season advances and the compaction is accentuated by wetting and drying cycles. At Samaru all modifying effects were found to disappear by the end of the growing season possibly because there was no incorporation of organic matter during ploughing.

(b) *Effect on root growth.* The ploughing of Savanna soils has a large effect on root development encouraging better ramification of roots in the soil and increasing the length and width of the root canopy. It increases density of roots particularly at deeper layers of the soil profile. Nicou, Seguy and Haddad (1970) and Charreau and Nicou (1971) have shown a very high negative correlation between soil bulk density and root density.

(c) *The effect on crop yield.* Results from cultivation experiments in the West African Savanna (Poulain and Tourte 1970, Charreau and Nicou 1971, Charreau 1974a) show convincingly the positive yield response of crops to ploughing or deep tillage as contrasted with shallow hoe tillage. The range of yield increases attributed to ploughing or deep cultivation (20-30 cm) as compared with hoe or shallow cultivation varied from 20-70 per cent with an average response of 24 per cent. It was concluded that the ploughing of land or deep tillage under the environmental conditions of the West African Savanna is one of the important means available for improving crop yields. The results are not surprising since the loosening of soil through deep tillage leads to the increase in root growth and therefore to an exploitation of greater volume of soil for nutrients and water.

Mould-board or disc ploughing with the incorporation of organic materials, such as crop residues, green manures or straw, into the soil results in a more lasting modification of soil physical properties and in substantial yield increases of crops. The residual effect of ploughing with incorporation of organic materials into the soil as compared with yields where plant residues were burned and soil not ploughed were as high as 40-50 per cent after two years and 16-20 per cent after three years.

(d) *The effect on water supply to crops.* The effects of tillage methods on crop growth and yields are to a large degree attributable to differences in soil moisture status brought about by improved infiltration, changes in soil water retention characteristics, or reduction of evaporation and better conservation of water.

It is a matter of common observation that crops on ploughed soils with deep soil tilth can withstand periods of water stress much better than the same crops on unploughed soil, particularly when it is ridged.

Ploughing, particularly when a rough surface is left intact, increases rainfall infiltration into the soil by at least 20 per cent, reduces the number of run-off periods and minimizes crust formation. This effect is particularly pronounced if ploughing is done immediately after harvest and before the soil is too dry to work. Ploughing can serve as a practical and significant means of conserving water stored in the soil profile if tillage is done before the end of the rainy period or immediately after the harvest of crops that are not greatly dependent on soil moisture reserves for maturation. It is estimated that between a quarter to half the available water in 1 m soil depth can be thus conserved by reduction of evaporation during the dry season (Gaudefroy-Demomoynes and Charreau 1961). The thin layer of loose surface soil protects the lower soil layers from evaporation. The water thus conserved may be a significant factor the following rainy season in dry years.

Finally, the increase in the range of available water by deep cultivation and the greater exploitation of the volume of soil by roots following ploughing, might benefit crops in areas of low or irregular rainfall.

(e) *Effect on run-off and erosion.* There is no experimental evidence in the Savanna regions that ploughing when compared with other forms of cultivation increases soil erosion. The danger of accelerated soil erosion lies in the exposure of large unprotected tracts of land to rainfall impact and surface run-off. The effect of ploughing usually encourages infiltration and the retention of large amounts of water by the soil thus reducing run-off. Consequently erosion risks are reduced. Further if the rough surface produced on ploughing is not deliberately smoothed, turbidity and solid content of run-off water is greatly reduced and erosion is much less.

(f) *Time of tillage operation.* The modification of the physical properties of soil by tillage is greatly influenced by the soil moisture status at the time of cultivation. During the dry season when surface soil is air dry, mechanical cultivation has a shattering effect on soils, destroying most aggregates and turning the soil into hard clods or fine dust. The soil so treated has an adverse effect on crop production, is very easily eroded by wind or water and is prone to compaction. During the rains in the middle of the wet season the soil is often too wet for the working of heavy equipment and, if cultivated, soil compaction results, often accompanied by a cloddy condition.

In contrast with temperate environments where soil moisture conditions are regularly and frequently favourable for mechanical tillage, in the Savanna environment the ideal conditions of soil moisture for tillage operations are comparatively rare. Under a Savanna environment, tillage operations commence with the onset of rains since delayed planting can result in a drastic reduction of yields. A delay in planting has a more pronounced effect on the decline in yields at higher latitudes. For this reason Francophone workers emphasize the advantages of tillage at the end of the rainy season. In addition to reducing the load of work during the planting time, this tends to give additional benefits. It may conserve soil moisture for the critical period of crop establishment, encourage better sanitation and reduce surface run-off and erosion during the early period of the rainy season. Finally, when ploughing takes place at the end of the rainy season, *hardening* of the soil does not occur during the dry season and the undesirable desiccation of the soil profile is avoided.

### 4.8 The control of soil fertility

All the nutrients with the exception of carbon are drawn by crop plants from the soil. The soil solution or liquid phase is the most important source of nutrients for absorption by roots although legumes can assimilate nitrogen via the soil atmosphere. The ability of the soil to supply nutrients to the growing crop depends on the availability of nutrients and moisture in the root zone. The subject of control of soil fertility is therefore basically related to methods employed to create a favourable physical and chemical environment in the soil so that the nutrient and moisture availability is adequate to obtain the desired optimum yields.

When losses of nutrient elements in soil erosion and run-off are negligible, the available soil nutrients are depleted by crop removal and leaching. These must be counterbalanced if the chemical fertility is to be maintained or enhanced. Removal of nutrients by a crop is influenced by factors such as cultivar, climate, soil nutrient status, and cultural practices. Also, different crops remove different amounts of nutrients and their proportions vary both within and between crops. Approximate amounts of nutrients removal in kg per tonne of produce of some important crops in the West African Savanna are shown in Table 4.15. Little can be done about the removal of nutrients in the economic products. However, total losses can be minimized if the nutrients contained in the non-economic products are returned to the soil. Ploughing crop residues into the soil is not feasible in the present hand tool system of cultivation where residues not removed are burnt resulting in the loss of nitrogen and sulphur. The range in potassium contained in crop residues is large reflecting the fact that there is always a risk of 'luxury' uptake of potassium, but the return of crop residues would keep the loss to a minimum.

**Table 4.15**

*Approximate amounts of nutrients removed in kg per tonne of produce of some important crops in the West African Savanna (Charreau 1974a)*

| Crop | Produce | N | P | K | Ca | Mg | S |
|---|---|---|---|---|---|---|---|
| Rice | Grain | 10–15 | 2·6–3·5 | 2·0–2·6 | 0·4–0·6 | 0·2–1·5 | – |
|  | Stover | 5–12 | 0·9–1·3 | 5–29 | 1·1–2·5 | 1·5–3·4 | 1·2–2·5 |
| Maize | Grain | 16–19 | 1·7–3·5 | 2·5–3·9 | 0·1–0·4 | 0·6–1·2 | 1·2–2·2 |
|  | Stover | 6–10 | 0·4–1·1 | 5·4–21 | 1·8–4·2 | 1·5–3·3 | 1–1·5 |
| Sorghum | Grain | 14–20 | 1·7–3·1 | 2·5–3·3 | 0·1–0·6 | 1·0–1·9 | 1·6 |
|  | Stover | 3–6 | 0·4–1·3 | 5·8–24 | 1·2–3·2 | 0·6–2·1 | 1 |
| Pearl millet | Grain | 18–25 | 1·5–3·1 | 3·3–5 | 0·2–0·6 | 0·8–1·1 | 1–2·5 |
|  | Stem | 5–9 | 0·2–0·4 | 8·3–27 | 1·1–2·1 | 0·8–2·7 | 0·6–3 |
|  | Leaf | 7–10 | 0·4–0·9 | 8·3–25 | 2·9–7·9 | 3–6 | 0·8–4 |
| Groundnut | Kernel | 20–50 | 3·3–4·8 | 6·7–8·3 | 0·3–0·9 | 1·5–2·1 | 2·2–2·7 |
|  | Shell | 5–11 | 0·3–1·1 | 5–15 | 0·5–2·9 | 0·5–1·2 | 0·7–1·7 |
|  | Haulm | 8–20 | 1·1–3·1 | 10–25 | 5–9·3 | 3·6–6·6 | 1·7–2 |
| Yam | Tuber | 12–20 | 1·0–2·0 | 15–21 | 3·9–6·1 | 0·8–1·2 | – |
|  | Top | 7–14 | 0·4–1·0 | 8·3–25 | 8·9–13·2 | 1·7–3·6 | – |

Leaching is a common feature in the Savanna regions during the humid period when precipitation exceeds evapotranspiration, and nutrient ions in the soil solution are leached beyond the root zone in drainage water. The amount of nutrients removed by leaching depends on a number of factors such as the volume of through drainage, crop cover, soil type and amount and type of fertilizer added. There is a general lack of information on nutrient losses by leaching in the different Savanna regions. Some values reported from lysimeter studies at Bambey, Senegal, are shown in Table 4.16. Average rainfall at Bambey is about 660 mm and about 120–140 mm is lost in drainage. The amount of phosphorus lost in drainage is very small and appears to be unaffected by the type of cropping. Losses of other nutrients appear to vary depending on the crop although losses are generally lower compared with those under bare soil. It is

**Table 4.16**

*Annual loss (kg/ha) of nutrients by leaching at Bambey, Senegal,
measured with drainage lysimeters*

| Treatment | Ref† | N | P | K | Ca | Mg |
|---|---|---|---|---|---|---|
| Bare soil | 1 | 45·6 | 0·13 | 11·5 | 55·4 | 23·3 |
| Grass fallow | 1 | 6·4 | 0·09 | 5·8 | 22·0 | 12·1 |
| Pearl millet (green manure) | 1 | 1·6 | 0·04 | 3·3 | 17·9 | 2·6 |
| Crop rotation over 12 years | 2 | 5·0–13·0 | 0·09–0·13 | 7·5–10·0 | 30·0–31·4 | 6·0–13·2 |

† Sources are: 1. Tourte *et al.* (1964); 2. Charreau (1972).

not possible at this stage to provide an accurate assessment of leaching losses under different situations. However, losses of nutrients by leaching are a regular annual feature of the Savanna. Apart from attempting to minimize these losses, it will be necessary to balance those which do occur if a long-term view of fertilizer use is taken. Losses of calcium and magnesium are particularly important for Savanna soils which are weakly buffered with low amounts of exchangeable calcium and magnesium. The soil $pH$ can drop rapidly if leaching losses are not minimized or counterbalanced. As nitrate and sulphate ions in soil solution are accompanied by calcium and magnesium ions they are leached with the cations. The situation is aggravated particularly when ammonium sulphate is added to the soil as a source of nitrogen. The ammonium ions replace the exchangeable calcium and magnesium which are leached with sulphate ions. However, it is true that the loss of nitrogen can be smaller when ammonium sulphate is used as compared with potassium nitrate. Thus, Blondel (1971a) at Bambey found that an application of 300 kg N/ha as potassium nitrate led to a leaching loss of nitrogen of 69 kg N/ha whereas the loss was 9 kg N/ha when a similar amount of nitrogen was applied as ammonium sulphate. The amounts of nutrient lost by leaching are likely to vary greatly depending on the situation. For Senegal, Charreau (1972) has reported that leaching losses under cropping are likely to be in the range N, 5–30; P, 0·04–0·22; K, 8–16; Ca, 29–107; Mg, 9–24; S, 3–30 kg/ha.

The full realization of the climatic potential in the West African Savanna for crop production depends on the control of fertility, water and erosion. The soils are chemically and physically very fragile. The cultivated layer is light, and easily erodible due to the high energy load of rainstorms. The CEC, organic matter content, and buffering capacity are low. The store of native soil nutrients cannot match the high climatic potential for crop growth, and must be supplemented by an application of wide-spectrum fertilizers (including major and minor nutrients) in amounts sufficient to meet crop requirements for higher yields, taking into account losses in crop removal and leaching.

Deficiency of phosphorus is widespread throughout the Savanna region and phosphate fertilization must be aimed at increasing the labile pool and rate of release into the soil solution to meet crop requirements. In the long run, application of phosphate will have to be regarded as a long-term investment because of its reaction with the soil and the significant residual effects. The acidifying effects of nitrogenous fertilizers must be taken into account if problems with soil acidity are to be avoided. The use of ammonium sulphate and urea should be accompanied by liming or application of other fertilizers containing calcium.

The return of crop residues must be regarded as part of management offering advantages in terms of conservation of nutrients, improvement in soil physical conditions, and control of run-off and erosion. The soil structure of most soils is weak and unstable, which leads to soil compaction, surface crust formation, run-off and erosion. The main concern should be to create a favourable soil environment for optimum root growth and absorption of rainfall. The change from the present bush fallow rotation to continuous cropping greatly increases the erosion hazards and degradation of soils. Soil conservation measures therefore must be included in any viable farming system.

To obtain high crop yields on a sustained basis in the Savanna area would eventually require an integrated approach towards the control of fertility. Implicit in the approach would be the concept of basal and maintenance fertilization developed by the Francophone workers (Charreau and Fauck 1970, Chaminade 1972, Morel and Quantin 1972, Charreau 1974a). Here a basal or initial dose of fertilizer is applied to correct the initial soil nutrient deficiencies, particularly phosphate, and bring the soil closer to its potential fertility; and then to manipulate the basal fertility by maintenance fertilization. Basal fertilization will have to be adapted to the nature of the soil and not to the nature of the crop. On the other hand maintenance fertilization must counterbalance all causes of nutrient losses which are mainly due to crop removal and leaching when erosion is kept under control.

# 5 Water resources — a hydrological appraisal

In modern societies water is not only a necessity to sustain the normal requirements of life but also a dominant commodity of industrial, economic, and social value. The amount of water used by a community can serve as a reliable measure of its productivity and the resulting standard of living.

In the West African Savanna regions, water is the limiting resource and determines the extent to which other resources can be developed or efficiently utilized. The pronounced wet and dry seasons and their intensities, corresponding to period of water availability and scarcity, affect every aspect of the Savanna environment, including human activity and the productivity of its main industry, agriculture. When water is abundant it generates high human activity; when it is scarce or lacking, it results in a period of comparative inactivity. The actual and potential productivity of rain-fed agriculture is closely related to the water availability periods (Kowal and Davies 1974). It is estimated, for example, that the potential production of plant dry matter for the whole rainy season at the 760 mm isohyet is only half of that at the 1500 mm isohyet.

Modern industrial development is conspicuously lacking in the Savanna regions. This can be largely attributed to a lack of reliable water supply to sustain industrial production throughout the year. In the drier parts of the Savanna regions poor availability of water is largely responsible for the low density of population. Similarly, a lack of adequate supply of water particularly during the dry season results in slow growth of urban population. The average domestic water consumption in the Savanna regions is estimated to vary from about 14 litres per person per day in the rural areas to about 60 litres per person per day in the urban areas. In the Sahel region, the domestic water consumption is less than 14 litres per person per day. The minimum quantity of water required for adult survival at 25 °C while performing hard work in the sun is 7 litres per day but only half that amount when resting in the shade. In comparison, average total consumption in London is about 160 litres per day per person (Barbour 1972).

Agriculture makes a very heavy demand on water resources, and returns in terms of productivity are low. It is estimated that in the developed countries the quantity of water required to provide 2700 kcal protein balanced diet per day is equivalent to 11 000 tonnes of water per adult per year. However, this amount depends greatly on the quality of food consumed and particularly on the amount of animal proteins in the diet as illustrated in the Table 5.1. Under subsistence conditions of low yields, and diet often low in animal proteins, the water requirement to sustain a human life throughout the year is much lower, amounting to about one-fifth of the amount quoted above. For example,

## Table 5.1

*Total amount of water needed to produce various products*

| Product | Water need (litres) |
|---|---|
| 1 orange | 500 |
| 1 egg | 900 |
| 1 pint beer | 1500 |
| 1 kg bread | 2400 |
| 1 litre milk | 3300 |
| 1 kg chicken | 10 000 |
| 1 kg beef | 110 000 |

assuming the average yield of local sorghum is 590 kg/ha, a sorghum crop water requirement of about 800 mm (Kowal and Andrews 1973), and an average starchy daily diet of 2700 kcal, the amount of water required to sustain life per person per annum is about 3350 tonnes.

The productivity value of water used in industry, mining, recreation, and particularly in generating hydroelectric power is much higher than in agriculture (UN 1964, Olivier 1967). In the United States, for example, the water that will support one worker in arid land agriculture will support 60 workers in the industry (Koening 1956).

The need for water in the West African Savanna region is increasing at a much faster rate than the growth of population to meet irrigation needs and high water demand for urban and industrial expansion. The rate of increase for water demand in the U.K. has been reported to be between 4 and 5 per cent annually (Lowe-McConnell 1966). In the West African Savanna in general, and in Nigeria particularly, the present high rate of expansion in irrigation, industry and growth in urban population has resulted in an unprecedented demand for water. This high rate of water demand cannot be easily met to satisfy demands particularly at higher latitudes, and a choice of priorities will have to be defined. For instance, it is seldom appreciated that the major constraint in expansion of urban growth in the Savanna regions is due to lack of water for domestic and industrial use. Most of the aquifers are poor and large quantities of water can only be secured by damming river flow and constructing artificial lakes. However, there are only few rivers with continuous flow throughout the year, and evaporation losses from lakes are very high. In the final analysis, therefore, large amounts of water can be conserved in comparatively few selected places but these will have a very low efficiency of conservation due to high evaporation during the main periods of storage. Under such circumstances it might not be wise to utilize water reserves at higher latitudes for irrigation with its low returns in terms of productivity. At lower latitudes, particularly south of the 1380mm isohyet which marks a boundary of annual precipitation matching annual potential evapotranspiration demands, there are much larger amounts of water that can be conserved in sufficient amounts and used for all purposes.

The existing storage of water supply in the drier parts of the Savanna region does not imply a total lack of water resources to sustain normal domestic and industrial requirements. For example, in Nigeria, in almost every part of the

Sudan and Northern Guinea Savanna, potential water resources are fairly high and at present these are being rapidly developed. Thus in the most arid parts of the country a large artesian area in the Chad basin is being developed as a source of drinking water for humans and livestock. Pressure water also occurs in the Gongola, Sokoto, and Benue basins. Good aquifers occur in the sedimentary formations present in the Benue, Gongola, Niger, and Sokoto basins and in the flood plains of the large rivers. Although areas underlain by the Basement Complex rocks constitute a poor source of groundwater, some limited quantities of good quality drinking water can be extracted from relatively shallow depths.

However, the greatest potential in development of water resources lies in the integrated river basin development and construction of large water reservoirs. The most important recent development in water conservation in West Africa was the construction of the Volta River and Kainji dams. These were primarily designed for the provision of hydroelectric power, but also for the development of irrigation agriculture, river navigation, fisheries and flood control. Large irrigation/hydroelectric projects are also being developed in the drier parts of the Savanna, notably at Tiga on the Kano river and Hadeja in Kano State, and in the Sokoto-Rima valley. Numerous small dams have been constructed throughout the Savanna as water reservoirs for urban needs and rural settlements. However, due to the flat topography and high evaporative environment, the efficiency of storing water during the dry season is very low. For example, the Bomo dam at the Institute for Agricultural Research, Samaru, erected across *fadama*, with storage capacity of 24·7 ha m (200 acre feet) and area at full capacity of 18·2 ha (45 acres), holds only sufficient water to irrigate some 2·5 ha during the five months of the dry season. Sixty five to seventy per cent of the stored water is lost in evaporation and presumably some in seepage. The small dams are therefore more suitable for providing drinking water for the urban areas, villages and livestock. They are inefficient when employed for irrigation purposes unless the dams are situated in sites which ensure a favourable ratio of storage depth to surface area of stored water.

### 5.1 Principal drainage basins

The main drainage systems of the West African Savanna are formed by the Niger, Senegal, Gambia, and Volta rivers. The inland Chad basin in the Sahel-Sudan region also constitutes an important hydrological unit. However, the bulk of the Savanna is dominated by the complex system of the Niger river with its principal affluents the Beni river in Mali, and the Kaduna and Benue rivers in Nigeria. The Niger basins extend over most of the countries within the Savanna belt namely Guinea, Mali, parts of Upper Volta, Niger, Dahomey (Benin), and Nigeria. The Niger is the greatest river of West Africa, 4200 km long; it has abundant water all the year round, average flow being 7000 cubic metres per second with about 30 000 cubic metres per second at the time of the maximum flood. The Niger has a tropical system of water flow: high water in the summer, associated with the rainy season from April to September, but because the water course is relatively flat, the flood spreads downstream slowly and the river has a very slow passage, averaging about 11 km/day. The Niger head waters receive vast quantities of water between May and August, and the peak of the flood (8 m above the low-water level) reaches Koulikoro near Bamako in Mali in October. By the end of December the peak flood reaches Timbuktu, by the following February it has travelled to Niamey in the Niger Republic, and then into Nigeria where the flood lasts up to May.

The river Niger provides poor access to the interior. It is navigable only at high water and only in stretches between Kourouisa and Bamako, Koulikoro and Ansongo, Tillabery and Gaya, and Jebba and the delta. However, its hydro-electric potential is enormous, and the flood plains are utilized for irrigation agriculture: in Macina and all the middle valley, irrigation permits the use of several million hectares. For certain arid areas, as in Mali where the river forms an inland delta, the economic importance of the river is very significant allowing commercial production of crops such as rice, cotton, and more recently tobacco, sugar cane, and tea. However, the full water storage potential for the development of irrigation and fisheries has so far been hardly realized.

The Senegal, Gambia, and Volta rivers although much smaller are nevertheless of similar economic importance as the Niger. The Sene-Gambia basin is drained by three rivers, the Senegal, Gambia, and Casamance, flowing all the year round. However, the northern and southern rivers of the Senegal basin flow only in the rainy season. The Senegal and Gambia rivers are flat plain rivers with broad valleys lending themselves to irrigation agriculture. Their lower courses are flooded by the tides.

The Chad basin, occupying the arid north eastern area of the Savanna region, is sparsely populated due to the pronounced deficiency of water. The most depressed section of this basin in the west is occupied by Lake Chad. The size of Lake Chad varies from 10 000 to 25 000 sq km during the year, due to the heavy evaporation losses and uneven water supplies. The lake is shallow with an average depth of 3–5 m in the south and 4–8 m in the north. About one third of the lake is covered by floating *Papyrus* and anchored vegetation. The lake level is lowest in July/August and highest in late December. The annual fluctuation in the level of the lake is between 65 and 130 cm. Rainfall over the lake varies from 160 to 400 mm. The only perennial river system supplying the lake is that of Chari (1200 km) and Logone (970 km) which receive water from the southern mountains of the Ubangi and Cameroon. The Chari river has an estimated flow of $38 \times 10^9$ m$^3$ and supplies 95 per cent of water to the lake. Yobe and Ebedji rivers flow seasonally with peak flow in November/December. The lake has a very high evaporation loss, about 2000 mm/year. The Chad basin has important artesian and sub-artesian groundwater supplies. Drilling has shown that the depth of pressure water occurs within inclined strata towards Lake Chad, ranging from about 100 to 400 m. Depending on the size of bore-hole the yield ranges from 10 000 to 90 000 litres/hour.

## 5.2 Catchment basin studies

The problem of conservation and utilization of water reserves in the Savanna is of major importance and closely related to the total productivity of the region. It is of particular importance at higher latitudes where lack of water is the main constraint limiting total industrial and agricultural productivity, agricultural activity in the wet season and the population growth.

There is little man can do to improve existing water supply until the start of rains. From then on what happens to the rainfall water can be greatly influenced by management. Some of the rain water runs rapidly over the surface to the nearest river and out to the sea; some sinks into the soil where it is stored as soil water or groundwater; some feeds the springs and the seepages which keep streams flowing when there is no rain, and supply open wells and bore-wells. Part of the rain water is lost in evaporation. To improve supplies of water in the dry season, it is of fundamental importance to know the components of the total water budget in the catchment basin under consideration.

The main components of the water budget for Ferruginous soils derived from the Basement Complex rocks in Northern Guinea Savanna have been studied at Samaru by Kowal (1970b), and the results are discussed in the following pages:

The water budget was estimated from the equation

$$P - Q - \Delta W - ET = 0 \qquad (5.1)$$

by measuring the total rainfall ($P$) received over the catchment basin (607 ha), and the total amount of run-off ($Q$) comprising of the surface run-off ($r$) and the seepage ($s$) draining into the lake. Changes in soil moisture status ($\Delta W$) were eliminated from the equation by computing the water budget over a period of 'water year' clearly identified by the rise in the dry season water table when the soil moisture deficit is small and of similar magnitude in different years. Evapotranspiration ($ET$) was estimated by difference.

The magnitudes of the water budget components of the catchment basin during the six years of experiment together with the relevant hydrological data are presented in Table 5.2.

(i) Rainfall: The average precipitation over the catchment basin was 1039 mm, about 7 per cent lower than the long term average. The duration of the total rainy period was 172 days, counting the first and last rainy day in the season. The average number of occasions the rain was recorded in each year was 82. The amount of cumulative rainfall required to raise the dry season water table was 444 mm.

(ii) Run-off and seepage: Measured amounts of surface run-off and seepage accounted for about 32 per cent (327 mm) of the rainfall received. Except for the exceptionally wet years, the seepage losses were greater than surface run-off. The average magnitude of seepage was about 20 per cent of the rainfall (202 mm), the remaining 12 per cent of the rainfall (125 mm) was lost in the surface run-off. The average duration of the seepage flow was about 87 days.

The average amount of water that could be conserved was 32 per cent of the rainfall (327 mm). This estimate compares closely with an annual average 'water surplus' of 364 mm derived from the water budget accounting (Kowal and Knabe 1972), assuming 100 mm soil water deficit. Expressed as percentage of rainfall these values are remarkably similar (32%), although they have been obtained for different years and by different methods.

(iii) Evapotranspiration: The difference between the precipitation and the combined loss of rainfall in the surface run-off and seepage represents the

**Table 5.2**

*Water balance account for the Samaru catchment basin (Kowal 1970b)*

| Water year | 1966 | 1967 | 1968 | 1969 | 1970 | 1971 | Average |
|---|---|---|---|---|---|---|---|
| | 30/9/65–12/10/66 | 13/10/66–28/9/67 | 29/9/67–3/10/68 | 4/10/68–29/10/69 | 30/10/69–29/9/70 | 27/9/70–21/5/71 | 7/10–6/10 |
| Duration (days) | 377 | 350 | 371 | 390 | 330 | 360 | 363 |
| Rainfall over catchment (mm) | 1382 | 990 | 998 | 1196 | 884 | 775 | 1039 |
| Rainy period | 6/4–12/10 | 22/3–28/9 | 18/4–3/10 | 3/4–29/10 | 7/5–26/9 | 15/5–21/9 | 16/4–5/10 |
| Rainfall duration (days) | 190 | 191 | 169 | 209 | 143 | 129 | 172 |
| Number of rainy days | 95 | 83 | 77 | 88 | 77 | 70 | 82 |
| Date of rise in the dry season water table | 11/7 | 15/7 | 27/7 | 29/6 | 30/7 | 31/7 | 19/7 |
| Cumulative rainfall (*CP*) at the time of the rise in water table level (mm) | 506 | 419 | 516 | 381 | 460 | 391 | 444 |
| Start of flow over spillway | 11/8 | 17/7 | 15/8 | 25/7 | 25/8 | 26/8 | 9/8 |
| End of flow over spillway | 12/12 | 12/11 | 16/10 | 15/11 | 19/10 | 20/10 | 5/11 |
| Duration of flow over spillway (days) | 124 | 118 | 62 | 113 | 56 | 54 | 87 |
| Total spillway discharge (mm) | 429 | 239 | 130 | 450 | 275 | 257 | 297 |
| Lake deficit (mm) | 30 | 30 | 30 | 30 | 30 | 30 | 30 |
| Total run-off and seepage (*Q*) (mm) | 459 | 269 | 160 | 480 | 305 | 287 | 327 |
| Run-off (*r*) (mm) | 259 | 168 | 8 | 180 | 81 | 49 | 125 |
| Seepage (*s*) (mm) | 200 | 101 | 152 | 300 | 224 | 238 | 202 |
| Annual evapotranspiration (*ET*) (mm) | 923 | 721 | 838 | 716 | 599 | 488 | 712 |
| *ET* − *CP* (mm) | 417 | 302 | 322 | 335 | 119 | 97 | 268 |

amount of water used in evapotranspiration during the 'water year'. The average annual evapotranspiration value was 712 mm or about half the annual potential evapotranspiration, and averaging 4·1 mm/day during the 172 days of the rainy period.

Hydrologically, the most significant point that has emerged from these studies is the magnitude of the combined loss of rainfall in the surface run-off and seepage. The value represents an average amount for annual rainfall that can be conserved. Further, it can be calculated with adequate precision for any station or region in the West African Savanna.

## 5.3  Groundwater

In order to deal satisfactorily with underground water resources it is important to have a clear appreciation of the conditions under which water enters and is stored in the earth's mantle or permeable rocks, and the conditions under which it is released.

By definition groundwater exists in the soil pores, crevices, joints and fissures of the earth's mantle rock, having entered them chiefly as rain water percolating through from the surface. The property of rocks or earth's mantle to contain interstices is known as porosity, and the capacity of the porous medium to transmit under pressure the water held in pores is known as permeability. Porosity and permeability are of practical importance in groundwater problems as they control the amount of water that can be stored and the rate of flow of groundwater in a given area. These two parameters determine the specific capacity of wells, expressed as yield per unit draw-down, i.e., the number of litres of water produced at a pumping well for each metre that the water level in the well is lowered or 'drawn down'.

On entering the soil, the rain water infiltrates into deeper strata of the subsoil of the porous rock material until it reaches the impermeable layer. Here it accumulates by filling up all the pores and forms a saturation layer or underground water storage from which water can be extracted. The upper limit of the saturation layer usually occurs at not too great a distance from the soil surface and is referred to as the water table.

The water bearing formations or aquifers vary considerably in the capacity to store groundwater due to differences in porosity and permeability. The range of porosity for various formations is given in Table 5.3. The porosity of well-

**Table 5.3**

*Porosity of rocks (Meinzer 1923)*

| Rock type | Porosity (per cent by volume) | | |
|---|---|---|---|
| | Minimum | Maximum | Average |
| Granite, schist and gneiss | 0·22 | 0·56 | 0·16 |
| Shale and slate | 0·49 | 7·55 | 3·95 |
| Limestone and dolomite | 0·53 | 13·36 | 4·85 |
| Sandstone | 4·81 | 28·28 | 15·89 |
| Sand (uniform) | 26·0 | 47·0 | 35·0 |
| Sand (mixture) | 35·0 | 40·0 | 38·0 |
| Clay | 44·0 | 47·0 | 45·0 |

sorted uncemented sediments ranges from about 16 to 38 per cent while that of clay is about 45 per cent. Theoretically a saturated layer of sandstone of 10 per cent porosity and 10 m thick contains about $1 \times 100$ m $\times$ 100 m = 10 000 cubic metres of water per hectare. Such a comparatively coarse grained rock is not only porous but also permeable, and most of the water it contains may be withdrawn by means of wells. In contrast a clay absorbs up to 47 per cent of water, but remains more or less non-water yielding and impermeable due to the small size of the pore space which holds water tightly through the capillary forces.

### 5.3.1  *Groundwater resources of the Savanna region*

The mode of occurrence and distribution of groundwater is controlled by the geology of the area concerned. It will be recalled that the geology of the southern half of the Savanna consists mostly of igneous and metamorphic rocks but much of the northern half is covered by consolidated or poorly consolidated sands with stretches of alluvium along rivers and valleys. In the west in Mali, Senegal, and Mauritania, there are extensive areas of marine deposits, sandstones and clays.

Areas underlain by the Basement Complex rocks are a very poor source of groundwater. The mantle of weathered rock is on the average about 20 m thick although it may be weathered to depths of up to 50 m (Du Preez and Barber 1965). The mantle of weathered material is therefore too thin to be able to store large quantities of water and is usually too clayey to serve as an efficient aquifer. The average yield of water from bore-holes and wells is about 4000 litres/ hour. The maximum yield reported in Nigeria is 14 000 litres/hour. In contrast, areas underlain by sandstones form excellent aquifers and good groundwater reservoirs. Bore-holes sunk 100–250 m deep yield on average 10 000 litres/hour but maximum yields of about 22 000 litres/hour have been recorded in Nigeria. Shales and marine formations with thickness of 250–350 m are also good aquifers, yielding on the average 10 000 litres/hour.

Throughout the Savanna, there are areas where artesian and sub-artesian groundwater occurs. The largest artesian water resource is in the Chad basin. At Maiduguri, water flow of 16 000 litres/hour with pressure head of 9 m has been obtained through 10 cm diameter casing. The depth of the aquifer was at 500 m. It is estimated that the 146 artesian wells completed in 1961 in the Bornu and Dikwa Emiriates are capable of producing 9100 million litres of water per year, if allowed to run uncontrolled (Du Preez 1961). Only one-tenth of this amount is needed to meet the present requirements of the people and livestock in the area.

### 5.3.2  *Quality of groundwater*

Average analytical values of groundwater in the Basement Complex rocks are given in Table 5.4. The quality of groundwater is good for domestic and industrial uses. Calcium, sodium and potassium constitute the principal cations, and biocarbonate and chloride are the chief anions. The water has usually less than 500 ppm of total soluble solids and a $p$H range of 6·5–8·8.

The Chad basin artesian water has mainly calcium and sodium bicarbonate but no carbonate. The chlorides are generally low at concentrations less than the

**Table 5.4**

*Average analytical values of groundwater from the Basement Complex rocks Nigeria (Average values from 30 wells; Du Preez 1961)*

| Constituents | Concentration (ppm) | |
|---|---|---|
| | Range | Average |
| Ammonium ($NH_4^+$) | 0·002–0·01 | 0·004 |
| Magnesium ($Mg^{2+}$) | 0·4–7·0 | 0·4 |
| Calcium ($Ca^{2+}$) | 2·0–31 | 20·5 |
| Aluminium ($Al^{3+}$) | – | < 0·01 |
| Ferric and Ferrous ($Fe^{2+}$, $Fe^{3+}$) | 1·3–0·09 | 0·12 |
| Copper ($Cu^{2+}$) | – | 0·2 |
| Zinc ($Zn^{2+}$) | – | 0·1 |
| Manganese ($Mn^{2+}$) | – | 0·02 |
| Sodium ($Na^+$) | 0–30 | 11·0 |
| Potassium ($K^+$) | Trace–15 | 6·0 |
| Flouride ($F^-$) | 0·1–0·6 | 0·2 |
| Chloride ($Cl^-$) | Trace–13 | 6·0 |
| Nitrite ($NO_2^-$) | Trace–0·3 | 0·06 |
| Nitrate ($NO_3^-$) | Trace–44 | 10·5 |
| Phosphate ($PO_4^-$ | < 0·1–0·5 | 0·1 |
| Sulphate ($SO_4^{2-}$) | – | Trace |
| Bicarbonate ($HCO_3^-$ | 4–120 | 43 |
| Carbonate ($CO_3^{2-}$) | 0 | |
| Silica ($SiO_2$) | 16–80 | 50 |

maximum concentrations permissible for drinking. The pH varies from 6·2 to 9·8. The water contains considerable free carbon dioxide which, aided by high temperature of the water (38–44°C), causes erosion of bore-hole casings.

*5.3.3 Seasonal fluctuation in the height of water table*

The groundwater in the Savanna region shows pronounced seasonal fluctuations in its storage capacity as reflected by the changes in the height of the water table. This is particularly pronounced in the areas underlain by the Basement Complex rocks characterized by a shallow mantle of porous material (Kowal and Omolokun 1970). Consequently, in such areas the considerable surplus of precipitation over evapotranspiration during the height of the rains leads to percolation through the profile, raising the water table nearer to the surface. This has an adverse effect on efficient conservation of surplus rain water and may directly affect crops by waterlogging of the rooting zone thus affecting adversely the physiology of crops, the nutrient status of soils, and the soil microbiological activity.

It should be appreciated that groundwater is not static but always in a state of flow due to inclination and unevenness of impervious base rock as well as due to differences in permeability and rainfall distribution over the catchment area. This creates variation in pressure or hydraulic gradient. The water level is not horizontal but resembles the inclination of the topography (Fig. 5.1). The slope of the water table is the result of the movement of the groundwater from levels of higher energy to levels of lower energy due to the differences in elevation and

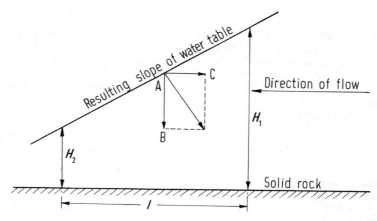

Fig. 5.1. Vector parallelogram of forces acting on the horizontal flow of groundwater (Kowal and Omolokun 1970).

pressure. During its flow, groundwater experiences a loss of energy due to friction along its path. This loss of energy per unit length of distance travelled is known as the hydraulic gradient, $(H_1 - H_2)/l$. This is best represented in a graphical form by constructing a water parallelogram of forces acting on the horizontal flow of water (Fig. 5.1). If AB represents the force of gravity and AC the resistance of the porous medium through which flow of water occurs, then the resulting slope of the water table will be represented by the perpendicular line to the diagonal of the parallelogram at point A. It is clear that if there was no water movement the water table would be horizontal. The slope of the water table in the catchment basin at any time is therefore the result of an equilibrium between the amount of rain water percolating into the lower depths of the soil, which causes a rise in the hydraulic head, and the natural drainage. The cross section of the Samaru catchment basin showing the position of the dry season water table in relation to rock surface and topography is given in Fig. 5.2.

During the height of the rains, the large amount of surplus rain water over evapotranspiration that percolates into the soil raises the height of water table, and causes an increase in the hydraulic gradient. This in turn greatly increases the amount of discharge of groundwater into streams, the discharge of groundwater as stream flow being proportional to the gradient of the water table (Kowal and Omolokun 1970). At Samaru, the rise in the water table and stream flow occurs towards the end of July when precipitation reaches about 40 per cent of the annual rainfall. Depending on the amount of annual rainfall and on the gradient of water table, stream flow stops between the middle of October and December (or soon after). Clearly, the normal methods of improving water supply for dry season use, by reduction of surface run-off and encouragement of infiltration (Arnon 1972) so as to increase the groundwater storage, do not apply under the environmental conditions of large water surplus and restricted depth of soil mantle. Under these conditions the limit for safe or useful ground-

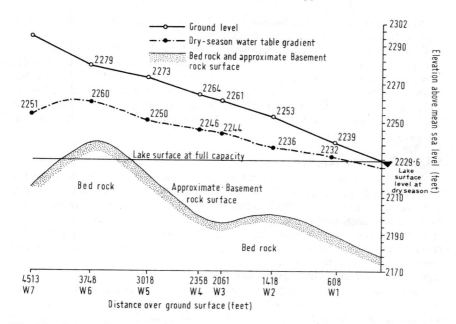

Fig. 5.2. Cross section of the Samaru catchment basin showing the position of the dry season water table in relation to rock surface and topography (Kowal and Omolokun 1970).

water storage in soils is reached rapidly even in the absence of management that encourages reduction in the surface run-off. Thus, water conservation techniques such as tie-ridging, introduced to conserve water in the drier environments or in soils underlain by a deep mantle to absorb excess water, at Samaru have led to an increase in the water table gradient, stream discharge, soil leaching, and often the extent of waterlogged areas. Under these conditions, which are representative of large areas of Northern and Southern Guinea Savanna, a compromise has to be struck between conservation of soil and water by run-off control and avoidance of too high a water table rise, waterlogging, and excessive leaching.

At higher latitudes, in the Sudan and Sahel Savanna, the amount and distribution of rainfall results in less excessive water surpluses; and in certain areas water surplus may be entirely absent. Under such environmental conditions, all management techniques to conserve and retain rainfall through improvement of infiltration and prevention of run-off are likely to benefit agricultural production. Francophone workers (Charreau 1974a) have demonstrated amply the benefits of soil water conservation in terms of crop yields. Also, in the Sahel and Sudan Savanna, the presence of groundwater relatively near the surface, and relatively easy and inexpensive to develop as the main source of water supply for humans and livestock, is of great economic importance. Further, it plays an important role in afforestation, and shelter belt establishment and survival. For example, in the most arid parts of northern Nigeria certain *Eucalyptus* spp. flourish throughout the long and serve dry season when water table depths are up to 10 metres (Kowal 1975).

Finally, it is pointed out that groundwater reservoirs are the largest and most efficient means of storing water, and represent renewable resources of great economic importance at our disposal. According to Arnon (1972), the volume of stored water at depths of less than 10m on a global basis is estimated to be 3000 times greater than that contained in all the rivers of the world. In the Savanna the contribution of the groundwater reserves to the total water resources is even greater.

## 5.4  Surface water supplies

Apart from Lake Chad, there are no natural surface water reservoirs in the West African Savanna region. Those which exist have been constructed by man and include some of the world's largest water reservoirs on rivers Niger and Volta. These large lakes were principally built for hydroelectric power supply and include the dams at Kainji in Nigeria, Akosombo in Ghana, Ayame in the Ivory Coast, and Kinkon and Teut Falls in Guinea. However, there are numerous small water reservoirs throughout the West African Savanna constructed to supply water for urban and agricultural needs.

Storage of surplus water in the surface reservoirs is of extreme importance for the water economy of the region, control of floods, livestock production, and market gardening. It is of equal importance in the industrial sector and for urban use. However, considerable amounts of rain water are annually lost from catchments unless they are directed to storage in surface water reservoirs. Surface reservoirs serve to conserve water during periods of high run-off, and regulate and conserve seasonal stream flows which often are characterized by torrential flows or floods, thus serving as the only means of conserving surface water for periods when there is no rainfall. Further, the importance of surface water storage in the water economy of the Savanna can be judged by the high percentage of the annual rainfall that is temporarily stored in the raised water table but eventually lost in stream flow. Thus, for instance, assuming 100 mm soil water deficit at the end of the dry season, the amount of rain water percolating into aquifers or lost in surface run-off in the Savanna region can be estimated by the following equation:

$$\text{Amount of surface water lost} = 949 - 60 \cdot 9(LA) - 3 \cdot 0(LO)\text{mm} \qquad (5.2)$$

Thus, at the 1160 mm isohyet or at 10°N latitude and zero meridian about 340 mm or 29 per cent of the annual rainfall could be conserved in surface water storage.

Unfortunately, although this high proportion of rain water could be diverted to surface water storage, the surface water reservoirs have low efficiency of water conservation. The main factors contributing to the low efficiency of storage in surface water reservoirs are as follows.

The reservoirs are usually shallow with extensive evaporation area in relation to the total amount of water stored. The topography of the region is such that construction of deep reservoirs is seldom possible. The evaporation rates of the water during the storage period are high. During the period of the Harmattan, evaporation is increased considerably because of the advective energy generated from the hot arid grounds surrounding the reservoirs. The contribution of the aerodynamic component to total evaporation (Fig. 3.17) is increased by the Harmattan wind; and the surface wave action caused as a result makes it impossible to reduce evaporation by application of surface films (hexadecanol and octadecanol multi- or mono-molecular films). Most reservoirs are fed directly by stream flow that are usually high in sediment load so that siltation risks in reservoirs are high. Consequently storage capacity of reservoirs is reduced with time.

Little direct work has been done in the Savanna to measure evaporation losses from surface water reservoirs, in spite of its great practical importance. In general the magnitude of water loss during the dry season storage period is directly proportional to the length of the dry season. Both the rate of evaporation and the duration of the dry season increase with increase in latitude but the water surplus that can be stored decreases.

Results of work conducted at the Makwaye lake, Samaru, representing a typical surface water reservoir in the Savanna, indicate that the average evaporation loss during the Harmattan period is about 7 to 8 mm/day. The Makwaye lake has storage capacity of 335 000 m³ and surface area at full capacity of about 21·4 ha. With average duration of the dry season of about 150 days, the evaporation loss may amount to 120 cm representing 42 per cent of the storage capacity. These high evaporation losses are mainly due to the unfavourable ratio of surface areas to storage capacity. The relationship between the area of reservoir and its storage capacity is presented graphically in Fig. 5.3.

Evaporation from Makwaye reservoir during the early part of the dry season was estimated using Penman's formula, with data obtained from a meteorological station on the lake, situated about 2/3 the distance from the windward shore where the advection and edge effects were minimal (Fig. 5.4). Mean values of the radiation balance *measured directly* over the lake surface together with other relevant information necessary to calculate Penman's open water evaporation are given in Table 5.5.

The short-wave radiation absorbed by the evaporation surface of the lake, $(1 - \alpha)R_i$, was equivalent to 8·5 mm/day, and the net radiation was 7·1 mm/day. The long-wave radiation estimated by difference was 1·4 mm/day ($-81\cdot6$ cal cm$^{-2}$ day$^{-1}$). The relative magnitudes of the energy and aerodynamic terms in the Penman formula were 7·1 and 6·3 mm/day respectively. The estimated evaporation, assuming negligible change in the heat storage capacity of the lake, was 6·9 mm/day. However, this estimated rate does not take into account the advective flow of energy which contributes to the latent heat throughout the 24 hours of the day. The measurement of the changes in the level of the lake during the period under study showed that actual evaporation from the lake as a whole was greater than 6·9 mm/day and that an additional 1·2 mm/day was lost. Further, these estimates of evaporation losses during the early part of the dry season increase considerably as the dry season advances.

There is a pronounced variation across surface reservoirs in the effect of advection on evaporation. Over the lake Makwaye the relative evaporation from

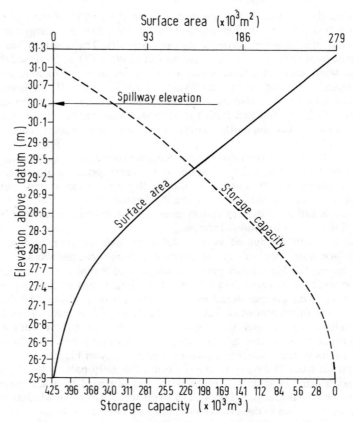

Fig. 5.3. Surface area and storage capacity in relation to the elevation of the water level for the Makwaye lake, Samaru, Nigeria (Naylor and Beredugo 1969).

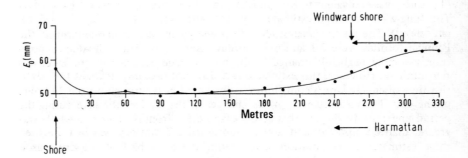

Fig. 5.4. Relative evaporation loss from evaporimeters along the transect across the lake Makwaye, Samaru.

**Table 5.5**

*Radiation balance and mean meteorological data* measured *over the lake during the period 22 October to 10 November 1975*

| Observations | Value | Instruments |
|---|---|---|
| $R_i$ (cal cm$^{-2}$ day$^{-1}$) | 543 | Kipp solarimeter |
| $R_n$ (cal cm$^{-2}$ day$^{-1}$) | 418 | Net radiometer |
| $R_n/R_i$ | 0·77 | Kipp solarimeter |
| $\alpha$ (albedo) | 0·08 | Kipp solarimeter |
| Relative humidity (%) | 25·2 | Wet- and dry-bulb thermometers |
| Wind speed (km/h) | 4·0 | Anemometer |
| Temperature (°C) | 23·7 | Maximum and minimum thermometer |

the lake surface near the windward shore was considerably greater than the evaporation in the middle of the lake (Fig. 5.4). The fetch over the lake necessary to minimize the effect of higher-than-normal evaporation was 60–75 m from the windward shore.

The practical implication of the above results is that a considerable saving in evaporation loss might be achieved by choosing dam sites which will ensure a favourable surface area to depth ratio and orientation in respect to advection during the dry season.

## 5.5 Notional water budget of the Savanna region

Quantitative appraisal of water resources in the dry regions is fundamental to those concerned with economic and social development. It is of particular practical interest to efficient agricultural development of the Savanna region where efficient utilization of water resources is the dominant contributing factor to increased agricultural productivity.

The relationship that exists between the latitudinal and longitudinal position and many environmental characteristics of the Savanna allows a quantitative description of the physical environment to be made in terms of multiple regression equations, and provides an opportunity for a quantitative evaluation of the water resources through the use of a notional water budget.

The basis of the following assessment is the comparison of the amount and distribution of rainfall and evapotranspiration, in consecutive short interval periods of the year, by means of a simple water balance account. The components of the water budget were quantified in terms of multiple regression equations relating each component of the water budget to the latitudinal and longitudinal position. The data used in processing the various regression equations were taken from the published works of Cocheme and Franquin (1967) and Kowal and Knabe (1972).

The regression equations of the water budget components are listed in Table 5.6. For the annual water budget, i.e., $P - ET + WD - WS = 0$, the assessment excludes the water supplied by rivers flowing into the region from outside the area or water supplies which could be drawn from the Lake Chad or certain artesian wells such as those in the Chad basin. The sample population representing the whole region consists of only 52 stations, but judging from the high

## Table 5.6

*Regression equations of the water budget components
for the West African Savanna region*

| Components | Regression | Correlation coefficient |
|---|---|---|
| Precipitation (P), mm | $2470 - 130 \cdot 9(LA) - 8 \cdot 6(LO)$† | −0·91 |
| Effective precipitation (EP), mm | $1614 - 81 \cdot 2(LA) - 6 \cdot 6(LO)$ | −0·90 |
| Potential evapotranspiration ($\alpha = 0 \cdot 25$) ($E_t$), mm | $758 + 74 \cdot 5(LA) + 3 \cdot 5(LO)$ | +0·70 |
| Water deficit (WD), mm | $-598 + 138 \cdot 3(LA) + 9 \cdot 5(LO)$ | +0·87 |
| Water surplus (WS), mm | $1116 - 66 \cdot 9(LA) - 3 \cdot 1(LO)$ | −0·72 |
| Groundwater storage (AW), mm | $949 - 60 \cdot 9(LA) - 3 \cdot 1(LO)$ | −0·75 |
| Start of rains (OP), coded decade | $-1 \cdot 16 + 1 \cdot 3(LA) - 0 \cdot 07(LO)$ | +0·94 |
| Termination of rains (TP), coded decade | $35 \cdot 2 - 0 \cdot 57(LA) - 0 \cdot 07(LO)$ | −0·84 |
| Duration of rains (DP), days | $363 \cdot 4 - 19 \cdot 1(LA) - 1 \cdot 4(LO)$ | −0·94 |
| End of growing season (ES), coded decade | $40 \cdot 6 - 0 \cdot 82(LA) - 0 \cdot 06(LO)$ | −0·89 |
| Length of growing season (LS), days | $418 - 21 \cdot 6(LA) - 0 \cdot 1(LO)$ | −0·94 |

†$LO$ is algebraically positive east of Greenwich and negative west of Greenwich.

values of the correlation coefficients which range from 0·70 to 0·94, it is probably an adequate representation of the region for the purpose of broad generalizations. The results of the notional water budget are presented and discussed for each bioclimatic region separately.

### 5.5.1  Sahel bioclimatic region

The boundaries of this region are defined by the 0 and 600 mm isohyets and are described by the equations:

$$\text{Northern boundary } LA\ (0) = \frac{2470 - 8 \cdot 6(LO)}{130 \cdot 9} \tag{5.4}$$

$$\text{Southern boundary } LA\ (600) = \frac{1870 - 8 \cdot 6(LO)}{130 \cdot 9} \tag{5.5}$$

The magnitude of the water budget components within the Sahel region are shown in Table 5.7.

Within the boundaries delineated by the 0 and 600 mm isohyet lies a belt of arid country, some 500 km wide with an average precipitation of 300 mm. The effective precipitation, i.e., actual rainfall available for crop production (assuming 100 mm soil water deficit at the beginning of rains), averages 230 mm, although at the southern boundary it averages 450 mm.

The amount of rain water that may contribute to groundwater storage, above the assumed 100 mm soil storage deficit, averages 40 mm for the whole region with a maximum of 80 mm at the southern boundary.

The average duration of the rainy period for the whole region is about 45 days with an average maximum of 90 days at the southern boundary. The

**Table 5.7**

*Magnitudes of the water budget components within the Sahel region*

| Components | Northern boundary | Southern boundary | Average for the region |
|---|---|---|---|
| $P$ (mm) | 0 | 600 | 300 |
| $EP$ (mm) | 0 | 453 | 227 |
| $E_t$ (mm) | 2152 | 1824 | 1988 |
| $WD$ (mm) | 2152 | 1380 | 1766 |
| $WS$ (mm) | 0 | 159 | 80 |
| $AW$ (mm) | 0 | 79 | 40 |
| $OP$ (coded decade) | 0 | $18 \cdot 0 - 0 \cdot 06(LO)$ | $21 \cdot 1 - 0 \cdot 06(LO)$ |
| $TP$ (coded decade) | 0 | $27 \cdot 0 - 0 \cdot 07(LO)$ | $25 \cdot 8 - 0 \cdot 07(LO)$ |
| $DP$ (days) | 0 | 90 | 45 |
| $ES$ (coded decade) | 0 | $28 \cdot 9 - 0 \cdot 06(LO)$ | $27 \cdot 0 - 0 \cdot 06(LO)$ |
| $LS$ (days) | 0 | 109 | 55 |

average duration of the growing period, assuming 100 mm storage capacity of soils, is 55 days with a maximum of 109 days at the southern boundary.

The dividing line between the northern Sahel, where the amount and distribution of rainfall is insufficient to sustain arable farming, and the southern Sahel, where arable farming is possible at high risk, was previously estimated to run along the 350 mm isohyet.

The notional water budget components of the two Sahel sub-regions are given for comparison in Table 5.8. The northern Sahel sub-region is a belt of very arid territory some 300 km wide with an average rainfall of 175 mm and the effective precipitation of only 150 mm. There is a negligible rain water surplus and groundwater storage. The duration of rainy periods is only some 29 days.

The southern Sahel sub-region, a belt of some 200 km wide, has an average precipitation of 475 mm and the effective rainfall of 376 mm. The average dura-

**Table 5.8**

*Water budget components of the two Sahel sub-regions*

| Components | Average for the northern sub-region | Boundary separating the northern and southern Sahel (isohyet 350 mm) | Average for the southern sub-region |
|---|---|---|---|
| $P$ (mm) | 175 | 350 | 475 |
| $EP$ (mm) | 150 | 299 | 376 |
| $E_t$ (mm) | 2059 | 1965 | 1895 |
| $WD$ (mm) | 1897 | 1642 | 1511 |
| $WS$ (mm) | 16 | 32 | 96 |
| $AW$ (mm) | 19 | 37 | 58 |
| $OP$ (coded decade) | $22 \cdot 3 - 0 \cdot 07(LO)$ | $20 \cdot 6 - 0 \cdot 07(LO)$ | $19 \cdot 3 - 0 \cdot 07(LO)$ |
| $TP$ (coded decade) | $25 \cdot 2 - 0 \cdot 07(LO)$ | $26 \cdot 0 - 0 \cdot 07(LO)$ | $26 \cdot 5 - 0 \cdot 07(LO)$ |
| $DP$ (days) | 29 | 54 | 72 |
| $ES$ (coded decade) | $26 \cdot 2 - 0 \cdot 6(LO)$ | $28 \cdot 0 - 0 \cdot 06(LO)$ | $28 \cdot 0 - 0 \cdot 06(LO)$ |
| $LS$ (days) | 40 | 68 | 89 |

tion of the rainy period for the sub-region is 72 days and average growing season of about 89 days. The average range of precipitation (350–600 mm) and duration of the rainy period (54–90 days) within the sub-region are sufficient for crop production but the unreliability of the amount and distribution presents high risks to the farmer. The average annual amount of rainfall that may contribute to groundwater storage for the sub-region is about 58 mm with a range of 37–70 mm at the northern and southern boundaries respectively. These amounts are of course insufficient for the exploitation of groundwater for irrigation purposes but are sufficient for human and livestock utilization.

### 5.5.2  Sudan bioclimatic region

This region extends in a belt of some 240 km wide between the 600 and 880 mm isohyets. The northern boundary is described by the equation (5.5); the southern boundary is described by the equation:

$$\text{Southern boundary } LA \ (880) = \frac{1590 - 8 \cdot 6(LO)}{130 \cdot 9} \qquad (5.6)$$

The magnitudes of the water budget components within the Sudan region are given in Table 5.9.

### Table 5.9

*Magnitudes of the water budget components within the Sudan region*

| Components | Northern boundary | Southern boundary | Average for the region |
|---|---|---|---|
| $P$ (mm) | 600 | 880 | 740 |
| $EP$ (mm) | 453 | 624 | 539 |
| $E_t$ (mm) | 1824 | 1667 | 1746 |
| $WD$ (mm) | 1380 | 1089 | 1235 |
| $WS$ (mm) | 159 | 299 | 229 |
| $AW$ (mm) | 79 | 207 | 143 |
| $OP$ (coded decade) | $18 \cdot 0 - 0 \cdot 06(LO)$ | $15 \cdot 1 - 0 \cdot 07(LO)$ | $16 \cdot 6 - 0 \cdot 07(LO)$ |
| $TP$ (coded decade) | $27 \cdot 0 - 0 \cdot 07(LO)$ | $28 \cdot 3 - 0 \cdot 07(LO)$ | $26 \cdot 5 - 0 \cdot 07(LO)$ |
| $DP$ (days) | 90 | 132 | 100 |
| $ES$ (coded decade) | $28 \cdot 9 - 0 \cdot 06(LO)$ | $30 \cdot 6 - 0 \cdot 06(LO)$ | $29 \cdot 7 - 0 \cdot 06(LO)$ |
| $LS$ (days) | 109 | 155 | 132 |

The average effective rainfall over the region is 540 mm, ranging from 453 to 624 mm at the northern and southern boundaries respectively. The average rainy period for the whole region is 100 days with a range of 90 and 132 days at the northern and southern boundaries respectively.

Both the amount of effective rainfall and duration of the rainy period are sufficient for arable production of short-season crops. The risk of crop failure due to water storage is greatly reduced particularly if one bears in mind that the length of the growing season ranges from 109 to 155 days at the northern and southern boundaries respectively, averaging 132 days for the whole region.

The estimated groundwater storage for the whole region averages 143 mm with a range of 79 to 207 mm at the northern and southern boundaries respectively. These amounts contribute to a temporary flow of streams and cannot be conserved without open water storage reservoirs. If all the run-off water in the region could be conserved the amount of water would be sufficient to irrigate 143 × 100/1235 = 11 per cent of the area in the region. Assuming a loss of 60 per cent in water storage and conveyance, the amount of water would be sufficient to irrigate only 5 per cent of the region.

### 5.5.3 Guinea bioclimatic region

The boundaries of this region are defined by the 880 and 1600 mm isohyets. The northern boundary is described by the equation (5.6); the southern boundary is described by the equation:

$$\text{Southern boundary } LA\ (1600) = \frac{870 - 8 \cdot 6(LO)}{130 \cdot 9} \tag{5.7}$$

The region extends in a belt of some 600 km wide. The magnitude of the water budget components within the Guinea bioclimatic region are given in Table 5.10.

**Table 5.10**

*Magnitudes of the water budget components within the Guinea region*

| Components | Northern boundary | Southern boundary | Average for the region |
|---|---|---|---|
| $P$ (mm) | 880 | 1600 | 1240 |
| $EP$ (mm) | 624 | 1074 | 849 |
| $E_t$ (mm) | 1667 | 1254 | 1460 |
| $WD$ (mm) | 1089 | 322 | 705 |
| $WS$ (mm) | 299 | 671 | 485 |
| $AW$ (mm) | 207 | 544 | 375 |
| $OP$ (coded decade) | $15 \cdot 1 - 0 \cdot 07(LO)$ | $7 \cdot 7 - 0 \cdot 07(LO)$ | $11 \cdot 4 - 0 \cdot 07(LO)$ |
| $TP$ (coded decade) | $28 \cdot 3 - 0 \cdot 07(LO)$ | $31 \cdot 4 - 0 \cdot 07(LO)$ | $29 \cdot 8 - 0 \cdot 07(LO)$ |
| $DP$ (days) | 130 | 237 | 184 |
| $ES$ (coded decade) | $30 \cdot 6 - 0 \cdot 06(LO)$ | $35 \cdot 1 - 0 \cdot 06(LO)$ | $32 \cdot 9 - 0 \cdot 07(LO)$ |
| $LS$ (days) | 155 | 274 | 215 |

It will be noted that the difference between the average annual precipitation in the region and the annual evapotranspiration is greatly narrowed. The effective rainfall over the whole region averages 850 mm with a range of 525 to 1075 mm at the northern and southern boundaries respectively. On average there is thus a very considerable excess of effective precipitation over crop water requirements of most crops. The duration of the rainy period, ranging from a minimum of 130 days at the northern boundary to 237 at the southern boundary and averaging 184 days for the whole region, is sufficient for the production of a wide range of crops and at the southern boundary for production of two crops per year.

The average amount of rainfall that may contribute to groundwater storage for the region is 375 mm, ranging from 207 to 544 mm at the northern and southern boundary respectively. The 375 mm average run-off represents a very substantial water resource that could be used for irrigation. Assuming a 60 per cent loss in storage and conveyance, the available run-off is sufficient to irrigate $375 \times 0{\cdot}40 \times 100/705 = 21$ per cent of the Guinea region.

The unimodal and bimodal patterns of rainfall distribution in the region can be distinguished north and south of the 1300 mm isohyet. Although the change in the pattern is not sharp, and in places there are considerable deviations, the 1300 mm isohyet is taken here as a convenient boundary separating the region into distinct sub-regions, the northern and southern Guinea sub-regions. It will be noted that in addition to the two distinct patterns in rainfall distribution, the 1300 mm isohyet very approximately separates the region into areas where $P < ET$ and $P > ET$. The actual latitude at which $P = ET$ is $[1712 - 12{\cdot}1(LO)]/205{\cdot}4$ that is, about $8\frac{1}{2}°N$, or along the 1384 mm isohyet. However, it will be appreciated that no exact boundary separating the two sub-regions exists and a transitional boundary for all practical purposes is taken as the 1300 mm isohyet. The two sub-regions are agriculturally and hydrologically distinct but particularly in respect of matching the growth cycles of crops to water availability periods, and the management of crops and land.

The average water budget components of the two sub-regions are given in Table 5.11.

### Table 5.11

*Water budget components of the two Guinea sub-regions*

| Components | Average for the Northern Guinea sub-region | Boundary separating the Northern and Southern Guinea sub-regions (isohyet 1300 mm) | Average for the Southern Guinea sub-region |
|---|---|---|---|
| $P$ (mm) | 1090 | 1300 | 1450 |
| $EP$ (mm) | 756 | 888 | 981 |
| $E_t$ (mm) | 1545 | 1424 | 1339 |
| $WD$ (mm) | 864 | 638 | 480 |
| $WS$ (mm) | 409 | 518 | 595 |
| $AW$ (mm) | 306 | 405 | 475 |
| $OP$ (coded decade) | $13{\cdot}0 - 0{\cdot}07(LO)$ | $10{\cdot}8 - 0{\cdot}07(LO)$ | $9{\cdot}3 - 0{\cdot}07(LO)$ |
| $TP$ (coded decade) | $29{\cdot}2 - 0{\cdot}07(LO)$ | $30{\cdot}1 - 0{\cdot}07(LO)$ | $30{\cdot}8 - 0{\cdot}07(LO)$ |
| $DP$ (days) | 162 | 193 | 215 |
| $ES$ (coded decade) | $31{\cdot}9 - 0{\cdot}06(LO)$ | $33{\cdot}3 - 0{\cdot}06(LO)$ | $34{\cdot}2 - 0{\cdot}06(LO)$ |
| $LS$ (days) | 190 | 225 | 249 |

(a) *The Northern Guinea Savanna bioclimatic sub-region.* This comprises of a belt of territory extending 350 km between the 880 and 1300 mm isohyets. The northern boundary is described by the equation (5.6); the southern boundary is described by the equation:

$$\text{Southern boundary } LA \ (1300) = \frac{1170 - 8 \cdot 6(LO)}{130 \cdot 9} \qquad (5.8)$$

The sub-region is regarded as the most productive (actually and potentially) and the most important of all the West African Savanna bioclimatic regions. The sub-region is particularly suitable for cereal production. The average rainfall is 1090 mm and the effective precipitation is 756 mm. Experience has shown that this area rarely suffers from severe drought hazards although occasionally the rainless periods during the growing season are longer than 10 consecutive days. The duration of the rainy period averages 162 days and is more than sufficient for production of most annual crops.

The high rainfall receipt and unimodal characteristic of the precipitation results in high percolation and run-off, averaging 306 mm or 28 per cent of the annual rainfall. This is responsible for the high soil nutrient losses due to leaching and accelerated soil erosion. In areas underlain by the Basement Complex rocks with shallow mantle of subsoil, the groundwater rises significantly above its dry season level causing stream flow which usually continues some 6–8 weeks after the termination of rains.

The main climatic disadvantage of the sub-region in respect of agricultural production and hydrology is the comparatively long, unproductive and arid dry season. Conservation of run-off water and stream flow losses by open water reservoirs can contribute substantially to useful water resources in the dry season. It is estimated that the average run-off is sufficient to bring 14 per cent of the area within the sub-region under irrigation, assuming a 60 per cent loss in open water evaporation and conveyance.

(b) *The Southern Guinea Savanna bioclimatic sub-region.* This sub-region extends some 250 km between the 1300 and 1600 mm isohyets. The northern boundary is described by the equation (5.8); the southern boundary is described by the equation (5.7).

It should be noted that the southern boundary of the area is very irregular and ill-defined in terms of natural vegetation and climatic parameters. It is also true that the sub-region is the least investigated in comparison with other areas of the West African Savanna.

The main characteristics of the sub-region are determined by the bimodal distribution of the precipitation and by excess of rainfall over annual evaporation demands. The average effective precipitation of the sub-region is 981 mm distributed over a period of 215 days. Because of its prolonged growing season, averaging 250 days, the region is potentially most suitable for livestock production (Kowal and Davies 1975), if tse-tse fly and endemic livestock diseases could be effectively controlled. Further, the long rainy period and distribution of rains allows production of two crops per year.

Apart from the very substantial percolation and run-off (475 mm), the sub-region is well supplied with a network of streams and rivers, some of which are perennial or carry water from regions outside the Savanna. The hydropotential of the sub-region is exceptionally high with much higher efficiency of open

# Table 5.12

The notional water budget components (mm) of the Savanna region in Nigeria (Kowal, 1973)

| Polygon | Latitude and Longitude | Area Sq km | Area % of total | $P$ | $E_t$ | $WD$ | $WS$ | $IP$† | $AW$ | $EP$ |
|---|---|---|---|---|---|---|---|---|---|---|
| Makurdi | 7°44'N, 8°32'E | 40 948 | 5·6 | 1363 | 1394 | 560 | 529 | 26 | 428 | 909 |
| Lokoja | 7°44'N, 6°44'E | 35 677 | 4·9 | 1310 | 1366 | 552 | 497 | 33 | 396 | 882 |
| Ibi | 8°11'N, 9°45'E | 65 786 | 9·0 | 1216 | 1528 | 706 | 394 | 45 | 292 | 878 |
| Ilorin | 8°29'N, 4°35'E | 18 153 | 2·5 | 1264 | 1283 | 470 | 451 | 30 | 349 | 885 |
| Bida | 9°06'N, 6°01'E | 16 739 | 2·3 | 1272 | 1236 | 579 | 614 | 29 | 513 | 730 |
| Yola | 9°14'N, 12°28'E | 59 002 | 8·1 | 984 | 1520 | 835 | 300 | 16 | 198 | 770 |
| Mokwa | 9°18'N, 5°04'E | 23 328 | 3·2 | 1104 | 1589 | 789 | 303 | 25 | 202 | 878 |
| Minna | 9°37'N, 6°12'E | 15 669 | 3·5 | 1408 | 1430 | 694 | 672 | 18 | 571 | 819 |
| Jos | 9°52'N, 8°54'E | 31 282 | 4·3 | 1423 | 1333 | 662 | 753 | 20 | 652 | 752 |
| Bauchi | 10°17'N, 9°49'E | 46 560 | 6·4 | 1072 | 1463 | 858 | 468 | 14 | 366 | 693 |
| Kaduna | 10°36'N, 7°27'E | 26 205 | 3·6 | 1259 | 1455 | 790 | 595 | 23 | 494 | 742 |
| Yelwa | 10°53'N, 4°45'E | 50 178 | 6·9 | 1108 | 1415 | 800 | 493 | 23 | 391 | 694 |
| Samaru | 11°11'N, 7°38'E | 15 322 | 2·1 | 1042 | 1462 | 863 | 444 | 18 | 342 | 682 |
| Potiskum | 11°42'N, 11°02'E | 45 436 | 6·2 | 891 | 1612 | 1040 | 319 | 19 | 217 | 655 |
| Maiduguri | 11°51'N, 13°05'E | 75 995 | 10·4 | 708 | 1564 | 1061 | 204 | 34 | 103 | 571 |
| Kano | 12°03'N, 8°32'E | 32 061 | 4·4 | 797 | 1770 | 1254 | 295 | 17 | 194 | 600 |
| Gusau | 12°10'N, 6°42'E | 35 234 | 4·8 | 977 | 1455 | 948 | 470 | 29 | 368 | 580 |
| Nguru | 12°53'N, 10°28'E | 27 135 | 3·7 | 567 | 1815 | 1377 | 129 | 22 | 28 | 518 |
| Sokoto | 13°01'N, 5°15'E | 45 876 | 6·3 | 760 | 1671 | 1121 | 211 | 33 | 109 | 618 |
| Katsina | 13°01'N, 7°41'E | 13 229 | 1·8 | 789 | 1618 | 1103 | 274 | 24 | 173 | 593 |
| Total | | 729 815 | 100 | | | | | | | |
| Average | | | | 1043 | 1511 | 853 | 421 | 25 | 319 | 722 |

†Ineffective precipitation

**Table 5.13**

*The notional water budget components (mm) of the Nigerian Savanna
in ten-day periods*

| Period | | $P$ | $E_t$ | WD | WS | IP | GC | CC | AW | EP |
|---|---|---|---|---|---|---|---|---|---|---|
| Jan | 1–10 | 0·3 | 35·6 | 37·3 | | 0·3 | | | | |
| | 11–20 | 0·5 | 38·4 | 37·8 | | 0·5 | | | | |
| | 21–31 | 0·8 | 43·2 | 42·4 | | 0·8 | | | | |
| Feb | 1–10 | 0·5 | 46·0 | 45·5 | | 0·5 | | | | |
| | 11–20 | 0·8 | 45·7 | 45·0 | | 0·8 | | | | |
| | 21–28 | 1·5 | 38·6 | 37·1 | | 1·5 | | | | |
| Mar | 1–10 | 3·3 | 50·3 | 47·0 | | 3·3 | | | | |
| | 11–20 | 5·0 | 50·0 | 45·0 | | 5·0 | | | | |
| | 21–31 | 7·1 | 56·6 | 49·5 | | 7·1 | | | | |
| Apr | 1–10 | 10·7 | 54·4 | 43·7 | | 10·7 | | | | |
| | 11–20 | 17·0 | 50·6 | 33·5 | | | | | | 17·0 |
| | 21–30 | 20·6 | 50·0 | 29·5 | | | | | | 20·6 |
| May | 1–10 | 28·2 | 49·5 | 21·3 | | | | | | 28·2 |
| | 11–20 | 31·2 | 48·8 | 17·5 | | | | | | 31·2 |
| | 21–31 | 41·7 | 53·6 | 11·9 | | | | | | 41·7 |
| Jun | 1–10 | 47·0 | 46·5 | | 0·5 | | +0·5 | 0·5 | | 46·5 |
| | 11–20 | 49·3 | 41·2 | | 8·1 | | +8·1 | 8·6 | | 41·2 |
| | 21–30 | 48·5 | 40·4 | | 8·1 | | +8·1 | 16·8 | | 40·4 |
| Jul | 1–10 | 55·1 | 38·6 | | 16·5 | | +16·5 | 33·3 | | 38·6 |
| | 11–20 | 60·5 | 36·1 | | 24·4 | | +24·4 | 57·7 | | 36·1 |
| | 21–31 | 81·3 | 37·1 | | 44·2 | | +42·4 | 100 | 1·9 | 37·1 |
| Aug | 1–10 | 70·6 | 32·6 | | 38·1 | | | 100 | 38·1 | 32·6 |
| | 11–20 | 77·7 | 32·5 | | 45·2 | | | 100 | 45·2 | 32·5 |
| | 21–31 | 94·0 | 34·0 | | 59·9 | | | 100 | 59·9 | 34·0 |
| Sep | 1–10 | 75·7 | 33·5 | | 42·2 | | | 100 | 42·2 | 33·5 |
| | 11–20 | 71·9 | 35·6 | | 36·3 | | | 100 | 36·3 | 35·6 |
| | 21–30 | 54·1 | 37·6 | | 16·6 | | | 100 | 16·6 | 37·6 |
| Oct | 1–10 | 39·1 | 38·6 | | 0·5 | | | 100 | 0·5 | 38·6 |
| | 11–20 | 24·1 | 39·9 | | | | −15·8 | 84·3 | | 39·8 |
| | 21–31 | 14·0 | 45·2 | | | | −31·2 | 53·0 | | 45·2 |
| Nov | 1–10 | 4·3 | 38·9 | 34·5 | | | −34·5 | 18·5 | | 38·9 |
| | 11–20 | 2·3 | 39·4 | 37·1 | | | −18·5 | | | 20·8 |
| | 21–30 | 0·8 | 39·6 | 38·9 | | | | | | |
| Dec | 1–10 | 0·8 | 36·3 | 35·6 | | | | | | |
| | 11–20 | 0·5 | 36·1 | 35·6 | | | | | | |
| | 21–31 | 0·5 | 39·4 | 38·9 | | | | | | |
| Total | | 1041·3 | 1510·4 | 764·6 | 340·6 | 30·5 | | | 240·7 | 767·7 |

water conservation due to the relatively lower evaporation losses and reduced
period of the dry season.

## 5.6 Notional water budget of the Nigerian Savanna

Kowal (1973) estimated the notional water budget of the Savanna region in
Nigeria, using Thiessen's method (Thiessen 1911) and data from 148 rainfall

stations and 20 evapotranspiration stations. The method permits one to assess at a glance magnitudes of the various water budget components within each polygon (Table 5.12). Depending on the polygon area and the number and reliability of rainfall data within each polygon, accurate information on the magnitudes of the water budget components may be obtained to serve local agricultural development. The technique may also be used to describe notional water budget for the region as a whole as represented by all the polygons. This has been done for the whole Nigerian Savanna in ten-day periods (Table 5.13). From this assessment the following points of interest emerge:

(i) The average precipitation over the Nigerian Savanna is 1040 mm per annum, while the potential evapotranspiration $(E_t)$ averages 1510 mm per annum. $E_t$ therefore exceeds precipitation by 470 mm or 45 per cent.

(ii) The wettest ten-day period occurs during the 1st decade in August, with about 94 mm of precipitation and 61 mm of water surplus over $E_t$.

(iii) The average period of water surplus occurs from 1 June to 10 October, averaging 340 mm or about one-third of the annual precipitation.

(iv) The recharge of the assumed 100 mm soil water deficit and the rise in the dry season water table occurs during the last ten-day period in July.

(v) The period during which leaching occurs is about 80 days, from 21 July to 10 October. The estimated amount of rainfall lost in deep drainage is about 240 mm.

# 6 Rangeland, livestock, and forest resources

This agro-ecological account of the West African Savanna would be incomplete without some reference to rangeland, livestock, and forest resources. These are, of course, closely related and in some instances are interdependent with the devleopment of arable agriculture. Unfortunately, relatively much less research has been carried out on these topics for a full quantitative assessment to be made and for this reason only a very brief appraisal is possible.

## 6.1 Rangeland resources

In the West African Savanna vast areas of rangelands unsuitable for crops are utilized for livestock production. These rangelands are an important resource to the economy of the regions because the future of the meat supplies in West Africa as a whole hinges basically on utilizing them on a permanently productive basis. At present the main source of food for the domesticated livestock is the natural rangeland vegetation. However, the future demand for livestock feed will depend on an integrated use of natural rangeland vegetation, artificial pastures, fodder crops and surplus grain. At present information on this subject is meagre and fragmentary.

Natural Savanna rangeland vegetation consists of grassland in competition with trees and shrubs forming an unstable association or proclimax, which is very sensitive to environmental changes. However, the dominant factor controlling the composition and productivity of rangeland is climate.

The management of natural Savanna vegetation may be directed either towards forest production, with the main objective of excluding grass species and encouraging the growth of trees or towards encouraging grass growth and the complete or partial exclusion of trees and shrubs. Therefore the primary aim when considering the productivity of rangeland as a main source of food for livestock, must be understanding and quantifying climatic limitations. The second aim is to consider the means of improving the productivity through management. Of particular interest here is knowledge of floral composition, of agronomic characteristics of the more important components of grass cover, and of the significance of changes in the botanical composition in response to fertilizer application, intensity of grazing, cutting, or burning.

### 6.1.1 Climatic influence and the relative productivity of natural rangeland

Livestock production depends closely on the availability of animal food whose production and quality is influenced by climatic conditions, the level of inputs and management.

Considering the productivity of natural rangeland without any inputs, the yield of rangeland vegetation comprising of grass and herbs is very low irrespective of species composition (Table 6.1). The annual yield at Samaru (11·18°N, 7·63°E) of natural range vegetation composed of annual and perennial grasses and herbs listed in Table 6.2 is estimated to be only about 2750 kg/ha dry matter in fire protected vegetation and about 2950 kg/ha in annually burned vegetation (J. M. Kowal and P. N. de Leeuw, unpublished 1974). These low amounts compare with about 18 600 kg/ha and 22 500 kg/ha dry matter produced maize and millet crop respectively under good management (Kowal and Kassam 1973a, Kassam and Kowal 1975). In terms of energy conversion efficiency this 6- to 8-fold disparity in productivity is even greater due to a longer period of growth for natural vegetation. Thus the average energy conversion efficiency for a 117 day maize crop at Samaru is about 1·3 per cent of the

### Table 6.1

*Grassland communities and their yield under natural environment*

| Main genera | DM yield tonne/ha | Bioclimatic region | Remarks |
|---|---|---|---|
| *Andropogon–Aristida* | 1·0–2·0 | Southern Sahel | Well developed grass cover, 1–2 m tall, annual and perennial spp. |
| *Aristida–Cenchrus* | 0·2–1·0 | Southern Sahel | Sparse annual grass cover, *Cenchrus* in fallows |
| *Brachiaria* | 0·5–1·0 | Sahel/Sudan | Low, sparse, annual grass with many weeds |
| *Schizachyrium–Schoenefeldia* | 0·5–1·0 | Sudan | Low open grass cover, annuals, many weeds, often in fallows |
| *Schizachyrium–Loudetia* | 0·5–2·0 | Northern Guinea (Northern parts) | Open to fairly dense grass cover, mainly annuals |
| *Schoenefeldia* | 0·5–1·0 | Northern Guinea (Northern parts) | Low, sparse, annual grass cover |
| *Loudetia* | 0·1–2·0 | Northern Guinea (Northern parts) | Open to dense, 1–1·2 m tall grass cover, annual and perennials |
| *Pennisetum–Schizachyrium* | 1·0–2·0 | Northern Guinea (Central parts) | Open, mainly annual grass cover with many weeds |
| *Hyparrhenia* | 2·0–3·5 | Northern Guinea (Central parts) | Open to dense grass cover up to 2·4 m tall, annuals and perennials |
| *Andropogon* | 1·6–4·5 | Northern Guinea (Central parts) | Tussock grassland up to 2·4 m tall with mainly perennial spp. |
| *Loudetia–Aristida* | 1·0–2·0 | Northern Guinea (Southern parts) | Open to dense grass cover, annuals and perennials |
| *Hyparrhenia (dissoluta)* | 2·0–3·5 | Northern Guinea (Southern parts) | Open to dense grass cover 1·2–1·8 m tall, annuals and perennials |

**Table 6.2**

*Composition of the vegetation measured in the erosion plots
at Samaru, 1972 (J. M. Kowal and P. N. de Leeuw, unpublished)*

| Species | % plant cover | |
| --- | --- | --- |
| | Protected | Burned |
| Tall perennial grasses: (> 2 m) | | |
| *Andropogon gayanus* | 10·5 | 17·6 |
| *Cymbopogon giganteus* | 9·7 | 3·0 |
| *Hyparrhenia rufa* | 1·5 | – |
| *Hyparrhenia subplumosa* | – | 10·2 |
| | 21·7 | 30·8 |
| Other perennial grasses: | | |
| *Setaria anceps* | 9·2 | 2·5 |
| *Sporobolus pyramidalis* | 1·0 | 2·2 |
| *Hyparthelia dissoluta* | 11·8 | 12·2 |
| *Schizachyrium sanguenium* | 1·0 | – |
| *Brachiaria jubata* | 0·7 | 1·0 |
| *Elyonurus hirtifolius* | 6·3 | 4·2 |
| *Sporobolus festivus* | – | 0·5 |
| | 30·0 | 22·6 |
| Annual grasses: | | |
| *Hyparrhenia involucrata* | 17·7 | 27·8 |
| *Hyparrhenia bagrimica* | 2·3 | 6·5 |
| *Pennisetum polystachyon* | 1·5 | – |
| *P. pedicellatum* | 4·0 | 0·5 |
| *Andropogon fastigiatus* | 1·2 | 0·3 |
| *Andropogon pseudopricus* | 1·0 | 2·5 |
| | 27·7 | 37·6 |
| Important herbs: | | |
| *Indigofera pulchra* | 5·8 | 0·2 |
| *Tephrosia bracteata* | 1·7 | 0·5 |
| *Aspillia africana* | 2·3 | – |
| *Stylosanthes mucronata* | 2·5 | – |
| *Lepidagathis colona* | – | 3·0 |
| Other herbs | 8·3 | 9·0 |
| Total | 100·0 | 100·0 |

total incoming radiation while that for natural rangeland is estimated to be in
the order of between 0·15–0·16 per cent during the 160 days period of the
average growing season at Samaru.

The level of *potential productivity* of rangeland under the West African
Savanna environment is dominated by the length of the growing period, and
there are large differences in respect of water availability and radiation income
during the growing period in various bioclimatic regions. The *relative productivity* of rangeland can be estimated for any locality or bioclimatic region of the
Savanna given the energy conversion efficiency ($\epsilon$) and the amount of total
incoming radiation during the growing period (equation 3.2).

By definition      $\epsilon = \dfrac{\text{Total dry matter production (DM)} \times 4000}{\text{Total solar energy input}}$      (6.1)

Hence      $\text{DM} = \dfrac{\epsilon(163591 - 7686\,LA - 376\,LO)\ \text{kg/ha per season}}{400}$      (6.2)

The magnitude of $\epsilon$ depends largely on chosen inputs and management. Assuming that under a natural environment without any inputs the $\epsilon$ is 0·0015, the estimated relative rangeland productivity per season of various bioclimatic regions is as follows:

| | |
|---|---|
| Northern Sahel | 1082 kg/ha |
| Southern Sahel | 1742 kg/ha |
| Sudan | 2324 kg/ha |
| Northern Guinea | 3097 kg/ha |
| Southern Guinea | 3889 kg/ha |

It will be noted that the average relative productivity of rangeland in the Sahel and Sudan bioclimatic regions is only 40 and 66 per cent respectively as compared with the Guinea region. The Guinea region, but particularly the southern part with a binominal rainfall distribution that cannot be easily matched to support two crops per season, is well suited to rangeland and livestock production.

In the higher and upper middle latitudes of the Savanna the climate lends itself to more intensive grain production since crops and crop varieties may be more efficiently matched to the length of the rainy period, thereby utilizing more efficiently the available water and relatively higher radiation income. As the rainy season is relatively short, very large amounts of fodder per unit area would have to be produced and conserved to support the food requirement of livestock during the dry season. Water harvest and conservation at higher latitudes are limited in amount for a large scale extension of the growing period.

At lower latitudes of the Guinea Savanna, where there is a much extended rainy period, much larger water resources, and a comparatively higher total dry matter production during the whole season, livestock production would be easy to accommodate. Here, under a much longer growing period, conditions for grass and fodder production are more favourable for the efficient utilization of climatic resources. Obviously much less fodder for dry season feeding has to be conserved, thus easing management problems and reducing the costs of livestock production during the short dry season. Assuming an effective control of trypanosomiasis and other health hazards more prevalent in the southern parts, livestock production at lower latitudes should be less costly, easier to manage and more productive. However, it may be stressed that when these areas are opened to year round grazing, their management must ensure a proper balance between herbaceous and woody species in order to prevent erosion and rangeland deterioration.

*6.1.2 Composition of natural pastures in different bioclimatic regions*

(a) *Sahel*. The value of the Savanna grazing resources is nowhere economically as important as in the Sahel region where arable production is at high risk and animal production is the major source of livelihood. The vegetation cover of the Sahel reflects more than anywhere else the extreme severity of climatic constraints. Competition between plant species is intense, because a given surface area can support only a limited number of individual plants. In these conditions, the spontaneous plant cover, with its regular distribution of tufts, resembles greatly an extensive pasture land in appearance, and is in fact invariably exploited as such (Gillet 1975).

In the Northern Sahel a steppe-like herbaceous vegetation is very sparse. Each tuft is separated from its neighbour by a bare ground and the vegetation cover represents less than 30 per cent of the total land surface. The most important species are: *Panicum turgidum*, a tall grass with the ability to grow very fast and provide fodder within a few days after the onset of rains, and *Cyperus conglomeratus* and *Aristida longiflora* which form pastures of poorer quality but constitute a relatively abundant source of forage. The latter two species preserve well during the dry season, and provide standing hay *in situ*. The species also provide good fodder for camels, sheep, and goats.

There is no control pattern of grazing. However, during the rainy season, areas in topographical depressions and close to temporary ponds are grazed. In the beginning of the dry season, grazing is in the vicinity of groundwater holes, where water is only 4–8 m below the ground surface. During the main part of the dry season the stock is shifted south and grazing is near the rivers or near deep water holes with water 80–100 m below the surface. *Fadama* areas and the flood plains of rivers provide most of the grazing during the dry season.

The Southern Sahel landscape shows a marked increase in tree cover particularly along water courses, with much increased annual herbaceous stratum which may form continuous ground cover during the rainy season. The area can be described as a 'region of seasonal extremes' since the contrast between the rainy and the dry seasons could not be more striking. Here is the centre of livestock breeding for the whole of the West African Savanna.

During the rainy season there is a rapid growth of grasses composed mainly of annual species, e.g., *Echinochloa clona*, *Panicum laetum*, endowed with a vitality that produces sufficient seeds to ensure survival under heavy grazing and drought. *Brachiaria* spp., and to a certain extent *Cenchrus biflorus* also cover extensive pasture areas. Extensive areas between southern Senegal and Chad support *Aristida mutabilis/Eragrostis tremula*, a grass association that is of particular value as dry fodder. The average biomass of this association is reported to be 590 kg/ha in Senegal (Morel and Bourliera 1962) and 600 kg/ha in Chad (Gillet 1967). *Schoenefeldia gracilis*, much relished by livestock and yielding more than one tonne/ha of dry straw, is more sensitive to water stress than the *Aristida/Eragrostis* association.

Of special interest in the southern Sahel are flood water pastures fed by the waters of the Senegal, Niger and Chari rivers. These pastures are of particular importance in the inland Niger delta where they are used as a main source of fodder for stock breeding. The most important species of flood water pasture is

*Echinochloa stagnina* which provides an abundance of leafy, highly nutritive, fodder on which young stock is reared.

Amongst the Sahel vegetation, forage trees, such as *Balanites aegyptiaca* and the thornless *Maerua crassifolia*, provide a highly palatable, protein-rich leaf fodder throughout the year. Deciduous trees such as *Commiphora africana* and *Combretum* spp., lose their leaves at the beginning of the dry season but provide a highly nutritious and protein rich source of food during the rainy season. A special mention must be made of *Acacia albida*. This leguminous tree has an active vegetative period during the dry season while during the rainy season the tree is entirely defoliated and nearly dormant. The pods of *Acacia albida* are traditionally used as protein rich fodder. It has been calculated that on average a tree yielding 125 kg of pods could provide feed for the production of 90 litres of milk or 12·5 kg of meat. At a medium population of 20 trees/ha the pods of the *A. albida* yield 2500 kg/ha dry matter and 175 kg/ha of digestible protein and compare very favourably with other fodders such as groundnut tops or meadow hay yielding 3000 kg/ha dry matter and 160 and 90 kg/ha digestible protein respectively (Charreau 1974a).

The average annual yield of pasture in the southern Sahel (e.g., Dara, Senegal) is about 1300 kg/ha, sufficient to support a live weight increase of 70 kg/ha per year (Boudet 1975). Depending on the stocking rate, the increase in live weight varies seasonally. Thus for instance the all-year-round grazing with 2–2·5 year old Zebu cattle shows the following pattern of growth.

| | |
|---|---|
| August–September: | daily weight gain 900 g, stocking rate 50 kg/ha |
| October–December: | daily weight gain 400 g, stocking rate 300 kg/ha |
| January–June: | daily weight *loss* 170 g, stocking rate 90 kg/ha |

These fragmentary results indicate the existence of a difficult period (January to June) during which losses in weight are inevitable without an addition of supplementary feed, particularly protein (Boudet 1975).

(b) *Sudan.* A large proportion of this region, mainly supporting perennial grasses and deciduous shrubs, falls within the tse-tse fly free belt of the Savanna. The area provides an excellent environment for the rearing and breeding of cattle, sheep, goats, horses, donkeys, and camels. However, the economic importance of the region lies in production of arable crops, particularly groundnut.

Perennials which grow vigorously include *Andropogon gayanus, Anthephora nigritane, Aristida* spp., *Hyparrhenia* spp. However, burning and heavy grazing has resulted in the disappearance of perennial grasses from many areas to be replaced by annuals that include *Andropogon pseudapricus, Aristida kershingii, A. longifora, Cenchrus biflorus, Schizachyrium* spp., and many others. The grassland is at present in a degraded condition and the productivity is low, ranging from 500 to 2000 kg/ha dry matter. The nutrient value of grasses is low and particularly deficient in proteins (Miller and Rains 1963). Assuming that the beef animal requires about 2500 kg dry matter per annum, the carrying capacity of rangeland is very low. Estimates of year round carrying capacity (de Leeuw and Brinckman 1975) vary from 12 ha per beast on the *Aristida* grassland yielding less than 500 kg dry herbage per ha to 3 ha per beast on the annual *Hyparrhenia* type with a yield of 3000 kg/ha. However the critical feeding period during the later part of the dry season is supplemented by the utilization of crop residues as fodder. Sorghum, cotton, groundnuts, and cowpeas supply the bulk of crop residues that are used as fodder (van Raay and de Leeuw 1970). The most critical period is after February when fodder becomes increasingly scarce and herds have to move southwards in search of new feeding grounds.

(c) *Northern Guinea*. This is a perennial grass zone in which *Hyparrhenia* spp. are dominant. During the rainy season cattle are excluded from this region because of the presence of tse-tse fly. The appearance of this region differs greatly from the Sahel and Sudan regions. During the rainy season the whole area is covered with tall grass which grows very rapidly, reaching maturity rapidly, and then becoming fibrous and tough. During the dry season the dry vegetation is burnt, clearing the ground and leaving occasional trees. Immediately after burning there is a green flush of young *Isoberlinia doka* which is not eaten by livestock.

The productivity of the Northern Guinea Savanna and grasslands in Nigeria was reviewed by Rains (1963) and by van Raay and de Leeuw (1974). The area ranks among the least productive grazing land in Nigeria (de Leeuw and Brinckman 1975). The main constraint is the seasonal fluctuations in herbage quality and quantity in the natural Savanna that cannot be controlled sufficiently or improved by simple management such as shrub cutting, burning and the adjustment of stocking rates. These measures failed to change the composition of the species, and the low quality of fodder, and resulted in a live weight gain of only 50 kg per annum even when supplemented with concentrates during the dry season.

Recent work by de Leeuw and Brinckman (1975) indicates that a substantial improvement in livestock production can be expected from the spectacular increase in productivity of sown pastures as compared with natural rangeland productivity. However, this is not likely to be relevant without a change towards a system of settled herd management.

(d) *Southern Guinea*. The prolonged rainy period in this region favours the lush growth of vegetation which varies from light forest to open Savanna woodland. Under shaded conditions ground flora includes a number of grasses such as *Streptogyne crinita* and *Andropogon tectorum*. In open situations *Andropogon gayanus*, *A. schirensis* and *Hyparrhenia* spp., form most prevalent perennials, while commonly occurring annuals include *Andropogon pseudapricus* and *Hyparrhenia chrysargyrea*. These species, but particuarly *A. gayanus*- dominated grassland, is preferred by stock in contrast with *Hyparrhenia* spp., occurring in the Northern Guinea.

The livestock production potential of the region is high since the total yield of herbage for the whole season is comparatively high and of better quality and palatability. Moreover the length of the dry season is moderate so that a loss in live weight during the dry season is not pronounced and can be much easier to prevent or eliminate. Thus for example the *Andropogon gayanus* grassland at Mokwa, in the Southern Guinea Savanna in Nigeria, produces 40–45 kg/ha live weight gain while in Fashala, in the Derived Savanna region with a prolonged rainy season, up to 115 kg/ha gains are produced. However, the health hazards in the region are very high and strict veterinary control is necessary for successful production.

### 6.1.3  Traditional extensive range management

The traditional management of livestock in the West African Savanna is based on a system evolved over centuries of trial and error and appears to be reasonably well adjusted to environmental demands, although at present it does not meet the requirements brought about by rapid changes on the agricultural, social, and economic scene. Above all the system resists the strong efforts of integration with arable agriculture and the necessity for improving efficiency and quality of production.

The bulk of Savanna livestock is managed by the nomadic Fulani although increasing numbers are being kept by settled stock owners in towns and villages. In Nigeria, herds of over 50 head of cattle, with accompanying flocks of sheep and goats, form mobile units tended by the groups of Fulani families. The units are in constant search of pastures and water. Their movement is closely adjusted to the seasonal fluctuation in herbage quantity and quality. Thus they move south in the dry season and north in the wet season. The annual cycle of migration follows a distinct orbit which over the years has proved able to meet most adequately the seasonal variation in the distribution of fodder, easy access to water, location of markets, and the avoidance of human and bovine disease. The migratory unit is self-sufficient in labour and feed in all seasons, its men tending the common herd and its women milking, trading, and preparing food.

Throughout the centuries, a set of rules has evolved for guaranteeing cattle tracks, the use of water supplies, and the pasturing of cattle on fallow land and stubble. The farmer benefits from the increased soil fertility in fields where livestock is kraaled and from crop residue grazing which results in the clearing of plant material and the breaking up of ridges. It also provides the farmer with the opportunity of obtaining milk in exchange for farm produce.

The cattle are usually kraaled at night and are not turned out to graze until late in the morning after milking is completed. They are then watered and spend the remainder of the day being driven slowly across the fields or bush, browsing and grazing as they go. Grazing areas, fixed by agreement with farmers, are well defined and herds cover grazing circuits on a rather flexible rotation. Tse-tse infested dense bush is avoided. The grass is burnt in patches to ensure a multiplicity of burnt areas of different sizes and stages of growth. Regrowth is rapid in moist sites and these areas may be grazed as early as a week or two after burning. The advantages of burning are well appreciated by herdsmen. Its chief aim is to produce flush of green herbage, to even up the grassland, to clear it of fibrous unpalatable stubble, and to discourage the encroachment of woody species. Some interesting accounts on the migrating Fulani and their pastoral habits are given by de St. Croix (1945), Hopen (1958), Fricke (1964) and van Raay (1973).

### 6.1.4  Improved range management

There are no major areas of rangeland under modern management, and little experience on which to base generalizations although some minor schemes, e.g., at Mokwa in the Southern Guinea Savanna, have been launched with moderate success. The fact is that the natural Savanna rangeland has an inherently low productivity imposed by the seasonal fluctuations in herbage quantity and quality. The grassland is composed of tufts of grass with sparse sward, forming unstable vegetation associations with a natural tendency to be invaded by woody species. This tendency is much encouraged when fire is excluded, and bush encroachment must be therefore constantly checked. Furthermore in many grassland associations early burning has in fact encouraged the growth of more palatable and productive species such as for instance *Andropogon gayanus*. The exclusion of fire and introduction of frequent light grazing causes the pastures to revert to much less productive species, e.g., *Aristida* spp., and *Heteropogon* spp., both almost useless form the grazing point of view.

Many of the pastures are dominated by coarse grasses that are palatable and nutritious only when young. Legumes are scarce. The growth of vegetation stops abruptly with the end of the rains and the grass dries out rapidly to form very poor quality hay, posing a major management problem in supplying supplementary food for the duration of the dry season. The objectives of range management have been enumerated by Webster and Wilson (1973) to be as follows:

(i) To provide, as far as possible, a uniform and year-round supply of herbage for a maximum number of stock.

(ii) To utilize the herbage at a stage which combines a good nutrient quality with high yield.

(iii) To maintain the pasture in its most productive condition by encouraging its best species and by promoting as full a ground cover as possible.

These objectives can be met by suitable grazing management ensuring timely and controlled defoliation by grazing and cutting, and adjusted stock rates and by the use of fertilizers particularly phosphate and nitrogen.

### 6.1.5 Seasonal changes in yield and feeding value

The seasonal changes in the yield and quality of natural Savanna grassland are pronounced. In general, the total yield of herbage increases steadily up to a fairly advanced stage of maturity and may produce a reasonable yield even under low fertility conditions but this greatly depends on the length of the rainy period. The quality of herbage, however, quickly deteriorates after flowering and may often limit animal production. This is particularly so in respect of crude protein. Young grass is usually low in crude fibre and relatively high in crude protein. As it grows towards maturity the crude protein, phosphate, and potash content decreases and crude fibre content increases. The crude protein of dried up vegetation rarely exceeds 2–3 per cent of the dry matter and cattle are reluctant to eat this low quality straw unless some form of supplementary feed, rich in nitrogen, is provided. Concentrate feeds such as cotton seed and groundnut cake locally available are very useful for this purpose, while another traditional source of protein is found in groundnut haulm and cowpea hay. A further possible source of nitrogen is urea and investigations at Samaru indicate the value of urea in supplementary low quality roughages as a means of increasing livestock gains (Haggar 1972).

Quantitative data on seasonal changes in yield components and chemical composition of *Andropogon gayanus*, obtained at Shika in the Northern Guinea Savanna of Nigeria (Haggar 1970, Haggar and Ahmed 1971) may serve as an example of general growth and quality trends. The results show the following:

(i) Dry matter yield: the yield of dry matter increased throughout the wet season reaching a maximum of about 3350 kg/ha in October (Fig. 6.1). There was a relatively rapid growth at the beginning of the rainy season reaching a maximum of about 32 kg/ha per day in late August, and falling rapidly during September with a termination of growth in early October.

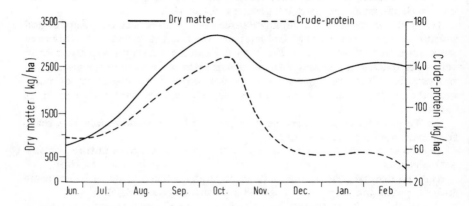

Fig. 6.1.  Dry matter and crude protein yield from *Andropogon gayanus* at Shika in 1964 (Haggar 1970).

(ii) Crude protein: the crude protein yield (Fig. 6.1) increased throughout the wet season but decreased shaprly at the beginning of the dry season. The crude protein content of the dry matter was highest at the beginning of the wet season falling to a low level in August, leaves contributing to the bulk of the crude protein.

(iii) Fibre: the percentage of fibre ranged from 31 to 37 per cent increasing during plant maturity in September–October. The percentage fibre in leaf was compartively lower ranging from 28 to 32 per cent as compared with 36 to 42 per cent in stem.

(iv) Minerals: the phosphorus and calcium content of leaves was higher than in the stems. The mean percentage values for the whole plant were 0·056 P and 0·23 Ca. Potassium content in the leaves was significantly lower than in the stem and the mean percentage K for the whole plant was 1·6.

Haggar concludes: 'The results demonstrate the inverse relationship between herbage quality and yield. During the early part of the wet season, when growth is in the vegetative phase, herbage quality as represented by the crude protein, crude fibre, and chemical content is at its highest due to the high proportion of leaf. Cutting for hay at this time would give a high quality product, although yield would be low and weather conditions would be unfavourable for making hay. The proportion of stem increases during August and September so that although herbage bulk increases, the overall quality decreases.' These conclusions are supported by earlier studies (Rains 1963) on undefoliated grassland in the Northern Guinea Savanna. However, the dry matter and protein yields reported by Rains (1963) and Haggar (1970) are low because little or no fertilizer was used.

### 6.1.6 Intensive management

Livestock production in the West African Savanna depends on a complex interaction of environmental factors but it is mainly a function of the availability and quality of fodder, particularly during the dry season, and the adequate control of animals' health. The relatively low productivity of natural rangeland vegetation as compared with the actual and potential dry matter yield of crops under intensive management, points to a possibility of obtaining adequate amounts of high quality fodder that could be grazed and/or conserved for dry season use by means of an intensive system of production, i.e., establishment of artificial pastures (leys), and forage production with high inputs including fertilizer.

Work on the evaluation of productivity of forage species for establishing sown pastures and leys in northern Nigeria was initiated as early as 1945, and involved the screening of hundreds of grasses and legumes (Foster and Mundi 1961, Rains 1963). Further evaluation, related to nutritive value, e.g., crude protein content, feed intake and digestibility (Haggar 1969) resulted in a selection of species that are most productive and adaptable to the Savanna environment. Summarizing these results, de Leeuw and Brinckman (1975) conclude that *Digitaria smutsii* and *Brachiaria brizantha* are the most suitable species for intensive wet season grazing, *Pennisetum purpureum* for silage and *Chloris gayana* for hay production. For less intensive systems of forage production, *Andropogon gayanus* was found most adapted, thus a considerable volume of work was done on this species (Haggar 1970, Haggar and Ahmed 1970, 1971, Zemmelink, Haggar, and Davies 1972). The level of yield obtained from these species is greatly affected by the level of nitrogen application and is only moderately high (Table 6.3).

It will be appreciated that the establishment of sown pastures requires considerable inputs, supporting services, and managerial skill. It is entirely unrelated to the traditional extensive livestock production and since there is no experience or tradition in either the establishment and management of sown pastures nor in the management of stock under these conditions it currently presents high financial risks.

In spite of the much greater productivity of sown pastures as compared with unimproved Savanna grassland, their economic justification needs much careful consideration, bearing in mind that sown grass pastures provide only feeding requirements during the growing period. Further, the increased productivity of sown pastures must be sustained over a prolonged period of time by correct management and costly inputs that are essential to avoid pasture deterioration.

**Table 6.3**

Dry matter (DM) and crude protein (CP) yield of sown pastures (de Leeuw and Brinckman 1975)

| Species | N = 0 | | N = 100 kg/ha | | N = 200 kg/ha | | Remarks | |
|---|---|---|---|---|---|---|---|---|
| | DM tonne/ha | CP kg/ha | DM tonne/ha | CP kg/ha | DM tonne/ha | CP kg/ha | No. of cuts/year | $P_2O_5$ kg/ha |
| *Andropogon gayanus* | 1·4 | 84 | 4·7 | 349 | 5·6 | 455 | 2 | 53 |
| *Andropogon gayanus* | 6·2 | 384 | 9·0 | 613 | 9·6 | 752 | 3 | 67 |
| *Chloris gayana* | 6·3 | 260 | 9·2 | 685 | 11·2 | 850 | 4 | 67 |
| *Chloris gayana* | 7·7 | 359 | 10·6 | 758 | 12·0 | 1133 | 1 | – |
| *Digitaria smutsii* | 4·7 | 196 | 5·8 | 385 | 6·7 | 530 | 1 | – |

Recently, large areas of unproductive Sudan region shrub Savanna have been improved with sown *A. gayanus* as the only suitable species for the low level of management and fertility. It is expected that the present average 500 kg/ha dry matter yield and the carrying capacity of 12 ha per beast will be substantially improved and depending on the level of fertilizer application will increase the carrying capacity to at least 3 ha per beast.

Increase in pasture and rangeland productivity through the introduction of perennial legumes into the sward has received considerable attention. Although many species have been tested, emphasis has been placed mainly on *Stylosanthes* spp., which appears to be the best adapted to the Savanna environment. Following the successful oversowing of *S. humilis* (Townsville stylo) in native grassland in Australia, similar techniques were tried at Shika in the Northern Guinea Savanna and in the Sudan region. Establishment of Townsville stylo in natural Savanna vegetation is a slow and hazardous process requiring judicious intermittent grazing and brush cutting during the wet season to reduce competition. Experimental results indicate that in the Sudan region with the open cover of annual plants, seeding without cultivation is successful. In the Northern Guinea region with large proportion of perennial grasses composition is too strong for successful establishment. There is high confidence in the successful establishment of Townsville stylo into the grassland vegetation of the Sudan region, and the Nigerian Government is in the process of oversowing 32 000 ha of rangeland with this legume. The project is based on aerial sowing and the application of 125 kg/ha single superphosphate that will be applied biannually (de Leeuw and Brinckman 1975).

The well established Townsville stylo pastures at Shika yield between 4·5 and 5·0 tonne/ha dry matter with legume content in the range of 50–60 per cent. It is widely accepted that the introduction of Townsville stylo into the Sudan region will double the average stocking capacity which is at present about 4 ha per animal

*S. guyanensis* (stylo) was found highly adaptable to the Savanna environment although it is difficult to establish in perennial grassland with limited seed-bed preparation. The main value of the species is that it continues to grow far into the dry season and can be utilized either in a mixture with grass or as a pure stand legume. It can be established by feeding the seed to cattle; who spread it through their dung, or by being broadcast on hoed or disc-harrowed strips of burnt Savanna. In general, however, stylo does not seed well in perennial grassland. Trials with these methods of seeding were not .successful because the legume could not stand competition from grasses. However, the establishment of stylo as sown pasture with cultivation and high management inputs seems more promising. During the 5 months of wet season one hectare stocked with about 500 kg live weight produced a gain of between 100 and 150 kg. Such stocking rate is lenient in order to leave a dense and leafy sward for dry season use and to permit a stocking of some 250 kg over a 7 month period with a live weight gain of about 45 kg/ha. Recrrrent inputs are low and yields can be sustained with a dressing of 125 kg/ha single superphosphate per annum.

The most efficient utilization of the natural resources of the Savanna is linked with the production of cultivated fodder crops for stall feeding or ensilage.

Elephant grass *Pennisetum purpureum* and high yielding varieties of maize are the major crops for silage production. Recently, however, millet and sorghum have also been found to be suitable for silage (Miller 1969, Couper and de Leeuw 1971, Haggar and Couper 1972, Couper 1972, de Leeuw and Brinckman 1975).

Dense newly established stands of elephant grass in the Northern Guinea, dressed with 150 kg N/ha per cut has been shown to produce 78 tonne of fresh material per ha in two cuts per year. Maize dressed with 700 kg/ha compound fertilizer (20:10:10) has been reported to yield 60–65 tonne fresh weight per ha when cut 73 days after sowing. Late millet (Maiwa) has been found to yield about 70 tonne/ha in two cuts at about 8 weeks interval with an initial compound fertilizer (20:10:10) application of 750 kg/ha.

These fodders are very palatable and although bulky (about 36 kg of fresh herbage is required to provide maintenance of one 450 kg cow) are highly nutritious and require only a low supplement of proteins. Of leguminous crops lucerne (*Medicago sativa*) and soya bean (*Glycine max*) are probably best suited for intensive production in the Savanna.

A valuable experience on the large scale use of cultivated fodder crops under the Savanna environment has been provided by the cattle fattening ranch at Mokwa, Nigeria (Nigerian Livestock and Meat Authority Ranch). Here the management almost entirely relied on high arable inputs (maize for silage, sorghum and soya for grain) with very limited use of the natural Savanna grassland.

Finally we would like to emphasize that there is a comparatively large potential in utilizing crop residues as fodder and surplus grain in the intensive system of livestock production. Little experimental work on this is available.

## 6.2  Livestock resources

Compared with other world environments the domestic livestock of the Savanna has a low population and low productivity, being at a distinct disadvantage because of its exposure to the destructive influences of the vectors of diseases such as tse-tse and ticks, and various other pests and diseases. The pronounced duration of the dry season linked with exposure and malnutrition during the dry season (when the quantity and quality of dry matter available may be insufficient to maintain energy requirements) prevent a steady growth and normal maturation, thus resulting in low productivity. In cattle the reproductive rates are low and the rate of development is slow, maturity occurring in 5–6 years. The dimensions and weight are often small and the conformations usually poor. Unless the animals are given better feeding and veterinary attention and more systematic management than normally provided, productivity and quality will remain poor.

Domestic livestock of the Savanna region comprises of cattle, goats, sheep, donkeys, horses, camels, poultry, and a limited number of pigs. Remarkable progress has been made in more recent years in the control of diseases, the improvement of food supplies and access to water. This and the improvement of indigenous or acclimatized stock by selection or by crossing and a better understanding of ecology, bears high promise in accelerated livestock production.

Detailed accounts on livestock in the tropics and West Africa are given by Epstein (1957), Williamson and Payne (1965), Oyenuga (1967), Webster and Wilson (1973). Here, only an abbreviated account is given that is relevant to the Savanna ecology.

### 6.2.1 Domestic animals

(a) *Cattle.* The Savanna region provides the bulk of the cattle population in West Africa, supplying a high demand for beef not only for its own region but also for southern humid areas supporting a high human population.

The main breeds and types of cattle in the Savanna can be broadly divided into two groups:

1. The humpless, long- and short-horned animals constituting the beef types.

2. The humped Zebu types which are dual purpose animals, providing milk and later being fattened for beef. These types are also suitable for use as work animals.

The humpless types are most numerous and have had centuries of ancestral residence in areas where trypanosomiasis is endemic, and many of them have developed a high degree of tolerance/immunity to this disease. Historical factors, such as the rise and fall of the West African Kingdoms, the development and decline of trade, tribal migration, local isolation, etc., are responsible for the marked variations within this group. The most important breeds of this group are the dwarf Short-horn, N'Dama, and Kuri.

The dwarf Short-horn is one of the most common breeds in the West African Savanna, found mainly in the southern West parts of the Savanna which is infested with tse-tse fly. The animals have a high resistance to trypanosomiasis. They are hardy compact animals often standing no more than 1 m high. Their milk yield is very poor, barely sufficient to rear a calf. The mature bullock produces a live weight of up to about 180–200 kg in about three years with a killing-out ratio of about 40 per cent.

The N'Dama breed is preferred in the tse-tse infested areas of the southern Savanna where it has shown promising performance as a range cattle on ranches. N'Dama calves suck for an average period of 13 months and mature at just over five years. The average live weight attained in one year is about 130 kg and in two years 190 kg, while the average live weight of mature animals is 250–270 kg (Oyenuga·1967).

The Kuri (Lake Chad cattle) is the heaviest breed of cattle in West Africa, attaining a weight in range of 300–800 kg. They are found around the Lake Chad and the animals are excellent swimmers often immersing themselves in water, with only the tip of their nostrils above surface, for a considerable part of the day.

The humped Zebu types, whose ancestors originated in trypanosomiasis-free Asia but have been exposed to rinderpest for centuries, are resistant to rinderpest but have a low resistance to trypanosomiasis. They are owned almost exclusively by the nomadic Fulani and grazed in areas free from tse-tse fly.

The most common breed in the humped Zebu group is the White Fulani or Bunaji. The value of Zebu lies in their big size and greater productivity. For example the mature Bunaji is a large animal, approximately 130 cm high. The cow weighs about 340 kg and the bull about 520 kg. The animals are truly dual purpose, producing milk and a good quality carcase. At Shika, the average milk yield during the 305 days lacatation period is about 1450 kg with elite cows producing as much as 2240 kg. The mean butter fat percentage is about 7·5. The weight increases under good management are of the order: 135 kg at one year, 210 kg at two years, 285 at 3 years and 350 kg at 4 years. The animals are docile and can be used for work.

The humped Zebu group also includes the Red Fulani or Rahaji, the Sokoto Gudali and the Shuwa Arab or Wadara breed. The Red Fulani is a breed similar to the White Fulani but used mainly for beef. The Gudali thrives under the dry conditions of the Sahel and Sudan Savanna and is used for milk and beef production as well as for farm work. The Wadara is widely distributed in the north eastern area of Nigeria, Niger and Chad, and is used for milk, farm work and as a beast of burden.

(b) *Sheep and goats.* These are widely distributed throughout the Savanna and are reared principally for their meat and skin. The majority of sheep produce little or no wool, nor indeed could the Savanna regions ever provide habitats congenial for wool breeds. Both animals are well known for their scavenging habits and are a menace to vegetation and soil under low input and poor management. They live unconfined and tend for themselves eating all available vegetation including plants and residues that no other animal would eat. In order that the animals may flourish and their destructive influences on vegetation and soils may be reduced, the animals require careful management. Indeed, when properly managed they may even be used to control unwanted vegetation but such management in the Savanna is rare.

Herds of sheep and goats are kept by many people who are unable to afford cattle and serve often as a first step towards becoming cattle owners. In the Sahel region, Fulani and Touareg herdsmen tend flocks which often are ruinous on already degraded vegetation, accelerating the destruction of the plant cover. The average live weight of mature goats is in the range of 25–35 kg and that of sheep 20–30 kg. The animals are often used in religious ceremonies and are traditionally eaten at certain festivals.

(c) *Camels.* These animals are still of economic importance in the Sahel region. The animals require little attention. They prefer to browse woody vegetation and the leaves of *Acacia raddiana* are their favourite food. If obliged to eat dry food and cover 25–30 km/day the camel needs to be fed daily but requires water every 3–4 days. In addition to its use as a pack and riding animal the camel provides milk and its hair is a useful commodity.

(d) *Horses.* Horses are the least robust of all the domesticated animals in the Savanna region. They are kept only for riding and for prestige and are treated with care and affection. The most luxuriant pastures are reserved for their use. South of the Sudan region horses are seldom kept in large numbers because of their susceptibility to trypanosomiasis, tick, and other parasitic infestations.

(e) *Pigs.* The religious objections of Muslims to pig rearing is responsible for an almost complete lack of native land races in the Savanna regions. Exotic pigs are easily acclimatized and under good management perform exceptionally well. Hygienic housing, a balanced diet and the control of worms and parasitic infections is all that is required for the production of pork animals that can be exceptionally productive and profitable.

(f) *Poultry.* The indigenous chickens and ducks are hardy birds. They are left to tend for themselves without any provision for food. For this reason they are unproductive and the eggs they produce are small. Poultry in the Savanna is susceptible to 'Newcastle disease' which in recent years has reduced the stock.

However, in many parts of the Savanna farmers are adopting exotic breeds of birds under intensive systems for both eggs and table production. Poultry farming is encouraged by some governments who provide assistance such as veterinary service and the provision of central feed depots from which farmers can purchase well-balanced mashes.

### 6.2.2 Diseases and pests of stock

The major constraint to livestock production in the West African Savanna is the exposure of stock to numerous pests and diseases that are either endemic or frequent in the region, resulting in a loss of production or death.

The economically most important endemic diseases of the region affecting cattle production are Protozoan-induced trypanosomiasis conveyed to animals through the saliva of the tse-tse fly (*Glassinia* spp.), and the rinderpest virus disease. Mass anti-rinderpest immunization by routine vaccination gives a satisfactory control of rinderpest but a satisfactory control of tse-tse still remains a most challenging problem. A good response follows the treatment of animals with Antrycide or Dimidium bromide, but much remains to be learnt about the application of these drugs and other aspects of the retention of livestock in infested areas. Trypanosomiasis tends to be a reducing rather than a killing disease, and if animals are well fed and tended, production loss my be avoided even in infested herds.

Ticks are the major parasties of livestock in the Savanna region causing discomfort, blood loss, and injection of toxins. They are the major vectors in the transmission of *Theileria mutans* and *Cowdria ruminantium* which causes heartwater fever in ruminants. They also transmit anaplasmosis and are important vectors of bovine babesiosis (Mohamed and Leeflang 1975). Periodical dipping and spraying the host animals with chemicals such as Toxaphene or gamma-BHC will control infestation.

Other common diseases affecting livestock production are:

Virus induced: Foot and mouth, rabies, swine-fever, horse-sickness, heartwater (in cattle, sheep and goats). Several forms of fowl-pest of which the notorious Newcastle disease causes great losses in poultry.

Bacteria induced: Anthrax is fatal but stock can be vaccinated against it. Several forms of Brucellosis causing contagious abortion, Malta fever causing much loss in sheep and goats, contagious bovine pleuro-pneumonia and Spirochaetosis in pigs and poultry are fairly common. The Anthrax and bovine pleuro-pneumonia may be controlled by means of vaccines, while calves can be vaccinated against contagious abortion.

Protozoan induced: They are less numerous but include, in addition to try-panosomiasis, tick-transmitted prioplasmosis (red water) and anaplasmosis (gall-sickness) in cattle and Theileria induced and tick transmitted disease.

Various parasites: These include roundworms, flatworms, flukes, tapeworms, hookworms which are responsible for a serious reduction in the vitality of live-stock and a loss of production.

No attempt is made here to present details of the biology of pathogens, disease symptoms and control methods but the interested reader is referred to Dunne (1959), Lapage (1956) and Whitlock (1960).

## 6.3  Forest resources

Until recently the development of forest resources in West African has been mainly concerned with the management and controlled exploitation of the lowland High Forest regions where high value timber such as the 'African Maho-ganies' and similar kinds are produced for veneers, cabinet woods, etc. This is not surprising in view of the high economic incentives, excellent rates of re-generation, and simple not too expensive or labour-demanding silvicultural management resulting in a comparatively rapid volume of increments.

In contrast, the Savanna forest resources have been much neglected because of the low value of the timber, the slow rates of growth and regeneration, fire hazards, and a relatively much higher cost of management. Consequently, for-estry activities in the Savanna have beem mainly limited to the maintenance of established 'Forest Reserves' as a means of the conservation of natural vegetation amounting to protection against fire, cutting and grazing. More recently, small firewood plantations and shelter belts have been established, but these have no appreciable impact on the development of forest resources or on the economy of the Savanna region to any significant degree.

Because of the very low productivity of the Savanna in its natural state, the present policy for the development of Savanna forest resources is to place emphasis on the establishment of plantations of exotic species specific to bio-climatic regions. The aim is to increase productivity, meet high fuel demands, and improve the effectiveness of soil protection as well as restoring soil fertility.

### 6.3.1  Natural woodland

The close interrelation of climate and biotic phenomena is the most striking characteristic of the West African Savanna resulting in distinct bioclimatic units. These bioclimatic units are characterized by definite seasonal patterns in the amount and intensity of climatic elements influencing plant growth. The quanti-tative description of bioclimatic elements within the major bioclimatic regions has been already dealt with indicating the limitations, risks and the potential of agricultural and related forms of production within a natural region.

From the point of view of vegetation each bioclimatic region represents a stage in the development of natural vegetation which is in equilibrium with the climate. The ultimate stage is the *climax* vegetation but this is rarely in exist-ence because of the strong disturbing influence or interference by man's many activities. Consequently within the bioclimatic units there is a range of natural vegetation communities at various stages of development resembling the climax, but gradually replaceable by it when the climatic control is not inhibited by human disturbance. This situation in the West African context is referred to as *proclimax* in preference to *subclimax*, a form referring specifically to the succesional stage immediately preceding the climax. Our present knowledge of succession in the Savanna vegetation is too slight to warrant its use.

The main bioclimatic regions vary in their composition, stocking and vigour of woody trees in a general matrix of grass and other non-woody vegetation. The woody species of the natural Savanna vegetation of interest to forestry are as follows:

The relatively dry areas of the Sahel and Sudan Savanna are dominated by *Acacia* spp., of low stature, small-leaves, widely dispersed trees with some *Combretum, Anogeissus, Sclerocarya* and occasional *Terminalia* species. In the Sahel *A. raddiana* is the most common species. *A. senegal* is the most important forest species in the Sudan region, as a source of gum, together with *A. nilotica*, used in tanning. *A. albida* is also important and it retains its leaves during the dry season providing leaf fodder and shade. Another important economic species in this dry zone is *Anarcardium occidentale*, the cashew tree.

In the Guinea region *Acacia* spp., are relatively rare giving way to *Isoberlinia, Daniellia, Afzelia, Uapaca, Terminalia*, and the *Pterocarpus* species. Their height ranges from 10 to 15 m and their crowns may be far apart or almost touching. At the southern fringes of the Guinea Savanna *Isoberlinia* and *Brachystegia* species are dominant with a much higher stocking capacity.

In general both the tree stocking and growth increment of natural woodland Savanna are very low. The yield of wood from native Savanna rages from 0·07 to 0·7 $m^3$/ha per annum (McComb and Jackson 1969). The average stocking of the Northern Guinea Savanna was found to be only 425 trees per hectare of stems 30 cm girth at breast height with a growth increment of only 70 $cm^3$/ha per annum (Kemp 1963). In addition to this very poor rate of growth, much of the indigenous tree species have poor quality timber unacceptable for any use other than fuel. The main defects in quality are lack of length, straightness and durability. The majority of timber is hard and heavy, difficult to season and unsuitable for saw mill production.

Some of the better quality woods such as *Khaya senegalensis* (dry zone mahogany), *Anogeissus leiocarpus, Afzelia africana, Maesopsis eminii, Pterocarpus angolensis* and *Isoberlinia doka* are unsuitable for plantations because of their establishment difficulties and slow growth (Iyamabo 1971).

The very low yields of woodland Savanna do not meet the ever-growing demand for even the crudest kinds of forest produce for firewood and building materials, and the large Savanna population does not have access to wood supplies which it can afford. The average villager does not have a bed, a table, chairs, benches, and many other items which would be constructed with simple tools if suitable wood were available. This is in contrast with the High Forest areas where most houses have furniture and where carpentry and wood working is well developed and saw mills are fairly common.

### 6.3.2  Forest plantations

The exceptionally low productivity of the natural forest Savanna and the low quality of its produce are far below the theoretical climatic potential of the Savanna region. Any improvement in productivity and quality of timber can only be achieved by drastic control of the environment and through the introduction of species both native and exotic that are specific to production needs and sufficiently adaptable to the climate and to other environmental constraints.

This entails the destruction of all natural vegetation and the establishment of pure stands of tree plantation, usually by the planting of seedlings previously raised in the nursery. The choice of species, and the mangement of decisions relating to land clearing, all subsequent soil management, nutrition, spacing, land cover, control of diseases, pests and weeds, labour utilization, etc., will greatly affect the productivity and economy of the plantation. There is as yet comparatively little experience on which to base the most efficient management decisions relating to plantation establishment. However, there is sufficient experimental information to provide the foundations for large scale afforestation, and the more important factors relating to management will now be considered.

(a)  *The establishment and the post-establishment phases of plantation management.*  It is important to distinguish between the phase relating to the establishment of the plantation and phase following the establishment, concerned with the growth of maturing stands and a yield of timber. There is no sharp distinction between the two phases, but for practical purposes recognizable changes in the physical environment occur at the time when stands form a closed or near closed canopy and when grass vegetation is excluded and leaf fall forms mulch. Correct management during the establishment phase is most critical. It is labour-consuming and expensive, and greatly affects the future productivity and economy of the plantation.

It should be appreciated that much of the present grassland-dominated Savanna vegetation is considered to comprise of vegetation climaxes induced by fire and man, and adversely affecting the total environment including soil fertility and macro- and micro-climate. Consequently there is considerable resistance to upgrading in what is at present a greatly reduced environmental potential for afforestation. This resistance is particularly severe during the initial phase of plantation establishment. However, once the full plantation canopy is formed, the natural regeneration of the chemical and physical properties of the soil occurs fairly rapidly, and the micro-climate changes sufficiently to favour tree growth. Biotic activity increases and consequently, the environmental resistance to changes into a forest dominated environment diminishes. One is under the impression that once the canopy cover has been established, there is a tendency in the aerial, edaphic, biotic, and hydrological factors to favour forest production without a supply of expensive inputs. In contrast with agricultural production where high inputs are essential in order to achieve a moderately high efficiency of energy conversion, well established forests can achieve this in time with relatively little inputs in terms of fertilizers, labour, equipment, and control of diseases, pests and weeds.

The major inputs in Savanna plantations seem therefore to be limited to the establishment phase which should be at least partially regarded as an investment for site amelioration and the improvement of damage brought about by fire and mismanagement in the past.

(b) *Potential productivity and rates of growth.* The rate of growth of a tree plantation is determined by both environmenal and plant factors. It is now possible to estimate the potential production of various tree plantations as a function of the controlling environmental factors.

The main factor controlling the production of the dry matter of economic plants in the Savanna is the climate but particularly those climatic (and edaphic) elements which control the availability of water to plants. Differences in the radiation-dependent factors in various areas such as light and temperature have a relatively minor influence on productivity. It should, however, be appreciated that if water and nutrients were not limiting, the humid High Forest areas would have a much lower annual potential productivity than the Savanna areas. This is so because the lower annual radiation income and higher night temperature in the High Forest areas result in lower net assimilation rates.

However, under the prevailing conditions of water regimes and particularly due to the drastic shortening of the water availability periods with increasing latitude as well as due to the decline of natural soil fertility northwards, the trend in the potential productivity is reversed. Productivity in the Savanna under natural conditions gradually diminishes with the increase in latitude and the potential dry matter production is clearly related to the period of water availability (Kassam and Kowal 1973, Kowal and Davies 1975).

The productivity of plantation forest as compared with the productivity of natural woodland Savanna is at least 10 times and often as much as 40–50 times greater. According to Jackson and Ojo (1975) the mean annual increment from natural woodland in the Savanna zones of Nigeria is between 0·35 and 1·0m$^3$/ha. Plantations in the same zones yield from 1·7 m$^3$/ha annually for very poor quality Neem plantation to over 42 m$^2$/ha for fast growing *Eucalyptus* on the Jos Plateau. Except from the Sudan zone, most plantation species can be expected to yield 14 m$^3$/ha per annum.

whole dry matter production of the trees, shrubs and ground vegetation of the forest (if present). There are no data available on the proportion of the useful yield of timber as compared with the primary production of Savanna woodland and forest plantations. Judging by the estimates reported by Greenland and Kowal (1960) on the weight composition of a 50-year old standing High Forest in Ghana, of the total amount of 359 820 kg/ha oven dried vegetation only 173 180 kg/ha comprised of stem timber (48 per cent of commercially useful timber). Under the conditions of Savanna plantation supporting *Eucalyptus* spp., the proportion of useful timber is much greater probably amounting to at least 65 per cent of total vegetation. On this basis, the primary production of a *Eucalyptus* plantation yielding 42 m$^3$/ha per annum at 0·89 g/cm$^3$ specific density would be of the order of 33 600 kg/ha per annum of timber and 11 760 kg/ha per annum of 'waste' or 45 360 kg/ha per annum of total dry matter. This compares very favourably with the total dry matter yield of arable crops under conditions of high inputs (e.g., maize: 20 000 kg/ha). In terms of energy conversion efficiency, i.e., energy content of the total net primary production/

total solar energy input, the estimated efficiency is of the order of 1·13 per cent. cent.

(c) *Seasonal growth patterns.* The growth patterns in plantation and indigenous woodland species in Nigeria have been studied by McComb (1968, 1970), and McComb and Ogigirigi (1970). The results indicate (Figs. 6.2 and 6.3) that accelerated growth occurs during the wet season decreasing rapidly after the onset of the dry season. Depending on the species, the growth may terminate at some point in the dry season or continue at a greatly reduced rate throughout the dry season. Thus, for example, in the Northern Guinea environment the weekly height growth of the *Eucalyptus citrodara* (Fig. 6.2) during the dry season was reduced to 12–23 per cent of that during the wet season; the corresponding reduction in growth for the pine (*Pinus caribaea*) was 41–46 per cent (McComb 1970). Measurements with Fritts dendrograph (Fig. 6.3) in a 9 year old *E. citrodora* stand showed the reduction in the rate of the dry season growth of 17–60 per cent as compared with the maximum rate of growth during the wet season. In conrast the radial growth of *Tectona gradnis* (Teak) and *Gmelina arborea* (Gumbar) which are deciduous and *Isoberlinia doka* an indigenous evergreen, virtually stops during the dry season. Evidence from several root excavations showed that *Eucalyptus* spp., have deeper roots than *Isoberlinia* spp., a factor which would affect water availability and may explain the difference in the dry season growth. In general, the growth rates appear to be closely and positively correlated with the actual evapotranspiration rates.

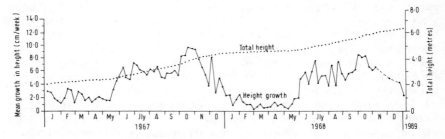

Fig. 6.2. Total height and height growth of *Eucalyptus citriodora* (22 trees) planted in 1966 at Afaka (McComb 1970).

(d) *Water availability.* The seasonal growth pattern indicates that the availability of water is the dominant factor in the Savanna environment controlling the growth and production of forest plantation. Clearly, the productivity of a plantation in a given bioclimatic region will largely depend on the length of the growing season, the amount of available water stored in the soil, the ability of roots to penetrate the deeper parts of the soil profile and draw on water reserves, and on the potential evapotranspiration rates.

The soil water characteristics studied by Samie (1973) in seven profiles at Afaka, in the Northern Guinea Savanna of Nigeria, showed that the total amount of water held in storage within the depth of 500 cm profile is in the order of

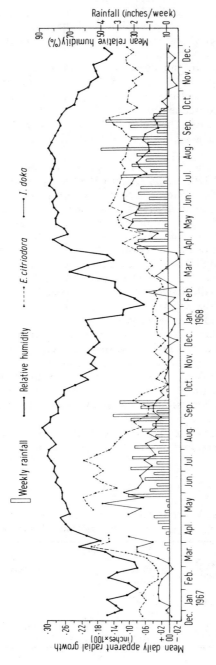

Fig. 6.3. Apparent radial growth of *Eucalyptus citriodora* and *Isoberlinia doka* in relation to mean relative humidity and rainfall at Afaka (McComb and Ogigirigi 1970).

130–165 cm. Out of this total storage within the 500 cm rooting depth about 36 to 46 cm is removed during the dry season. Laboratory investigation indicated that the average amount of water held within the range 0·33–15 atmosphere tension is about 1 cm per 10 cm of soil depth, but most of it is held at higher tensions and therefore is less available to plants.

Contrary to expectation, the depletion of soil water in relation to time occurred fairly uniformly throughout the 500 cm depth of profiles investigated. This suggests that there is a strong preference by vegetation to utilize only 'the easily available water'. Consequently roots must extend to a great depth in order to meet water requirements. This of course results in a poor efficiency in the utilization of the total soil available water, and probably constitutes a serious limiting factor for perennial vegetation.

Furthermore, the decline in the rates of growth during the dry season observed by McComb (1970) would support the theory that either ramification of the soil profile by roots is insufficiently developed to extract water held in higher ranges of tensions or the unsaturated conductivity of the soil is so low as to constitute a major stress in plants once the 'easily available water' reserves have been exhausted. This would be responsible for the development of high water stress in the plant tisue, the closure of stomata, and a consequent reduction of transpiration and net assimilation rates. The further evidence in support of the above theory comes from observations at Malam Fatore, in the northern part of the Sudan zone of Nigeria, where trees under irrigation maintain high rates of growth during the dry season and result in some of the highest yields (although of poor quality) so far recorded.

The magnitude of water requirements to meet plantation evapotranspiration needs during the period of the dry season may be evaluated for any locality in the Savanna, from the regression equation (3.34) which describes the total amount of $E_t$ during the dry season. The equation has already been discussed in Chapter 3 dealing with climatic resources. Estimates of the magnitude of available water storage in the soil profiles required to fully meet evapotranspiration demands during the dry season based on equation (3.34) are given in Table 6.4.

Only in the Southern Guinea region is precipitation sufficient to meet fully the annual evapotranspiration demands. Consequently the growth of plantations

**Table 6.4**

*Magnitude of available water storage in the soil to meet evapotranspiration demands in the dry season in different bioclimatic regions*

| Bioclimatic region | Mean $P$ (mm) | Mean $E_t$ (mm) | | $P-E_t$ wet season (mm) | % surplus rainfall to meet dry season $E_t$ |
|---|---|---|---|---|---|
| | | Wet season | Dry season | | |
| Southern Sahel | 475 | 500 | 1400 | −25 | — |
| Sudan | 740 | 670 | 1130 | 120 | 11 |
| Northern Guinea | 1090 | 780 | 770 | 310 | 40 |
| Southern Guinea | 1450 | 940 | 410 | 510 | 124 |

in this region is unlikely to be affected by water shortage and therefore a realization of the climatic potential is likely to be achieved far more easily.

In the Northern Guinea and the Sudan regions the amount of surplus rainfall
over the wet season evapotranspiration demands is sufficient to contribute only
some 40 and 11 per cent respectively to the dry season evapotranspiration
demands. Consequently, irrespective of other environmental and technical constraints, the rate of plantation growth cannot be fully maintained in the dry
season and some reduction in productivity must be accepted. Under these condi-
tins a careful selection of sites allowing for exploitation of the groundwater
within reach of tree roots may contribute to increased productivity.

In the Southern Sahel region, precipitation is only sufficient to match 95 per
cent of the wet season evapotranspiration demands. Because of pronounced
aridity and the fact that minor changes in environmental parameters produce
disproportionate effects on productivity (e.g., drought in 1972–74) the region is
not suitable for large scale high output afforestation. However, the major
interest to forestry in this region is the establishment of shelter belts and windbreaks to control wind erosion and to ameliorate to some extent the harshness
of the environment. There is as yet little practical experience or experimental
evidence on which to base generalizations. However, from the personal observations of authors an impression is gained that the introduction of shelter belts
and small plantations to utilize groundwater is not only possible but likely to be
an economical proposition in addition to a number of ecological advantages. The
success will largely depend on finding species that will not only survive the harsh
environment but be able to show a relatively rapid growth. It is possible that
certain species of *Eucalyptus* will meet these requirements.

(e) *Soil and nutritional aspects.* The research on soils and their fertility in the
Savanna of West Africa has a long history, mainly based on research centres at
Samaru (IAR) or at Bambey, Senegal (IRAT/OSTROM). Most of this work is
relevant in its application to forestry and is well documented. A review of the
research work on the Savanna soils and their fertility was recently compiled by
Jones and Wild (1975). In general terms the Savanna soils are being degraded
through burning, leaching, erosion, and man's mismanagement (through cultivation, overgrazing, tree destruction, and a lack of inputs to replace nutrients
removed by crops). Little is returned to the soil in terms of crop residues which
are used as building material, fuel, or animal feed.

In afforestation there are two important aspects of practical interest concerning soils. The first concerns the depth of soil profile. Since a lack of water during
the dry season constitutes the main constraint to production it is essential that
sites supporting plantation should have a deep profile free of plinthite layers to
allow the exploitation of a large volume of soil water by roots. The improvement
of the water-holding capacity by management (to any significant extent) is not
possible except during the initial phase of establishment. It may be useful to
remember that very approximately the depth of 1 cm soil holds about 1 mm of
available water. This may serve as a rough basis on which to estimate the
minimum depth of soil profile required by a plantation. For example, if the total
amount of evapotranspiration during the dry season is 500 mm, then the soil

should be at least 500 cm deep to provide fully for the storage of water requirements during the dry season if growth is to remain unaffected.

The second factor concerns plant nutrition. The soil are low in organic matter
and nutrient status and are deficient in phosphate, nitrogen and minor and trace
elements. The importance of the adequate provision and adequate fertilizer inputs during the critical period of plantation establishment cannot be over-
emphasized. The application of phosphate and nitrogen must be generous to
stimulate rapid growth, and in the case of *Eucalyptus*, boron must be added. In
fact the cost of fertilizer input during this initial stage should be viewed as a
price to be paid for the rehabilitation of the soils and environment and should
not be measured in terms of initial growth response.

There are no extensive data on which to base fertilizer recommendations for
the post-establishment phase of afforestation. However, it is abundantly evident
that once the canopy has been established, there are rapid changes in the
environment and micro-climate favouring a build up of the soil organic matter
and soil nutrient status as a result of soil protection by canopy and the accumulation of plant nutrients in a closed cycle of growth-decay-reabsorption. To what
extent the nutrition of a highly productive plantation forest needs to be supplemented by fertilizer treatments is largely unknown.

### 6.3.3  Choice and performance of species

The main considerations in choosing species for Savanna afforestation are
motivated by economical and environmental criteria. The economic factors
include the utility and quality of produce, the relative rate of growth, yield
potential, and management costs, while the environmental criteria include the
adaptability of different tree species to various degrees of aridity, exposure, and
edaphic limitations.

At present there is a very high demand for wood to supply towns and settlements with a source of fuel but also for sawn-wood and poles which have to be
brought in large quantities from outside the Savanna regions. Governments are
also anxious to develop wood industries and to lessen their ever growing demand
for paper by producing pulp for paper making. In addition to these normal
forest products the more arid areas of the Savanna are climatically equipped to
produce gum arabic, tanning materials, and cashew nuts.

An account on the performance of various tree species in the Savanna regions
has recently been published (FAO 1974). Here only a brief summary is given.
The most important species that perform well and are adaptable to a range of
environmental conditions of the West African Savanna include *Acacia* spp., and
*Eucalyptus* spp., in the most arid regions, *Eucalyptus* spp., and *Callitris* spp.,
in the less arid regions, *Eucalyptus* spp., and *Pinus* spp., in the more humid areas
while *Gmeliùm* spp., and *Tectone* spp., are suitable for areas with prolonged
rainy period. A list of the most successful species that show promise to Savanna
afforestation is given in Table 6.5.

### 6.3.4  Management

The management of forest plantaiton is a very specialized art that requires
knowledge of land clearing and preparation, nursery work and planting techn-

## Table 6.5

*Important species for afforestation of Savanna*

| Species | Remarks |
|---|---|
| Sahel and Sudan bioclimate: | |
| *Acacia senegal* | Gum arabic, hard wood |
| *Acacia albida* | Vigorous growth, readily coppices, prolific growth of leaves and pods for fodder |
| *Acacia nilotica* | Used for sawn-wood and poles. Poor coppicing |
| *Azadirachta indica* (Neem) | Fuel wood |
| *Eucalyptus camaldulensis* *Eucalyptus microtheca* *Eucalyptus tereticornis* | Fast growing species attaining height of 10–12 m in 3 years and yielding 63 m$^3$/ha at that age |
| *Anarcardium occidentale* (Cashew nut) | Used as windbreaks, no timber value |
| Guinea bioclimate: | |
| *Callitris* spp. (Cypress pine) | Good termite resistant poles and fine timber |
| *Eucalyptus* spp. | Range of species, very vigorous growth, very high incremental growth of the order of 15–30 m$^3$/ha per annum or more |
| *Pinus caribaea* *Pinus kesiya* *Pinus merkusii* *Pinus oocarpa* | Excellent growth rates although performing better at higher elevations, growth affected by mycorrhizal fungus, sensitive to presence of grass, mean annual increment in Nigeria 15–24 m$^3$/ha |
| *Gmellina arborea* (Gumbar) | Very high rate of growth, annual growth increment in Nigeria 16–28 m$^3$/ha |
| *Tectona grandis* (Teak) | Excellent and durable timber, mean annual increment 10 m$^3$/ha |

iques, skill of establishing seedlings, nutrition, weeding, pruning, fire protection, and general tending. These are beyond the scope of this book. The interested reader is advised to consult various forestry books and numerous publications of the Department of Forestry but in particular the FAO (1974) publication 'Tree planting practices in the African Savannas' that provides a summary of relevant information and references.

# 7 Crop resources

In a subsistence setting the farmer's main concern is not how to obtain the maximum possible yield but how to secure an adequate and a dependable harvest of his food crops. Consequently, traditional cultivars and cropping systems used by the farmer have evolved over a long period of time to satisfy his security motive. Although subsistence farmers are profit conscious (Norman 1972), cash crops fit into cropping systems in such a manner as will ensure that enough food is produced for the coming year. Yields of crops are small not because of any overriding disadvantages in the natural environment but because farmers do not have either resources or methods to manage the environment productively, and very often they would have no markets to sell to if they did.

The length of the growing season is determined by external limitations imposed by climate. However, the crop resources which the traditional farmer uses during the time available for crop production are influenced by the following factors: his food supplies at the beginning of the season are low; his crops largely or completely rely on natural soil fertility; diseases, pests, and weeds have to be kept under control without the use of biocides; and all farming operations are performed by hand using family labour. For most farmers the most crucial resource is labour at the beginning of the season, when it is essential for their survival that sufficient land should be seeded and weeded before the mineralized nitrogen is lost by leaching or taken up by weeds, and to secure the earliest possible crop from a part of their land, to break or shorten the 'hungry gap'. Bunting (1975) has illustrated some of the ways in which traditional crop cultivars and traditional farming systems are precisely adapted both to their social use and to the timetable imposed by the environment.

For a crop to be successful, it is necessary that its growth cycle as a whole should be of such a length that it is comfortably contained within those proportions of the year which are favourable for growth, and that the crop should use as much as possible fo the favourable season for yield-forming activities. However, whatever the environment may have to offer, different crops are obliged, by their structure, to accumulate yield at different stages of their life cycles. The structure of the plant is determined by the rate at which nodes and internodes are produced in space and time, and at some point in this sequence, yield-forming organs are differentiated. In respect of the numbers and location of node–internode units, and so the proportion of their life span, which can be used to form yield, crops fall into three broad phenological classes.

In the first, yield may be produced throughout much or all of the period in which growth is possible because it consists of, or is accumulated in, the vegetative parts of a sufficiently long-lived, and often a perennial or a biennial crop. In this group are the fodder grasses and other forage and silage plants, sugar cane, many root and tuber crops (potato, yam, cassava, sweet potato, cocoyam), and tobacco.

The second group includes the botanically indeterminate-flowering plants in which yield is produced, during a greater or smaller fraction of the life of the crop, in fruits and seeds borne on lateral inflorescences which may begin to be formed early in the crop's life. This group includes the leguminous pulses and oilseeds, tomato and cotton.

In the third group yield is produced in terminal or late-formed inflorescence as the last phase in the life of an annual crop or of the annual shoots of a perennial crop. This group includes the cereal crops—sorghum, millet, maize, rice and wheat. In these crops no more leaves can be formed once the apical bud of the shoot has become reproductive.

Clearly, therefore, plant structure imposes limitations on the use of time by crops to form yield. At the same time, however, phenological differences offer the farmer a choice of crops and cultivars which can make the best possible use of the time between whatever sowing date fits into his seasonal pattern of resource use and constraints, and the environmentally determined end of the growing season. It is indeed the phenological variation which the farmer uses to locate the yield-forming activities of his crops, at a particular stage of the season, appropriate to the environmental circumstances and to the technology of the farming system (Bunting 1975).

Except in the southernmost parts of the West African Savanna, the basic foods are cereals—mainly sorghum and pennisetum millet. In the drier, northern parts of the cereal area, where the start, the amount and the end of the rains are all unreliable, day-neutral types of both sorghum and millet are grown as main crops. Because they are day-neutral, they come into ear after a fixed number of leaves have been formed, and so they mature in the minimum possible time after sowing. Ecologically, these are desert ephemerals, escaping drought by completing their life cycles rapidly.

In the wetter parts of the cereal area, the first crop to be sown, on the first light rain, day-neutral pennisetum millet of types similar to those grown as main crops further north, and these flower at a fixed leaf number, and mature early to break the hungry gap. The main crops, sown when the rains are felt to be established, are cultivars of sorghum which are generally sown between the rows already planted with early millet. These sorghums flower at dates related to the average dates of the end of the rains in their home localities, more or less independent of the time they are sown. If they were to flower too soon, insects and moulds would damage the panicles; if they were to flower too late, there would be too little water left in the soil profile to see them through the grain-filling period. Because the rains end progressively earlier from south to north the mechanism is short-day photoperiodic, and because the isolines of average date of the end of the rains run with the lines of latitude, the local sorghums of any latitude all flower at much the same time.

Into these crops of sorghum, after weeding and generally after harvesting the early millet, farmers usually sow a long-season, spreading, short-day photoperiodic type of cowpea. As the development of inflorescences in these cowpeas is controlled by changing daylength, the inflorescence initials expand and flower at about the time when the panicles of the surrounding sorghum crop have emerged and its leaf area is starting to decline. The early millet is generally har-

vested before the sorghum has initiated its panicle, and often the millet crop has
no or little detrimental effect on the yield of sorghum which is formed much
later. Therefore, the phenological time-tables of the millet, sorghum and the
associated cowpea are closely co-ordinated in a system of mixed cropping which
provides a better control of late weeds, protects the soil surface from erosive
rains, helps to spread the labour load, makes a fuller use of the environmental
resources, and produces a yield of starch and protein with an LER of more than
one.

To the south of the cereal zone the main staple energy foods are starchy
tubers, particularly yams and cassava. These crops are perennial, and cassava at
least is often left unharvested in the soil as a good reserve. Therefore, the main
shortage in the hungry gap period is protein, which further north is supplied,
along with calories, by the cereal itself. So the crop sown early, in these wetter
regions, to break the hungry gap is a cultivar of early-flowering cowpea which
behaves as a day-neutral photoperiodic type.

The above example of the staple food crops, taken from Bunting (1975),
clearly shows that many of the features of the traditional crop cultivars and
traditional farming systems are closely adapted to help the farmer achieve his
goals. They are conssistent with the constraints of his total environment, including economic and social factors, a subject which is further discussed in Chapter
8. On the other hand, however, if farming in the West African Savanna is to
become more productive and lead farmers into a more commercial economy,
high yielding cultivars of crops with appropriate cultural practices will have to
be used. There is no doubt that the application of simple but improved technology can result in increased levels of crop production in the West African
Savanna. Accumulated knowledge from past and current research on crop
science in the West African Savanna indicates that improved resources of seeds,
fertilizers, and crop production technology, and the knowledge of how best to
use them within the available natural resources of climate and soil are sufficiently advanced to enable vast increases to be made in productivity of crops.

This chapter deals with three aspects, ecology, cultivation, and diseases and
pests, related to the crop resources of the West African Savanna. The information presented has an agronomic bias to it because of its practical importance.
Accurate statistics on distribution and production of crops in the West African
Savanna do not exist. FAO estimates of production on country basis and other
sources have been used to indicate the present production and mean yields of
crops. Only those crops which are extensively grown or whose potential has been
established by research work in West Africa and elsewhere are considered here.
Readers are referred to Purseglove (1975, 1975) for a comprehensive account of
tropical crops and Irvine (1974) for a general account of the crops in West
Africa.

## 7.1 Cereals

### 7.1.1 Sorghum (Sorghum bicolor)

The crop appears to have been domesticated in Ehtiopia some 5000 years
ago and was taken to West Africa at an early date across the Sudan to the Upper
Niger river (Doggett 1970). Sorghum is grown primarily for grain for human con-

sumption, as a thin porridge, or thick paste, or in beer. White or yellow corneous grains without a sub-coat are preferred for flour, which is prepared by pounding the seed in a mortar to remove the pericarp and further pounding or grinding to produce a fine granular powder. Sorghums with red or brown bitter grains are preferred for brewing beer. Local cultivars are typically large, and tall plants and crop residues are used as building material, fuel, and feed. Sorghum has a number of other uses including silage and grain for livestock. Accounts of sorghum as a world crop are given in Doggett (1970), Wall and Ross (1970) and Rao and House (1972).

Estimated total production of sorghum in West Africa in 1971 was about 5·8 m. tonnes from an area of about 9·7 m. ha, corresponding to a yield of about 500 kg/ha. However, yield figures from individual countries vary between about 420 kg/ha in Senegal and Togo and 750 kg/ha in Cameroon and Ghana. Within a country yields vary between 300 and 1500 kg/ha depending on soil fertility and moisture conditions. Generally yields are higher in the Guinea Savanna than in the Sudan Savanna because of the longer growing season and higher soil fertility. Good experimental yields of local sorghums under improved cultural practice is about 1 tonne/ha in the Sudan Savanna and about 2 tonne/ha in the Guinea Savanna: those of improved photosensitive sorghums about 2 tonne/ha and 3·5 tonne/ha respectively; and of improved short-season photoinsensitive sorghums about 2·5–3·0 tonne/ha and 4–4·5 tonne/ha respectively (Webster 1970, Barry 1970, Andrews 1970a, 1970b, Le Conte 1970, Robledo 1970).

(a) *Ecology*. Sorghum is one of the principal sources of food in the Sudan and Northern Guinea Savanna, but it remains an important cereal in the Southern Guinea and Derived Savanna. Sorghum production reaches its greatest concentration where rainfall varies from 600–1000 mm or more per year.

In the drier northern parts where the growing season is short and rainfall unpredictable, nonphotoperiodic cultivars are grown. However, in areas where rainfall is greater than 600 mm, the local cultivars are photoperiodic and because they flower at the end of the rains their growth cycles range from 120–135 days in the notherly areas in the Sudan Savanna to 240 days or more in the southern areas. The number of nodes and height therefore varies between 15 and 30 and 3 and 6 m respectively depending on the length of the growth cycle (Curtis 1967, Kassam and Andrews 1975). However, sensitivity to photoperiod is modified by temperature (Cocheme and Franquin 1967).

An important adaptive feature of local sorghums is that by means of photoperiodism, the date of heading is closely related to the average date of the end of local rains (Curtis 1968a, Bunting and Curtis 1968) so that seed set occurs as the weather becomes dry. In this way the grains are not attacked by moulds and insects as they would be if heading was earlier in the rains. Local cultivars were therefore found to yield better in their own region than in regions north or south, because heading in the new locality was still related to the average date of the end of the rains in its original locality (Curtis 1968b). This behaviour could not be explained entirely by responses to photoperiod in terms of a critical daylength requirement, and Bunting and Curtis (1968) have suggested that the stimulus may have been the number of successively shortening days after

June 21 rather than their absolute length which controlled the date of heading in local sorghums.

Date of sowing has a marked effect on yields of local and improved photosensitive sorghums. Because heading is at the end of the rains the crop forms its yield largely on the moisture stored in the soil. However, if heading is late due to late sowing or if there is an earlier than normal cessation of rains, grains fail to fill completely. Under indigenous practice, local sorghums are sown as early as possible though often after millet so as to capture most of the mineralized nutrients and to minimize the possible damage from shoot-fly, stem-borers and weeds. The effect of delay in sowing on delay in heading in a normal season is comparatively small in local and improved photosensitive sorghums but can have a signficant influence on yield particularly when rains start or end earlier or both. The grain filling phase of local sorghum is about 35–40 days and those of improved photosensitive sorghums 45–50 days. When sowing is late, not only is the plant size and its root system smaller, but because of the delay in heading, grain filling occurs that much later and under relatively worse soil moisture conditions, which can cause a shortening of the grain filling period. Thus, at Samaru the date of heading in local Farafara in an average season was linearly related to the date of sowing over an 8–10 week spread in sowing date. Heading was on 6 October when the crop was sown during 12–16 May but then onwards each week's delay in sowing caused a delay in heading of about 0·9–1·3 days (Curtis 1968a, Andrews 1973). The delay in heading was about 2 days per week's delay in sowing during the season when rains ended earlier than normal while the earliest sown crop on 16 May still headed on 6 October with a consequent progressive decline in yield from later sowings of about 200 kg/ha (about 12·5 per cent of the maximum yield) per week's delay in sowing after 30 May (Andrews 1973). In the improved dwarf and tall photosensitive sorghums each week's delay in sowing has been shown to delay heading date by 2 days or more. In the Northern Guinea Savanna Andrews (1973) showed that each week's delay in sowing after the optimum sowing date in May and early June decreased the yield at the rate of about 300–600 kg/ha, corresponding to about 15 per cent of the maximum yield. Similarly a decrease of about 360 kg/ha (10 per cent of the maximum yield) per week's delay in sowing after 26 May over a 10-week spread in sowing date at Samaru was found by Kassam and Andrews (1975). In the Southern Guinea Savanna where the normal growth cycle of local sorghums is 200 days or more, experiments (Andrews 1975a) exploring the possibility of using improved photosensitive cultivars from more northerly areas by mid-season sowing have shown that each week's delay in sowing delayed heading date by about 2 days and yield decreased at the rate of 810 kg/ha (25 per cent of maximum) per week's delay in sowing after 2 August with insecticide control of stem-borers. Without insecticide control the rate was about 375 kg/ha (17 per cent of maximum) per week's delay in sowing after 26 July.

Later sowing of improved photosensitive sorghum SK 5912 has been shown (Kassam and Andrews 1975) to reduce the normal length of vegetative period of 98 days from sowing to floral initiation by about 4·5 days per week; the normal length of the head development period of 42 days from floral initiation to heading by about 0·4 day per week; and the normal length of the grain-filling period of 48 days from heading to physiological maturity by about 0·9 days per week, corresponding to a total reduction of the normal growth cycle of 188 days by about 6 days per week. Further, both total dry weight and leaf area index decreased with later sowing, contributing to the observed decreases in the number of heads per plant and number of grains per head. The delay in heading, reduction in grain-filling period and smaller root system contributed to the observed decreases in the grain size and grain to head ratio. It is likely that some of the decrease in yield due to the decrease in head number per plant and grain number per head could be reduced by sowing the crop at higher densities when sown late.

In general, when moisture and nutrient supplies are adequate, about 110–120 days are required to produce a high yield. Cultivars with longer growth cycles produce lower yields or show no extra yield advantages because the increase in the length of the growth cycle is mainly in the length of the vegetative phase. Further, the longer the crop occupies the land the greater the risks of attack from pathogens and pests. Yields drop sharply if the growth cycle is less than 80 days but with 90–100 days to maturity yields are lower by about 20 per cent to those obtained at 110–120 days. By virtue of photoperiodism, local sorghums at present escape head mould attack and produce grain of good quality despite the variation in sowing date from region to region and within a region from season to season. However, their yield potential is low and they occupy the land for a period longer than that required to produce a high yield per unit of input per unit time within the period when soil moisture supply is most favourable Yields of local sorghums drop severely when rains end earlier than normal; and in years when rains commence late also, they may fail to produce a yield. The use of cultivation techniques to conserve rainfall, by preventing run-off, and to improve the soil surface infiltration rate have been found to be beneficial to the yields of sorghum crops. Thus, Lawes (1966) from a series of field experiments over six seasons, found that mulches of groundnut shells and dead grass increased yields by 270–400 kg/ha and 190–415 kg/ha respectively; tying all ridges and leaving alternate furrows open increased yields by 113–216 kg/ha and 103–157 kg/ha respectively during dry years; and deep vertical mulching in all furrows, and alternate furrows left open, at high level of fertility increased yields by 295–302 kg/ha while deep and shallow vertical mulch in all furrows at low level of fertility increased yields by 423–436 kg/ha.

For improved grain yields, cultivars responsive to high fertility at increased plant population are required. However, for improved photosensitive cultivars, to minimize the effects of soil moisture deficit during the grain-filling period when higher plant densities are used, the crop should flower as early as possible consistent with maintaining acceptable grain quality. High-yielding, mould-resistant photoinsensitive cultivars do not exist at present but high-yielding, photosensitive cultivars which flower 8–14 days earlier than local sorghums have been produced for the Guinea Savanna (Andrews 1970a, 1970b). These produce a high yield of good quality under improved practice when sown at normal sowing dates common in the indigenous practice in the Sudan and Northern Guinea Savanna. In the Southern Guinea Savanna these cultivars when sown appropriately late have been shown to produce yields of over 3 tonne/ha in about 120–140 days which is 2–3 months less than the length of growth cycles of local cultivars (Andrews 1975a). Further, experimental photosensitive hybrids have produced yields up to 6 tonnes/ha in the Guinea Savanna (Andrews 1975b). High-yielding photoinsensitive cultivars of 90–120 days to maturity have been produced which if sown appropriately late will flower earlier than local cultivars and set seed with little trouble from mould and soil moisture deficit (Goldsworthy 1970a, Andrews 1970b). These improved cultivars are most suitable for one crop per season in the Sudan Savanna and for multiple cropping as a second late-sown crop in the Guinea Savanna. However, in the Guinea Savanna late sowing of short-season cultivars leads to problems with crop establishment due to pest attack, requiring chemical control, and very wet soil conditions. The eco-physiological aspects related to crop growth, development, and yield of local, improved photosensitive and short-season photoinsensitive sorghums in Nigeria have been discussed by Goldsworthy (1970a, 1970b, 1970c) and Goldsworthy and Tayler (1970), while Eastin (1972) has reviewed the physiology of yield in sorghum in general.

Sorghum is adapted to a wide range of ecological conditions. It can tolerate hot and dry conditions better than maize and can withstand periodic waterlogged conditions which occur in the months of August and September in much of the West African Savanna. It has a marked degree of drought endurance and can tolerate a wide range of soil conditions. It grows well on heavy soil including the black soils but will grow satisfactorily on lighter sandy soils. It has an advantage over maize because of its better ability to endure drought and soil acidity but in the Savanna areas, including the Sudan Savanna, where soil moisture regime is favourable, maize produces higher yields per unit of input. Sorghum can be grown in soils of $pH$ ranging from 5·0–8·5 and can tolerate salinity better than maize.

Total crop water use of a 180-day long-season sorghum between sowing and harvest in the Guinea Savanna has been reported to be 657 mm (Kowal and Andrews 1973), corresponding to water use efficiency of about 270 g water per g total dry matter. Response to fertilizer depends on the region (Goldsworthy 1967) and cultivar. However, an improved sorghum crop yielding 4066 kg/ha in Senegal has been reported to remove N, 132 kg/ha; P, 12·4 kg/ha; K, 57·5 kg/ha; Ca, 40·7 kg/ha (IRAT 1972). Growth and nutrient uptake in high yielding sorghums has been discussed by Vanderlip (1972).

(b) *Cultivation.* Sorghum is grown as a rain-fed crop but some is produced as a dry season crop on residual moisture on the flood plains of Lake Chad. The indigenous practice is to sow it as early as possible, but after millet, in the wet season. Seeds are sown on ridges, or on the flat and often ridged later, at about 30–45 days after sowing. Most of the sorghum is grown in mixture with other crops in 2–5 crop combinations involving early millet (Gero), late millet (Maiwa), groundnut, cowpea and cotton, but the most common combinations are those involving early millet, cowpea and groundnut. About 25 per cent of the total area under sorghum was found to be sole crop sorghum in village studies in the Guinea Savanna (Norman 1972) while sorghum in mixtures is sown in intricate patterns with other crops (Fig. 7.1). When grown sole the spacing is generally about 0·60–0·90 m (about 12 000–18 000 stands/ha) while in 2–3 crop combinations stand population is in the range about 12 000–15 000 per ha, and in 4–5 crop combinations about 6750–7000 (Norman 1972). Usually early millet is sown first, followed by sorghum. In the sorghum/millet/cowpea mixture, cowpea is undersown on the same ridge as sorghum when the millet is harvested; the millet is sown in the furrows between the ridges sown with sorghum. The time of sowing is governed by the time of arrival of rains and sowing is therefore later in the Sudan Savanna than in the Guinea Savanna. Sorghum is generally grown in the fields closer to the villages and often on a continuous basis. The fields receive a certain amount of manure but little or no fertilizer is used. Cultivation, sowing, thinning, weeding, and harvesting is done by hand. Early sowing and control of weeds is most important to enable the crop to capture most of the mineralized nutrients before they are leached or taken up by weeds. It has been suggested that undersowing of the legume in the latter part of the season may contribute some nitrogen to the system beneficial to the standing sorghum crop (Bunting 1972b). As the heading date of local sorghum is related to the date of the end of the rains, days to maturity and harvest time varies from region to region: sorghum in the Sudan Savanna being harvested first. The grain after harvest is often stored in the head in simple storage structures (Bugundu 1970, Hill 1972) and is very subject to insect attack. The grain to head weight ratio is about 70–75 per cent while the grain to total dry weight ratio (harvest index) is 7–15 per cent (Goldsworthy 1970a).

Improved long-season photoperiodic cultivars and short-season photoinsensitive cultivars are sown when the rains are established, or sown appropriately late so that the crop is harvested soon after the rains have ended. Treated seeds are sown at a spacing in the range $0\cdot1$–$0\cdot3 \times 0\cdot45$–$0\cdot90$ m depending on the cultivar and days to maturity. Semi-dwarf photosensitive cultivars are generally sown at a density of about 40 000–80 000 plants/ha while dwarf, photosensitive, long-season and photoinsensitive, short-season, cultivars at 100 000 plants/ha or more. Responses to nutrients vary from area to area (Goldsworthy 1967, Vaille 1970, Heathcote 1972b) but for yields over 3 tonne/ha, experimental rates of 60–140 kg/ha of N and 15–40 kg/ha of P are applied.† Chemical control of shoot-fly and stem-borers can be necessary particularly when the crop is sown late in the Guinea Savanna. Harvest index of improved sorghum is 20–40 per cent (Goldsworthy 1970a). Improved sorghums show extra yield advantages when grown in mixtures with millet under high management but responses have been shown to vary with cultivars (Andrews 1974). Yield advantages of up to 55 per cent have been reported (Andrews 1972a, 1974, Baker 1974) while a greater total nitrogen uptake has been reported in a sorghum/millet mixture compared to sole sorghum (Kassam and Stockinger 1973).

(c) *Diseases and pests*. Sorghum diseases in West Africa have been discussed by Delassus (1970), Sauger, Bilquez, Doggett, Le Conte, Moorman, and Webster (1970), and S. B. King (1972). Of the numerous diseases which attack sorghum, the smuts are of the greatest economic importance. Covered smut (*Spacelotheca sorghi*) and loose smut (*S. cruenta*) are seed-borne and can be effectively con-

---

† The experimental fertilizer rates quoted are not necessarily the recommended economic rates unless stated otherwise.

*Crop resources*

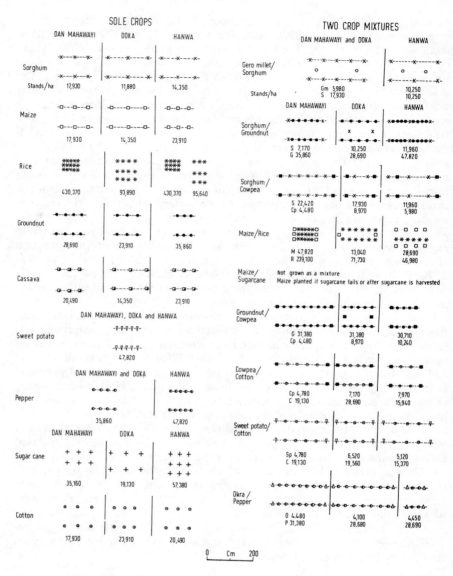

trolled by seed treatment at little cost and effort. Losses due to head smut (*S. reiliana*) and long smut (*Tolyosporium ehrenbergii*) are less severe and generally localized. Breeding for resistance is the only feasible approach to controlling these two smuts. Downy mildew (*Sclerospora sorghi*) is one of the serious foliar diseases of sorghum. Local cultivars have adequate resistance to it which should make incorporation of genetic resistance possible in the improved culti-

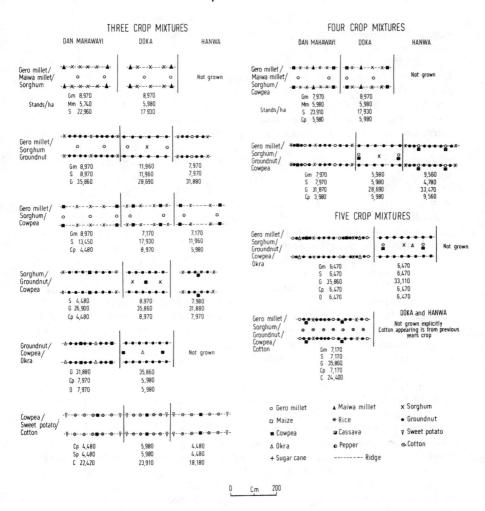

Fig. 7.1. Spatial arrangement of some common sole crops and crop mixtures in the survey villages, Dan Mahawayi Doka, and Hanwa, near Zaria, Nigeria (Norman 1972).

vars. Charcoal rot (*Macrophomina phaseolina*) can be serious in the Sudan Savanna particularly during drought conditions. Head mould, caused by a complex of organisms, is most prevalent in sorghum which matures during the rains, rendering the grain unfit for human consumption. The incidence of these moulds is related to the atmospheric humidity and compactness of the panicle. Improved, long and short-season cultivars can escape a serious attack if sowing is timed so as to enable the crop to mature as the rains are ending.

Damage in sorghum by shoot-fly (*Atherigona soccata*), stem-borers (*Busseola fusca, Sesamia* spp.) and midge (*Contarinia sorghicola*) is relatively unimportant under the indigenous practice of early sowing/late harvest, while local cultivars have adequate tolerance to stem-borer attack (Sauger *et al.* 1970). However, in the case of midge, Harris (1961) has reported that midge attack can be severe particularly in the southern, wetter areas where the growing season is longer and alternate hosts more abundant. It appears that growing sorghums of different growth cycle in one area may change the dynamics of these insect populations. Consequently, early maturing cultivars, sown later and harvested earlier than the long-season cultivars, may suffer from a severe shoot-fly and stem-borer attack while the long-season cultivars may suffer severely from midge due to population build-up from crop to crop. Incorporation of genetic resistance against these insects in the future seems promising but at present high yielding cultivars are very susceptible. Chemical control of *Busseola* (Barry and Andrews 1974) and shoot-fly is effective but no effective control measures exist for *Sesamia* spp.

Sorghum, stored in simple granaries as threshed grain or in the head, is very susceptible to a large number of storage pests and losses can be high (Giles 1964a, 1964b). Hard grains with corneous endosperm are less liable to attack. The most common pests include the rice weevil (*Sitophilus oryzae*), and flour beetles (*Tribolium* spp.) in threshed grain; the grain moth (*Sitotroga cerealella*) in grain stored in the head; and the grain borer (*Rhizopertha dominica*). Other storage pests include the grain beetle (*Oryzaephilus surinamensis*) and the khapra beetle (*Trogoderma granarium*). Ambient storage temperature and humidity conditions and grain moisture content are critical factors influencing the extent of damage. Grain moisture content must be less than 10–12 per cent (Giles 1964a).

Damage to sorghum by Quelea (*Quelea quelea*) is a major problem particularly in the Sudan Savanna. At present no effective and economical technology exists for the control of Quelea (Crook and Ward 1968).

*Striga* is a semi-parasitic weed which can cause serious damage to sorghums. Only *S. hermontheca* and *S. senegalensis* have been reported in West Africa. *Striga* seed requires stimulation by root exudates from the host to germinate. However, the moisture content of the soil environment appears to have a considerable influence on *Striga* emergence (Ogborne 1972a). Although a moist pre-treatment is necessary for germination, *Striga* seeds appear to undergo dormancy during wet conditions. In the Savanna regions severe *Striga* emergence occurs towards the end of the rainy season when the local cultivars are heading and forming their yields. However, in early maturing cultivars *Striga* emergence often occurs earlier. Several different methods of control have been tried with varying degree of success. These include hand weeding, trap cropping, high fertility, foliar and soil active herbicides, and host resistance. Until very recently only hand weeding could be recommended to small farmers but now a foliar herbicide has been recommended: it must be directed at the weed with a cheap water pistol (Ogborne 1972b). Some pre-emergent herbicides for sole crop of sorghum have been shown to be promising but in crop mixture involving sorghum more specific herbicides are required. Host resistance appears promising in the future although the host-parasite relationship is not fully understood.

### 7.1.2 *Millet* (Pennisetum typhoides)

The crop is native to Africa and probably originated in the West African Savanna (Chevalier 1934, Stapf and Hubbard 1934). Millet in West Africa is grown primarily for grain for human consumption. The grain is ground into flour after removing the husk and mainly eaten as a porridge but some is malted and made into beer. Lustrous, grey or slate-blue, corneous, seeds are preferred for flour. The husk is fed to poultry while crop residues are used as building material, fuel and feed. Millet has been used successfully as a green manure and forage crop. Both short-season, nonphotoperiodic millet (Gero millet) and long-season photoperiodic millet (Maiwa millet) are grown, although the former is always dominant, probably accounting for about 80 per cent of the total area under millet (D. J. Andrews, personal communication 1975). Transplanted millet (Dauro millet), considered to be a specialized type of Maiwa, is also grown but on a very restricted scale. Maiwa millets are larger and taller (3–6 m) than Gero millets (1·5–3 m).

Estimated total production of millet in West Africa in 1971 was about 6·7m. tonnes from an area of about 11·5m. ha, corresponding to a yield of about 580 kg/ha. However, yield figures from individual countries vary between about 290 kg/ha in Mauritania and 690 kg/ha in Mali. Good experimental yields of local millets under improved practice is about 1–1·5 tonne/ha; those of improved millets about 2–2·5 tonne/ha in the Sudan and Southern Guinea Savanna, and about 2·5–3·5 tonne/ha in the Northern Guinea Savanna.

(a) *Ecology.* Millet is the most important cereal in the Sudan and Northern Guinea Savanna but it remains an important cereal in the Southern Guinea Savanna. Gero millets are of 75 to 100 days to maturity while Maiwa millets 120–280 days. Like the local sorghums, Maiwa millets appear to be adapted to flower at the end of the rains. At Samaru the date of heading in a Maiwa millet (ex-Mokwa) was linearly related to the date of sowing over an 8-week spread in sowing date. Each week's delay in sowing delayed the heading date by about one day. This effect, although small, can lead to decreases in yields when the crop is sown late or rains cease earlier than normal or both, for reasons similar to those explained in the case of photoperiodic sorghums. The main reason why the area under Maiwa millet is small is because Gero millet is higher yielding and produces a yield much more quickly. Also, farmers prefer to grow photoperiodic sorghums whose duration is similar to Maiwa millets but are higher yielding. However, on lighter soils farmers prefer to grow Maiwa millets rather than sorghums. Further, Maiwa millets mature slightly earlier than sorghum because of its shorter grain filling period; and this appears to enable the farmer to spread his labour demand for harvesting the late-season crops.

Gero millets are resistant to head mould attack and have a better ability to ripen good grain in wet conditions than Maiwa millets. Consequently, Gero millet is usually the first crop sown because the farmer's food supply is very low at the end of the dry season and he needs a crop as soon as ever possible. A 90-day Gero millet crop normally sown in May in the Northern Guinea Savanna therefore matures and is harvested in August, the wettest month, without a great deal of difficulty from pests and diseases.

The northern limit of millet in West Africa is around the 200–250 mm isohyets in the Sahel Savanna where sorghum can no longer be safely grown as a rain-fed crop. Here, millets of 55–65 days to maturity are grown. However, it is in the Sudan Savanna where millet reaches its greatest concentration, occupying equal status with sorghum. Agronomic and eco-physiological aspects of millet have been reviewed by Ferraris (1973). In general, millets are known to be well adapted to conditions of lighter soils, high temperature, and high solar radiation and can have a very high rate of growth and water use of efficiency for total dry matter under favourable rain-fed conditions (Begg, Bierhuizen, Lemon, Misra, Slatyer, and Stern 1964, Kassam 1972). Thus, Kassam and Kowal (1975) reported that total water used by an 85-day crop of Gero millet was 330 mm equivalent to water use of efficiency of 148 g water per g total dry weight. Furthermore, once the millet crop has established itself, it has a marked degree of drought endurance. Millet is grown on both light and heavy soils but it thrives best on light loams. Unlike sorghum it cannot tolerate waterlogged conditions. Millets are less susceptible to damage from stem-borers, *Striga* and weeds but they suffer badly from bird attack.

Millets in general are able to take up large quantities of nutrients because of their high growth potential. However, as a grain crop, local millets are inefficient users of nutrients because of the low harvest index. There is a very large scope for improving millet for intensive grain and forage production. Indeed crop improvement research in West Africa, particularly in Senegal, has achieved a large measure of success in breeding high yielding dwarf cultivars which can utilize nutrients more efficiently. These experimental cultivars have a harvest index of 40–50 per cent and mature in 75–100 days (Bilquez 1970, Jacquinot 1970, Etasse 1970, OSTROM-IRAT 1970–71). An improved recommended cultivar yielding 3130 kg/ha in the West African Savanna has been reported to remove N, 132 kg/ha, P, 27·5 kg/ha; K, 65 kg/ha; Ca, 56 kg/ha (IRAT 1972) which is greater than for an equivalent yield of maize.

(b) *Cultivation*. Millet is grown as a rain-fed crop and the indigenous practice is to sow it as early as possible in the wet season although some is sown dry followed by transplanting or second sowing to fill the gaps. Seeds are sown on the flat and occasionally ridged later or in the furrows. Nearly all the Gero millet is sown in mixture with other crops in 2–5 crop combinations involving late millet, sorghum, cowpea, groundnut. Maiwa millet is sown as a sole crop to some extent and about 28 per cent of the total area under Maiwa millet was found to be sole crop millet in village studies in the Guinea Savanna (Norman 1972). On the light soils, in mixtures, millet is sown in the furrow between the ridges sown to sorghum (Fig. 7.1) but on heavy soils it is often sown on ridges with sorghum in the furrows. The spacing is generally about 1–2 × 1 m while the stand population for Gero millet varies between 7500–8500 per ha in 2–4 crop combinations and 7000 per ha in 5 crop combinations (Norman 1972); and for Maiwa millet between about 8500 per ha when grown sole and 5800 per ha in 3–4 crop combinations. Gero millet is harvested in July and August in the Guinea Savanna and August and September in the Sudan Savanna, while Maiwa millets are harvested in the dry season before the harvest of the sorghum crop. Because of heavy basal tillering, generally two or more harvests are taken. The grain to head weight ratio is about 50-60 per cent while the harvest index is 10-20 per cent.

Improved Gero millets as sole crops are sown when the rains are established. Treated seeds are sown at spacings of 0·1-0·3 × 0·45-0·90 m, depending on the cultivar and days to maturity. Tall Maiwa millet and semi-tall Gero millet cultivars are generally sown at a density of 40-80 000 plant/ha while with dwarf Gero millet cultivars over 100 000 plant/ha or more are necessary. Responses to nutrients vary from area to area but for yields over 2·5-3·0 tonne/ha, experimental rates of 60-125 kg/ha of N and 15-35 kg/ha of P are applied. Harvest index of improved Gero millets is 20-35 per cent. Improved Gero millets show extra yield advantages when grown in mixtures with sorghum under high management and yield advantages of up to 80 per cent have been reported (Kassam and Stockinger 1973, Andrews 1972a, Baker 1974).

(a) *Diseases and pests.* At present general disease and pest problems in millet are relatively minor in the Savanna areas (Sauger *et al.* 1970, King, S.B. 1970a, 1970b). Green ear (*Sclerospora graminicola*), a downy mildew, is the most serious disease of millet although susceptibility of a cultivar varies considerably with environmental conditions. In Nigeria average yield losses in Gero millet are reported to be about 10 per cent. Maiwa millet seem to be less severely attacked by the disease, though yield losses of about 8 per cent have been reported. However, downy mildew occurs almost annually in some parts of West Africa and it is not uncommon to find symptoms on 50 per cent of the plants in a farmer's field. Symptoms of downy mildew are extremely variable but infection generally becomes systemic and infected plants commonly show both foliar and green ear symptoms. The primary source of downy mildew inoculum is apparently soil-borne oospores which enter through roots. Leaves of infected plants are generally pale in colour and sporangia appear on the surfaces of leaves. The importance of sporangia in spreading the pathogen from one plant to another is not clearly understood but sporangia are not considered to be as important in infection as are oospores. Environmental conditions, particularly during the first few weeks of plant growth, greatly influence the incidence of the disease, and high atmospheric humidity greatly favours infection. The only practical way to control downy mildew is through the development of resistant cultivars and sources of tolerance and resistance have been reported. Grain smut (*Tolyposporium penicillariae*) is a common disease, but it is not of economic importance at present although it can be serious on occasions. The primary source of inoculum is the sporidia produced by spore balls surviving in the soil. Sporidia become air-borne and infection occurs through the flowers, which are most susceptible immediately before stigmas emerge. The fungus grows in the ovary and as the head matures the fungal spore-sacs are produced. Some or all the grains on the head are replaced by shiny green smut spore-sacs, which are usually larger than the grain and have smooth rounded apex. As the millet head matures, the spore-sac membranes become brown and brittle, and can be easily broken to reveal the black smut spores. Many of the spores adhere tightly to form spore-balls. Smut is commonly found at the lower portion of those heads which do not fully emerge from the flag leaf. Little can be done at present to control this disease but strict sanitary measures can help in its control. Ergot (*Claviceps microcephala*) commonly occurs in millet but the incidence is generally not of economic significance. Infection occurs through the flowers. The primary source of inoculum is believed to be soil-borne sclerotia which produce air-borne spores during the month of July. Insects are important in spreading spores produced duing the honey-dew phase of the disease from one spike to another. The fungus grows inside the grain and produces sclerotia of purple to black in colour. Cultural practice of timely sowing, use of cultivars with synchronous heading and burning infected heads do help in its control but no effective control measure exists at present. Other diseases include the rust (*Puccinia penniseti*) which occasionally becomes severe on late millet but is usually not found on early millet, leaf spots (*Gleocercospora* spp., *Pyricularia* spp., *Cercospora* spp.) which are commonly observed, and the stem rot (*Fusarium moniliforme*). However, these diseases are unimportant at present.

Normally pest damage to pearl millet is minimal. However, Coutin and Harris (1968) have reported that the millet grain midge (*Geromyia penniseti*) is widely distributed in the Savanna areas, and has the potential of becoming a serious pest. Further, since the abnormally low rainfall period of 1971–73, a lepidopterous insect, *Masalia* sp., has become very common throughout the northern Savanna areas, and has been reported from Nigeria, Niger, Upper Volta, and Senegal. This pest causes severe damage to the panicle.

In store, the usual cereal pests, *Sitotroga cerealella* and the small strain of *Sitophilus oryzae*, can be very damaging if storage is prolonged.

Damage to millet by Quelea is a major problem, particularly in the Sudan Savanna.

Millet is attacked by *Striga* but the extent of attack and losses are not as serious as in sorghum. Gero millet generally escapes *Striga* attack as it is harvested during the wettest part of the rainy season when *Striga* seeds undergo dormancy. However, *Striga* attack on Maiwa millet is comparatively greater.

### 7.1.3  Maize (Zea mays)

Central America is considered to be the origin of this crop which reached West Africa probably during the early sixteenth century. It appears that the hard-seeded flint types were introduced into West Africa from the north across the Sahara while the soft-seeded, flour types came from South America (Porteres 1955). At present maize reaches its greatest concentration in the humid Forest areas and Derived Savanna areas of West Africa. The lack of a high-yeilding cereal which could be grown more extensively than rice in the Forest and southern Savanna areas, and historical reasons, resulted in research work being concentrated early on growing maize in the Forest areas of West Africa. In the north, maize has never become a major grain crop because of the importance of sorghum and millet in the Guinea and Sudan Savanna. Local land races in the Savanna areas are grown in backyards or close to the houses as a garden crop, in upland field, and in the lowland *fadama* areas. Maize grown in the Forest areas is largely consumed green on the cob as a vegetable while in the Savanna areas it is made into flour and consumed as a thick paste. Maize has been used successfully for silage in the Savanna areas (Couper and de Leeuw

1971, Couper 1972, Haggar and Couper 1972) while elsewhere in the world maize has a wide variety of uses. Full accounts of various aspects of the crop are available (Berger 1962, Aldrich and Leng 1965, Miracle 1966, Cunard 1967, Milbourn 1971).

Production figures for the Savanna areas alone are not available. Estimated total production of maize in West Africa both in the Savanna and Forest areas in 1971 was about 2·7m. tonnes from an area of about 3·4m. ha, corresponding to a yield of about 800 kg/ha. However, yield figures for individual countries vary between about 500 kg/ha in Dahomey (Benin) and 1100 kg/ha in Ghana. Under local practice yields are larger in the Forest and Derived Savanna areas than in the Guinea and Sudan Savanna. However, under improved practice at high fertility highest yields are obtained in the Guinea Savanna: yields in the Sudan and Derived Savanna and Forest areas are lower by 30–50 per cent than those in the Guinea Savanna (Kassam *et al.* 1975a). Good experimental yields of maize are 3–4 tonne/ha in the Sudan and Derived Savanna and 5–8 tonne/ha in the Guinea Savanna (Craig 1967–72, Webster 1969, Tatum 1971, IITA 1973a), although experimental yields of 10 tonne/ha or more are commonly obtained in the Northern Guinea Savanna.

(a) *Ecology.* Production of maize in the Savanna areas is expanding and it promises to replace a considerable portion of the current area under sorghum where moisture supply is dependable. Research has shown that the environment in the Savanna areas is suitable for intensive production of maize and recently considerable effort has been made in popularizing maize as a grain crop in the Guinea and Sudan Savanna where sorghum is normally grown. Major reasons for this are:

(i) Average experimental yields of maize in the Savanna area are consistently greater by two to three times than the average experimental yields of improved cultivars of sorghum and millet.

(ii) Experiments in the Guinea Savanna have shown that the yield potential of maize is much greater than that of either sorghum and millet; yields of 8–10 tonne/ha or more have been obtained with maize in the Guinea Savanna, whereas 4–5 tonne/ha appear to be the maximum yield obtainable from improved millet and long-season sorghum. (It appears that the theoretical yield potential of short-season, nonphotoperiodic sorghum is just as high as that of maize. However, the low quality of grain, lack of resistance to head mould and shoot-fly, and difficulties with sowing and harvesting under wet conditions make it unacceptable at present as an alternative sorghum grain crop.)

(iii) Maize ears are protected by the husk against insects and from damage by rain during the ripening period.

(iv) Maize is resistant to bird damage.

The main reason for higher yields in the Guinea Savanna is because the pattern of water requirement of maize matches the pattern of water availability better than the long-season sorghum or millet (Kassam *et al.* 1975a). However, short-season sorghum of similar growth cycle with harvest index of 40–50 per cent is likely to produce a performance similar to that of maize and would not have to rely on residual soil moisture at the end of the season for grain filling.

Short-season millet, although maturing before the end of the rains, produces lower yields because of its shorter growth duration and lower harvest index. In the low-altitude Guinea Savanna areas 110–120 days growth cycle appears to be adequate to produce the highest yields. No advantage is obtained with cultivars having a longer growth cycle. Yields are lower in cultivars with growth cycles of less than 100 days, and this is one of the reasons why relative yields of maize in the Sudan Savanna are lower than in the Guinea Savanna. However, in the Derived Savanna and Forest areas yields are lower than in the Guinea Savanna because the rainfall pattern is bimodal, solar radiation receipts during the growing season are 20–30 per cent lower, the incidence of pests and diseases is greater, and night temperatures are high leading to greater respiratory losses and poor dry matter distribution and harvest index. For example, at Ibadan on the Forest/Derived Savanna border the annual rainfall is about 1140 mm spread over 9 months from March to November in a bimodal pattern resulting in a two crop season. The first season is long enough for 120-day maize crop but the balance between crop water requirement and water availability is tight with consequent periodic water stress. In the second season crop water requirement can be met without high soil moisture deficits only for 80–90 days. A 120-day maize crop therefore suffers severe water stress during the grain filling period. On the other hand, at Samaru in the Northern Guinea Savanna the annual rainfall is about 1120 mm spread over 5 months from May to September in a unimodal pattern. Once the rains are established, precipitation soon exceeds crop water requirement and water requirement of a 120-day maize is fully met (Kowal and Kassam 1973a, Kassam *et al*. 1975a).

Local land races in the Savanna areas vary in days to maturity between 80 and 140 days. Some of these have been found to have retained their high yield potential under local practices because they have been grown under relatively higher soil fertility. In the Guinea Savanna 90–100 day local maize has produced over 6 tonne/ha under improved practice (Andrews 1972b, E. F. I. Baker, unpublished 1975) while early hybrids from local maize and early U.S. maize have produced yields of 7 tonne/ha in 90 days (Andrews 1972b). In the Sudan Savanna 80-day local maize have produced 3–4 tonne/ha (Barry, King, Stockinger, and Kassam 1973). Improved maize produces higher yields but breeding efforts so far have concentrated more on adapted types for the Guinea Savanna than the Sudan Savanna, so that high yielding maize adapted to Sudan Savanna conditions has yet to be bred.

Maize is considered to be either a short-day or day-neutral plant (van Eijnattan 1965). Date of sowing has been shown to have a great influence on yields of maize in West Africa (van Eijnattan 1965, Akinbode 1966, de Geus 1970, Koli 1970, Jones and Stockinger 1972, Stockinger 1972). In the Northern Guinea Savanna yields decrease if sowing is after about mid-June. Sowing in May either shows no advantage or lower yields depending on the rainfall conditions, than sowing during early to mid-June. Later sowing results in a decrease in cob number per plant, number of grains per cob and grain size. Eco-physiological causes behind this date of sowing effect are not clearly understood. But van Eijnattan (1965) found that tasselling was earlier when the crop was sown earlier, and although there was significant negative correlation between tasselling time and minimum temperature both at Ibadan and Samaru, the significance of this in relation to the sowing date effect on yield could not be established either in terms of daylength or temperature. At Samaru, Jones and Stockinger (1972) found that before silking there was no significant difference in the cob number per plant and the number of potential seeds on each cob at different sowing dates. However, both the number of cobs and seed number per cob at maturity decreased in later sowings. Further, total dry weight did not differ significantly with sowing date. They therefore concluded that the yield decrease with lateness of sowing seemed to be related to conditions at or subsequent to silking; and in addition to poor soil moisture conditions during grain filling due to late sowing, other factors such as poor pollination or inefficient transfer of dry matter to the cob probably as a result of an imbalance in the minor nutrient status in the plant may be involved. Generally, leaf concentrations of iron and manganese have been found to increase in maize with decreasing soil aeration, as a result of waterlogging or a high water table (Lal and Taylor 1970). However, in the study of Jones and Stockinger (1972) minor nutrient availability including those of iron and manganese decreased with later sowing indicating perhaps that excess moisture was not the cause of declining yields at Samaru. On the other hand in East Africa the date of sowing effect often seems to be associated with the rainfall pattern and water stress (Semb and Garberg 1969). However, at Kitale in Western Kenya, A. Y. Allan (1970) found that a date of planting effect existed even when rainfall was not limiting, and under these circumstances poor yields from later sown crops were related to excess moisture and impeded growth in the early stages of growth. However, Allan's (1970) hypothesis was not based on actual measurement of soil aeration, and later work by Cooper (1975) has shown that at Kitale the aeration status of the soil under young maize never reaches critical levels, even for late planted maize. Other work by Cooper (1974) and Law (1974) at Kitale suggests that the natural seasonal variation in soil temperature may be the primary factor responsible for the observed reduction in yield of late planted maize. In the Sudan Savanna where the growing season is shorter and matches the crop growth cycle tightly, the delay in sowing causes yield losses principally due to a shortage of water during silking and grain filling. The reproductive processes and parts of maize are more sensitive to water stress than those of sorghum and millet. High temperatures and water stress at tasselling and silking result in pollen being shed before the silks are receptive, or in the death of the tassel and drying out of silk. This defect is one of the major reasons for poor yields of maize in the Sudan Savanna in years with a mid-season drought despite a high total dry matter production in such years. There is some evidence that an adequate boron nutrition is necessary for good pollination in hot and dry conditions.

Maize can be grown on a wide range of soil types but it prefers well drained loams. Maize can be grown successfully on soil with $p$H ranging from 5–8. With soil of low fertility, maize often fails to produce a yield, unlike sorghum and millet. High yields of maize are not possible without adequate nutrition. Response to fertilizer varies from area to area (Goldsworthy 1968) but a crop yielding 5440 kg/ha in Senegal has been reported to remove N, 138 kg/ha; P, 28 kg/ha; K, 95 kg/ha; Ca, 11 kg/ha (IRAT 1972). Growth and nutrient uptake in maize have been described by Hanway (1965).

Total crop water use of a 120-day maize between sowing and harvest in the Guinea Savanna has been reported to be 486 mm corresponding to crop water use efficiency of 253 g water per g total matter (Kowal and Kassam 1973a). Eco-physiological aspects of growth and yield in maize have been reviewed by Duncan (1975).

(b) *Cultivation.* Maize is grown as a rain-fed crop but in the *fadama* areas it may rely on residual soil moisture in the dry season. The local practice on the upland areas is to sow it as early as possible but after millet and sorghum have been sown. In the *fadama* areas it is generally sown after sugar cane either when the latter fails to establish or after it has been harvested. Maize is grown as a sole crop as well as in mixtures and the proportion of the area under each varies considerably. In village studies in the Northern Guinea Savanna about 27 per cent of total area under maize was found to be grown sole while about 70 per cent under 2–4 crop mixtures and about 3 per cent under 5–6 crop mixtures (Norman 1972). Maize is intercropped with a large variety of crops including cereals, legumes, vegetables, root crops, and cotton. In the *fadama* areas it is commonly intercropped with rice. It is sown on ridges particularly in the *fadama* areas or on the flat. When grown sole (Fig. 7.1) it is sown at a sapcing of about 0·45–0·80 × 0·90 m while the stand population varies between about 14 000 and 24 000 per ha. In mixtures, it is sown at a variety of spacing depending on the crops involved and local practice. For example in the maize/rice intercrop (Fig. 7.1) the crop is sown on the flat at spacings in the range 0·25–0·45 × 0·75–1·7 m (about 35 000–48 000 stands/ha). Harvest time varies with area, sowing date, and cultivar, and generally it is harvested after millet but before sorghum. The late sown crop in the *fadama* areas is harvested in the dry season. The grain to head weight ratio is about 75–80 per cent while the harvest index is about 25–35 per cent.

Improved maize cultivars are sown when the rains have established. Treated seeds are sown at a spacing of about 0·3 × 0·7–1·0 m, corresponding to plant densities of about 30–50 000 plants/ha. Responses to nutrients vary from area to area but for yields over 5 tonne/ha in the Guinea Savanna, experimental rates of 100–175 kg/ha of N and 25–65 kg/ha of P are applied. In the Sudan Savanna for yields over 3 tonne/ha, experimental rates of 60–120 kg/ha of N and 17–44 kg/ha of P are applied. Harvest index of improved cultivars is 40–50 per cent.

Extra yield advantages have been shown to accrue in maize when intercropped under improved management and increases up to 40 per cent have been recorded depending on the cultivar and crop combination (Baker 1974).

(c) *Diseases and pests.* Rust (*Puccinia sorghi*) is indigenous to West Africa but causes little damage. *P. polysora*, a rust of Central American origin caused considerable damage in the fifties (Cammack 1953, 1956a, 1956b, 1958a, 1958b) but it is not a serious problem at present as improved cultivars have adequate resistance. Corn smut (*Ustilago maydis*) and head smut (*Sphacelotheca reiliana*) are not serious and generally localized. Leaf blight (*Helminthosporium maydis*) is widespread and has been known to cause considerable damage in the southern humid areas (Cammack 1956a). Sources of genetic resistance to blight are available. Leaf spot (*Physoderma* spp.) is not serious but can become so under continuous cropping. Streak virus disease transmitted by leaf-hopper (*Cicadulina* spp.) has become more serious in recent years. The incidence varies from year to year and area to area but recently in northern Nigeria fields with 40–50 per cent infected plants have been observed. Other diseases of maize in West Africa have been discussed by van Eijnattan (1965).

The most important pests of stored maize are the grain moth (*Sitotroga cerealella*), the grain beetle (*Oryzaephilus surinamensis*) and the grain weevil (*Sitophilus oryzae*).

Maize is attacked by *Striga* and improved cultivars are very susceptible. Further, *Striga* can cause serious damage in maize before it emerges above the soil surface.

### 7.1.4  *Rice* (Oryza sativa)

Rice of the species *O. glabberima* has been cultivated for centuries in the West African Savanna. However, much of the present rice is derived from strains of *O. sativa* introduced from Asia. *O. glabberima* and *O. sativa* closely resemble each other and are both considered to have a common ancestor. The consumption of rice is increasing in the Savanna areas and the total area under rice is probably greater than the area under maize. Rice is usually cooked by boiling in water while the crop residues are used as feed. It has been reported (NAS 1974) that non-paddy rice in West Africa accounts for at least two thirds of the total area under rice. Production and yield figures for non-paddy rice are not available. However, Norman (1972) reports average yields of about 500 kg/ha and 357 kg/ha for sole crop and mixed crop respectively for non-paddy rice in the *fadama* areas in the Guinea Savanna while Bourke (1965) reports yields between 700–1000 kg/ha for the flood plains of rivers in the Sudan and Sahel Savanna. Estimated total production of paddy rice in West Africa in 1971 was about 1·87m. tonnes from an area of about 1·55m. ha, corresponding to a yield of about 1200 kg/ha. Yield figures from individual countries vary between 800 kg/ha in Cameroon and 1700 kg/ha in Nigeria. If non-paddy rice is two thirds of the total area under rice then its area would appear to be just over 3m. ha. At a yield of 500 kg/ha, its production would be about 1·5m. tonnes which together with the similar average total production of paddy rice amount to more than that of maize. Yield potential of local strains of rice is low under improved practices (Porter 1964). However, improved cultivars of paddy rice under proper management have produced over 8 tonne/ha in the dry season and 6–7 tonne/ha in the rainy season while upland cultivars 3–4 tonne/ha (de Geus 1970, IITA 1973a). Recently, at Kou Valley near Bobo-Dioulasso in the Northern Guinea Savanna in Upper Volta three crops of paddy rice per year grown on a large scale have produced yields of 12–14 tonne/ha. Similar yields have also been reported from Ghana (Kowal 1962). General accounts on rice as a world crop are given by Grist (1965) and Purseglove (1975).

(a) *Ecology.* Rice in the Savanna areas is grown as a non-paddy crop in the upland areas and in the *fadama* areas with a high water table, as a paddy crop in the *fadama* areas and on the river banks which are seasonally flooded, and in paddies in which rainfall or irrigation water is impounded, while floating rice is grown on a restricted scale. Rice has a high degree of plasticity to the ecological conditions in the Savanna areas, but the chief limiting factor to its growth is the water supply which is the major factor influencing yields of upland rice during the wet season. Yields of paddy rice are higher in the dry season than in the wet season because of higher solar radiation and lesser pest problems. In the Sudan Savanna low temperatures during the dry season can lead to retarded seedling devleopment and head sterility.

Success in paddy cultivation depends greatly on how well the water supply is controlled. Paddy crops relying on rainfall are greatly influenced by the variation in rainfall characteristics. Similarly, paddy crops on flood plains of rivers where water supply is largely uncontrolled are always vulnerable. High yields are only possible when the water supply is adequate and under controlled management. The eco-physiological basis of yield in paddy rice has been recently reviewed by Murata and Matsushima (1975). Rice breeding has led to the development of erect-leaved, short-strawed, heavy tillering cultivars (Tanaka, Yamaguchi, Shimazaki, and Shibata 1968, Ito and Hayashi 1969, Chandler 1969). These make a more efficient use of solar radiation and nutrients with minimum lodging.

Rice is grown on many types of soil but heavy alluvial soils of river valleys are better suited than lighter soils. Heavier soils permit better puddling for paddy cultivation and greater return per unit of water and nutrients supplied as losses are relatively smaller compared to those on lighter soils. Optimum $pH$ for paddy rice appears to be about 7 but upland rice will perform satisfactorily at 5–6 while on black soils where conditions are alkaline, paddy rice performs satisfactorily under $pH$ of 8–9.

The soil conditions in paddy fields have been described by Grist (1965) and Russell (1973). Nitrogen is fixed by blue-green algae and the autotrophic bacteria in the soil and rhizosphere. Although the exact amounts are not known, it appears that in good paddy soils in Asia these sources of nitrogen are adequate to maintain yields of rice at low levels almost indefinitely. To what extent this is true for West Africa is not clear. However, for high yields adequate nutrition is essential. Improved photoinsensitive cultivars of paddy rice have been reported to remove N, 19 kg/ha; P, 4·3 kg/ha; K, 47 kg/ha; Ca, 7·2 kg/ha; Mg, 5·3 kg/ha; Fe, 2·6 kg/ha; Mn, 2·6 kg/ha; Si, 178 kg/ha for each 1 tonne of yield (IRII 1963) while rain-fed rice crops in Senegal have been reported to remove N, 24 kg/ha; P, 5·2 kg/ha; K, 28 kg/ha; Ca, 7 kg/ha for each 1 tonne of yield (IRAT 1972).

Some of the local cultivars of rice appear to be photoperiodic and flower under short days. Little is known about their adaptability to daylength in Savanna areas. High-yielding, improved cultivars are nonphotoperiodic and allow sequential cropping when water is available.

(b) *Cultivation.* Under indigenous practice dryland rice in the upland areas or non-paddy rice in the *fadama* areas is cultivated in a manner similar to other rain-fed cereals. In village studies in the Guinea Savanna, about 73 per cent of the rain-fed rice was found to be grown as sole crop. The remaining was grown in 2–4 crop mixtures involving late millet, sorghum, and groundnut on the upland areas and maize, yam, and sweet potato in the *fadama* areas (Norman 1972). Sole crop non-paddy rice is sown at various spacings (Fig. 7.1) while the stand population varies in the range of 94 000–430 000 per ha. The seed is often broadcast at the rate of about 50 kg/ha to provide similar plant populations. In mixtures, various spacings are used (Norman 1972). For example, average stand population in the rice/maize mixture is about 47 000–240 000 per ha (Fig. 7.1). Sowing is done when the rains are established in May or June, for harvesting in September or October. In the *fadama* areas a second crop or a dry-season crop is often grown; seeds are sown in nurseries in September or October and seedlings are transplanted in November. On average the crop is in the ground for 120–160 days depending on the region.

Paddy rice in the flood plains and *fadama* areas depend on both rainfall and flooding during the rainy season and gradual drying-off at the end of the rains. The times of sowing and transplanting vary according to the region and the time of the highest floods. The rice fields and paddies remain flooded during the rainy season from June to September or October. Paddy rice grown under irrigation under local practice is sown in March and harvested in July and August and the next crop is sown in September for harvesting in January. Here nonphoto-periodic cultivars of 120–140 days to maturity are used. For paddy rice in some areas, a wet nursery is a common method followed by transplanting when seedlings are 25–50 days old while in other areas direct sowing of pre-germinated seed is common. Little or no fertilizer is used under indigenous practice. Harvest index and grain to head weight ratio under local practice is 10–20 per cent and 65 per cent respectively.

For high yields paddy rice must be grown under controlled irrigation conditions with proper nutrition. Maturity in the high yielding cultivars varies between 90–120 days and three crops per year are possible with transplanted or pre-germinated rice. These cultivars have a harvest index of 40–50 per cent and grain to head weight ratio of 70–75 per cent. For yields over 4 tonne/ha experimental rates of about 60–125 kg/ha N and 17–39 kg/ha P are applied. However, in cultivars where the grain ripens before the straw is dry, mechanical harvesting has often been difficult while the necessity of rapid drying of grain after harvesting for safe storage can be a real constraint in the wet season.

(c) *Diseases and pests.* Diseases of rice in West Africa have been reported by Williams and Abifarin (1973) and R. J. Williams (1973a), and Ou (1972) has presented a fuller account of rice diseases. Blast (*Pyricularia oryzae*) is one of the most serious diseases of rice. As it is both seed and air-borne, seed treatment provides only a partial control. Chemical control is effective but not economic at low levels of production. Recently tests conducted by IITA at the International Blast Nursery in Sierra Leone have produced a number of promising resistant types. However, it appears that new physiologic races are continually evolving and immunity based on the action of single genes is therefore likely to be shortlived. For example, of the 104 lines which were immune at IITA in 1970, only 15 remained immune in 1971 (Williams, R. J. 1973a). Cultivars with quite a high degree of what appears to be horizontal resistance have been developed but these have relatively low yield ceiling, with poor plant type and poor grain quality. The brown leaf spot (*Cochliobolus miyabeanus*) may cause considerable damage in cooler season or when there is a nutrient deficiency or in soils in a much reduced condition in which toxic substances accumulate (Ou 1972). However, the disease is not serious at present and is not likely to be an important disease in adequately fertilized rice. Sources of resistance to brown leaf spot have been found but as the disease is seed-borne, seed treatment assists in control. Leaf scale (*Rhynchosporium oryzae*) was first observed in Nigeria in 1969; and subsequently observed in Ivory Coast in 1970 and Ghana in 1971 (Lamey and Williams 1972). Leaf scald has shown the potential to spread rapidly and be as destructive as the blast disease. The occurrence of leaf scald is not as widespread as the blast disease, however, and periods of rapid spread of leaf scald are frequently interrupted by periods of almost no spread. Narrow brown leaf spot (*Cerospora oryzae*) is common but not serious. Cultivars resistant to it exist. Other rice diseases encountered in West Africa are false smut (*Ustilaginoidea virens*), bakanae (*Gibberella fujikuroi*), stackburn disease (*Trichoconis padwickii*), sheath blight (*Corticium sasakii*) and white tip (*Aphelenchoides besseyi*). These are not serious diseases.

Stem-borers (*Chilo zacconius, Sesamia calamitis*), white-borers (*Maliarpha separatella*) and stalk-eyed flies (*Diopsis thoracica, D. apicalis*) are serious insect pests of rice in West Africa. Recently at IITA sources of resistance have been isolated while chemical control under experimental conditions has been effective. Some cultivars with a high silica content in the stem have considerable resistance to borers. Other insect pests are considered minor and these include cotton stainers (*Dysdercus superstitiosus*), coreid bugs (*Leptocorisa* spp. *Mirperus dentipes*), green shield bugs (*Nezara viridula*), spittle bugs (*Locris maculata*), mole crickets (*Gryllotalpa africana*), shield bugs (*Aspavia armigera*) and stem beetles (*Heteronychus oryzae*).

The most serious damage in storage is caused by the rice weevil (*Sitophilus oryzae*), the grain-borer (*Rhizopertha dominica*), the grain beetle (*Oryzaephilus surinamensis*), the grain moth (*Sitotroga cerealella*) and the khapre beetle (*Trogoderma granarium*).

Damage to rice by *Quelea quelea* is a major problem and damage by rodents can be serious.

The most serious weeds of paddy rice are the hydrophyte grasses and species of *Cyperus* but perennial grasses such as *Paspalum* spp., *Echinochola pyramidalis* can become persistent. Cultural and chemical methods for control of these grasses have been described by Bullen (1971). In upland rice *Striga* has become a serious problem in some areas.

### 7.1.5  *Wheat* (Triticum aestivum)

Wheat (*Triticum* spp.) has been traditionally cultivated in the Sahel and Sudan Savanna and around the shores of Lake Chad for unknown length of time, but certainly for centuries. Cultivars used under indigenous practice were introduced from North Africa and these have been grown on dry season irrigated gardens, usually on bunds between beds and on the edges of irrigation channels (Curtis 1965, Andrews 1968, 1969). Production of local wheat is very small, the grain being sold in the local markets as a luxury product. The type of wheat which has been grown locally, known as 'Ble de Kanem', closely resembles a durum wheat (*T. durum*) but cytological investigation (Zeven, 1974) has shown it to be a hexaploid bread wheat (*T. aestivum*). The grain is used for making bread and during the last two decades there has been a rapid increase in the consumption of bread in the Savanna areas. Since 1960, locations have been developed in the northern Savanna areas to grow wheat under irrigation in the dry season.

Estimated total production of wheat in 1971 was about 19 000 tonnes from an area of about 12 000 ha, corresponding to a yield of about 1600 kg/ha although yield figures from individual countries vary between 900 and 2500 kg/ha. Some local wheat cultivars have the ability to produce good yields and over 4 tonne/ha have been recorded on a field scale (Andrews 1968) but they are susceptible to stem and leaf rusts. Improved cultivars including the Mexican wheats from CIMMYT have a higher yield potential and some carry resistance to many sources of stem rust. Yields of over 5 tonne/ha have been obtained with improved cultivars in northern Nigeria (Andrews 1972c, Andrews and Palmer 1972).

(a) *Ecology.* The eco-physiological basis of growth and yield in wheat has been recently reviewed by Evans, Wardlaw, and Fischer (1975). Wheat requires cool weather during the tillering and early growth stages. These conditions are met during the months of November and December in the Sudan and Sahel Savanna. During this time humidity ranges 0–10 per cent, day temperatures 32–38°C and night temperatures 8–15°C. Also, a constant wind (Harmattan) blows from the north-east and this, coupled with the very low humidity, lowers the surface temperatures of the soil to about 4°C.

Time of sowing has a strong effect on yield and the best time to sow is early in the dry season—late October or November—so that the crop matures in the coolest months—January and February. The reason for decrease in yield when sowing is delayed is partly eco-physiological (J. L. Palmer, personal communication 1974) and partly because of severe incidence of diseases particularly stem rust (Andrews 1968).

Wheat can be grown on a variety of soils but prefers soils with reasonable drainage. However, in West Africa some of the areas selected for irrigated wheat production are near the rivers and on black soils with a high clay content and poor drainage. These areas are likely to create problems with alkalinity and salinity if drainage is not managed properly

(b) *Cultivation.* At the start of the dry season the ground is cultivated by hand hoeing. Beds for flood irrigation are formed and fertilizer is commonly broadcast just before sowing. The seed is commonly broadcast at rates between 90 and 135 kg/ha. Clumps of seeds in hills spaced 25–30 cm on the square may be sown on sites where weed problem is severe but clump sowing reduces the yield potential. A subsidized cultivation, sowing, and fertilizing operation by tractor can be purchased by farmers in some areas in northern Nigeria. Irrigations (4–5 cm) are given once every week or 10 days. Harvesting and threshing are done by hand.

For yields over 4 tonne/ha, experimental rates of 60–125 kg/ha N and 17–39 kg/ha of P are applied. At these levels of fertility, local cultivars lodge badly.

Along the shores of Lake Chad in the Republic of Chad wheat is grown in the recesses in the shore line (D. J. Andrews, personal communication, 1976). Because of the undulating shore line, water flows into the lower areas forming recesses where *Papyrus* grows freely. After a few years of growth, the water is impounded. Surface water is lost through evaporation and the dead *Papyrus* provides a large amount of organic matter which may be up to 45 per cent in the surface soil. Wheat is grown for a number of years until yields decline when the cycle is started again by letting water in.

(c) *Diseases and pests.* The stem rust (*Puccinia graminis*) is one of the most destructive diseases of wheat and has appeared in West Africa particularly in 1962–64 causing up to 70 per cent of crop losses in some areas. A large number of physiological races are found and new races appear to be continually evolving. Early sowing avoids much of the infection but where the infection comes from is not known. Wheat is not sown in the wet season and alternate hosts have not been found. The attacks do not occur annually and this suggests that the rust may be brought in by the prevailing northeasterly winds (Andrews 1968). Brown leaf rust (*Puccinia recondita*) is frequently recorded, mostly on late sown crops but it does not cause serious losses.

At present there are no serious insect pest problems in wheat in the field while storage pests have not been studied in any detail.

## 7.2  Legumes

### 7.2.1  *Cowpea* (Vigna unguiculata)

Cowpea, probably domesticated in Ethiopia (Steele 1972) is the major grain legume crop in the West African Savanna, serving as both cash and food crop. It is exported from Savanna areas to the Forest areas in the south (Oyenuga 1967, Gilbert 1969). Estimated total production of cowpea in 1971 in Mauritania, Niger, Nigeria, Senegal, and Upper Volta was about 1·1m. tonnes from an area of about 4·6m. ha, corresponding to a yield of about 240 kg/ha. Yield figures from individual countries vary between 220 kg/ha in Nigeria and 550 kg/ha in Niger. Good experimental yields of improved cultivars under improved management in the Savanna areas are between 1·5–2·5 tonne/ha of grain and yields over 3 tonne/ha have been obtained in the Guinea Savanna. Summerfield, Huxley, and Steele (1974) have reviewed the current status of this crop.

(a) *Ecology.* Cowpea is considered to be either a short-day or day-neutral plant (Steele 1964). The seed yield is largely dependent on the total number of nodes produced before the onset of flowering and the number of pods subsequently produced and retained at these nodes. The absolute size of plants at first flower and hence the number of nodes produced, is mainly dependent upon the extent to which cultivars are sensitive to night temperature and/or daylength. According to Summerfield (1975a) higher night temperatures in photoperiodic and nonphotoperiodic cultivars and/or longer daylength in photoperiodic cultivars result in greater vegetative growth rates and larger plants at the time of first flower. Day temperatures experienced in the Savanna areas have little effect. Photoperiodic plants flower earlier in shorter days while high temperature can drastically hasten the onset of flowering in both photoperiodic and nonphotoperiodic plants. Consequently, the effects of longer days in delaying flowering in photoperiodic plants and the higher night temperatures in hastening can in some cases almost exactly offset one another. High day temperatures, despite having little effect on vegetative growth and time to first flower, can reduce grain yield after flowering has begun. Leaves senesce much faster in warmer days and the duration and efficiency of grain filling is considerably reduced. Under warmer day and night temperatures the abscission of young peduncles and flower buds is increased considerably.

Plants with effective nodules do not appear to show significant increase in seed yields from application of nitrogen. Under controlled conditions nodulated plants grown without nitrogen have produced yields only 10 per cent less than non-nodulated plants supplied with nitrogen equivalent to 480 kg/ha (Summerfield 1975b).

Cultivars vary in maturity between 80 and 160 days or more. Improved cultivars with erect and determinate growth habit do produce a high yield within 80–100 days and two or more harvests may be taken. Local cultivars are generally photoperiod sensitive, and late maturing with spreading and indeterminate growth habit, and therefore are more adapted to the lower light intensities in the intercrop canopies under local practice where crops in mixtures are largely superimposed on each other (Norman 1972). With an early maturing cultivar of indeterminate growth habit two or more harvests are taken. Yields of cowpea are drastically reduced when intercropped with sorghum and millet, and the relative yield reduction compared to sole crop is greater in upright cultivars than in spreading cultivars. Yields may be reduced by as much as 75 per cent of that obtained when grown sole, but generally yield reductions are between 45–55 per cent (Andrews 1972a). However, cowpea as an intercrop in the indigenous practice is a bonus crop in a number of mixtures where it is undersown late and does not reduce yields of the standing crops. Further, without chemical control of pests sole crop cowpea generally fails to produce a yield whereas intercropped cowpea without chemical control of pests produces about 25–50 per cent of the yield.

In the southern parts where the growing season is long two crops of cowpea are grown. However it is not known with certainty whether the cultivars grown as the first crop are truly day-neutral types or whether they are in fact short-day photoperiodic types but appear insensitive to daylength because of the interaction between the effect of long days in delaying flowering and the effect of high night temperature in hastening it (R. I. Summerfield, personal communication 1977).

Cowpea is grown under a wide range of soil and climate conditions in the Savanna areas, and can tolerate hot and relatively dry conditions in the Sudan Savanna. It prefers well drained soils and will perform satisfactorily on acid soils. A crop yielding 1·5 tonne/ha removes about N, 85 kg/ha; P, 6·5 kg/ha; K, 25 kg/ha.

(b) *Cultivation.* Cowpea is rarely grown as a sole crop in the indigenous practice. It is generally grown in mixtures of 2–6 crop combinations involving sorghum, millet, maize, groundnut, cotton, and root crops (Norman 1972).

Without chemical control of insects, sole crop cowpea produces very low yields, but when grown in mixture with other crops, the incidence of pests is drastically reduced and a higher yield is obtained. The spacing varies greatly (Fig. 7.1) depending on the crop mixture (Norman 1972) and stand population varies between 6000 and 7500 per ha. Sowing time under local practice varies with region. In the Sudan and Northern Guinea Savanna it is undersown in July or August and harvested in November and December. In the Southern Guinea and Derived Savanna it is sown in April or May and harvested in August or it is sown in September and harvested in November and December. However, in the Sudan Savanna a dry season crop is grown in the *fadama* areas where it is sown in December and harvested in March or April. Pods are harvested and threshed by hand.

Sole cropping of cowpea with improved cultivars requires chemical control of pests for the high yield potential to be realized (Booker 1965, Raheja and Hays 1975). The crop is sown on ridges or on the flat at a spacing of about 0·15–0·3 × 0·75–1·0 m, (30 000–90 000 plants/ha). In the Sudan and Northern Guinea Savanna the crop is sown in June or July while in the Southern Guinea and Derived Savanna April or May for the early crop and August or September for the late crop. For yields over 1·5 tonne/ha, experimental rates of 15–30 kg/ha P are applied to the crop. A starter dose of 5–10 kg/ha N has been found beneficial for crop establishment prior to the development of effective nodules.

(c) *Diseases and pests.* The fungal, bacterial, and viral diseases of cowpea in Nigeria are described with information on their importance and control by R. J. Williams (1975a). In general, problems in cowpea are greater in the Derived and Southern Guinea Savanna than in the areas further north.

The major seedling pathogens are *Pythium aphanidermatum* and *Corticium solani*. Both pre- and post-emergence mortality occur. At the beginning of the rains when the soil has been hot and dry for several months and rainfall is sporadic the incidence is low; whereas during the cool, wet, overcast weather in the June to September period the incidence is high (Williams, R. J. 1975b). It appears unlikely that resistance can be found to these unspecialized soil-borne pathogens at the seeding stage. Seed treatment with fungicides provides effective control. Other principal fungal diseases are *Septoria* leaf spot (*Septoria vignae*), *Cercospora* leaf spot (*Cercospora canescens, C. cruenta*), rust (*Uromyces appendiculatus*), stem rot (*Pythium aphanidermatum*) and *Corynespora* leaf spot or target spot (*Corynespora cassiicala*). Sources of resistance to *Septoria* leaf spot, *Cercospora* leaf spots and rust are known. Chemical control of these fungal diseases is effective. Pod and seed mould (*Aspergillus flavus*) can be serious in cowpea which matures in the wet season. Other fungal diseases of minor importance in the Savanna areas are web blight (*Corticium solani*), powdery mildew (*Erysiphe polygoni*), stem rot (*Corticum rolfsii*), premature senescence (*Rhizoctonia bataticola*), zonate leaf spot (*Dactuliophora tarrii*), and lambs-tail pod rot (*Choanephora infundibulifera*).

Two most important bacterial diseases of cowpea in Nigeria (Williams, R. J. 1975a) are bacterial pustule (*Xanthomonas* spp.) and bacterial blight (*Xanthomonas vignicola*). Many lines immune to bacterial pustule have been identified and cultivars resistant to bacterial blight exist.

The effect of viral diseases can be devastating in cowpea and they remain a major constraint to large scale cowpea production particularly in the southern Savanna areas (Williams, R. J. 1975a). Yellow mosaic virus, transmitted by a leaf-eating beetle (*Ootheca mutabilis*), is common and can be serious. It has also been reported that several other insects including two thrips (*Sericothrips occipitalis* and *Taeniothrips sjostedti*), the chrysomelid beetle (*Paraluperodes quaternus*), the curculionid beetle (*Nematocerus acerbus*) and two grasshoppers (*Cantatops spissus spissus* and *Zonocerus variegatus*) are capable of transmitting cowpea yellow mosaic virus (Whitney and Glimer 1974). Possible methods of control include vector control with insecticides, and the use of resistant varieties. Sources of resistance have been identified (Williams, R. J. 1975a). Cowpea mottle virus is another important virus (Robertson 1963a) whose effect on the yield of susceptible cultivars can be of the same order as that due to cowpea yellow mosaic virus (Williams, R. J. 1975a). Tolerant cultivars do exist and tolerance appears to be dominant to susceptibility (Bliss and Robertson 1971). Cowpea aphid-borne mosaic virus was reported by Raheja and Leleji (1974) in cowpea grown under irrigation. The virus is transmitted by an aphid (*Aphis craccivora*). Crop losses can be high and for irrigated crop it is of great potential importance to cowpea production in the Savanna areas. Bean southern mosaic virus has been recently reported (Shoyinka 1974) but its importance remains to be determined.

*Maruca testulalis* is the major pest of cowpea in the Savanna areas. It attacks both flowers and pods, causing them to drop. Yield losses of 70–80 per cent have been reported (Booker 1965, Raheja 1974). Coreid bugs (*Acanthomia brevirostris, A. horrida, Anoplocnemis curvipes* and *Mirperus jaculus*) are serious pests. They feed on green pods, causing them to shrivel and dry prematurely. *Piezotrachelus varium* damages the seeds within the pod and losses can be high. *Ootheca mutabilis*, a leaf-eating beetle, can cause yield losses when young plants are attacked by a very large population. Normally, plants are able to withstand a considerable degree of defoliation without adverse effect. Stem girdler (*Alcidodes leucogrammus*) can cause yield losses when present in large numbers but it is not usually serious (Raheja 1975). Chemical control of most of the insect pests is effective and economical under improved practice (Raheja and Hays 1975).

Losses in storage are generally very high. The most important pests are the beetles (*Callosobruchus maculatus* and *Bruchidius atrolineatus*). These insects are present in cowpea fields at harvest and delay in harvest is one of the reasons for heavy losses in storage under local practice (Caswell 1968). Cowpea stored in shell suffers less damage than when stored threshed.

### 7.2.2 Groundnut (Arachis hypogaea)

Groundnut is of South American origin. It is the major cash crop in the West African Savanna and reaches its greatest concentration in the Sudan and Northern Guinea Savanna. It is also an important part of the diet and is consumed in stews, roasted meat preparations, and as roasted or boiled kernels, while groundnut oil is used in cooking. Local oil pressing mills recently set up in the Savanna areas are increasingly absorbing a considerable proportion of the current produc-

tion. Internal and export trade therefore involves kernels including confection-
ary types, oil, and cake. Crop residues are used mainly as feed. Estimated total
production of groundnut in shell in the West African Savanna was about 3·2m
tonnes from an area of about 4·5m. ha, corresponding to a yield of about 710
kg/ha or about 500 kg/ha of kernel at a shelling percentage of 70. Pod yields
from individual countries vary from just over 1 tonne/ha (700 kg/ha of kernel)
in Ghana and Cameroon to 400 kg/ha (280 kg/ha of kernel) in Togo. Good
experimental yields of improved cultivars with proper management and pest
control are about 3–3·5 tonne/ha of kernel while 4 tonne/ha have been obtained
in the Sudan Savanna and over 5 tonne/ha in the Northern Guinea Savanna
(Rotimi 1970, C. Harkness, personal communiction 1975, Kassam *et al.* 1976).
Crop culture and uses have been described by APREA (1973) while Sigafus
(1973) has briefly reviewed the current worldwide status of the crop.

(a) *Ecology*. Groundnut is generally considered to be a day-neutral plant
although some work suggests that sensitivity to daylength depends on temperature (Wynne, Emery, and Downs 1973). However, daylength is not a critical factor influencing yields and in the Savanna areas the number of days to first flower
is largely independent of the daylength and depends on the cultivar. Two broad
groups of groundnut cultivars are grown in West Africa. These are the alternately
branched cultivars belonging to the Virginia and Castle Cary Group (subspecies
*Hypogaea*), and the sequentially branched cultivars belonging to the Spanish and
Valencia Group (subspecies *fastigiata*) (Bunting 1955, 1958, Gibbons, Bunting,
and Smartt 1972). The alternately branched cultivars vary in maturity from
120–145 days while the sequentially branched cultivars from 90–105 days.
Hybrids between these two types have produced promising cultivars with
115–120 days to maturity (C. Harkness, unpublished).

Detailed studies on the influence of temperature on groundnut have been
conducted by de Beer (1963) who found that a temperature of 28 °C may be
considered as an optimum, whereas below 24 °C or above 33 °C growth and
development is adversely affected. By altering the temperature from 24 °C to
33 °C and vice versa at various stages during the development of the plant,
it was shown that vegetative growth and flowering were complements in development; in combination, however, they constitute an opposing factor to fruit
development. The temperature during the vegetative phase of development
has little or no influence on the later reproductive development, but the rate of
flowering and some flower characteristics, e.g., length of hypanthium, pollen
viability, is greatly influenced by temperature during the flowering stage.
Groundnut plants flower abundantly at 38 °C, but they produce very few pods,
and de Beer (1963) found that at high temperatures smaller quantities of pollen
are produced and set free and those produced have a low viability. Further, the
hypanthia are longer and the distance the pollen tube has to travel in order to
effect fertilization is therefore longer. However, pollen character was not
seriously influenced by the temperature during the day of flowering, but by the
temperature 36–96 hours before the opening of the flowers. Boron was found
essential in production of active pollen.

The development of the groundnut fruit has been described by Schenk

(1961). Pod yield per unit area depends on the number of pods per unit area and weight per pod. The number of pods depends on the proportion of total flowers which produce pegs and pods within the time available for filling, while the rate of pod growth and development to mature kernel depends on the supply of carbon. Therefore, although yield in a given cultivar depends on pod number and weight, these yield components in themselves do not determine yield *per se*. The eco-physiological factors which control the pattern and intensity of flower production, fertilization, and survival on the one hand and the flow of carbon to support peg and pod growth on the other determine yield. High yields are obtained when a favourable balance is achieved between the early, concentrated, establishment by the plant of flowering nodes which can contribute to yield and the subsequent photosynthetic capacity to supply and develop them. In terms of supply of photosynthates yields in the Savanna areas are severely limited by *Cercospora* leaf spot leading to premature loss of leaf area. Large yield increases are obtained by spraying against the disease. The extra yield in a given cultivar is largely accounted for by more pods per stand and to a lesser extent by increased kernel weight (Elston, Harkness, and McDonald 1976). Sequentially branched cultivars have been found to produce higher yields with leaf spot control than do the alternately branched cultivars. Studies on high-yielding cultivars in the Sudan and Guinea Savanna (C. Harkness, also O. Rotimi, also A. H. Kassam and C. Harkness, all unpublished) have indicated some of the differences in the flowering pattern and components of yield which are responsible for the present difference in yield between the sequentially and alternately branched cultivars (Table 7.1).

In general breeders in the past have concentrated on exploiting local and exotic germplasm by selection (mass and single plant) rather than hybridization. Indeed, considerable progress has been made by this method. For example, the cultivars Samaru 38 and Samaru 61 recommended in northern Nigeria were improved through pedigree selection from local material. However, further progress in yield and resistance to pest and diseases in the future is likely to come from hybridization of the subspecies *fastigiata* and *hypogaea*. In northern Nigeria selections made from such crosses have shown considerable promise. The results from a trial conducted at Samaru in 1973, a dry year with earlier than normal cessation of rains, to compare the performance of cultivars from *fastigiata, hypogaea* and intervarietal crosses between the subspecies are shown in Table 7.1. The crop was lifted after 107 days from sowing. Although highest yields were obtained from T47-56 and Spanish 205, the intervarietal selections F439.4 and F452.4 outyielded Samaru 38 and Samaru 61.

Groundnut crop is relatively more difficult to produce in the Derived and Southern Guinea Savanna than in the areas further north because of the greater incidence of pests and diseases particularly *Cercospora* leaf spot, the aphid-borne rosette virus disease and aflatoxin produced by the *Aspergillus flavus* fungus. For the Savanna region as a whole, good and clean crops are produced when the crops mature as the rains are ending. If the crop ripens too soon before the end of the rains, the wet harvest leads to problems with aflatoxin and drying of pods. If the crop ripens after the end of the rains, it experiences water stress at the critical stage in the last two or three weeks during pod filling (Kowal and

## Table 7.1

*Flower production, yield, and yield components in groundnut cultivars with sequential, intermediate, and alternate branching habit in 1973 at Samaru, northern Nigeria (A. H. Kassam and C. Harkness, unpublished)*

| Type | Sequential | | Intermediate | | Alternate | |
|---|---|---|---|---|---|---|
| Cultivar | T47-56 | Spanish 205 | F439.4 | F452.4 | Samaru 61 | Samaru 38 |
| Normal days to maturity | 90–100 | 95–105 | 115 | 115–120 | 120 | 120 |
| Days to first flower | 27 | 27 | 34 | 34 | 34 | 34 |
| Flowering period (days) | 67 | 67 | 56 | 56 | 63 | 63 |
| Total flowers produced/stand | 273 | 371 | 231 | 233 | 229 | 247 |
| Pegs/stand | 168 | 200 | 166 | 157 | 180 | 181 |
| Pegs as % of total flowers | 62 | 54 | 72 | 68 | 79 | 74 |
| Pod bearing pegs/stand | 93 | 146 | 103 | 111 | 98 | 95 |
| Pod bearing pegs as % of total flowers | 34 | 39 | 45 | 48 | 43 | 38 |
| Pegs without pods | 75 | 54 | 63 | 46 | 82 | 86 |
| Pegs without pods as % of total flowers | 28 | 15 | 28 | 20 | 36 | 35 |
| % flowers not producing pegs | 39 | 46 | 28 | 33 | 21 | 26 |
| Days after sowing to produce 50% of total flowers | 46 | 53 | 60 | 61 | 63 | 64 |
| Days after start of flowering to produce 50% of total flowers | 18 | 26 | 26 | 27 | 29 | 30 |
| Days after sowing to produce flowers equal to total peg number | 48 | 56 | 70 | 68 | 77 | 74 |
| Days after start of flowering to produce flowers equal to total peg number | 21 | 29 | 36 | 34 | 43 | 40 |
| Days after sowing to produce flowers equal to total pod numbers | 42 | 48 | 56 | 60 | 61 | 58 |
| Days after start of flowering to produce flowers equal to total pod number | 15 | 21 | 24 | 26 | 27 | 24 |
| Pod yield (kg/ha) | 5425 | 4961 | 5071 | 4660 | 4085 | 3775 |
| Kernel yield (kg/ha) | 3727 | 3397 | 3191 | 2856 | 2612 | 2497 |
| Shelling % | 69 | 69 | 61 | 61 | 64 | 66 |
| Harvest index (%) | 35·0 | 32·4 | 29·3 | 24·7 | 24·1 | 20·5 |
| Kernel weight/stand (g) | 78 | 71 | 67 | 60 | 55 | 52 |
| Kernel number/stand | 231· | 225 | 192 | 125 | 167 | 165 |
| Weight/kernel (g) | 0·337 | 0·315 | 0·349 | 0·375 | 0·328 | 0·316 |
| Kernel number/pod | 2·49 | 1·54 | 1·72 | 1·55 | 1·69 | 1·74 |

Kassam 1973b, C. Harkness, unpublished). Crop water use of a 120-day ground-nut crop in the Northern Guinea Savanna has been reported to be about 440 mm corresponding to crop water use efficiency of about 520 g water per g total dry matter (Kassam *et al.* 1975b).

A large number of trials on fertilizer including minor and trace elements have been conducted on groundnut in West Africa (Gillier and Prevot 1960, Bockelee-Morvan 1963-6, 1968, Goldsworthy and Heathcote 1963, Evelyne and Thornton 1964, Goldsworthy 1964, Meredith 1964, Gusten 1965). Although response varies in different regions with cultivar, ridge or flat planting, spacing and population, adequate phosphorus, calcium, and sulphur is essential for good yields and except for nitrogen, deficiencies of other elements are likely to be-come important under long-term intensive cultivation. Nutrient uptake has been studied by Gillier (1964, 1966) and Thornton (1964), and mineral removal by the crop for each tonne of pod yield is generally N, 51-63 kg/ha; P, 3·9-4·8 kg/ha, K, 17-21 kg/ha; Ca, 8-11 kg/ha (FAO 1965, IRAT 1972) while a crop yielding 2·5 tonne/ha of pods and 5 tonne/ha of tops has been reported to remove N 157 kg/ha; P, 12 kg/ha; K, 96 kg/ha; Ca, 47 kg/ha; Mg, 20 kg/ha (Godin and Spensley 1971).

The most suitable soils for groundnut are the well drained, light sandy loams. Soil which crust or cap easily can lead to difficulty with peg penetration. Groundnut tolerates a wide range of *p*H but prefers slightly acid soils. Ground-nut does not tolerate waterlogging and in heavier soils harvesting is more diffi-cult as the soil sticks to the pods.

(b) *Cultivation.* Small farmers under indigenous practice sow much of the crop in mixture of 2-6 crop combinations involving millet, sorghum, cowpea, cotton, vegetables, and even root crops. However, the most common mixtures involve millet, sorghum, and cowpea. In village studies in the Northern Guinea Savanna about 16 per cent of the total area under groundnut was in sole crop while about 70 per cent was in 2-4 crop mixtures (Norman 1972). On the other hand a much larger proportion of the groundnut crop in Senegal, where it occu-pies about 45 per cent of the total cultivated area, is grown sole. Spacing under local practice varies greatly particularly in mixtures (Fig. 7.1). The crop is largely sown on ridges. Under sole cropping the spacing is about 0·3-0·4 × 1·0 m while the stand population is about 28 000 per ha. In mixtures, ridges are about 1 m apart while the stand population is about 33 000 per ha. In the northern Guinea and Sudan Savanna the crop is sown in June and harvested in September or October. In the Southern Guinea and Derived Savanna two crops are often taken, the first crop being sown in April or May and harvested in August while the second crop is sown in August or September and harvested in November. Local cultivars and improved recommended cultivars grown under indigenous practice are the alternately branched types which have some tolerance to *Cerco-spora* disease.

Groundnut when grown in mixtures with sorghum, millet and maize produces lower yields per stand because of shading. The local practice is to keep the cereal population low, about 3000-6000 stands/ha, and raise the population of ground-nut. In village studies stand populations of groundnut in sole crops were found to be about 28 000 per ha while those in mixture about 33 000 per ha. Respective yields per stand were about 21 g and 14 g while yields were 587 kg/ha and 438 kg/ha, a reduction of about 25 per cent (Norman 1972). However, an application of fertilizer to mixtures with groundnut in local practice has given yield increases of about 45 per cent compared to groundnut in the unfertilized mixtures (Norman, Buntjer and Goddard 1970). Despite the decrease in yield in groundnut, mixtures involving groundnut and cereals still produce a greater total yield/ha per season than one sole crop, both in the indigenous practice, and in experiments at higher levels of management. In intercropping experiments with improved cultivars at several population densities, groundnut grown with maize or sorghum has shown reduced yields but again total production in the mixtures were greater than those of the respective sole crops. With sorghum, reduction in yields were smaller with dwarf cultivars than tall cultivars (J. L. Palmer, unpublished results, 1967–72).

Sole cropping of groundnut with improved cultivars, both sequentially and alternately branched types, requires chemical control of *Cercospora* for the high yield potential to be realized (McDonald 1970a). However, yields of 1·5–2·5 tonne/ha are possible with the alternately branched cultivars without *Cercospora* control. This is not possible with the sequentially branched types which are highly susceptible to the disease. The crop is sown on ridges at a spacing of about 0·15–0·25 × 0·6–0·9 m (45 000–110 000 plants/ha). For alternately branched types 45 000–60 000 plants/ha are adequate to produce high yields but higher plant population is desirable for the sequentially branched types. With square sowing on the flat, greater yields are possible with higher plant populations particularly with the sequentially branched types which have produced maximum yields at plant populations of 200 000 plants/ha or more with *Cercospora* control (Rotimi 1970).

For yields over 2·5 tonne/ha, experimental rates of 17–35 kg/ha P are applied. Calcium deficiency can cause seriously low yields due to 'blind nuts'. A crop with effective nodules can supply all the nitrogen required for high yields.

(c) *Diseases and pests.* Pest control in groundnut as a world crop is given in Feakin (1973). A wide range of soil-inhabiting fungi are capable of causing disease in groundnut (McDonald 1968, 1969, 1970b, c, d). Some are known as casual agents of wilt and stem and root rots (e.g., *Sclerotium rolfsii, Rhizoctonia bataticola, Pseudomonas solanacearum*) while others attack the pod. Fungi which infect shells and kernels are of great importance as they reduce the quality of crop produce rendering it toxic and unacceptable for export and human consumption. Aflatoxin (*Aspergillus flavus*) and concealed damage (*Macrophomina phaseoli* and *Botryodiplodia theobromae*) are the most serious problems. Moisture content of the fruit and the environment is the most important factor in the development of these diseases. According to McDonald (1968) simple means of reducing the chance of fungal infection of fruits include cultural practices aimed at use of seed treatment and prevention of disease in the growing crop, timing of harvest to avoid inclusion of too many over-mature fruits, and rapid post-harvest drying of the pods and kernels. Investigations by McDonald and Harkness (1963) have shown that harvested pods are virtually free from aflatoxin toxicity except when pods are broken or damaged. Slow drying of moist pods and kernels is particularly conducive to fungal growth and Burrell, Grundey and Harkness (1964) have shown that rapid and complete drying of pods prevents their growth. Leaf spot (*Cercospora arachidicola, C. personata* and *C. canescens*) is the major foliar disease of great economic importance. For example, in northern Nigeria losses up to 60 per cent have been estimated from disease control trials (Fowler 1970) and it is probable that no rain-fed crop or even plant remains free of these diseases. The alternately branched cultivars are more tolerant to leaf spot than the sequentially branched cultivars but genetic resistance does not seem promising. Chemical control of *Cercospora* is effective and economical under improved practice (Fowler and McDonald 1975). Resistance to *Cercospora* has been found in wild groundnut species but its inclusion into adapted types has not yet been possible. Rosette virus is another serious disease particularly in the Derived and Southern Guinea Savanna (Hayes 1932, Porterçs and Leglęu 1937, Greenwood 1951, Tourte and Fauche 1954, Booker 1963, A'Brook 1964, 1968, Hull 1969). The vector is *Aphis craccivora* and the principal host of the vector during the dry season is *Euphorbia hirta*. The infected plant is severely stunted and leaves are chlorotic and mottled (Storey and Ryland 1955, 1957). The level of infection is less at higher plant populations and late sowing results in greater infection. High seed rate and early sowing have therefore been recommended in much of Africa as a standard control measure (Storey and Bottomley 1928, Hayes 1932, Soyer 1939, Evans, A. C. 1954). Work conducted in East Africa has shown that chemical control of the vector is effective (Davies and Kasule 1964, Davies, J. C. 1975a, b). Studies conducted on the relationships between plant density and rosette disease incidence under sprayed and unsprayed conditions in Uganda (Davies, J. C. 1970) have shown that during growth the number and percentage of plants showing symptoms of rosette disease was significantly greater at low plant densities under sprayed and unsprayed conditions. At harvest the numbers attacked in unsprayed plots were still greater at low plant densities but in sprayed plots the number of plants attacked was greater at high densities although the percentage of plants attacked was higher at low densities. Plant density did not affect quality of the groundnuts obtained, but yields were highest under both sprayed and unsprayed conditions at the highest plant densities. Resistance to rosette has been found in wild and cultivated species. In Senegal resistant cultivars have been developed subsequent to the discovery of the sources of resistance (Daniel and Berchoux 1965).

Except for the *A. craccivora* which feeds on young leaves and stems, and spreads the rosette virus, no serious insect pests attacks the groundnut crop. However, fruit damage by millipede (*Peridontopyge* spp.) has been reported while termites have been known to cause premature death of plants (Perry 1967).

Groundnut is seriously affected by pests in store. The groundnut bruchid (*Caryedon fuscus*) is important in that it causes severe damage to nuts in shell. Both the khapra beetle (*Trogoderma granarium*) and the flour beetle (*Tribolium castaneum*) attack nuts which have been shelled.

### 7.2.3 *Soya bean* (Glycine max)

This crop is thought to be of Asian origin. Attempts to introduce and extend the cultivation of the crop in the West African Savanna have met with limited success. However, there appears to be a good potential for soya bean in the Guinea and Derived Savanna. At present, the crop is grown to some extent, largely in northern Nigeria where the total annual production is about 15 000 tonnes covering an area of about 53 000 ha. This corresponds to a yield of about 280 kg/ha. Experimental yields of 2·5–3·0 tonne/ha have been obtained with improved cultivars under proper management in the Derived and Guinea Savanna, and over 3 tonne/ha has been obtained by IITA (1973b). A recent account of improvement, production, and uses of soya bean is given in Caldwell (1973).

(a) *Ecology*. The eco-physiological basis of yield in soya bean has been reviewed by Shibles, Anderson, and Gibson (1975). Soya bean is considered to be either a short-day or day neutral plant. The seed yield is largely dependent on the total number of nodes produced before the onset of flowering and the number of pods subsequently produced and retained at these nodes. The effects of temperature and daylength on seed yield in soya bean are similar to those in cowpea (Summerfield 1975a). Similarly, plants with effective nodules under adequate nutrition can meet the nitrogen requirement for high yields (Summerfield 1975b) although often responses to nitrogen application have been obtained in different parts of the tropics. Recently, Kang (1975) in Nigeria found that inoculation alone was inadequate to supply the nitrogen need of the crop, 30 kg/ha of N being needed with inoculation, and 60 kg/ha of N without inoculation for maximum yield. However, the strain of *Rhizobium japonicum* is specific to soya bean, so that inoculation is essential when the crop is grown in a new area.

Cultivars vary in maturity between 80 and 180 days or more. However, high yields can be produced with improved, nonphotoperiodic, cultivars in 90–110 days. Cultivars presently grown are photoperiodic and late maturing. Work in Nigeria in the Guinea Savanna has shown that sowing date has a strong effect on yield. In the nonphotoperiodic cultivars, the effect of later sowing on yield is less marked unless the sowing is delayed to the extent that the crop has to mature partly or completely on the residual moisture in the soil at the end of the wet season. In the photoperiodic cultivars, delay in sowing results in a smaller plant at the time of first flower and fewer pod-bearing nodes. Further, the crop matures under relatively worse soil moisture conditions when sowing is delayed until July or August, in the Northern Guinea Savanna.

Soya bean can be grown on a wide range of soil types but sandy or clay loams with high calcium content are preferred. Optimum $pH$ is in the range 5·7–6·2. Response to fertilizer depends on the cultivar and plant population but little work has been conducted on fertilizer requirements under intensive production in the West African Savanna. However, responses to phosphorus and sulphur have been reported (Goldsworthy and Heathcote 1964) while nutrient removal for 1 tonne/ha of yield has been reported to be N, 60 kg/ha; P, 15 kg/ha; K, 67 kg/ha (Godin and Spensley 1971).

(b) *Cultivation*. With improved cultivars of 90–110 days to maturity, high yields are obtained when the crop is sown at a population of 140 000–300 000 plants/ha or more and square planting produces slightly greater yields than rectangular planting. Yields in the range 2–3 tonne/ha have been obtained at spacings of 0·07–0·10 × 0·45–0·75 m. In the Northern Guinea Savanna, the crop should be sown in June, for harvesting in September. In the Southern Guinea and Derived Savanna two crops are possible with crops sown in April and May and again in August or September. For high yields experimental rates of 15–30 kg/ha of P are applied.

(c) *Diseases and pests.* At present soya bean crops in the Savanna areas are relatively free from diseases and insects although damage by leaf-hoppers (*Empoasca* spp.) and pod borer (*Laspeyresia ptychora*) has been reported. Chemical control of these pests is effective.

### 7.3  Roots and tubers
*7.3.1  Cassava* (Manihot esculenta)

Cassava is of South American origin and was introduced into West Africa in the sixteenth century. Initially it was grown in the Forest areas but since the turn of this century it has been slowly moving into the Savanna areas. More recently it has become a common crop in the Northern Guinea and Sudan Savanna in areas of high population density. The cassava plant has many uses and it is grown as a source of carbohydrate and consumed in a variety of ways (Oyenuga 1967, Irvine 1974). Estimated total production of cassava in West Africa in 1971 was about 16m. tonnes from an area of about 1·93m. ha, corresponding to a yield of about 8·3 tonne/ha fresh tubers. Production figures for the Savanna areas are not available but in northern Nigeria the crop is estimated to occupy about 0·5 per cent of the total cultivated area. Yields in the Forest areas are about 9·5–10 tonne/ha, and in the Savanna areas, about 5–8 tonne/ha. Local cultivars have a low yield potential under improved practice, although improved local cultivars have produced experimental yields of 15–25 tonne/ha of fresh tubers or about 4·6–8·1 tonne/ha of dry yield in 12 month period (Ekandem 1965, IITA 1973c). Improved long season cultivars can produce 40–50 tonne/ha of fresh tuber in 18–24 months. Recently, crop improvement research at CIAT and IITA has achieved a large measure of success and experimental yields of 25–30 tonne/ha in 7 months (Wholey and Cock 1974) and 40–50 tonne/ha in 10–12 months have been obtained with improved cultivars. Kay (1973) has reviewed the status of cassava while Jennings (1970) and Coursey and Haynes (1970) have discussed the potential of cassava in Africa and the tropics.

(a) *Ecology.* The growth period of cassava is generally from 9–24 months depending on the cultivar and growing conditions. Normally, cassava is considered to be a long-term root crop which can be harvested between nine months and two years, depending on whether the roots are to be consumed as a fresh vegetable or processed for flour or starch. A few quick-growing cultivars can be harvested in 6–7 months, but good yields are normally obtained after 9–12 months. When utilized as a vegetable the tubers are harvested within 12 months, otherwise they become very fibrous. For processing they are left to reach full maturity, 18–24 months after planting.

Cassava appears to be a highly plastic plant and is grown in the Savanna areas with rainfall of 800 mm and above. In the West African Savanna, cassava reaches its major concentration·in the Southern Guinea Savanna. Cassava is a hardy plant with a marked degree of drought endurance and can endure hot and dry conditions once it is established. Indeed, the crop under indigenous practice survives the dry season when it sheds all its leaves except the top few and resumes growth rapidly as the rains begin the following season. Optimum mean temperature conditions for cassava are in the range 25–29°C. Growth stops at mean temperatures below 10°C while yields are reduced at mean temperatures above 29°C. Cassava grows best on sandy or sandy loam soils but will perform satisfactorily on any soil with pH of 5–9 provided it is not saline, and not waterlogged. When grown on heavy clay soils, the plant produces stem and leaf growth at the expense of the roots and many cultivars give poor yields.

Cassava is a short-day plant and less productive of tuberous roots in daylengths greater than 10–12 hr. Both the number of days to flower and the height to branching decrease with decreasing daylength but there is a certain minimum vegetative growth requirement for flowring to be induced which varies with cultivars (IITA 1973c). Flowering appears to be associated with yield and yields are lower in non-flowering plants. Short-days are required for tuberization (Bolhuis 1966) and there is some evidence that tuberization is stimulated by low temperature (Arraudeau 1967). C. N. Williams (1974) has discussed the process of tuberization in cassava. Tuberization is the result of a change in the nature of the differentiation of xylem cells in the secondarily thickened roots and involves the change from lignified xylem cells to parenchymatous xylem cells. This change is probably affected by the supply of assimilates and a hormonal factor which could suppress lignification and promote cell differentiation, the hormone (probably IAA) being transported from the tops under short-day conditions.

Studies on yield components, tuber weight and tuber number, in three high, medium, and low yielding cultivars by C. N. Williams (1972, 1974) have indicated that tuber size contributes most to the differences in yield and the diameter of the tubers, rather than their length, is the main yield component. Wholey and Cock (1974) studying the onset and rate of root bulking found that the differences in the root yield in the cultivars studied were caused by the variations in rate of root bulking, and were not associated with differences in onset of root bulking, which occurred during the second month of growth. Root growth studies (Williams, C. N. 1974) have shown that bulking rate and canopy assimilation are strongly connected, since differences in assimilation and bulking rate could not be accounted for by properties of the assimilation apparatus alone. Radial expansion of the storage cells, and the deposition of starch within them, appears to be the centre of sink activity which affects assimilation and bulking rate. Further, there is a strong internal competition for assimilates within the root system itself at the time of onset of bulking, since tuberization brings about a slowing down or cessation of growth in root length. However, tuberization does not reduce the growth of the stem, which forms an alternative sink for assimilates during tuber filling.

On the whole, relatively little crop improvement research has been conducted on cassava until very recently. Local cultivars have a low yield potential under improved practice mainly because' high fertility results in excessive vegetative growth. Improved local cultivars produce higher yields but again these have a low harvest index (20–30 per cent) and long growing period. In the last 6–8 years research into changing the plant structure and developmental pattern has produced cultivars responsive to fertilizer at high plant densities. These cultivars produce a higher yield more rapidly and have a higher harvest index (40–60 per cent). One of the major difficulties in achieving longer and higher rates of tuber filling has been the short duration of active life of leaves. For Savanna areas, short duration (5–8 months) cultivars with high root bulking rates are needed. These are likely to become available in the future and may have a good potential as a both food and cash crop because tubers and tops can be used for purposes other than for human consumption. The main advantage of cassava in the indigenous cropping pattern is that the crop can be grown with little labour while the tubers can be kept in the ground until required. Cassava can tolerate soils of low fertility better than yams and other food crops, especially if the feeder roots can penetrate to depths of 40–60 cm or more. Further, cassava plays an important role in the local diet during periods of seasonal food shortage; and in a year with poor and erratic rainfall or severe attack from locust, cassava has proved to be the most valuable famine reserve crop. It is likely that cassava can be introduced into the northern parts of the Sudan Savanna and the southern parts of the Sahel Savanna in the *fadama* areas as a famine reserve crop. However, there is acute shortage of domestic water in these areas and cassava with very low HCN content, which require minimum washing, will be needed.

(b) *Cultivation.* Cassava under local practice is grown both as a sole crop and in mixtue of 2–6 crop combinations involving sorghum, maize, groundnut, cowpea, yam, sweet potato, vegetables, and kenaf. In the village studies in the Northern Guinea Savanna about 65 per cent of the cassava crop was found to be sole crop while about 30 per cent in 2–3 crop mixtures (Norman 1972). The common spacing of the sole crop is $0.45–0.7 \times 0.9–1.1$ m, equivalent to about 13 000–24 000 plants per ha at one plant/stand (Fig. 7.1). In mixture the spacing is wider. Cassava is planted on ridges and on the flat but ridge planting is more common. Cuttings of about 20–30 cm long are inserted for about half their height often at an angle of 30–45 degrees. Cuttings sprout after 7–14 days after planting while root bulking begins during the second month after planting (Doku 1969). The time of rapid bulking varies depending on the time of planting. Under local practice, planting and harvest dates vary considerably. The crop is planted either in May to June and harvested the following September to December, or planted in late September to December and harvested the following October to December, although some is harvested before. Cassava is more popular than yam in the northern Savanna areas because it requires less labour and produces a greater yield in relatively poor soils.

For intensive production of short-season cassava, early planting at higher fertility will be required. Work elsewhere has shown that a yield of 40 tonne/ha at a harvest index of 50 per cent removes about N, 285 kg/ha; P, 57 kg/ha; K, 383 kg/ha; and Ca, 161 kg/ha. Cassava has a high requirement of potash, otherwise yields are very much reduced and the tubers have a low starch content and higher HCN content.

Harvesting is done by digging up the tubers by hand after detopping the plant. With large scale production they can be mechanically ploughed up, but yields are often reduced because a higher percentage of tubers is left in the ground. The difficulty with machine harvesting is because tubers are spread 120 cm or more and their depth of penetration in the soil is 45–60 cm. Once harvested, the tubers deteriorate rapidly and begin to rot after 48 hours. Coating with a fungicidal wax has been found to extend the storage life to at least 16 days while cold storage at 0–2°C and 85–90 per cent relative humidity has been reported to extend the storage life for periods up to six months.

(c) *Diseases and pests.* Leaf mosaic, a virus disease, is the most serious disease of cassava (Williams, R. J. 1973b). It can be spread by infected cuttings. It is transmitted by vectors of white flies (*Bemisia* sp.), probably *B. tabaci*. Genetic resistance appears promising at present. Bacterial blight, a new and potentially disastrous disease, was first identified in West Africa in 1972 (Williams, Agboola, and Schneider 1973). It appears that resistance to cassava bacterial blight is associated with resistance to cassava mosaic disease (IITA 1972–73). Root disease known as white thread (*Fomes lignosus*) has been reported to cause losses of 20 per cent or more in Ghana. Other minor diseases are brown leaf spot (*Cercospora hennigsii*), white leaf spot (*Cercospora caribaea*) and anthracnose (*Glomerella cingulata*).

The most serious insect pests are the white flies (*Bemisia tabaci*). Other common insect pests include the bugs (*Pseudotheraptus devastens, Anoplocnemis* spp., *Planococcus citri, Ferriseana virgata*), variegated grasshopped (*Zonocerus erythrinae*) in Togo. Various species of termites have been known to cause in West Africa, *Meloidogyne incognita* in the Ivory Coast and Nigeria, the lesion nematode (*Pratylenchus brachyurus*) and the spiral nematode (*Helicotylenchus erthrinae*) in Togo. Various species of termites have been known to cause damage to cassava while rodents and wild animals often attack cassava roots.

### 7.3.2 *Yam* (Dioscorea *spp.*)

Yams provide the staple carbohydrate food in the yam zone of West Africa. They are consumed in a variety of ways. There are six main types of cultivated yams in West Africa and of these *D. rotundata* (white yam), *D. cayenensis* (yellow yam) and *D. alata* (greater yam) are the most important. Only these are considered here. *D. esculenta* (lesser yam), *D. bulbifera* (potato yam) and *D. dumetorum* (bitter yam) are in use but on a limited scale. Readers are referred to Coursey (1967a), Ayensu and Coursey (1972), Irvine (1973) and Kay (1973) for a detailed account of various cultivated yams. *D. rotundata* and *D. cayenensis* are of West African origin while *D. alata* is of Asian origin. Yam production in West Africa is considered as declining because the crop requires a large input of manual labour for cultivation and food preparation, is attacked by several pests which limit yields, and spoils easily in storage. These problems have tended to persist because little concentrated research has been conducted into yam improvement in the past. In the Savanna areas, particularly the Northern

Guinea and Sudan Savanna, cassava produces a better and higher return than yam. However, in the Derived and Southern Guinea Savanna, the climate is more suitable for yam production and yields equal or surpass those from cassava under indigenous practice. The area under yam in the Savanna region is greater than under cassava, probably occupying about 2–4 per cent of the total cultivated area. Estimated production of yam in 1971 in West Africa was about 20m. tonnes from an area of about 2m. ha, corresponding to a yield of about 10 tonne/ha of fresh tubers. However, yields in the Savanna areas are probably about 7 tonne/ha in the Derived and Southern Guinea Savanna and about 3–5 tonne/ha in the Northern Guinea and Sudan Savanna. Crop improvement research conducted in West Africa in general and more recently at IITA has indicated that the yield potential of yam in favourable climate conditions is between 30–50 tonne/ha, and yields greater than 60 tonne/ha have been obtained (Gurnah 1974). Yields greater than 50 tonne/ha under commercial production have been reported from elsewhere. However, in the Northern Guinea and Sudan Savanna the potential for yam cultivars presently available is low unless short-season cultivars of 5–7 months duration with early onset of bulking and rapid bulking rate become available. The past and future of the yams as crop plants has been discussed by Coursey and Martin (1970).

(a)  *Ecology.*  In West Africa the yam zone extends from about 4°N to about 10°N. Further north the dry season is too long. However, yam is grown in the Northern Guinea and Sudan Savanna but yields are low compared with those in the Derived and Southern Guinea Savanna. Optimum temperature for growth appears to be in the range 25–30°C. Growth is poor below 20°C while temperatures much above 30°C have an adverse effect, especially if accompanied by dry conditions. Yams require adequate moisture throughout their growing period and there is a positive correlation between moisture supply, vine growth, and tuber yield. The critical period is during 14–20 weeks of growth when the food reserves of the sett are almost exhausted and the shoots are making rapid growth before new tubers have been formed. Later, they can endure periods of drought but yields are reduced. In West Africa yams reach their highest concentration in areas where there is a dry season of 2–4 months and a rainfall of 1150 mm or more during the growing season. Good drainage is essential for high yields and quality. Yams perform best in deep well drained loams. In heavy soils tubers are susceptible to rotting while in very sandy soils favourable moisture conditions are difficult to maintain.

   *D. rotundata* is better adapted to a long dry season and can complete its life cycle in 6–7 months, although about 8 months growing period is required for good yields. It can be grown farther north in the Savanna areas than most other yam species. For good yields, however, white yam requires a rainfall of 1000–1500 mm evenly distributed over 6–7 months. It grows best on heavy loams and can tolerate a higher clay content than most other yams. *D. cayenensis* can only withstand a short dry period, 2–3 months. It therefore performs best in the Forest areas. On average it requires about 10 months or more to complete its life cycle. When grown in the Savanna areas it is lifted prematurely. It is more tolerant of sandy soils than most other species. *D. alata* requires 9–10 months to reach full maturity and grows satisfactorily in the Derived and Southern Guinea Savanna. It will tolerate poorer soils better than most other cultivated yams.

Yams are influenced by photoperiod. However the relationships between daylength and vine and tuber growth have not been fully studied. Long days (greater than 12 hours) favour the growth of the vine and short days (less than 10–11 hours) favour tuber development. Planting date has a strong effect on yield because the size of the vine at the time of onset of tuber development and the length of the bulking period are both affected by it. Delay in sowing reduces yields and generally, the earlier the planting, the greater the yield. The time of planting varies considerably in different areas. In the Derived and Southern Guinea Savanna, yams are often planted in the dry season from November to March, so that they sprout with the early rain. In areas further north where the dry season is severe, this practice is not followed because yams tend to shrivel or decay or are attacked by termites. Yams are therefore planted just before or immediately after the rains have started. However, in general most of the yams in the Savanna areas are planted towards the end of the dry season and beginning of the rainy season. In the Northern Guinea and Sudan Savanna yams are often planted in June or July after the staple cereals have been sown.

Traditionally, yams are planted in hills or mounds which are between about 0·6–1·3 m high and 0·9–1·3 m apart. Hills are often made at the end of the rains when the soil is still soft. Various methods of mechanizing the crop have been tried and good results have been obtained from ridges about 0·45–0·6 m high and 0·6 m wide at the base. The average size of yam tends to be smaller than those grown in mounds but the total yield is greater. For propagations farmers use either seed yams or setts. Most yams produce one or two tubers larger than the rest and these are generally used as food. They are cut off near the top leaving the crown with the green stem attached. This is replanted and gradually grows again producing two or more small seed tubers. In the Northern Guinea and Sudan Savanna the growing season is not long enough to produce seed yams. Some farmers in the southern areas specialize in the production of seed yams but generally the available quantity of seed yam is insufficient. Large yams are therefore cut into pieces known as setts which are then used for planting. On average, seed yams or setts weigh between 170 and 400 g. Most farmers cut their yams into two or three pieces. The 'tops' are at the stem end, the centre part is the 'middle', and the other end the 'bottom'. Whole seed yams and tops generally sprout at the same time, but for equal weight, seed yams produce slightly heavier yield than tops. Middles and bottoms generally sprout later but their yields are often lower than seed yams or tops. The weight of planting sett has a considerable effect on yield. For white yam Miege (1957) found that an increase in sett weight from 50 to 250 g linearly increased yield and decreased mean sprouting time. Baker (1964) also found similar relations between set weights and yield that enabled him to deduce a mathematical relation between yield per plant, sett weight, and plant population. Recently, Gurnah (1974) found that in white yam sett weight in the range 203–608 g had a large effect on yield, heavier setts producing the greatest weights of tubers. Further, increasing sett weight increased the average number of tubers produced per plant, possibly because the heariver setts had more buds from which new tubers could be initiated. However, sett weight did not appear to affect average tuber weight in this study, although Coursey (1967a) has observed that heavier setts are used when extra large tubers are required for festivals and shows.

The plant population used by farmers is about 7000–10 000 plants/ha. However, studies in West Africa and elsewhere have shown that higher yields are possible at much higher plant populations with adequate fertility. Thus, Gurnah (1974) in Ghana found that the relation between plant population and yield in white yam was linear up to the highest population tested, 35 000 plants/ha. However, spacing has a considerable effect on yield of tubers, and Gurnah (1974) found that the best yields over the four square spacings tested (0·31, 0·61, 0·91, and 1·22 m) were produced with the narrowest spacing (highest plant population). The number of tubers per plant was not affected but the average tuber weight was, the heaviest being in the widest spacing (lowest plant population). However, a higher plant population entails the use of more setts. Cheaper methods of propagation are likely to contribute greatly towards growing yams at higher populations economically as husbandry practices improve. It has been demonstrated with several yam species that it is possible to propagate yams from vine cuttings. Recently seed propagation of white yam at IITA has met with some considerable success although the method needs much more research (IITA 1973c). One of the major advantages of denser planting is that the small yams produced could be more easily lifted mechanically—the local consumers do not appear to object to smaller tubers.

Most yams are grown as the first cop in the rotation or on land after it has been cleared from bush or fallow because yams under local practice, unlike cassava, perform poorly on soils which has already been cropped in the previous seasons. Little or no fertilizer is used on yams and there is a wide response to treatment, particularly to the application of phosphorus and potassium. In their review on the response of yams to fertilizers and manures, Ferguson and Haynes (1970) noted that there were generally low but positive responses to nitrogen and organic matter. In some cases low levels of potassium gave small increases, but phosphorus did not affect yield. The growth, development, and nutrient uptake in white yam in Nigeria was studied by Sobulo (1972a and b). It was estimated that a yam crop of 29 tonne/ha removed 133, 10, and 85 kg/ha of N, P, and K respectively. This pattern of nutrient usage may explain why yams often respond to nitrogen and sometimes to potassium but not to phosphorus. For example, trials conducted in West Africa under the Freedom from Hunger Campaign (FFHC 1965) showed that in the Forest areas compound fertilizer containing about 45 kg/ha each of N, $P_2O_5$, and $K_2O$ increased yields, whereas in the Savanna regions nitrogen was the only element which gave a response. Sobulo (1972b) and Gurnah (1974) obtained similar results in the Savanna area of Nigeria and in the Forest area of Ghana, respectively.

Seed yams or setts are planted in the middle of the hills in holes 15 cm deep. In some areas yams are planted 5–10 cm deep while some farmers plant them almost at ground level. However, it appears that it is better to plant too deeply than too near the surface. Shallow planting may dry out the sett before sprouting. After planting the hills are capped by a layer of dried grass or weeds about

30 cm in diameter on the top of the hill and kept in position by a thin layer of soil. Experiments have shown that the percentage of sprouting and the final yield from capped hills are double those from uncapped hills. In the Savanna areas failure to cap hills can result in almost complete loss of the crop and in direr areas capping preserves the tubers throughout the dry season by preserving the moisture. In general protected yams sprout more quickly than unprotected yams as they do not dry out. However, if left too long the caps and even the tubers may be eaten by termites. Capping is thought to create steady temperature conditions and also protects the tubers from the sudden spells of dry weather and scorching sun, and also from the heavy rain and wind during the wet season.

As young shoots appear, long yam poles from hard wood trees are put in 1–2 m deep on the windward side of the hills. Soft wood poles rot or are attacked by termites at ground level, or at the end of the season may break under the weight of the foliage. Living poles are also used. In the drier Savanna areas where trees are scarce, yam poles are sometimes only 1 m high, although experiments have shown that yams grown on 2 m poles yield almost double those on 1 m poles. Further increase in pole length does not increase yields appreciably. In the Derived and Southern Guinea Savanna, yams are planted after late maize and sorghum and when these crops have been harvested the dried stalks are bent over 1 m above the ground in rows. As the yam vines grow they are trained along the dried stalks thus avoiding the use of poles in areas where wood is scarce. In Forest areas yams are grown around trees left when the bush is cleared and strings are attached to the outer branches and to short stakes. Sometimes tree or four mounds may have strings leading to one tree. An experiment conducted to study the effect of staking and changing plant canopy structure by pruning yam stems to 50 cm and 100 cm heights (IITA 1973c) showed that pruning in white yam resulted in bushy plants with sturdy main stems minimizing the requirement for staking especially when the plants were pruned to 50 cm. Staking, pruning, and their interactions had no significant effect on the number of tubers per hills but significantly affecred tuber size and yield. Staking improved tuber size and yield when the stems were not pruned. When the stems were pruned, staking made little difference while yield reduction was proportional to the severity of pruning.

Aspects related to storage problems and losses, storage practices, and post-harvest technology and processing have been discussed by Coursey (1967a and b).

(b) *Cultivation.*   White, yellow, and greater yams are grown as rain-fed crops. The indigenous practice is to grow them on hills and mounds which are prepared at the end of or early in the wet season. They are planted sole or in mixture with other crops in 2–4 crop combinations involving millets, sorghum, maize, rice, cowpea, groundnut, sweet potato, and cassava. In village studies in the Northern Guinea Savanna about 30 per cent of the total area under yams was found to be sole crop while about 48 per cent was in two crop mixtures (Norman 1972). The crop is sown during the dry season or at the beginning of the rains depending on the region. Seed yams or setts are planted in the mounds which are 0·6m high or more. When setts are used the cut part always points upwards with the buds or eyes downwards. After sowing the hills are protected by capping. A wide range of planting distances is used depending on the species, growing conditions, and whether grown sole or in mixture. Common spacings used are about 0·6–1·2 × 1·2–1·8 m at one plant per stand (about 9000–14 000 plants/ha) and corresponds to about 1·5–2·5 tonne/ha of setts. During the growing season cultivation operations include weeding, hilling, and setting poles. Harvesting is done in the dry season but often yams planted in October or November in the southern areas are lifted in July or August. Fertilizer is not commonly used on yams but organic manure is often used. Lifting is done by hand.

For high yields whether on hills or ridges, good fertility at much higher plant population is necessary. Mechanical harvesting is possible on ridges but lifting is difficult at low plant densities because of the large size of tubers which can vary in weight up to 20 kg or more. Staking is necessary for high yields but adds to the cost of production.

(c) *Diseases and pests*. Of the various diseases which can affect yams shoestring and die back (*Glomerella cingulata*), an anthracnose type of disease, are of major importance. Recently sources of resistance to these diseases have been found (IITA 1973c). Witches' broom (*Phylleutypa dioscorea*) has been known to cause damage to yams in West Africa. Several leaf spot diseases have been reported and those caused by *Cercospora* spp. are the commonest. A virus disease of the mosaic type has been recorded while susceptibility appears to vary with species and cultivars. It is believed that both leaf spot and virus diseases cause relatively little yield losses.

Storage losses from various fungal rot diseases are generally severe, particularly when the tubers are damaged. The commonest and most important is *Botryodiplodia theobromae* which also causes a rot in the field. It has been shown to be responsible for wet rot, soft rot and brown rot. Other fungal rot diseases in storage causing considerable damage are *Rosellinia bunodes, Penicillium* spp., and *Fusarium* spp. Chemical control of these diseases is effective to some extent.

Yam tuber beetles (*Heteroligus meles, H. appius, Prionoryctes rufopiceus, P. caniculus*) are by far the most serious pests in West Africa but *H. meles*, the greater yam beetle, is the most common and widespread species and is found in the Savanna areas. These beetles do not breed in the yam fields but in swampy areas. The eggs are deposited in moist soil during November and December. The three larval instars and the pupal stage are completed by March or April when the beetles emerge. Beetles fly to the yam fields with the advent of rains and remain until the end of the rain. In November and December the beetles return to the breeding areas completing the 1 generation a year cycle (Libby 1968). Chemical control is effective. A beetle (*Crioceris livida*) is known to cause damage. Both larvae and the beetle attack the leaves soon after the rains begin, but can be controlled chemically or by hand-picking. Scale insects (*Aspidella hartii* and *A. destructor*) are common pests of which *A. hartii* is the worse. *A. hartii* mainly attacks stored yams but when large colonies are built up on the tubers, sprouting is prevented. *A. destructor* builds up large colonies and feeds on the underside of leaves causing the leaves to become distorted and wilted.

Chemical control of scale insects is effective. In parts of Nigeria considerable damage is occasionally caused by the cricket (*Gymnoryllus lucens*) and, in association with ants of the genus *Camponotus*, the citrus mealy bug (*Planococcus citri*). Chemical control of these is effective. The variegated grasshopper (*Zonocerus variegatus*) has been reported to cause loss of stand or reduced yield. Nymphs and adults defoliate the plants and may kill young plants. Yam tubers are also subject to attack by several species of termites both when growing and during storage, while rats and other large animals can also cause damage. Nematodes can cause considerable damage, seriously reducing yields, increasing storage losses and affecting tuber sprouting. The most important is the yam nematode (*Scutellonema bradys*) while root-knot nematode (*Meloidogyne* spp.) and root-lesion nematodes are of importance. Little work has been done on the control of nematodes but chemical control is partially effective.

### 7.3.3  *Sweet potato* (Ipomoea batatas)

The sweet potato is of South American origin and was introduced into West Africa by the Portuguese. Although it is considered a minor root crop in West Africa, it is widely grown in the Savanna areas. Total estimated production of sweet potato in 1971 in West Africa was about 0·9m. tonnes from an area of about 0·22m. ha, corresponding to a yield of about 4 tonne/ha of fresh tubers. Yields between countries vary widely from about 0·5 tonne/ha in Mauritania to about 9 tonne/ha in Mali. Although figures are not available, it appears that a large proportion of the crop is grown in the Savanna areas, particularly in the Derived and Guinea Savanna. The popularity of the crop under indigenous practice seem to rest on its dependability of producing some yield regardless of the season and thereby providing valuable reserves during the dry season and in times of famine. There are three recognized West African types, white, red and yellow. The crop is grown as a source of carbohydrate and tubers are consumed boiled or baked while young terminal shoots and leaves are used as spinach. In West Africa, flour, starch, syrup, and spirit are made from sweet potato tubers while crop residues are used as stock feed. However, the crop can be processed in a variety of other ways (Kay 1973). Crop improvement research conducted in West Africa and more recently at IITA has shown that the yield potential of sweet potato under favourable conditions is between 20–30 tonne/ha, and experimental yields greater than 40 tonne/ha have been obtained (IITA 1973c). The highest experimental yields obtained elsewhere are of the order of 50–70 kg/ha (Chadha and Dakshinamurthy 1965, Lowe and Wilson 1975a) and yields of 20 tonne/ha or more under commercial production have been reported.

(a) *Ecology.* Sweet potato, although a perennial, is normally cultivated as an annual crop. The crop under indigenous practice is harvested from 3–8 months after planting, depending upon the cultivar and climatic conditions. It can be successfully grown under irrigation in the dry season and experimental yields of 30–40 kg/ha have been obtained at IITA. Because the crop can be harvested in 3–4 months, sweet potato is grown in the northern areas, in the Sudan Savanna, where rainfall is only 500 mm. However, for good yields an annual rainfall of 750–1250 mm is necessary, with dry weather as the crop reaches maturity. The best area for sweet potato in West Africa is therefore the Guinea Savanna and southern areas of the Sudan Savanna. Sweet potato can tolerate dry periods of considerable length once it is established. However, yields are drastically reduced if severe water stress occurs at the time when tuber initiation has begun, 40–60 days after planting. Sweet potato thrives best under temperatures around 24 °C or more with abundant sunshine. Growth is poor in cool weather and temperatures below 10 °C damage the plant.

Sweet potato is a short-day plant and short days promote both flowering and root development. A photoperiod of 11 hours or less hastens flowering while at 13·5 hours flowering ceases, but tuber yields do not appear to be affected. Little work has been done on the effect of planting date on the physiology of yield of the rain-fed crop. However, early planting results in higher yields mainly because the plant size at the time of onset of tuber development and the length of the bulking period are greater. Consequently, both the mean number of tubers per plant and mean weight per tuber decrease with delay in planting. Under adequate moisture and temperature conditions, however, dry season yields are often greater than wet season. The crop takes longer to mature in the wet season and has fewer tubers per plant. During the dry season solar radiation receipts are considerably greater than in the wet season and may partly contribute to the difference in the yield.

Studies on the eco-physiological basis of yield conducted elsewhere in the tropics have shown the importance of aspects related to dry matter accumulation such as crop growth rate, net assimilation rate and leaf area index (Haynes, Spence and Walter 1967) as well as the distribution of assimilates (Fujise and Tsuno 1967, Austin and Aung 1973). However, the terminal components of yield in sweet potato and other tuber crops are the number and mean weights of tubers per plant. Consistent production of both high tuber number and mean tuber weights is therefore a major characteristic of a high yielding cultivar. Further, reciprocal graft experiments with high and low yielding cultivars (Wilson 1967, Hozyo 1970, Hozyo, Murata, and Yoshida 1971) have shown that the capacity of tuber development in root stocks was an important determinant of yield, emphasizing the importance of the process of tuberization relative to dry matter production in the development of tuber yield. Studies on contribution of yield components to tuber yields in six cultivars (Wholey and Haynes 1969, Wilson and Lowe 1973, Lowe and Wilson 1974, 1975a) showed that there were significant negative correlations between tuber number and mean tuber weight in five of the six cultivars, and positive correlation between these yield components and yield. Lowe and Wilson (1975a) have suggested that these cultivars may be grouped into 'tuber number—tuber weight' and 'tuber weight' types, as well as a 'random type' in which yield is related to neither component because of the existence of a strong compensatory relation between yield components. In general, sweet potato crops show a high degree of variability in tuber yield, both total and marketable (Haynes and Wholey 1971). This has been found to be related to either or both yield components. The sources of variation in yield components, and hence yield, have been attributed to planting material (i.e., number of nodes on terminal cuttings used for planting since tubers are produced on root developed from subterranean nodes), tuber development (i.e., time of onset, and rate and period of bulking), and season (Wilson 1970, Wilson and Lowe 1973, Lowe and Wilson 1974, 1975b).

Considerable variation in $CO_2$ compensation point has been found in sweet potato, a $C_3$ plant (Sadik 1973). However, growth analysis experiments on cultivars with low and high compensation points under field conditions have not revealed any consistent difference in total biological yield and components of the biological and economic yield between the two categories, suggesting that in addition to compensation point, other yield determining physiological factors are involved (IITA 1973c).

Response to application of fertilizer depends on the cultivar and growing conditions. However, a crop yielding 15 tonne/ha of fresh tubers has been reported to remove about N, 70 kg/ha, P, 9 kg/ha; K, 92 kg/ha (Samuels 1967, Yong 1970, Kay 1973). For good growth and yield, sweet potato has a high requirement for other nutrients particularly calcium, boron, and magnesium. Good drainage is essential for high yields although the crop can be grown in a wide range of soils. A sandy loam of *p*H 5·6–6·6 with a permeable clay subsoil is considered best for the crop. As the crop does not tolerate waterlogging, it is commonly grown on ridges or mounds. It is sensitive to saline and alkaline conditions.

(b) *Cultivation.* Sweet potato is grown largely as a rain-fed crop in the Savanna areas although some is grown in the low-lying areas and *fadama* areas on residual moisture. The indigenous practice is to grow the crop on ridges or sometimes on the flat, but in areas which are liable to flood it is grown on mounds. It is mainly grown in mixture in two to six crop combinations involving sorghum, millet, maize, rice, cowpea, groundnut, yam, cassava, potato, vegetables, cotton, and tobacco. About 16 per cent of the total area under sweet potato was found to be in sole crop in village studies in the Northern Guinea Savanna while about 85 per cent was in 2–3 crop mixtures (Norman 1972). The crop is generally sown in May and June in the Derived and Southern Guinea Savanna and in June and July in the Northern Guinea and Sudan Savanna. The plant may be propagated either by tubers (whole or part of a tuber), slips, or vine cuttings, the last method being the one in common use. In slip propagation tubers are planted in a nursery bed. The new plants which sprout from the various buds of the tubers are known as slips. They are separated and planted as such. Vine cuttings are preferred as they are relatively cheaper, the plants are free from soil-borne diseases and the tubers produced are of a more uniform shape and size. Apical cuttings are generally used as they produce better growth and yield than basal or middle cuttings. Vine cuttings 20–45 cm long with 7 or more nodes are planted half to two-thirds of their length in the soil. In some areas the crop is grown in large flat-topped mounds varying in area from 3 to 5 $m^2$ with several cuttings planted on mounds. In other parts mounds are small, round-topped, and 30 to 60 cm apart, with one plant on each mound. When planted on ridges or rows, the spacing varies considerably depending on whether grown sole or in mixture (Fig. 7.1). Common spacing in sole crop is about 0·25 × 0·9 m at one plant per stand (about 48 000 plants/ha). In two to three crop mixtures, the common spacing is about 2·3 × 0·9 m (about 3700–5500 plants/ha). Roots sprout from the subterranean nodes within 5-14 days depending on the quality of the planting material and moisture conditions. Once the crop is established, it requires minor weeding if the land has been properly prepared initially and is not over-infested with weeds, since the creeping stems spread quickly, covering the soil. At maturity the stems turn from green to brown while the growing period generally varies between 4 to 6 months depending on the cultivar, although often, tubers are harvested as required from 3 months after planting, the crop being finally harvested in the dry season in November or December. The crop responds well to manures while results from fertilizer trials are conflicting for reasons explained earlier with yam. Jacob and Uexkull (1963) have discussed the fertilizer application rates for the crop.

For yields of over 20 tonne/ha on soils of adequate fertility, common spacings appear to be between 0·25–0·4 m apart in rows, or ridges 0·6-1·1 m apart (24 000-72 000 plants/ha) depending on the cultivar, days to maturity, fertility, and purpose for which the crop is grown. Mechanical harvesting of the crop is possible but losses can be high. Sweet potato tubers are very perishable and methods used to harvest the crop have a very considerable effect upon the market quality and storage life of tubers. Aspects related to harvesting, storage and processing have been discussed by Gooding and Campbell (1964), Keleny (1965), Kushman and Wright (1969), Austin (1970), Austin and Bell (1970), Austin and Graves (1970), and Francois and Law (1971).

(c) *Diseases and pests.* In general diseases in the field are of minor importance at present. Black rot (*Ceratocystis fimbriata*) and soft and dry rot (*Rhizopus* spp.) which affects the growing crop can be controlled by planting healthy tubers and by crop rotation. Leaf spot (*Colletotrichum capsici*) has been reported but little work has been conducted on this disease.

Storage or black rot (*Botryodiplodia theobromae*) can be a serious disease in stored tubers which have been damaged during harvesting. A soft rot (*Rhizopus* spp.) is also known to attack the tubers in storage while the black rot (*Ceratocystis fimbriata*) can also develop in stored tubers. With the indigenous method of harvesting, storage losses are considered small at present.

The sweet potato weevil (*Cylas puncticollis*) is the major insect pest, the larva feeding on the roots and tubers. The crop is not usually severely attacked before July or August so that early harvest may avoid infestation. It is particularly serious on the late planted or dry season crop. Proper crop rotation helps in its control while sources of resistance have been isolated recently (IITA 1973c). Chemical control is effective. Leaf feeding caterpillar of hawk moth (*Herse convolvuli*) and tortoise beetle (*Aspidomorpha* spp.) have been reported on the wet season crop but they appear to be sporadic pests. Variegated grasshopper (*Zonocerus variegatus*) and flee beetle (*Halticus tibialis*) have been reported to attack the crop, damaging the leaves.

### 7.3.4 Cocoyam (Colocasia esculenta *and* Xanthosoma sagittifolium)

There is a considerable confusion in the taxonomy of the cultivated edible species of *Colocasia* and *Xanthosoma*. Here the various reported species are grouped into one polymorphic species each as suggested by Purseglove (1975), namely, *C. esculenta* and *X. sagittifolium*, although Dalziel (1955) considers that *X. mafaffa* is the species currently cultivated in West Africa. *C. esculenta* is of Asian origin but has been grown in West Africa for centuries. It is known as the old cocoyam distinguishing it from *X. sagittifolium*, the new cocoyam of tropical American origin, introduced into West Africa in the middle of the nineteenth century. Cocoyam is the third most important cultivated root crop in West Africa following yam and cassava, although in the Savanna areas the production is less than of sweet potato. Since it was introduced, *X. sagittifolium* has been gradually displacing *C. esculenta* and in Ghana and Cameroon its cultivation is greater. Some of the reasons for increasing preference for the new cocoyam are that it is resistant to *Phytophthora* blight, it is easier to prepare and cook, more tolerant to lower rainfall conditions, and less of a health hazard. Cocoyams are mainly consumed baked, boiled, pounded, or mashed, and as flour in stews and soups. Young leaves and shoots are used as spinach. Accurate production figures are difficult to find but cocoyam is a major root crop in the Forest areas where probably 75–85 per cent of the total crop is grown. Much of the remaining crop is grown in the Derived and Southern Guinea Savanna although some is grown in the *fadama* areas in the Northern Guinea and Sudan Savanna. Separate production figures for new and old cocoyam are not readily available but combined annual production from Nigeria, Ghana, Cameroon, and Ivory Coast during the period 1966–70 was about 0·31 m tonnes (Kay 1973). Yields under indigenous practice in the Forest areas appear to be in the range 3–5 tonne/ha while in the Savanna areas 1·5–2·5 tonne/ha. In general little crop improvement research has been done on cocoyam although experimental yields of 15–30 tonne/ha of fresh tubers have been obtained in the Forest and Derived Savanna areas. Elsewhere in the tropics, experimental yields of 20–40 tonne/ha in the upland areas, and 35–55 tonne/ha in the lowland areas with adequate moisture have been obtained from crops of 9–12 months in duration, and yields up to 75 tonne/ha have been reported for 12–15 months crop at high fertility. The crop is only briefly considered here because it is a very minor crop in the Savanna areas. Readers are referred to Kay (1973) for a fuller account.

(a) *Ecology.* The old cocoyam is perennial but its life cycle in the field varies from 6 to 18 months according to the cultivar and growing conditions. In the Forest areas the crop is often in the ground for 12 months or more while in the Savanna areas about 5–9 months. With the new cocoyam the tubers are considered to be mature in 10 to 12 months but the crop will continue to grow for 18 months or more if moisture permits. In the Savanna areas the crop is harvested in 5–9 months after planting depending on the region. Highest yields are obtained when the crop is grown for 12–15 months and generally the earlier the crop is harvested the lower the yield. Also, because of the fact that cocoyams thrive under warm and humid conditions with long and moist growing season, the region best suited for intensive production in Savanna areas is the Derived and Southern Guinea Savanna although its natural potential lies in the Forest areas. *Colocasia* is adapted to moist environments but will grow well under irrigation in upland areas provided temperature does not limit growth. *Xanthosoma* is also adapted to high rainfall conditions but can be grown satisfactorily in areas with rainfall of 1000–1200 mm if it is evenly distributed or under irrigation. In general, yield improvement in the Savanna areas will depend on the availability of high-yielding, quick-maturing cultivars. For good growth mean temperatures in the range 20–30 °C is required.

Cocoyam can be grown on a wide variety of soils but deep, well-drained, loams with *p*H of 5·5–6·6 are considered best. Yields are low in very sandy or hard clay soils. The new cocoyam unlike the old cocoyam is very sensitive to waterlogging and saline conditions. Indeed, the old cocoyam has been used elsewhere in the tropics as a first crop in the reclamation of saline, sandy, soils. Little is known about the nutritional requirements of cocoyams. In the tropics, good responses to nitrogen have been obtained but responses to K and P have been variable. Recommended rates for 9–12 month crop are in the range N, 40–100 kg/ha; P, 15–40 kg/ha; K, 50–110 kg/ha but higher rates are used for longer duration crops. The old cocoyam has a high calcium requirement and liming has been found to be beneficial.

(b) *Cultivation.* Cocoyam is grown as a rain-fed crop. Small corms, or cormels, or pieces of corms, or the top of the main root stock with part of the original corm with cormels attached are used for propagation. These are planted at 0·6–0·9 × 0·6–0·9 m (12 000–28 000 plants/ha) but spacing varies widely. The crop is grown sole or in mixture with maize, rice and vegetables (Norman 1972). Planting usually takes place during the rainy season in May to July on ridges or mounds. Sprouting occurs 7–15 days after planting and the crop is harvested at the end of the rains when the leaves turn yellow.

Higher yields of cocoyams in the Derived and Southern Guinea Savanna are possible if soil fertility can be improved. Successful,mechanized, commercial production under irrigation and rain-fed conditions exist elsewhere in the tropics.

(c) *Diseases and pests.* In general the new cocoyam is relatively free from severe attacks by pests. Leaf spot (*Cladosporium ternuissimum, Cercospora xanthosomatis*) have been reported on *Xanthosoma*. Leaf blight (*Phytophthora colocasiae*) is prevalent on *Colocasia* in the lowland. Wilt (*Sclerotium rolfsii*) has been reported to attack the roots and collar in very moist conditions. Root rot in *Xanthosoma* although not so severe now is still common but the causal agent is not known.

Root-knot nematodes (*Meloidogyne* spp.) can cause damage in upland areas if the soil is heavily infested.

## 7.3.5 *Potato* (Solanum tuberosum)

The potato originated in South America and although in the tropics it is grown in highland areas, and at low altitudes during the cool season, it is not a tropical crop because of its very specific temperature requirements. In the West African Savanna it is grown in areas of high altitude. During the dry season, however, when temperature conditions are moderate it is grown in the lowland and *fadama* areas, although some farmers grow it as a rain-fed crop. The potato was introduced at the beginning of the century to the Cameroons and the Jos plateau in northern Nigeria but production remained small until the outbreak of the Second World War when there arose the need to feed troops stationed in

West Africa (Williams, G. G. 1962). Although production declined immediately after the war, the crop remained of some importance and there has been a considerable expansion in recent years particularly in the Cameroons, Nigeria, Senegal, and Mauritania. Estimated combined production from these countries in 1971 was about 0·1m. tonnes from an area of about 13 000 ha, corresponding to a fresh yield of about 7·7 tonne/ha. However, experimental yields of 15–30 tonnes in the highland areas of West Africa have been obtained. The potato is growing in importance in West Africa and a potato-growing industry is developing around several metropolitan centres in the Savanna areas. It has been reported that the potential for growing the potato in climates warmer than those in which it thrives are considerable (NAS 1974). Crop improvement research at the International Potato Centre (CIP) in Peru is attempting to increase the tolerance of the crop to high temperatures, and if successful it is likely that large areas of West Africa will be open to production. Since it is a short-season crop of 3–4 months duration, the potato can compete well with other root and tuber crops that require much longer growing season. However, in the highland areas of West Africa the potential of the potato crop has been well established. Full account of this crop is not given here as detailed accounts are available in Ivins and Milthorpe (1963), Burton (1966), Deanon and Cadiz (1967), O. Smith (1968), Hawkes and Hjerting (1969), Simmonds (1971), Booth and Proctor (1972), Meijers (1972), and Kay (1973).

(c) *Ecology.* Eco-physiological basis of yield in potato has been reviewed by Moorby and Milthorpe (1975). High yields of temperate potato cultivars are obtained in areas where the average temperature during the growing season ranges 15°–18°C and these conditions in the Savanna areas of West Africa prevail in the highlands at elevation above 1300–1500 m, and are approached in the lowlands during the dry season in the Sudan and Northern Guinea Savanna. In temperate cultivars, day temperatures above 21°C have an adverse effect upon yields while cool nights with an average temperature of 10°–14°C are essential. Tuber formation is retarded when the soil temperature rises above 20°C and above 29°C little or no tuberization occurs. Although young potato plants are very susceptible to frost, most cultivars once established will tolerate light frosts. In West Africa, potatoes produce tubers satisfactorily in seasons with mean temperatures below 24°C, and cultivars suited for the tropics have a much wider temperature tolerance than temperate cultivars. However, day temperatures in the highlands or during the dry season at lower altitudes are still too high while night temperatures not low enough to allow the present tropical cultivars to produce yields approaching those in the temperate areas. Generally, therefore, average yields in the tropics are about half of those obtained in the temperate areas where commercial yields of 20–30 tonne/ha are commonplace.

Potatoes originated in the Andes in tropical areas of high altitude, a region characterized by short daylengths (12–13 hours). Early cultivars bred in temperate conditions require a daylength of 15–16 hours while the late cultivars produce reasonable yields under long or short day conditions. For the tropics therefore cultivars which tolerate short-days at high temperatures are required and crop improvement research is directed towards developing cultivars that will widen the climatic adaptation of the crop (Upadhya, Purchit, and Sharda 1972). Some of the present late maturing temperate cultivars are best suited to elevations above 1500 m where temperature conditions are adequate for good growth and tuber development. At lower elevations these cultivars are acceptable in the dry season when mean temperatures drop to 24 °C or below. One of the reasons why satisfactory tuberization does occur at higher temperatures in the tropics is that the effect of daylength and temperature is modified by radiation intensity. Radiation receipts are higher in the high altitude areas and during the dry season and it appears that higher the radiation intensity, the higher the maximum temperature permitting tuberization. Recently, potato cultivars adapted to a range of tropical conditions have been developed and better adapted cultivars are likely to become available in the future.

Potatoes require a continuing supply of moisture. Dry periods, even of short duration, can drastically reduce tuber yields while seriously affecting the quality of the crop when moisture supply becomes limiting or irregular towards the final stages of bulking. Generally, it is considered that a short duration crop requires 500–700 mm of evenly distributed moisture supply either from rainfall or irrigation and a long duration crop about 750–900 mm.

The crop can be grown on all types of soils, except heavy waterlogged clays. A deep, well drained, loam or sandy loam with a $p$H of 5·5–6 is considered best. $p$H in the range 4·8–5·5 is tolerated but above 6 m, tubers are liable to suffer from scab.

Potatoes respond well to manures and fertilizers, and good yields can be obtained only with adequate fertility. Fertilizer requirements vary greatly depending on the cultivar and growing conditions but a crop yielding 25 tonne/ha removes N, 115–120 kg/ha; P, 20 kg/ha; K, 167 kg/ha, and Ca, 71 kg/ha. In the tropics good yields are generally in the range 10–18 tonne/ha and the nutrient removal is about N, 50–80 kg/ha; P, 9–13 kg/ha, K, 67–117 kg/ha.

(b) *Cultivation.* The crop is grown sole or in mixture with sorghum, millet, maize, cowpea, groundnut, sweet potato, vegetables, and tobacco. In village studies in the Northern Guinea Savanna about 22 per cent of the crop was found to be grown sole while the remaining in mixture of 2–5 crop combinations (Norman 1972). Propagation is done using tubers, either whole or cut, although whole tubers are less liable to develop rots in the soil. Tubers have a dormancy period of at least 8–12 weeks after being harvested depending on the cultivar and environmental conditions. Dormancy can be broken artificially but naturally broken dormancy produces a more uniform crop and better growth. Nondormant planting material weighing about 40–60 g of regular shape is considered best. It is essential that the planting material is free from diseases, pests and damage and certified 'seed' tubers free from virus disease should be used when possible. When cut pieces are planted immediately, it is recommended that they are chemically treated to prevent disease, or else stored for a period of 7–10 days for the cut surfaces to heal or suberize before planting. Potatoes may be planted by hand or mechanically and the crop is usually planted on ridges at a depth of 5–15 cm. As the crop is shallow rooted, a seed-bed cultivated to a depth of about 25–30 cm to produce fine deep tilth is necessary for good yields. Common plant spacing is 0·92–0·3 m in rows 0·75–1·2 m apart but optimum spacing depends on the cultivar, fertility and growing conditions, and spacing between rows of 0·4–0·6 m may be required for a short-duration crop at high fertility. For fertilizers to be most effective, these should be placed in bands somewhat below the 'seed' pieces and separated by a 5–8 cm layer of soil. This avoids the hazards of chemical 'burning', minimizes the inactivation of phosphate by interaction with soil, and ensures that the fertilizer will be promptly available to the young plant as well as the growing crop. Potatoes compete weakly with weeds and timely, efficient, weeding by pulling, hoeing, or tillage is essential. In temperate areas the crop is often repeatedly hoed, up to 5 times during the season, to control weeds while ridges are earthed up to avoid greening of the tubers. Normally the crop is mature for harvest in 3–4 months. Harvesting should be done on a dry day and when the tubers are mature. The crop is lifted by hand but mechanical harvesting is possible. It is recommended that the tubers are harvested when the three-quarters of the crop leaves have turned yellow or brown. The tubers should be stored temporarily in a shaded, dry, well-ventilated place for 7–10 days to allow time for the skin to become well suberized before they are prepared for market or long term storage.

(c) *Diseases and pests.*  The potato crop is subject to a number of diseases some of which are of great economic importance in West Africa. Brown rot or bacterial wilt (*Pseudomonas solanacearum*) is the most serious disease of potato in West Africa (Robinson, R. A. 1967, 1968). Cultivars bred and selected in temperate regions are extremely susceptible, as bacterial wilt does not occur there. The disease is carried by seed tubers. There is considerable evidence that the ability of the bacteria to survive the dry season as saprophytes in the soil is very limited and the bacteria survive the dry season in alternative hosts in the weed flora. In recent years sources of resistance to bacterial wilt have been discovered. Other bacterial diseases include soft rot (*Eriwinia carotovora*) and ring rot (*Corynebacterium sepedonicum*). In the early sixties the potato industry in West Africa suffered a severe setback because of severe losses due to late blight (*Phytophthora infestans*). All parts of the plant are affected and infested tubers develop dry or wet rots either before or after harvest. There is no cultivar completely resistant to late blight, although some have a high degree of resistance for several years. In addition, there are other diseases of considerable importance and potential threat to the crop. Early blight or target spot (*Alternaria solani*) can be of considerable economic importance, although it is easier to control than late blight. Scab (*Streptomyces scabies*) often affects potatoes grown in soils of pH above 6, causing raised corky areas, on the tubers. Black scurf or stem canker (*Rhizoctonia solani*) has the potential of causing serious damage, attacking the stems and tubers at or below the soil level. The fungus has a wide host range and can survive as a saprophyte in the soil, which can make its control difficult. *Verticillium* wilt (*Verticillium albo-atrum*) is another potentially serious disease with a wide host range. Several types of tuber rots are caused by *Fusarium* spp. which also cause wilting of plants.

There are several virus diseases which can cause severe crop losses and virus-free planting stock is essential since there are no effective treatments for these diseases. Some of these viruses are transmitted by aphids and the only effective control method is to grow virus-free seed tubers from special aphid-free areas in the highlands in West Africa. Locally grown seed tubers are heavily contaminated with viruses.

Potatoes are attacked by aphids which are widespread and spread virus diseases. Flee beetles (*Podagrica sjostedti, P. uniforma*) and mole crickets (*Gryllotalpa africana*) have been known to attack the crop and can cause considerable losses when young plants are attacked by a large number of these insects. A number of nematodes are capable of causing serious losses. These include the root-knot nematodes (*Meloidogyne* spp.), the reniform nematode (*Rotylenchulus reniformis*) and root-lesion nematodes (*Protylenchus* spp.). Root eating ants (*Dorylus orientalis*) can be troublesome.

## 7.4 Vegetables

### 7.4.1 *Tomato* (Lycopersicon esculentum)

The tomato plant is of South American origin (Rick 1956) and it appears that little was cultivated in Africa until the end of the nineteenth century. At present it is one of the most important vegetable crops in West Africa. Its use raw as a salad is rare in the traditional patterns of consumption and much of the tomato produced locally is eaten cooked in local dishes. Further, it has never been available in large quantities and because of its low keeping quality, it is used more as a condiment. To cater for extensive dispersion and reduce the seasonality of supply, it has been ground, usually together with other similar components such as onions and peppers (Quinn and McLean 1975). Recently, the consumption of canned tomato paste has increased considerably to meet the growing demand. In rural areas, it is readily accepted and used when supplies of fresh and dried fruits are unavailable. However, much of the tomato used in the paste industry is imported. For example Senegal, Ivory Coast, Ghana, and Nigeria together import nearly 20 000 tonnes of concentrated paste (28–30 per cent) annually while the figure for West Africa as a whole probably may be over 30 000 tonnes. Estimated production of fresh tomato in West Africa in 1971 was about 332 000 tonnes from an area of about 44 000 ha, corresponding to a yield of about 7500 kg/ha. Yield figures vary greatly between countries from about 670 kg/ha in Togo to about 10 tonne/ha in Ivory Coast and Nigeria. The market and scope for processing of local tomatoes in the West African Savanna is very large and recently commercial production for making canned tomato paste has been encouraged. Crop improvement research has shown that improved cultivars can produce fresh marketable yields of 50–80 tonne/ha (Quinn 1974) while experimental yields of over 90 tonne/ha have been recorded in the Northern Guinea Savanna (J. G. Quinn, unpublished). Indeed, in commercial plantings yields of 40–50 tonne/ha have been obtained (Quinn 1973a).

(a) *Ecology.* Tomato is grown throughout the Savanna areas in both the upland areas and *fadama* areas where it often receives supplementary irrigation. In general, experimental yields of rain-fed and irrigated dry season crops are greater in the Northern Guinea and Sudan Savanna than in the Southern Guinea

and Derived Savanna. Detailed research into field problems resulting from variations in climatic conditions and pest environment in the Savanna areas have con-
firmed that if a tomato industry were to be established, it would have to be in
the drier areas of the West African Savanna (Quinn 1971). The lower yields of
rain-fed crops in the Southern Guinea and Derived Savanna can be largely attributed to the greater incidence of foliage and stem diseases and to some extent to
the relatively lower solar radiation and higher night temperatures (Kassam and
Kowal 1973) leading to excessive vegetative growth at the expense of fruiting.
Observations have shown that the build-up of root-knot nematodes, bacterial
wilt and virus diseases is more severe where the dry season is short. Indeed,
where there is a long desiccating dry season, these problems are greatly reduced
in subsequent wet season cropping on the upland areas.

Tomato is a day-neutral plant. However, planting date investigations at
Samaru (Quinn 1971, 1974, Quinn and McLean 1974) have revealed a strong
effect of temperature on yield. Tomatoes transplanted at 3–4 week intervals
throughout the year produced average yields of about 35 tonne/ha from crops
established during the June to December period, while yields from crops established during the January to May period averaged about 8 tonne/ha. This difference is largely attributed to temperature extremes. Night temperatures often
decrease below 15 °C during December and January and, from late February to
May day temperatures frequently exceed 33 °C, while night temperature above
21 °C are common. Such extremes cause an imbalance in the relationship
between vegetative and reproductive growth processes while high day and night
temperatures accompanied by relatively greater energy load leads to decrease in
photosynthesis, increase in plant water deficit and early leaf senescence (Went
1944, 1949, Calvert 1965, L. T. Evans 1969). Evaporation demands in March
and April at Samaru often exceed 7–8 mm/day, with much greater day-time
values, which leads to plant water deficits high enough to cause plants to wilt
under irrigated conditions.

During the wet season, high relative humidity favours heavy attacks of leaf
and stem diseases, although in the Northern Guinea and Sudan Savanna where
rainfall is lower, these diseases are easier to control with chemical means.
Marketable yields can be doubled or trebled as compared with an unsprayed
crop (Quinn 1971). However, rains frequently occur in torrential storms of short
duration accompanied by violent winds. Unprotected crops under such
conditions suffer considerably and plants are beaten to the ground, often breaking lateral branches heavy with fruits. Further, the resulting contact with the
soil causes rotting to both fruit and foliage, while soil splash extends rotting
further up the plant. Experiments at Samaru (Quinn 1973b) using either stakes
or a heavy mulch of grass or groundnut shells, have shown average increases of
over 90 per cent in marketable yields. Successful wet season production may
therefore need disease control by spraying and mulching, while crops planted
late in the wet season may need supplementary irrigation to finish them to maturity. However, the dry season crop needs full irrigation and insect control against
fruit worm but no disease control, mulching, or support (Quinn and McLean
1974).

Tomatoes can be grown on a variety of soils but a well drained, light loam
with a *p*H of 5–7 is preferred.

(b) *Cultivation.* Most of the tomato under indigenous practice is grown in mixture of 2–6 combinations involving other vegetables, sweet potato, maize, cowpea, and sorghum. In the village studies in the Northern Guinea Savanna about 18 per cent of the crop was found to be grown sole while about 80 per cent was in 2–4 crop mixture (Norman 1972).

For efficient production, Quinn (1971) recommends that seeds should be sown in nurseries and later transplanted. The recommended practice is for seeds to be sown in rows approximately 10 cm apart and 0·5 cm deep in well prepared nursery beds. These beds are about 2 m wide to facilitate hand-sowing, weeding and thinning (Schneider and Quinn 1972). A seed bed area of about 80 $m^2$ is required to supply one hectare of transplants. For the first planting during the wet season, seed-bed nurseries should be on raised bed about 15–25 cm high. Later seed-beds established in the dry season should be arranged so that the margins are surrounded by an irrigation channel. Seedlings should be planted on the water line along each side of the 90 cm ridge to give a population of about 41 000 plants/ha. Phosphate, about 11 kg/ha P should be applied during cultivation before transplating while three and six weeks after transplanting an equally split side dressing, of 65 kg/ha of N has been found to produce optimum yields. For high yields during the wet season the crop must be sprayed to control diseases and it is necessary to stake or mulch the crop. Disease control is not necessary during the dry season but one or two applications of insecticides are required to control fruit worm. Time to maturity varies between 10 and 14 weeks after transplanting depending on the cultivar.

(c) *Diseases and pests.* Bacterial wilt (*Pseudomonas solanacearum*) is one of the most serious diseases of tomatoes, particularly in the Southern Guinea and Derived Savanna and when strict rotation is not followed. Genetic resistance so far has not been promising. Early blight (*Alternaria solani*), leaf spot (*Septoria lycopersici*), and leaf mould (*Cladosporium fulvum*) are the most serious diseases of the wet seaon crop. Fungicide spraying is effective. During the dry season only early blight is the major disease but is not of economic importance at present. Tomatoes can be seriously attacked by various virus diseases particularly in the southern areas.

A number of insects attack tomatoes but at present they are of minor importance and can be controlled effectively by spraying. These include the fruit worm (*Heliothis armigera*), mites (*Hemitarsonemus latus*), the flower midge (*Contarina lycopersici*) and the leaf miner (*Liriomyza stricata*). Root-knot nematodes (*Meloidogyne* spp.) are very common, particularly when strict rotation is not practised.

### 7.4.2 Onion (Allium cepa)

The onion is believed to have originated in the Near East in an area which includes Iran, Afghanistan and West Pakistan. It has been grown in the West African Savanna for a very long time for both food and cash. Its use as a salad is rare and much of it is consumed cooked in local dishes and fried bean cakes. Although it is commonly eaten, it has never been available in large quantities. Availability is at its lowest in July–August and highest in March–April. However, onions are traditionally a very important vegetable in the Savanna areas and would probably constitute an ingredient of one meal per day if supplies were available (Green 1971a). Although no figures are available, average yields quoted are about 40–50 tonne/ha or more under improved husbandry (Green 1971b), and marketable yields of over 90 tonne/ha have been obtained (Green 1972a).

(a) *Ecology*. Observations suggest that most onion production in the West African Savanna is located in the Northern Guinea and Sudan Savanna. The main commercial crop is grown during the dry season because of disease problems associated with conditions of high relative humidity during the wet season. Thus, the main sites of onion production are the *fadama* areas where irrigation is possible.

The common onion under normal conditions forms a food storage organ in the first season of growth and flowers in the second season. The production of bulbs is controlled by photoperiod. The critical daylength varies from 11–16 hours, depending on the cultivar. Long-day cultivars developed in temperate countries will not form bulbs in the shorter days of the tropics, for which short-day cultivars are required. Bulbing is influenced by temperature and plant size; it takes place more quickly at warm than at cool temperatures provided the photoperiodic requirements have been met. Good vegetative growth is necessary before bulbing is initiated to produce good yields, although excessive vegetative growth particularly due to excess nitrogen can slow down the bulbing process.

The conditions required to initiate flowering are low temperatures (below 14°C) and a certain minimum size of bulb since small bulbs show almost no tendency to flower when exposed to low temperatures (Jones and Mann 1963). If plants have attained a certain size and are subject to low temperatures, they may flower in the first season. This is commonly referred to as bolting, and is not influenced by photoperiod. Environmental conditions which will induce bolting occur in the Northern Guinea and Sudan Savanna during the dry season (October–April) when the main commercial bulb crop is grown. Surveys conducted in northern Nigeria have shown that bolting is a serious problem and the percentage of bolters is generally high (Green 1970). Part of the reason for this is probably the undesirable practice of saving seed from the previous year's bolters. Cultivars vary in their susceptibility to bolt and a high percentage of bolters can be expected from imported cultivars not adapted to local conditions. However, assessment of indigenous strains of onion at Samaru and observations in other areas have shown that the numbers of bolters generally exceed 50 per cent. According to Green (1970) it appears that many farmers are not aware of the detrimental effect bolting has on yield and quality of the ware crop. The farmers seem to feel that if they can harvest seed and bulbs from the same crop, then it may be more profitable than growing separate crops.

Seed for both wet and dry season plantings is produced by farmers in the previous dry season. The traditional method is to select a mother bulb of good quality that was grown in the previous wet season or dry season. A transverse cut is made between a third and halfway from the neck of the bulb, and the lower portion of the bulb is then planted in a nursery bed. Axillary buds, formed during the growth of the mother bulb, sprout and they are separated from the cluster when 10–15 cm in height and transplanted as individuals to produce seed during the dry season. Some 15-20 plants are obtained from one bulb of 8-10 cm diameter. This method is used by many farmers and produces seed whch will give a good quality bulb crop with a low percentage of bolters (Green 1970). However, Green (1972b), studying the influence of bulb cutting and separation of axillary shoot on seed production, found no evidence to suggest that the local method of onion seed production was superior in any way to the method commonly employed elsewhere in the world using uncut bulb. In Niger, where bulb cutting is practised, Nabos (1971) reported that cutting and shoot separation was decidedly disadvantageous, the seed yield per unit area being depressed by 35-62 per cent. The reduced seed yields are due to loss of food reserve for growth when the mother bulb tissue is removed, because larger bulbs produce more inflorescence, more seed per inflorescence, and a greater weight of seed per original mother bulb (Jones and Emsweller 1939, Woodbury and Dietz 1942, Green 1972b).

Planting date has a strong effect on yield and crop maturity. Highest yields are obtained from crops transplanted during October–November. Yields decrease sharply and maturity is delayed in later planted crops which produce green bunching onions from August onwards.

A large proportion of the main crop bulbs harvested during March–April is stored to fetch a higher price during the wet season. During storage there is frequently a loss of over 50 per cent of bulb within 12 weeks, and this is thought to be partly due to storing bulbs which have bolted (Green 1970). The necks of such bulbs do not cure properly because of the wide hole left by the emerging scape, allowing ease of access to pathogens. Storage of bolted bulbs is not recommended (Jones and Mann 1963). Storage losses depend on a number of factors including the cultivar, storage conditions, bulb quality at harvest, and how well the bulbs were cured. In northern Nigeria, Green (1972c) has made suggestions to achieve improved storage.

Onions can be grown under a wide range of climatic conditions but they are not suited to regions with heavy rainfall. Cool conditions, with an adequate moisture supply, are most suitable for early growth, followed by warm, drier conditions for maturation, harvesting and curing. These conditions prevail between October and April in the Northern Guinea and Sudan Savanna in the *fadama* areas. Onions grow best in well drained soils, a good fertile loam of $pH$ 6-7 being the best.

(b) *Cultivation*. Of the three main types, white, red, and purple skinned, the red is most common and has a longer storage life. The wet season onion crop under indigenous practice is largely intercropped in 3-6 crop combinations involving cowpea, potato, sweet potato, peppers, okra, tomato, millet, sorghum, and groundnut (Norman 1972). In the village studies in the Northern Guinea Savanna about 13 per cent of the crop was found to be grown sole while about 73 per cent in 2-4 crop mixtures (Norman 1972). The wet season crop is planted in June and harvested in August about 90 days. The dry season crop is grown sole or in mixtures with other vegetables. The normal spacing under improved practice is about 0·7–0·1 × 0·3–0·4 m when planted either from seed, dry sets or transplants. For yields of over 25–35 tonne/ha, 70–100 kg/ha N, and 13–22 kg/ha

P are applied to the crop. Nitrogen in split application, two-thirds applied after transplanting and one-third when bulbing commences, reduces excessive leaf growth. The crop matures 90–150 days after planting, depending on the cultivar. After harvesting the bulbs are cured which takes 5–10 days, and well cured bulbs are hard with firm necks. For longer storage life, dry conditions with good air circulation are necessary.

(c) *Diseases and pests.* A wide variety of diseases attack the crop, particularly in the wet season. These include purple blotch (*Alternaria porri*), powdery mildew (*Peronospora destructor*), pink rot (*Pyrenochaeta terrestris*), and white rot (*Sclerotium cepivorum*). Yellow dwarf virus disease is also common.

The most serious pests of onion are thrips (*Thrips tabaci, Podothrips* spp.) which can cause serious losses of the dry season crop. A heavily infested crop can lose 50 per cent of its yield. In general, thrips do not thrive in conditions of heavy rain, and the damage caused by them in the wet season is small. Work at Samaru (Raheja 1973) has shown that thrips in the dry season crop appear soon after transplanting. The population gradually builds up and reaches a peak about 50 days after transplanting when thrips per plant can be about 40.

### 7.4.3  *Pepper* (Capsicum *spp.*)

Pepper is of South and Central American origin. It is widely grown in the West African Savanna. The two species of pepper grown are *C. annuum* and *C. frutescens*. The former is also grown for export, as in northern Nigeria, the latter for local consumption, *C. annuum* includes the chilli and sweet peppers, but most of cultivars grown are the chilli type which are very pungent. *C. frutescens* are the birdseye peppers which are very hot. Accurate production figures do not exist but average yields under local practice are probably around 400 kg/ha of fresh fruits because most of the crop is grown in mixture. Yields of sole crop or in two crop mixture may be about 700–900 kg/ha. Improved cultivars under good management can produce yields of 2–3 tonne/ha of fresh fruit.

(a) *Ecology.* Peppers grow well in most areas and under a variety of soils. They are usually grown as a rain-fed crop but heavy rainfall and wet conditions are detrimental, as they lead to poor seed set and rotting of the fruit. Peppers are very sensitive to waterlogging and perform best in light loamy soils which are well drained. It is best to sow the crop appropriately late in the wet season so that the fruits mature as the weather becomes dry, but not so dry or hot that they shrivel before they are ripe. Days to first picking vary between cultivars but generally flowering begins 1–2 months after planting and it takes another month to the first picking of green fruits. From then on ripe fruits are picked at intervals of 1–2 weeks and harvesting continues over a period of 3 to 5 months depending on the region. Heavy rain during flowering results in flower shedding and poor fruit set. Flowers remain open for about 2–3 days while the percentage of fruit set is 40–50. *C. annuum* usually grows more quickly that *C. fructescens* and is more suitable for areas in the Northern Guinea and Sudan Savanna. *C. fructescens* is usually grown in the Derived and Southern Guinea Savanna where some cultivars survive the dry season and bear fruits in the following season.

(b) *Cultivation.* Under indigenous practice the wet season crop is grown mainly in mixture of 2–6 crop combinations involving other vegetables, cowpea, groundnut, millet, sorghum, maize, kenaf, and root crops. In the village studies in the Northern Guinea Savanna about 19 per cent of the crop was found to be grown sole while about 62 per cent in 2–3 crop mixtures and the rest in 4–6 crop mixtures (Norman 1972). The crop is planted during May to July and finally harvested in November or December, 130–180 days after planting. Seedlings are transplated at 4–5 weeks when they are about 10–15 cm high. The crop is grown on ridges or on the flat at a variety of spacings (Fig. 7.1) at 1 plant/stand. The stand population varies from about 38 000 plants/ha when grown sole to about 29 000 plants/ha when grown in 2–3 crop mixtures. Fruits are picked over several months after the first picking, 2–3 months after planting. Harvested fruits, if not consumed fresh, are spread out thinly and dried in the sun for 1–2 weeks. Crops grown for export are not stored for too long as the fruits lose colour. The main harvest is during October to December, and fruits are picked with their stalks to reduce fruit rotting. Dried fruits store well for long periods.

For high yields, improved cultivars require good fertility at spacings of about 0·65 m on the square or on rows 0·75–0·9 m apart and 0·45–0·75 m between plants.

(c) *Diseases and pests.* Leaf curl and mosaic, both virus diseases, cause serious damage to the crop. It is probable that they are transmitted by the thrip (*Scirtothrips dorsalis*). Powdery mildew (*Leveillula taurica*) and bacterial wilt (*Pseudomonas solanacearum*) are known to attack the crop while the damping-off disease can be serious in the southern areas. Other serious diseases are fruit-rot (*Colletotrichum capsici*) and anthracnose.

Eelworm can reduce yields if there is a heavy infestation. Strict rotation helps in its control. Stored peppers are liable to infestation by the grain moth (*Cadra cautella*) and the grain beetle (*Oryzaephilus mercator*). Chemical control is effective.

### 7.4.4 *Okra* (Hibiscus esculentus)

Okra is of African origin and is grown as a vegetable on almost all West African farms. The fruits are consumed dry, ground with other vegetables, or fresh, in soups and stews. Young shoots and leaves are used as spinach while leaves and stems provide fodder for sheep and goats. Stem fibre can be used for domestic purposes. Production figures are not available but average yields under local practice are probably around 200 kg/ha of fresh pods because most of the crop is grown in mixture. Yields of sole crop or in two crop mixture may be about 1 tonne/ha. Improved cultivars under good management can produce yields of 4·5–5·5 tonne/ha of fresh pods.

(a) *Ecology.* Okra is tolerant to wide range of soil and rainfall conditions and grows well during both wet and dry seasons. Some cultivars are sensitive to excessive soil moisture. Days to maturity varies considerably depending on the cultivar and whether young or mature pods are required. The first batch of pods are ready for picking in 2–3 months after sowing while the plant continues to bear fruit for several months afterwards until the dry season, when they become fibrous and set seed.

(b) *Cultivation.* Under indigenous practice the wet season crop is grown mainly in mixture of 2–6 crop combinations involving other vegetables, cowpea, groundnut, maize, millet, sorghum, kenaf, and root crops. In the village studies in the Northern Guinea Savanna about 3 per cent of the crop was found to be grown sole while about 78 per cent in 2–4 crop combinations (Norman 1972). The crop is sown during April to June depending on the onset of rains and finally harvested in October or November, 130–180 days after sowing. The crop is grown on ridges or in the furrow or on the flat at a variety of spacings (Fig. 7.1). The stand population varies from about 11 000 per ha and 7600 per ha in 2 and 3 crop mixtures respectively to about 6275 per ha in 5 crop mixtures. Pods are picked over several months after the first picking, 2–3 months after sowing. Harvested pods, if not consumed fresh, are dried and stored. For production of seeds for the next planting, selected pods are allowed to ripen and these are dried and seeds extracted from them.

Improved cultivars grown for high yields are sown at a spacing of 0·30 X 0·3–0·9 m under good fertility.

(c) *Diseases and pests.* Leaf curl and mosaic, both virus diseases, often attack okra. Strict rotation, use of disease-free seed and proper sanitation help in controlling these diseases. Powdery mildew and black leaf mould have been reported to cause damage to okra. There appears to be no known control for either.

Leaf-eating beetles and sucking insects including the cotton stainer are often found on the leaves and can cause serious damage. Eelworm or root-knot nematodes may cause a serious reduction in yields where the crop is grown continuously without rotation.

### 7.5  Fibres

#### 7.5.1  *Cotton* (Gossypium hirsutum)

The origin of cotton is still uncertain (Purseglove 1974). However, several species of short staple, diploid, cotton were grown in the West African Savanna for many centuries. These were almost completely displaced in the sixteenth century by the medium staple, tetraploid, American cotton of the species *G. hirsutum.* Cotton is second only to groundnuts in importance as a cash crop. Until recently it was a major export crop, but large textile industries developed within the countries in the West African Savanna are increasingly absorbing a considerable proportion of the current production. Virtually all surplus seed is exported, but crushing mills now being established locally will produce edible oil, and seed cake for the livestock industry and export. Cotton reaches its major concentration in the Northern Guinea and Sudan Savanna and only a small amount is produced in the areas further south. Estimated total production of seed cotton in the West African Savanna in 1971 was about 0·54m. tonnes from an area of about 1·06m. ha, corresponding to a yield of about 510 kg/ha (180 kg/ha of lint at ginning percentage of 35). Experimental yields of 1·5–2·0 tonne/ha seed cotton are generally obtained under proper management while yields of 2·5–3·0 tonne/ha of seed cotton have been obtained in the Northern

Guinea Savanna on long term maximum yield plots. A full account on cotton as a world crop is given by Prentice (1972).

(a) *Ecology.* The eco-physiological basis of yield in cotton has been reviewed by McArthur, Hesketh, and Baker (1975). The crop is grown under a wide range of climatic conditions and on various soil types. In the West African Savanna, the crop is entirely rain-fed, except for a small amount in the extreme north of the Sudan Savanna where cotton is grown in riverain alluvial soils. Most of the cotton crop is produced in the Northern Guinea and Sudan Savanna with rainfall of 700–1100mm and the rainy season of 120–180 days. Only a small amount (about 5 per cent) of cotton is grown in the Derived and Southern Guinea Savanna where rainfall is 1100–1500 mm and the rainy season is 190–250 days. The rainfall distribution is bimodal so the choice of an optimum sowing date is more difficult than in the unimodal rainfall regime further north. Insect pest attack, boll rotting and the risk of rain damage at harvest are far greater in the Derived and Southern Guinea Savanna than in the northern areas. Although good yields have been obtained in the southern areas by the use of fertilizers and efficient pest control, the cost of production is higher and quality of the crop lower than elsewhere. Another minor area of production is situated in the extreme north of the Sudan Savanna where cotton is grown on riverain alluvial soils. Here the annual rainfall is only 500–600 mm in a rainy season of 90–100 days, but some supplementary irrigation is provided and the cotton produced is of good quality.

Under indigenous practice the farmer gives priority to the production of food crops and the sowing of cotton is delayed until labour can be spared. For example, in the Northern Guinea Savanna the rainy season begins in May but most of the cotton crop is not sown until late July or early August (Norman 1972, Norman, Hayward, and Hallam 1974). Flowering does not start until the end of the rains in late September or early October, and continues in the dry season. Very little fertilizer or insecticide is used on the crop at present. It has been generally recognized that the late sowing is the main factor limiting the yields of the farmers' crop and that the application of fertilizers or pesticides under these conditions is not worthwhile. High yields are only possible when sowing is early together with the use of fertilizers and insecticides (Lawes 1968, Lyon 1970, Palmer and Goldsworthy 1972). Further, it appears that use of nitrogen on the crop without adequate pest protection may lead to greater losses and uneconomic returns (Hayward 1972). Indeed, Palmer and Heathcote (1970) reviewing cotton agronomy work in northern Nigeria pointed out that results from trials conducted in many areas suggest that farmers should not be encouraged to fertilize unsprayed cotton.

As cotton has an undeterminate habit of growth, the length of its growth cycle in the West African Savanna is controlled primarily by the availability of water. The amount of water available at the end of the rainy season has been shown to have a considerable effect on late-sown cotton. Thus H. E. King (1957), examining the production statistics in the main cotton growing areas in Nigeria, found a positive correlation between the amount of October rainfall and yield. However King also found a poor relationship between the yield of early sown cotton and the date when the rains ended, while King and Lawes (1959, 1960) found that supplementary irrigation after the end of the rains increased the yield of late sown cotton but not of early sown cotton.

Studies on flower production, crop phenology, and crop water relations (Kowal 1970b, Kowal and Faulkner 1975, Smithson and Hayward 1977) have shown that the period between the time to first flower and when evapotranspiration exceeds rainfall controls the number of bolls which are eventually retained and harvested. The length of the period is strongly dependent on sowing date and the later the sowing the shorter it becomes. For example, when the crop in the Northern Guinea Savanna is sown early, in June, the number of days to first flower after sowing (Phase I) is about 60, the duration of the flowering period before the onset of the rainfall deficit period (Phase II) about 40–50 days, and the maturation period (Phase III) about 55–60 days. When the crop is sown late, Phase II is reduced. This results in a reduction in flowers and bolls produced and retained, and a reduction in plant size and root system which further leads to less efficient use of water stored in the soil after the rains and shortening of Phase III (Kowal and Faulkner 1975). An extension of Phase II therefore improves yield, provided that plant nutrition and pest control are adequate, by lengthening the flowering period before the onset of water stress and by improving the use of water in Phase III. Work elsewhere has drawn similar conclusions and in Uganda, Farbrother and Munro (1970) showed that the yield was strongly correlated with the length of time from sowing to the end of Phase II. Other indirect evidence to support this hypothesis is provided by work in Nigeria where increase in yields resulting from earlier sowing, or from supplementary irrigation at the end of the rains can be interpreted as due to an extension of Phase II. Similarly, the greater productivity of the farmers' late sown crops in years when the rains continue beyond the end of September can also be attributed to a delay in the onset of water stress and a lengthening of Phase II.

It is clear that in absence of irrigation, the principal method of extending Phase II in relation to growth must be early sowing. Sowing at the beginning of the rainy season would give the longest possible duration of Phase II, but there are practical considerations limiting the extent to which the sowing date can be advanced. In order to avoid reducing the quality of the crop, it is desirable that boll opening should not begin until near the end of the rainy season. For the improved cotton cultivars currently in use in the West African Savanna, the period from sowing to the start of flowering is about 60 days and the boll maturation period is about 55–60 days. It therefore follows that the optimum length of Phase II, consistent with maintaining lint quality, would be achieved by sowing crops about 120 days before the start of the rainfall deficit period. By applying these arguments to the different regions where cotton is grown, some tentative conclusions may be drawn. In the Derived and Southern Guinea Savanna where the rainy season is about 200 days, optimum sowing date would be in early July and trials have indicated that further delay leads to a reduction in yield (Faulkner and Smithson 1972). In the Northern Guinea Savanna where the rainy season is about 150–180 days, optimum sowing date would be early to mid-June. In all these regions there is a lengthy period of rainfall before the optimum sowing date, which gives adequate time for land preparation and, in some cases, the possibility of growing a preceding crop. In the Sudan Savanna, however, the rainy season is no longer than the optimum growing period (Phase I + II), 120 days. Here, the cotton crop requires the whole rainy season for maximum production, and should be sown as soon as possible after the beginning of the rains in May. In the extreme north the rainy season of less than 100 days is inadequate for good cotton production, which justifies the local practice of sowing the crop in the river valleys at the beginning of the rains and extending the growing period by supplementary irrigation at the end of the season.

Thus, earlier sowing of cotton becomes increasingly important from south to north. In the Northern Guinea Savanna in Nigeria, the main area of production, the sowing date currently recommended is mid-June. However, the rainy season of 150–180 days suggests that a sowing date earlier (i.e., beginning of June) than now recommended (i.e., mid-June) would lengthen the growth Phase II and allow the crop to develop its full potential (Brown 1971). However, Kowal and Faulkner (1975) have pointed out that many of the difficulties that now prevent farmers from adopting the present recommendation would apply even more strongly to very early sowing when the cotton crop would compete directly with food crops. Furthermore, the period in which the crop is exposed to pest attack would be lengthened, and the additional protection required would increase the cost of production.

Another approach to the problem of lengthening Phase II of growth would be to produce earlier varieties, which start flowering earlier. Such cultivars would be most valuable in the more northerly areas of production, but might have little or no advantage in southern areas, although it could be argued that longer term cultivars would make better use of the extended rainy season. Recent work in Nigeria on okra-leaf cotton (Smithson and Hayward 1977) indicate that further improvement in yield may be possible. Okra-leaf cotton, an unadapted recent introduction, flowers and matures earlier than normal-leaf cotton. Further, because of its smaller size, more synchronized vegetative and reproductive growth, higher harvest index, better ability to accept closer spacing and canopy structure, better suited to efficient pest control with chemical spray, okra-leaf cotton may prove more advantageous than normal-leaf cotton in the future as farmers become more serious of the need for improved practice. The optimum population of normal-leaf cotton is about 100 000 plants/ha while of okra-leaf cotton about 200 000 to 300 000 plants/ha.

Cotton can be grown on a variety of soils from light sandy to heavy alluvium. However, good drainage and aeration are important, and as the crop matures on residual moisture, loam soils are preferred as they allow a greater proportion of the available water to be used by the crop. For well drained soils in the Savanna area, the amount of available water between field capacity and −15 bar soil water potential in the 120 cm soil profile is about 140–200 mm. Deficits of 160–180 mm at harvest have been reported (Kowal 1970b, Kowal and Faulkner 1975). At Samaru, in the Northern Guinea Savanna, an early sown crop was shown to remove 87 per cent of the available water while a late sown crop removed 74 per cent (Kowal and Faulkner 1975). The amounts withdrawn from the upper half of the profile by the two crops were similar, the main difference occurring below 75 cm. This showed that the cotton was efficient in using available soil moisture, but the late-sown crop was less efficient than early sown crop in using water from the lower parts of the soil profile. The crop water use of cotton sown at the end of June at Samaru has been reported to be about 480 mm (Kowal and Faulkner 1975) while minerals removed by a crop producing 1 tonne/ha seed cotton in Senegal have been reported as N, 48 kg/ha; P, 7·5 kg/ha; K, 27 kg/ha; Ca, 8·5 kg/ha (IRAT 1972).

(b) *Cultivation.* Small farmers under indigenous practice sow most of the crop in mixture of 2–5 crop combinations involving groundnut, cowpea, sweet potato, millet, and sorghum. However, the most common mixtures involve cowpea, groundnut and sweet potato. In village studies in the Northern Guinea Savanna about 20 per cent of the total area under cotton was found to be grown sole while about 45 per cent was in 2–4 crop mixtures (Norman 1972). Generally, except for cotton grown in settlement schemes where support facilities for spraying and extension exist, unsprayed cotton is grown in mixtures (Norman *et al.* 1974). Spacing under local practice varies greatly particularly in mixtures (Fig. 7.1). The crop is largely sown on ridges. Under sole cropping the spacing is about 0·5 × 1 m while the stand population is about 20 500 per ha. In mixtures, ridges are about 1 m apart while the stand population varies from about 19 000 per ha in two crop mixtures to 24 000 per ha in five crop mixtures (Norman 1972). The crop is sown in July or August and harvested in December. Much of the crop is cultivated by hand but a few farmers do use ox-drawn implements on schemes which are government assisted where farmers are encouraged to spray the crop and follow recommended practice. Harvesting is done by hand.

Sole cropping with improved cultivars requires early sowing at adequate population and crop nutrition and efficient spraying regime to control pests for the high yield potential to be realized. For intermediate levels of fertility and pest control, spacing is generally about 0·4 × 0·9 m at two plants/stand (55 500 plants/ha) while at high fertility and efficient pest control, optimum plant population is about 100 000 plants/ha either on square planting at about 0·932 × 0·32 m at one plant/stand or on rectangular planting at about 0·03 × 0·6 m at two plants/stand.

For yields over 1·5 ton/ha, experimental rates of 40–80 kg/ha N and 13–22 kg/ha P are applied to the crop. Recently widespread boron deficiency has been reported in farmers' fields while large responses to applications of boron have been reported (Smithson 1972, Heathcote and Smithson 1974, Smithson and Heathcote 1974).

(c) *Diseases and pests.* The cotton plant is particularly subject to attack from diseases and insects. Bacterial blight (*Xanthomonas malvacearum*) is a common disease which affects all parts of the plant including bolls. It is carried by seed and plant debris but not by soil. Seed treatment and proper sanitation gives effective control. Genetic resistance is available and is used in breeding. Leaf curl, a virus disease carried by white flies (*Bemisia* sp.), can be serious but control is possible with strict sanitation, crop rotation and the use of genetic resistance. *Fusarium* wilt (*Fusarium oxysporum*) and *Verticillium* wilt (*Verticillium dahliae*), both soil-borne, are minor diseases and genetic resistance is available. Anthracnose (*Glomerella gossypii*) affects all parts of the plant but the disease is not serious at present. Crop sanitation and rotation provides partial control. Grey mildew (*Ramularia gossypii*) is a minor disease of little importance. There are various species of fungus which gain entrance to bolls which have been damaged by insects.

Bollworms (*Diparopsis castanea, Pectinophone gossypiella, Cryptophlebia leucotreta, Eria* spp.) are the most serious pests of cotton. They feed in the bolls, damaging lint and seed, and cause large reductions in yield and quality. Proper sanitation, crop rotation and early maturing crop can provide some measure of control, but never sufficiently complete. Sources of genetic resistance have been found and may be transferred to cultivated types. Cotton stainers (*Dysdercus* spp.) are very common and serious. They attack the opening bolls, leaving a rust colour stain on the lint. They feed on the seeds and are vectors of the fungi, *Nematospora* spp., which cause internal boll-rot. Sucking bugs (*Empoasca facialis, Helopeltis* spp., *Aphis gossypii*) can cause considerable damage as they feed on all parts of the plant and cause boll shedding. Chemical spraying is effective against most of these insects.

### 7.5.2 *Kenaf* (Hibiscus cannabinus)

Kenaf, a plant probably of African origin, is grown in much of the West African Savanna on a very small scale to provide fibre. The retted fibre from the stem is used for rope and cordage and can be woven to make coarse bags. The young leaves are sometimes used as a pot-herb. No reliable production statistics exist for the crop. However, limited research in Nigeria has indicated that considerable potential exists for kenaf in the Savanna areas. Although the fibre is coarser than that from jute, it is comparable to jute in lustre and is more resistant to rotting. The seed contains oil which is suitable for industrial uses. An account of the crop on a world basis is given by Kirby (1963).

In preliminary trials in the Guinea Savanna, yields of over 2 tonne/ha of dry fibre have been obtained with the crop growing on 90 cm ridges (Abdullahi 1970), although potential yields at closer spacings on the flat appear to be considerably greater, about 3 tonne/ha.

(a) *Ecology*. The climate in the Northern Guinea and southern parts of the Sudan Savanna are most suitable for intensive production of kenaf. It is a short-day plant and early sowing therefore produces greater and longer stem growth before flowering begins. Fibre strands of 3–4 m require about 4–5 months growth period. Delay in sowing therefore results in shorter fibres due to effects of photoperiod and earlier moisture stress at the end of the rainy season. Kenaf prefers well drained, neutral, sandy loams and does not tolerate waterlogging.

(b) *Cultivation*. Under indigenous practice about a quarter of the crop in the village studies was found to be grown sole while the rest was in mixtures of 2–3 crop combinations involving sorghum, maize, cassava and vegetables such as okra and peppers (Norman 1972). Seed rates under sole cropping and in mixture is about 10 kg/ha equivalent to a plant population of about 200 000 plants/ha. The crop is harvested 3–5 months after sowing.

For fibre production under improved practice, a higher plant populations of about 700 000–800 000 at a spacing of 0·05–0·08 × 0·2 m appears to produce the highest yields, over 3 tonne/ha of dry fibre (E. F. I. Baker, unpublished). For seed production a spacing of 0·3 × 0·6 m is optimum. The longer the vegetative phase the greater the yield and early sowing in May or June is necessary for high yields. For high quality fibre, the best time to harvest is when about 8–12 flowers are in bloom. Delay in harvesting leads to coarser fibre or lower lustre and lower retting per cent. Retting of stems in water takes about 8–10 days after which the bark is stripped and beaten gently to separate the fibres. Wet fibre is washed in water and dried. Generally, the fibre yield is about 16 per cent of the weight of dry stem while dry fibre as percentage of dry ribbon is about 61–67 per cent (Abdullahi 1970). Mechanical decortication with retting is effective while recently, decortication of dry stems without retting has given good results at Samaru in Nigeria.

(c) *Diseases and pests.* The most common diseases are dry rot (*Macrophomina phaseolina*), anthracnose (*Colletotrichum hibisci*), leaf burn (*Corticum solani*) and stem and root rot or wilt (*Phytophthora nicotianae*).

The most common insect pests are flea beetles (*Podagrica* spp.) which attack the leaves particularly of late sown crops, stem girdler (*Alcidodes brevirostries*) and cotton stainers (*Dysdercus* spp.).

### 7.5.3 Roselle (Hibiscus sabdariffa)

Roselle is probably indigenous to West Africa. It is grown in much of the West African Savanna on a very small scale to provide fibre while the succulent calcyes and young leaves and stems are used as pot-herbs. No reliable statistics exist for the crop. However, limited research in Nigeria has suggested that considerable potential exists for roselle in the Savanna areas. A brief account of the crop is given by Kirby (1963).

In preliminary trials in the Guinea Savanna yields of about 2 tonne/ha of dry fibre have been obtained with the crop growing on 90 cm ridges, although potential yields at closer spacings on the flat appear to be considerably greater, about 3 tonne/ha.

(a) *Ecology.* The climate in the Guinea Savanna is suitable for intensive production of roselle. It is a short-day plant and early sowing therefore produces greater and longer stem growth before flowering begins. Fibre stands of 3–5 m require about 5–7 month growth period. It prefers well drained, neutral, sandy loams and does not tolerate waterlogging.

(b) *Cultivation.* Under indigenous practice much of the crop is grown in mixture with vegetables. The crop is grown at a very low plant population for fruit production and is harvested 3–5 months after sowing.

For fibre and seed production under improved practice, the husbandry and retting is similar to that in kenaf. However, dry fibre as percentage of dry ribbon is generally lower than in kenaf, about 49–63.

(c) *Diseases and pests.* Pests which attack kenaf have been reported also to attack roselle but little research work has been conducted to date.

## 7.6 Other crops

### 7.6.1 Sesame (Sesamum indicum)

Sesame or benniseed is believed to have originated in Africa, probably Ethiopia. It is a well established crop in parts of the African Savanna, grown for its edible seeds which are a rich source of sesame oil. A large proportion of the crop is exported for industrial and domestic use elsewhere while locally ground or cooked seeds are eaten in soups and sweetmeat. Young leaves are used as potherb and stems are burnt as fuel. There are a number of other uses for sesame products (Weiss 1971, van Rheenen 1973, Purseglove 1974). Estimated total production of sesame in 1971 in West Africa was about 88 000 tonnes from an area of about 0·3m. ha, corresponding to a yield of about 290 kg/ha. About 70 per cent of the total production is in Nigeria where most of the crop is grown in the Southern Guinea Savanna. Although the crop is grown largely for export, there are no large scale commercial growers. The yield reflects the low standard of crop husbandry because, under proper management in parts of America, yields of about 2 tonne/ha are obtained under commercial production of rain-fed crops; and yields in the range of 0·7–1·2 tonne/ha have been reported for other areas in Africa (Litzenberger 1974). In general, little crop improvement research has been done on sesame and high yielding cultivars adapted to the conditions in the West African Savanna have yet to be bred and introduced. However, work conducted by van Rheenen (1973) in Nigeria has shown that yields of up to 0·8 tonne/ha are possible with local improved cultivars under improved practice. Further improvements in the yield potential will depend largely on breeding plant types whose structure and developmental physiology is adapted to local environmental conditions but responsive to high fertility at high plant densities.

(a) *Ecology.* Sesame is adapted to growing in hot and dry conditions but in West Africa it is grown in areas where rainfall ranges from 500 mm, in the Sudan Savanna, to 1100–1500 mm in the Southern Guinea and Derived Savanna. Once established, it has a marked degree of endurance to drought of short periods. About 80 per cent of the crop in West Africa is grown in the Southern Guinea and Derived Savanna although environmental conditions are suitable for production in the Northern Guinea and Sudan Savanna where the remaining crop is grown. The crop is sown early in the wet season, but in the Southern Guinea Savanna, a late crop sown two or three months before the end of the wet season is common.

Sesame is basically a short-day plant but long-day types exist while some appear to be less sensitive to photoperiod. Yield is greatly influenced by photoperiod, and temperature can have a considerable modifying effect. Effect of photoperiod and temperature interactions have not been fully studied although Weiss (1971) has summarized the work conducted in various areas of the world. It appears that in short-day cultivars such as those grown in West Africa, flowering is delayed and vegetative grown increases with longer photoperiods, while capsule and seed produced may be positively or negatively affected depending on the cultivar (Ghosh 1955, Matsuoka 1959, 1960, Smilde 1960). Sesame normally requires fairly hot conditions during growth to produce maximum yields. A temperature of 25°–27°C encourages rapid germination, initial growth and flower formation while temperatures below 18°–20°C inhibit germination and growth. Low temperatures at flowering can cause pollen sterility and flower drop, while temperatures above 40°C reduces fertilization and capsule set. In some African cultivars, studies by Matsuoka (1959, 1960) have shown that the number of days from sowing to flowering, the height to the first capsule, and the number of branches per plant is greater under higher temperatures than normal, although the number of capsules per plant is less. Under controlled conditions Smilde (1960) found that the optimum germination temperature ranged 32°–35°C while vegetative growth increased as the average temperature was raised from 24°C to 33°C. A constant temperature of 24°C–27°C induced early flower initiation, whereas high (33°C) and low (15°C) night temperature caused a delay. However, the retarding effect of low and high night temperature was more or less counteracted by high and low day temperature respectively. Further, the delay in flowering due to long photoperiod is offset by high temperatures. In non-African cultivars, different kinds of sensitivity and responses to temperature and photoperiod have been reported (Weiss 1971).

Cultivars grown in West Africa have a growth cycle of about 120–160 days, but cultivars of 180 days to maturity are also grown. Date of sowing has a great influence on yield. Delay in sowing causes decreases in yields in all areas (Stonebridge 1963, van Rheenen 1973). Highest yields are obtained when the crops are sown in March and April in the Southern Guinea Savanna and May and June in the Northern Guinea and Sudan Savanna. Each week's delay after the optimum sowing time has been found to decrease yield by about 15 per cent. In the Southern Guinea Savanna where a late crop is sown, August sowing was found to produce the best yield with about 8 per cent decrease in yield per week's delay in sowing subsequently. Effects of sowing date on growth, development and yield of sesame in Nigeria have been discussed by van Rheenen (1973). Factors thought to affect yields in different sowing dates were daylength, temperature, soil moisture stress, leaching of nitrogen, soil capping by rainfall, waterlogging, solar radiation, and disease and pest incidence.

The optimum plant population varies with cultivar, fertility, and growing conditions. Although sowing on 0·90 m ridges is recommended in West Africa, maximum yields at adequate fertility have been obtained at a spacing of about 0·13 × 0·22 m (about 350 000 plants/ha). Generally, local cultivars at low fertility produce their best yields at wider spacings, improved cultivars at closer spacings (van Rheenen 1973).

Most of the local cultivars are characterized by open or dehiscent capsules. This character has the advantage that it simplifies threshing, but the disadvantage that it increases seed loss. The discovery in 1943 of the indehiscent character led to the possibility of complete mechanized production. Recently, a somewhat similar mutant (paper capsule) has appeared to be more promising. Losses due to seed shattering can be high under local practice if harvesting is delayed. However, experiments by van Rheenen (1973) have shown that seed loss should not exceed 2 per cent if a good harvesting method is applied.

Recommended cultivars in West Africa respond only to a low level of fertilizer application but for high yields of 1–2 tonne/ha cultivars responsive to fertilizer must be used. Estimated removal of nutrients by a crop yielding 0·5 tonne/ha is N, 25 kg/ha; P, 3 kg/ha; K, 25 kg/ha. However, a crop yielding 2·2 tonne/ha removes about N, 120 kg/ha; P, 30 kg/ha; K, 133 kg/ha (Bascones and Lopez Ritas 1961a, 1961b). Aspects related to crop nutrition have been discussed by Weiss (1971).

Sesame prefers sandy loam soils and it is grown in well drained soils of pH 6·0–6·5. It is very sensitive to waterlogging although it will grow reasonably on poor soil under indigenous practice. In West Africa sesame is grown as the third or fourth and last crop in the rotation, frequently after sorghum and yams, but also following maize, groundnut, cotton, millet, or beans. Exceptionally it takes the first or second place in the rotation.

(b) *Cultivation.* The crop is grown during the rainy season. The local practice is to grow the crop without fertilizer at a wide range of spacings and plant densities. Sowing is done on widely spaced ridges about 4 m apart and about 1·5 m between stands (1650 stands/ha) with about 16 plants per stand (27 500 plants/ha) or by broadcasting the seed either over the whole flat field or on the low, fairly wide ridges. In the latter the average amount of seed used is 4·5–9·0 kg/ha. No thinning is done after sowing, and the plant population varies from 360 000 to 900 000 plants/ha (Steele 1960, van Rheenen 1973). Interplanting of melons which creep in the furrows is not uncommon. When leaves begin to drop off and the remaining have turned yellow, and when the lowest capsules on the stem are about to split open, sesame is ready for harvest. Plants are uprooted or cut and either left in the windrow for one or two days or immediately bundled and tied. The plant bundles are placed in shocks or put to racks until sufficiently dry for threshing which is done by beating gently with sticks.

If yields in the order of 1–2 tonne/ha are to be obtained, cultivars responsive to fertilizer must be grown at adequate fertility. Deficiency of one major nutrient has been shown to reduce uptake of other nutrients and phosphate deficiency in particular can reduce uptake of nitrogen, potassium, calcium, sulphur and magnesium (Pal and Bangarayy 1958, Sen and Lahiri 1959). Spacing and plant density can vary from 0·5–0·10 × 0·6–0·90 m to 0·15–0·45 × 0·15–0·34 m depending on the cultivar and harvesting method. Sesame crop does not compete well with weeds and timely weed control is essential for good yields.

(c) *Diseases and pests.* Sesame is attacked by a number of diseases during the wet season. It appears that foliage diseases in West Africa occur as a complex and not as individual diseases. Identification work in Nigeria has isolated a number of organisms from leaves of diseased plants (i.e., *Alternaria sesami, Cercospora sesami, Curvularia lunata, Cylindrosporium sesami, Fusarium semitectum, Helminthosporium halodes, Macrophomina phaseoli, Oidium* spp., *Pestalotiopis mayumbensis* and *Pseudomonas sesami*). However, it appears that the pathogens *Cylindrosporium sesami, Cercospora sesami, Alternaria sesami* and *Pseudomonas sesami* are possibly the main members of the disease complex and cause leaf spot symptoms described by van Rheenen (1973). Root rot (*Corticium solani*) has been reported on crops grown continuously or too often on the same place. Virus diseases reported for sesame are mycoplasma and leaf curl. Damage caused by mycoplasma is negligible at present but can become of some importance in the dry season crop under irrigation. Leaf curl (*Nicotiana virus 10* or *Tobacco leaf-curl virus*) transmitted by the white fly (*Bemisia tabaci*) can do much damage to sesame and it has become a disease of major importance since 1964 in Nigeria (Bailey 1966). It was not reported before that (Robertson 1963b).

Main insect pests are the leaf roller or webber (*Antigastra catalaunalis*) and the gall midge (*Asphonydylia sesami*). Larvae of the former eat the young flower buds, flowers and young fruits but can be controlled effectively with insecticides, while the effect of climatic factors on the pest incidence has been reported (Chadha 1974). The gall midge lays eggs in the ovaries and gall develop before the flowers open. The maggots feed on the surrounding tissue and pupate inside the gall. Capsules may be partly or totally affected and in extreme cases all or nearly all capsules of all plants in the field show galls. Chemical control is difficult but resistance against the gall fly has been found recently (S. S. Chadha, unpublished 1970–73). Resistance to the gall midge has also been observed in the species *Ceratotheca sesomoides* which is indigenous to Africa, and crosses with *Sesamum indicum* (van Rheenen 1970). Other insects which are known to attack sesame are grasshoppers, *Agonoscelis versicolor*, and the seed bug (*Rhyparochromus*).

### 7.6.2 *Tobacco* (Nicotiana tabacum)

Tobacco is believed to have originated in South America. *N. tabacum* is the source of commercial tobacco and it is one of the very few crops whose trade is on a leaf basis. Tobacco is an important cash crop in West Africa where most of it is used in cigarettes and some in snuff, chewing, and pipe smoking. Although figures are not available, a large proportion of the crop is grown in the Savanna areas. Estimated total production of cured tobacco leaves in 1971 in West Africa was about 33 000 tonnes from an area of about 66 000 ha, corresponding to a yield of about 500 kg/ha. Average yields vary widely from 300 kg/ha in Ivory Coast to about 1700 kg/ha in Mali, depending on the level of husbandry, growing conditions, fertility and area under cultivation. About 55 per cent of the total production in West Africa is in Nigeria where average yields are about 460 kg/ha. Recently, there has been quite a rapid expansion of commercial tobacco in many of the West African countries. Although quantities grown are small by world standards, an increasing proportion of the commercial crop is being grown under conditions of improved management, and pesticides and low to medium levels of fertilizers are applied. Here, yields of 0·8–1·0 tonne/ha are obtained but at a higher level of management yields of 1·5–2·0 tonne/ha are possible and have been obtained under experimental conditions. Elsewhere in the tropics commercial yields under high level of management are in the range 2·2–2·6 tonne/ha. A full account of growing and processing of tobacco as a world crop has been given by Akehurst (1971).

(a) *Ecology*. Most of the crop in West Africa is grown in the Derived, Guinea and Sudan Savanna where the tobacco types grown are principally the flue-cured Virginia and the air-cured Burley. Cigar and oriental types have been reported to be minor. The optimum growing temperatures are between 20° and 30°C, but tobacco will tolerate temperature up to 35°C. The crop requires about 90–120 days from transplanting to final harvesting and for good yields about 500–750 mm well distributed rainfall during its growth. In the Derived and Southern Guinea Savanna rainfall and the length of the rainy season are adequate for two crops. In the Sudan and Northern Guinea Savanna the rainy season is long enough for one crop but during the dry season a sizable proportion of the total crop (about 30–40 per cent) is grown in the *fadama* areas and a small amount under irrigation (Coppock 1966, Irvine 1974). There are considerable season to season variations in yields of rain-fed crops and differences in weather, especially in duration, frequency, and intensity of the rains, are the principal causes. Also, disease, especially leaf curl, has an important influence. Dry weather is required for ripening and harvesting. Continual rains towards the end of the crop's life leads to diseases and thin, light-weight leaves. A prolonged dry period when the crop is nearing maturity causes premature ripening, while heavy rains after a long dry period during ripening leads to secondary growth. In both cases the leaves are difficult to cure. Further, after harvest, if weather is too dry during air-curing, it may cause leaves to dry out too rapidly and remain green; too high a humidity may cause leaf rot.

Cultivated tobacco is day-neutral although short-day types, the 'Mammoth' cultivars, only flower when exposed to short days. Because leaf expansion is greatly influenced by temperature, leaf thickness under a given temperature regime depends on the solar radiation intensity. High temperature and low radiation intensity can lead to production of thin leaves which may be difficult to cure.

Both yield and quality are very sensitive to soil conditions and they determine the type and use of the leaf produced. Collectively, all tobaccos cover a wide range of soil conditions; but for a specific tobacco type, the requirements are somewhat exacting for production of high quality cured leaf. Different types of tobacco make effective use of a wide range of soils. A light sandy loam is essential for flue-cured bright tobacco; air-cured brown tobacco grows best on heavier silt or clay loam soils; air-cured bright tobacco is grown on soils intermediate between the two. In general, the crop requires adequate drainage, soil moisture retention and aeration. Tobacco is very sensitive to waterlogging, while strongly acid or strongly alkaline soils do not produce good crops. Soils with a $pH$ of 5·0–6·5 are considered satisfactory.

The three principal cured tobaccos at present produced in West Africa vary in accordance with the method of curing which also varies with climatic conditions in the area in which the crop is grown. The air-cured tobacco is produced by allowing the leaves to dry in natural air. However, since the humidity in the Derived and Southern Guinea Savanna is high, the curing period is extended and results in a change of leaf colour from green to yellow and finally to dark brown. This is in contrast to the bright colour produced from the air-cured crop in the Sudan and Northern Guinea Savanna where drier conditions result in rapid drying and curing of the leaf. Air-curing is done by either hanging the leaves outside in the open (i.e., sun-cured tobacco) or in barns (i.e., shade-cured tobacco) which are simple open-sided or drop-sided sheds with thatched or tin roofs.

Drop-sided barns are necessary in the humid areas as the sides can be lowered at night. Curing in the humid areas takes 5–6 weeks or more while in the drier areas as short as 3–7 days. The rain-fed crop in the Northern Guinea and Sudan Savanna is harvested in October and November and leaves are hung up to dry until the rising humidity of the first rains makes it possible to handle the leaves again in June or July. Much of the crop grown in the *fadama* areas during the dry season is planted from mid-September to mid-November depending on the area and recession of the floods. Some may be continued to be planted until February, but its contribution is very small. The crop is harvested in January to March and the harvested leaves are cured but not handled until June or July when the leaves are moist enough. However, for the production of high quality bright tobacco in the dry season in the *fadama* or under irrigation, it is advisable to plant as early in September as possible to take advantage of the very dry conditions which are essential to produce a bright yellow, air-cured leaf. Because of low temperatures during the first half of the dry season, crop growth both in the nursery stage and in the field is slow and a late planted dry season crop may reach maturity when the very dry conditions are on the wane, leading to slower curing and less bright tobacco (Winter 1965). In the flue-cured tobacco, artificial heat is applied during curing and the whole process is completed in 5–7 days. Curing, particularly flue-curing, requires considerable skill and experience and it must be done with great care because imperfect curing can destroy the potential good qualities in the leaf. The various methods of curing have been described by Akehurst (1971) and Purseglove (1974). The process basically involves starving the leaves slowly. During the yellowing process circulation of the sap is necessary, followed by killing and drying the leaf. If water is lost too quickly the leaf remains green, if lost too slowly the leaf becomes sponged and may rot. In West Africa some tobacco is sun-cured for home consumption.

Good yields are only obtained under adequate fertility and an air-cured crop yielding about 1·9 tonne/ha removes N, 101 kg/ha; P, 11 kg/ha; K, 121 kg/ha. The fertilizer type and amount must be adjusted to the kind of tobacco grown, the soil type, and the yield level being aimed at. Flue-cured bright tobacco should be grown under fertility conditions relatively low in nitrogen but high in phosphate and potash. For air-cured tobacco the fertilizer should be more balanced as to the nutrients. In the tropics for medium to high yields of 1·5–2·0 tonne/ha under commercial planting, nitrogen is usually applied at the rate of 20–45 kg/ha to flue-cured, and 50–110 kg/ha to air-cured. Phosphate and potash are applied at the rate of P, 25–50 kg/ha and K, 90–140 kg/ha after transplanting.

(b) *Cultivation.* Commercial tobacco growing in West Africa is an example of integrated management (Hunter and Bottrall, 1974) where commercial firms provide full control of the complete process. In Nigeria, for example, this includes research, extension service, inputs including seed, credit, graded marketing, and processing of the crop (Norman 1974). Mechanization is becoming increasingly important in many areas in the preparation and cultivation of the land, and tractors and implements can be hired in some regions at a fixed price per unit area. The commercial crop is usually grown sole, while for home consumption tobacco is often grown in mixture. In the village studies in the Northern Guinea Savanna, about 72 per cent of the crop was found to be grown sole while the remaining in 2–3 crop combinations involving sorghum, maize, sweet potato, okra, and onion (Norman 1972). Nursery seed beds are prepared during the middle of the rainy season for the second crop. Seed beds are shaded and mulched, and 12:14:7 compound fertilizer at the rate of 540 kg/ha with pesticides is recommended. After about 40–50 days, the seedlings are transplanted to the field, usually on ridges or, when the land is suitable, to the flat. Ridges are more satisfactory because of good drainage and better root growth. When large areas are planted, crops are often successively planted to spread out the work of harvesting and drying. In commercial plantings, 10:13:10 compound fertilizer at the rate of 112 kg/ha is recommended at present and this is applied at the time of transplanting, placed inside the ridge about 20 cm deep, or side-placed few days after transplanting. Spacing is usually 0·6–0·75 × 0·9–1·2 m (about 11 000–18 500 plants/ha) but seedlings may be planted at closer spacings 0·3–0·6 × 0·5–0·9 m (18 000–66 500 plants/ha) depending on the cultivar and soil fertility. Weeds can influence both yield and quality and the field is generally cultivated two to three times to control them. When flower buds are formed, about 50–70 days after transplanting, the inflorescences and the topmost leaves are broken off by hand, an operation which improves the yield and quality. The time and height of topping depends on the type of tobacco grown and soil, the level of fertility, and the spacing. Topping therefore requires considerable skill and judgement for achieving best results. Soon after topping, suckers are produced in the axils of the leaves and are removed weekly until harvest, otherwise the advantages of topping are lost. About 15–25 days after topping or 65–95 days after transplating, the lowest leaves begin to ripen and these are picked singly from the bottom. Two or three leaves are taken at each picking, which is continued at weekly intervals. The leaves are strung back to back in alternate pairs on each side of sticks and hung in the barn for curing. The sequential picking of leaves for the flue-cured tobacco is essential but for the air-cured tobacco whole plants may be harvested by cutting the stem near the ground when the greatest number of the best leaves are at the proper stage of ripeness, which is usually 90–125 days after transplanting. This method is used elsewhere in the tropics and the leaves may be cured on the stems, which are tied to the poles and the leaves are wilted before transfer to the curing barn. Complete stalk-curing is not done in West Africa. Occasionally, when half the leaves have been taken from the plant if the remaining leaves show a uniform ripening, plants are cut and the remaining leaves are then stalk-cured, thus saving labour. Usually, however, the remaining leaves do not ripen simultaneously.

In West Africa at present there are five grades of flue-cured tobacco, and three grades of air-cured, with graded prices (G.A.F. Rand, personal communicatin 1976). The grades of flue-cured tobacco are: (1) Clean yellow leaves without blemish; (2) Yellow/orange leaves with spots and some degree of blemish or sponging; (3) Yellow leaves with under-ripe greenish centres; (4) Burnt leaves; (5) Green leaves. The grades of dark air-cured tobacco are: (1) Clear light to dark brown leaves without blemish, usually from the middle of the plant; (2) Clear light to dark brown leaves but with a degree of blemish and coarseness and darker colour; (3) Short tip leaves with medium to dark brown colour, and those leaves not fitting into grades (1) and (2). The grades of bright air-cured tobacco, from the *fadama* areas in the northern Savanna regions, are: (1) Clear bright leaves without blemish, usually from the middle of the plant, (2) Clear bright leaves but with a degree of blemish and coarseness and duller colour; (3) Short tip leaves with medium to bright colour and those leaves not fitting into grades (1) and (2). Quality of tobacco is determined by the genetic make-up, environment, cultural practice, curing, and aging. In countries where tobacco growing is advanced, cured leaves are sorted into many different grades and in assessing leaf quality all the following elements are taken into account: size and shape of leaf, mid-rib, leaf venation, thickness, density of structure and texture, weight per unit area, elasticity, aroma, taste and hygroscopic properties. In West Africa in general, however, quality does not yet seem to be a major agronomic objective, but it is likely to become more important as the tobacco industry advances and the volume of production increases, necessitating finer grading. When this stage is reached more attention will have to be paid to a number of aspects of cultural practice, in particular the nitrogen-potash balance in the nutrition of the crop.

(c) *Diseases and pests.* Tobacco suffers from many diseases of the leaf, stem, and root, and is attacked by several insect pests. Damping-off disease (*Pythium* spp., *Rhizoctonia* spp.) is a condition of young seedlings in which the stem at soil level becomes soft and rotten, killing the seedling. The fungus is present in the soil, entering and softening the tissues which are then invaded by a large number of soil organisms, especially bacteria (Keay and Quinn 1967). Chemical control is effective while good drainage, avoidance of over-watering or over-crowding, and seed-bed sterilization also help in its control. Black shank (*Phytophthora parasitica*) is primarily a disease of the roots and the basal part of the stem, but the pathogen is capable of attacking any part of the plant at any stage of growth (Amile 1972). Symptoms vary according to the age of the plant and organ affected, weather conditions, and the degree of host resistance. On young seedlings, early attack results in damping-off. Environmental conditions greatly influence the severity of this disease. Black shank is a warm weather disease and soil temperature below 20 °C drastically reduces field infection. Excessively wet soil conditions favour the disease. There is some evidence that the severity of the disease is increased in the presence of nematodes, especially the root-knot nematodes; and most black-shank resistant cultivars appear to lose some of their resistance in the presence of this nematode. Previously it was thought that tobacco was the only natural host for the black shank fungus. However, Allen (1971) reported that the fungus causes Zebra disease on *Agave* spp. Tomato, egg plant, sweet potato, castor bean, and peppers have been infected with the disease by means of artificial inoculation. However, these crops when grown on heavily infested soil in field do not show any evidence of disease attack, although they can play a role in the perpetuation of the fungus. There is no adequate chemical treatment for control. Resistant cultivars are available while soil sterilization, rotation, and strict sanitation help considerably in its control. Black root rot (*Thielaviopsis basicola*) has been reported on tobacco and the fungus can live in the soil for a long time. It attacks other plants such as groundnut and cowpea. Soil sterilization helps in its control but resistant cultivars exist. Southern stem rot (*Sclerotium rolfsii*) has been reported (Irvine 1974) attacking the plant in its later stages of growth. The fungus appears to have a wide host range so that crop rotation does not lead to its control. Frog-eye leaf spot (*Cercospora nicotianae*) can be a serious disease under wet and humid conditions. It is mainly found on the older leaves in the field but can cause spotting during the early stages of curing.

Tobacco mosaic virus disease is very common but recently sources of genetic resistance have been found. Several mosaic virus strains appear to be involved and these are transmitted mechanically in handling plants and the use of infected tobacco. Other major virus disease is leaf curl, transmitted by white flies (*Bemisia tabaci*).

Several insect pests in addition to white flies have been reported (Libby 1968). These include green shield bugs (*Nezara viridula*), mealy bugs (*Planococcus citri*), budworms (*Heliothis umbrosus*), leaf worms (*Spodoptera littoralis*) and mole crickets (*Gryllotalpa africana*).

Nematodes, particularly the root-knot nematode (*Meloidogyne* spp.) and the reniform nematode (*Rotylenchulus reniformis*), have the potential of causing serious losses. Other crops such as vegetables, sweet potato, potato, cowpea, wheat, cotton, melon are also affected by these nematodes. Tobacco should not therefore be grown near these crops, and land infected through these crops should be avoided. Control of nematodes is effective through the use of nematicides while high fertility, fallow, flooding, and soil sterilization also help in their control.

### 7.6.3 *Sugar cane* (Saccharum *spp.*)

Sugar cane originated in Asia and the original cane (*S. officinarum*) probably evolved in New Guinea from *S. robustum*, and introgression from *Erianthus maximus* may have been involved. *S. robustum* is believed to have evolved from strains of the wild species *S. spontaneum*, which, although indigenous to India, is thought to have become isolated in New Guinea, and introgression also may have occurred from *Miscanthus floridulus* (Grassl 1969, Purseglove 1975). Cultivars of *S. officinarum* are known as the 'noble' canes, because of their fine thick stems, to differentiate them from the thin canes of *S. barberi* and *S. sinense* which have long been cultivated in India and Asia and thought to be hybrids between *S. spontaneum* and *S. officinarum*. Up to the end of the nineteenth century, only a few clones of the noble canes had been used to establish the major portion of the world sugar cane industry. With the rediscovery of seed and seedlings in sugar cane in 1898, genetic variability was increased to some extent by using new cultivars and breeding within *S. officinarum*. Many of these noble canes were high yielding but their resistance to pests and pathogens was low. These continued as the main commercial cultivars until higher yielding interspecific hybrids with greater and wider resistance to pests and pathogens were produced from crosses with *S. spontaneum* and back-crossing to the noble canes, the process being known as nobilization. Almost all the commercial cultivars grown today are interspecific hybrids of *Saccharum* spp., specially bred during the present century, and these have a complex ancestry (Purseglove 1975). It has been recorded that sugar cane was introduced into West Africa by the Portuguese during the early fifteenth century. Whether the spread to the deep interior took place form the coast or from the Mediterranean is not known. Sugar is a popular item in the diets of the people in West Africa, and consumption far exceeds the supply from local production. Sugar imports into West Africa are currently estimated at about 0·3m. tonnes annually, equivalent to about 2·93m. tonnes of cane. Estimated total production of cane in West Africa in 1971 was about 1·3m. tonnes (about 0·17m. tonnes of sugar) from an area of about 51 000 ha, corresponding to a yield of about 25 tonne/ha. In other words, about two-thirds of the sugar consumed in West Africa is imported. Sugar cane is therefore an important crop commodity in West Africa not only because of its present demand on the foreign exchange but also for its domestic and industrial potential within West Africa and for export, both of sugar and various by-products. Although sugar cane is widely distributed in West Africa, in the past it has nowhere been grown on a large scale. It was mainly grown in small patches for chewing, and for production during the dry season of 'jaggery' and alcohol by local methods. Recently, however, large plantations have been established for commercial production. The setting up of the commercial sugar industry in Nigeria has been discussed by Barnes (1974). About 50 per cent of the total sugar in West Africa is produced in Nigeria where cane yields under local practice, with about 8-12 months growing period, average about 20-25 tonne/ha. Large scale experimental yields in the range 130-170 tonne/ha have been obtained in 12 months (Kowal 1962, Kowal and Hill 1965); and yields from commercial production with about 11-14 months growing period are likely to be about 90-120 tonne/ha or more—this compares favourably with other areas in the tropics where production is advanced. Detail accounts of the cultivation and processing of commercial sugar cane are available (King, Mungomery, and Hughes 1965, Humbert 1967, Barnes 1974, Purseglove 1975).

(a) *Ecology*. Sugar cane thrives under conditions of high temperature and solar radiation. For a crop of 12-14 months duration about 1500-1700 mm of water is needed. For good yields, soil of high fertility with good drainage is essential. The ideal climate is one with a long warm growing season (24°-27°C or more) and a fairly dry, sunny, and cool ripening and harvesting season. In the Savanna these conditions prevail in the *fadama* areas and flood plains, and on the upland under supplementary irrigation. Elsewhere in the tropics the duration of the crop ranges from about nine months to two years, but most sugar cane is grown for 14-18 months for the plant crop and 12 months for the ratoon crop.

The crop is propagated from stem cuttings called setts. Each node has an axillary bud and a band of root primordia and is capable of producing a new plant. The germinating bud is initially dependent on the sett and sett roots for nutrients and water, but develops its own root system after about 2-3 weeks in favourable conditions. The optimum temperature for the sprouting of stem cuttings is 32-38°C. Below 20°C, growth is slow and fails at lower temperatures. The short roots arise from underground nodes, and the axillary buds at these nodes give rise to tillers. As many as 144 stalks have been recorded in a stool arising from a one bud sett. The development of the cane plant from germinating sett has been reviewed in detail by van Dillewijn (1952).

Various eco-physiological aspects related to crop growth, development and yield have been reviewed by Bull and Glaszion (1975). A 12-month crop has a quadratic growth curve, while a 20 to 24 month crop has a cubic growth curve because, after the bloom stage in the first year, growth slows down as the cane stalks approach maturity. However, the exact shape of both the 12 and 24 month crop depends greatly on cultivar, temperature, solar radiation, availability of nutrients, and moisture. On average, total dry matter production of a 12-month crop is about 50 tonne/ha while a 24-month crop produces about 75 tonne/ha, equivalent to about 100 tonne/ha and 150 tonne/ha of cane respectively. Experiments in Hawaii and Queensland have shown that the linear relationship between total dry matter production and water use (about 125 g water per g dry matter) is not greatly affected by temperature or the stage of growth of the plant (Mongelard and Mimura 1971, 1972, Bull and Glaszion 1975). Provided prolonged periods of water stress do not occur during the wet season the potential cane yield is roughly 2–4 tonne/ha per 2·5 cm of evapotranspiration. It may thus be possible to use evaporation and water budget figures to estimate the potential yields in different regions.

Most *Saccharum* cultivars will not flower under daylength longer than about 13 hours or shorter than about 12 hours, nor if given light in the middle of the dark period. There are exceptions, however. Some of the *S. spontaneum* cultivars flower regardless of the nature of the photoperiod. Coleman (1968) has discussed the physiology of flowering in sugar cane. Generally, a daylength of 12·5 hours and night temperatures between 20°C and 25°C will induce floral initiation if enough inductive cycles are given, once the plant has reached a certain stage in its development. However, there is a great variation in the sensitivity to photoperiod depending on the cultivar, and the response is modified by the age of the plant, temperature, water stress, nutrition and weed infestation prior to full cover. Flowering has a considerable negative effect on growth and yield and several methods with varying degrees of success have been used to prevent flowering during the first season. In West Africa, sugar cane flowers in the dry season, October to December. The sugar in the stalk is capable of being mobilized and transported elsewhere in the plant to support growth requirements in excess of that provided by current photosynthesis. Conditions which favour sugar storage in stalks include maturity of the plant, and a check to internode elongation rates in the stalk by cold, nutritional, or water stress (which is effective provided canopy photosynthesis is maintained at a sufficient rate).

Sugar cane can be grown on a wide variety of soil types, but heavy soils are usually preferred. The crop is a gross feeder and exhausting to the soil. The nutrient requirements and fertilizer practices vary widely between countries depending on local climate, soil and economic conditions (Davies and Viltos 1969) and on whether or not the crop is irrigated and ratooned. Sugar cane removes large quantities of nutrients from the soil. A crop yielding about 28 tonne/ha, of cane is reported to remove N, 30 kg/ha; P, 9 kg/ha; K, 50 kg/ha, while a crop yielding about 74 tonne/ha removes N, 107 kg/ha; P, 26 kg/ha; K,

250 kg/ha. Aspects related to crop nutrition have been reviewed by Purseglove (1975).

In the West African Savanna, sugar cane under indigenous practice is grown in the *fadama* areas and the flood plains of streams and rivers which flow strongly in the rains and shrink or dry up during the dry season. These lands are subject to annual flooding and waterlogging and in the dry season the water table is high. There is considerable variation in texture, and 60–70 per cent of clay is frequently present in the upper soil overlying silty or sandy clay below. These soils are usually acid, and often rich in nitrogen.

(b) *Cultivation.* Under indigenous practice, the land is prepared for planting by deep hoeing soon after the end of the rains, and un-arrowed tops or stem segments are planted during the period October to March. The predominant cultivars are the noble cane Bourbon (*S. officinarum*) and thinner Creole cane (*S. barberi*). The planting material is often sprouted before being planted, by making bundles which are placed with their cut ends in shallow water. Cuttings are put into the soil at an angle. Sugar cane is usually planted on the flat but where the land is liable to flood, they are grown on ridges and sometimes on hills. About 3–4 tonne/ha of setts are planted. Spacing varies considerably (Norman 1972) and spacings of 0·7 × 0·8–0·9 m (16 000–19 000 stands/ha), 0·55 × 0·55 m (34 000 stands/ha) and 0·4 × 0·45 m (57 000 stands/ha) have been reported. The crop is largely grown sole but a tiny amount (2–3 per cent) has been reported to be grown in mixture of 2–3 crop combinations involving cowpea, rice, cassava, sweet potato, and vegetables (Norman 1972). In favourable weather, setts root in about two weeks and new growth appears soon after. The crop is harvested from October to February, 8–14 months after planting depending on the region. In the northern Guinea and Sudan Savanna the crop duration is often about 8–10 months while in areas further south about 12–14 months. Ratoon crops are rarely taken. The cane is harvested by pulling the ripe stalks form the stool using a twisting action which causes the break to occur below the ground level or by cutting at the ground level. Yields in terms of sucrose are unknown but the yield of 'jaggery' or crude sugar is about 8–10 per cent of the weight of cane crushed.

Commercial crops in West Africa are generally planted directly in the field, either in setts on ridges or cuttings laid horizontally in the base of a shallow furrow which is earthed up as the plants grow. The planting material is chemically treated before planting. With mechanized cultivation and irrigation, spacing is about 0·30–0·60 m in rows 1·30–1·60 m apart. Commercial planting is done in October to February and harvested by hand using cutlasses the following December to February, after 12–14 months. The cut cane soon begins to deteriorate and it is transported to the factory within 48 hours. Ratoon crops are taken but as elsewhere in Africa their yields are lower than the planted crop. Fertilizers are applied but amounts generally vary in the range N, 50–220 kg/ha; P, 10–40 kg/ha; K, 30–170 kg/ha.

(c) *Diseases and pests.* Commercial crops grown on large scale elsewhere in the tropics are attacked by a number of pests. In West Africa, because of the recent commercial nature of the crop, and because areas involved are small, disease problems are relatively mild. However, a severe outbreak of red rot (*Colletotrichum falcatum*), of which the perfect stage is *Physalospora tucumanensis*, occurred in Nigeria in 1952. This was the first record of the disease in epidemic proportion, though it had possibly been present for a long time previously in a mild form. Dark red lesions occur on the midrib, reddish discolouration occurs near the base of the stem in one or more internodes, interspersed with whitish spots. The conidial stage of the fungus can sometimes cause the whole plant to die. Most noble canes are very susceptible, but sources of resistance exist in some clones of *S. spontaneum*. Other diseases include ring spot (*Leptosphaeria sacchari*) and eye spot (*Helminthosporium* spp.). These fungus diseases are of little importance at present. The ratoon stunting disease (RSD) has been observed in local cultivars and in ratoon of some of those recently introduced, but not in the plants of the latter. Infected canes show depressed growth, particularly in ratoon crops, resulting in thin canes. Diseased plants have orangered vascular bundles at the nodes, and pink discolouration of the growing point. The disease is spread by diseased setts and infected cutting knives. Hotwater treatment of setts is effective in its control, together with sterilization of knives used for cutting setts.

Of the several insect pests recorded on sugar cane in West Africa, cane borers (*Busseola fusca, Sesamia* spp., *Eldana saccharina, Coniesta ignesfusalis*) are the most numerous and can become of economic importance. These borers are found on other crops such as sorghum, millet, maize, and rice. The eggs are usually deposited by the moths on the young leaves and the larvae burrow into the stem, subsequently emerging as adults. This results in a loss of sucrose, stem strength and young tillers. The tunnel provides an entrance for other diseases such as red rot. Various species of termites have been known to cause serious damage to the crop, particularly in the dry season, and small fields are often completely destroyed. Irrigated crops appear less liable to be attacked. Chemical control on the newly planted cane is effective. Other insect pests reported include cotton stainers (*Dysdercus superstitiosus*), spittle bugs (*Locris maculata, Poophilus adustus*), stem beetles (*Heteronychus oryzae*), sap beetles (*Carpophilus* spp.) and maize beetles (*Heteronychus licas*). The beetle attack is often followed by secondary attacks from other beetles and rot organisms (Libby 1968).

# 8 Farming systems and problems of improving them

## by D. W. NORMAN

Bunting (1971) has defined a system as 'a set of relations in which inputs give rise to, or are engaged in, processes leading to outputs'. In agricultural or farming systems the inputs result in processes 'occurring over time in assemblages of living organisms which occupy space'. There are a number of factors responsible for influencing the farming system that will evolve. Earlier chapters have stressed the fundamental importance of the physical environment (i.e., soil, water, temperature, etc.) and the necessity of ensuring that the physiological requirements of the living organisms (i.e., usually plants) are compatible with it. A study of these factors can give a valuable idea of what is technically and potentially possible in terms of a farming system. The potential farming system can, however, often be improved greatly (i.e., in terms of total production) as a result of intervention by man in terms of modifying the environment (e.g., lengthening the period during which water is available through irrigation, use of improved seed, development of fertilizers, herbicides, seed dressing, insecticides, etc.).

### 8.1 General patterns and local systems

Since farming systems are harnessed by man to fulfil particular objectives, what actually evolves is invariably only a subset of what is technically feasible. A farmer has certain specified quantities of the four factors of production (i.e., land, capital, labour, and managerial ability) at his disposal. With these he can undertake a variety of farming enterprises. The skill of the farmer lies in combining the factors of production to produce a mix of farming enterprises which gives a result consistent with the goal he is pursuing. The farming systems that tend to evolve are therefore extremely complex and go far beyond physical and biological factors to encompass economic, social (Charreau 1974b), and sometimes even political elements also. Therefore, even within the West African Savanna area, there is a considerable diversity in the farming systems that have evolved, due in part to the human factor. As a result, generalizations are extremely difficult (Helleiner 1976).

However, although farming systems may tend to be somewhat location specific, it is possible to make three general points. These are:
   (i) The farming systems that exist at the present time reflect manipulation by man over long periods of time (Okigbo 1974).
   (ii) These farming systems are in general well adapted to the environment in which they are operating (De Wilde 1967, Bunting 1972b). At the same time, however, it should be emphasized that these systems could often be improved as a result of a change in quantities, qualities and/or

ratios of factors of production available to the farmer, injection of new man-made inputs, etc.

(iii) Because of the dynamic nature of agriculture and the activities of man, changes in farming systems are continuously taking place, not only because of changes in population density (Charreau 1974b), and the availability of new markets for cash crops (Charreau 1974b, Okigbo 1974) but also because of many other reasons (e.g., changes in education, goals, income, credit institutions, availability of inputs, etc.).

The genralizations mentioned above imply that man himself is the central character in determining the farming system within the boundary conditions established by the physical and biological factors. The central thesis underlying this chapter is that, since the farmer within fairly wide limits has a choice over the farming system he adopts in West African Savanna areas,† it is important that changes are suggested which respond to the felt needs and constraints of farmers. Otherwise he is unlikely to be convinced of the value of changing, and therefore little progress is likely to be made. Therefore the objectives of this chapter are two-fold:

(i) To provide a brief overview of farming in the West African Savanna with the aim of delineating the major constraints to change.

(ii) Arising out of the above, to delineate in broad terms the types of technology that might be relevant to farmers in the Savanna together with an indication of the possible conditions (i.e., infrastructural development) that will be necessary to encourage their adoption.

Since, as mentioned earlier, farming systems tend to be somewhat location specific, it is impossible to provide a general description, or for that matter, a general prescription in the form of possible improvements, for the whole Savanna area of West Africa. Consequently details will be given relevant to the Zaria area (11°11′N, 7°38′E) which, it is believed, are exemplified to some extent elsewhere in the Savanna area. At the same time reference is made whenever possible to findings obtained elsewhere in the Savanna area.

## 8.2 Farming systems in the Zaria area

### 8.2.1 Background

The study area, within 160 km of Zaria, is characterized by an average rainfall of 1090 mm, which falls during the period April to October and results in a severe water deficit during the dry season and surplus during the rainy season. Mean monthly temperatures fluctuate from 22 °C in January to 29 °C in April.

The landform is generally a gently undulating plain at an altitude of 600 to 900 m. In certain areas inselbergs rise above the plain while broad valleys are common. Leached Ferruginous Tropical soils are most common and have well developed textural B horizons which contain 30 to 40 per cent clay. They are well to somewhat poorly drained. A typical feature of the upland (i.e., *gona* fields) soils which support crops only during the rainy season, is their high silt content, which causes the surface to cap. In the limited valleys (i.e., *fadama* fields) are found Hydromorphic soils which are normally of clay texture and

---

†This choice is fairly wide both in the technical and political senses. Most West African countries do not force farmers to change.

therefore poorly drained, which support crops throughout the year. The natural vegetation of the Northern Guinea Savanna ecological zone, which is Savanna woodland, has been largely replaced by parkland, as a result of human activities.

Agriculture forms the principal means of livelihood for 75 per cent of the working population in the Zaria area. The predominantly illiterate population† consists of two main segments: the nomadic pastoral Fulani with their herds of cattle, and the settled, primarily crop farming population of both Hausa and Fulani origins. Attention here is confined to the biggest group of people, that is, those settled farmers belonging to the Muslem faith, who tend to live in nucleated villages or well defined hamlets. The traditional society is strongly auto-cratic with village heads exercising considerable authority.

Many of the figures quoted in the following two sections were derived from a study of 124 farming families from whom data were collected twice weekly for a time of one year. These farmers were randomly selected in three villages differ-ing in ease of communciation with Zaria, while at the same time care was taken to ensure as far as possible that the villages were representative of other villages in the same general location. It was perhaps not surprising that ease of com-munication (i.e., accessibility) with Zaria also proved to be positively related to the population density (Table 8.1). The location of the village therefore proved to be important in influencing the farming system. Detailed results con-cerning the study are presented elsewhere (Norman 1972, 1973). In this chapter these are only presented in summary form.

## 8.2.2　*Availability and utilization of inputs of land, labour, and capital*

(a) *Amount and distribution of land.* As would be expected the average amount of land possessed by farming families is inversely related to population density (Table 8.1). Although in many parts of West Africa land is a communal asset, and individuals only possess usufructuary rights to it, considerable inequal-ities still arise in its distribution. The average size of farm was found to be 3·9 ha, but the range was from 0·2 to 21·7 ha. In fact, in the Zaria study it was found that 50 per cent of the farmers farmed only 27 per cent of the land. A similar result was found in the Sokoto area (Norman, Fine, Goddard, Kroeker, and Pryor 1976a). Nevertheless as population density increases the relative variation in the area farmed by families decreased. The opportunity cost of leaving land fallow in such areas is relatively high and farmers are thereby encouraged to surrender their usufructuary rights. Since additional income can be earned from renting, pledging, and leasing land, it is rarely left fallow and the more mobile types of tenure become increasingly popular (Table 8.1).

It has been noted by P. Hill (1972) that in Hausa land, the traditionally pre-ferred system has been the establishment of permanently cultivated fields near residential areas where fertility is maintained through the application of organic manure, while fields more remote tend to be fallowed. As population density increases, length of fallow and frequency of fallowing will become increasingly less. Charreau (1974b) in fact has reported that in some regions of Senegal where the population is more than 70 to 80 persons/sq km, fallow land has virtually

---

†Because of informal Koranic schooling many are literate to some extent in Arabic script. Literacy in Roman script which is taught in primary schools is less common.

**Table 8.1**

*Availability of land and labour, Zaria, 1966–67*

| Variable specification in terms of an average farming family | Dan Mahawayi village | Doka village | Hanwa village | | Average of the three villages† |
|---|---|---|---|---|---|
| | | | Non-cattle owners | Cattle owners | |
| Location | 11°19′N 7°35′E | 11°22′N 7°47′E | 11°8′N 7°43′E | | |
| Ease of accessibility | Poor | Good | Very good | | |
| Population density per sq km | 32 | 153 | 274 | | 153 |
| Farm land per resident (ha) | 0·8 | 0·5 | 0·2 | 0·3 | 0·5 |
| **Land:** | | | | | |
| Farm size (ha)‡ | ·4·8 | 4·0 | 2·2 | 3·7 | 3·9 |
| Coefficient of variation in size | 88·4 | 78·9 | 70·2 | 47·8 | 76·3 |
| Composition of farm (ha): | | | | | |
| Upland | 4·4 | 3·5 | 1·9 | 3·6 | 3·6 |
| Lowland | 0·4 | 0·5 | 0·3 | 0·1 | 0·3 |
| Per cent of hectares that were: | | | | | |
| Inherited or a gift | 80·1 | 93·7 | 31·5 | 18·7 | 65·9 |
| More 'mobile' types of tenure§ | 19·9 | 6·3 | 68·5 | 81·3 | 34·1 |
| **Labour:** | | | | | |
| Family size‖ | 6·8 | 8·0 | 10·3 | 11·6 | 8·6 |
| Age of family head (years) | 42·9 | 43·1 | 45·0 | 40·7 | 43·0 |
| Composition of families (per cent): | | | | | |
| *Iyali* | 57·1 | 59·1 | 55·0 | 16·7 | 57·1 |
| *Gandu* | 42·9 | 40·9 | 45·0 | 83·3 | 42·9 |

†Each village is weighted equally. The same applies to Tables 8.2, 8.3, 8.5 and 8.8. The total number of families surveyed was 124, 42 in Dan Mahawayi, 44 in Doka, and 20 non-cattle owners and 18 cattle owners in Hanwa. No cattle were owned by farmers in the other two villages. Cattle owners were separated out in the analysis since many of the characteristics of their farming systems were different from the other families.

‡A field was defined as a contiguous piece of land farmed by one family. The sum of the areas of fields left fallow or farmed by members of the family during the survey year constituted the farm.

§For example, land that has been obtained through renting, pledging and purchasing. The latter is in this context considered mobile since there are no titles to the land and consequently land thought to be purchased is often pledged.

‖A family was defined as 'those people eating from one pot'.

disappeared. This has serious implications for modifying farming systems in such a way as to ensure that soil fertility is maintained.

Although as mentioned above, the average size of farm is low, it is still highly fragmented, even in areas where population density is lower and most of the land is inherited. Fragmentation tends to be accentuated by the practice of dividing each field among the heirs on the death of the family head. There are problems of mechanization when farms are highly fragmented. However, for the majority of farmers this may not be a major problem since in order to support a team of oxen it has been estimated that between 4 to 8 ha of cultivated arable land are required in Senegal (Ramond 1971) or 12 ha including pasture land are required in northern Nigeria (J. H. Davies, personal communication). However, even under hand farming conditions in the close settled zone of Sokoto, Goddard (1970) has found evidence of farmers attempting to consolidate their fields. Presumably this is an attempt to overcome the inconveniences of working in several different locations during the same time period.

Two types of land can be differentiated: the upland or *gona* fields which support, during the rainy season, crops of relatively low value per hectare such as millet, sorghum, groundnuts, cowpeas, and cotton, and lowland or *fadama* fields which support, throughout the year, more labour-intensive, higher value crops such as sugar cane. The possibility of year-round cultivation of the limited amounts of *fadama* land (Tables 8.1 and 8.2) should logically induce a premium on such land. However, for a number of reasons, a high proportion of this type of land can be left fallow in particular villages. Reasons can include the unavailability of the high labour inputs required for its cultivation (Table 8.3), alternative employment opportunities during the dry season, and low value per unit weight of the crops produced which makes transport costs high, thereby discouraging production in less accessible villages.

**Table 8.2**

*Use of land, Zaria, 1966–67*

| Variable specification in terms of an average farm | Dan Mahawayi village | Doka village | Hanwa village Non-cattle owners | Hanwa village Cattle owners | Average of the three villages |
|---|---|---|---|---|---|
| Fallow (per cent): | | | | | |
| Total | 21·2 | 26·8 | 2·6 | 2·3 | 16·8 |
| Upland | 19·2 | ·28·5 | 2·8 | 2·4 | 16·8 |
| Lowland | 42·1 | 12·4 | 1·0 | 0·0 | 18·4 |
| Adjusted† cultivated hectares devoted to (per cent): | | | | | |
| Cereals‡ | 51·6 | 47·1 | 50·8 | 58·8 | 51·4 |
| Grain legumes § | 23·7 | 22·1 | 28·6 | 12·0 | 21·5 |
| Starchy roots and tubers‖ | 6·1 | 5·3 | 13·6 | 8·3 | 7·3 |
| Vegetables¶ | 3·0 | 7·3 | 1·8 | 4·1 | 4·5 |
| Sugar cane | 3·7 | 12·0 | 4·6 | 0·1 | 5·9 |
| Non-food†† | 11·8 | 6·3 | 0·6 | 16·7 | 9·4 |
| Cultivated hectares devoted to (per cent) | | | | | |
| Sole crops | 23·7 | 29·3 | 16·1 | 13·3 | 22·5 |
| Crop mixtures | 76·3 | 70·7 | 83·9 | 66·7 | 77·5 |

†In calculating adjusted area, area of each crop in the mixture is calculated by dividing the area of the crop mixture by the number of crops in the mixture. For example, a two-hectare millet/sorghum mixture was recorded as one hectare millet and one hectare sorghum.

‡Early millet (Gero), late millet (Maiwa), sorghum, maize, rice, and *iburo*.
§Groundnut, bambara-nut, and cowpea.
‖Cassava, Irish potato, sweet potato, yam, and cocoyam.
¶Okra, onion, pumpkin, pepper, garden egg, and tomato.
††Henna, cotton, deccan hemp, tobacco.

## Table 8.3

*Utilization of labour, Zaria, 1966–67*

| Variable specification in terms of an average farm | Dan Mahawayi village | Doka village | Hanwa village Non-cattle owners | Hanwa village Cattle owners | Average of the three villages |
|---|---|---|---|---|---|
| **Composition of work on farm:** | | | | | |
| Total man-hours[†] | 1516·3 | 1634·2 | 2109·4 | 2405·5 | 1800·0 |
| Composition of farm work (per cent of total man-hours): | | | | | |
| Family: Male adults | 62·9 | 82·7 | 76·5 | 65·4 | 72·2 |
| Female adults | 0·1 | 0·3 | 0·7 | 0·6 | 0·4 |
| Large children | 8·3 | 10·9 | 9·9 | 5·0 | 8·9 |
| Hired | 28·7 | 6·1 | 12·9 | 29·0 | 18·5 |
| **Man-hours per cultivated hectare:** | | | | | |
| Total | 399·2 | 560·8 | 972·6 | 660·6 | 581·6 |
| Upland[‡] | 370·1 | 477·6 | 864·3 | 664·5 | 523·0 |
| Lowland[‡] | 1132·2 | 1142·9 | 1842·8 | 620·7 | 1265·8 |
| **Work per family male adult per annum:** | | | | | |
| Hours per day worked [§] | 4·9 | 4·9 | 5·4 | 5·7 | 5·1 |
| Days worked: | | | | | |
| Family farm | 140·1 | 158·7 | 124·6 | 117·9 | 140·1 |
| Off-farm occupations | 122·6 | 39·5 | 86·5 | 123·9 | 88·6 |
| **Composition of work by male adults in off-farm occupations (per cent):** | | | | | |
| Traditional: Primary[‖] | – | – | – | 84·4 | 15·5 |
| Manufacturing[¶] | 21·2 | 29·3 | 11·3 | 2·1 | 18·9 |
| Services[††] | 40·1 | 27·2 | 20·9 | 9·8 | 27·4 |
| Trading | 35·0 | 24·7 | 3·4 | 0·1 | 20·4 |
| Modern: Services[‡‡] | 3·7 | 18·8 | 64·4 | 3·6 | 17·8 |

[†]The physical productivity of individuals varies according to age and sex. On the basis of this, one hour of work by different individuals was evaluated in terms of man-hours as follows: Small children 0–6 years old = 0·00, large children 7–14 years old = 0·50, male adults 15–64 = 1·00, female adults 15–64 = 0·75 and men and women 65 years old or more = 0·50. The figure does not include time spent travelling to and from the fields.

[‡]Does not include fields that are partly upland and partly lowland.

[§]Including travel time to and from fields.

[‖]Includes looking after cattle.

[¶]Includes blacksmiths, tailors, carpenters, spinning, leather working and making pots, cigarettes, mats and sugar, etc. An average remuneration per day worked was ₦0.28.

[††]Includes tending own houses (fencing, building, thatching, cutting grass and firewood), barbers, butchers, hunting, begging, washermen, public officials, Koranic teachers, etc. Trading can also be classified as a traditional service. Average remuneration per day worked was ₦0.21.

[‡‡]Includes commission agents, messengers, labourers, nightwatchmen, bicycle repairers, buying agents, etc. Average remuneration per day worked was ₦0.41.

(b) *Labour: family size and organization.* The size of family varied from two to thirty persons with the average size being nearly nine persons. It was possible to divide families into two types of units: a simple unit or *iyali* which consists of an individual married adult with his wives and dependent children, and a composite unit or *gandu* which is composed of two or more male adults, usually married, together with their wives and children.

In general, simple units were found to be more common than complex units. Indeed Goddard (1973) in Sokoto and Buntjer (1970) in Zaria have found that the simple farming family unit is becoming more common although traditionally the complex family unit was preferred. Whether or not such a change takes place will be based on non-economic as well as economic reasons (Norman, Pryor, and Koreker 1976b). With reference to non-economic reasons both M. G. Smith (1955) and Goddard (1973) mention that death and migration often necessitate the presence of simple family units. More recently this tendency has been reinforced by the notion that the complex family unit is no longer as prestigious as it used to be and because subordinate males in complex family systems are increasingly questioning the authority (which is based on age and seniority) of the complex family, particularly if the head is a brother rather than a father. However, although non-economic reasons are important in creating preconditions necessary for the maintenance or breakdown of the complex family unit system it is likely that economic reasons play a vital and decisive role in actually influencing the type of family structure that will result. Complex family units in the manner described by M. G. Smith (1955) now rarely exist (Goddard 1973). For example, taxes on male adults organized in complex family units are now very often paid by each male adult rather than by the family head, thereby leading over time to a weakening of the authority of the latter. Two other examples of economic factors that will influence the form of family organization that will evolve are: firstly the ownership of cattle by settled farming families, which partly because there are economies of scale in herding supervision, will encourage the maintenance of a complex system of family organization (Buntjer 1970, Goddard 1973); and secondly the type of improved technology available to the farmer will be of considerable influence in determining whether or not the larger farms organized under the complex family system will give way to the smaller farms that tend to exist with a simple family unit. In the Zaria study, for example, the average size of farm for a complex family unit was 2·91 ha compared with 1·9 ha for a simple family unit (Norman *et al.* 1976b).

In order to maximize profits farmers need to maximize the return to the most limiting factor.† In the case of large farms, labour-augmenting technology in the form of ploughs and oxen is most relevant to farmers' needs. It is therefore not surprising that Tiffen (1973), working in the Gombe area, found complex family systems associated with farmers using oxen. In contrast, as was mentioned earlier, farms in the Zaria area are in general too small to permit mechanization. Therefore land intensification technology, which exhibits no economies of scale, becomes more relevant thereby encouraging the formation of simple family units.

(c) *Work on the farm.* In general in the Savanna areas of West Africa, there is not a large class of landless labourers in rural areas. As a result, the bulk of labour on the farm is derived from family sources although, as expected, within

---

†However, as will be emphasized later in the chapter, this is in most parts of the West African Savanna likely to be constrained by the desire for security in the form of sufficient food.

villages the contribution of hired labour did increase on larger farms (Norman 1973)

On an average farm in the Zaria study about 82 per cent of the labour on the family farm was contributed from family sources (Table 8.3). Of this, family male adults contributed by far the greatest proportion (i.e., 89 per cent). The insignificant participation of women in farm work is related to the partial or complete seclusion of Moslem wives (Smith, M. G. 1955). The same constraint has been observed in other parts of the Savanna areas of West Africa (Monnier and Ramond 1970) and must be taken into account when suggesting changes in farming systems which might involve adjustments in the labour requirements.

Hired labour can take three forms: work paid by the hour, contract work paid by the job, and communal work which is often contributed free of charge but may be rewarded with a meal or drink. All three types of labour are often remunerated in kind rather than explicitly in terms of cash. Work paid by the hour and contract work are more productive, and were by far the most common, accounting for 50 and 45 per cent of the hired labour, respectively. As mentioned above, the lack of a supply of landless labourers, together with the limited availability of cash, inhibits the hiring of much increased quantities of labour even if it was justified by the farming system adopted.

(d) *Work undertaken by family male adults.* The amount of work individuals will undertake is determined by many factors such as health, nutrition, climate, size of family and farm, subsistence needs, incentives, presence and accessibility of markets, attitude and educational level, availability of financial resources to pay for hired labour, off-farm employment opportunities, etc. On average in the Zaria study, a male adult was found to work about 226 days per year at an average of about five hours per day worked. These figures compared closely with those derived in other parts of West Africa, for example, Gambia (Haswell 1963), North Cameroon (Guillard 1958), Senegal (Monnier and Ramond 1970) and other parts in the Savanna areas of Nigeria, for example, Katsina (Luning 1963) and Sokoto (Luning 1967, Norman *et al.* 1976a).

The seasonal nature of the rainfall was mentioned earlier in the chapter. Largely because of the long dry season and the relatively limited amounts of irrigated and *fadama* land a fairly substantial proportion of a farmer's time in the Savanna areas of West Africa tends to be devoted to off-farm occupations. The month by month distributions of time devoted to farm and off-farm occupations tend, as would be expected, to be negatively correlated.† In the Zaria study an average male adult spent about 39 per cent of his time working on occupations other than working on the family farm.

The opportunities for income from off-farm sources depend to some extent on the location or accessibility of the village although in some parts of the Savanna, such as the Sokoto area (Norman *et al.* 1976a) farmers go on short-season migration (i.e., *cin rani*) to find work during the long dry season. However, apart from these exceptions, the composition of off-farm employment can also be partially explained in terms of location. Off-farm occupations can

---

†The correlation coefficient was −0·71 which is significantly different from zero at the five per cent level.

be ascribed to two main sectors (i.e., traditional and modern). Employment in the traditional sector consists of those jobs that are fairly independent of the developmental process; in other words they are jobs that have been undertaken for many generations. In contrast jobs in the modern sector have arisen directly or indirectly as a result of improved communications and the development of large cities, commercial firms, and government bodies. In the case of the village most accessible to Zaria, jobs are found more commonly in the modern sector which is generally more remunerative than work in the traditional sector. The difficulty of access to Zaria precludes individuals in the most isolated village seeking jobs in the modern sector (Table 8.3). However, this relative isolation does have a beneficial influence in that some traditional services and crafts are still undertaken by villagers, in contrast to the most accessible village which has suffered from competition with full time specialists in Zaria. In the intermediate villages, employment opportunities in the modern sector are very limited, while at the same time traditional activities also suffer because of easier accessibility. However, on the positive side, accessibility to a main road has encouraged farmers to cultivate the remunerative sugar cane on the *fadama* land rather than relying on less certain sources of income provided from off-farm activities.

In introducing changes into the farming system, it is important to take cognizance of time devoted to off-farm employment by farmers in Savanna areas of West Africa. Whether or not such individuals will be prepared to forego such alternative employment opportunities will depend on a number of factors such as the pleasure in terms of tangible and intangible rewards they obtain from such occupations compared with the alternative of becoming full-time farmers. Too often development programmes plans have been formulated which either assume the farmer is a full-time farmer, or assume he will obviously choose, if possible, to become a full-time farmer. Such assumptions are obviously not valid.

(e) *The problem of the seasonal nature of farming.* The seasonal farming pattern in the Zaria area (Table 8.4), due to the uneven rainfall distribution, is emphasized by the fact that on an average farm, about 50 per cent of the annual input of man-hours occurs during the May through August period with June and July being the busiest months. Conversely the four-month period from December to March accounted for less than 17 per cent of the total annual labour input. The concentration on rain-fed agriculture is a characteristic of agriculture in the Savanna areas of West Africa. For example in Senegal it has been noted that 90 per cent of agricultural activity occurs during the rainy season (Monnier and Ramond 1970).

There is ample evidence throughout the Savanna area of West Africa that the main seasonal peak in terms of labour requirements is for weeding and cultivating during June to August and sometimes for planting (Anon undated, Monnier and Ramond 1970, Norman 1970, Bunting 1971). This leads to the conclusion that the amount of labour a family can contribute or hire during this period determines to a large extent the family's land requirements and level of agricultural activity during the rest of the year (Monnier and Ramond 1970). For example, in the Zaria study, various linear programming models showed that labour availability during the June to August period was usually the most limit-

## Table 8.4

*Seasonality of farming and off-farm occupations, Zaria, 1966–67*

| Variable specification | Total | Per cent of total man-hours or man-days | | | | | | | | | | | |
|---|---|---|---|---|---|---|---|---|---|---|---|---|---|
| | | Apr | May | June | July | Aug | Sept | Oct | Nov | Dec | Jan | Feb | Mar |
| Work on average farm (man-hours): | | | | | | | | | | | | | |
| Family | 1467·0 | 5·8 | 10·4 | 11·1 | 10·5 | 9·1 | 7·0 | 7·0 | 7·5 | 5·0 | 3·8 | 2·7 | 1·7 |
| Hired | 333·0 | 1·5 | 2·0 | 2·1 | 2·5 | 2·2 | 1·7 | 1·8 | 1·3 | 1·5 | 0·9 | 0·4 | 0·5 |
| Work per male adult (days): | | | | | | | | | | | | | |
| Farm | 140·1 | 4·4 | 7·0 | 7·4 | 7·1 | 6·4 | 5·2 | 5·4 | 5·8 | 4·1 | 3·3 | 2·7 | 1·9 |
| Off-farm | 88·6 | 3·7 | 3·0 | 2·9 | 3·0 | 2·9 | 2·9 | 2·7 | 2·8 | 3·1 | 3·9 | 4·0 | 3·4 |
| Seasons of year: | | | | | | | | | | | | | |
| Weather | | ← Rainy → | | | | | | | | ← Dry → | | | |
| Farming | | ← Planting → | | | | ← Harvesting → | | | | | | | |
| (gona) | | ← Weeding → | | | | | | | | | | | |

ing factor and often resulted in land being left fallow (Ogunfowora 1972). Marginal value productivities of labour during this period were found to be at least four times higher than the wage rate paid for hired labour (Norman 1970). There is, then, considerable evidence that this labour bottleneck is an important constraint on the expansion of agricultural activity in the Savanna areas. There are at least three possible ways of ameliorating the effect of this labour constraint.

Firstly, it is possible to increase the availability of family members for work on the family farm by reducing the time spent on off-farm activities. As mentioned earlier, there is a significant negative relationship between the days spent per month by family adults in family farm work and off-farm employment. However, even during the bottleneck period of June and July, over six days per month, or 29 per cent of an average adult male's working days, were spent in off-farm employment. One possible reason is that, in order to be reasonably successful in the occupation during the dry season, it is necessary to provide some continuity throughout the whole year. This would be particularly true in the case of occupations that involve patronage by clientele (e.g., crafts and services such as trading). Another possible reason is that the immediate need for money to buy food may compel family members to devote some time to off-farm occupations which yield an immediate monetary return†. Cash and food resources tend to be low at the peak period in farming activities, since most crops are harvested between August and December and little additional income is obtained from farming activities until after the bottleneck period.

A second way of relieving labour constraints is through the hiring of labour. One would expect that since labour is in such demand during the June–July period, this would also be the period when the bulk of non-family labour is hired. In fact, it was found that in the Zaria study that 25 per cent of the total man-hour input of non-family labour was employed during this period, corresponding to the 26 per cent of total man-hour input by family members on the family farm. Results of a test for significant difference between the monthly man-hour input of family labour and non-family labour on the family farm when each monthly total was expressed as a percentage of each annual total supported the hypothesis of no difference‡. Hired labour is used throughout the year and is therefore apparently not reserved for the June–July period. Hiring of labour during the latter period may be limited for two reasons. Firstly, there is no class of landless labourers. Therefore the period hired labour is most in demand is the time when the individuals who could do it are busiest on their 'own farms. Secondly, the low level of cash resources during this period imposes a practical restriction on the amount of labour that can be hired. Contrary to expectations, the wage-rate for non-family labour remained almost the same throughout the year. Norman (1972) discusses reasons for this.

A third approch to the problem of labour constraints is to introduce

---

†Smaller farmers have in particular mentioned this problem. Examples were indeed found that farmers were forced to neglect their own farms because of the more pressing need for ready cash.

‡The correlation coefficient between the two variables was 0·94 which is significantly different from zero at the five per cent level.

improved technology specifically designed to overcome the labour bottleneck. One that is often mentioned is that of mechanization, particularly using oxen. The potential of this will be considered later in the chapter. Another possibility which as yet generally still requires adaptive research is the use of herbicides. These intrinsically have advantages over mechanization because they involve less capital investment. They have the characteristic of being neutral to scale and therefore of being capable of more widespread use and of being effective in weed control both between and within rows.

(f) *Capital goods.* The two main inputs of traditional agriculture are labour and land. The amount of capital and the proportion of income invested are very low. Mellor (1967) has, however, emphasized that savings and investment are a function of two main factors: first the attitudes toward saving, investment, and consumption (i.e., the position of the supply schedule for saving) and secondly the marginal returns available to further investment. Consequently, capital formation in traditional agriculture tends to be low, not necessarily because the capacity for saving is low, but because the returns to investment tend to be low. Mellor gives two reasons for the low rates of return on investment. These are, first, that many forms of capital goods are directly formed from labour (e.g., simple tools, land improvements, etc.), so that the returns are low because of low returns to labour, and second, that the low level of technology greatly reduces the productivity of capital (e.g., investment in fertilizer, improved seeds, etc.) compared with the returns in agriculture practised at a higher level of technology.

It is not surprising therefore to find that investment in durable farm capital goods (i.e., livestock excluding cattle, buildings, and equipment) was low (Table 8.5). The dependence on hand tools together with the absence of farm buildings, other than grain stores, resulted in an average inventory value of investment in these items of only ₦4.50 per farm in the Zaria study in the 1966–67 year. A relatively larger investment in livestock (i.e., mainly chickens, sheep, and goats, but also a few guinea fowl, donkeys, and horses) arises in spite of the fact that livestock do not play an important role in the farming activities and incomes of most households. However, livestock do provide a form of investment that can readily be translated into cash†. Investment in livestock is considerably higher when families own cattle, and in the case of oxen, this investment is made for the purpose of partially substituting for hand labour in the farming system—though in the Zaria study, the eighteen farmers who owned cattle did not use them as a source of power. However, in relation to other items constituting durable capital, the magnitude of the investment in oxen plus complementary equipment is so high that without some kind of institutional credit programme it is beyond the grasp of the majority of farmers.

The problems of the seasonality of farming have been emphasized in the preceding section. It was noted that during the peak period in farm activities (i.e., June–July) cash resources tend to be at their lowest level. The same problem pertains, though perhaps less acutely, to the two months immediately prior to

† Since land is not individually owned in most parts of the Savanna no value has been placed on it.

## Table 8.5

*Farm capital goods and cash expenses (₦), Zaria, 1966–67*

| Variable specification in terms of an average farm | Dan Mahawayi village | Doka village | Hanwa village | | Average of the three villages |
|---|---|---|---|---|---|
| | | | Non-cattle owners | Cattle owners | |
| Value of durable capital goods (April 1966): | | | | | |
| Livestock | 11·36 | 16·72 | 18·85 | 621·09 | 110·73 |
| Buildings, tools and equipment | 4·54 | 5·68 | 3·04 | 3·55 | 4·51 |
| Total | 15·90 | 22·40 | 21·89 | 624·64 | 115·24 |
| Imputed expenditure on capital goods (April 1966–March 1967): | | | | | |
| Durable | 4·41 | 6·58 | 1·49 | 2·48 | 4·32 |
| Non-durable: Seed | 14·94 | 14·24 | 12·90 | 10·16 | 13·59 |
| Fertilizer | 2·97 | 2·64 | 5·94 | 17·41 | 5·57 |
| Total | 22·32 | 23·46 | 20·33 | 30·05 | 23·48 |
| Per cent of total value of: | | | | | |
| Seed which was purchased | 24·3 | 15·7 | 21·6 | 20·3 | 20·3 |
| Organic manure which was purchased | 2·5 | 2·8 | 16·3 | 0·8 | 3·5 |
| Cash expenses: | | | | | |
| Total | 35·17 | 16·71 | 24·57 | 35·87 | 27·27 |
| Composition of cash expenses (per cent of total): | | | | | |
| Land | 6·2 | 2·3 | 4·8 | 3·1 | 4·1 |
| Hiring labour | 65·2 | 38·4 | 61·0 | 79·2 | 58·4 |
| Capital goods: Durable | 15·4 | 34·7 | 18·4 | 10·1 | 21·3 |
| Non-durable | 12·5 | 17·9 | 15·3 | 6·2 | 13·5 |
| Marketing costs | 0·7 | 6·7 | 0·6 | 1·4 | 2·7 |

this (i.e. April and May) when most of the main crops are being planted. This is also the time when the demand for non-durable capital is greatest (e.g., for fertilizer and seeds). Under such circumstances, the input of fertilizer particularly suffers and, in fact, very little inorganic fertilizer is used, although often organic manure is obtained free of charge†. Although as population density increases there is evidence that the application of organic manure becomes more concentrated (Mortimore and Wilson 1965, Norman *et al.* 1976a), there does remain some concern that this is not completely replenishing the soil fertility which has suffered as a result of the inevitable reduction or even elimination of the fallow period (Monnier and Ramond 1970). Certainly farmers in the Sokoto area have complained about the declining fertility of the land in spite of the application of relatively high amounts of organic manure (Norman *et al.* 1976a). The ownership of cattle does, as expected, result in much use of organic manure (Table 8.5). The shortage of fertilizer in recent years in many parts of the Savanna,

† Apart from the few settled cattle owners, most of the organic manure applied is produced as a result of the cattle owned by the nomadic Fulani being corralled on the field after harvesting has been completed. Often this arrangement is undertaken without monetary cost on either side; the crop residues provide food for the cattle which produce manure.

coupled with its relatively high cost to the farmers in relation to their incomes, has prevented it from performing the role it could in maintaining soil fertility and improving production.

The other major components of non-durable capital, seed, is often umimproved and is saved from the previous year's harvest. The exception is cotton seed, which is often issued free by governmental agencies or their representatives. Once again, as with fertilizer, the unavailability of improved seed together with a lack of ready cash at the relevant time often preclude farmers from purchasing improved seed varieties.

Improved technology developed at research stations usually involves substantial investment in capital goods, sometimes of a non-durable type. Therefore an assessment of the practicability of expecting this to occur without some external support (e.g., in the form of an institutionalized credit programme) must be included when considering suggested substantial changes in the farming system at present used by farmers.

(g)  *Cash expenses.*  As far as farming activities are concerned, cash expenses or goods valued in terms of cash are used to obtain the services of inputs either on a temporary basis (e.g., renting, pledging, or leasing land, hiring labour etc.), or on a more permanent basis (e.g. purchasing the usufructuary rights to land, equipment, seeds, fertilizer, etc.). Cash expenses on farming were found to be relatively small and amounted on average to only 13 per cent of gross farm income in the Zaria study (Table 8.5). As would be expected in an areas where the dominant right to land is that which is inherited, only 5 per cent of the total cash expenses was spent on obtaining the rights of use to additional land. With respect to seed and organic manure, which accounted for an average of 13 per cent of the farm cash expenses per family, the importance of sources of supply other than the market place has earlier been emphasized. Costs of marketing were also relatively insignificant, both because of the relatively low proportion of total production that is sold, and because of the operation of middlemen or traders who purchase products directly from the farmers and arrange for their transport to market.

Earlier in the chapter it has been emphasized that labour is often an important constraint, particularly during the weeding period. Therefore it is not surprising that in the Zaria study it was found that a family spent an average of 58 per cent of its total farm cash expenses on hiring labour. In the Sokoto area this percentage was found to be 30 (Norman *et al.* 1976a). King (1975a, 1975b), in studies in Kano and Bauchi states, found that traditionally the most important use of credit in farming was for hiring labour.

The relatively low level of cash expenses incurred by farmers is a cause for some concern, particularly when viewed on a monthly basis. As mentioned above, the demand for cash in terms of purchasing or hiring inputs is likely to be highest when the supply of cash is at its lowest (i.e., May to July). This could be a problem when introducing improved technology, most of which requires more rather than less in the way of cash expenses. The implications of this have been discussed in the preceding section.

(h)  *Land and labour relationships.*  As would be expected, the magnitude of the labour input per cultivated hectare in the Zaria study proved to be inversely related to the number of cultivated hectares on the farm (Table 8.1 and 8.3). Although the use of hired labour increases with a rise in the size of farm (Norman 1973), this increase was not sufficient to offset the decline in the total man-hour input per hectare. The results also indicated that the labour input per hectare was considerably lower than that on the more productive lowland.

The greater intensity of cultivation on smaller farms, both in terms of more man-hour per unit area, and lower frequency and length of fallow, does raise the problem alluded to earlier, that is the question of maintenance of soil fertility. Because of their relatively lower incomes and therefore lower potential cash expenses, this eventually can become a severe constraint in terms of sustaining a living. This would have become even more exaggerated if complementary relationships had not been established with nomadic cattle owners. As population density increases it is likely that such cattle owners are likely to find it increasingly difficult to maintain their way of life and therefore the significance of organic manure is likely to decrease, necessitating the maintenance of soil fertility by other means.

## 8.2.3 Production

Crop production is the main source of income for farmers in most parts of the Savanna, although livestock, particularly cattle when owned by such farmers, can play a very significant role.

The Zaria study identified a total of 25 crops being grown, with a family growing on average eight crops. This indicates a desire for diversification on the part of the farmer. As the rain-fed growing season becomes shorter on moving north, the number of crops that can be grown becomes less. However, even around Sokoto, this desire for diversification was still apparent with a total of 21 crops being grown and farmers on average growing six (Norman *et al.* 1976a).

In the Savanna area of West Africa the main crops tend to be cereals (particularly millet, sorghum and increasingly maize), grain legumes (cowpeas and groundnuts), starchy roots and tubers (yams and cassava), and cotton. This finding is supported by the results found in the Zaria study (Table 8.2), although it is recognized that the emphasis will change from one area to another depending on variations in physical, social, and economic conditions. For example, in the drier Sokoto area, millet is more significant and sorghum less significant than in the Zaria area (Norman *et al.* 1976a).

The method and rationale of growing these crops has provoked much research and analysis (Andrews 1972a, Kassam 1973, Baker 1974, Baker and Norman 1975) and consequently need not again be discussed in detail. The interest has arisen because of the fact that throughout the Savanna areas of West Africa, crops are planted in mixtures (Charreau 1974b). For example in the Zaria study (Norman 1972), the 24 crops found on *gona* land were grown in a total of 174 different crop enterprises (e.g., sole crop sorghum, millet/sorghum mixture, millet/sorghum/groundnut mixture, etc.). Sole crops accounted for only 18 of these or less than 17 per cent of the total cultivated area of 360 hectares. Although 156 different crop mixtures were noted, seven accounted for 61 per cent of the area devoted to mixtures. Of these a millet/sorghum mixture was most common. Mixtures aided by the traditional system of ridge cultivation are usually planted in a systematic pattern.

With reference to individual crops, millet and cowpeas are very rarely found in sole stands (Table 8.6). Logical reasons account for this. For example, to maximize the use of the land and to enable the maximum return to be reaped from past labour (e.g., labour involved in preparing and ridging the land) it would appear reasonable to grow them in mixtures with other crops since millet is harvested in the middle of the growing season (i.e. August), while cowpeas are planted rather late (i.e. July). In addition cowpeas grown in mixtures appear to be less prone to insect attack.

In terms of labour requirements it was found that the annual man-hour input of crop mixtures required 62 per cent more labour per hectare than sole crops. However this differential was reduced to 29 per cent in the months when labour was truly limiting (i.e., June and July), therefore implying that crop mixtures help alleviate the labour peak emphasized earlier in the paper.

In terms of output it was found that although the individual physical yields of sorghum, groundnuts and cotton were depressed when grown in mixtures rather than sole stands (Table 8.6), the presence of yields from other crops in the mixture more than compensated for this decrease.† As a result when the returns were expressed in monetary terms (in order to permit comparisons) the average value of production per hectare was almost 62 per cent higher for crop mixtures (Table 8.7). The average value of production per man-hour for crop mixtures was 15 per cent lower than for sole crops indicating that the higher labour input for mixtures was not quite compensated by the higher return. However, if labour is used in the period when it is truly limiting (i.e., June and July), the average value of production per unit of labour put in during that period is 20 per cent higher for crop mixtures.

The figures given above make a good case in themselves for growing crops in mixtures under indigenous conditions. However, when asked why they grow crops in mixtures, farmers articulated a number of reasons. Two were amenable to empirical testing (i.e., profit maximization and security). The results indicated that in general the profitability of crop mixtures was 60 per cent higher than that from sole crops and that farmers were rational in pursuing mixed cropping because there was either a lack of land or labour (Table 8.7). In terms of a security strategy it was shown, as with a profit maximization goal, that under indigenous conditions growing crops in mixtures was superior to sole stands. In the case of the security goal the results indicated that there was a greater probability of obtaining a higher gross return per unit of input from growing crops in mixtures rather than in sole stands.‡ In general, similar conclusions were obtained from an analysis of indigenous cropping systems in the Sokogo area (Norman *et al.* 1976a).

---

†Possible reasons for this are given elsewhere (Baker and Norman 1975, Andrews and Kassam 1975).

‡In more recent analysis of the same data Abalu (1977) has laid more emphasis on the risk aversion or income stability aspects. He concludes that crop mixtures grown by farmers fulfil this objective.

**Table 8.6**

Physical data on crop enterprises, Zaria, 1966–67

| Type of enterprise | Labour input (man-hours/ha) | | Adjusted area (ha) | | | | | Yield (kg/ha) | | | | |
|---|---|---|---|---|---|---|---|---|---|---|---|---|
| | Annual | Jun–Jul | Millet | Sorghum | Groundnut | Cowpea | Cotton | Millet | Sorghum | Groundnut | Cowpea | Cotton |
| Sole crop | 362·3 | 122·3 | 0·2 | 30·1 | 6·6 | 0·9 | 11·3 | – | 786 | 587 | – | 213 |
| Mixtures: | | | | | | | | | | | | |
| 2 crops | 582·2 | 150·0 | 47·9 | 54·2 | 10·8 | 12·7 | 13·6 | 370 | 726 | 437 | 97 | 215 |
| 3 crops | 556·7 | 151·0 | 13·7 | 16·8 | 13·0 | 17·0 | 8·0 | 359 | 536 | 389 | 138 | 161 |
| 4 crops | 669·9 | 223·1 | 8·0 | 9·2 | 8·5 | 9·4 | 2·6 | 365 | 374 | 429 | 139 | – |
| 5–6 crops | – | – | 3·6 | 3·4 | 3·3 | 3·6 | 1·4 | – | – | – | – | – |
| All mixtures | 586·4 | 157·9 | 73·2 | 83·6 | 35·6 | 42·7 | 25·6 | 366 | 644 | 412 | 132 | 189 |

**Table 8.7**

*Financial data on crop enterprises under indigenous conditions, Zaria, 1966–67*

| (a)<br>LEVEL OF RETURN | Value of production (₦) | | | Net return (₦/ha) | | |
|---|---|---|---|---|---|---|
| | Per ha | Per man-hour | | Labour | | |
| | | Annual | Jun–Jul | Not<br>costed | Jun–Jul<br>costed | All<br>costed |
| Type of enterprise: | | | | | | |
| Sole crop | 37·95 | 0·13 | 0·35 | 36·79 | 33·04 | 18·31 |
| Mixtures: | | | | | | |
| 2 crops | 59·45 | 0·11 | 0·43 | 58·24 | 50·58 | 28·54 |
| 3 crops | 56·81 | 0·10 | 0·42 | 54·42 | 46·70 | 26·02 |
| 4 crops | 84·23 | 0·11 | 0·40 | 79·79 | 68·40 | 45·62 |
| All mixtures | 61·36 | 0·11 | 0·42 | 59·50 | 51·45 | 29·60 |

| (b)<br>DEPENDABILITY OF RETURN | Value of production | | |
|---|---|---|---|
| | per<br>hectare | per man-hour | |
| | | Annual | Jun–Jul |
| Probability (in per cent) that value of<br>production per unit of input is: | | | |
| Higher from crop mixtures than sole crops | 71·5 | 55·6 | 59·2 |
| Lower from crop mixtures than sole crops | 28·5 | 44·4 | 40·8 |

The indigenous cropping systems with their emphasis on mixed cropping are therefore well attuned to the physical, social, and economic environment. A balance has been achieved by matching satisfactory attainment of profit maximization and security goals by maximizing yields subject to the very real physical environmental constraints of a limited growing season. In general, maintenance of soil fertility levels is also achieved (although admittedly often at a rather low level) through minimal inputs of organic manure and fertilizer. Any changes which are introduced need to be examined to ascertain whether this balance, which is of proven stability, is not replaced by a new relationship which could conceivably have serious deleterious effects in the long run.

### 8.2.4 Income

Under indigenous conditions incomes are low. For example, in the Zaria study the average disposable income per family, including a value for home consumption of products produced on the farm, was only about ₦206 in 1967, if income from cattle was excluded (Table 8.4). Twenty-two per cent of this income was derived from off-farm employment. Size of farm proved to be an important factor in differentiating incomes from farming. This was reflected in the substantially higher incomes derived from the larger farms which resulted from larger net farm incomes per resident (Norman 1973). However, even for these, incomes were low compared with those in institutional positions in urban centres (Monnier and Ramond 1970, RERU 1972). It is therefore not surprising that the savings potential is somewhat limited and therefore the ability to over-

## Table 8.8

*Composition of farm and family income (₦), Zaria, 1966–67*

| Variable specification in terms of an average farming family | Dan Mahawayi village | Doka village | Hanwa village Non-cattle owners | Hanwa village Cattle owners | Average of the three villages |
|---|---|---|---|---|---|
| Gross farm income: | | | | | |
| Crops[†] | 194·35 | 183·27 | 181·72 | 245·69 | 196·58 |
| Livestock | 4·58 | 6·74 | 2·21 | 363·25 | 61·48 |
| Cost of production[‡] | 42·70 | 24·30 | 31·33 | 41·73 | 34·42 |
| Net farm income | 156·23 | 166·71 | 152·60 | 567·21 | 223·64 |
| Off-farm income | 48·65 | 23·46 | 79·40 | 10·40 | 39·61 |
| Total income | 204·88 | 189·17 | 232·00 | 577·61 | 263·25 |
| Net farm income per hectare | 35·41 | 48·33 | 75·17 | 152·22 | 69·15 |
| Net farm income per resident | 22·38 | 23·00 | 16·07 | 50·28 | 25·89 |

[†]Includes value of products from the farm which were consumed by the family. On average it was estimated that 40 per cent of the value of products produced on the farm was sold for cash.

[‡]Includes depreciation of tool, equipment and buildings, costs of acquiring usufructuary rights to land, value of seed planted, and costs of fertilizer, hired labour and marketing.

come adverse circumstances is severely curtailed. This therefore is likely to result in low investment in inputs for the farm.

## 8.3 Implications for bringing about change

The typical farmer in the Savanna area is small in the sense that he has 'very limited access to political power, productive services, productive assets, and/or income streams in the society' (Adams and Coward 1972). This observation is supported by empirical evidence presented earlier in the chapter. As a result the small farmer tends to be caught in a vicious cycle or low productivity trap (Zandstra, Swanberg, and Zulberti 1975). Two implications arising from this problem are:

(i) Because farmers' incomes are low, their actual levels of living tend to be close to the minimum subsistence level of living (Wharton 1968). As a result they are likely to be somewhat reluctant to adopt radical changes in their farming system, which in the past has at least enabled them to survive.

(ii) Because of their low incomes, savings available for investment are likely to be low. Therefore, even although they may have the desire to change their farming systems, they may be unable to do so since, as was emphasized earlier, most changes involve additional monetary resources to purchase the improved technology.

Bearing in mind these points, it is possible to derive in general terms what is required in order to create conditions conducive to the adoption of changes in the farming systems of farmers. The change is likely to be attractive to them if it provides for felt needs and overcomes felt constraints[†]; if it is technically feas-

[†]There is in general justification for assuming that the felt needs or constraints reflect the actual constraints.

ible, economically profitable and dependable, and socially acceptable; and providing the requisite infrastructural support systems are available, if it is within the capacity of the farmer to adopt.

Therefore in order to develop relevant technology it is important to understand and analyse the existing farming system (Monnier and Ramond 1970). In terms of infrastructure, relevance is defined in terms of understanding the deficiencies of the present system relative to what will be required to ensure that the technology is adopted. Programmes will need to be implemented to rectify these deficiencies if changes are to be successfully adopted. The relevance of technology and infrastructure will, to a great extent be location specific (Norman 1970, Charreau 1974b, Norman 1976). Elements of infrastructural support systems that will be necessary (e.g. market for product, convincing or extension input, need for credit, distribution system for inputs, etc.) will vary according to the location and the technology being advocated. Failure to recognize the interdependences between the present farming systems, the proposed improved technology, and the necessary infrastructural support system has often been responsible for the lack of changes in indigenous farming systems (Norman 1976).

## 8.4 Relevant technology

In general terms there are two types of technology that are relevant to farmers. For most farmers in the Savanna area labour augmenting technology particularly that which is designed to overcome the seasonal labour peak of June and July, is most relevant. In other parts of the area where higher population densities exist, land intensification is more appropriate. In this section these two basic types of technology will be briefly discussed using as specific examples data collected concerning improved technology at the farmers' level in the Daudawa (11°38'N, 7°9'E) area located fairly close to Zaria.

### 8.4.1 Labour-augmenting technology

It was mentioned earlier that under practical farming conditions growing crops in mixtures rather than in sole stands has helped to ameliorate the weeding bottleneck of June and July. However, in terms of improved technology, oxen and the use of herbicides have to date been the main strategies designed to overcome this problem.

The use of oxen has been advocated in many parts of the Savanna. Indeed there is some justification for this. Parts (a) of Figs. 8.1 and 8.2 show that under practical farming conditions, the use of oxen in fact results in the peak labour period being shifted to harvesting.† Consequently oxen can be of considerable value. Nevertheless there are a number of problems which limit their being always relevant.

Firstly, the problem of the tse-tse fly, carrier of trypanosomiasis, limits their use in many parts of the Savanna.

Secondly, because of the overheads involved in keeping them, oxen are not

---

†For example it was found that labour requirements for millet were reduced by more than two thirds when this technique was used instead of hand labour, STRC/OAU-JP26 (1972a).

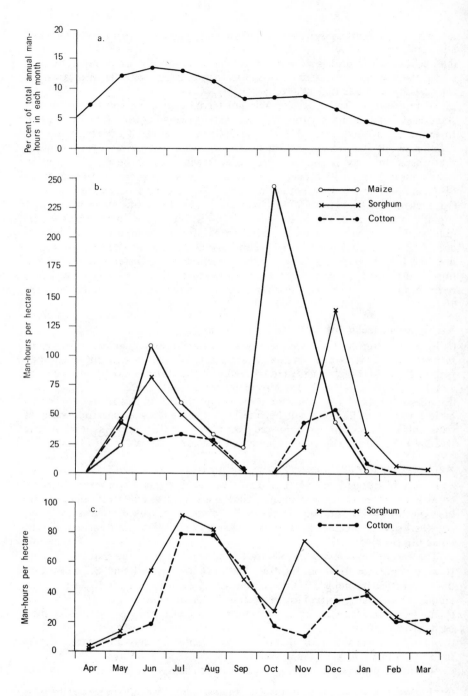

Fig. 8.1. Seasonal labour requirements using hand power; (a) all farming activities; (b) improved crop enterprises; (c) indigenous crop enterprises.

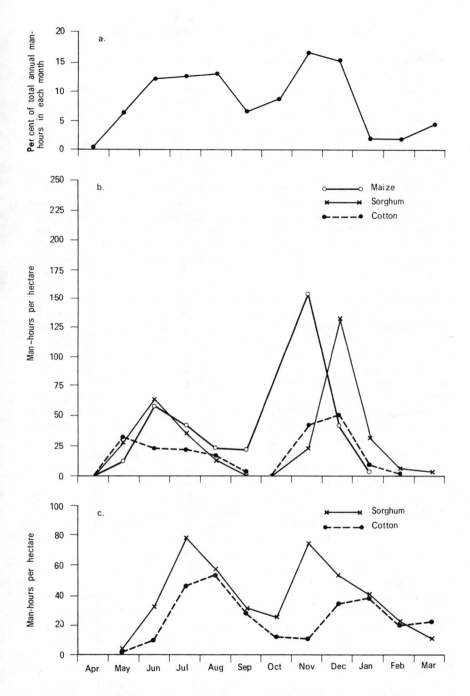

Fig. 8.2. Seasonal labour requirements using oxen; (a) all farming enterprises; (b) improved crop enterprises; (c) indigenous crop enterprises.

a viable proposition for farms smaller than four or preferably eight hectares of cultivated land (Ramond 1971).

Thirdly, although the use of oxen does help overcome the bottleneck of June and July, they are not as effective as they potentially could be. Much of the equipment used has been developed with land preparation in mind. This can also be used for ridging-up operations (i.e., inter-row cultivation). However, the problem of intra-row cultivation remains and consequently hand weeding is still a major operation even when oxen are utilized (Beeden *et al.* 1976a, Norman *et al.* 1976c and d). Nevertheless the use of oxen does, in terms of total man-hour input, or in terms of labour input during June and July, substantially increase its productivity (Table 8.12). Further increases in productivity per man-hour on an annual or June and July basis could however be brought about if the problem of hand weeding within rows could be reduced and the oxen more fully utilized during the rest of the year. With reference to intra-row weeding Charreau (1974b), STRC/OAU-JP26 (1972a), and others have indicated that in certain areas (e.g., certain parts of Senegal) it is possible to grow crops on the flat and use row tracing (i.e., cultivate in both directions by planting on the square).† Another possible strategy which is receiving a good deal of attention at Samaru at the present time is the application of herbicides along the ridge (i.e., within the row). In terms of more fully utilizing oxen throughout the year it does seem that it has not received the attention it deserves. As noted earlier, the use of oxen has shifted the labour peak to the harvesting period. Results in Table 8.12 confirm that the bulk of the reduction in labour requirements for growing crops using oxen and traditional technology results from operations other than harvesting. Evacuation of the crop from the field, which is a very time-consuming operation, could be substantially reduced by the use of oxen (Tiffen 1974). Unfortunately this is often not feasible since oxen farmers frequently do not own ox carts. Another problem inhibiting their more efficient utilization is that oxen are often in poor physical condition at the beginning of the rain-fed farming year. This unfortunately is precisely the time when their workload is most demanding. To overcome this problem, supplementary foods need to be available in addition to pasture improvement and the incorporation of such land into the farming system (J. H. Davies, personal communication).

Yet another aspect is that the practice of mixed cropping creates problems for the use of oxen. However, there is evidence that farmers owning oxen tend to simplify their cropping patterns to facilitate the utilization of animal power. In addition Andrews (1972a) has in fact demonstrated that alternate row cropping is quite easily adaptable to a cropping system using oxen.

Finally there is the problem of availability of funds to purchase oxen plus equipment (Ramond 1971) and the necessity of training farmers in their utilization. This has been recognized for a long time in many parts of the Savanna (e.g., Senegal, northern parts of Nigeria) and institutional credit and training programmes have been. set up to encourage the adoption of ox mechanization systems (e.g., Mixed Farming Scheme in northern Nigeria; Alkali 1969). Al-

†For example it was found that labour requirements for millet were reduced by more than two thirds when this technique was used instead of hand labour STRC/OAU-JP26 (1972a).

## Table 8.9

*Costs and returns on sole crop enterprises, Daudawa, 1973–74†*

| | | | Physical terms | | | Monetary terms | | | | | | Return (₦) man-hour | | |
| Crop | Type of power | Type of Technology | Yield (kg/ha) | Fertilizer (N:P:K) | Labour (man-hours) | Gross income (₦) | Non-labour costs (₦) | Labour costs (₦) | | Net return† (₦/ha) | Total | Excluding harvesting | Jun–Jul§ |
| | | | | | | | | Actual | Value of family labour | | | | |
|---|---|---|---|---|---|---|---|---|---|---|---|---|---|
| Sorghum | Hand | Indigenous | 641 | 0: 0: 0 | 240·9 | 77·25 | 1·18 | 11·46 | 13·37 | 51·24 | 0·21 | 0·37 | 0·81 |
| | | Improved | 1345 | 95: 46: 0 | 400·5 | 157·26 | 41·13 | 21·39 | 19·82 | 74·92 | 0·17 | 0·34 | 0·53 |
| | Oxen | Indigenous | 641 | 0: 0: 0 | 199·2 | 77·25 | 11·71 | 11·46 | 9·07 | 45·01 | 0·21 | 0·43 | 0·93 |
| | | Improved | 1345 | 95: 46: 0 | 337·4 | 157·26 | 40·92 | 21·39 | 13·33 | 81·62 | 0·22 | 0·52 | 0·74 |
| Cotton | Hand | Indigenous | 358 | 1: 0: 0 | 384·2 | 52·31 | 1·42 | 14·11 | 18·50 | 18·28 | 0·04 | 0·06 | 0·17§ |
| | | Improved | 736 | 27: 22: 0 | 516·9 | 107·80 | 22·61 | 27·56 | 15·76 | 41·87 | 0·07 | 0·12 | 0·25§ |
| | Oxen | Indigenous | 358 | 1: 0: 0 | 275·8 | 52·31 | 9·22 | 14·11 | 9·30 | 19·68 | 0·06 | 0·11 | 0·31§ |
| | | Improved | 736 | 27: 22: 0 | 430·4 | 107·80 | 31·00 | 27·56 | 8·51 | 40·73 | 0·08 | 0·16 | 0·31§ |
| Maize | Hand | Improved | 2897 | 189: 49: 49 | 526·3 | 292·58 | 55·16 | 19·91 | 34·09 | 183·42 | 0·33 | 0·79 | 1·05 |
| | Oxen | Improved | 2897 | 189: 49: 49 | 354·0 | 292·58 | 65·90 | 19·91 | 16·41 | 190·36 | 0·51 | 1·29 | 1·68 |

†The results for the hand labour system should be treated with caution since they were derived from other studies were used in converting tractor and oxen hours to hand labour terms. For land preparation (i.e., ploughing) 1 man-hour using an oxen team was found to be equivalent to 3·60 man-hours using hand labour. Similarly 1 man-hour using a tractor = 21·57 man-hours using hand labour for the same operation. For ridging after sowing 1 man-hour using an oxen team = 3·61 man-hours using hand labour. For evacuation of the harvested crop it was assumed that a donkey could evacuate twice as much in the same time as doing it by head load. For oxen a ratio of 10:1 was used and for a tractor a ratio of 20:1 was assumed.

‡The calculation of the numerator was based on the method used elsewhere (Norman *et al.* 1974). An opportunity cost of capital of 12 per cent was assumed. Briefly it involved the following operation: gross income—(non-labour costs) (1·12)—(actual labour costs) (1·12)—value of family labour = return.

§If the figures per unit of labour put in during June are considered only these figures are (i.e., reading downwards) 0·86, 0·66, 1·63 and 1·05. This is more reasonable in the case of cotton where under indigenous conditions planting is undertaken in July.

# Table 8.10

*Variability in return from sole crop enterprises using oxen, Daudawa, 1973–74*

| Crop | Year | Length of growing season (days) | Indigenous practices | | | | | | Improved practices | | | | | |
|---|---|---|---|---|---|---|---|---|---|---|---|---|---|---|
| | | | Days between planting and end of growing season | Yield (kg/ha)† | Net return (₦/ha) | Per cent of farmers who | | | Days between planting and end of growing season | Yield (kg/ha) | Net return (₦/ha) | Per cent of farmers who | | |
| | | | | | | Covered costs | Net return more than | | | | | Covered costs | Net return more than | |
| | | | | | | | Average for indigenous practice | Average for improved cotton | | | | | Average for indigenous practice | Average for improved cotton |
| Sorghum | 1973 | 153 | 128 | 436±172 | 37·95 | 83 | 42 | 67 | 141 | 1161±385 | 80·77 | 100 | 53 | 74 |
| | 1974 | 185 | 185 | 845±112 | 52·07 | 89 | 44 | 22 | 179 | 1530±245 | 82·46 | 100 | 67 | 33 |
| Cotton | 1973 | 153 | 91 | 454±122 | 16·72 | 88 | 50 | 50 | 110 | 658±125 | 16·60 | 79 | 42 | 42 |
| | 1974 | 185 | 131 | 364±128 | 38·83 | 100 | 42 | 17 | 143 | 784±127 | 80·18 | 100 | 74 | 39 |
| Maize | 1973 | 153 | – | – | – | – | – | – | 129 | 2867±516 | 193·96 | 100 | – | 100 |
| | 1974 | 185 | – | – | – | – | – | – | 167 | 2927±589 | 186·75 | 100 | – | 75 |

†The definition of growing season used was the difference in days between the end of the preparatory period (i.e., when rainfall was more than the potential evaporation over a ten day period) and the ten day period in which soil storage capacity dropped below 102 mm (Beeden et al. 1976b, Norman et al. 1976c, 1976d).
‡Including 95 per cent confidence limits.

## Table 8.11

*Increase in labour requirement and net returns from adopting improved technology, Daudawa, 1973–74*

| Type of power | Crop | Increase in man-hours/ha | | | Percentage of total increase | | percentage increase in total man-hours | Increase in net return (₦/ha) | |
|---|---|---|---|---|---|---|---|---|---|
| | | Excluding harvesting | Harvesting | Total | Excluding harvesting | Harvesting | | Amount | Per cent |
| Hand | Sorghum | 61·2 | 98·4 | 159·6 | 38·4 | 61·6 | 66·2 | 23·68 | 46·2 |
| | Cotton | 40·2 | 92·5 | 132·7 | 30·3 | 69·7 | 34·5 | 23·59 | 129·1 |
| Oxen | Sorghum | 44·0 | 94·2 | 138·2 | 31·8 | 68·2 | 69·4 | 36·61 | 81·3 |
| | Cotton | 62·1 | 92·5 | 154·6 | 40·2 | 59·8 | 56·1 | 21·05 | 107·0 |

## Table 8.12

*Decrease in labour requirement from using oxen instead of hand power, Daudawa, 1973–74*

| Type of technology | Crop | Decrease in man-hours/ha | | | Percentage of total decrease | | Percentage decrease in total man-hours |
|---|---|---|---|---|---|---|---|
| | | Excluding harvesting | Harvesting | Total | Excluding harvesting | Harvesting | |
| Traditional | Sorghum | 38·3 | 3·4 | 41·7 | 91·8 | 8·2 | 17·3 |
| | Cotton | 108·4 | – | 108·4 | 100·0 | – | 28·2 |
| Improved | Sorghum | 55·5 | 7·6 | 63·1 | 88·0 | 12·0 | 15·8 |
| | Cotton | 86·5 | – | 86·5 | 100·0 | – | 16·7 |
| | Maize | 81·6 | 90·7 | 172·3 | 47·4 | 52·6 | 32·7 |

though Tiffen (1974) has presented a somewhat different viewpoint, it is probably true that only in very special circumstances will it be possible for the numbers of oxen farmers to expand rapidly without an explicit programme on the part of government.

Although oxen have considerable potential in many parts of the Savanna, herbicides have, as was mentioned earlier, several advantages, which potentially give them far more general applicability. The major problem at the present time is in terms of adaptive research to screen suitable herbicides, assess methods of application (e.g., herbilizers versus spraying, etc.), determine doses required for effective weed control, and assessing their potential use in a mixed cropping framework. As yet no firm recommendations are available but the potential pay-off of this research is very high, especially in an area where a seasonal weeding bottleneck is one of the major problems.

### 8.4.2  Land intensification technology

Land intensification technology or the derivation of a greater output per unit of land usually revolves around the use of improved seed and fertilizer. This invariably results in higher labour inputs compared with indigenous technology. Using the ideas mentioned earlier, a number of comments can be made about the relevance of the technologies presented in Figs. 8.1 and 8.2 and Tables 8.9 and 8.10. Detailed discussions on the technologies are presented elsewhere (Hayward and Norman 1976b, Norman *et al.* 1976c and d). Very briefly a few points are as follows:

(a) *Technical feasibility.*  The technology must be physically or technically feasible. For example, it is obvious the S 123 composite maize with a growing period of 120 days fits well into the growing season and it was tested even in the unusually dry year of 1973. As a result the yields obtained in each year were very similar. However, in the case of the SK 5912 sorghum variety with a 160 day requirement, the results were not so promising. The average yield was 32 per cent higher in the case of the more favourable 1974 year. It is apparent that the sorghum variety is not so well adapted to the environment in any year which is shorter than normal. Because of the greater variability in yield of SK 5912 it is likely all other things being equal, that farmers would prefer to grow the more dependable maize. Another point which pertains to cotton and is not apparent from the figures presented is the use of the ULV system of spraying in contrast to the previous water-based methods. The elimination of the need for water, the considerable reduction in the time required for spraying plus the relative cheapness of the ULV spraying machine and its ease of operation, are all factors which make this technology much more technically feasible for the small farmer.

(b) *Level and dependability of profit.*  In terms of profitability the improved technologies for all the crops were substantially higher than under indigenous conditions. However, a question mark pertains to the dependability part. In terms of maize which gave by far the best results, there is potentially a problem over the market for the product. Maize is traditionally not grown in large quantities in the Savanna area. Will rurual communities in these areas be willing to consume more maize at the expense of millet and sorghum thereby increasing the size of market? Alternatively, is there a market for the product outside the Savanna area? These questions would need to be answered to assess the potential desire for farmers to grow this product. No such problem is attached to sorghum which has an established market. In spite of the difference in yields in the two years, the profitability of sorghum was similar in both years because of the substantially higher price for sorghum in the drought year of 1973. This gives some idea of the depth of the market for sorghum and certainly may appeal to farmers in spite of the substantially lower profits obtained from growing it compared with maize. The example of cotton provides another implication concernin the market side. The price offered by the Marketing Board for seed cotton in 1974 was substantially higher and resulted in profits comparable with the returns obtained from improved sorghum technology.

(c) *Compatibility with farming system.* Another question as to whether the proposed technology is economically and socially acceptable is whether or not it fits into the farming system. Thus it is not sufficient to assess its profitability by simply comparing it with the same crop using indigenous technology. In deciding whether or not to adopt it, the farmer will consider whether it is the best way to use his limited resources (i.e., land, labour, capital, and management) consistent with his goal. Therefore he will, in his decision, take into account the possibility of producing other crops, as well as the possibility of using different technological levels for the same crop. For example, for farmers with a goal of profit maximization and no labour or cash constraint, the rational enterprise to produce would be the one with the highest net return per unit area. However, for most farmers, including those in the Savanna, the decision-making process is somewhat more complex. Firstly, the goal as mentioned earlier is not usually simply one of profit maximization but is also constrained by a security strategy. Secondly, when potential labour is viewed on a monthly basis it can become severely limiting in certain months (e.g., June and July). An examination of the figures indicates that the introduction of improved technology involves both an increase in total labour requirements compared with indigenous technologies and a change in its distribution. With the use of hand labour the most marked effect is the increase in the time required for harvesting the extra crop resulting. In actual fact, this accounted for an average of 65 per cent of the increased labour requirements for growing sorghum and cotton under improved technological conditions. Fortunately this is probably not too serious a bottleneck since, for most crops, the rains are usually over and timing of this operation is not so critical as with some of the pre-harvest operations. However, problems do apply to increases in labour requirements earlier in the year as a result of higher amounts of fertilizer applications, (e.g. with cotton, increased labour is required for weeding and spraying). These problems further exaggerate the peak in June and July. In the case of cotton it is further accentuated by the fact that until recently, the recommendation for growing cotton under improved technological conditions stipulated planting in June instead of July. Is the additional labour required justified in terms of the yield resulting? It is beyond the scope of this chapter to discuss it in detail, but a somewhat crude idea can be obtained from Table 8.9. The returns per annual man-hour are as expected highest for maize and lowest for cotton. Apart from cotton, the net return per man-hour was substantially higher than the wage rate (i.e., ₦0.10 per man-hour). However, when the labour input applied during the peak June and July period is considered by itself it is apparent that the improved technologies for sorghum and cotton† suffer in comparison with the indigenous methods of growing these crops. It is however impossible without further analysis to ascertain whether as a result they would be excluded from the farming system adopted by the farmer. Nevertheless the results do show that on the basis of return per unit of either labour or land, maize does appear to be a very promising crop. Finally, while on the subject of labour requirements, the figures do show the potential advantages of combining labour-augmenting and land intensification technologies. The results in Tables 8.9 and 8.12 show that the man-hour requirement is substantially lowered by introducing oxen into the farming system as a source of power. Because, as mentioned earlier, they tend to be used mainly on land preparation and ridging they in effect accentuate the harvesting peak relative to the June-July period (i.e., parts (b) and (c) of Figs. 8.1 and 8.2). This is also apparent from the results in Table 8.12 where the relative decrease in labour requirements is greater under indigenous systems of technology where yields are lower. However, the ability of oxen to reduce effectively the labour requirements in June and July results in increasing the productivity of labour (Charreau 1974b) both during that period and as a result on an annual basis (Table 8.9). It has also been noted that the deeper ploughing possible with oxen allows better incorporation of residues, and therefore aids in the maintenance of soil fertility (Monnier and Ramond 1970, STRC/OAU–JP26, 1972b).

(d) *Compatibility with infrastructure.* The final comment on the relevance of the technologies pertains to whether or not there is an infrastructure developed which is necessary to ensure their adoption. The possible problems of markets for the products have already been mentioned. However, equal concern needs to be emphasized on the input side. Two elements that would immediately appear to be of crucial importance are the necessity of an efficient fertilizer distribution system to ensure that the large supplies required are available, and the likelihood of having to set up an institutional credit programme to enable farmers to purchase it and perhaps hire the extra labour required. There is also the necessity of having a greater concentration of extension workers than are generally available at the present time. This is because the adoption of the improved technology involves a drastic change from mixed to sole cropping, and it is sensitive to timing in terms of the operations and in the case of spraying cotton, a relatively complex technology both of which require expertise in managing the improved technology which can be imparted to some extent through the extension worker. This latter point is reinforced by the fact that the risk of a low pay-off attached to the high investment in terms of money and hours needs to be minimized. Therefore to ensure that the improved technologies briefly reviewed here do have some chance of adoption it would appear that a relatively high infrastructural commitment has to be made on the part of governmental agencies. This is in fact being done in the IBRD integrated agricultural development

† See footnote § in Table 8.9.

project located at Funtua in the same general area. However, because of limited financial and manpower sources it will not be possible for governmental agencies to provide similar concentrations of infrastructural development in all areas. Therefore pleas are increasingly being made for the development of improved technologies which accept these limitations. These can be termed intermediate compared with advanced practices which were discussed earlier in this section. Relevant intermediate technology would therefore be types that:

(i) Do not involve a strong 'convincing' element, or in other words, a concentration of extension workers. These would be types that would not involve radical changes in the farming system (e.g., could be used in the traditionally popular intercropping system,† such as improvement with late sown cotton), would be simple to adopt, would be flexible as to timing, and would involve little risk.

(ii) Would not involve high investment in improved inputs (Charreau 1974b), therefore necessitating only low levels of such inputs.

Faced with these constraints it is unlikely that the research worker will be able to evolve technological improvements which will result in spectacular payoffs. However a farmer is more likely to adopt a technology with a low profit if it has the above characteristics.

## 8.5 Conclusion

This chapter has attempted to provide a brief description of the characteristics of farming systems in the Savanna areas of West Africa. Using this as a backdrop, it has assessed the relevance of certain types of technology to small farmers in the area. In doing so, it has been argued that the synthesis of improved farming systems must be based on the analysis of existing indigenous farming systems if there is to be any real hope of relevance—and relevance is defined not only in physical but also in economic and social terms. The synthesis stage also needs to take account of any additional infrastructural support systems that might be necessary to create conditions conducive to its acceptance by farmers. In doing so, research workers must be realistic as to what might reasonably be expected to be provided and, if necessary, in the light of this modify their objectives. Finally it has been emphasized that farming systems tend to be somewhat location specific. Therefore the synthesis of improved farming systems is also likely to be somewhat location specific, often necessitating substantial adoptive research.

†Work at present being undertaken by Baker (1974) at the Institute for Agricultural Research, Samaru, Zaria is providing very promising results along these lines.

# List of organizations

| | |
|---|---|
| APREA (Virginia, U.S.A.) | American Peanut Research and Education Association Inc. |
| ASA (Wisconsin, U.S.A.) | American Society of Agronomy |
| CIAT (Cali, Colombia) | Centro Internacional de Agricultura Tropical |
| CIMMYT (El Batan, Mexico) | Centro Internacional de Mejoramieto de Maiz y Trigo |
| CIP (Lima, Peru) | Centro Internacional de la Papa |
| CSIRO (Canberra, Australia) | Commonwealth Scientific and Industrial Research Organization |
| CSSA (Wisconsin, U.S.A.) | Crop Science Society of America |
| FAO (Rome, Italy) | Food and Agriculture Organization of the United Nations |
| IAR (Samaru, Nigeria) | Institute for Agricultural Research |
| ICRISAT (Hyderabad, India) | International Crops Research Institute for the Semi-Arid Tropics |
| IITA (Ibadan, Nigeria) | International Institute of Tropical Agriculture |
| IRAT (Paris, France) | Institut de Recherches Agronomiques Tropicales |
| IRRI (Los Banos, Philippines) | International Rice Research Institute |
| NAS (Washington D.C., U.S.A.) | National Academy of Sciences |
| ORSTOM (Paris, France) | Office de la Recherche Scientifique et Technique Outre-Mer |
| RERU (Samaru, Nigeria) | Rural Economy Research Unit |
| STRC/OAU | Scientific, Technical and Research Commission of the Organization of African Unity |
| TPI (London, U.K.) | Tropical Products Institute |
| UNDP (Vienna, Austria) | United Nations Development Programme |
| UNESCO (Paris, France) | United Nations Educational, Scientific and Cultural Organization |
| USAID | United States Agency for International Development |
| USDA | United States Department of Agriculture |
| WARDA (Monrovia, Liberia) | West African Rice Development Association |
| WMO (Geneva, Switzerland) | World Meteorological Organization of the United Nations |

# References

Abalu, G. O. I. (1977). A note on crop mixtures under indigenous conditions in northern Nigeria. *J. Develop. Studies*, (in press).

Abdullahi, A. (1970). Fibre research. *Samaru agric. Newslet.*, 3, 57–60.

A'brook, J. (1964). The effect of planting date and spacing on the incidence of groundnut rosette disease at Mokwa, northern Nigeria. *Ann. appl. Biol.*, 54, 199–208.

—— (1968). The effect of plant spacing on the number of aphids trapped over the groundnut crop. *Ann. appl. Biol.*, 61, 289–94.

Adams, D. W. *and* Coward, E. W. (1972). *Small farmer strategies: a seminar report*. Agricultural Development Council, New York.

Ahn, P. M. (1974). *West African Soils*. Oxford University Press, London.

Akehurst, B. C. (1968). *Tobacco*. Longman, London.

Akinbode, B. O. (1966). Late maize variety/planting date trial in western Nigeria. *Afr. Soils*, 11, 224–33.

Aldrich, S. R. *and* Leng, E. R. (1964). *Modern Corn Production*. Farm Quarterly, Cincinnati

Alkali, M. (1969). Mixed farming—need and potential, *Livestock development in the dry and intermediate Savanna Zones*, pp. 36–41. Institute for Agricultural Research, Samaru, Nigeria.

Allan, A. Y. (1970). A review of maize agronomy research in Western Kenya. *Seminar on maize research in West Africa*, Ibadan, 1970.

Allen, D. J. (1971). Control of Zebra disease of *Agave* hybrids by breeding for resistance to *Phytophthora* spp. *PANS*, 17, 42–4.

Amile, S. (1972). Black shank disease on tobacco. *Samaru agric. Newslet.*, 14, 26–30.

Andrews, D. J. (1968). Wheat cultivation and research in Nigeria. *Niger. agric. J.*, 5, 67–72.

—— (1969). Wheat in Nigeria. *Samaru agric. Newslet.*, 11, 50–3.

—— (1970a). Breeding and testing dwarf sorghums in Nigeria. *Exp. Agric.*, 6, 41–50.

—— (1970b). Progress in sorghum breeding in Nigeria. *Afr. Soils*, 15, 449–60.

—— (1972a). Intercropping with sorghum in Nigeria. *Exp. Agric.*, 8, 139–50.

—— (1972b). Early maize yield trials, Samaru. (Mimeo.). Institute for Agricultural Research, Samaru, Nigeria.

—— (1972c). The wheat variety situation 1971/72. (Mimeo.), Institute for Agricultural Research, Samaru, Nigeria.

—— (1973). Effects of date of sowing on photosensitive Nigerian sorghums. *Exp. Agric.*, 9, 337–47.

—— (1974). Responses of sorghum varieties to intercropping. *Exp. Agric.*, 10, 57–63.

—— (1975a). Sorghum varieties for the late season in Nigeria. *Trop. Agric., Trinidad*, 52, 21–30.

—— (1975b). Sorghum grain hybrids in Nigeria. *Exp. Agric.*, 11, 119–27.

—— *and* Kassam, A. H. (1975). Importance of multiple cropping in increasing world food supplies. *Agron. Soc. Am. Multiple Cropping Sympos.* Knoxville, Tennessee, 24–29 Aug., 1975.

—— *and* Palmer, J. L. (1972). Wheat research and production; Notes for the National Accelerated Food Production Survey Team. (Mimeo.), Institute for Agricultural Research, Samaru, Nigeria.

Angstrom, A. (1924). Solar and terrestrial radiation. *Quart. J. Roy. Met. Soc.,* **50**, 121–6.

Anon (undated). Study of farming systems in French-speaking Africa and Madagascar. (Mimeo.).

APREA (1973). *Peanuts—culture and uses.* American Peanut Research and Education Association Inc., Roanoke, Virginia.

Arnon, I. (1972). *Crop production in dry regions. Vol. I. background and principles.* Leonard Hill, London.

Arraudeau, M. (1967). Cassava in the Malagasy Republic. *Proc. 1st Int. Sympos. Trop. Root Crops,* (*eds.* E. Tai *et al.*), **1**, 180–4. University of West Indies, Trinidad.

Auberville A. (1959). *Vegetation map of Africa south of the Tropic of Cancer.* Oxford University Press, London.

Austin, M. E. (1970). Various methods of harvesting sweet potatoes. *2nd Int. Sympos. Trop. Root and Tuber Crops,* (*ed.* D. L. Plucknett), **1**, 45–8. Hawaii.

—— *and* Aung, L. H. (1973). Patterns of dry matter distribution during development of sweet potato. *J. Hort. Sci.,* **48**, 11–17.

—— *and* Bell, J. B. (1970). Evolution of hand and mechanical harvest of sweet potatoes. *2nd Int. Sympos. Trop. Root and Tuber Crops,* (*ed.* D. L. Plucknett), **1**, 48–51. Hawaii.

—— *and* Graves, B. (1970). Mechanical harvesting of sweet potatoes. *2nd Int. Sympos. Root and Tuber Crops,* (*ed.* D. L. Plucknett), **1**, 44–5. Hawaii.

Ayensu, E. S. *and* Coursey, D. G. (1972). Guinea yams. *Econ. Bot.,* **26**, 301–18.

Bache, B. W. (1965).The harmful effects of ammonium sulphate on fine sandy soils at Samaru. *2nd Meet. on Soil Fertility and Fertilizer Use in West Africa,* **1**, 15–20.

—— *and* Heathcote, R. G. (1969). Long-term effects of fertilizers and manure on soil and leaves of cotton in Nigeria. *Exp. Agric.,* **5**, 241–7.

—— *and* Rogers, N. E. (1970). Soil phosphate values in relation to phosphate supply to plants from some Nigerian soils. *J. agric. Sci., Camb.,* **74**, 383–90.

Bailey, A: G. (1966). A check-list of plant diseases in Nigeria. *Memor. Fedl. Dept. Agric. Res. Nigeria No. 96.* Moor Plantation, Ibadan, Nigeria.

Baker, E. F. I. (1964). Plant population and crop yield. *Nature, (London),* **204**, 856–7.

—— (1974). Mixed cropping with cereals—A system for improvement. *Int. Workshop on Farming Systems,* pp. 287–302. ICRISAT, Hyderabad, 18–21 Nov., 1974.

—— (1975). Effects and interactions of 'package deal' inputs on yield and labour demand of maize. *Exp. Agric.,* **11**, 295–304.

—— *and* Norman, D. W. (1975). Cropping systems in northern Nigeria. *Cropping Systems Workshop,* pp. 334–61. Los Banos, IRRI, 18–20 Mar., 1975.

Barber, R. G. *and* Rowell, D. L. (1972). Charge distribution and the cation exchange capacity of an iron-rich kaolinitic soil. *J. Soil Sci.,* **23**, 135–46.

Barbour, K. M. (1972). *Planning for Nigeria: a geographical approach.* University Press, Ibadan.

Barnes, A. C. (1974). *The Sugar Cane.* Leonard Hill, London.

Barry, J. (1970). Millet and sorghum in the Niger—present state of research. *Ford Foundation/IRAT/IITA Seminar on Sorghum and Millet Research in West Africa.* IRAT, Bambey, Senegal, 31 Aug.–4 Sep., 1970.

Barry, B. D. and Andrews, D. J. (1974). A sprayer for control of *Busseola fusca* in the whorl of sorghum. *J. econ. Ent.,* 67, 310–311.

—— King, S., Stockinger, K. R., and Kassam, A. H. (1973). Report on and expedition to Niger, Upper Volta, and Ivory Coast. *Samaru agric. Newslet.,* 15, 89–91.

Bartholomew, W. V. (1972). Soil nitrogen and organic matter. *In Soils of the Humid Tropics,* pp. 63–81, National Academy of Sciences, Washington.

Bascones, L. and Lopez Ritas, J. (1961). La nutricion mineral del ajonjoli. *Agron. Trop. Venezuela,* I (1961a), 2, 17–32; and II (1961b), 2, 93–101.

Bean, A. G. and Wells, D. A. (1953). Soil capping by water drops. *National Institute of Agricultural Engineering Rep. No. 23.* Silsoe, England.

Beeden, P., Norman, D. W., Pryor, D. H., Kroeker, W. J., Hays, H. M. and Huizinga, B. (1976a). The feasibility of improved sole crop cotton technology for the small-scale farmer in the Northern Guinea Savanna Zone of Nigeria. *Samaru misc. Paper No. 61.* Institute for Agricultural Research, Samaru, Nigeria.

—— Hayward, J. A. and Norman, D. W. (1976b). A comparative evaluation of ultra low volume insecticide application on cotton farms in the North Central State of Nigeria. *Niger. J. Pl. Protec.,* (in press).

Beer, J. F. de (1963). *Influences of temperature on* Arachis hypogaea *L. with special reference to its pollen viability.* Versl. Landbouwk. Onderz. NR. 69.2, Wageningen.

Beevers, H. (1061). *Respiratory metabolism in plants.* Harper and Row, New York.

Begg, J. E., Bierbuizen, J. F., Lemon, E. R., Misra, D. K., Slatyer, R. O. and Stern, W. R. (1964). Diurnal energy and water exchanges in bullrush millet. *Agric. Met.,* 1, 194–312.

Bennett, H. H. (1939). *Soil conservation.* McGraw-Hill, New York and London.

Berger, J. (1962). *Maize production and the manuring of maize.* Centre d'Étude de l'Azote, Geneva.

Berger, J. M. (1964). Profils culturaux dans le centre de la Côte d'Ivoire. *Cah. ORSTOM, Ser. pedol.,* 1, 49–69.

Berkum, P. van, Dart, P. J., Day, J. M., Jenkinson, D. S. and Witty, J. F. (1975). Nitrogen fixation other than by nodules. *Rothamsted Subject Day 1975: Nitrogen,* (eds. J. Ashworth and P. J. Dart), pp. 43–6. Rothamsted Experiment Station, Harpenden, England.

Bertrand, R. (1967). Étude de l'erosion hydrique et de la conservation de eaux et du sol en pays Baoule (Côte d'Ivoire). *Colloque sur la fertilité de sols tropicaux,* 2, 1281–1295. Tananarive, 19–25 Nov., 1967.

Bilquez, A. F. (1970). General features of the research on millets in Africa. *Ford Foundation/IRAT/IITA Seminar on Sorghum and Millet Research in West Africa.* IRAT, Bambey, Senegal, 31 Aug.–4 Sept., 1970.

Birch, H. F. (1958). The effect of soil drying on humus decomposition and nitrogen availability. *Pl. Soil,* 10, 9–31.

—— (1959). Further observations on humus decomposition and nitrification. *Pl. Soil.,* 11, 262–86.

—— and Friend, M. T. (1956). The organic matter and nitrogen status of East African soils. *J. Soil Sci.,* 7, 156–167.

Black, C. C. (1971). Ecological implications of dividing plants into groups with distinct photosynthesis production capacities. *Adv. ecol. Res.,* 7, 87–114.

Bliss, F. A. *and* Robertson, D. G. (1971). Genetics of host reaction in cowpea to cowpea yellow mosaic virus and cowpea mottle virus. *Crop Sci.,* 11, 258–62.

Blondel, D. (1965). Premiers élements sur l'influence de la densité apparente du sol sur la croissance racinaire de l'arachide et du sorgho. Les consequences sur les rendements. *OAU/STRC Sympos. on the Maintenance and Improvement of Soil Fertility,* pp. 173–181. Khartoum, 8–12 Nov., 1965.

—— (1967). Importance réelle des pertes par volatilisation de l'ammoniaque en sol sableux (dior). *Colloque sur la fertilité des sols tropicaux,* pp. 189–97. Tananarive, 19–25 Nov., 1967.

—— (1971a). Contribution à l'étude du lessivage de l'azote en sol sableux (dior) au Senegal. *Agron. trop., Paris,* 26, 687–696.

—— (1971b). Contribution à l'étude de la croissance—matière sèche et de l'alimentation azote des céreals du culture sèche au Sénégal. *Agron. Trop., Paris,* 26, 707–20.

—— (1971c). Contribution à la connaissance de la dynamique de l'azote minéral en sol sableux (dior) au Sénégal. *Agron. Trop., Paris,* 26, 1303–33.

—— (1971d). Contribution à la connaissance de la dynamique de l'azote en sol ferrugineux tropical à Sefa (Sénégal). *Agron. Trop., Paris,* 26, 1334–54.

—— (1971e). Contribution à la connaissance de la dynamique de l'azote minéral en sol ferrugineux tropical à Nioro-du-Rip (Sénégal). *Agron. trop., Paris,* 26, 1354–61.

—— (1971f). Rôle de la plante dans l'orientation de la dynamique de l'azote en sol sableux. *Agron. trop., Paris,* 26, 1362–71.

Bockelee-Morvan, A. (1963). Étude expérimentale et pratique du placement des engrais. *Oleagineux,* 18, 687–8.

—— (1964). Études sur la carence potasique de l'arachide au Sénégal. *Oleagineux,* 19, 603–9.

—— (1965). Appliction des engrais sur l'arachide au Sénégal. *Oleagineux,* 20, 589–90.

—— (1966). Efficacité des diverses formes d'apports de élements minéraux sur l'arachide. *Oleagineux,* 21, 163–6.

—— (1968). Fumure annuelle et fumure de fond en zone arachidiere du Sénégal. *Oleagineux,* 23, 179–84.

Bolhuis, G. G. (1966). Influence of length of illumination period on root formation in cassava. *Nether. J. agric. Sci.,* 14, 251–4.

Bonner, J. (1962). The upper limit of crop yield. *Science,* 137, 11–15.

Booker, R. H. (1963). The effect of sowing date and spacing on rosette disease of groundnut in northern Nigeria, with observations on the vector, *Aphis craccivora. Ann. appl. Biol.,* 52, 125–31.

—— (1965). Pests of cowpeas and their control in northern Nigeria. *Bull ent. Res.,* 55, 663–72.

Booth, R. H. *and* Proctor, F. J. (1972). Considerations relevant to the storage of potatoes in the tropics. *PANS,* 18, 409–31.

Boudet, G. (1975). Pastures and livestock in the Sahel. *The Sahel: ecological approaches to land use,* pp. 29–34. MAB Technical Notes. The UNESCO Press, Paris.

Bourke, D. O'D. (1965). Rice in the West African Sahel and Sudan zones. *Afr. Soils,* 10, 43–70.

Bouyer, J. (1970). Essai de synthese de connaissances acquises sur les facteurs de fertilité des sols en Afrique intertropicale francophone. (Mimeo.), ORSTOM, Paris.

Bouyer, S. (1958). Correlation entre les résultats culturaux et les teneurs en phosphore dans le sol, dans le cas des sols ferrugineux tropicaux du Sénégal, *AISS, Congres de Hambourg*, **2**, 244–50.

—— and Damour, N. (1964). Les formes du phosphore dans quelques types de sols tropicaux, *8th Int. Congr. Soil Sci.*, **4**, 551–61.

Bovill, E. W. (1933). *Caravans of the Old Sahara*. Penguin, Harmondsworth.

—— (1955). *The golden trade of the Moors*. Penguin, Harmondsworth.

Braud, M. (1967). La détermination des formules d'engrais en culture cotonniere. *Colloque sur la fertilité des sols tropicaux*, **1**, 862–73. Tananarive, 19–25 Nov., 1967.

—— (1969). Sulphur fertilization in cotton in tropical Africa. *Sulphur Inst.*, **5**, 3–5.

——, Fritz, A., Megie, C. and Ossillon, P. J. (1969). Sur la déficience en bore du cotonnier. Observations préliminaries du cotonnier. *Coton et Fibres trop.*, **24**, 465–7.

Brichambaut, C. P. de (1956). Notes sur les pluies en A. E. F. *La Météorologie*, **4**, 215–41.

Bromfield, A. R. (1972). Sulphur in northern Nigerian Soils. *J. agric. Sci., Camb.*, **78**, 465–70.

—— (1973). Uptake of sulphur and other nutrients by groundnuts in northern Nigeria. *Exp. Agric.*, **9**, 55–8.

—— (1974a). Report on sulphur research project R 2122 in Nigeria. Overseas Development Administration, U.K.

—— (1974b). The deposition of sulphur in the rainwater in northern Nigeria. *Tellus*, **26**, 408–11.

—— (1974c). The deposition of sulphur in dust in northern Nigeria. *J. agric. Sci., Camb.*, **83**, 423–5.

—— (1974d). The deposition of sulphur on soil. *J. agric. Sci., Camb.*, **83**, 567–8.

Brooks, F. A. (1959). *An introduction to physical microclimatology*. University of California Press.

Brouwer, R. (1962). Nutritive influences on the distribution of dry matter in the plant. *Nether. J. agric. Sci.*, **10**, 361–76.

Brown, K. J. (1971). Plant density and yield of cotton in northern Nigeria. *Cotton Grow. Rev.*, **48**, 255–66.

Brown, L. H. and Cocheme, J. (1969). *A Study of the agroclimatology of the highlands of East Africa*. FAO/UNESCO/WMO Interagency Project on Agroclimatology. Rome, FAO.

Brown, L. R. and Finsterbusch, G. W. (1972). *Man and his environment: food*. Harper and Row, New York.

Brunt, D. (1941). *Physical and dynamical meteorology*. Cambridge University Press.

Bugundu, L. M. (1970). The storage of farm products by farmers in my village. *Samaru agric. Newslet.*, **12**, 2–10.

Bull, T. A. and Glaszion, K. T. (1975). Sugar cane. In *Crop physiology: some case histories*, (ed. L. T. Evans), pp. 51–72. Cambridge University Press.

Bullen, M. J. (1971). Weed control in rice. *Samaru agric. Newslet.*, **13**, 51–53.

Bunting, A. H. (1955). A classification of cultivated groundnuts. *Emp. J. exp. Agric.*, **23**, 158–70.

— (1958). A further note on the classification of cultivated groundnuts. *Emp. J. exp. Agric.*, **26**, 254–8.

— (1971). Research needs and capabilities concerning agricultural systems. (Mimeo.). Department of Agricultural Development Overseas, Reading University, England.

— (1972a). Pests, population, and poverty in the developing world. The John Curtis 'Woodstock' Lecture. *J. Royal Soc. Arts.*, March, 1972, 227–39.

— (1972b). Effects of environmental differences on the transfer of agricultural technology between temperate and tropical regions. (Mimeo.), Department of Agricultural Development Overseas, Reading University, England.

— (1975). Time, phenology and the yields of crops. *Weather*, **30**, 312–25.

— *and* Curtis, D. L. (1968). Local adaptation of sorghum varieties in northern Nigeria. *UNESCO Natural Resource Studies. VII. Proceedings of the Reading Symposium*. Reading University, England.

—, Dennett, M. D., Elston, J. F. *and* Milford, J. R. (1976). Rainfall trends in the West African Sahel. *Quart. J. R. Met. Soc.*, **102**, 59–64.

Buntjer, B. J. (1970). The changing structure of *gandu. Zaria and its Region: a West African Savanna city and its environs*, (ed. M. J. Mortimore), pp. 157–69. Ahmadu Bello University, Zaria, Nigeria.

Burrell, N. J., Grundey, J. K. *and* Harkness, C. (1964). Growth of *Aspergillus flavus* and production of aflatoxin in groundnuts. *Trop. Sci.*, **6**, 74–90.

Burton, W. G. (1968). *The potato*. H. Veenman and Zonen N.V., Wageningen.

Byers, H. (1959). *General meteorology*. McGraw-Hill, New York.

Caldwell, B. E. (1973). *Soybeans: improvement, production and uses*. Agronomy Monograph No. 16. Amer. Soc. Agron., Madison, Wisconsin.

Calvert, A. (1975). Flower initiation and development in the tomato. *NAAS Quart. Rev.*, **70**, 79–88.

Calvin, M. *and* Bassham, J. A. (1962). *The photosynthesis of carbon compounds*. Benjamin, New York.

Cammack, R. H. (1953). Observations on *Puccinia polysora* Underw. in West Africa. *Rep. West Afr. Maize Res. Unit, 1953*. Moor Plantation, Ibadan, Nigeria.

— (1956a). Notes on the more important fungi affecting maize in Nigeria. *Memor. West Afr. Maize Res. Unit, No. 6*. Moor Plantation, Ibadan, Nigeria.

— (1956b). Notes on the introduction of *Puccinia polysora* Underw. into Africa. *Memor. West Afr. Maize Res. Unit, No. 7*. Moor Plantation, Ibadan, Nigeria.

— (1958a). Factors affecting infection gradients from a point source of *Puccinia polysora* in a plot of *Zea mays. Ann. appl. Biol.*, **46**, 186–97.

— (1958b). Studies on *Puccinia polysora* Underw. I. The World distribution of forms of *P. polysora. Trans. Brit. Myc. Soc.*, **41**, 89–94.

Caswell, G. H. (1958). The storage of cowpea in the northern States of Nigeria. *Proc. Agric. Soc. Nigeria*, **5**, 4–6. Ibadan, 2–6 July, 1968.

Chadha, S. S. (1974). Effect of some climatic factors on the fluctuation of population of *Antigastra catalaunalis* Dupon. *Samaru misc. Paper No. 48*. Institute for Agricultural Research, Samaru, Nigeria.

Chadha, Y. R. *and* Dakshinamurthy, J. (1965). Sources of starch in Commonwealth territories: sweet potato. *Trop. Sci.*, **7**, 56–62.

Chaminade, R. (1972). Recherches sur la fertilité et la fertilisation des sols en régions tropicales. *Agron. trop., Paris*, **27**, 891–904.

Chandler, R. F. (1969). Plant morphology and stand geometry in relation to nitrogen. In *Physiological aspects of crop yield*, (eds. J. D. Eastin, F. A.

Haskins, C. Y. Sullivan, *and* C. H. M. van Bavel), pp. 265–85. ASA & CSSA, Madison, Wisconsin.

Chang, Jen-Hu. (1968). The agricultural potential of the humid tropics. *Geogr. Rev.*, **58**, 333–61.

—— (1970). Potential photosynthesis and crop productivity. *Ann. Ass. Am. Geogr.*, **60**, 92–101.

Charreau, C. (1972). Bilans mineraux étudiés en cases lysimetriques sur 3 sols du Sénégal. IRAT, Sénégal, Arch. Agropedologie.

—— (1974a). *Soils of tropical dry and dry-wet climatic areas and their use and management.* A series of lectures, Spring Semester, Cornell University.

—— (1974b). Systems of cropping in the dry tropical zone of West Africa with special reference to Senegal. *Int. Workshop Farming Systems,* pp. 287–302. ICRISAT, Hyderabad, 18–21 Nov., 1974.

—— *and* Fauck, R. (1970). Mise au point sur l'utilisation agricole des sols de la région de Sefa (Casamance). *Agron. trop., Paris,* **25**, 151–91.

—— *and* Nicou, R. (1971). L'amelioration du profil cultural dans les sols sableux et sabloargileux de la zone tropicale sèche Ouest Africaine et ses incidences agronomiques (d'après les travaux des chercheurs de l'IRAT en Afrique de l'Ouest). *Agron. trop., Paris,* **26**, 209–55; 565–631; 903–78; 1183–1237.

—— *and* Poulain, J. (1963). La fertilisation des mils et sorghos. *Agron. trop., Paris,* **18**, 53–63.

—— *and* Tourte, R. (1967). Le rôle des facteurs biologiques dans l'amelioration du profil culturel dans les systèmes d'agriculture traditionnel de zone tropicale sèche. *Colloque sur la fertilité de sols tropicaux,* **2**, 1498–1517. Tananarive, 19–25 Nov., 1967.

Chauvel, A. *and* Tobias, C. (1967). Quelques données sur les caracteristiques physiques et le pedoclimat des sols de sefa. (Mimeo.), ORSTOM, Dakar, Senegal.

Chevalier, A. (1900). Les zones et les province botanique l'A.O.F. *C. r. Acad. Sci. Paris,* 130.

—— (1934). Étude sur les prairies de l'Ouest Africian. *Rev. Bot. appl. et Agric. trop.,* **14**, 17–48.

Chi-Bonnardel, R. van (1973). *The Atlas of Africa.* Jeune Afrique, Paris.

Clayton, W. D. (1958). A preliminary survey of soil and vegetation in northern Nigeria. (Mimeo.), Institute for Agricultural Research, Samaru, Nigeria.

Cocheme, J. *and* Franquin, P. (1967). *A study of the agroclimatology of the semi-arid areas south of the Sahara in West Africa.* FAO/UNESCO/WMO Interagency Project on Agroclimatology. FAO, Rome.

Coleman, R. E. (1968). Physiology of flowering in sugar cane. *Proc. int. Soc. Sug. Cane Technol.,* **13**, 795–812.

Coleman, N. T., Weed, S. B., *and* McCracken, R. J. (1959). Cation-exchange capacity and exchangeable cations in Piedmont soils of North Carolina. *Soil Sci. Soc. Am. Proc.,* **23** 146–9.

Combeau, A. *and* Quantin, P. (1964). Observations sur les relations entre stabilité structurale et matieère organique dans quelques sols d'Afrique Centrale. *Cah. ORSTOM, Ser. pedol.,* **2**, 3–9.

Cooke, G. W. (1967). *The control of soil fertility.* Crosby Lockwood, London.

Cooper, P. J. M. (1971). *Organic sulphur fractions in northern Nigerian soils.* Ph. D. Thesis, Unviersity of Reading, England.

—— (1974). Soil temperature under maize and bare fallow in Western Kenya. *5th E. Afr. Cereals Res. Conf.,* Malawi.

—— (1975). Studies on the soil atmosphere composition under maize, grass and bare fallow in Western Kenya. *E. Afr. Agric. For. J.,* **40**, 313–31.

Coppock, J. T. (1966). Tobacco growing in Nigeria. *Samaru agric. Newslet.*, 8, 48–56.

Couper, D. C. (1972). The cost of silage production at Shika Agricultural Station. *Niger. agric. J.*, 8, 77–84.

—— and Leeuw, P. N. de (1971). The cost of dry season forage feeding at Shika Agricultural Research Station. *Samaru agric. Newslet.*, 13, 110–14.

Coursey, D. G. (1967a). *Yams*. Longman, London.

—— (1967b). Yam storage: a review of yam storage practices and of information on storage losses. *J. Stored Prod. Res.*, 2, 229–44.

—— and Haynes, P. H. (1970). Root crops and their potential as food crops in the tropics. *Wld. Crops*, 22, 261–5.

—— and Martin, F. W. (1970). The past and future of the yams as crop plants. *2nd Int. Sympos. Trop. Root and Tuber Crops*, (ed. D. L. Plucknett), pp. 87–90, Hawaii.

Coutin, R. and Harris, K. M. (1968). The taxonomy, distribution, biology and economic importance of the millet grain midge, *Geromyia penniseti* (Fett.). *Bull. ent. Res.*, 59, 259–73.

Craig, J. (1967–72). Major cereals in West Africa. *Annual Report of the AID/ARS Project (STRC JP 26)*.

Crook, J. M. and Ward, P. (1968). The Quelea problem in Africa. *The Problems of Birds as Pests*, (eds. R. K. Murton and K. N. Wright), pp. 211–29. London, Academic Press.

Crowder, M. (1962). *The Story of Nigeria*. Faber and Faber, London.

Cunard, A. C. (1967). Maize agronomy. *Wld. Crops*, 19(1), 20–7; 19(3), 24–8; 19(4), 50–60; 19(6), 45–56.

Curtis, D. L. (1965). The cultivation and utilization of wheat in the Republic of Chad, 1964–65. *Samaru agric. Newslet.*, 7, 43–7.

—— (1967). The races of sorghums in Nigeria: their distribution and relative importance. *Exp. Agric.*, 3, 275–86.

—— (1968a). The relationship between the date of heading of Nigerian sorghums and the duration of the growing season. *J. appl. Ecol.*, 4, 215–26.

—— (1968b). The relation between yield and the date of heading in Nigerian sorghums. *Exp. Agric.*, 4, 93–101.

Dagg, M. (1965). A rational approach to the selection of crops for areas of marginal rainfall in East Africa. *East Afr. Agric. For. J.*, 30, 296–300.

—— (1968). Evaporation pans in East Africa. *4th Specialist Meet. Appl. Met. in East Africa* University College, Nairobi, Kenya.

—— (1970). A study of the water use of tea in East Africa using a hydraulic lysimeter. *Agric. Met.*, 7, 303–20.

Dalby, D. and Harrison Church, R. J. (1973). *Drought in Africa*. Centre for African Studies, School of Oriental and African Studies, Unviersity of London.

Dalziel, J. M. (1955). *The useful plants of West Tropical Africa*. Crown Agents for the Colonies, London.

Dancette, C. and Poulain, J. F. (1968). Influence de l'*Acacia albida* sur les facteurs pedoclimatiques et les rendements des cultures. *Sols Africains*, 13, 197–239.

—— —— (1969). Influence of *Acacia albida* on pedoclimatic factors and crop yields. *Afr. Soils*, 14, 143–84.

Daniel, I. and Berchoux, C. de (1965). Sur la résistance au virus dans la rosette de l'Arachide. *Oleagineux*, 2, 373–6.

Dart, P. J. *and* Day, J. M. (1975). Nitrogen fixation in the field other than by nodules. *Soil microbiology: a critical review*, (*ed.* N. Walker), pp. 225–52. Butterworths, London.

——, Day, J. M. *and* Harris, D. (1972). Assay of nitrogenase activity by acetylene reduction. In *Use of isotopes for study of fertilizer utilization by legume crops*, pp. 85–100. International Atomic Energy Agency, Vienna.

Davies, J. A. (1967). A note on the relationship between net radiation and solar radiation, *Quart. J. Roy. Met. Soc.*, **93**, 109–115.

Davies, J. C. (1970). *A study of the chemical control and bionomics of* Aphis craccivora *Koch. and their effects on rosette disease attack and yield of groundnuts*. Ph.D. Thesis, University of East Africa.

—— (1975a). Insecticides for the control of the spread of groundnut rosette disease in Uganda, *PANS*, **21**, 1–8.

—— (1975b). Menazon control of rosette disease of groundnuts, *Trop. Agric., Trinidad*, **52**, 359–67.

—— *and* Kasule, F. K. (1964). The control of groundnut rosette disease in Uganda, *Trop. Agric., Trinidad*, **41**, 303–9.

Davies, W. N. L. *and* Vlitos, A. J. (1969). Fertilization of sugar cane. *Proc. Int. Soc. Sug. Cane Technol.*, 68–83.

Day, J. M. *and* Dobereiner, J. (1976). Physiological aspects of $N_2$-fixation by a *Spirillum* from *Digitaria* roots. *Soil Biol. Biochem.*, **8**, 45–50.

Deanon, J. R. *and* Cadiz, T. G. (1967). Irish potato. *Vegetable Production in South-East Asia*, (*eds.* J. E. Knott *and* J. R. Deanon), pp. 221–44. Laguna, University College, Los Banos, Philippines.

Delassus, M. (1970). Sorghum diseases of economic importance in West Africa. *Ford Foundation/IRAT/IITA Seminar on Sorghum and Millet Research in West Africa*. IRAT, Bambey, Senegal, 31 Aug.–4 Sept., 1970.

D'Hoore, J. L. (1964). *Soil Map of Africa*. Joint Project No. 11, Commission for Technical Cooperation in Africa, Lagos.

Dillewijn, C. van (1952). *Botany of sugar cane*. Chronica Botanica Co., Waltham, Mass.

Dixey, F. (1963). Geology, applied geology and geophysics in Africa. In *A review of the natural resources of the African continent*, pp. 51–100. UNESCO, Paris.

Dobereiner, J., Day, J. M. *and* Dart, P. J. (1972a). Nitrogenase activity and oxygen sensitivity of the *Paspalum notatum–Azotobacter paspali* association. *J. gen. Microbiol.*, **71**, 103–16.

—— —— —— (1972b). Nitrogenase activity in the rhizosphere of sugar cane and some other tropical grasses. *Pl. Soil*, **37**, 191–6.

Doggett, H. (1970). *Sorghum*. Longman, London.

Doku, E. V. (1969). *Cassava in Ghana*. University Press, Accra.

Dommergues, Y. (1963). Les cycles biogéochimiques des elements minéraux dans les formations tropicales. *Bois et Forêts des Tropiques*, **87**, 9–25.

—— (1966). Symbiotic fixation of nitrogen by *Casuarina*. *Soils Fertil.*, **30**, 344–53.

——, Balandreau, J. P., Rinaudo, G. *and* Weinhard, P. (1973). Non-symbiotic nitrogen fixation in the rhizospheres of rice, maize and different tropical grasses. *Soil Biol. Biochem.*, **5**, 83–9.

Du Preez, J. M. (1961). The distribution of groundwater in northern Nigeria. *Geological Survey of Nigeria Rep. No. 1188*. Lagos.

— *and* Barber, W. (1965). The distribution and chemical qualities of ground-water in northern Nigeria. *Geological Survey of Nigeria Bull. No. 36.* Govt. Printer, Lagos.

Duncan, M. G. (1967). Model building in photosynthesis. *Harvesting the Sun,* (*eds.* A. San Pietro, F. A. Grear, *and* L. J. Army), pp. 309–20. Academic Press, London.

— (1975). Maize. In *Crop physiology: some case histories* (*ed.* L. T. Evans), pp. 23–50. Cambridge University Press.

Dunne, L. E. (1959). *Diseases of Swine.* Iowa State University Press.

Eastin, J. D. (1972). Photosynthesis and translocation in relation to plant development. *Sorghum in the Seventies,* (*eds.* N. G. P. Rao *and* L. R. House), pp. 214–44. O.U.P. and IBM Publishing Co., New Delhi.

Eijnatten, C. L. M. van (1965). *Towards the improvement of maize in Nigeria.* Meded. Landbouwhogeschool Wageningen 65.3. H. Veenman & Zonen N.V., Wageningen.

Ekandem, M. J. (1965). Cassava investigations carried out in northern Nigeria, 1958–62. *Samaru agric. Newslet., 7,* 22–28.

Ellison, W. D. (1944). Studies of raindrop erosion. *Agric. Eng., 25,* 131–6.

— (1952). Raindrop energy and soil erosion. *Emp. J. exp. Agric., 20,* 81–6.

Elston, J. F., Harkness, C., *and* McDonald, D. (1976). The effects of *Cercospora* leaf disease on the growth of groundnuts in Nigeria. *Ann. appl. Biol., 83,* 39–51.

Elwell, H. A. *and* Stocking, M. A. (1973). Rainfall parameters for soil loss estimation in a sub-tropical climate. *J. agric. Eng. Res., 18,* 169–77.

Enwezor, W. O. (1967). Soil drying and organic matter decomposition. *Plants and Soil, 26,* 269–76.

— *and* Moore, A. W. (1966). Phosphorus status of some Nigerian soils. *Soil Sci., 102,* 322–8.

Epstein, H. (1957). The origin and history of African cattle. *The indigenous cattle of the British dependent territories in Africa.* HMSO Publication No. 5, London.

Etasse, C. (1970). Millet breeding objective for intensive agriculture. *Ford Foundation/IRAT/IITA Seminar on Sorghum and Millet Research in West Africa.* IRAT, Bambey, Senegal, 31 Aug.–4 Sept., 1970.

Evans, A. C. (1954). Groundnut rosette disease in Tanganyika. *Ann. appl. Biol., 41,* 189–206.

Evans, L. T. (1969). *Induction of flowering: some case histories.* Macmillan, London.

—, Wardlaw, I. F., *and* Fischer, R. A. (1975). Wheat. In *Crop physiology: some case histories,* (*ed.* L. T. Evans), pp. 101–49. Cambridge University Press.

Evelyne, S. H. *and* Thornton, I. (1964). Soil fertility and the response of groundnuts to fertilizers in the Gambia. *Emp. J. exp. Agric., 32,* 153–160.

FAO (1965). *Fertilizers and their uses.* FAO, Rome.

FAO (1974). *Tree planting practices in African Savannas.* FAO, Rome.

Farbrother, H. G. and Munro, J. (1970). Water. In *Agriculture in Uganda,* (*ed.* J. D. Jameson), pp. 3–42. Oxford University Press, London.

Fauck, R. (1956), Évolution des sols sous culture mechanise dans les régions tropicales. *6th Int. Congr. Soil Sci., E.,* pp. 593–6.

— (1960). Matière organique et azote des sols de la Moyenne Guinea et relations avec les rendements des cultures. *C. r. Acad. Agric. Fr., 46,* 152–5.

—— (1963). The sub-group of leached Ferruginous tropical soils with concretions. *Afr. Soils*, **8**, 407–27.

——, Moureaux, C., *and* Thomann, C. (1969). Bilans de l'évolution des sols de Sefa (Casamance, Sénégal) après quinze années de culture continue. *Agron. trop., Paris*, **24**, 263–301.

Faulkner, R. C. *and* Smithson, J. B. (1972). *Cotton Res. Rept. Northern States Nigeria*, 1970–71. Cotton Research Corporation, London.

Feakin, S. D. (1973). *Pest Control in Groundnuts*, PANS Manual No. 2, Centre for Overseas Pest Research, London.

Ferguson, T. V. *and* Haynes, P. H. (1970). The response of yams to nitrogen, phosphorus, potassium, and organic fertilizers. *2nd Int. Sympos. Root and Tuber Crops*, (*ed.* D. L. Plucknett), **1**, 93–6. Hawaii.

Ferraris, R. (1973). *Pearl Millet.* Review Series No. 1/1973. Commonwealth Bureau of Pastures and Field Crops, Hurley, Maidenhead, England.

FFHC (1965). *Progress during the first four years, fertilizer programme.* Freedom From Hunger Campaign. FAO, Rome.

Fogg, G. E. (1968). *The growth of plants.* Penguin, Harmondsworth.

Foster, W. H. *and* Mundi, E. J. (1961). Forage species in northern Nigeria. *Trop. Agric., Trinidad.* **38**, 311–18.

Fowler, A. M. (1970). The epidemiology of *Cercospora* leaf-spot disease of groundnuts. *Samaru agric. Newslett.*, **12**, 66–9.

—— *and* McDonald, D. (1975). The response of different groundnut varieties to control of *Cercospora* leaf spot disease in northern Nigeria. African Groundnut Council, Council of Representatives, 24th Ordinary Session, 13th Session of Scientific and Technical Committee, Bamako, Mali, Nov., 1975.

Francois, C. F. *and* Law, J. M. (1971). *Sweet potato storage.* Louisiana State University, Baton Rouge, DAE Res. Rep. La No. 429.

Frederick, S. E. *and* Newcomb, E. H. (1969). Microbody-like organelles in leaf cells. *Science.* **163**, 1353–5.

Frere, M. (1972). A method for the practical application of the Penman formula for the estimation of potential evapotranspiration and evaporation from a free water surface. FAO, Rome.

Fricke, W. (1964). Cattle husbandry in northern Nigeria. *The cattle and meat industry in northern Nigeria*, (*eds.* W. Werhahn, W. Fricke, F. Hunger, F. Weltz, H. Gottschalk, *and* H. Saager). Frankfurt/Main.

Fujise, K. *and* Tsuno, Y. (1967). The effect of potassium on dry matter production of sweet potato. *1st Int. Sympos. Trop. Root Crops*, (*eds.* E. Tai *et al.*), **2**, 20–33. University of West Indies, Trinidad.

Furon, R. (1963). *Geology of Africa* (*trans.* H. Hallam *and* L. A. Stevens). Oliver and Boyd, London.

Gaudefroy-Demomoynes, P. *and* Charreau, C. (1961). Possibilité de conservation de l'humidité dans le sol pendant la saison sèche; influence correlative sur le degré d'ameublissement du sol. *Agron. trop., Paris*, **26**, 238–54.     .

Gavaud, M. (1968), Les sols bien drainés sur matériaux sableux du Niger. *Cah. ORSTOM, Ser. pedol.*, **6**, 277–307.

Geus, J. G. de (1970). *Fertilizer guide for foodgrains in the tropics and subtropics.* Centre d'Étude de l'Azote, Zurich.

Ghosh, B. N. (1955). Photoperiodic response in til (*Sesamum indicum* L.) *Curr. Sci.*, **24**, 170–5.

Gibbons, R. W., Bunting, A. H., *and* Smartt, J. (1972). The classification of varieties of groundnut. *Euphytica*, **21**, 78–85.

Gilbert, E. H. (1959). *Marketing of staple foods in Northern Nigeria. A study of the staple food marketing systems, Kano City.* Ph.D. Thesis, Food Research Institute, Stanford University.

Giles, P. H. (1964a). The storage of cereals by farmers in northern Nigeria. *Trop. Agric., Trinidad,* 41, 197–212.

— (1964b). The insect infestation of sorghum stored in granaries in northern Nigeria. *Bull. ent. Res.,* 55, 573–88.

Gillet, N. (1967). Essai d'evaluation de la biomass végétable en zone sahélienne (végétation annuelle). *J. Agric. trop. et Bot. appl.,* 14, 123–58.

— (1975). Plant cover and pastures of the Sahel. *The Sahel: ecological approaches to land use,* pp. 21–7. MAB Technical Notes. The UNESCO Press, Paris.

Gillier, P. (1960). Fumures minérales de l'arachide au Sénégal. *Oleagineux,* 15, 783–91.

— (1964). Les exportations en élements minéraux d'une culture d'arachide dans les différentes zones de Sénégal, *Oleagineux,* 19, 745–6.

— (1966). Les exportations en élements mineraux d'une culture d'arachide dans les différentes zones du Sénégal. *Oleagineux,* 21, 13–15.

— and Prevot, P. (1960). Fumers minérales de l'arachide au Sénégal. *Oleagineux,* 15, 783–91.

Goddard, A. D. (1970). Land tenure and economic development in Hausaland. *Samaru agric. Newslet.,* 2, 30–3.

— (1973). Changing family structures amongst the rural Hausa. *Africa,* 43, 207–18.

Godin, V. J. and Spensley, P. C. (1971). *Oils and Oilseeds.* TPI Crop and Product Digest No. 1. Tropical Products Institute, London.

Goldswrothy, P. R. (1964). Methods of applying superphosphate to groundnuts in northern Nigeria. *Emp. J. exp. Agric.,* 32, 231–4.

— (1967). Responses of cereals to fertilizers in northern Nigeria. I. Sorghum. *Exp. Agric.,* 3, 29–40.

— (1968). Responses of cereals to fertilizers in northern Nigeria. II. Maize. *Exp. Agric.,* 3, 263–73.

— (1970a). The growth and yield of tall and short sorghums in Nigeria. *J. agric. Sci., Camb.,* 75, 109–22.

— (1970b). The canopy structure of tall and short sorghum. *J. agric. Sci., Camb.,* 75, 123–31.

— (1970c). The sources of assimilate for grain development in tall and short sorghum. *J. agric. Sci., Camb.,* 74, 523–31.

— and Heathcote, R. G. (1963). Fertilizer trials with groundnuts in northern Nigeria. *Emp. J. exp. Agric.,* 31, 351–366.

— and Heathcote, R. (1964). Fertilizer trials with Soya beans in northern Nigeria, *Emp. J. exp. Agric.,* 32, 257–62.

— and Tayler, R. S. (1970). The effect of plant spacing on grain yield of tall and short sorghum in Nigeria. *J. agric. Sci., Camb.,* 74, 383–90.

Gooding, H. J. and Campbell, J. S. (1964). The improvement of sweet potato storage by cultural and chemical means. *Emp. J. exp. Agric.,* 32, 65–75.

Goudie, A. S. (1972). *The concept of post-glacial progressive dessication.* School of Geography, Oxford.

Grassl, C. O. (1969). *Saccharum* names and their interpretation. *Proc. Int. Soc. Sug. Cane Technol.,* 868–75.

Green, J. H. (1970). Selection of onion seed by farmers and its effect on ware crops in the northern States. *Samaru agric. Newslet.,* 12, 18–19.

— (1971a). Cultivar trials with onion in the northern States of Nigeria. *Niger. agric. J.*, **8**, 169–74.

— (1971b). The potential for the bulb onion crop in the northern States of Nigeria. *Samaru agric. Newslet.*, **13**, 54–60.

— (1972a). Preliminary trials with herbicides in irrigated onions at Samaru, Nigeria. *Hort. Res.*, **12**, 119–25.

— (1972b). The influence of bulb size, bulb cutting and separation of axillary shoots on seed production of onion. *J. hort. Res.*, **47**, 365–8.

— (1972c). Suggestions for improved storage of onions in northern Nigeria. *Samaru agric. Newslet.*, **14**, 56–7.

Greenland, D. J. (1975). Contribution of micro-organisms to the nitrogen status of tropical soils. *Conf. on Biological Nitrogen Fixation in Farming Systems of the Tropics*. IITA, Ibadan, 20–23 Oct., 1975.

— and Kowal, J. M. (1960). Nutrient content of the moist tropical forest of Ghana. *Pl. Soil.*, **12**, 1954–74.

— and Nye, P. H. (1959). Increases in the carbon and nitrogen contents of tropical soils under natural fallows. *J. Soil Sci.*, **10**, 284–99.

Greenwood, M. (1951). Fertilizer trials with groundnuts in northern Nigeria. *Emp. J. exp. Agric.*, **19**, 225–41.

— (1954). Sulphur deficiency in groundnuts in northern Nigeria. *5th Int. Congr. Soil Sci.*, **3**, 245–51.

Gribbin, J. (1973). Planetary alignments, solar activity and climatic change. *Nature, (London)*, **246**, 453–4.

Griffiths, J. F. (1960). Bioclimatology and the meteorological services. *Tropical meteorology in Africa*, (*ed.* D. J. Bargman), pp. 283–301. Munitalp Foundation, Nairobi.

— (1966). *Applied climatology: an introduction*. Oxford University Press, London.

Grist, D. H. (1965). *Rice*. Longman, London.

Grove, A. T. (1973). Desertification in the African environment. *Drought in Africa*, (*eds.* D. Dalby *and* R. J. Harrison Church), pp. 33–45. Centre for African Studies, University of London.

Guillard, J. (1958). Essai de mesure de l'activité d'un paysan Africaine le Toupouri, *Agron. trop., Paris*, **13**, 418–28.

Gurnah, A. M. (1974). Effects of spacing, sett weight and fertilizers on yield and yield components in yams. *Exp. Agric.*, **10**, 17–22.

Gusten, R. (1965). Die Rentabilital der Verwenclung von Mineraldunger bei Erdnussen in Senegal, Nordnigeria and Niger. *Z. Auslandische Landwirtsch.*, **4**, 149–53.

Haggar, R. J. (1959). Improved pastures in the northern States of Nigeria, *1st Livestock Conf.*, pp. 86–92. Institute for Agricultural Research, Samaru, Nigeria.

— (1970). Seasonal production of *Andropogon gayanus*. I. Seasonal changes in yield components and chemical composition. *J. agric. Sci., Camb.*, **74**, 487–94.

— (1972). The intake and digestibility of low quality *Andropogon gayanus* hay supplemented with various nitrogenous feeds, as recorded by sheep. *Samaru Res. Bull. No. 151*. Institute for Agricultural Research, Samaru, Nigeria.

— and Ahmed, M. B. (1970). Seasonal production of *Andropogon gayanus*. II. Seasonal changes in digestibility and feed intake. *J. agric. Sci., Camb.*, **74**, 369–73.

—— *and* Ahmed, M. B. (1971). Seasonal production of *Andropogon gayanus*. III. Changes in crude protein content and *in vitro* dry matter digestibility of leaf and stem portions. *J. agric. Sci., Camb.,* 77, 47–52.

—— *and* Couper, D. C. (1972). Effects of plant population and fertilizer nitrogen on the growth and components of yield of maize grown for silage in Nigeria. *Exp. Agric.,* 8, 251–63.

Hall, D. A. *and* Rao, K. K. (1972). *Photosynthesis.* Institute of Biology's Studies in Biology No. 37. Edward Arnold, London.

Hanway, J. J. (1965). Growth and nutrient uptake by corn. *20th Ann. Hybrid Corn Industry Res. Conf.,* pp. 106–10.

Hardy, R. W. F., Burns, R. C. *and* Holsten, R. D. (1973). Application of the acetylene assay for measurement of nitrogen fixation. *Soil Biol. Biochem.,* 5, 47–81.

Harris, K. M. (1961). The sorghum midge, *Contarina sorghicola* (Cog.) in Nigeria. *Bull. ent. Res.,* 52, 129–46.

Haswell, M. R. (1963). *The changing pattern of economic activity in a Gambia Village.* Overseas Research Publication No. 2, Department of Technical Cooperation, HMSO, London.

Hatch, M. D. (1970). Chemical energy costs for $CO_2$ fixation by plants with differing photosynthetic pathways. *IBP/PP Tech. Meet. on Prediction and Measurement of Photosynthetic Productivity,* pp. 215–20. Trebon, 14–21 Sept., 1969.

—— *and* Slack, C. R. (1966). Photosynthesis by sugar cane leaves. A new carboxylation reaction and the pathway of sugar formation. *Biochem. J.,* 101, 103–11.

——, Osmond, C. B., *and* Slatyer, R. O. (1970). *Photosynthesis and photorespiration.* Wiley-Interscience, New York.

Haughton, S. M. (1963). *The stratigraphical history of Africa south of the Sahara.* Oliver and Boyd, London.

Hawkes, J. G. *and* Hjerting, J. P. (1969). *The potatoes of Argentina, Brazil, Paraguay and Uruguay: a biosystematic study.* Clarendon Press, Oxford.

Hayes, T. B. (1932). Groundnut rosette disease in the Gambia. *Trop. Agric., Trinidad,* 9, 211–20.

Haynes, P. H. *and* Wholey, D. W. (1971). Variability in commercial sweet potatoes in Trinidad. *Exp. Agric.,* 7, 27–32.

——, Spence, J. A., *and* Walter, C. J. (1967). The use of physiological studies in the agronomy of root crops. *1st Int. Sympos. Trop. Root Crops.* (*eds.* E. Tai *et al.*) 1, 1–17. University of West Indies, Trinidad.

Hayward, J. A. (1972). Relationship between pest infestation and applied nitrogen in cotton in Nigeria. *Cotton Grow. Rev.,* 40, 224–35.

Heathcote, R. G. (1972a). The effect of potassium and trace elements on yield in northern Nigeria. *Afr. Soils,* 17, 85–9.

—— (1972b). Potassium fertilization in the Savanna zone of Nigeria. *Samaru Res. Bull. No. 170.* Institute for Agricultural Research, Samaru, Nigeria.

—— (1973). The use of fertilizer in the maintenance of soil fertility under intensive cropping in nothern Nigeria. *10th IPI Colloquium.* Abidjan, Ivory Coast, Dec., 1973.

—— *and* Fowler, A. M. (1977). Molybdenum deficiency in groundnuts in northern Nigeria. *Samaru misc. Paper.* Institute for Agricultural Research, Samaru, Nigeria (in press).

— *and* Smithson, J. B. (1974). Boron deficiency in cotton in northern Nigeria. I. Factors influencing occurrence and methods of correction. *Exp. Agric.,* **10**, 199–208.

— *and* Stockinger, K. R. (1970). Soil fertility under continuous cultivation in northern Nigeria. II. Responses to fertilizers in the absence of organic manures. *Exp. Agric.,* **6**, 345–50.

Helleiner, G. K. (1976). *Small-holder decision making: tropical African evidence.* (in Reynolds, L. G., *ed., Agriculture in development theory*. New Haven, Yale University Press).

Henin, S., Monnier, G. *and* Combeau, A. (1958). Methode pour l'étude de la stabilitie structurale des sols. *Ann. Agron.,* **9**, 73–92.

Hill, P. (1972). *Rural Hausa: a village and a setting.* Cambridge University Press.

Hill, R. (1970). Bioenergetics of photosynthesis at the chloroplast and cellular level, *IBP/UNESCO Meeting on Productivity of Tropical Ecosystems,* Makerere University, Uganda, Sept., 1970.

Holm, L. (1969). Weed problems in developing countries. *Weed Sci.,* **17**, 113–18.

Hopen, C. E. (1958). *The pastoral Fulbe family in Gwandu.* Oxford University Press, London.

Hozyo, Y. (1970). Growth and development of tuberous root in sweet potato. *2nd Int. Sympos. Trop. Root and Tuber Crops,* (ed. D. L. Plucknett), **1**, 22–3. Hawaii.

—, Murata, T., *and* Yoshida, T. (1971). The development of tuberous roots in grafting sweet potato plants, *Bull. Natn. Inst. Agric. Sci., Tokyo (Ser. D), No. 22.* pp. 165–91.

Hudson, N. W. (1971). *Soil conservation.* B. T. Batsford Ltd, London.

— *and* Jackson, D. C. (1959). Results achieved in the measurement of erosion and run-off in Southern Rhodesia, *3rd Inter-Afr. Soils Conf.,* Dalaba.

Hull, R. (1969). Rosette and other diseases of groundnuts. *Samaru agric. Newslet.,* **11**, 22–5.

Humbert, R. P. (1967). *The growing of sugar cane.* Elsevier, Amsterdam.

Hunter, G. *and* Bottrall, A. F. (1974). *Serving the small farmer: policy choices in Indian agriculture.* Croom Helm, London.

Hurault, J. (1971). The erodibility of overgrazed soils in the Adamawa high plateaux. *Bull Assoc. Fr. Étude Sol.,* **1**, 23–56.

IITA (1972–73). *International Institute of Tropical Agriculture Report 1972–73.* IITA, Ibadan, Nigeria.

— (1973a). *Cereal Improvement Programme 1973 Report.* IITA, Ibadan, Nigeria.

— (1973b). *Grain Legume Improvement Programme 1973 Report.* IITA, Ibadan, Nigeria.

— (1973c). *Root and Tuber Improvement Programme 1973 Report.* IITA, Ibadan, Nigeria.

Ipinmidun, W. B. (1972). Organic phosphorus in some northern Nigerian soils in relation to soil organic carbon and as influenced by parent rock and vegetation. *J. Sci. Fd. Agric.,* **23**, 1099–1105.

IRAT (1972). *Rapport annue d'activité 1971–72.* IRAT, Bambey, Senegal.

IRRI (1963). *Annual Report 1963.* International Rice Research Institute, Los Banos, Philippines.

Irvine, F. R. (1974). *West African Crops.* Oxford University Press, London.

Ito, H. *and* Hayashi, K. (1969). The changes in paddy field rice varieties in Japan. *Sympos. Optimization of Fertilizer Effect in Rice Cultivation,* pp. 13–23. Agric. For. and Fisher, Res. Council, Min. Agric. and For., Japan.

Ittersum, A. van (1972). A calculation of potential rice yields. *Nether. J. agric. Sci.*, **20**, 10–21.

Ivins, J. D. *and* Milthorpe, F. L. (1963). *The growth of the potato*. Butterworth, London.

Iyambo, D. E. (1971). Species introduction and growth in African Savanna. *Savanna For. Res. Stn. Res. Paper No. 8*. Samaru, Nigeria.

Jackson, J. K. *and* Ojo, G. O. A. (1973). Productivity of natural woodland and plantations in the Savanna zones of Nigeria. *Fdl. Dept. For. Res. Paper No. 20*. Ibadan, Nigeria.

Jacob, A. *and* Uexkull, H. von (1960). Sweet Potatoes. *Fertilizer use: nutrition and manuring of tropical crops*, pp. 159–63. Hannover: Verlagsgesellschaft fur Ackerbau mbH.

Jacquinot, L. (1970). Potentialities of millet yield and quality. *Ford Foundation/IRAT/IITA Seminar on Sorghum and Millet Research in West Africa*. IRAT, Bambey, Senegal, 31 Aug.–4 Sept., 1970.

—— (1973). Effects de la nature de l'alimentation azotée et du pH sur la croissance et la productivité du mil (*Pennisetum typhoides*). *Afr. Soils*, **17**, 95–8.

James, W. O. (1953). *Plant Respiration*. Oxford University Press, London.

Jenkinson, A. F. (1973). A note on variations in May to September rainfall in West African marginal rainfall areas. *Drought in Africa*, (eds. D. Dalby *and* R. J. Harrison Church), pp. 31–2. Centre for African Studies, University of London.

Jennings, D. L. (1970). Cassava in Africa. *Fld. Crop Abstr.*, **23**, 271–8.

Jenny, H. (1941). *Factors of Soil Formation*. McGraw Hill, New York.

—— *and* Raychaudhuri, S. P. (1960). *Effect of climate and cultivation on nitrogen and organic matter reserves in Indian soils*. Indian Council of Agric. Res., New Delhi.

Joachim, F., Bulow, W. von *and* Dobereiner, J. (1975). Potential for nitrogen fixation in maize genotypes in Brazil. *Proc. Nat. Acad. Sci., USA*, **72**, 2389–93.

Jones, H. A. *and* Emsweller, S. L. (1939). Effect of storage, bulb size, spacing and time of planting on production of onion seed. *Bull. Calif. Agric. Expt. Stn. No. 628*.

—— *and* Mann, L. K. (1963). *Onions and Their Allies*. Leonard Hill, London.

Jones, M. J. (1971). The maintenance of soil organic matter under continuous cultivation at Samaru, Nigeria. *J. agric. Sci., Cambridge*, **77**, 473–82.

—— (1973). The organic matter content of the Savanna soils of West Africa. *J. Soil Sci.*, **24**, 42–53.

—— (1975). Leaching of nitrate under maize at Samaru, Nigeria. *Trop. Agric., Trinidad*, **52**, 1–10.

—— *and* Bromfield, A. R. (1970). Nitrogen in the rainfall at Samaru, Nigeria. *Nature, London*, **227**, 86.

—— *and* Stockinger, K. R. (1972). The effect of planting date on the growth and yield of maize at Samaru, Nigeria. *Afr. Soils*, **17**, 27–34.

—— *and* Wild, A. (1975). *Soils of the West African Savanna*. Tech. Comm. No. 55. CAB, Harpenden.

Jung, G. (1967). Influence de l'*Acacia albida* sur la biologie des sols 'Dior'. (Mimeo.), ORSTOM, Dakar, Sénégal.

Kadeba, O. (1970). Organic matter and nitrogen status of some soils from the Savanna zone of Nigeria. *Inaugural Conf. For. Ass. Nigeria*, Ibadan.

Kang, B. T. (1975). Effects of inoculation and nitrogen fertilizer on soya bean in Western Nigeria. *Exp. Agric.*, **11**, 23–31.

Kassam, A. H. (1972). Water use and efficiency of energy conversion of crops at Samaru. *Samaru agric. Newslet.,* 14, 52–5.
—— (1973). In search of higher yields with mixed cropping in northern Nigeria—a report on agronomic work. (Mimeo.), Institute for Agricultural Research, Samaru, Nigeria.
—— (1977). Net biomass and yield of crops. Project on a global assessment of present and potential land use by agro-ecological zones. Land and Water Development Division, FAO, Rome.
—— *and* Andrews, D. J. (1975). Effects of sowing date on growth, development and yield of photosensitive sorghum at Samaru, northern Nigeria. *Exp. Agric.,* 11, 227–40.
—— *and* Kowal, J. M. (1973). Productivity of crops in the Savanna and Rain Forest zones in Nigeria. *Savanna,* 2, 39–49.
—— *and* Kowal, J. M. (1975). Water use, energy balance and growth of Gero millet at Samaru, northern Nigeria. *Agric. Met.,* 15, 333–42.
—— *and* Stockinger, K. R. (1973). Growth and nitrogen uptake of sorghum and millet in mixed cropping. *Samaru agric. Newslet.,* 15, 28–33.
——, Kowal, J. M., Dagg, M., *and* Harrison, M. N. (1975a). Maize in West Africa: and its potential in the Savanna areas. *Wld. Crops,* 17, 75–8.
——, Kowal, J. M., *and* Harkness, C. (1975b). Water use and growth of groundnut at Samaru, northern Nigeria. *Trop. Agric., Trinidad,* 52, 105–12.
——, Kowal, J. M., *and* Sarraf, S. (1977). Climatic adaptability of Crops. Project on a global assessment of present and potential land use by agro-ecological zones. Land and Water Development Division, FAO, Rome.
——, Dagg, M., Kowal, J. M., *and* Khadr, F. (1976). Improving food crop production in the Sudan Savanna zone of northern Nigeria. *Outlook on Agric.,* 8, 341–7.
Kay, D. E. (1973). *Root Crops.* TPI Crop and Product Digest. Tropical Products Institute, London.
Keay, M. A. *and* Quinn, J. G. (1967). Damping-off disease. *Samaru agric. Newslet.,* 9, 42–5.
Keay, R. W. S. (1959). *An outline of Nigerian vegetation.* Govt. Printer, Lagos.
Keleny, G. P. (1965). Sweet potato storage. *Papua New Guin. agric. J.,* 17, 102–8.
Kemp, R. H. (1963). Growth rates and regeneration of Northern Guinea Savanna Woodland. *Dept. For. Res. Techn. Note No. 24.* Ibadan, Nigeria.
King, H. E. (1957). Cotton yields and weather in northern Nigeria. *Emp. Cotton Grow. Rev.,* 34, 153–4.
—— *and* Lawes, D. A. (1959). *Progr. Rept. Expt. Stas. Northern Nigeria, 1957–58,* Cotton Res. Corp., London.
—— *and* Lawes, D. A. (1960). *Progr. Rept. Expt. Stas. Northern Nigeria, 1958–59,* Cotton Res. Corp., London.
King, J. W. (1973). Solar radiation changes and the weather. *Nature, (London),* 245, 443–6.
King, N. J., Mungomery, R. W. *and* Hughes, C. G. (1965). *Manual of cane growing.* Elsevier, New York.
King, R. (1975a). Experiences in the administration of cooperative credit and marketing societies in northern Nigeria. *Agric. Admin.,* 2, 195–208.
—— (1975b). Capital credit and savings in northern Nigerian agriculture: questioning the conventional wisdom. (Mimeo.). Institute for Agricultural Research, Samaru, Nigeria.

King, S. B. (1970a). Millet diseases, *Ford Foundation/IRAT/IITA Seminar on Sorghum and Millet Research in West Africa*, IRAT, Bambey, Senegal, 31 Aug.–4 Sept., 1970.
— (1970b). Millet diseases in Nigeria, *Samaru agric. Newslet.*, 12, 87–89.
— (1972). Sorghum diseases and their control, *Sorghum in the Seventies*, (*eds.* N. G. P. Rao *and* L. R. House), pp. 411–34. O.U.P. and IBH Publishing Co., New Delhi.
Kirby, R. H. (1963). *Vegetable fibres, botany, cultivation and utilization.* Leonard Hill, London.
Koening, L. (1956). The economics of water resources. In *The future of arid lands*, (*ed.* G. F. White), pp. 320–30. Amer. Assoc. Adv. Sci., Washington D.C.
Kohler, M. A. (1954). Lake and pan evaporation. *U.S. Geol. Survey Profess. Paper No. 269.*
—, Nordensen, T. J. *and* Fox, W. E. (1955). Evaporation from pans and lakes. *U.S. Dept. Comm. Res. Paper No. 38.*
Koli, S. E. (1970). The optimum planting date for maize in Ghana. *Ghana J. agric. Sci.*, 3, 73–81.
Kowal, J. M. (1954). *Some studies of soil fertility in southern Nigeria.* M.Sc. Thesis, University of Wales.
— (1962). *The agricultural development of the black clay soils of the Accra plains*, Ph.D. Thesis, London University.
— (1968a, b). Physical properties of soil at Samaru, Zaria, Nigeria: Storage of water and its use by crops, parts I and II. *Niger. agric. J.*, 5, 13–20; 49–52.
— (1969). Some physical properties of soil at Samaru, Zaria, Nigeria: Storage of water and its use by crops, part III. *Niger. agric. J.*, 6, 18–29.
— (1970a, b, c, d). The hydrology of a small catchment basin at Samaru, Nigeria, parts I–IV. *Niger agric. J.*, 7, 27–40; 41–52; 120–33; 134–47.
— (1970e). Effect of an exceptional storm on soil conservation at Samaru, Nigeria. *Niger. geog. J.*, 13, 163–73.
— (1972a). Radiation and potential crop production at Samaru, Nigeria. *Savanna*, 1, 89–101.
— (1972b). Study of soil surface crusts in the loess plain soils of northern Nigeria. *Niger. J. Sci.*, 6, 93–100.
— (1973). Notional water budget in the six nothern States of Nigeria. *Sympos. on Hydrology and Water Resources Development in Nigeria.* Institute for Agricultural Research, Samaru, 4–9 Sept., 1972.
— (1975). Report on research proposals for the soil physics and soil chemistry sections of the Savanna Forestry Research Station, Samaru, Nigeria. UNDP/FAO, Rome.
— *and* Adeoye, K. B. (1973). An assessment of aridity and severity of the 1972 drought in northern Nigeria. *Savanna*, 2, 145–58.
— *and* Andrews, D. J. (1973). The pattern of water availability and water requirement for grain sorghum production at Samaru, Nigeria. *Trop. Agric., Trinidad,* 50, 89–100.
— *and* Davies, J. H. (1975). Water resources and dry matter production for livestock in northern Nigeria. *Agric. Environ.*, 1 339–55.
— *and* Faulkner, R. C. (1975). Cotton production in northern states of Nigeria in relation to water availability and crop water use. *Cotton Grow. Rev.*, 52, 11–29.
— *and* Hill, P. R. (1965). Some preliminary observations on the performance of sugar cane at Agricultural Irrigation Research Station, Kpong, Ghana.

*Samaru misc. Paper No. 13.* Institute for Agricultural Research, Samaru, Nigeria.

—— *and* Kassam, A. H. (1973a). Water use, energy balance and growth of maize at Samaru, northern Nigeria. *Agric. Met.,* **12**, 391–406.

—— *and* Kassam, A. H. (1973b). An appraisal of drought in 1973 affecting groundnut production in the Guinea and Sudan Savanna areas of Nigeria. *Savanna,* **2**, 159–64.

—— *and* Kassam, A. H. (1975). Rainfall pattern in the Sudan Savanna region of Nigeria. *Weather,* **30**, 24–8.

—— *and* Kassam, A. H. (1976). Energy load and instantaneous intensity of rainstorms at Samaru, northern Nigeria. *Trop. Agric., Trinidad,* **53**, 185–97.

—— *and* Knabe, D. (1972). *An agro-climatological atlas of the northern states of Nigeria.* Zaria, Ahmadu Bello University Press.

—— *and* Omolokun, A. O. (1970). Hydrology of a small catchement basin at Samaru. II. Seasonal fluctuation in the height of the groundwater table. *Niger. agric. J.,* **7**, 27–40.

—— *and* Stockinger, K. R. (1973a). Construction and performance of weighing lysimeter. *Samaru misc. Paper No. 44.* Samaru, Institute for Agricultural Research.

—— *and* Stockinger, K. R. (1973b). The usefulness of ridge cultivation in Nigerian agriculture. *J. Soil Wat. Conser.,* **28**, 136–7.

——, Kijewski, W. *and* Kassam, A. H. (1973). A simple device for analysing the energy load and intensity of rainstorms.*A gric. Met.,* **12**, 271–80.

Kushman, L. J. *and* Wright, F. S. (1969). Sweet potato storage. *USDA Agric. Handbk. No. 38.*

Lal, R. (1973). Effects of seed bed preparation and time of planting on maize in western Nigeria. *Exp. Agric.,* **9**, 303–13.

—— *and* Taylor, G. S. (1970). Drainage and nutrient effects in a field lysimeter study. II. Mineral uptake by corn. *Soil Sci. Soc. Am. Proc.,* **34**, 245–8.

Lamb, H. H. (1972). *Climate: present, past and future.* Methuen, London.

Lamey, H. A. *and* Williams, R. J. (1972). Leaf scald of rice in West Africa. *Pl. Dis. Rep.,* **56**, 106–7.

Lapage, G. (1956). *Veterinary Parasitology*, Chas. C. Thomas, Springfield.

Larsen, S. (1967). Soil Phosphorus. *Adv. Agron.,* **19**, 151–210.

——, Gunary, D. *and* Sutton, C. D. (1965). The rate of immobilization of applied phosphate in relation to soil properties. *J. Soil Sci.,* **16**, 141–8.

Law, R. L. (1974). Investigations of the important growth stages of maize. *5th E. Afr. Cereals Res. Conf.,* Malawi.

Lawes, D. A. (1961). Rainfall conservation and the yield of çotton in northern Nigeria. *Emp. J. exp. Agric.,* **29**, 307–18.

—— (1964). *Rainfall, run-off and soil surface infiltration rates at Samaru, Northern Nigeria.* M.Sc. Thesis, University of Wales.

—— (1965). A note on the soil moisture storage capacity of the Samaru Soils, northern Nigeria. *Samaru misc. Paper No. 5.* Institute for Agricultural Research, Samaru, Nigeria.

—— (1966). Rainfall conservation and the yields of sorghum and groundnuts in northern Nigeria. *Exp. Agric.,* **2**, 139–46.

—— (1968). Crop husbandry and the yield of cotton in northern Nigeria. *Cotton Grow. Rev.,* **45**, 1–16.

Lawton, K. (1945). The influence of soil aeration on the growth and absorption of nutrients by corn plants. *Soil Sci. Soc. Am. Proc.,* **10**, 263–8.

Le Conte, J. (1970). The state of sorghum research conducted by IRAT. *Ford Foundation/IRAT/IITA Seminar on Sorghum and Millet Research in West Africa.* IRAT, Bambey, Senegal, 31 Aug.–4 Sept., 1970.

Leeper, G. W. (1947). The forms and reactions of manganese in the soil. *Soil Sci.,* **63**, 79–94.

Leeuw, P. N. de *and* Brinckman, W. L. (1975). Pasture and rangeland improvement in the Northern Guinea and Sudan zone of Nigeria. *Samaru Conf. Paper No. 5.* Institute for Agricultural Research, Samaru, Nigeria.

Lemon, E. R. (1966). Energy conversion and water use efficiency. *Plant Environment and Efficient Water Use.* Amer. Soc. Agron., Wisconsin, Madison.

—— (1967). Aerodynamic studies of $CO_2$ exchange between the atmosphere and the plant. *Harvesting the Sun,* (*eds.* A. San Pietro, F. A. Grear, *and* T. J. Army), pp. 291–309. Academic Press, London.

—— (1970). Mass and energy exchange between plant stands and environment. *IBP/PP Tech. Meet. on Prediction and Measurement of Photosynthetic Productivity,* pp. 199–206. Trebon, 14–21 Sept., 1969.

Libby, J. L. (1968). Insect pests of Nigerian crops. *Coll. of Agric. and Life Sciences Res. Bull. No. 269.* The University of Wisconsin.

Litzenberger, S. C. (1974). *Guide for field crops in the tropics and the subtropics.* Technical Assistance Bureau, USAID, Washington, D.C.

Loomis, R. S. *and* Williams, W. A. (1963). Maximum crop productivity: an estimate. *Crop Sci.,* **3**, 67–72.

Lowe, S. B. *and* Wilson, L. A. (1974). Comparative analysis of tuber development in six sweet potato cultivars. *Ann. Bot.,* **38**, 319–26.

—— *and* Wilson, L. A. (1975a, b). Yield and yield components of six sweet potato cultivars, parts I and II, *Exp. Agric.,* **11**, 39–48; 49–58.

Lowe-McConnell, R. H. (1966). *Man-Made Lakes.* London.

Luning, H. A. (1963). *An agro-economic survey of Katsina Province.* Govt. Printer, Kaduna.

—— (1967). *Economic Aspects of low labour-income farming.* Ph.D. Thesis, Wageningen.

Lyon, D. J. de B. (1970). Cotton research and its application in Nigeria. *Change in Agriculture,* (*ed.* A. H. Bunting), pp. 191–7. Duckworth, London.

McArthur, J. A., Hesketh, J. D., *and* Baker, D. N. (1975). Cotton. *Crop physiology: some case histories,* (*ed.* L. T. Evans), pp. 297–326. Cambridge University Press.

McComb, A. L. (1968). Report on tree physiology. *Savanna Forestry Research Station Semi-annual Report, June 1968.* Samaru, Nigeria.

—— (1970). Tree physiology. *FO:SF/NIR 16, Technical Report 3.* Rome, FAO.

—— *and* Jackson, J. K. (1969). The role of tree plantation in Savanna development. *Unasylva,* **23**, 8–18.

—— *and* Ogigirigi, M. (1970). Features of the growth of *Eucalyptus citriodora* and *Isoberlinia doka* in the Northern Guinea Savanna zone of Nigeria. *Savanna For. Res. Stn. Res. Paper No. 3.* Samaru, Nigeria.

McDonald, D. (1968). Soil fungi and the fruit of the groundnut. *Samaru misc. Paper No. 28.* Institute of Agricultural Research, Samaru, Nigeria.

—— (1969). Groundnut pot diseases. *Rev. appl. Mycol.,* **38**, 465–74.

—— (1970a). Field trials for control of *Cercospora* leaf-spot diseases of groundnuts. *Samaru agric. Newslet.,* **12**, 70.

—— (1970b). Investigations on the mycoflora of the groundnut fruit. *Samaru agric. Newslet.,* **12**, 71.

— (1970c). Fungal infection of groundnut fruit before harvest. *Trans. Brit. mycol. Soc.*, **54**, 453–60.

— (1970d). Fungal infection of groundnut fruit after maturity and during drying. *Trans. Brit. mycol. Soc.*, **54**, 461–72.

— and Harkness, C. (1963). Growth of *Aspergillus flavus* and production of aflatoxin in groundnuts. *Trop. Sci.*, **5**, 208–14.

Manning, H. L. (1951). Confidence limits of expected monthly rainfall. *J. agric. Sci., Camb.*, **40**, 169–76.

— (1956). The statistical assessment of rainfall probability and its application in Uganda agriculture. *Proc. Roy. Soc., London (B)*, **144**, 460–80.

Martin, G. (1963). Dégradation de la structure de sols sous culture mecanisé dans la vallée du Niari. *Cah. ORSTOM, Ser. pedol.*, **1**, 8–14.

— and Fourier, P. (1965). Les oligoélements dans la culture de l'arachide au Nord Sénégal. *Oleagineux*, **20**, 287–91.

Matsuoka, K. (1959). Studies on the sesame varieties, 7. *Japan J. Ecol.*, **9**, 39–45.

— (1960). Studies on the sesame varieties, 9. *Japan J. Ecol.*, **10**, 22–8.

Meijers, C. P. (1972). *Potato storage in warm countries.* Dutch Inform. Cent. for potatoes, The Hague.

Meiklejohn, J. (1962). Microbiology of the nitrogen cycle in some Ghana soils. *Emp. J. exp. Agric.*, **30**, 115–26.

Meinzer, O. E. (1923). The occurrence of groundwater in the United States. *U.S. Gw. Ser. Water Supply Paper No. 489.*

Mellor, J. W. (1967). *The economics of agricultural development.* Cornell University Press, Ithaca.

Meredith, R. M. (1964). The effect of planting desntiy and manuring on the yield of bunch-type groundnuts. *Emp. J. exp. Agric.*, **32**, 136–40.

— (1965). A review of the responses to fertilizers of the crops of northern Nigeria. *Samaru misc. Paper No. 4.* Institute for Agricultural Research, Samaru, Nigeria.

Miege, J. (1957). Influence de quelques caracters des tubercules semences sur la levée et le rendement des ignames cultivées. *J. Agric. trop. Bot. appl.*, **4**, 315–42.

Milbourn, G. M. (1971). *Maize for grain.* Home-Grown Cereals Authority, London.

Miller, T. B. (1969). Forage conservation in the tropics. *J. Brit. grassl. Soc.*, **24**, 158–62.

— and Rains, A. B. (1963). The nutritive value and agronomic aspects of some fodder in northern Nigeria. 1. Fresh herbage. *J. Brit. grassl. Soc.*, **18**, 158–67.

Miracle, M. P. (1966). *Maize in tropical Africa.* University of Wisconsin Press, Madison.

Mohamed, A. N. and Leeflang, P. (1975). Cattle tick control at Shika Agricultural Research Station. *Samaru agric. Newslet.*, **17**, 75–7.

Mongelard, J. C. and Mimura, L. (1971). Growth studies on the sugar cane plant. I. Effects of temperature. *Crop Sci.*, **11**, 795–800.

— — (1972). Growth studies on the sugar cane plant. II. Some effects of root temperature and gibberellic acid and their interactions on growth. *Crop Sci.*, **12**, 52–8.

Monnier, G. (1965). Action des matières organiques sur la stabilité structural des sols (deuxième partie). *Ann. Agron.*, **16**, 471–534.

— and Ramond, C. (1970). A study of intensive production systems in Senegal.

*Seminar on traditional African agricultural systems and their improvement.* University of Ibadan, 16–20 Nov., 1970.

Monteith, J. L. (1965). Light distribution and photosynthesis in field crops. *Ann. Bot.*, **29**, 17–37.

— (1972). Solar radiation and productivity in tropical eco-systems. *J. appl. Ecol.*, **9**, 747–66.

— (1973). *Principles of environmental physics.* Edward Arnold, London.

— and Elston, J. F. (1971). Microclimatology and crop production. In *Potential crop production*, (eds. P. F. Wareing and J. P. Cooper). Heineman, London.

Moorby, J. and Milthorpe, F. L. (1975). Potato. In *Crop physiology: some case histories*, (ed. L. T. Evans), pp. 225–8. Cambridge University Press.

Morel, P. C. and Bourliere, F. (1962). Relations écologiques des avifaunes sédentaires et migratrices dans une savana sahélienne. *La terre et la vie*, 109.

Morel, R. and Quantin, P. (1972). Observations sur l'évolution a long terme de la fertilité des sols cultivés à Grimari (Republique Centrafricaine). Resultats d'essais de culture mecanisée semi-intensive, sur des sols rouges ferrallitiques moyennement désatures en climat soudano-guineen d'Afrique centrale. *Agron. trop., Paris*, **27**, 667–739.

Morgan, W. B. and Pugh, J. C. (1969). *West Africa.* Methuen & Co. Ltd., London.

Mortimore, M. J. and Wilson, J. (1965). Land and people in the Kano close-settlement zone. *Dept. of Geogr. Occasional Paper No. 1.* Ahmadu Bello University, Zaria, Nigeria.

Moureaux, C. (1967). Influence de la température et de l'humidité sur les activités biologique de quelques sols Ouest-Africaine. *Cah. ORSTOM, Ser. Pedol.*, **5**, 393–420.

Murata, Y. and Matsushima, S. (1975). Rice. In *Crop physiology: some case histories*, (ed. L. T. Evans), pp. 73–99. Cambridge University Press.

Nabos, J. (1971). The onion in the Niger. *Seminar Veg. Crops.* Ibadan, Nigeria.

Naegele, A. F. (1967). Végétation du Sénégal. In *A study of the agro-climatology of the semi-arid area south of the Sahara in West Africa*, (ed. J. Cocheme and P. Franquin), pp. 15–19. FAO/UNESCO/WMO Interagency Project on Agro-climatology. FAO, Rome.

NAS (1974). *African Agricultural Research Capabilities.* National Academy of Sciences, Washington.

Naylor, A. H. and Beredugo, Y. O. (1969). The design and construction of the Makwaye Dam, Samaru. *Niger. Eng.*, **5**, 21–9.

Nicou, R. and Thirouin, H. (1968). Mésures sur la porosité et l'enracinement— premiers résultats. (Mimeo.), IRAT, Sénégal.

—, Seguy, L. and Haddad, G. (1970). Comparaison de l'enracinement de quatre varietés de riz pluvial en precence ou absence de travail du sol. (Mimeo.). IRAT, Sénégal.

Nofziger, D. L. (1974). Root growth of maize and sorghum at Samar, Nigeria. Mimeo. Institute for Agricultural Research, Samaru, Nigeria.

Norman, D. W. (1967). An economic study of three villages in Zaria Province. I. Land and labour relationships. *Samaru misc. Paper No. 19.* Institute for Agricultural Research, Samaru, Nigeria.

— (1970). Initiating change in traditional agriculture. *Proc. Agric. Soc. Nigeria*, **7**, 6–14.

— (1972). An economic study of three villages in Zaria Province. II. Input-output study. Vol. 1 Text. *Samaru misc. Paper No. 37.* Institute for Agricultural Research, Samaru, Nigeria.

—— (1973). Economic analysis of agricultural production and labour utilization among the Hausa in the north of Nigeria. *African Rural Employment Paper No. 4.* Michigan State University, East Lansing.

—— (1976). The organizational consequences of social and economic constraints and policies in dry-land areas. (In Hunter, G., Bunting, A. H., and Bottrall, A., *Policy and practice in rural development.* London, Croom Helm). pp. 168–86.

——, Buntjer, B. J., *and* Goddard, A. D. (1970). Intercropping observations plots at the farmers' level. *Samaru agric. Newslet.,* 12, 97–101.

——, Hayward, J. A., *and* Hallam, H. R. (1974). An assessment of cotton growing recommendations as applied by Nigerian farmers. *Cotton Grow. Rev.,* 51, 266–80.

——, Fine, J. C., Goddard, A. D., Koreker, W. J., *and* Pryor, D. H. (1976a). A socio-economic study of three villages in the Sokoto close-settlement zone. Part 2. Input-output study. Vol. 1. Text. (Mimeo.), Institute for Agricultural Research, Samaru, Nigeria.

——, Pryor, D. H., *and* Koreker, W. J. (1976b). A comment on the relationship between family organization and improved farming practices in Hausaland. (Mimeo.), Institute for Agricultural Research, Samaru, Nigeria.

——, Beeden, P., Kroeker, W. J., Pryor, D. H., Hays, H. M. *and* Huizinga, B. (1976c). The production feasibility of improved sole crop maize production technology for the small-scale farmer in the Northern Guinea Savanna Zone of Nigeria. *Samaru misc. Paper No. 59.* Institute for Agricultural Research, Samaru, Nigeria.

——, Koreker, W. J., Pryor, D. H., Huizinga, B., *and* Hays, H. M. (1976d). The feasibility of improved sole crop sorghum production technology for the small-scale farmer in the Northern Guinea Savanna Zone of Nigeria. *Samaru misc. Paper No. 60.* Institute for Agricultural Research, Samaru, Nigeria.

Nuttonson, M. V. (1947). Agro-climatology and crop ecology of Palestine and Trans-Jordan and climatic analogues in the United States. *Geogr. Rev.,* 37, 436–56.

Nye, P. *and* Bartheux, M. H. (1957). The distribution of phosphorus in Forest and Savanna soils of the Gold Coast and its agricultural significance. *J. agric. Sci., Camb.,* 49, 141–59.

—— *and* Greenland, D. J. (1960). *The soil under shifting cultivation.* Tech. Com. No. 51. Commonwealth Bureau of Soils, Harpenden.

Obihara, C. H., Badwen, M. G. *and* Jungerius, P. D. (1964). The Anambra-Do rivers area. *Soil Survey Memoir No. 1.* Min. of Agric., Eastern Nigeria.

Odu, C. T. I. (1967). *Aerobic nitrogen transformations in some soils of the Derived Savanna.* Ph.D. Thesis, University of Ibadan, Nigeria.

Ogborn, J. (1972a). The significance of the seasonal pattern of emergence of *Striga hermontheca* Benth. *Sorghum in the seventies,* (eds. N. G. P. Rao and L. R. House), pp. 562–71. O.U.P. and IBH Publishing Co., New Delhi.

—— (1972b). The control of *Striga hermontheca* in peasant farming. *11th Brit. Weed Control Conf.,* pp. 1068–77.

Ogunfowora, O. (1972). *Derived resource demand, product supply and farm policy in the North Central State of Nigeria.* Ph.D. thesis, Iowa State University, Ames.

Oguntoyinbo, Y. S. (1974). Land use and reflection coefficient map for southern parts of Nigeria. *Agric. Met.,* 13, 227–37.

Okigbo, B. N. (1974). Traditional farming systems in eastern Nigeria. *2nd Int. Seminar on Change in Agriculture.* University of Reading, 9–19 Sept., 1974.

Olivier, H. (1967). Irrigation as a factor in promoting regional development. *Water for Peace*, pp. 266–81. U.S. Govt. Printing Office, Washington.

Olson, R. A. *and* Engelstad, O. P. (1972). Soil phosphorus and sulphur. *Soils of the Humid Tropics*, pp. 82–101. National Acad. of Sciences, Washington.

ORSTOM-IRAT (1970–1971). Improvement of millet. Fed. Project 215-015.25 Report of activity Nov. 1970–Nov. 1971. (Mimeo.), ORSTOM/IRAT, Senegal.

Ou, S. H. (1972). *Rice diseases*. Commonwealth Mycological Institute, London.

Oyenuga, V. A. (1967). *Agriculture in Nigeria*. FAO, Rome.

Pal, N. L. *and* Bangarayy, A. (1958). Deficiency symptoms in *Sesamum indicum*. *Indian J. agric. Sci.*, 28, 607–11.

Palmer, J. L. *and* Goldworthy, P. R. (1972). Fertilizer trials with sprayed and unsprayed cotton in Nigeria. *Exp. Agric.*, 7, 281–7.

— *and* Heathcote, R. G. (1970). Cotton agronomy. *Samaru agric. Newslet.*, 12, 50–1.

— (1968). *Some aspects of the effects of fluctuating water tables on the growth of sorghum and maize at Samaru, Northern Nigeria*. M.Sc. Thesis, Ahmadu Bello University, Zaria, Nigeria.

Penman, H. L. (1948). Natural evaporation from open water, bare soil and grass, *Proc. Roy. Soc., London (A)*, 193, 120–45.

— (1968). The earth's potential. *Science*, May, 1968, Special issue, pp. 42–7.

Pereira, H. C. (1955). Soil structure criteria for tropical crops. *5th Int. Congr. Soil Sci.*, 2, 59–64.

Perry, D. A. (1967). Premature death of groundnut plants in northern Nigeria. *Exp. Agric.*, 3, 211–14.

Phillips, J. (1959). *Agriculture and ecology in Africa*. Faber and Faber, London.

Pichot, J. *and* Roche, P. (1972). Phosphore dans les sols tropicaux. *Agron. trop., Paris*, 27, 939–65.

Pieri, C. (1974). L'acidification des terres de cultures exondées au Sénégal. Mimeo. IRAT, Sénégal.

Porter, C. B. (1964). Introduction of *Oryza sativa* in Sokoto-Rima valley. *Samaru agric. Newslet.*, 6, 171–3.

Porteres, R. (1955). L'introduction du mais en Afrique. *J. Agric. trop. et Bot. appl.*, 5, 6.

— *and* Legleu, R. (1937). La rosette de l'arichide. Connaissances actuelles, rélations avec la date des semis dans le pays du Basule-Nord, methods prophylactiques à appliquer. *Ann. Agric., A.O.F.*, 1, 332.

Poulain, J. F. (1967). Résultats obtenus avec les engrais et les amendements calciques. Acidifcation des sols et correction. *Colloque sur la fertilité des sols tropicaux*, 1, 469–489. Tananarive, 19–25 Nov., 1967.

— *and* Tourte, R. (1970). Effects of deep preparation of dry soil on yields from millet and sorghum to which nitrogen fertilizers have been added (sandy soil from a dry tropical area). *Afr. Soils*, 15, 553–86.

Prentice, A. M. (1972). *Cotton: with special reference to Africa*. Longman, London.

Purseglove, J. W. (1974). *Tropical crops: Dicotyledons*. Longman, London.

— (1975). *Tropical crops: Monocotyledons*. Longman, London.

Quantin, P. (1965). *Les sols de la République Centrafricaine*. ORSTOM.

Quinn, J. G. (1971). *Factors affecting the production of tomatoes for the processing industry during different seasons in the Northern States of Nigeria*. M.Sc. Thesis, Ahmadu Bello University, Zaria, Nigeria.

— (1973a). Nigeria: prospects for a tomato paste industry. *Span*, 6, 1–3.

—— (1973b). An evaluation of methods of mulching and staking tomatoes grown during the rains at Samaru, Nigeria. *Hort. Res.,* **13**, 97–104.

—— (1974). Environment and the establishmentof an industrial tomato crop in northern Nigeria. *EUCARPIA Meet. of the Tomato Working Group.* Valenzano, Bari, Italy, International Centre for Advanced Mediterranean Agronomic Studies, 26–30 Aug., 1974.

—— *and* McLean, K. (1974). Production marketing and processing of tomatoes in the semi-arid regions. *Samaru agric. Newslet.,* **16**, 40–2.

Raay, J. G. T. van (1973). Animal husbandry in the Zaria area. *Samaru Res. Bull. No. 179.* Institute for Agricultural Research, Samaru, Nigeria.

—— *and* Leeuw, P. N. de (1970). The importance of crop residues as fodder. *Samaru Res. Bull. No. 139.* Institute for Agricultural Research, Samaru, Nigeria.

—— *and* Leeuw, P. N. de (1974). Fodder resources and grazing management in a Savanna environment. An ecosystem approach. *Samaru Res. Bull. No. 224.* Institute for Agricultural Research, Samaru, Nigeria.

Raheja, A. K. (1973). Onion thrips and their control in northern Nigeria. *Samaru agric. Newslet.,* **15**, 82–6.

—— (1974). A report on the insect pest complex of grain legumes in northern Nigeria. *1st IITA Grain Legume Improv. Workshop,* pp. 295–303. IITA, Ibadan, 29 Oct.–2 Nov., 1973.

—— (1975). Notes on *Alcidodes leucogrammus* as a pest of cowpea. *Trop. Grain Legume Bull.,* **1**, 8.

—— *and* Hays, H. M. (1975). Sole crop cowpea production by farmers using improved practices. *Trop. Grain Legume Bull.,* **1**, 6.

—— *and* Leleji, O. I. (1974). An aphid-borne virus disease of irrigated cowpea in northern Nigeria. *Pl. Dis. Rep.,* **58**, 1080–4.

Rains, A. B. (1963). Grassland research in northern Nigeria, 1952–1963. *Samaru misc. Paper No. 1.* Institute for Agricultural Research, Samaru, Nigeria.

Ramond, C. (1971). Introduction of intensive schemes in traditional farms—economic consequences. (Mimeo.), Centre National De Recherches Agronomiques, Bambey, Senegal.

Ramsey, D. M. (1968). Land use in Nigeria. *Samaru agric. Newslet.,* **10**, 73–80.

Rao, N. G. P. *and* House, L. R. (1972). *Sorghum in the seventies.* O.U.P. and IBH Publishing Co., New Delhi.

RERU (1972). Farm income levels in the northern states of Nigeria. Rural Economy Research Unit Report to the Salaries and Wages Review Commission of 1970. *Samaru misc. Paper No. 35.* Institute for Agricultural Research, Samaru, Nigeria.

Rheenen, H. A. van (1970). Intergeneric hybridization between *Ceratotheca sesamoides* Endl. and *Sesamum indicum* L. *Niger. J. Sci.,* **4**, 251–4.

—— (1973). *Major problems of growing sesame in Nigeria.* Ph.D. Thesis, Wageningen.

Richards, L. A. and Wadleigh, C. H. (1952). Soil water and plant growth. In *Soil physical conditions and plant growth,* (ed. B. T. Shaw), p. 73–252. Academic Press, New York.

—— *and* Weaver, L. R. (1943). Fifteen-atmosphere percentage as related to the permanent wilting percentage. *Soil Sci.,* **56**, 331–40.

Rick, C. M. (1956). Cytogenetics of the tomato. *Adv. Genetics,* **3**, 267–392.

Rijks, D. A. (1967). Water use by irrigated cotton in Sudan. I. Reflection of short-wave radiation. *J. appl. Ecol.,* **4**, 561–8.

Rinaudo, G., Hamad-Fares, I., *and* Dommergues, Y. R. (1975). $N_2$ fixation in the rice rhizosphere: methods of measurement; practices suggested to enhance the process. *Conf. on Biological Fixation in Farming Systems of the Tropics.* IITA, Ibadan, 20–23 Oct., 1975.

Robertson, D. G. (1963a). Cowpea virus research in Nigeria. *1st Nigerian Grain Legume Conf.* Institute for Agricultural Research, Samaru, Nigeria.

—— (1963b). Plant virus diseases in Nigeria. *Memor. Fedl. Dep. Agric. Res. Nigeria No. 47.* Moor Plantation, Ibadan, Nigeria.

Robinson, D. H. (1965). *Fream's elements of agriculture.* John Murray, London.

Robinson, R. A. (1967). Bacterial wilt of Irish potatoes. *Samaru agric. Newslet.,* 3, 70–71.

—— (1968). Bacterial wilt of Irish potatoes on the Jos plateau. *Samaru agric. Newslet.,* 4, 81–4.

Robledo, C. (1970). The problem of improving the production of sorghum and millet in Upper Volta. *Ford Foundation/IRAT/IITA Seminar on Sorghum and Millet Research in West Africa.* IRAT, Bambey, Senegal, 31 Aug.–4 Sept., 1970.

Roose, E. (1967). Dix années de mésure de l'érosion et du ruissellement au Sénégal. *Agron. tropic., Paris,* 22, 123–52.

—— *and* Bertrand, R. (1971). Contribution à l'étude de la méthode des bandes d'arrêt pour lutter contre l'érosion hydrique en Afrique de l'Ouest. Résultats expérimentaux et observations sur le terrain. *Agron. tropic., Paris,* 26, 1270–83.

Rose, C. W. (1966). *Agricultural Physics.* Pergamon Press, Oxford.

Rotimi, O. A. (1970). Increasing yields of groundnuts by planting on the flat. *Samaru agric. Newslet.,* 12, 102.

Russell, E. W. (1973). *Soil conditions and plant growth.* Longman, London.

Sadik, S. (1973). Screening sweet potato for low $CO_2$ compensation point. *3rd Int. Sympos. Trop. Root Crops.* IITA, Ibadan, Nigeria.

Samie, A. G. A. (1973). Contribution of rainfall to the moisture storage in some soils at the Afaka Forest Reserve. *Min. Agric. Nat. Resor. Res. Paper No. 25.* Nigeria.

—— (1974). Soil-water-tree relationship in the Savanna region of Nigeria. *FAO Project Working Document FO: NIR 64/516.*

Samuels, G. (1967). The influence of fertilizer ratios on sweet potato yields and quality. *1st Int, Sympos. Trop. Root Crops,* (eds. E. Tai *et al.*), 1, 86–93. University of West Indies, Trinidad.

Sauger, L., Bilquez, A., Doggett, H., Le Conte, J., Moorman, F. R., *and* Webster, O. J. (1970). A summary of the discussion. *Ford Foundation/IRAT/IITA Seminar on Sorghum and Millet Research in West Africa.* IRAT, Bambey, Senegal, 31 Aug.–4 Sept., 1970.

Sceicz, G. (1974). Solar radiation for plant growth. *J. appl. Ecol.,* 11:617–636.

Schenk, R. V. (1961). Development of the peanut fruit. *Georgia Agric. Expt. Stn. Tech. Bull. NS 22.* Athens, Georgia.

Schneider, R. M. *and* Quinn, J. G. (1972). The design of an implement for making seed drills in tomato nurseries. *Samaru agric. Newslet.,* 14, 43–4.

Semb, G. *and* Garberg, P. K. (1969). Some effects of planting date and nitrogen fertilizer in maize. *E. Afr. agric. For. J.,* 34, 371–6.

Sen, P. K. *and* Lahiri, A. (1959). Studies on the nutrition of oilseed crops. IV. Effects of phosphorus and sulphur on the uptake of nitrogen and growth and yield of sesame. *Indian Agric.,* 23, 6–10.

Sestak, Z., Catsky, J., *and* Jarvis, P. G. (1971). *Plant photosynthetic production. Manual of methods.* Dr. W. Junk NV. Publishers, The Hague.

Shantz, H. L. *and* Turner, B. L. (1958). Photographic documentation of vegetational changes in Africa over a third of a century. *Coll. Agric. Res. No. 169.* University of Arizona.

Shibles, R. M., Anderson, I. C., *and* Gibson, A. H. (1975). Soybean. In *Crop Physiology: some case histories,* (ed. L. T. Evans), pp. 151–89. Cambridge University Press.

Shoyinka, S. A. (1974). Status of virus diseases of cowpea in Nigeria. *1st IITA Grain Legume Improv. Workshop.* IITA, Ibadan, 29 Oct.–2 Nov., 1973.

Siband, P. (1972a). Étude de l'évolution des sols sous culture traditionelle en Haute-Casamance. Principaux résultats. *Agron. trop., Paris.,* 27, 574–91.

—— (1972b). Premiers résultats de la recherche sur riz pluvial en Casamance, en agropedologie pour l'année 1971. (Mimeo.), IRAT, Senegal.

Sigafus, R. E. (1973). *Peanuts: a limited review of some worldwide laboratory and field research.* University of Kentucky, Thailand Project, College of Agriculture, Lexington.

Simmonds, N. W. (1971). The potential of potatoes in the tropics. *Trop. Agric., Trinidad,* 48, 291–9.

Slatyer, R. O. (1967). *Plant-water relationships.* Academic Press, New York.

Smilde, K. W. (1960). *The influence of some environmental factors on growth and development of* Sesamum indicum *L.* Meded. Landbouwhogeschool Wageningen 60(5), BP 70.

Smith, M. G. (1955). *The economy of Hausa communities of Zaria,* Colonial Research Studies No. 16, HMSO, London.

Smith, O. (1968). *Potatoes: production, storing, processing,* AVI Publishing Co. Inc., Westport, Conn.

Smithson, J. B. (1972). Differential sensitivity to Boron in Cotton in the northern States of Nigeria. *Cotton Grow. Rev.,* 49, 350–3.

—— *and* Hayward, J. A. (1977). The effect of plant density and insecticide on super okra and normal leaf cotton in the northern States of Nigeria. *Cotton Grow. Rev.,* (in press).

—— *and* Heathcote, R. G. (1974). Boron deficiency on cotton in northern Nigeria. II. The effect of variety. *Exp. Agric.,* 10, 209–18.

SMT (1951). *Smithsonian Meteorological Tables.* The Smithsonian Institution, Washington.

Sobulo, R. A. (1972a, b). Studies on white yam *Dioscorea rotundata,* parts I and II, *Exp. Agric.,* 8, 99–106; 107–15.

Soyer, D. (1939). La 'rosette' de l'arachide. recherches sur les vecteurs possibles de la maladie. *INEAC Serie Scientifique No. 21.*

Stanton, W. *and* Cammack, R. H. (1953). *West African Maize Rust Research Unit First Annual Report, 1953.* Moor Plantation, Ibadan, Nigeria.

Staph, O. *and* Hubbard, C. E. (1934). Pennisetum. *Flora of tropical Africa,* (ed. D. Prain), Vol. 9. London.

St. Croix, F. W. de (1945). *The Fulani of Northern Nigeria.* Government Printer, Lagos.

Steele, W. M. (1960). *Sesame and soya bean.* Internal Report, Mokwa Agricultural Research Station, Nigeria.

—— (1964). The yield of cowpea in northern Nigeria. *Samaru agric. Newslet.,* 6, 181–6.

—— (1972). *Cowpeas in Africa.* Ph.D. Thesis, University of Reading, England.

Stiles, W. *and* Leach, W. (1960). *Respiration in plants.* Methuen, London.

Stirk, G. B. (1957). Physical properties of soils in the lower Burdekin Valley, Northern Queensland. *Divisional Rept. 1/57.* CSIRO, Australia.

Stockinger, K. R. (1972). Annual report, major cereals in West Africa, OAU/ STRC JP 26. (Mimeo.), Institute for Agricultural Research, Samaru, Nigeria.

Stonebridge, W. C. (1963). Benniseed variety and sowing method trials. *Tech. Rept. Inst. Agric. Res. Northern Nigeria,* 28, 1–9.

Storey, H. M. *and* Bottomley, A. M. (1928). Rosette disease of the peanut. *Ann. appl. Biol.,* 15, 26–45.

— *and* Ryland, A. K. (1955). Transmission of groundnut rosette virus. *Ann. appl. Biol.,* 43, 423–32.

— *and* Ryland, A. K. (1957). Virus causing rosette and other diseases in groundnuts. *Ann. appl. Biol.,* 45, 318–26.

STRC/OAU-JP 26 (1972a). Cereal problems in Senegal. Liaison Document No. 4/72. (Mimeo.), Institut de Recherches Agronomiques Tropicale et des Cultures Vivrières, Dakar, Senegal.

— (1972b). Agronomic necessity and economic interest of intensive farming systems in Senegal. (Mimeo.), Institut de Recherches Agronomiques Tropicale et des Cultures Vivrières, Dakar, Senegal.

Summerfield, R. J. (1975a). Effects of tropical daylengths and day-night temperatures on vegetative growth, reproductive ontogeny and seed yield of cowpea and soya bean: a general model. *Physiology Workshop.* IITA, Ibadan, Nigeria.

— (1975b). Some aspects of the nitrogen nutrition of cowpea. *Grain Legume Workshop,* IITA, Ibadan, Nigeria.

—, Huxley, P. A., *and* Steele, W. (1974). Cowpea (*Vigna unguiculata* (L.) Walp.). *Fld. Crop Abstr.,* 27, 301–12.

Tanaka, A., Yamaguchi, J., Shimazaki, Y., *and* Shibata, K. (1968). Historical changes of rice varieties in Hokkaido viewed from the point of plant type. *J. Sci. Soil and Manure, Japan,* 39, 526–34.

Tatum, L. (1971). Maize as a grain crop in northern States of Nigeria. *Samaru agric. Newslet.,* 13, 87–90.

Thiessen, A. H. (1911). Precipitation for large areas. *Mon. Weather Rev.,* 39, 1087–94.

Thornthwaite, C. W. (1948). An approach towards a rational classification of climate. *Geog. Rev.,* 38, 85–94.

Thornton, I. (1964). The effect of fertilizers on the uptake of nitrogen, phosphorus and potassium by the groundnut. *Emp. J. exp. Agric.,* 32, 235–40.

— (1965). Nutrient content of rainwater in the Gambia. *Nature, London,* 205, 1025.

Tiffen, M. (1973). Relationshiops between age, family size, and progressive farming in Moslem areas of northern Nigeria. *Savanna,* 2, 165–172.

— (1974). Economic and administrative influences on successful agricultural development: a Nigerian case study. *J. Admin. Overseas,* 13, 449–61.

Tolbert, H. E. *and* Yamazaki, R. K. (1969). Leaf peroxisomes and their relation to photorespiration and photosynthesis. *Ann. N.Y. Acad. Sci.,* 168, 325–41.

Toupet, C. (1965). Les éléments annuels du climat. *International Atlas of West Africa.* OAU/STRC, Dakar, Senegal.

Tourte, R. *and* Fauche, J. (1964). La 'rosette' de l'arachide. *Bull. Agron. Fr. d'Out. Mer.,* 13, 155.

——, Vidal P., Jacquinot, L., Fauche, J., *and* Nicou, R. (1964). Bilan d'une rotation quadriennale sur sole de régénération au Sénégal. *Agron. Trop., Paris*, **19**, 1033–72.

U.N. (1964). *Water Desalination in Developing Countries.* United Nations, New York.

Upadhya, M. D., Purchit, A. N. *and* Sharda, R. T. (1972). Breeding potatoes for tropical and subtropical areas. *Wld. Crops.*, **24**, 314–16.

Vaille, J. (1970). Sorghum fertilization in the north Cameroons. *Ford Foundation/IRAT/IITA Seminar on Sorghum and Millet Research in West Africa.* IRAT, Bambey, Senegal. 31 Aug.–4 Sept., 1970.

Vaille, J. *and* Goma, H. (1972). Mise en evidence d'une déficience en bore sur arachide dans le Nord-Cameroun. (Mimeo.), IRAT, Nogent.

Vanderlip, R. L. (1972). How a sorghum plant develops. Contribution No. 1203, Agronomy Dept., Kansas Agric. Expt. Stn., Manhattan, 66502.

Veihmeyer, F. J. *and* Hendrickson, A. H. (1949). Methods of measuring field capacity and permanent wilting percentages of soils. *Soil Sci.*, **68**, 75–95.

Vidal, P. *and* Fauche, J. (1962). Quelques aspects de la dynamique des éléments minéraux d'un sol dior soumis a différentes jachères. Premiers résultats. *Agron. trop., Paris*, **17**, 828–40.

Walker, H. D. (1962). Weather and climate. In *Agriculture and land use in Ghana*, (*ed.* J. B. Wills), pp. 7–50. Oxford University Press, London.

Wall, J. S. *and* Ross, W. M. (1970). *Sorghum Production and Utilization.* The AVI Publishing Co., Inc., Westport, Connecticut.

Webster, C. C. *and* Wilson, P. N. (1973). *Agriculture in the Tropics.* Longman, London.

Webster, O. J. (1969). Report of maize investigation. (Mimeo.), Institute for Agricultural Research, Samaru, Nigeria.

—— (1970). Sorghum and millet research in West Africa. *Ford Foundation/ IRAT/IITA Seminar on Sorghum and Millet Research in West Africa.* IRAT, Bambey, Senegal, 31 Aug.–4 Sept., 1970.

Weiss, E. A. (1971). *Castor, sesame and safflower.* Leonard Hill, London.

Went, F. W. (1944). Plant growth under controlled conditions. II. Thermoperiodicity in growth and fruiting of the tomato. *Am. J. Bot.*, **31**, 135–50.

—— (1949). The effect of temperature upon translocation of carbohydrates in tomato plant. *Pl. Physiol., Lancaster*, **34**, 505–26.

Westlake, D. F. (1963). Comparison of plant productivity. *Biol. Rev.*, **38**, 385–425.

Wharton, C. R. (1968). Risk, uncertainty and the subsistence farmer. *Joint Meet. of the American Economic Association and the Association for Cooperative Economics.* Chicago, Dec., 1968.

Whitlock, J. d. (1960). *Diagnosis of veterinary parasites.* Kempton, London.

Whitney, W. K. *and* Glimer, R. M. (1974). Insect vectors of cowpea mosaic virus in Nigeria. *Ann. appl. Biol.*, **77**, 17–21.

Wholey, D. W. *and* Cock, J. H. (1974). Onset and rate of root bulking in cassava. *Exp. Agric.*, **10**, 193–8.

—— *and* Haynes, P. H. (1969). *Root Crop Programme. Half Yearly Report, 1968/69.* Faculty of Agriculture, University of West Indies, Trinidad.

Wijk, W. R. van (1966). *Physics of plant environment.* North-Holland Publishing Co., Amsterdam.

Wild, A. (1971). The potassium status of soils in the Savanna zone of Nigeria. *Exp. Agric.*, **7**, 257–70.

—— (1972a). Nitrate leaching under bare fallow at a site in northern Nigeria. *J. Soil Sci.*, 23 315–24.

—— (1972b). Mineralization of soil nitrogen at a Savanna site in Nigeria. *Exp. Agric.*, 8, 91–7.

Wilde, J. C. de (1967). *Experiences with agricultural development in tropical Africa. Vol. I. The synthesis.* John Hopkins Press, Baltimore.

Wilkinson, G. E. (1975). Effect of grass fallow rotation on the infiltration of water into a Savanna zone soil of nothern Nigeria. *Trop. Agric., Trinidad*, 52, 97–103.

Williams, C. N. (1972). Growth and productivity of tapioca (*Manihot utilissima*). I. Crop ratio, spacing and yield, *Exp. Agric.*, 8, 15–23.

—— (1974). Growth and productivity of Tapioca (*Manihot utilissima*). IV. Development and yield of tubers, *Exp. Agric.*, 10, 9–16.

Williams, G. G. (1962). Potato growing in Plateau Province, *Samaru agric. Newslet.*, 5, 2–11.

Williams, R. J. (1973a). Major diseases of rice in West Africa and their control, *WARDA Seminar on plant protection for the rice crop*, West Afr. Rice Dev. Assoc., Monrovia, 21–29 May, 1973.

—— (1973b). Cassava mosaic workshop, International Institute of Tropical Agriculture, December 1972, *PANS*, 19, 580–2.

—— (1975a). Diseases of cowpea in Nigeria, *PANS*, 21, 253–67.

—— (1975b). Control of cowpea seedling mortality in southern Nigeria, *Pl. Dis. Rep.*, 59, 245–8.

—— *and* Abifarin, A. O. (1973). Blast and other diseases of rice in West Africa, *Int. Rice Res. Conf.*, IRRI, Philippines, April 1973.

——, Agboola, S. D., *and* Schneider, R. W. (1973). Bacterial wilt of cassava in Nigeria. *Pl. Dis. Rep.*, 57, 824–7.

Williamson, G. *and* Payne, W. J. A. (1965). *An Introduction to Animal Husbandry in the Tropics.* Tropical Agricultural Series. Longman, London.

Wilson, L. A. (1967). The use of rooted leaves and grafted plants for the study of carbohydrate metabolism in Sweet Potato. *1st Int. Sympos. Trop. Root Crops*, (*eds.* E. Tai *et al.*), 1, 46–55. University of West Indies, Trinidad.

—— (1970). The process of tuberization in sweet potato. *2nd Int. Sympos. Trop. Root and Tuber Crops*, (*ed.* D. L. Plucknett), 1, 24–6. Hawaii.

—— *and* Lowe, S. B. (1973). The anatomy of the root system in West Indian Sweet Potato cultivars. *Ann. Bot.*, 37, 633–43.

Winstanley, A. F. (1973). Rainfall pattern and general atmospheric circulation. *Nature, (London)*, 245, 190–4.

Winter, J. D. (1965). Irrigated tobacco observation in Kano. *Samaru agric. Newslet.*, 7, 29–31.

Wischmeier, W. H. *and* Smith, D. D. (1960). A universal soil-loss estimating equation. *7th Int. Congr. Soil Sci.*, 1, 418–25.

Wit, C. T. de (1959). Potential photosynthesis of crop surfaces. *Nether J. agric. Sci.*, 7, 141–9.

—— (1965). Photosynthesis of leaf canopies. *Inst. for Biol. and Chem. Res. on Fld. Crops and Herbage Res. Rept. No. 663*, Wageningen.

—— (1965). Photosynthesis of leaf canopies. *Inst. for Biol. and Chem. Res. on the sun*, (*eds.* A. San Pietro, F. A. Grear, *and* T. J. Army), pp. 315–20. Academic Press, London.

Woodbury, G. W. *and* Dietz, C. (1942). Onion seed production in Idaho. *Bull. Idaho agric. Exp. Stn. No. 247.*

Wynne, J. C., Emery, D. A., *and* Downs, R. J. (1971). Photoperiodic responses of peanuts. *Crop Sci.*, **13**, 511–14.

Yong, C. W. (1970). Effects of length of growing season and NPK fertilizers on the yield of five varieties of sweet potatoes on peat. *Malay. agric. J.*, **47**, 453–64.

Zandstra, H. G., Swanberg, K. G. *and* Zulberti, C. A. (1975). Removing constraints to small farm production. *Ann. Meet. Canadian Agric. Econ. Soc.* Brandon, Manitoba, 22–25 Jun., 1975.

Zeven, A. C. (1974). Indigenous bread wheat varieties from northern Nigeria. *Acta. Bot. Neevl.*, **23**, 137–44.

Zelitch, I. (1971). *Photosynthesis, photorespiration and plant productivity.* Academic Press, New York and London.

Zelitch, I. (1975). Improving the efficiency of photosynthesis. *Science*, **188**, 626–32.

Zemmelink, G., Haggar, R. J., *and* Davies, J. H. (1972). A note on the voluntary intake of *Andropogon gayanus* hay by cattle. *Anim. Prod.*, **15**, 85–8.

# Author index

# Subject index

Page numbers in italics refer to Figures and Tables